Uncle John's Endlessly ENGROSSING BATHROOM READER

By the Bathroom Readers' Institute

Bathroom Readers' Press
Ashland, Oregon

OUR "REGULAR" READERS RAVE!

"I love the *Bathroom Reader*. My whole family loves your books, too—by far the most-read book in my house. They always give us something to talk about. Everything I know I learned from the BRI."

—Jack

"I have read and collected almost every one of your wonderful books. Even my boys, a 10-year-old and 20-year-old (in the Navy), can't resist grabbing one and reading any chance they get. Thanks for the many years of pleasure and education."

—Kerry

"I am a huge fan and spend hours buried in the interesting stories and facts. Keep up the awesome work."

—Liz

"I want to let you now how much I enjoy your books. I not only enjoy them in their intended venue, but on the job as well. I am a tour bus driver in Kentucky, which involves a lot of waiting around. Some of that waiting is for very short periods of time, and so *Bathroom Readers* are perfect to fill it in. I also get a lot of 'I love those books!' from passengers who spot them sitting on the dash."

—Anne D.

"I love your books because they make me feel smarter and crack me up! I buy two each time and save the second one to give as a gift. I can't part with my *Bathroom Readers*."

—Anita

"I love your books. They are my favorite things to read!"

—Kristyn

"Your *Unsinkable Bathroom Reader* actually is unsinkable. How do I know? Because my copy survived a fall into a toilet!"

—Lucas

UNCLE JOHN'S ENDLESSLY ENGROSSING BATHROOM READER®

For information, write:
The Bathroom Readers' Institute, P.O. Box 1117,
Ashland, OR 97520
www.bathroomreader.com • 888-488-4642

Cover design by Michael Brunsfeld, San Rafael, CA
(*Brunsfeldo@comcast.net*)
BRI "technician" on the back cover: Larry Kelp

ISBN-13: 978-1-60710-036-2 / ISBN-10: 1-60710-036-3

Library of Congress Cataloging-in-Publication Data
Uncle John's endlessly engrossing bathroom reader.
    p. cm.
  ISBN 978-1-60710-036-2 (pbk.)
  1. American wit and humor. 2. Curiosities and wonders. I.
Bathroom
Readers' Institute (Ashland, Or.)
  PN6165.U5337 2009
  081.02'07—dc22

                                            2009022950

First Printing
1 2 3 4 5 6 7 8 9 13 12 11 10 09

Hiya, Sophie! Hiya, Jesse!

THANK YOU!

The Bathroom Readers' Institute sincerely thanks the people whose advice and assistance made this book possible.

Gordon Javna	Claudia Bauer
John Dollison	Claire Breen
Brian Boone	JoAnn Padgett
Jay Newman	Melinda Allman
Thom Little	Lisa, Monica & Amy
Amy Miller	Ginger Winters
Michael Brunsfeld	Maggie Javna
Angela Kern	Tom "Honey" Mustard
Lorraine Bodger	Sydney Stanley
Jolly Jeff Cheek	David Calder
Jef Fretwell	Karen Malchow
Megan Todd	Elise Gochberg
Judy Plapinger	Julie Bégin
Jack Mingo	Julia Papps
Erin Barrett	Media Masters
Malcolm Hillgartner	Brendan & Avery, B.R.I.T.
Jahnna Beecham	*Instant Genius*
Jeff Bahr	The Nation of Canada
William Dooling	Eddie Deezen
Valerie Harrison	Publishers Group West
Michael Kerr	Bloomsbury Books
Christine DeGueron	Trish & Tony
James Greene Jr.	Raincoast Books
Scarab Media	Porter the Wonder Dog
Amelia & Greta Zeve	Thomas Crapper

CONTENTS

Because the BRI understands your reading needs, we've
divided the contents by length as well as subject.

Short—a quick read
Medium—2 to 3 pages
Long—for those extended visits, when something
a little more involved is required
* Extended—for those leg-numbing experiences

WE KEEP GOING...AND GOING...AND GOING...

The question I'm most often asked (other than, "When are you coming out of there?") is, "Uncle John, what is it about this series that makes it so popular?" The answer, I believe, comes down to the fact that when you pick up a *Bathroom Reader*, you're not just reading *one* book, but several—even dozens. How so? Within these 540 pages you'll find a history tome, a weird news anthology, a science text, a dictionary, a how-to manual, a sports magazine, a joke book, a business primer, a quotations collection, and the list goes on. You could say it's...endless.

Just flip to any page and you'll find something new to entertain you—it may make you laugh, think, or just shake your head in amazement. For example:

• **Weirdness:** Alfonzo the Slobberer and other oddly named rulers, beef-scented cologne, and trees that paint pictures.

• **History unleashed:** The story of a flag called "Old Glory," the handgun that fired rockets, and the great moon hoax...of 1835.

• **Myths and Legends:** Totem polls, Pecos Bill, Sciopod the one-legged monster, the rebirth of Jack in the Box, and the scariest ghost story we've ever told.

• **That's entertainment:** Musicians who snubbed the music industry (to great success), the future of 3-D television, Rocky Balboa's climb to the top, and Jar Jar Binks' plunge to the bottom.

• **Good sports:** How Indiana changed basketball, how to talk NASCAR, and Haaaaai-YA!—the history of judo.

• **Wordplay:** More of your favorites—including Tom Swifties, flubbed headlines, tongue twisters, cosmic questions from comedians, and endangered words on the brink of exuviation.

• **Life's BIG instruction book:** How to get furniture dents out of your carpet, how to successfully pull off the short con, and how to tell if you've been abducted by aliens.

Before you dive into this bottomless bowl of fun, I'd like to give a special round of applause to Amy for keeping everything together with such poise and good humor. To Brian, John, Jay, and Thom for continuing to create amazing bathroom reading treasures. To Claudia and Claire for declunking our clunky copy. To Angie for providing us with those endlessly engrossing little facts we call running feet. (Flame throwers are legal in 40 states. Who knew?) To Michael B., who recently advised us that he has now been designing *Bathroom Reader* covers for more than half of his life.

But the biggest round of applause goes to you, our readers. And to answer another question I'm often asked, "What makes a typical *Bathroom Reader* fan?" We've learned that after more than 20 years of making these books, there's really no such thing as a typical fan—our readers come from all walks of life and span generations. Some grandparents have told us that our books help them connect with their grandkids. Younger readers have thanked us for helping them get through high school. Older readers have thanked us for helping them get through college. (One parent even told us that our books helped her son get *into* college.)

In the end, there's one thing that every *Bathroom Reader* fan (the BRI included) has in common: an insatiable appetite to know our world better—the good, the bad, the ugly, and the amazing. So no matter who you are, you'll find a whole lot to love in these pages. So get reading, and reading, and reading…

And as always,

Go with the Flow!

—Uncle John, the BRI Staff,
and Porter the Wonderdog

YOU'RE MY INSPIRATION

*It's always interesting to find out where the architects of
pop culture get their ideas. These may surprise you.*

FERRIS BUELLER. One of writer/director John Hughes's
models for the title character of his 1986 film was his childhood friend Edward McNally. Like Ferris, McNally was tormented by a school official over his frequent absences, impersonated
his father to sneak his friends out of school, and tried to reverse
the odometer on a "borrowed" sports car. Ferris's shy, nerdy friend
Cameron was based on Hughes himself.

IRON MAN. In the early 1960s, comic book writer Stan Lee got
the inspiration for the superhero and his alter ego—wealthy industrialist Tony Stark—from wealthy industrialist Howard Hughes,
who, like Stark, constructed bizarre aircraft.

HALLE BERRY. The Oscar-winning actress was named after the
landmark Halle Building, home of the Halle Brothers department
store, in Berry's hometown of Cleveland, Ohio.

THE WONDER YEARS. The 1989–93 sitcom, set from 1969 to
'73, depicted a teenager (Fred Savage) growing up in the suburbs.
The title of the show wasn't a reference to the "wonder" a kid
feels as he discovers the world—it came from a 1960s ad campaign
from the 1960s for Wonder Bread, which told kids to eat it
through their "wonder years" of adolescence.

MICHAEL JORDAN. When Jordan's older brother Larry played
high-school basketball, his jersey number was 45. When Jordan
started playing, he picked #23—that's half of 45, rounded up.
Why? Because he hoped to be half the player that Larry was.

TWILIGHT. One of author Stephanie Meyer's favorite books is
the 1813 Jane Austen classic *Pride and Prejudice*, which concerns a
lonely young woman who falls in love with a seemingly out-of-
reach sophisticated gentleman. That provided the inspiration for
Twilight, a novel about a lonely teenage girl who falls in love with
a seemingly out-of-reach sophisticated…vampire.

WARNING LABELS

Some things in life go without saying...but there's always the occasional genius who has to be told not to hold the moving end of a chain saw.

On Cadbury Whole Nut Milk Chocolate bar: "Contains nuts, milk."

On a massager: "Do not use while unconscious."

On shin guards: "Cannot protect any part of the body they do not cover."

On a fireplace lighter: "Do not use near flame or sparks."

On a hot beverage cup: "Caution: Hot beverages are hot!"

On a Frisbee: "May contain small parts."

On an electric cattle prod: "For use on animals only."

On a cordless phone: "Do not put lit candles on phone."

On cat litter: "Safe for use around pets."

On an iPod shuffle: "Do not eat iPod shuffle."

On a lottery ticket: "Do not iron."

On a Jet Ski: "Never use a lit match or open flame to check fuel level."

On sunglasses: "Not suitable for driving under conditions of poor light."

On a bottle of mineral water: "Suitable for vegetarians."

On PMS relief medicine: "Do not use if you have prostate problems."

On a bottle of champagne: "Remove label before placing in microwave."

On a Slush Puppie: "Ice may be cold."

On a chain saw: "Do not hold the wrong end of a chain saw."

On a toilet plunger: "Do not use near power lines."

On baby lotion: "Keep away from children."

On a 500-piece puzzle: "Some assembly required."

On a superhero costume: "You cannot save the world!"

If you gave birth on a plane flying over the U.S., your child would automatically be a U.S. citizen.

MYTH-CONCEPTIONS

*"Common knowledge" is frequently wrong. Here are some
examples of things that many people believe...but
that, according to our sources, just aren't true.*

Myth: The Wild West was a violent, lawless wasteland where murder and gunfights occurred every day.

Truth: It's portrayed that way in Western movies because it's dramatic. But during the heyday of the Old West (1870–85) the five major towns of Dodge City, Ellsworth, Caldwell, Abilene, and Wichita had a combined total of 45 murders. That's a rate of 1 per 100,000 residents. The present day is far deadlier than the Wild West. The 2007 murder rate in the United States was 5.6 per 100,000—more than five times as dangerous as the "Wild" West.

Myth: Eighteenth-century composer Antonio Salieri hated his rival, Wolfgang Amadeus Mozart, and may even have poisoned him.

Truth: The common perception of Salieri comes from the play and movie *Amadeus*, which took a lot of dramatic license. Salieri wasn't as gifted as Mozart (who is?), but he was a respected musician who wrote more than 40 popular operas and tutored Schubert and Beethoven. Salieri and Mozart even collaborated on the cantata *Per la ricuperata salute di Ophelia* in 1785, a few years before Mozart died...of rheumatic fever, not poison.

Myth: Holland is another name for the Netherlands.

Truth: Holland is a region of the Netherlands, not another name for the country itself. Today, the region is split into two provinces: North Holland and South Holland. From the 10th to the 16th century, it was an autonomous country, but ever since has been part of the Netherlands.

Myth: Mice love cheese.

Truth: Sure, they'll eat it if it's in a mousetrap, but the fact is that mice will eat pretty much anything—they're scavengers. They actually prefer sweets. The reason cheese is used in mousetraps is because it's fragrant, which lures the mouse to the trap.

Adding marigold petals to chicken feed will make egg yolks a brighter yellow.

BUTTERFLY FACTS

How odd—when we first wrote this page, it was called "caterpillar facts."

- There are around 24,000 known species of butterflies (and about 140,000 species of moths).

- Butterflies can't see the full color spectrum—they see reds, greens, and yellows, but not blues or greens. They can, however, see ultraviolet (UV) rays, which are invisible to humans.

- World's largest butterfly: the Queen Alexandra's birdwing from New Guinea, with a wingspan of 11 inches.

- When they emerge from their cocoons, butterflies are fully grown and remain that size until they die.

- The average butterfly weighs about as much as two flower petals.

- Butterflies don't pee. They drink enough liquid for subsistence. Any extra is emitted as a pure water mist from their abdomens.

- Most butterflies live for two to three weeks. The Brimstone lives the longest—up to 10 months.

- World's fastest butterfly: the Monarch. It can fly at speeds of up to 17 mph.

- If a butterfly loses part of a wing, it can still fly.

- Butterflies don't have lungs. They inhale oxygen directly into their bodies through small openings in their abdomens called *spiracles*.

- Butterflies are among the world's most prominent pollinators, second only to bees.

- Where do butterflies sleep? Between large blades of grass or underneath leaves.

- Few butterfly species fly at night. The Northern Pearl Eye does, and it has extra ears on its wings to help it detect nocturnal predators, such as bats.

- Butterflies clean themselves in mud puddles.

- Butterflies are cold-blooded; they can't produce internal heat like mammals. They warm up their flying muscles by lying in the sun. Once their internal temperature reaches 86°F, they're off.

OOPS!

It's always fun to read about other people's blunders.
So go ahead and feel superior for a few minutes.

STAYING ON TRACK

A Toronto police officer reporting to a robbery in January 2008 parked his squad car next to a convenience store, which was adjacent to some train tracks. While investigating the crime, a train rumbled past the store and demolished his squad car. "Maybe it was a little bit *on* the tracks," the officer admitted.

THE LONG AND SHORT OF THINGS

Due to a birth defect, a Swedish police officer's right leg was slightly longer than his left leg. So in 2008, he found a surgeon who agreed to shorten the right one so that his legs would be equal. But the surgery was botched: The knee joint was put back in the wrong position, and one of the screws they used to hold the joint together came loose. During a second surgery, the doctor discovered another problem with the first surgery, which required a third one. That one was slightly botched, too, requiring a fourth. Each time, the surgeon had to take a little more off of the patient's right leg—which had been two and a half centimeters longer than the left. Now it's five centimeters shorter than the left.

FIRE SAFETY 101

While firefighters in Honolulu, Hawaii, were at the scene of a traffic accident in 2009, they received a call about a fire...back at their firehouse. The cause: They'd been cooking food on the stove and had forgotten to turn it off when the emergency call came in for the traffic accident. The firehouse fire caused $25,000 in damage.

CSI: OOPS

Police in southern Germany feared that a female serial killer was running loose. After comparing evidence gathered over a period of 15 years, they noticed the same woman's DNA was present at 40 crime scenes, linking her to dozens of robberies and three murders. It wasn't until 2009 that police made a major breakthrough in the

---

case: The matching DNA samples didn't come from the evidence, they came from the cotton swabs that had been used to collect it. They concluded that a batch of cotton had been accidentally contaminated by a female worker at the factory many years earlier. The crimes remain unsolved.

LOWER EDUCATION

At the end of the 2008–09 school year, a fifth-grade teacher in California (her name was not released to the press) decided to make a present for her students: a DVD featuring the year's best class moments. When some of the kids (and their parents) watched it at home, they were shocked when footage of a class field trip suddenly cut to a very naughty scene featuring the teacher and a man in one of *their* best moments. The teacher was mortified when she found out; she apologized profusely and got all of the DVDs back. Because the teacher is otherwise well respected, school officials called it an "honest mistake" and let her keep her job.

MAN VS. DRYER

In 2009, 42-year-old Dave Chapman was doing a load of laundry at a friend's house in Waipopo, New Zealand. That evening, thinking his friend had put his laundry in the dryer earlier, Chapman went to the laundry room to change. "By then, I'd had a fair bit to drink," he later said. Chapman removed all his clothes except his T-shirt, and then looked inside the front-loading dryer for a clean pair of underwear. He couldn't find any, so he stuck his head inside. Still no underwear. So he climbed in even farther, past his shoulders...and got stuck. And the dryer was still hot. Chapman started thrashing about but couldn't get out. He did manage to dislodge the dryer from on top of the washer, however, and dryer and drunken man crashed down onto the floor. His friends rushed in but were unable to free him (or stop laughing). So they called for help. A few minutes later, rescue personnel arrived to free the half-naked man, whom they described as "agitated." It took two firefighters to hold onto the dryer and two more to pull Chapman out by his legs. He was bruised and had mild burns, but was otherwise okay. Only then did he find out that his underwear was still in the washing machine.

TECH SUPPORT

Believe it or not, all of these calls are real.

Caller: I'm having a problem with my mouse. It's squeaking.
Tech: I'm sorry, did you say squeaking?
Caller: That's right. The faster I move it across the screen, the louder it squeaks.
Tech: Are you pressing your mouse up against the screen?
Caller: Well, sure! The message says, "Click here to continue."

Caller: My computer has locked up, and no matter how many times I type "eleven," it won't unfreeze.
Tech: What do you mean, "type eleven?"
Caller: The message on my screen says, "Error Type 11."

Tech: Type "fix," with an "f."
Caller: Is that "f," as in "fix"?

Tech: Click on "cancel."
Caller: Capital?
Tech: "Cancel."
Caller: Sorry, it only says "OK" and "cancel."

Caller: I was printing something.
Tech: From before you called?
Caller: No, from Microsoft Word.

Tech: I need you to right-click on the Desktop.
Caller: Okay.
Tech: Did you get a pop-up menu?
Caller: No.
Tech: Okay. Right click again. Do you see a pop-up menu?
Caller: No.
Tech: Sir, can you tell me what you have done up until this point?
Caller: Sure. You told me to write "click" and I wrote "click."

Tech: Okay ma'am, do you see the button on the right-hand side of your mouse?
Caller: No, there's a printer and a phone on the right-hand side of my mouse.

Caller: Now what do I do?
Tech: What is the prompt on the screen?
Caller: It's asking for "Enter Your Last Name."
Tech: Okay, so type in your last name.
Caller: How do you spell that?

Tech: Tell me, is the cursor still there?
Caller: No, I'm alone right now.

What did the *Apollo 17* crew use to repair a fender on the lunar rover? Duct tape.

FOOD ORIGINS

History that's good enough to eat (or drink).

LATTE

If you ordered a *caffe latte* in Italy, you'd get a cup of coffee with some milk in it. (In Italian, it literally means "coffee with milk.") You *wouldn't* get espresso combined with steamed milk. That's an American latte, a variation on cappuccino that was created in 1959 in Berkeley, California. Lino Meiorin, owner of Caffe Mediterraneum, came up with it when customers who were unfamiliar with Italian coffee drinks ordered a cappuccino and, disliking the strong taste, asked for extra milk. Meiorin served his first lattes in bowls and pint glasses.

FAST FOOD KIDS' MEAL

The first fast-food chain to offer a combo meal of kid-size portions (with a free toy) was Salt Lake City-based Arctic Circle, a burger joint popular on the West Coast from the 1960s to the '80s. Introduced in 1961, the Arctic Circle Kids' Meal consisted of a hamburger, fries, soda, and a toy prize, all inside a brightly colored box with games and puzzles on it. The format became a standard part of every fast-food restaurant's menu. Examples: Burger King's Kids Club Meal, McDonald's Happy Meal, and Sonic's Wacky Pack.

THE SHIRLEY TEMPLE

In the 1930s, child actress Shirley Temple was the biggest star in Hollywood and she frequently went to dinner at Chasen's, a restaurant popular with the film industry. In 1938, on the occasion of her 10th birthday, the bartenders at Chasen's concocted a drink just for her—alcohol-free and caffeine-free. The original recipe: two parts ginger ale, one part orange juice, a tablespoon of grenadine syrup, and a maraschino cherry garnish. Today, the drink is more commonly made with 7-Up instead of ginger ale, and without orange juice. Temple was such a big star that the drink caught on. Today there are alcoholic variations, such as the Shirley Temple Black, which adds Johnnie Walker Black Whiskey or Kahlua and plays on the star's married name.

Madonna and Celine Dion are both distant cousins of Prince Charles's wife, Camilla.

WHY ARE THEY CALLED "TANKS"?

And other interesting word origins to read on the tank.

TERM: Jerky
MEANING: Dried or cured meat
ORIGIN: It comes from the Quechua language, spoken in the Andes region of South America since before the time of the Incas. Their word *ch'arki* means "dried flesh." Spanish explorers, possibly as early as the 1500s, borrowed it and it became the Spanish word *charqui*. That migrated to English, and by the 1840s it had become "jerky."

TERM: Tank
MEANING: An armored, heavily armed military vehicle that moves on tracks
ORIGIN: During World War I, the British military started working on a new specialized combat vehicle. The project was so top-secret that the workers who were making the vehicles didn't even know what they were—the government told them that they'd be used to carry water during desert operations. The workers called them "water-carriers"…until someone pointed out that the name could be abbreviated to "WC"—meaning "water-closet" or "toilet." So they started calling them "water tanks," and then "tanks." (Tanks made their combat debut at the Battle of the Somme in Northern France in September 1916.)

TERM: Hush puppies
MEANING: A classic food from the American South
ORIGIN: Hush puppies are deep-fried balls of cornmeal batter, often seasoned with onions or pepper. The most common explanation for the name says that they were originally made around campfires (the story often has the campers being Confederate soldiers), where they were tossed to hungry, yelping dogs with the command "Hush, puppies!" Over time that became the name of

---

Collisions with birds cause more than a billion dollars' worth of damage to aircraft each year.

the food. The oldest documented use of the term goes back to a 1918 publication on American English called *Dialect Notes*.

TERM: Chestnut
MEANING: The nut from a chestnut tree, or the tree itself
ORIGIN: The Ancient Greek word for chestnut was *kastanea*. That could have meant either "nut from Castanea," a city in Turkey, or "nut from Castana," a city in central Greece. Both regions were (and still are) renowned for their chestnuts. *Kastanea* passed into Latin as *castanea*, which became *chastaigne* in Old French. That went to Middle English as *chasteine*, and around 1570 became *chestnut*.

TERM: Urban legend
MEANING: Modern folktales often thought to be factual
ORIGIN: Why are they called "urban" when they often don't involve cities in any way? Because they're named after Jeffrey Jack Urban, a farmer from Yankton, South Dakota. He was a notorious teller of wild, almost-believable stories in the 1930s. Local people started calling any such tales "Urban legends" after Jeffrey Jack. *(Just kidding. We made that up.)*

The truth is that in the 1940s and '50s, folklorists started collecting modern American legends and noticed that they had different characteristics than older, rural-based legends did. They called these legends "urban belief tales" or "city tales," the words "urban" and "city" indicating their darker, more modern themes, even though the stories weren't necessarily based in cities. The name evolved to become "urban legend" in the 1960s. The first recorded use is usually credited to folklorist Richard Dorson in the 1968 book, *Our Living Traditions*. (Dorson is also credited with popularizing the term "fakelore." For more on that, see page 435.)

*   *   *

"Of course I can keep secrets. It's the people I tell them to that can't keep them."

—Anthony Haden-Guest

EVERYDAY HEROES

*Here's something to think about: Every time you walk out your door,
you could be faced with an opportunity to save someone's life.
Are you ready for it? These people were.*

STEERED RIGHT

Nearly every weekday for 30 years, John Beatty drove his pickup truck across San Francisco's Golden Gate Bridge on his way to and from work. One morning in late 2007, the 50-year-old electrician suddenly came up on a slow-moving Jeep Grand Cherokee. He hit the brakes and went to pass the Jeep, only to see the driver slumped over the steering wheel. "It began to cross into the fast lane, and people were using that lane to pass her," Beatty later said. "On the other side of the road, traffic was flying northbound. I thought, 'I'm not letting this happen.'" He drove in front of the Jeep and let it hit his pickup. Displaying some impressive driving skills, Beatty was able to steer the SUV toward the right lane. At first, other drivers honked impatiently at the slow procession, but once they understood what was happening, they gave Beatty the space he needed to get the Jeep safely off the road. Sadly, the unconscious driver later died from her condition, but California Highway Patrol officers credit Beatty with preventing what could have been a deadly collision into oncoming highway traffic. "I lead a kind of low-key life," admitted Beatty. "Excitement's not my bag."

RAIL BRAVE

Veeramuthu Kalimuthu, known as Kali, stood on a subway platform during a busy New York City afternoon rush hour in 2008. A new train rolled in every three minutes, and Kali's was about a minute away. That's when he heard screams and saw that a man had fallen onto the tracks from the platform on the opposite side of the station. Kali watched and waited for someone to help, but no one did. Knowing time was running out, he jumped down from his own side onto the train tracks, and then jumped over the third rail, which carries 600 deadly volts of electricity. When he finally got across, Kali—at 5'5" and 150 pounds—realized the man was nearly twice his size…and unconscious (he'd been drinking). Kali tried to lift the man, but was unable to get him all the way up onto the platform. He did, however, lift him high enough so that people up on top could pull him to safety. Then, as bystanders applauded, Kali jumped back over the third rail and quickly scooted up to his own platform just in time to catch his train home. Kali's humble explanation of his good deed: "People should help people."

IT CAME FROM ABOVE

At around 11:00 a.m. on a Monday in April 2008, mail carrier Lisa Harrell walked into a front yard in Albany, New York, to deliver an Express Mail package. Harrell, a 13-year Postal Service veteran, stepped up onto the porch and rang the bell. All of a sudden, something brushed her shoulder. Without thinking, Harrell extended her arms and discovered that she was holding a baby. The one-year-old girl was crying but otherwise fine. Had Harrell not been there, the infant would have landed on the concrete. The mother ran outside, grabbed her daughter, thanked Harrell, and then ran off to her own mother's house down the street. (It was later revealed that the baby had been sitting on a bed next to an open window when she rolled out.) Making the story even stranger, normally Harrell wouldn't have been at that house until after 2:00 p.m., but because she was delivering an Express Mail package that day, she had to get there by noon. "I was pretty shaken up," said Harrell. "I couldn't finish the route."

DIDN'T SEE THAT ONE COMING

In Fenton, Missouri, a man who was later identified only as "Jerry" heard some strange noises coming from his neighbor's apartment. Aware that the woman who lived there wasn't home, he had a gut feeling that it was an intruder. So Jerry went outside and kicked open his neighbor's door. Whoever was inside slammed it shut again and locked it. So Jerry waited outside until his neighbor returned home. When she did, she told him that no one should have been inside her place. They called the police, who came and apprehended the intruder—later revealed to be an ex-con who'd planned to wait in the apartment and attack the woman when she arrived home. Police hailed Jerry as a hero. One other thing about him: He's legally blind.

BIONIC MEN

Part man, part machine—and all real stories of people with robot parts.

FINGER. Finnish computer programmer Jerry Jalava lost his ring finger in a motorcycle accident. He replaced it with a prosthetic finger of his own design—it's also a computer flash drive. It looks like a normal finger (a shiny plastic one), but Jalava can pull back the nail, plug it into the USB slot on his computer, and store data files. (Ironically, these drives are sometimes called "thumb drives.")

KNEE. Brad Halling served in the Army's Special Forces during the 1993 U.S. intervention in Somalia. A grenade hit his helicopter, and Halling lost his leg in the attack. In 2007 he received the most sophisticated joint replacement ever built: the Power Knee. Connected to two prosthetic leg parts, a microprocessor in the $100,000 device receives a signal from a small transmitter strapped to Halling's other leg. The microprocessor senses how he's moving and directs the robotic knee's electric motor to copy the muscle movements. In short, he can walk normally. The downsides: It makes a loud whirring noise and has to be charged every night.

EYE. Canadian filmmaker Rob Spence lost the use of his right eye in a childhood gun accident. So, inspired by the tiny camera on his cell phone, in 2009, Spence decided to make the ultimate first-person-POV film...by installing a prosthetic eye that is also a camera. A team from the University of Toronto is building the eye-camera (or "Eyeborg," as Spence calls it), which will record video and send it wirelessly to a computer.

BONES. Researchers in the U.S. military may have found a way to regenerate human limbs. They use a technique called *nanoscaffolding*, in which tiny, cell-sized nets made of fiber optics hundreds of times thinner than a human hair are attached to the end of a missing limb. This structure acts as a framework where cells can congregate and bond into bones and tissue, growing through tiny holes in the scaffolding. The procedure isn't quite ready to try out on humans yet, but scientists believe that one day it may also be used to generate new organs.

Blast off! NASA uses trampolines as part of its training regimen.

CONFESSIONS!

In their continuing quest to entertain us, today's hottest celebrities divulge their innermost secrets!

"I ate a bug once. It was flying around me. I was trying to get it away. It went right in my mouth. It was so gross!"

—**Hilary Duff**

"I used to think I actually *was* Batman."

—**Justin Timberlake**

"I'd kiss a frog even if there was no promise of a Prince Charming popping out of it. I love frogs."

—**Cameron Diaz**

"I always cry when I watch myself on-screen."

—**Clint Eastwood**

"I like cars and basketball. But you know what I like more? Bananas."

—**Frankie Muniz**

"What kills me is that everybody thinks I like jazz."

—**Samuel L. Jackson**

"I'm horrible to live with. I forget to flush the toilet."

—**Megan Fox**

"The kindest word to describe my performance in school was 'sloth.'"

—**Harrison Ford**

"I cheated a lot at school. I just couldn't sit and do homework. I usually sat next to someone extremely smart."

—**Leonardo DiCaprio**

"All reporters ask exactly the same questions, and I say exactly the same answers. I don't have to think; I can just stand there like a broken record going LALALA…."

—**Emma Watson**

"I don't keep track of paper that well. My desk is a mess."

—**Barack Obama**

"I've never seen a phone bill of mine in my life."

—**Paris Hilton**

"I used to use the name 'Mr. Stench.' It was funny to be in a posh hotel and hear a very proper concierge call out, 'Mr. Stench, please.'"

—**Johnny Depp**

The week that it debuted, *Cheers* finished dead last in the Nielsen ratings.

THAT'S AMORE?

Love is a many-splendored thing…except when it isn't.

STUPID CUPID

James Miller's girlfriend broke up with him in early 2009. So on Valentine's Day, the 19-year-old British carpenter dressed up like Cupid (wearing only boxer shorts) and ran across the field at a Premier League soccer match shooting roses with a bow and arrow toward his lost love, who was sitting in the stands. Did it work? "If he honestly thought I would be impressed, then he must be more stupid than he looks," she said. Adding insult to injury, Miller was banned from the stadium for three years and fired from his job. "That sort of behavior always works some romantic magic in the movies," he said. "Now I have no girlfriend and no job."

WHO'S SORRY NOW?

When police arrived on the scene in Palm City, Florida, in April 2009, Derick Culberson, 22, was sitting next to his truck—his hands and ankles bound with zip ties. He told them he'd been robbed at gunpoint by two men. More than a dozen officers began to canvass the area…until a cop happened to notice the same brand of zip ties in Culberson's truck. When confronted by cops, Culberson admitted he'd made the whole thing up. Why? His girlfriend had recently left him, and he wanted her to hear about his "ordeal" and feel sorry for him and take him back. (She didn't.)

SLEEP THE NIGHT AWAY

After working a 14-hour day as a courier in Christchurch, New Zealand, 18-year-old Tim Roberts wanted nothing more than to go to sleep, but his fiancée got upset when he tried to call off their movie date. So Roberts grudgingly showed up at the theater just as the romantic comedy was starting. He was fast asleep within minutes. When he awoke, he was all by himself in the dark, locked theater, the movie having long since ended. Upset that his fiancée had left him there, and still groggy from having been asleep, he stumbled out into the lobby…and tripped the security alarm. "It was this horrible, ear-piercing, screeching sound," he said. Roberts tried to leave, but the doors couldn't be opened without keys. The situation got scary when the police rushed the building with their guns drawn. Somehow, Roberts was able to communicate his dilemma, and finally got out via the fire escape. The episode convinced the couple that they weren't as compatible as they thought they were, and they made a "mutual" decision to call off their engagement.

OH, WHAT A TANGLED WEB SITE

In 2007 a married couple in Connecticut (names not released to the press) began receiving strange phone calls that were very sexually suggestive, and all for the wife. The husband did a Web search and discovered that his wife had posted several lewd profiles on adult dating sites. She flat-out denied it, so he asked around and found the real culprit: his ex-girlfriend, Pilar Stofega, who was hell-bent on breaking up the couple. Stofega, 34, was arrested and charged with second-degree harassment. When asked why she did it, she explained, "To be vindictive."

TRADING PLACES

Victoria Thorp, 19, was so desperate to see her boyfriend that she broke *into* a detention center in Gainesville, Florida, where he was being held on drug charges. Her boyfriend, 18-year-old Aquilla Wilson, was equally desperate to get *out*, so he jumped out of the window that she had come in through. When the guards arrived, he was gone, and she was still there. Thorp was charged for "aiding in a prisoner's escape." She was jailed; he remains at large.

I WANT HALF!

After 18 years of marriage, a Cambodian man named Moeun Sarim accused his wife, Vat Navy, of having an affair with a policeman in their town. She denied it, but he didn't believe her. He filed for divorce in October 2008, and in the settlement, he got half of their estate—literally. He and some of his relatives showed up at the 20-by-24-foot wooden house with saws in hand. Police tried to talk him out of it, but Sarim was adamant. The sawers started cutting the house right down the middle, loading the parts into pickup trucks. The remaining half of the house— although a bit draftier—was still structurally sound, so Navy kept living there. "Very strange," she said, "but this is what he wanted."

METROPOLIS CONFIDENTIAL

Random facts about Superman.

• In the comic books, when Clark goes into a phone booth to emerge as Superman, what does he do with his clothes? He has a small pouch hidden on the underside of his cape.

• Lois Lane is not Superman's first love. He once dated a girl named Lana Lang, who later became a superhero named Insect Queen.

• While Superman's city of Metropolis is obviously a stand-in for New York City, co-creator/artist Joe Shuster modeled the city's skyline off of his hometown of Toronto.

• Superman's popularity is almost entirely confined to the United States. In fact, Richard Lester, the director of *Superman III*, grew up in England and had never heard of the character.

• Little-known Kryptonite fact: After Superman succumbs to an individual piece of Kryptonite once, he's forever immune to that one piece.

• For the 1990s TV series *Lois and Clark,* the *Daily Planet* editor Perry White's catchphrase from the 1950's TV series *The Adventures of Superman* was updated from "great Caesar's ghost!" to "great shades of Elvis!"

• The first three movies did well at the box office, but the low-budget *Superman IV* did not, earning just $15 million in 1987. Assuming this meant that superhero movies were dead, the studio, Cannon, canceled a planned *Spider-Man* movie. (Oops.)

• According to *Superman III*, Kryptonite can be synthesized. Ingredients: 15% plutonium, 18% tantalum, 24% promethium, 28% xenon, 11% dialium, and 4% mercury.

• There was a Superman broadway musical. Staged in 1966, *It's a Bird...It's a Plane... It's Superman* was a campy take (a "ten-time Nobel Prize-losing scientist" wants to kill Superman; scenes are intercut

Average weight of a Macy's Thanksgiving Day Parade balloon: 500 pounds.

with go-go dancing), inspired by the *Batman* TV series of the day. It lasted just three months on Broadway.

• First-ever Superman: radio actor Bud Collyer on *The Adventures of Superman* from 1940–51. He received no on-air credit because producers wanted audiences to believe Superman was real. Collyer became better known as host of the TV game shows *Beat the Clock* (1950–61) and *To Tell the Truth* (1956–68).

• Though Superman first appeared in comics in 1938, creators Jerry Siegel and Joe Shuster came up with the original incarnation of Superman in 1932…as an evil, bald telepath who wants to take over the world.

• Actor Nicolas Cage is such a Superman fan that he named his son Kal-El (Superman's name on his home planet, Krypton).

• Superman had several pets from Krypton, including Krypto the Superdog, Kal-El's family dog who makes it to Earth; Beppo, a monkey who stows away on baby Kal-El's rocket; and Kelex, a robot who serves as the housekeeper in Superman's Fortress of Solitude.

A MINI-ENCYCLOPEDIA OF KRYPTONITE

Green Kryptonite: Deadly.

Red Kryptonite: Causes weird, erratic behavior.

Blue Kryptonite: Safe for Superman, but deadly to Bizarros, who live in an alternate universe where everything is the opposite.

X-Kryptonite: Gives Earthlings superpowers for a limited time.

Gold Kryptonite: Removes superpowers permanently.

White Kryptonite: Kills any plant life from any world.

Jewel Kryptonite: Pieces of Krypton's Jewel Mountains that allow residents of the Phantom Zone—a two-dimensional "prison dimension"—to focus their energy and make objects in the outside world explode.

Black Kryptonite: Effects unknown.

EATING CONTESTS TO AVOID

You'd think that with all the donut, hot dog, and pie eating contests there are in the world, there'd be no call for the competitions listed below. Try telling that to the International Federation of Competitive Eating (IFOCE), which has certified all of the following contests.

CRANBERRY SAUCE

Titleholder: Juliet Lee, who polished off 13.24 *pounds* of the sauce in eight minutes in November 2007.

Additional Accomplishments: Lee, who once taught chemistry at the University of Nanjing in China, also won first prize at the 2008 Ultimate Eating Tournament after she downed seven chicken wings, one pound of nachos, three hot dogs, two personal pizzas, and three Italian ices in 7 minutes, 13 seconds.

HAGGIS

Description: For the uninitiated, haggis is a traditional Scottish dish that consists of sheep's lungs, liver, and heart that are combined with oatmeal, onion, spices, and other ingredients, then stuffed into a sheep's stomach and boiled for three hours.

Titleholder: Eric Livingston, who ate three pounds of haggis in 8 minutes in 2008.

RAMEN NOODLES

Titleholder: Timothy Janus, who slurped down 10.5 pounds of noodles in 8 minutes in October 2007.

Additional Accomplishments: Janus, a day trader who uses the name "Eater X" and wears makeup to disguise his true identity, currently holds six eating records, including nigiri sushi (141 pieces in 6 minutes), tamales (71 in 12 minutes), and burritos (11.81 pounds in 10 minutes).

CHILI SPAGHETTI

Titleholder: "Humble" Bob Shoudt put away 13.5 pounds of

"Cincinnati Chili" (a thin, meaty chili flavored with oregano, cinnamon, and cloves, served over spaghetti) in 10 minutes in September 2008.

Additional Accomplishments: Shoudt also holds the record for beef brisket BBQ sandwiches (34.75 sandwiches in 10 minutes), and the miniature-hamburger two-minute speed-eating record—39 burgers. When he isn't competing, he's a vegetarian.

PICKLED BEEF TONGUE (WHOLE)

Titleholder: Dominic "The Doginator" Cardo, who consumed an entire 3-pound tongue, plus "a few bites" of a second tongue, in 12 minutes on Fox TV's prime-time *Glutton Bowl* in 2002.

BUTTER (¼-pound sticks)

Titleholder: Don Lerman, who goes by the name "Moses" and is another Glutton Bowl winner, downed seven ¼-pound sticks of salted butter in 5 minutes.

Additional Accomplishments: Lerman, an IFOCE Lifetime Achievement Award Winner, also holds records in baked beans (6 pounds in 1 minute, 46 seconds), bologna (2.76 pounds in 6 minutes), quarter-pound hamburgers (11 ¼ in 10 minutes), and other categories. He placed third in the *Glutton Bowl's* cow brain eating finals, losing to Takeru Kobayashi—the Tiger Woods of "gurgitation," as it's known in the trade. Kobayashi, who is most famous for winning the Nathan's Famous 4th of July hot dog eating contest six years in a row (2001–06), consumed 57 entire cow brains, or 17.7 pounds' worth, in 15 minutes to win first prize.

HARD-BOILED EGGS

Titleholder: In 2003 Sonya "The Black Widow" Thomas downed 65 eggs—more than five dozen—in 6 minutes, 40 seconds, smashing the old record of 38 eggs in 8 minutes. Thomas swallowed the eggs whole. So why'd she stop at 65? The organizers ran out of eggs.

Additional Accomplishments: Thomas, one of the biggest stars of the competitive eating world, holds 29 different world titles in foods as diverse as cheesecake (11 pounds in 9 minutes), chicken nuggets (80 nuggets in 5 minutes), crawfish jambalaya (9 pounds in 10 minutes), and oysters (46 dozen in 10 minutes). To keep her stomach in top form, Thomas eats one very large meal per day.

Technically, Christmas trees are edible. So why don't we eat them? They taste terrible.

When she worked as an assistant manager at Burger King, a typical daily meal consisted of one chicken Whopper, 20 chicken nuggets, three large orders of fries, and 64 ounces of diet soda, consumed over the course of a couple of hours. You might assume that Thomas is overweight, maybe even obese, but she's not. She exercises two hours a day, five days a week, to maintain her competitive edge. Her weight typically fluctuates between 98 and 105 pounds.

PICKLED JALAPEÑO PEPPERS

Titleholder: Richard "The Locust" LeFevre, a retired accountant, popped 247 pickled peppers at the Texas State Fair in 2006. (No word on who picked the peck of pickled peppers.)

Additional Accomplishments: Another living legend in the world of competitive eating, LeFevre, 63, has held records in 24-inch-diameter pizza slices (7 ½ extra-large slices in 15 minutes), birthday cake (5 pounds in 11 minutes, 26 seconds), chili (1 ½ gallons in 10 minutes), SPAM (6 pounds in 12 minutes), huevos rancheros (7 ¾ pounds in 10 minutes), and other categories. He weighs 132 pounds.

* * *

GURGITATION SECRETS OF THE PROS

Some tips we've collected from current and former IFOCE champs:

• Eat healthy in your daily diet. Avoid junk food.

• Eat fewer meals, but make each one larger to get your stomach used to accommodating large quantities of food. As a contest date approaches, eat larger and larger quantities of food.

• Exercise regularly, and lose weight! Belly fat surrounding your stomach can impair its ability to stretch out as needed when stuffed with hot dogs, beef tongue, hard-boiled eggs, etc. (This theory is especially popular with titleholders weighing under 125 pounds. It's much less popular with those weighing over 300 pounds.)

• Don't eat the night before an eating contest.

• If you start to feel sick during the contest, slow down! Gurgitators who regurgitate are disqualified on the spot.

• Kids, don't try this at home.

THE FIRST TRAIN ROBBERS

*Train robberies are such a common part of Western movies
that we forget that somebody had to be the first to do it.*

SOMETHING NEW

On October 16, 1866, brothers John and Simeon ("Sim") Reno and a third man, Frank Sparkes, boarded a train in Seymour, Indiana, and broke into the express car (where the money was kept) once the train was underway. After overpowering a guard, the men smashed open a safe and stole its contents—$10,000. They pushed a larger safe off the train at a spot where other members of the "Reno gang," including John and Sim's brothers Frank and Bill Reno, were waiting. An approaching posse forced the gang to flee before it could get the big safe open. Not the biggest haul in the world, but it was the very first train robbery in U.S. history.

END OF THE LINE

John Reno soon went to prison for robbing a courthouse; the rest of the gang kept robbing trains. Their second robbery netted $8,000; a third was thwarted by Pinkerton detectives. A fourth netted $96,000. Then the gang's luck ran out: While attempting a fifth train robbery, they were ambushed by Pinkertons, and though all but one of the robbers escaped, they were quickly rounded up. Three were arrested, then seized by vigilantes and hanged from a tree on July 20, 1868. A few days later three more gang members were captured and hanged from the same tree. Bill and Sim Reno were arrested at the end of July; then Frank Reno and another gang member named Charlie Anderson were caught in Canada and extradited to the U.S., where they were put in the same jail with Bill and Sim. All four men were hanged by a *third* lynch mob that stormed the jail on December 11, 1868.

The lynching of ten members of the Reno gang, which never numbered more than about 15 people, put it out of business for good. But newspaper coverage of the their exploits inspired other criminal gangs (the James-Younger gang, the Wild Bunch, the Dalton gang, etc.), who would soon follow in their footsteps. The era of Wild West train robberies had begun.

"Honest" Clint Reno was so named because he was the only brother not to join the Reno gang.

TITANIC, STARRING MACAULAY CULKIN

Some movie roles are so closely associated with a specific actor that it's hard to imagine he or she wasn't the first choice. But it happens all the time. Can you imagine, for example...

DRIVING MISS DAISY, STARRING LUCILLE BALL
Ball loved Alfred Uhry's Pulitzer Prize-winning play *Driving Miss Daisy*. In 1988, when she heard it was going to be turned into a movie, the 76-year-old actress went after the title role of the crotchety old Southern woman who develops a tender friendship with her African-American driver. Ball almost landed what would've been a career-capping comeback part, but right before producers Lili and Richard Zanuck made a decision, they got a phone call from her—she felt she was too ill to play the part. Indeed, by the time cameras rolled in early 1989, Ball had died.

TITANIC, STARRING MACAULAY CULKIN
By 1996 Culkin was a fading former child star (*Home Alone, Richie Rich*) who had pretty much quit show business, having not made a movie in three years. But in casting what would ultimately be the highest-grossing movie to date, *Titanic* producer/director James Cameron nearly hired Culkin for the male lead. When 20th Century Fox wanted him to cast Matthew McConaughey instead, Cameron compromised with a third option: critically acclaimed actor—and former child star—Leonardo DiCaprio.

CHARLIE'S ANGELS, STARRING ANGELINA JOLIE
As producers started work on this big-screen remake of the classic 1970s TV series, two of the three Angels were quickly cast: co-producer Drew Barrymore, who cast herself, and Cameron Diaz. The third slot proved more difficult to fill. It was first offered to Angelina Jolie, who turned it down because she didn't like the original TV show. Jada Pinkett Smith was also given a shot, but she decided to make Spike Lee's *Bamboozled* instead. Then producers considered (and rejected) Catherine Zeta-Jones, Liv Tyler,

two different Spice Girls, and singers Lauryn Hill and Aaliyah, who gave a good test performance but was ultimately considered too young. Nia Long landed the role, but backed out to film *Big Momma's House*, a less physically demanding movie than *Charlie's Angels*, because she was pregnant. British actress Thandie Newton replaced her, but had to drop out when filming for her previous movie, *Mission: Impossible 2*, ran over schedule. The role was finally offered to—and accepted by—*Ally McBeal* co-star Lucy Liu.

GREASE, STARRING HARRY REEMS

The family-friendly musical set in the squeaky-clean 1950s nearly co-starred a controversial, non-family-friendly figure of the 1970s. Adult-film actor Reems, best known for his part in the 1972 pornographic film *Deep Throat*, was cast to play Coach Calhoun, the Rydell High track coach. Reems had done legitimate theater before making porn films, which is how his agent was able to get him the role. But before the movie began filming, executives at Paramount Studios got nervous and fired Reems. Cast instead: real-life 1950s icon Sid Caesar.

THE CROW, STARRING CHRISTIAN SLATER

In *The Crow,* Eric Draven and his girlfriend are brutally murdered by a gang of street thugs, and a year later, he rises from the dead to avenge their deaths. Newcomer Brandon Lee, son of martial-arts legend Bruce Lee, was cast as Draven, but he wasn't the studio's first choice—they wanted Christian Slater. When Slater declined, Lee got the role. Sadly, Lee was killed on the set when a prop gun misfired. In a weird twist of fate, Slater's next role would come because of another premature death. He played the Interviewer in *Interview with the Vampire* after the original actor hired—Slater's friend River Phoenix—died of a drug overdose in 1993.

FORREST GUMP, STARRING DAVE CHAPPELLE

Chappelle auditioned for and won the role of Bubba Blue, the slow, backwoods-born, shrimp-loving soldier befriended by Forrest Gump during the Vietnam War. Even though he was a 21-year-old comedian struggling to land his first major acting job, Chappelle turned the part down because he thought it stereotyped blacks. The part went instead to Mykelti Williamson, who received an Oscar nomination for Best Supporting Actor.

THRASHINGS

The best games in sports are usually the ones that are close. But blowouts—legendary, record-breaking blowouts—are fun, too.

HORSE RACING

In more than 100 years of organized horse racing, only 11 horses have ever won the Triple Crown. The most impressive winner: Secretariat in 1973. While the horse's first two wins were definitive, they weren't phenomenal. In both the Kentucky Derby and the Preakness Stakes, Secretariat won by just two lengths both times—about 16 feet. For the third and final leg, the Belmont Stakes, it looked at first as if the race might actually end in a close, dramatic finish, as Secretariat and a horse named Sham were neck and neck out of the gates and around the first stretch. Then Secretariat pulled ahead…and kept pulling ahead…and kept pulling ahead. Ultimately, the horse won in a record 2 minutes and 24 seconds, ahead of Sham by a still-unmatched 31 lengths. Put another way, by the time Secretariat had finished the race, Sham was only two-thirds of the way done.

BASKETBALL

On March 2, 1962, the Philadelphia Warriors beat the New York Knicks 169–147, the largest combined point total in NBA history up to that point. But the most remarkable achievement belonged entirely to Warriors center Wilt Chamberlain. While he routinely scored more than 60 points in a game and held the single-game individual player record of 78 points, this night would be special. When Chamberlain reached 80 points in the second half, a hush overtook Philadelphia's Hershey Arena. Sensing a record-breaking night, his teammates decided to let Chamberlain carry the game, feeding him the ball whenever they could. Result: Of Philadelphia's 169 points, Chamberlain scored 100—the first, and so far only, time a player has made it to triple digits.

SOCCER

In a 2001 World Cup qualifying game against Tonga, Australia set a team record for most goals scored in a game, winning 22–0. Just two days later, the team broke its own record, playing American Samoa, at the time the lowest-ranked team in the world, at #203. Not surprisingly, Australia won the match. What is surprising is the final score: 31–0, the biggest blowout ever in a game sanctioned by FIFA, soccer's international governing body. Striker Archie Thompson scored 13 goals, the most ever scored by a single player in a game, shattering the mark of 10 by Sofus Nielsen of Denmark in the 1912 Olympics.

OLYMPIC HOCKEY

Hockey teams usually score between one and three goals per game. But in a 2008 qualifying match to determine which European teams would compete in the 2010 Winter Olympics, the women's hockey team from Slovakia proved that they belonged on the world's top athletic stage. They also proved that their competitor, the team from Bulgaria, did not. The Slovakians took 139 shots on goal, about seven times as many as in an average NHL game. What's uncommon was their rate of success: They scored 82 times. That's an average of one goal every 44 seconds. And while they dominated on offense, Slovakia's defense was equally astonishing. The Bulgarians didn't manage to score a single goal. Final score: 82–0.

GOLF

By 2000, four years after turning professional, Tiger Woods had already established himself as one of the best golfers of all time. In that year, he became the first golfer to win all four major PGA tournaments in a single 12-month period. The Masters, the British Open, and the PGA Championship were solid wins for Woods. But at the U.S. Open, it wasn't even close. After day two of the four-day tournament, he held a six-stroke lead—a record. After the third day, he led by 10—another record. His final score on day four: 272, or 12 strokes under par, destroying the previous record of finishing eight strokes under. He wasn't just well under par, he was way ahead of the competition. Ernie Els and Miguel Angel Jimenez tied for second place at three strokes *over* par, meaning Woods beat them by 15 strokes. That, too, was a record, topping the 138-year-old record for the largest margin of victory in *any* major golf tournament.

Andrew Johnson was drunk when he took the vice-presidential oath of office (1865).

DID YOU EVER NOTICE...

Sometimes, the answer is irrelevant—it's the question that counts.

"Why do people say, 'It's always the last place you look'? Of course it is. Why would you keep looking after you've found it?"

—**Billy Connolly**

"If 95% of accidents happen within the home, where do homeless people go to have 95% of their accidents?"

—**Strange de Jim**

"What's the deal with lampshades? If it's a lamp, why do you want shade?"

—**Jerry Seinfeld**

"Why are they called stairs inside but steps outside?"

—**Peter Kay**

"How come the dove gets to be the peace symbol? How about the pillow? It has more feathers than the dove, and it doesn't have that dangerous beak."

—**Jack Handey**

"Why do people say, 'It was more fun than a barrel of monkeys'? Have you ever *smelled* a barrel of monkeys?"

—**Steve Bluestein**

"Did you ever notice that people who say they don't care what other people think are usually desperate to have people think they don't care what people think?"

—**George Carlin**

"Did you know that the male sea horse has the baby? Why don't they just call that one the female?"

—**Jim Gaffigan**

"What's the shelf life of a shelf?"

—**Jason Love**

"Opening a can of worms? Do worms even come in cans?"

—**Ellen DeGeneres**

"Why do men have nipples? They're like plastic fruit."

—**Carol Leifer**

"At what age is it appropriate to tell a highway it's adopted?"

—**Zach Galifianakis**

"Ever notice the first thing you see at an airport is a big sign that says 'TERMINAL'? Have a nice flight."

—**Lewis Grizzard**

A single pond in Brazil can sustain a greater variety of fish than is found in all of Europe's rivers.

THREE AMAZING AFRICAN TREES

*Everybody hears about the lions and elephants
and zebras—but what about the trees?*

THE BIG BAOBAB

Baobab trees are native only to Australia, Madagascar, and Africa. The African species is the largest and is found in dry savannah land in much of the sub-Saharan region of the continent. They're known for their massive trunks and their odd appearance: They're often called "upside-down trees" because they look more like bulbous cylinders topped by a mass of tangled roots than typical trees. (Several African legends tell stories of how God became angry at the baobab trees, and pulled them up and jammed them back into the ground upside down.) There are many famous baobabs, the largest and best-known being the "Big Baobab" in Limpopo Province, South Africa. It's only about 72 feet tall, but its trunk is more than 150 feet around. It takes 45 people holding hands to circle it. And…you can buy a beer inside it. In 1990 Doug and Heather van Heerden purchased the farm where the tree stands, cleared the detritus from the hollows in the tree's base…and built a pub inside it. Its ceiling is more than 12' high, and it easily seats 15 people—though on one occasion 54 people crammed in for a party. Carbon dating indicates that the tree is around 6,000 years old.

THE MIRACLE TREE

Located near the northeastern South African city of Pretoria is the *Wonderboom*, or "Miracle Tree," Nature Reserve. (*Wonder* means "miracle" and *boom* means "tree" in Afrikaans.) The park is built around a wild fig tree that is believed to be more than 1,000 years old—and is considered a freak of nature. Why? First, this particular species of wild fig normally grows to about 30 feet in height. The Wonderboom is 70 feet tall. Secondly, over its long life some of its branches have drooped to the ground and sprouted new roots, from which new trunks sprouted. Those trees then grew new branches that later drooped to the ground and spawned more trunks. The Wonderboom now has 13 distinct daughter trunks around the original—and the tree's massive canopy now covers an area of about 170 feet by 170 feet, about ⅔ of an acre. Local legend says that the size of the tree is due to the fact that it grew on a spot where a great tribal leader was buried long ago.

THE TREE OF TÉNÉRÉ

Unfortunately, this is the story of an amazing tree that no longer exists. It was a small acacia tree, called the most isolated tree in the world. It was located on a caravan route in a vast, empty swath of the Sahara Desert in Niger known as the *Ténéré* ("desert" in the language of the nomadic Tuareg people), and there wasn't another tree within 120 miles in any direction. Dubbed *L'arbre de Ténéré* in French, or "the Tree of Ténéré," it was the last survivor of the dense forest that thrived in the region thousands of years ago, before the changing climate turned it into a desert. The tree was just 10 feet tall (about five feet up, it split into two branches, giving it a distinctive Y shape), topped by a tangle of thin branches. But it was legendary to desert nomads and other travelers in the region, who could spot it from miles away and probably wondered how the tree could survive in such a spot. In 1938 the French military decided to dig a well near the tree—and found that its roots were drawing water from a source more than 130 feet below the surface. The little tree came to a tragic end in 1973 when a Libyan truck driver on the caravan route did the improbable: He hit the only tree in a region larger than the state of Michigan. The dead tree was taken to the Niger National Museum in the capital of Niamey, where it remains today. An unknown artist erected a metal sculpture made of pipes and auto parts at the desert site, in honor of the lonely Tree of Ténéré.

*   *   *

OVERSHADOWED

Literary giants Aldous Huxley and C. S. Lewis both died on the same day, but their passings didn't receive much press. Why? It was November 22, 1963, the day John F. Kennedy was assassinated.

OFFICIAL STATE BUSINESS

Every state has a motto, a nickname, and even a traditional dish. But many states also have a few more "official" items.

- **The official neckware of Arizona** is the bolo tie.

- **The official possum of Georgia** is Pogo, the possum from Walt Kelly's long-running comic strip of the same name.

- **The official state beverage of Indiana** is water. (In Nebraska, it's Kool-Aid.)

- **The official state meal of Oklahoma** is barbecue pork, chicken-fried steak, fried okra, squash, cornbread, biscuits, corn, sausage and gravy, grits, black-eyed peas, strawberries, and pecan pie.

- **The official exercise of Maryland** is walking. (Maryland's official sport: jousting.)

- **The official children's book of Massachusetts** is Robert McCloskey's *Make Way for Ducklings* (1941). In 2003 a third-grade class from Canton pushed it through the state legislature as a class project. The official children's book author of Massachusetts, however, is Dr. Seuss.

- **The official cartoon character of Oklahoma** is Gusty, a raindrop-headed figure drawn nightly on the weather maps on a Tulsa news broadcast by weatherman Don Woods.

- **The official vehicle of Texas** is the chuck wagon.

- **The state beverage of Alabama** is Clyde May's Conecuh Ridge Alabama Style Whiskey. (The state bird of Alabama is the wild turkey, not to be confused with Wild Turkey, a beverage distilled in nearby Kentucky.)

- **The official state rock song of Washington** is "Louie Louie."

- **The official dinosaur of the District of Columbia** is the Capitalsaurus. Paleontologists still aren't sure it's actually a separate species—it's more likely some type of tyrannosaurus—but it's okay if the Capitalsaurus isn't real, because D.C. isn't really a state.

Square dancing is the official folk dance of 24 states.

NUMBERED FACTS

Big things come in small packages. (You can count on it.)

2 TWOS
• Shakespeare's *Two Gentlemen of Verona:* Valentine and Proteus.

• The twins of the astrological sign (and constellation) Gemini: Castor and Pollux (or Alpha Geminorum and Beta Geminorum).

3 THREES
• The Three Wise Men were Melchior, Gaspar, and Balthazar. Their gifts were, respectively, gold, frankincense, and myrrh.

• Aristotle's Unities—his criteria for a proper tragic play: unity of action (one plot), unity of place (one location), and unity of time (all action occurs in one day).

• *The Three Caballeros* from the 1944 Disney movie are Panchito Pistoles (a rooster), José Carioca (a parrot), and Donald Duck (a duck).

4 FOURS
• The four classes of ancient Japanese society: samurai, farmers, artisans, traders.

• The Quad Cities of the Midwest are Rock Island, Moline, and East Moline, Illinois; and Davenport, Iowa.

• Ernest Hemingway's "four things to do to be a man": write a book, plant a tree, fight a bull, have a son.

• The Four Horsemen of the Apocalypse represent the four plagues of pestilence, war, famine, and death.

5 FIVES
• The five events of the Olympic pentathlon: fencing, horseback riding, shooting, long-distance running, and swimming.

• The five stages of grief: denial, anger, bargaining, depression, acceptance.

• New York's five organized crime families: Gambino, Genovese, Lucchese, Colombo, Bonanno.

• The Channel Islands of Britain: Alderney, Guernsey, Herm, Jersey, Sark.

• Biology's five functions of life: respiration, reproduction, ingestion, digestion, excretion.

6 most common U.S. county names: Washington, Jefferson, Franklin, Lincoln, Jackson, Madison.

THE GREAT RACE, PART I

It involved only a half-dozen cars and 17 men, but this was one race that not only made history—it changed it.

GET A HORSE

In 1908 the promise of the automobile was just that—a promise. The industry was in its infancy, and most people still relied on horses or their own two feet to get from one place to another. Skeptics were convinced that the automobile was just an expensive and unreliable gimmick. So how could anyone prove to the world that the automobile was the most practical, durable, and reliable means of transport ever invented? Easy: Sponsor a race. But not just any race—it would have to be a marathon of global proportions, pitting the newfangled machines (and their drivers) against the toughest conditions possible on a course stretching around the world, with a sizable cash prize to the winner, say, $1,000. Then call it "The Great Race"…and cross your fingers.

MY CAR'S BETTER THAN YOURS

It's hard to comprehend the hold automobiles had on the public imagination at the turn of the 20th century. A similar frenzy of technological one-upmanship occurred during the race to the moon in the 1960s, as industrial nations competed fiercely to be considered the most modern and up-to-date technologically. When it came to cars, there had a been a few rally-style road races before 1908—most notably a Peking-to-Paris auto race in 1907, but nothing on a truly global scale. So the *New York Times* and the French newspaper *Le Matin* combined to organize a bigger, better competition designed to be the ultimate test of man and machine. Starting in New York City, the racers would cross the continental United States and the Alaskan territory, take a ferry across the Bering Strait, then drive from Vladivostok across Siberia to Paris—a trek of 22,000 miles.

Few paved roads existed anywhere at that time, and much of the planned route crossed vast roadless areas. And with few gas stations in existence, just completing the course would require every ounce of stamina and ingenuity on the part of the car and the driver, but the winner would own indisputable bragging rights to the claim of Best Car in the World.

GENTLEMEN, START YOUR ENGINES

To the cheers of a crowd of 250,000 people, six cars representing four nations pulled out of New York's Times Square on February 12, 1908, to begin the great adventure. France had three cars: a De Dion-Bouton, a Motobloc, and a Sizaire-Naudin. Germany was represented by a Protos, and Italy by a Zust. All but the American entry—a stock off-the-line Thomas Flyer driven by George Schuster—were custom built for the competition. (The Thomas was a last-minute entry because the sponsors couldn't bear the thought of a race of this magnitude not having an American representative.) All but the 1-cylinder Sizaire-Naudin had 4-cylinder engines ranging from 30–60 horsepower; the fastest, the Protos, could get up to 70 mph. The cars were heavy, boxy things, with open cockpits and no windshields (glass was considered too dangerous). Each team consisted of a principal driver, a relief driver/mechanic, and an assistant, usually a reporter who would travel with the team and send stories from the road via telegraph.

THEY'RE OFF!

Immediately upon leaving Manhattan, the cars drove into a fierce snowstorm that claimed the Sizaire-Naudin as the race's first victim. The 15-horsepower French two-seater broke down in Peekskill, New York, and was forced to quit. It had gone a mere 44 miles. Snow dogged the remaining cars all the way to Chicago, slowing their progress to a snail's pace. It took the Thomas Flyer eight hours to travel four miles in Indiana, and then only with horses breaking the trail in front of the car.

After Chicago, the cars headed across the Great Plains in sub-zero temperatures. To keep warm, the French Motobloc team rerouted heat from the engine into the cab (an innovation that found its way into future cars) but to no avail: The Motobloc had to quit the race in Iowa. Meanwhile, the winter weather had turned the plains to mud, which stuck to the chassis of the cars, adding hundreds of pounds of weight to each vehicle. Teams took

Once used as currency: kettle drums (Indonesia), eggs (France), and dogs' teeth (Solomon Islands).

to stopping at fire stations in every town they passed for a high-pressure rinse.

Unable to find usable roads across Nebraska, the drivers took to "riding the rails," straddling railroad tracks and bouncing along, tie to tie, for hundreds of miles. (Blowouts were frequent.) A Union Pacific conductor rode along with the American team to alert them to oncoming trains. In especially bad weather, one team member would straddle the radiator with a lantern and peer ahead of the car.

When there were no train tracks, the cars used ruts left by covered wagons years before. They navigated by the stars, sextants, compasses, and local guides, when they could hire them. And if they had to stop for more than a few hours, the radiators had to be completely drained—antifreeze hadn't been invented yet.

TAKING THE LEAD

After 41 days, 8 hours, and 15 minutes, the Thomas Flyer was the first entrant to reach San Francisco, becoming the first car ever to cross the United States in winter. The American team promptly boarded a steamer to Valdez, Alaska, the starting spot for the overland trip to the Bering Sea, and brought a crate of homing pigeons with them to send reports back to the States. Race organizers had hoped the ice across the Bering Strait would provide a bridge for the cars. But the Alaska leg had to be scrapped because the weather and driving conditions were even worse than they'd been in the United States. (The pigeon plan didn't work so well, either. The first bird sent aloft from Valdez was attacked and eaten by seagulls.)

The U.S. team was given a 15-day bonus for their Alaskan misadventure and told to return to San Francisco to join the other racers on the S.S. *Shawmutt*, bound for Yokohama, Japan. At the same time, the German team was penalized 15 days for putting their car on a train from Ogden, Utah, to San Francisco. Both decisions would bear heavily on the race's end.

Would rain or snow or roving bandits stop these racers from their course? To find out how the story ended, turn to page 269.

turn to page 269.

Food fight! The word "grenade" comes from the French word for pomegranate.

THE BEIJING TEA SCAM (AND OTHER CONS)

We like to think that most people are decent. But not everybody is—some people make a living by scamming any victim they can find, and someday, it could be you. So here are a few of the oldest tricks in the con artist's book…just in case someone tries one on you.

THE CON: The Antique Toy

HOW IT WORKS: The first con man, or "grifter," buys a worthless old toy from a secondhand store. He goes into a bar, sets it down, and buys a drink. He then pretends to take an important call on his cell phone and steps outside, leaving the toy on the bar. After a few moments, the grifter's accomplice enters. He excitedly notices the antique toy, and asks where it came from, because "it's a rare antique worth a fortune." The accomplice tells the bartender that he's going to get some money—because he'll pay the owner of the toy $500 for it. The first con man then returns to the bar. If all goes according to plan, the bartender gets greedy and offers to buy the toy off the first con man for a modest fee, thinking he can turn around and sell it to the accomplice for $500. The grifter accepts; the accomplice never returns.

THE CON: The Human ATM

HOW IT WORKS: The grifter places an "out of order" sign on the screen of an ATM. Then, wearing a security-guard uniform, he stands next to it, straight as a rod and looking ahead. Whenever anyone comes by to make a cash deposit, he tells them that he works for the bank and is taking deposits by hand. He writes out a receipt and takes their cash, but also asks for their account number and PIN to secure the transaction. It's amazing that anyone would fall for this, but there are frequent reports of it happening.

THE CON: The Melon Drop

HOW IT WORKS: While carrying a sealed package full of

broken glass, the con artist bumps into an innocent person and drops the package. When it hits the ground, it sounds like a precious glass object inside just broke into a thousand pieces (even though it was already broken). The con man angrily blames the clumsy bystander and demands money to replace the expensive item he's just broken. This ploy gets its name from a scam perpetrated on Japanese tourists. In Japan, watermelons are expensive, but in the United States they're cheap. So the scammer buys a watermelon at a grocery store, then deliberately bumps into a Japanese tourist, drops the watermelon, and demands a large amount of cash to replace it.

The Con: The Barred Winner
How It Works: A con man approaches the "mark" outside a casino, holding what he says is a bag of gambling chips worth several thousand dollars. The problem, he says, is that he was accused of cheating and thrown out of the casino without getting a chance to cash in his chips. He asks the victim to redeem them in the casino, promising a portion of the proceeds. When the mark agrees, the con man acts suspicious, afraid the mark will just walk away with all his money. (Oh, the irony!) The con man asks for collateral—his wallet or a piece of jewelry. The victim goes inside to cash in the chips, only to discover the the chips are fake and that the con artist has absconded with the collateral.

The Con: The Fake Mugger
How It Works: Two con artists spot an easy victim for a purse-snatching. The first one steals the purse and takes off running. The second one shouts, "Stop, thief!" and chases the mugger down the street as the mark looks on. The second con man wrestles the purse away, but in the melee, the "thief" escapes. The purse is returned to the mark, who gratefully gives the brave con man a cash reward. The two con men then split the haul.

The Con: The Beijing Tea Scam
How It Works: This tourist scam originated in China. Two young women approach, chat up, and befriend a traveler. After hitting it off with their new friend, the women will suggest that their new

friend accompany them to a traditional Chinese tea ceremony. The tourist thinks this is a great idea (an authentic cultural experience) and agrees. The three people then go to a small tea-house. They are never shown a menu—if asked, the two con women say that that is just how it's done. Then the tea is brewed, poured, and slowly consumed. At the conclusion, the tourist is given a bill for $100. The women hand over their money, and the tourist reluctantly does the same. The girls part ways with the tourist…then return to the teahouse, where they get their cut of the $100.

The Con: The Landlord Scam

How It Works: The con man takes a short-term sublet of an apartment, and then takes out a classified ad offering the apartment for rent at an amazing below-market rate. Potential tenants come to view the apartment, and since it's a great place for a great price, they are ready to sign a lease on the spot. The con man takes their deposit and first month's rent. And then he does this with another tenant, and another, and another. The con man tells each victim that they can move in on the first day of the following month. When all of the scammed tenants arrive at the same time with their furniture, ready to move in, the con man is long gone with their money.

The Con: The Street Mechanic

How It Works: At a stoplight or stop sign, the con artist flags down an expensive car. There's something wrong with the car, he tells the driver. There isn't, of course, but the con man says the problem is one that's difficult to see, like a "slightly crooked bumper," for example. He tells the victim that this kind of repair is usually very expensive, but he can fix it in just minutes—he's a mechanic—and the only payment he asks for is a ride to work. The con man "fixes" the bumper, and the victim drives him to work. While riding along, the con man "calls his boss" and a staged emotional conversation follows in which the con man is "fired" for being late again. The victim, feeling grateful (and guilty) that the man stopped to help him, offers up a hefty reward of thanks.

IRONIC, ISN'T IT?

*There's nothing like a good dose of irony to put the
problems of day-to-day life into proper perspective.*

HE WROTE THE BOOK. In 2009 Bernard Madoff was
found guilty of fraud after bilking investors out of billions
of dollars. One victim was University of Colorado professor Stephen Greenspan—he lost $250,000 to Madoff. The scandal
broke in early 2009, around the same time as the publication of
Greenspan's new book: *The Annals of Gullibility: Why We Get
Duped and How to Avoid It.*

HOW'S THE WEATHER? England's most powerful supercom-
puter—capable of 1,000 billion calculations per second—was
designed to predict climate change. After it was installed in 2009,
however, critics noted that the massive, hangar-sized machine
requires 1.2 megawatts of energy to operate. Using that much
power produces 12,000 tons of carbon dioxide per year, making it
one of Great Britain's single worst contributors to climate change.

WHO ARE YOU? In 2009 a man named Kevin Mitnick was
unable to access his Facebook account. Due to a temporary glitch,
the social networking site didn't accept his claims that he was who
he said he was. Ironically, Mitnick had previously spent time in jail
for impersonating other people in order to access their computers.
"I used to be very influential at proving I was someone else," he
said. "And now I can't even prove I'm the real Kevin Mitnick."

RIGHT UNDER THEIR NOSES. In 2006 England's Home
Office was embarrassed when five workers—hired to clean their
immigration department offices in London—were arrested for
being illegal immigrants.

WHO WASN'T WHERE? Cate Blanchett was not there for the
2008 Golden Globe Awards due to the Hollywood writers' strike
(actors boycotted the event). Had Blanchett been there, she could
have picked up her award for Best Supporting Actress for her role
in the film *I'm Not There.* "I wish circumstance would allow me to
be there," said Blanchett in a statement.

DINGLES AND BEEF

Every profession has its own slang. Here are
some everyday terms used by movie crews.

Walk a banana: Instruction to an actor to walk in a curvy pattern away from the camera for no other reason than to avoid blocking something that needs to be seen.

Barney: A cloth used to keep a camera warm in cold weather. It gets its name from *Barney Google*, a 1920s comic strip that featured a horse that always wore a thick blanket.

Buff and puff: Hair and makeup.

Futz: To degrade recorded dialogue so it sounds worse. Example: The sound would be "futzed" (distortion or static is added) if a character is speaking through a telephone or appearing on a TV set.

Bubbles: Lights.

Make the day: Successfully complete all scenes scheduled to shoot for that day.

Noncombatants: Anyone on set not involved in the shooting of a particular shot, such as extra crewmembers or actors not in that scene.

Gone with the Wind in the morning, Dukes of Hazzard after lunch: The production spent too much time getting everything right before lunch and doesn't have much to show for it, so they're going to have to speed through the rest of the day's scheduled scenes.

Beef: Lighting strength. "More beef" means that more-intense lighting is required.

C47: A wooden clothespin, a low-tech solution for a number of problems on a film set. Legend says that a studio accountant didn't want to have to justify a production's large order of clothespins, so he called them C47s to make them sound like sophisticated moviemaking equipment.

Shoe leather: Scenes or shots with no dialogue that exist only to move characters from one location to the next, such as walking to a taxi or boarding an airplane.

Fishpole: Boom microphone—the one on the long stick they keep just out of frame.

Dingle: A branch set in front of a light to cast creepy shadows.

McGarrett: A 50mm film lens. The name comes from the character played by Jack Lord on the TV series *Hawaii Five-O*.

Manmaker: Any prop, usually a wooden box, that an actor stands on to seem taller.

Balloon tires: Circles under an actor's eyes.

Century lights: Spotlights, so named because they were once made by the Century Lighting Company (which no longer exists).

Emily: A technical term for a floodlight is a "single broad." Legend has it that a lighting technician knew an unmarried woman named Emily.

Flamethrower: A cameraman who uses too much light—so much that the shot is saturated or impossible to see on film.

Honeywagon: The portable toilet truck.

Groveler: A soft pad for the camera operator to kneel on when a shot requires the camera to be very close to the ground.

Inky: A low-wattage (100- or 200-kilowatt) light. It's short for "incandescent."

Sheet metal: A prop car

Obie: A small light mounted on the camera, just above the lens, to shine directly onto an actor's face, invented by cameraman Lucien Ballard to show off the eyes of actress Merle Oberon (Ballard's wife).

Powder man: An explosives expert.

Mickey Rooney: Instruction to a cameraman to move the camera a few feet, but very slowly—in other words, a short creep.

Rhubarb: It adds realism to a scene when extras walk by having conversations. Since they don't have microphones, it doesn't matter what they say, so the actors usually say the word "rhubarb" repeatedly.

Snowshoes: When a clumsy person bumps into a light and knocks it out of position, or trips over a cord and unplugs something, they are sarcastically asked to "take off their snowshoes."

Martini: The last shot of the day.

UP IN A DOWN ECONOMY

*Here are a few examples of what economists call "countercyclical assets"
—products or industries that thrive while the rest of the economy tanks.*

COMIC BOOKS. Sales of vintage comic books from the 1950s and '60s were brisk in 2009, but not for their nostalgic value—they're an investment. Activity on the Silver Age Comic Book Pricing Index was up 14 percent. During the same period, Standard and Poor's 500 stock index was down 11 percent.

SHOE REPAIR. The average cost of a new pair of men's shoes is about $50. It costs less than half that to fix a pair of shoes, but cobbling is a dying profession. There were 120,000 cobblers in the U.S. in the 1930s; there are just 7,000 today. But the bad economy has been good for the industry. According to retail trade groups, cobbling is up 25 percent. Sales of new shoes: down 3 percent.

SEEDS. You can save money by growing vegetables at home instead of buying them, and the newly unemployed have more time to tend gardens. Result: Seed catalog businesses are actually enjoying the recession. Onion seed seller Dixondale Farms reports 40 percent growth; the organic Seeds of Change says sales have increased 30 percent.

VACATION RENTAL HOMES. Since the economy sank, many Americans who own vacation homes have tried unsuccessfully to sell them for quick cash. So they've turned to another option: renting them out for a week at a time to vacationers. Americans still want to take vacations, but they want to spend less money doing so, and renting a private home costs a lot less than seven nights in a hotel. HomeAway is a company that manages these kinds of properties. Since 2007 its business has increased 59 percent.

CHOCOLATE. In December 2008, cocoa futures hit their highest level in 25 years. It's partially because supply was down, but it's also because chocolate demand was way up during the recession—chocolate is a comfort food. In the London futures market, the price of cocoa rose 71 percent in a single year to $2,546 per ton.

Love and fear cause the same physical reactions: pupil dilation, sweaty palms, elevated heart rate.

RANDOM BITS ON '70s HITS

Pop songs are short, catchy, and memorable—just like these facts.

• **"My Sweet Lord," by George Harrison.** The Beatles broke up in 1970. This song hit #1 in '71—the first chart-topper for any solo former Beatle.

• **"Close to You," by Carpenters.** It's Carpenters (not "the" Carpenters), and this is their best-known song. But it's a cover. The original version was recorded in 1963 by Richard Chamberlain—TV's *Dr. Kildare*—as an attempt at a teen-idol singing career.

• **"Stairway to Heaven," by Led Zeppelin.** The bestselling rock song ever…in sheet music (more than a million copies were sold).

• **"Daniel," by Elton John.** As recorded, it's cryptically from the point of view of a man who misses his brother as he's "heading for Spain." John thought the song was too long, so he didn't record lyricist Bernie Taupin's final verse that explains the story—Daniel is a Vietnam vet who returns home blind and disillusioned and leaves America forever—for Spain.

• **"Take Me Home, Country Roads," by John Denver.** The backing singers on this recording were a vocal group known as Fat City, who later changed their name to the Starland Vocal Band and had a huge hit in 1976 with "Afternoon Delight."

• **"Morning Has Broken," by Cat Stevens.** Rick Wakeman, the keyboard virtuoso from the progressive rock band Yes, arranged the song and played piano. He wasn't paid for the session until 2000, when he received a check for $15.

• **"Sweet Home Alabama," by Lynyrd Skynyrd.** Three band members cowrote the song: Ronnie Van Zant, Gary Rossington, and Ed King. So who was from Alabama? None of them: Van Zant and Rossington were from Florida; King was from California.

• **"Night Fever," by the Bee Gees.** Drummer Dennis Byron

recorded the song shortly before leaving to attend his father's funeral. He wasn't around for the rest of the *Saturday Night Fever* sessions, so a portion of his work on this song was looped to provide the drums for "Stayin' Alive." And though "Stayin' Alive" is probably the most famous disco (and Bee Gees song) ever, "Night Fever" actually sold more copies and was a bigger hit.

• **"Bohemian Rhapsody," by Queen.** According to guitarist Brian May, the group did so many vocal and guitar overdubs that by the end of recording, the overused master tape was almost transparent.

• **"No Woman, No Cry," by Bob Marley and the Wailers.** Marley's first hit (in England) was also one of the few songs he recorded but didn't write. It was written by his friend Vincent Ford, who ran a soup kitchen in Jamaica. The royalties from this song kept the charity afloat for decades.

• **"Hotel California," by the Eagles.** The line "stab them with their steely knives" is a reference and homage to Steely Dan, whose 1976 song "Everything You Did" contains the lyric "Turn up the Eagles, the neighbors are listening."

• **"You're the One That I Want," by John Travolta and Olivia Newton-John.** This song was not in the original 1971 stage version of *Grease*. It was written specifically for the movie (but has since been included in the stage version).

• **"Alison," by Elvis Costello.** On this, Costello's first single, he was backed by the group Clover. The group had a harmonica player who wasn't needed for the session—Huey Lewis. Clover later became Huey Lewis and the News.

• **"Baker Street," by Gerry Rafferty.** The saxophone part by Raphael Ravenscroft was supposed to be filler—a placeholder until it could be overdubbed with a guitar solo later. But the sax part was never replaced, it became the song's signature element, and the record went to #2 on the charts. Ravenscroft was paid $50 for the session. (And the check bounced.)

• **"Le Freak," by Chic.** The songwriter conceived the opening lyric of "ah-h-h-h freak out" much differently from the way it appeared on the record. The word "freak" was substituted for a radio-unfriendly F-word, and "out" was used instead of "off."

DOWN THE HATCH!

Here's how folks around the world toast each other when they're having a drink.

India/Pakistan: *Aish karo!* (Enjoy!)

Slovakia: *Na zdravie!* (To health!)

Romania: *Noroc!* (Good luck!)

France: *Sante!* (To health!) or *Cul sec!* (Bottoms up!)

Arabic: *Shereve!* (To health!)

Finland: *Kippis!* (Cheers!)

China: *Gan Bei!* (Empty the glass!)

Swahili: *Afya!* (Health!)

Philippines: *Mabuhay!* (Long live!)

Sri Lanka: *Onna Ehenam?* (Shall we, gentlemen?)

Serbia: *Ziveli!* (For health!)

Portugal: *Saude!* (Cheers!)

Latvia: *Prieka* (To joy!)

Esperanto: *Je zia sano!* (Health!)

Germany: *Prosit!* (Cheers!)

Argentina: *Chin-Chin!* (Sound of clinking glasses)

Iceland: *Skal!* (The cup!)

Italy: *Cent' anni!* (A hundred years [of luck]!)

Turkey: *Serefe!* (To honor!)

Hawaii: *Hauoli maoli oe!* (To your happiness!)

Spain: *Salud!* (Health!)

Israel: *L'Chayim* (To life!)

Albania: *Gezuar!* (Cheers!)

Greece: *Yia Mas!* (To our health!)

Brazil: *Saude! Viva!* (To your health!)

Hungary: *Egészségére!* (To your health!)

Kenya: *Maisha Merefu!* (To good life!)

Estonia: *Terviseks!* (For health!)

Lebanon: *Kessak!* (Cheers!)

Iran: *Salahmatie!* (To good health!)

Indonesia: *Selamat minum!* (Cheers!)

Korea: *Ogung bai!* (Bottoms up!)

Yiddish: *Zol zon tzgezhint!* (To your health!)

A 2005 study found the United Nations was successful in two out of three peacekeeping efforts.

DO-IT-YOURSELF DISASTERS

Tackling a home project? Be careful...or it might just tackle you.

PROBLEM: Tone Pina's apartment in Citrus Heights, California, was infested by thousands of cockroaches.

FIX: Because there were so many roaches, Pina got a lot of bug bombs. He said about 8 to 10; the police later said there were probably as many as 18. (One or two is usually recommended.) Pina set them all off at the same time and rushed out of his house.

OUTCOME: A spark from his refrigerator ignited the fumes, triggering an explosion that separated the building's walls from its roof, caused three families to lose their homes, and cost more than $1 million to repair. Pina still has cockroaches.

PROBLEM: In 2007 a Brevard, North Carolina, teenager's Xbox 360 video game console kept turning off every five minutes.

FIX: The 14-year-old boy did some research online and found a Web site that the said the power supply was probably overheating. So, following the directions provided, he wrapped the power supply in plastic and tape and submerged it in a bowl of cool water... while it was still plugged in.

OUTCOME: The teen's mother walked into the room a few minutes later and found him lying unconscious on his back. She rushed him to the hospital, where he was treated for minor burns to his right hand and right foot.

PROBLEM: While trying to fix up his old Lincoln Continental, a 66-year-old man from South Kitsap, Washington, tried everything he could think of to get that last stubborn lug nut off the right rear wheel.

FIX: Frustrated, he went and got his 12-gauge shotgun. Holding the barrel only a few feet away from the lug nut, he fired.

OUTCOME: His plan backfired—literally. A police spokesman said the man's legs were "peppered with buckshot." He was taken to the hospital for serious (but not life-threatening) injuries.

Most abundant mammals in tropical rainforests: bats.

PROBLEM: Weeds were growing between the hedges at the home of a German gardener.

FIX: While it's not uncommon for gardeners to use a small blow-torch to clear weeds from cracks in a driveway or sidewalk, it's not recommended when the weeds are growing among giant hedges. But that's what this 54-year-old gardener tried to do.

OUTCOME: The hedges caught fire...then the toolshed...then the roof of his house. Unable to extinguish the blaze with his garden hose, the man called the fire department. By the time they put it out, his house was so damaged that it was uninhabitable.

PROBLEM: A 45-year-old man from Düsseldorf, Germany, found a hole in his inflatable air mattress.

FIX: He tried to seal the hole with tire solvent, which is flammable. Then he used an electric air pump to blow up the mattress.

OUTCOME: A spark from the pump ignited the solvent, and the explosion knocked out a wall and shattered all of the windows in the apartment. The man and his daughter were treated for burns, but were otherwise okay.

PROBLEM: The toilet in the master bathroom of Carol Taddei's Minneapolis home stopped working.

FIX: Taddei, a retired paralegal, wanted to save money on costly repairs, so she purchased a new toilet and tried to install it herself.

OUTCOME: The new toilet seemed to work fine at first...but Taddei didn't know that a pipe underneath it was leaking. A few days later, the bathroom floor gave out and the commode crashed down into the living room below. In Taddei's rush to get the hardware store for repair supplies, her car clipped a pole in the garage, dislodging the bumper and sending several shelves of flower pots crashing down. Total cost for repairs: $3,000.

*   *   *

"My theory on housework is, if the item doesn't multiply, smell, catch fire, or block the refrigerator door, let it be. No one else cares. Why should you?"

—Erma Bombeck

Energy food? One kernel of candy corn supplies enough calories for an adult to walk 150 feet.

KITCHEN Q&A

The top chefs at the Bathroom Readers' Institute are here to answer some basic questions about our second-favorite room in the house.

What is "freezer burn"? Is it bad for you?

You put your pound of hamburger or chicken breasts into a plastic bag and stick it in the freezer. When you take it out a few months later, it has dry-looking patches all over it. That's "freezer burn." It occurs when the water molecules in the food form ice crystals and migrate out of the food. The loss of water dehydrates the surface of the frozen food, creating those dry patches. Best way to avoid freezer burn: Wrap foods tightly in moisture-resistant packaging and keep the freezer temperature at a constant 0°F. (Tight packaging will also prevent oxygen molecules from creeping in and altering the food's flavor.) Freezer burn can make food (especially meat) *look* unappetizing and even taste a bit stale, but don't worry—it isn't harmful.

What's the reason for boiling live lobsters?

Any dead (but uncooked) crustacean will begin to deteriorate very quickly, so we've gotten into the habit of protecting ourselves from potential food poisoning by putting the live lobsters directly into boiling water. Seems like a good solution, since lobsters don't feel pain, right? Wrong. Scientific evidence shows the opposite: They actually suffer severely. A more humane way to deal with a live lobster is to freeze it for several hours to reduce nerve function and pain sensitivity *before* dropping it into the pot, or to practice the quick-kill technique of inserting a knife point into the back of the lobster's head, an inch below the eyes, in the middle of the back—and then put it immediately into the boiling water.

Why do they put wax (or whatever that stuff is) on cucumbers?

It is wax—edible food-grade wax. Growers apply it to retain moisture and protect against damage during shipping. For reasons of taste and aesthetics, most chefs recommend peeling waxed cukes before you eat them. If you don't want to peel it, a good scrub with soapy water will make an unpeeled waxed cucumber more

---

His way: Frank Sinatra always asked for chicken-and-rice soup before going on stage.

palatable...but it won't remove all the wax. Don't like wax on your cucumbers? Avoid it by buying local produce.

Is it true that you have to cook pork until it's well done?

No. Before 1980 it was legal in the U.S. to feed pigs garbage containing raw meat, which sometimes included animal parts infected with the *trichina spiralis* parasite, the cause of a deadly disease called *trichinosis*. It was thought that pork had to be cooked to 180°F (very well done) in order to kill the parasite. Two things have changed: First, in 1980 uncooked garbage was outlawed as pig food. And second, it was discovered that cooking pork to only 137°F will destroy the parasite. To be completely safe, the USDA recommends 160°F, which is medium doneness. Since 1980, cases of trichinosis have declined to about 10 per year in the U.S., most of which have been traced to undercooked game meats such as bear and boar.

There's mold on my cheese. Can I eat it anyway?

It depends. With most soft cheeses, such as Brie, Camembert, mozzarella, chèvre, Monterey Jack, Muenster, and ricotta, any unfamiliar mold growth means toss it—do not eat. But you *can* eat hard cheeses if you cut out the mold to a depth of one inch on all sides of it. Molds form threadlike roots that insinuate themselves into the foods on which they grow, and even though most molds are harmless (like the ones used to produce blue cheeses), some are not. If you can't cut away all of the mold, the safest thing to do is throw out the cheese. (Caution: Don't let the knife touch the mold or you'll end up cross-contaminating the cheese—and the mold may reappear.) Some hard cheeses that are generally considered safe to eat once the mold is removed: cheddar, Colby, Gruyère, Asiago, Parmesan, and Swiss.

Is that red juice oozing from the roast beef actually blood?

No. Blood is *hemoglobin*, found in arteries. That red juice is *myoglobin*, a purplish-colored protein found in the tissue cells of meat. When it combines with oxygen, it's called *oxymyoglobin* and looks bright red. That's why the surface of raw meat is bright red. It's also why the liquid that oozes from your roast beef is bright red: The myoglobin has been exposed to oxygen. Chicken and other "white" meats contain less myoglobin than red meats.

WHAT A CONCEPT!

If there's one thing Uncle John remembers about his school days (besides bad dorm food), it's all those different theoretical concepts he learned in history, science, economics, and other classes. Here's a sampling.

Concept: Meinong's Jungle (Philosophy)

What It Means: Alexius Meinong was a 19th-century Austrian philosopher who believed that since we have the ability to conceive of things that do not exist—unicorns, islands in the sky, square circles, the sound of one hand clapping, honest politicians—these things must exist in some sense. Meinong's jungle is the place where all the things that do not exist, exist.

Concept: Opportunity Cost (Economics)

What It Means: The sacrifice a person makes when choosing one product or service over another. If you spend $1,000 on a new transmission for your car instead of going on vacation, for example, you are giving up rest and relaxation in order to keep your car running. The lost rest and relaxation is part of the cost—the opportunity cost—of the transmission. Likewise, if you choose to watch an episode of *CSI* instead of an episode of *Law & Order* on another channel, giving up the opportunity to watch *Law & Order* is the price you pay to enjoy the episode of *CSI*.

Concept: Lullaby Effect (Psychology)

What It Means: It's the process by which humans and other organisms adapt and become desensitized to new—and frequently repeated—stimulus. If you move into a house next to the railroad tracks, for example, after a while you may not even notice the noise and the rattling caused by the trains passing by.

Concept: Motherese (Linguistics)

What It Means: Also known as Child-Directed Speech, motherese is what we think of as "baby talk"—the special language that a parent or other caretaker uses when addressing infants and young children. Characteristics can include shorter words and simpler sentences than in normal speech, a higher and more vari-

---

Most successful police dog: Trepp, a Florida golden retriever, has over 100 arrests to his credit.

able pitch, and a specialized vocabulary. Experts in child development and language acquisition are still debating whether baby talk enables babies to develop language skills more quickly.

Concept: NAIRU, the Non-accelerating Inflation Rate of Unemployment (Economics)
What It Means: The level of unemployment that does not affect the rate of inflation over time. Rates of unemployment *lower* than the NAIRU put upward pressure on inflation, as more people with more money bid up the price of goods. Rates of unemployment *higher* than the NAIRU put downward pressure on inflation as people who have lost or fear losing their jobs cut back on spending, causing prices to fall. When the unemployment rate is right at the NAIRU, the upward and downward pressures on inflation are equal, and the inflation rate remains steady…in theory, anyway.

Concept: The Least-Effort Principle (Psychology)
What It Means: This explains how rats learn to navigate mazes: When given a choice of tasks that result in the same reward, such as taking a long, circuitous route through a maze or the shortest, most direct route to a piece of cheese, rats instinctively seek out the choice that requires the least amount of effort.

Concept: Gresham's Law (Economics)
What It Means: Where coins minted from precious metals like silver and gold are concerned, "bad money will drive out good." If, for example, the value of the silver in a $1 coin rises above $1, speculators will remove the coins from circulation to melt down the silver and sell it at a profit, leaving only coins whose metal content is worth less than their face value. Now that precious metals are no longer used in coins, the theory no longer applies.

Concept: Fallibilism (Philosophy)
What It Means: It's the doctrine that nothing can be known with absolute certainty, although imperfect knowledge is still possible. Fallibilism is widely believed to be true…but can we really know for sure?

EVACUATE NOW!

No, it isn't an article on Ex-Lax. These are the stories of some of the most famous and infamous mass evacuations of people in history.

DUNKIRK, FRANCE

Trapped! In May 1940, nine months into World War II, several German Panzer divisions tore into France, then swooped north, and in just days reached the English Channel. In the mayhem, hundreds of thousands of British, French, and Belgian troops were trapped in a pocket around the harbor town of Dunkirk, France, surrounded by a much larger and better-equipped German army. If they were killed or captured, said British Prime Minister Winston Churchill, "the whole root, core, and brain of the British Army" would be lost, setting the stage for a Nazi invasion of Great Britain.

Evacuate! British leaders decided to evacuate as many soldiers as possible. They put out a call to all English citizens for private vessels—and more than 700 responded. On the night of May 26, an armada of 200 destroyers, along with the 700 fishing boats, yachts, barges, sloops, and private ships of every kind, poured across the English Channel. Those "little boats of Dunkirk," as they were later called, motored up to the shoreline, loaded soldiers aboard, and ferried them to the waiting destroyers. This went on for nine days, all amidst the din (and danger) of artillery fire from land and strafing bullets and bombs from Luftwaffe airplanes. When it was over, an astounding 338,226 soldiers had been carried safely back to England. The evacuation of Dunkirk was hailed as a "miracle," proved to be a huge morale-booster for the British, and may have thwarted the German invasion of Britain.

MISSISSAUGA, ONTARIO

Trapped! Minutes before midnight on November 10, 1979, an axle on a 106-car freight train in Mississauga, just outside Toronto, broke, derailing 23 cars. Their cargo: explosive and toxic chemicals. The derailment immediately caused several propane tanker cars to explode and spilled the contents of several more—caustic soda, styrene, and toluene—onto the tracks. The fire from the

propane tanks ignited vapors from the chemicals, causing a massive explosion with a fireball nearly 5,000 feet high. (People 50
miles away saw it.) Among the derailed cars, officials found a
tanker carrying 81 tons of chlorine. And it was leaking. If it blew
up, it could create a cloud of chlorine gas that could wipe out the
entire city.

Evacuate! The entire city—including six nursing homes and
three large hospitals—would have to be evacuated. Thousands of
police, firefighters, emergency medical technicians, doctors, nurses, bus drivers, and other volunteers worked around the clock
driving people to makeshift evacuation centers outside of town.
When it was over, more than 218,000 people were moved in less
than 48 hours, and not a single life was lost. Until the much less
successful post-Hurricane Katrina operation, it was the largest
peacetime evacuation in North American history. (It took five
days to get the site under control and, thankfully, the chlorine
tank never blew.)

THE SS REPUBLIC

Trapped! On the morning of January 24, 1909, the RMS *Republic*, a 570-foot luxury ocean liner, was heading from New York
toward the Mediterranean with 742 passengers and crew aboard.
At the same time, the SS *Florida*, a smaller ship, was headed *into*
New York with more than 800 Italian immigrants aboard. In
deep fog about 50 miles off Nantucket, Massachusetts, the two
ships collided, killing three people on each ship. The *Republic*
lost all power and was taking on water; the *Florida* was seriously
damaged but still had power and wasn't sinking. Luckily for all
involved, the *Republic* had a wireless radio onboard, and the
operator sent out a distress signal. (It was the first time in history
that a wireless had been used for a large disaster.) Another luxury liner in the area, the *Baltic*, got the signal and set out for the
scene.

Evacuate! The *Florida* quickly came about and was able to get
alongside the sinking *Republic*, a feat in itself, considering the condition of both ships and the fact that they were in thick fog. Over
the next several hours, everyone on the *Republic* was evacuated.
When the *Baltic* arrived twelve hours later, they did it again,
transferring passengers and crew from both ships—more than

World's oldest fire: A coal seam in Australia's Burning Mountain has been burning for 6,000 years.

1,500 people. And in eight-foot swells. It took eight hours, but they managed both evacuations without a single injury or death. The *Republic* went down while the rescue was still under way; the *Baltic* and the *Florida* made it safely back to New York.

Extra: The *Republic* was part of the White Star Line fleet and in its day called "unsinkable." Three years later, another White Star "unsinkable" went down in the North Atlantic: the *Titanic*.

Extra Extra: Among the items purported to have been on the *Republic* when she went down: $265,000 in cash belonging to the U.S. Navy; several hundred thousand dollars in silver ingots; passengers' jewelry worth hundreds of thousands of dollars; and a secret five-ton shipment of American Gold Eagle coins straight from the mint and meant for the Czar of Russia. The ship was located in 1981. Two salvage trips have so far found no treasure… but future trips are planned, so stay tuned.

PRIPYAT, UKRAINE

Trapped! You've heard of this town's more famous neighbor: Chernobyl, the city of 14,000 located about 10 miles southeast of the infamous nuclear power plant that experienced a massive meltdown on April 26, 1986. (See page 404.) Pripyat was much closer to the plant, just two miles away, and it was the home of nearly 50,000 people. Even worse, the prevailing winds at the time of the accident shifted, blowing the radiation straight into Pripyat. Within hours the entire city was contaminated with radioactive fallout. The people in the city were told nothing. The next day, 1,100 buses arrived from the Ukrainian capital of Kiev, about 70 miles away, but the drivers had to wait for an official order to do anything.

Evacuate! The order didn't come until midnight. When it finally did, those buses left with every man, woman, and child from every home, nursing home, and hospital—all 50,000 people—and in less than three hours the city was completely empty. Despite all the waiting and unnecessary exposure to radiation, the evacuation was an extraordinary success and without question saved many lives.

Extra: Today there is still an "exclusion zone" with a radius of about nine miles around the plant where people are not allowed to live. The city of Pripyat still stands outside the zone, but more than two decades later, it's still a ghost town.

UNCLE JOHN'S STALL OF FAME

*We're always amazed by the creative ways people (and animals)
get involved with bathrooms, toilets, toilet paper, etc.
That's why we created the Stall of Fame.*

Honoree: The 2009 Taste Festival in Hobart, Australia
Notable Achievement: Providing live entertainment for the festival's restroom users
True Story: In a bid to make the festival—which celebrates fine food and wine—as memorable as possible, every public restroom had its own poet, minstrel, singer, juggler, etc. Each performer was given two duties: to keep spirits high, and to hand out soap and towels to patrons. "This adds an extra dimension that people will appreciate," said Hobart mayor Rob Valentine.

Honoree: Roger Robinson, an American mountaineer
Notable Achievement: Inventing a go-anywhere toilet that you can take to the top of the world
True Story: As more adventurers than ever before ascend to the planet's highest peaks, garbage and, uh, human-generated pollutants are becoming a serious problem. With that in mind, Robinson conceived of the "Clean Mountain Can" in 2000. It consists of a plastic bucket and lid along with a gas-impervious bag that neutralizes foul odors. It's 11 inches tall, weighs 2.4 pounds, comes with straps that attach it to a backpack, and is completely leakproof. Capacity: 1.86 gallons, which covers 10 to 14 uses.

Honoree: Dawa Steven Sherpa, a Nepalese mountaineer
Notable Achievement: Taking Robinson's Clean Mountain Can (see previous entry) to the top of the world
True Story: In May 2008, 25-year-old Dawa led an "eco-expedition" up Mt. Everest to bring awareness to the impact of climate change in the Himalayas. At the same time, he wanted to put Robinson's portable toilet to the ultimate test. How did the CMC do? By all accounts, very well. Dawa's 18-member team was able

to pack out 143 pounds of their own "personal" waste, keeping it from contaminating Everest.

Bonus: Dawa's team carried out a lot more than #2. They also hauled down "2,100 pounds of garbage, including cans, gas canisters, kitchen waste, tents, parts of an Italian helicopter that crashed 35 years ago, and the remains of a British climber who died in 1972."

Honoree: Yasmin Mughal, from Sweden
Notable Achievement: Successfully potty-training her pet parrot
True Story: "I noticed that every time I took Emil out of his cage, he had to do a poo," said Mughal. One problem: The parrot kept doing it on the furniture. "So I placed him on the toilet and told him to make a poo, which he actually did!" Now Emil knows that if he wants to get out of his cage and play, he must first go to the loo. (No word on whether she taught the bird to flush.)

Honoree: Steve Oswald, a Michigan merchant
Notable Achievement: Cleaning his town's filthy public restrooms…for a price
True Story: August is the busiest time of year for the popular tourist destination of Saugatuck, a culture and arts mecca on the shores of Lake Michigan. But in 2008, Oswald received several complaints from out-of-towners about the state of the city's dirty restrooms. After looking at them, Oswald agreed: "I wouldn't have sat down there, either." He tried notifying the city council, but no one called him back. So he took matters into his own hands and cleaned up a few of the worst loos near his business himself. Then he sent a cleaning bill to the city for $156.94. The mayor thanked Oswald for his civic-mindedness, but refused to pay, saying it might set the "wrong precedent." That didn't surprise Oswald. He only sent the bill "as a matter of principle." He just wants the town to stop grossing out its most important economic stimulators—tourists. (The city council promised to hire more cleaners.)
Bonus: As a token of appreciation (and in lieu of payment), the mayor presented Oswald with Saugatuck's first ever "Golden Plunger Award" (a plunger spray-painted gold). "I will display this proudly in my window as a symbol that one person can make a difference," said Oswald at the ceremony.

SO, WHERE ARE THEY?

If there are other planets in the universe capable of supporting intelligent life—and astronomers speculate that there may be millions of them—how is it that no trace of alien life has ever been detected in space or here on Earth?

FERMI'S PARADOX

In the summer of 1950, a Nobel Prize-winning nuclear scientist named Enrico Fermi paid a visit to the Los Alamos National Laboratory in New Mexico. One afternoon he and some other physicists took a break from the project they were working on and went to lunch. Reports of flying saucer sightings had been in the news recently, and as the men walked, they chatted about the sightings.

The scientists all agreed that the UFO sightings in question were spurious. Nevertheless, it prompted Fermi to ask Edward Teller, one of the other physicists present, what he thought the odds were that a real alien spacecraft would be spotted in the next ten years. Teller thought the odds were about 1 in 100,000. Fermi disagreed: He thought the chances were 1 in 10, or 10 percent. As the conversation moved on to other topics, Fermi suddenly interjected, "Don't you ever wonder where everybody is?"

Fermi was talking about aliens. Given that there are 100 billion stars in our Milky Way galaxy, many of which are billions of years older than the sun, the odds seemed pretty high to Fermi that there must be advanced extraterrestrial life somewhere out there. Fermi's query, or the "Fermi Paradox," as it has become known, may have gotten a lot of laughs that day at lunch, but it's a serious question, and people still ask it today. If the aliens really are out there, why are they so hard to find? And if they haven't visited Earth, why not?

LOW PRIORITY

Part of the problem is at our end: If you want to find evidence of alien life in outer space, you have to look for it, and we haven't been looking very hard or for very long. The galaxy is a big place,

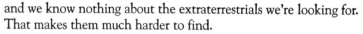

and we know nothing about the extraterrestrials we're looking for. That makes them much harder to find.

Programs to search for extraterrestrial intelligence (or SETIs, as they're called) date back only to 1960, and such programs as there are have been sporadic and very limited in scope. Most are privately funded, because using public money to search for space aliens is pretty controversial. Funding for NASA's last SETI program, for example, was cut in the early 1990s after politicians ridiculed it as "The Great Martian Chase."

A CONVENIENT SPACEGOAT

But could the aliens also be to blame? Here are four possible reasons that have been tossed around over the years:

1. We haven't been noticed yet. With billions upon billions of planets scattered all across the universe, it's possible that no one has visited us because no one realizes we're here.

2. We've been noticed...but we haven't attracted any interest. We may not be advanced enough or unique enough to interest a civilization that's millions of years ahead of us. When was the last time you hiked a mile uphill to get a better look at some moss growing in a crack in the pavement, or waved at a ladybug to see if it would wave back? We may be so inferior to the aliens that they hardly take notice of us, even though they know we're here.

3. The trip to Earth is too expensive. It's possible the aliens haven't landed here for the same reason that we canceled the last three Apollo moon landings and have no firm plans to travel to Mars anytime soon, even though we have the technology to do it. Maybe the aliens, like us, have limited funds and higher priorities.

4. They're already here—we just don't know it. Who can say for sure they *haven't* landed? If they're sophisticated enough to travel across one or more galaxies to get here, they're probably sophisticated enough to study us, perhaps even live among us, without attracting our attention—which, if true, raises another interesting question: *Why* don't they want to attract our attention?

SILENT TREATMENT

This part of the mystery has been referred to as "The Great

Silence," and there are numerous possibilities for why the extraterrestrials never bother to call or write. For example:

• **It takes too long.** Radio and laser signals travel at the speed of light, but the nearest habitable planets may be hundreds of light years away. It's pretty difficult to have a conversation with someone if you have to wait hundreds of years for a response.

• **They *did* call, but we didn't know how to answer the phone.** Centuries ago we would not have known how to detect alien communication signals even if they had been directed at Earth. It's possible that alien civilizations tried to contact Earth in 1000 B.C. or A.D. 1500, and when they didn't receive a response, either lost interest or died out before we could communicate back.

• **They don't want to disturb the animals.** According to the "Zoo Hypothesis," the aliens know we're here and are observing us without our knowledge. They don't want to interfere with our development, so they're treating us like a herd of elephants in a nature preserve and leaving us alone.

• **We're on probation.** The other worlds know we're here, but they're waiting to see if we can curb our warlike impulses and get past the age of nuclear weapons before they reveal themselves to us and risk spreading our barbarism to other worlds.

• **Alien civilizations self-destruct before they figure out how to to travel to or communicate with Earth.** So far, at least, the human race hasn't exhausted its natural resources, nuked itself back to the Stone Age, or polluted the planet to the point of extinction. Maybe the aliens haven't been so lucky: This possibility is known as the "Doomsday Argument"—civilizations advance to a certain stage of development, and then they destroy themselves.

• **The extraterrestrials are hiding from *other* extraterrestrials.** Human history is filled with tragic examples of primitive civilizations that get wiped out when they come in contact with more-advanced societies. Who's to say galactic history isn't just as tragic? It's possible that some alien civilizations choose to keep a low profile, out of fear of what might happen to them if an even more advanced civilization happens along and discovers them.

Q. How many times was the word "sex" spoken during the 5-year run of *The Brady Bunch?* A. Twice.

FUNERAL MISHAPS

A memorial service ought to be a solemn occasion in which the life of a loved one is remembered, and their loss mourned. But like everything else in life, it can easily be ruined by protestors, fires, lawyers, and monkeys.

HE LOOKS TERRIBLE IN THAT (LAW)SUIT

Harold St. John of New Jersey suffered from asbestos exposure, which he believed was caused by the brake linings he installed in Chrysler cars in the early 1960s. He sued Chrysler, and the suit was to go to trial on March 9, 2009. The only problem: St. John died on February 28, 2009. A trial delay motion was filed, and the family prepared for the funeral service at the Spotswood Reform Church in Jamesburg, New Jersey. But as they were praying by St. John's graveside, a process server arrived. He immediately called off the funeral—he had a subpoena from Chrysler demanding the *burial* be delayed (instead of the trial) so that St. John's body could be tested for asbestos, even though he'd already undergone extensive—and conclusive—testing while he was alive.

DO NOT SPEAK ILL OF THE DEAD

Orlando Bethel, a preacher from Loxley, Alabama, was scheduled to sing at the June 2002 funeral of Lish Taylor, his wife's uncle. Before he began singing hymns, however, Bethel wanted to say a few words about the departed—that he was a "drunkard" and a "fornicator," and was now "burning in Hell." Bethel never sang—mourners attacked him, beat him up, and threw him out of the church. Bethel later claimed that "the Holy Ghost" instructed him to speak out, and added that the angry mourners were "whoremongers."

BAD MONKEY

In 2009 several body viewings and funeral services were interrupted at Ang Yew Seng's funeral home in Singapore. The cause: an angry monkey. Ang spotted the stray monkey in his yard and, thinking it was hungry, offered it a bushel of bananas. Instead of taking the gift, it jumped on Ang's back and bit him. Ang pulled the monkey off himself, threw it on the ground, and ran away. The monkey, however, didn't leave. It smashed memorial urns, chewed up flowers, swiped food from funeral receptions, and bit five mourners. After four days of unsuccessful attempts, Singapore animal control finally captured the monkey and ended its reign of terror.

UNITED IN DEATH

Teamsters Local 727 represents Chicago undertakers and hearse drivers. By the 1990s, the funeral industry in Chicago was almost completely unionized—except for the small, family-run Donnellan Funeral Home. And the Teamsters had a problem with that. So in late 1999, union members began holding protests in front of the funeral home, quietly pacing back and forth while holding pro-labor picket signs. The marching never occurred while services were being held or mourners were inside...until January 2000, when they decided to picket a funeral. As the coffin was being carried out of the home, protesters started chanting at the hearse (and the deceased's family), "Who are we? We are Teamsters!" A Teamsters representative spoke to the media about the incident. Apology? No. If Donnellan refused to go union, he said, Teamsters would follow any mourners to churches and even to graveside services. Two weeks later, they reached an understanding. (Donnellan stayed non-union.)

DEATH AT A FUNERAL

In April 2008, 66-year-old church organist Brian Markland performed Beethoven's "Moonlight Sonata" at a funeral service in the Preston, England, church where he worked. Immediately after finishing the piece, Markland shut his eyes, collapsed, and fell to the floor, dead. An autopsy revealed he'd died of heart failure. Three days later, his funeral was held at the same church, where another organist played "Moonlight Sonata" (and lived).

*   *   *

FROM THE CLASSIFIEDS

• Fork, mangled, 50 cents. Also selling garbage disposal. Used once. Needs repair.
• Free Sundaes for Dads on Father's Day (Dads must be 15 or older).

ROBOTS IN THE NEWS

One day, they will enslave and/or kill us all. Until then, let's just enjoy these stories about (mostly) friendly and innocuous robots.

BUG-BOT

In 2007 a team of researchers at Free University in Belgium developed tiny robots the size of cockroaches. They sprayed the robo-roaches with cockroach pheromones and released them among real roaches. The goal: to see if the robots could lure the cockroaches into following them. But in the end, it was the robots who followed the cockroaches (into dark corners, which is where roaches like to congregate). The scientists say the result is a major development in creating robots that can understand, adapt to, and even mimic animal behavior.

SCIENCE-BOT

Robotics scientists at Aberystwyth University in Wales and Cambridge University in England have developed a robotic scientist. "Adam" is programmed to propose a scientific hypothesis and then prove it by conducting experiments. He's already conducted his first tests (on baker's yeast). Ross King of Aberystwyth thinks this could lead to teams of human and robot scientists working together in labs someday, with robots conducting the tedious experiments and keeping records, which human scientists don't like doing.

BARTENDER-BOT

London has more than 6,000 pubs, but as of 2007, it has only one that is robot-operated. The bartenders at Cynthia's Cyberbar are robots—named Cynthia and Rastus—that are programmed to pour pints and mix drinks in the perfect proportions. And like real bartenders, they engage in friendly conversation (although their responses are all prerecorded).

LIFTER-BOT

In June 2007, a worker at a factory in Bålsta, Sweden, was trying to repair an industrial robot used to lift and move heavy rocks. The man turned off the power supply and approached the robot.

German anatomist Wilhelm von Waldeyer coined the term "neuron" in 1891.

Well, he *thought* he'd turned off the power supply. As he came near, the robot, which is programmed to grab and lift whatever came near it, latched its "hands" around the worker's head and lifted him into the air. The man broke free, but suffered four broken ribs in the process. Swedish police investigated the incident and fined the factory the equivalent of $3,000.

PET-BOT

The most widely known robots in the United States today are probably Roombas, the commercial line of programmable robotic vacuum cleaners. Researchers at Georgia Tech University have published a study showing just how accepted Roombas have become. Despite lacking the humanoid structure of science-fiction robots (the Roomba is disc-shaped and six inches high), according to the study, owners commonly attribute human qualities to them and even name them (like pets) or dress them up in tiny outfits.

TEACHER-BOT

"Saya," the newest teacher at Kudan Primary School in Tokyo, is the world's first ultra-realistic robot teacher. Professor Hiroshi Kobayashi, who has been working on the project at the city's University of Science since 1994, created Saya, a robot that looks like an attractive Japanese woman in her early 20s. He's especially proud of her skin, which feels smooth and real because it's made out of a very fine latex. As she conducts preprogrammed lesson plans, Saya can simulate human facial expressions and give feedback to her students. One of her 10-year-old students told reporters that she's "pretty," while another said she's "scary, but fun."

RECYCLE-BOT

Each year since the mid-1980s, more than 150 robots of various types and sizes compete in an event called "Sweeping the Nation." In the Massachusetts Institute of Technology gymnasium, the robots pick up crushed soda cans and small piles of trash that have been scattered on the floor and place them in a "recycling center" (a milk crate). The objective: to see which robot can "recycle" the most trash in under a minute. It's the final project for an MIT sophomore class in mechanical engineering. The top eight finishers (the humans, not the robots) get T-shirts.

The University of Minnesota is older than the state of Minnesota.

PSEUDOCIDAL TENDENCIES

In America, faking your own death is called "pseudocide." In England it's called "doing a Reginald Perrin," after a 1970s British sitcom character who escaped from his boring job by faking his own drowning. Perrin eventually returned from the dead and took up his life again. But that's not quite the way it worked with these pseudocides.

JOHN STONEHOUSE. Stonehouse was a 49-year-old rising star in Britain's Labour Party when he went for a swim at a Miami beach in November 1974 and disappeared. He was presumed drowned, leaving a wife and daughter. But on Christmas Eve he was discovered in Melbourne, Australia, with a new identity...and his 28-year-old former secretary. Deported to England, Stonehouse was eventually convicted on 18 counts of theft, fraud, and deception relating to phony businesses he'd set up before going into hiding. He served three years of his seven-year sentence, married the secretary in 1981, and died in 1988 at the age of 62.

MARCUS SCHRENKER. Schrenker, a 38-year-old money manager from Indiana, was facing financial ruin in 2008 when authorities began to investigate him for theft (stealing from his clients) and securities fraud. What to do? First, Schrenker went to Alabama and stashed a flashy red motorcycle in a storage facility. Then he returned to Indiana and took off toward Florida in his Piper Malibu airplane. Over Huntsville, Alabama, he sent out a distress call, claiming that his windshield had imploded and he was bleeding badly, and then he parachuted 2,000 feet to safety. The plane, tracked by military aircraft trying to intercept it, flew on autopilot for another 200 miles before it crashed in a Florida swamp near several homes. It was assumed that Schrenker had been killed—but there was no blood in the plane and the windshield did not appear damaged. Schrenker, meanwhile, retrieved the motorcycle in Alabama and zoomed away toward the Florida Panhandle. He holed up in a remote campground, wrote a goodbye e-mail to a friend, and slit one wrist. By the time U.S. Marshals found him, days later, he had lost a lot of blood—but he survived. He pled guilty to federal charges and faces up to 26 years in prison.

STEVEN CHIN LEUNG. At the time of the World Trade Center attacks in 2001, 27-year-old Leung was under indictment for passport fraud in Hawaii. He saw the 9/11 tragedy as his chance to escape prosecution, so he decided to masquerade as his brother (he didn't really have a brother) and apply for his own death certificate. First, in a phone call to his own lawyer, he posed as "Jeffrey Leung" and claimed that Steven had been working at the brokerage firm of Cantor Fitzgerald and had died in the terrorist attacks. Next he posed as "William Leung" and told the NYC Law Department the same thing. He even concocted e-mails supposedly exchanged by Steven and a deceased manager at the brokerage firm and cited the e-mails as proof that he had been in the Twin Towers on that day. When U.S. Marshals caught up with him, Steven admitted that he'd never worked in the World Trade Center and had faked his own death to avoid federal prosecution for passport fraud. The judge threw the book at him, sentencing him to four years in jail—18 months more than federal guidelines recommend for passport fraud.

SAMUEL ISRAEL III. As owner of Bayou Group LLC, a phony hedge fund based in Stamford, Connecticut, Israel bilked investors out of $450 million. He was arrested in 2005 and eventually sentenced to 20 years in prison. But on June 9, 2008, the day he was supposed to begin his sentence at a federal prison hospital (he had severe back problems and was addicted to painkillers), the 49-year-old Israel disappeared. His RV was found abandoned near the Bear Mountain Bridge in New York with the words "Suicide is painless" written in the dust on the windshield. Investigators looked for his body in the Hudson River, but found nothing. A month later, Israel resurfaced when he drove a motor scooter to a Massachusetts police station and gave himself up. He was returned to New York, where the judge who had originally sentenced him said, "Welcome back, Mr. Israel," ordered his $500,000 bail forfeited...and added two more years to his sentence.

For more strange tales of "pseudocide," turn to page 344.

DER FARTENFÜHRER

What was it that caused Adolf Hitler's physical and mental health to collapse in the closing days of World War II? He was losing the war, of course—surely that had a great deal to do with it. But for more than 60 years, historians have wondered if there was more to it than that.

THE LEADER

On April 21, 1945, an SS physician named Ernst-Günther Schenck was summoned to Adolf Hitler's bunker in Berlin and ordered to stock it with food. By that time Germany's war was hopelessly lost—most of the country was already in Allied hands. Soviet troops had almost completely circled Berlin and were battling their way into the center of the city. Rather than flee, Hitler had decided to make his final stand in his *führerbunker* in the heart of the Nazi capital. He would remain there until the end, which for him was just nine days away.

Like all Germans, Dr. Schenck had been fed a steady diet of photographs, films, and propaganda posters of Hitler since the dictator had come to power in 1933. But the man he saw in the bunker looked nothing like those images. The 56-year-old Hitler "was a living corpse, a dead soul," Schenck remembered in a 1985 interview. "His spine was hunched, his shoulder blades protruded from his bent back, and he collapsed his shoulders like a turtle.... I was looking into the eye of death."

OLD MAN

Even more shocking than the way Hitler looked was the way he moved about the bunker. He walked with the slow, halting shuffle of a man 30 years older, dragging his left leg behind him as he went. He couldn't go more than a few steps without grabbing onto something for support.

Hitler's head, arms, and entire left side trembled and jerked uncontrollably. No longer able to write his own name, he signed important documents with a rubber stamp. He had always insisted on shaving himself—this murderer of millions could not bear the thought of another man holding a razor to his throat—but his trembling hands made that impossible, too. He could not lift food

Role reversal: Seals sometimes eat baby sharks.

to his mouth without spilling it down the front of his uniform and could not take a seat without help—after he shuffled up to a table, an aide pushed a chair behind him, and he plopped down onto it.

Hitler's mental state had deteriorated as well. His thinking was muddled, his memory was failing, and his emotions whipsawed back and forth between long bouts of irrational euphoria (especially irrational considering how close Germany was to defeat) and fits of screaming, uncontrollable rage that lasted for hours.

DIAGNOSES

Schenck remained in Berlin until the end. On April 29, Hitler married his longtime mistress, Eva Braun, and the following day the pair committed suicide in the führerbunker. Germany surrendered unconditionally on May 7.

After the war, Schenck spent a decade in Soviet prison camps. He never forgot what he saw at the führerbunker, and after his release he spent years poring over Hitler's medical records in an attempt to discover just what had caused the dictator's health to decline so rapidly in the final years and months of his life.

He was not alone in this effort—in the more than 60 years since the end of the war, many historians, physicians, and World War II buffs have done the same thing. What caused Hitler's collapse—was it Parkinson's disease? Tertiary syphilis? Giant cell arteritis? Countless theories have been advanced to explain Hitler's physical and mental decline, and after all this time the experts are no closer to agreeing than they were on the day he died.

THE CURE THAT ILLS

One of the most bizarre theories was advanced by some of Hitler's own doctors in July 1944. The diagnosis came about by chance, after a visiting ear, nose, and throat specialist named Dr. Erwin Giesing happened to notice six tiny black pills—"Doctor Koester's Anti-Gas Pills"—sitting on the Führer's breakfast tray next to his porridge, dry bread, and orange juice. After spotting the pills, Giesing did something that Hitler's own personal physician, an eccentric quack named Dr. Theodor Morell, had apparently never bothered to do: He examined the tin the pills came in and actually *read the label* to see what was in them. Giesing was stunned by what he read. Could it be? Was the Führer was being poisoned by the pills he took to control his *meteorism*—powerful attacks of uncontrollable farting?

GUT FEELING

Hitler had suffered from digestive problems his entire life. Since childhood he'd been prone to crippling, painful stomach cramps during times of emotional distress. By the time he reached his early 40s, the cramping had become more frequent, often accompanied by violent attacks of farting, along with alternating bouts of constipation and diarrhea.

The farting attacks are one of the reasons Hitler became a vegetarian in the early 1930s: He didn't trust doctors, so rather than seek professional help for his condition he tried to treat it himself by eliminating meat, rich foods, milk, and butter from his diet in favor of raw and cooked vegetables and whole grains.

STILL FARTIN'

Increasing the fiber in his diet did not improve Hitler's condition; if anything it made him even gassier than he'd been before. (But the vegetarian diet may have made his farts less smelly, and he may have been willing to settle for *that*.) By the mid-1930s, Hitler was the ruler of Germany...and still farting like a horse. His attacks were most severe right after meals; during dinner parties it was common for him to suddenly leap up from the table and disappear into his private quarters, leaving stunned guests to wonder why the Führer had gone and when he might be back. On many nights he did not return at all.

In 1936 Hitler happened to meet Dr. Morell at a Christmas party. After pulling the doctor aside Hitler poured out his problems, describing his intestinal distress and his eczema: itchy, inflamed skin on his shins, so painful that he could not put on his boots. By now Hitler had given up trying to cure himself and allowed Germany's best doctors to examine him. They put him on a diet of tea and dry toast, but all that did was leave him feeling weak and exhausted. Morell listened attentively...and then promised to cure both problems within a year. Hitler decided to give him a try.

So what kind of a doctor was Theodor Morell?
Part II of the story is on page 312.

CHEST HAIR: $7 MILLION

Sometimes a celebrity's livelihood depends solely on a single physical trait or talent. Should they suddenly lose their good looks or their lovely voices, their careers are just as suddenly over. Solution: insurance.

THE SCAR POLICY

You've probably heard stories about singers insuring their voices for large sums of money. It's for real. Technically, it's known as the "surplus lines" market, which covers any strange or specific risks not normally covered by life or disability insurance. It's also extremely expensive, and available only after all other insurance policies have been maxed out. So although anybody can get a policy, it's usually only the rich and famous who do.

Few American insurers deal in surplus lines, but foreign companies do—it's what made the British firm Lloyd's of London famous. Their first celebrity client: silent-film star Douglas Fairbanks Sr., who feared physical disfigurement that would end his career as a matinee idol. Fairbanks asked Lloyd's to write a "scar policy" for him.

FAME...

Here are some other celebrities with highly specific insurance.

• **Ben Turpin.** He is believed to have been the first celebrity to insure a trademark feature. Turpin was a vaudeville and silent film performer who had crossed eyes. Should they ever have straightened, he would have received a $20,000 payout.

• **David Beckham.** The English soccer star has insured his legs for $70 million.

• **Rod Stewart.** His singing voice is insured for $6 million. (He can't make a claim unless he loses it completely, so he can't collect yet—it's *supposed* to sound that gravelly.)

• **America Ferrera.** The star of *Ugly Betty* was hired by Aquafresh to promote teeth-whitening products. To protect the investment, the company insured Ferrera's smile for $10 million.

• **Tom Jones.** He's as famous for his machismo and sex appeal as for his songs "It's Not Unusual" and "What's New, Pussycat?" He will collect $7 million if an accidental, catastrophic occurrence ever destroys his most notable and macho asset—his chest hair.

• **Mariah Carey.** She has a five-octave singing range and she's one of the most successful solo recording artists of all time, with 18 #1 hit singles. But her image is apparently more important to her than her voice: Her legs, not her voice, are insured for $1 billion. Other stars with insured legs: Betty Grable (for $1 million in the 1940s), Angie Dickinson, Brooke Shields, Mary Hart, and Tina Turner (for $3.2 million).

• **Michael Flatley.** After starring in the touring Irish dance troupe Riverdance, he went on to start his own show, called *Lord of the Dance*. To ensure his livelihood, he bought a $39 million policy for his dancing feet.

• **Jimmy Durante.** In the 1940s, he had his highly recognizable nose insured for $50,000.

• **Keith Richards.** Should he ever accidentally cut off one of his guitar-playing fingers, he will receive $1.8 million.

...AND FORTUNE

Less-famous people who have taken out specific insurance policies:

• Food critic Egon Ronay has a $400,000 policy for his taste buds.

• In 1959 the 40 members of the Derbyshire Whiskers Club, a British "beard appreciation group," paid £20 each to insure their facial hair against fire and theft.

• A British soccer fan insured himself against "psychic trauma" in case England lost the 2006 World Cup. They didn't win—no word on whether the man had a mental breakdown or received a payout.

• Harvey Lowe, who won a national yo-yo contest in 1932 when he was 13, insured his hands for $150,000.

• In 2007 Florida woman Domitila Hunnicutt won a Most Valuable Legs contest sponsored by the maker of Jergens Lotion. Her prize: a one-year $2 million insurance policy for her legs. (After one year, she was on her own.)

THE 49TH STATE

2009 marked the 50th anniversary of Alaska becoming the 49th U.S. state. Here's a timeline of how it happened.

BACKGROUND
Alaska has been inhabited since about 12000 B.C., when nomadic tribes from Siberia first crossed over the Bering Land Bridge—now covered in water and called the Bering Sea—into Alaska. All natives who live there, including the Inuits and Aleuts, are descended from those nomads. Despite being just a few miles away (three miles at the closest point), white settlers from Russia didn't come to Alaska until the 1730s, when the area became known as "Russian America."

• **1859:** After losing the Crimean War in 1856, Russia needs money, so it offers to sell the territory to the United States. The U.S., however, is more concerned with trying to avert the impending Civil War, and declines the offer.

• **1867:** Russia offers Alaska to the U.S. again, and this time it accepts. Secretary of State William Seward agrees to purchase the 586,000-mile area parcel of land for $7.2 million, supposedly for use as a strategic point on the Pacific Rim. The purchase is widely criticized as "Seward's Folly" because Alaska is perceived as a useless, frozen wasteland. It's classified as the Department of Alaska and placed under the control of the War Department.

• **1884:** With a total population of about 30,000 people (natives and white settlers), a civic infrastructure to keep the peace becomes necessary, so the federal government appoints judges, clerks, and marshals to serve in Alaska. In order to have a body of laws to enforce, this coalition—a mere 13 people—adopts the legal code of Oregon.

• **1896:** Gold is discovered in Alaska. About 30,000 *more* people move there. Along with the economy, crime in Alaska grows, so in 1900 Congress sends more judges…and enacts a tax code.

• **1912:** Congress creates a territorial legislature of eight senators

South Korean scientists have cloned cats that glow red when exposed to ultraviolet light.

and 16 representatives, and one non-voting delegate to the House of Representatives for the newly renamed Alaska Territory.

• **1916:** Alaska's House delegate, a former territorial judge named James Wickersham, proposes the first bill to make Alaska a state. Congress doesn't need to rule on it because Alaskans themselves aren't interested—the majority of Alaska's 58,000 people feel no tangible connection to the United States.

• **1933:** Alaska's Congressional delegate Anthony J. Dimond petitions Congress to build military airfields and army garrisons in Alaska, as well as a highway to link the territory to the mainland U.S. The reason: Dimond believes Japan is a growing threat. He is convinced that the Japanese fishermen who work off Alaska's coasts are military spies gathering information about weak spots in Alaska's harbors. Dimond argues that Alaska is as much a key to the Pacific as Hawaii, especially since that's why the U.S. annexed it in the first place. Nevertheless, Congress declines the requests.

• **1942:** A few months after Japan bombs Pearl Harbor and the U.S. enters World War II, Congress allocates funds to build military facilities and a highway to Alaska through Canada.

• **1946:** The Alaska Territory's two highest-ranking politicians, Governor Ernest Gruening and Delegate Bob Bartlett, organize a territory-wide referendum on statehood. Due to frustration over "taxation without representation," at this point Alaskans are overwhelmingly in favor of statehood, and the referendum passes, 67 to 33 percent.

• **1948:** Based on that vote, Bartlett presents another statehood bill to Congress. It never makes it to the House floor, dying in the Public Lands Committee. Committee chairman Hugh Butler opposes statehood because he thinks Alaska's remoteness will make it a hotbed of Communism. He also thinks Alaska's low population, about 100,000, doesn't warrant statehood.

• **1949:** A grassroots group called the Alaska Statehood Committee forms to aggressively promote statehood. They solicit labor organizations, state governors, newspaper editors, and celebrities to join the cause. Among those who speak out in favor: James Cagney, Pearl S. Buck, and former First Lady Eleanor Roosevelt, who writes in her newspaper column, "It seems extraordinary that an area of North America as important to our country as Alaska is should not be admitted as a state."

• **1950:** Bartlett avoids Butler's Senate committee by submitting a statehood bill first to the House of Representatives. If it passes there, then it would *have* to get Senate approval, he figures. The bill passes the House 186–146. But in the Senate, the controlling coalition of Republicans and conservative Southern Democrats vote it down out of the fear that Alaska would send liberal Democrats to Congress, tipping the balance of power.

• **1952:** The Alaska Statehood Committee sends members of Congress bouquets of Forget-Me-Nots—the official flower of Alaska. Friends of ASC members in the continental U.S. receive Christmas cards that year that read

> Make Alaskans' future bright
> Ask your Senator for statehood
> And start the New Year right.

• **1955:** In an attempt to force Congress's hand, the Alaskan Constitutional Convention meets at the University of Alaska-Fairbanks to draw up a state code, even though Alaska isn't a state. It also organizes elections for one congressman and two senators to send to Washington, another attempt to force Congress into making it a state. Congress doesn't recognize or seat them, because Alaska *isn't* a state.

• **1957:** After two years of inactivity, the statehood debate is revived when Speaker of the House Sam Rayburn endorses the idea. When asked what changed his mind after years of opposition, Rayburn says, "Bob Bartlett," referring to the delegate's years of tireless lobbying for statehood. Senate Democratic leader Lyndon Johnson pledges the support of all Democrats (liberal and Southern) should Alaskan statehood come to a vote. It does, and passes the House 217–172, and the Senate 64–20.

• **1959:** On January 3, President Eisenhower signs an official declaration making Alaska the 49th state.

What does *propinquity* mean? Living close to your place of birth.

DUMB CROOKS

Proof that crime doesn't pay.

EGG ON HIS FACE

One night in July 2009, 18-year-old Daniel Barr of Strasburg, Pennsylvania, and a bunch of his friends were driving around and decided it would be fun to throw eggs at a police car. They found a parked cruiser and hurled a dozen eggs at it. They might have gotten away with the crime…had they not chosen a police car that was occupied by a police officer.

TAKE THE MONEY AND (DON'T) RUN

In January 2008, a 53-year-old man and his 20-year-old accomplice (names were withheld in police reports) set out to rob the Vernon, British Columbia, branch of the CIBC Bank. The older man went into the bank to commit the actual robbery, while the younger man stayed in the getaway car, listening to the radio. When the older man returned, the car wouldn't start—the battery was dead. They quickly got out of the car and ran down the street, but were apprehended a few minutes later. Why? The CIBC Bank is located next door to a police station.

KNIFE? CHECK. MASKS? CHECK. GAS? UH…

Lonnie Meckwood and Phillip Weeks robbed the Quickway Convenience Store in Kirkwood, New York, at knifepoint. They got away with the money and the clerk was unharmed. Here's the dumb part: Meckwood and Weeks were caught by police less than a mile away from the convenience store when they were spotted standing on the side of the road, next to their car… which had run out of gas. (The store they'd just robbed was also a gas station.)

LIQUID COURAGE

Thirty-three-year-old Shawn Lester stormed into a Charleston, West Virginia, convenience store, filled up a cup at the soda fountain, then demanded all of the money in the register, claiming he had a gun. But before the clerk could get any money out, Lester got cold feet and didn't want to go through with the robbery. He started

---

How serious are they? Each year, about 30 people attempt to commit suicide with BB guns.

to walk out of the store…with his drink. The clerk told Lester he had to pay for it, so he did—with his debit card. Even though he signed the receipt "John Doe" (and didn't actually steal any money), police easily traced the debit card and arrested Lester at his home.

HEY, I KNOW THAT GUY!

Donald Keene was at a New Chicago, Indiana, police station to report a crime when he happened to see a wall of photos of the area's most-wanted criminals. One of the photos looked familiar: It was a man wanted for breaking into a home and stealing jewelry, video games, and a shotgun. Keene instantly recognized the man— it was him. He casually mentioned it to the police officer he was speaking with…and was immediately arrested.

IT'S JUST POLITE TO LEAVE A NOTE

One day in June 2009, an employee at Ziggy's, a hardware store in Spokane, Washington, found a plastic bag filled with small, crystallized rocks on the floor near the checkout. Thinking that it was crystal methamphetamine, the employee called the police. But before they arrived, 34-year-old Christopher Wilson walked in and asked if anyone had found a bag of crystal meth he thought he may have lost in the store. The employee lied and told him they hadn't, so Wilson left his name and phone number, just in case the drugs turned up. Wilson returned home…where police arrested him a few minutes later.

CUFF 'EM, DAN-O

In 2009 a Massachusetts man showed up at a police station and asked to have a pair of handcuffs removed. Earlier that day, the man's sister had put the cuffs on him as a joke, but then lost the key. On a whim, the police decided to run the man's name through their computer and discovered that he had several outstanding warrants. (He was promptly given a brand-new set of handcuffs.)

*   *   *

"People who think they know everything are a great annoyance to those of us who do."

—Isaac Asimov

12 oz. of beer, 5 oz. of wine, and a 1.5-oz. shot of vodka all contain the same amount of alcohol.

INVENTED WORDS

Most English words took decades, even centuries, to achieve their modern form. But not these—they were invented overnight.

FACTOID
Coined by: Norman Mailer
Story: In 1973, while writing his biography of Marilyn Monroe, Mailer was trying to describe made-up facts that are believed because they're printed in a magazine or newspaper. He combined the word "fact" with the suffix *-oid*, which means "like." The term held this "invented fact" meaning until the 1990s, when CNN Headline News began displaying trivia and statistics on the screen beneath the title "Factoid." Result: Now it also means "little fact."

AGNOSTIC
Coined by: Thomas H. Huxley, 19th-century biologist
Story: Huxley's belief that people can only truly understand what they can see with their own eyes earned him the "atheist" label, and no matter how hard he tried, he couldn't distance himself from it. So one night at a party in 1860, "I invented the word 'agnostic' to denote people who, like myself, confess themselves to be hopelessly ignorant concerning a variety of matters." Huxley combined the prefix *a-*, meaning "without," and *gnostic*, a word derived from the Greek *gnostos*, meaning "knowable," and used by early Christian writers to mean a "higher knowledge of spiritual things." The definition has since changed subtly from "admitted ignorance of spiritual things" to the "questioning of spiritual things."

GROK
Coined by: Robert A. Heinlein, science-fiction writer
Story: It appears in Heinlein's 1961 novel, *Stranger in a Strange Land*, as a Martian word that means "to understand so thoroughly that the observer becomes a part of the observed—to merge, blend, intermarry, lose identity in group experience. It means almost everything that we mean by religion, philosophy, and science—and it means as little to us (because of our Earthly assumptions) as color means to a blind man." Although the humans in

Kitchen tip: Rubbing your hands on stainless steel will remove the smell of garlic.

the novel never really grokked the meaning of the word, it has since been adopted by popular culture "to understand a concept, opinion, or philosophy on a deep, profound level."

YES-MAN
Coined by: Tad Dorgan, American cartoonist
Story: In 1913 Dorgan drew a cartoon called "Giving the First Edition the Once-Over," which featured a newspaper editor and his assistants. Attempting to show how weak-kneed the assistants were, above each of them was the word "yes-man." The term quickly expanded to include any subordinate—in business, sports, or politics—who always agrees with the boss, regardless of whether it's justified. (Also credited to Dorgan: "23-skidoo," "cat's meow," "dumbbell," "for crying out loud," "hard-boiled," and "Yes, we have no bananas.")

REALTOR
Coined by: Charles N. Chadbourn, president of the Minneapolis Real Estate Board
Story: What do you call a person who sells homes? A realtor? Wrong—a real estate agent. Not all real estate agents are REALTORS®. The term is what's called a *collective membership trademark*, so only members of the National Association of Realtors (NAR) can legally use it. Chadbourn invented the word in 1916 after reading the headline: *Real Estate Man Swindles a Poor Widow.* "The advantage of a distinguishing mark," he said, "is so that the public may know the responsible, expert real estate man from the curbstoner who possesses no such qualifications." He sold the rights of the word to NAR for $1.

GOBBLEDYGOOK
Coined by: Maury Maverick, U.S. Congressman
Story: To Maverick, a straight-talking Texas politician (and grandson of Samuel Maverick, from whom we get the word "maverick"), most other politicians were like turkeys: "always gobbledy gobbling and strutting around with ludicrous pomposity." While chairman of Smaller War Plants Corporation in 1944, Maverick sent out a memo: "No more gobbledygook language! Anyone using the words 'activation' or 'implementation' will be shot."

TOM SWIFTIES

This classic style of pun was invented in the 1920s. They're atrocious and corny...so of course we had to include them.

"I never worry about blackouts," Tom said delightedly.

"What's my favorite song? 'I Got You Babe,'" Tom shared sunnily.

"I just ordered another of these terrific cutlets," Tom revealed.

"I had to come back to the marina," Tom reported.

"I'm wearing this ribbon around my arm," said Tom with abandon.

"Use your own toothbrush!" Tom bristled.

"Okay, you can borrow it again," Tom relented.

"This oar is broken," said Tom robustly.

"Would you like to buy some cod?" asked Tom selfishly.

"No, I won't give you a note saying you're excused," said Tom unwaveringly.

"So only one person arrived at the party before I did?" Tom second-guessed.

"I need an injection," Tom pleaded in vain.

"It's only average," said Tom meanly.

"What are these berries?" Tom rasped.

"This location looks kind of familiar," Tom said warily.

"I've caught Moby Dick!" Tom wailed.

"I would never give that a grade of A," Tom berated.

"That young insect is female," said Tom gallantly.

"I love Granny Smiths," said Tom applaudingly.

"Please don't point that arrow at me," said Tom, quivering.

"I flatly deny this," said Tom under pressure.

"The optician probably doesn't have my glasses ready yet," Tom speculated.

"I shot the gun, but there's no bullet hole," Tom said blankly.

"I'm dying," Tom croaked.

Most American ice cream trucks play "Turkey in the Straw." British trucks play "Greensleeves."

THE BESTSELLING...

Here are the top-selling LPs and CDs in the U.S. How many do you own?

...movie soundtrack: *The Bodyguard* (1992), 17 million.

...live album: Garth Brooks, *Double Live* (1998), 11 million.

...Beatles album: *The Beatles*, also known as "The White Album" (1968), 9.5 million.

...studio album: Michael Jackson's *Thriller* (1982), 28 million.

...album that never made the Top 10: Meat Loaf's *Bat Out of Hell* (1977) peaked at #14, but it went on to sell 14 million copies.

...debut album: The first, self-titled LP by the rock band Boston (1976) has sold 17 million copies.

...double album: Pink Floyd, *The Wall* (1979), 11.5 million.

...triple album: Bruce Springsteen and the E Street Band, *Live/1975–85*, four million.

...country album: Shania Twain, *Come On Over* (1997), 20 million.

...hard rock album: Led Zeppelin's untitled, fourth album (1971), 23 million.

...hip-hop album: MC Hammer, *Please Hammer, Don't Hurt 'Em* (1990), 10 million.

...instrumental album: Kenny G, *Breathless* (1992), 12 million.

...jazz album: Miles Davis's *Kind of Blue* (1959), four million.

...reggae album: Bob Marley & the Wailers' greatest-hits compilation, *Legend* (1984), 10 million.

...comedy album: Impressionist Vaughn Meader's Kennedy family parody, *The First Family* (1962), with seven million copies.

...solo debut album: After leaving Wham!, George Michael recorded *Faith* (1987), which sold 10 million copies.

...greatest-hits collection: Eagles, *Greatest Hits 1971–1975* (1976), 29 million. It's America's bestselling album of all time of any kind.

Aptly named: The Pentagon has five sides, five stories, and a five-acre courtyard.

THE DIGITAL CAMERA REVOLUTION, PART I

*For our Supremely Satisfying Bathroom Reader, we wrote an article about
the history of photography, ending with the introduction of Kodak's Instamatic
cameras of the 1960s, which we said "brought photography to the masses."
We didn't realize it at the time, but photography was about to undergo
a substantial—and revolutionary—change: the move to digital.*

A DEVELOPING STORY

Throughout photography's nearly 200-year history, camera makers have striven to make their products smaller, the images sharper, and the process faster and easier. Yet the advancements of the first century and a half took place at intervals of 5, 10, or even 20 years. Once the digital revolution got going in the 1990s, major advancements started taking place yearly. But it took a few decades of tinkering to get to that point.

The process of creating an electronic camera that could take pictures without film began in 1957 when Russell Kirsch, a computer engineer at the U.S. National Bureau of Standards, created the first scanned image that could be viewed on a TV screen. The grainy black-and-white image—named by *Life* magazine "one of the 100 photographs that changed the world"—was simply a photo of his three-month-old son. Kirsch had invented the scanner but, more importantly, he'd also invented the *pixel* (short for "picture element," and defined as "the smallest unit of an image displayed on a computer or television screen"). Kirsch's baby picture—just 176 pixels wide—marked the beginnings of home computing, satellite imaging, and digital photography.

SENSOR SHIP

In the 1960s, NASA scientists experimented with the new digital technology in order to, among other things, send images from space probes orbiting the moon back to Earth. In 1961 Eugene Lally, a scientist at the Jet Propulsion Laboratory, published the first description of what he called a *mosaic photosensor,* a device that would translate light into bits of information. Although the technology for Lally's idea didn't yet exist, it got other scientists in the field excited about digital imaging. Willard Boyle and George Smith, two developers at Bell Labs, added the next big piece of the puzzle in 1969: the *charged coupling device*. In simple terms, the CCD is a type of semiconductor that generates an electrical charge when hit by light. This would be the basis for the "sensor" that would later replace the film in digital cameras.

THE KODAK DIGITAL TOASTER

This new technology caught the attention of electronics companies such as Texas Instruments (TI) and Eastman Kodak. TI applied for a patent for a digital camera in 1972, but never actually built one. Three years later, in 1975, Kodak bosses charged a 25-year-old engineer named Steven Sasson with a task: Build a camera that utilizes a CCD. "I'd never built a regular camera. What made me think I could build anything with this CCD device?" recalled Sasson. "I decided to take a digital approach because my background was digital and I could avoid the mechanical complexities." He raided other departments for parts he needed, including an analog-to-digital converter adapted from Motorola components and a discarded movie camera lens. After a few months of experimenting, Sasson emerged with a contraption that resembled a big toaster with a lens on one side. It weighed eight pounds and took 23 seconds to produce its first picture: a 0.01 megapixel image of Sasson's lab assistant. The dark, blurry image could be displayed only on a specially made television screen, but it was the first truly digital photograph.

Sasson's superiors were impressed with the accomplishment (though less so with the poor image quality). They asked him how long he thought it would take for the digital camera market to take off. Sasson's answer: "About 15 or 20 years." Kodak patented the invention, but kept their focus on film cameras.

GOING COMMERCIAL

The first consumer electronic camera that required no film was the Sony Mavica (short for **M**agnetic **V**ideo **Ca**mera). Released in 1981, it wasn't a true digital camera, it was a video camera that

King James IV of Scotland was an amateur dentist. He paid people...

could freeze single frames and then transfer them onto a two-inch floppy disk. Just as with Sasson's digital camera, the pictures could be viewed only on a TV screen. The Mavica generated some interest among technology buffs, but at the time few people outside the industry paid much attention to a camera that didn't use film. As the 1980s unfolded, however, the desktop computer was starting to become a fixture in people's homes, and with it came the first widespread interest in a truly digital camera that *anyone* could use.

Kodak played a big part in this. In 1986 they developed a powerful new CCD that worked in *megapixels*. Whereas Sasson's digital toaster could display only 10,000 pixels, it was now possible to create a sensor that could display more than *a million* pixels of information, or one megapixel. (Today's cameras go up to about 15 megapixels…and counting.) After that, the innovations kept coming and coming—from the first photo CDs in 1990 to the first digital camera designed for professional photojournalists in 1991, a Nikon F3 that utilized a 1.3 megapixel sensor built by Kodak. Retail price: $13,000.

TAKING OVER

But the high cost wasn't the only reason that the digital camera was still considered a novelty in the early 1990s. It still couldn't come close to matching the image quality attained by conventional film cameras, which were still much less expensive. So the big camera makers—Nikon, Kodak, Canon, Pentax, Olympus, and Minolta—kept pushing film while they worked on increasing the quality of their digital lines. And as the costs began to fall, digital sales started rising—at about the exact time that Sasson had predicted they would back in 1975. "In the late '90s," he recalled, "I was vacationing with my family and was waiting for the next eruption of Old Faithful in Yellowstone Park. They have you sit around in a semicircle to watch, and I looked around and there were several digital cameras. I remember telling my wife, 'It's happening. It's really here.'"

For Part II, advance to page 204.

AERO-NUTS

*From our "Dustbin of History" files, here's the harrowing
tale of a little-known milestone in aviation history.*

LOADED
It was January 7, 1785, and two men were preparing for the
first ever balloon crossing of the English Channel. The one
who financed the adventure was John Jeffries, a well-to-do American doctor. The one with the aviation skills was Frenchman Jean-
Pierre Blanchard, one of the innovators of ballooning—which at
that point had only been around for two years. A crowd gathered
near the Dover cliffs to watch them lift off for France. At 1:00 p.m.,
Blanchard and Jeffries embarked on their 21-mile journey. But
there was one problem: They were too heavy.

They were carrying 30 pounds of ballast weights (used to keep
the balloon steady), plus steering gear, personal items, a bag of
mail to be delivered in France, and scientific equipment. And
then there were the four "wings." Made out of silk and extending
from the carriage, they served no real purpose except to make the
balloon look like a bird.

CHANNEL SURFING

Only a few miles into the crossing, it was apparent that the balloon was flying too low. The Channel loomed close, and neither
man could swim. Their only option: lose some weight.

First went the ballast bags, but the balloon didn't rise. As the
carriage skimmed 20 or so feet above the surface, Blanchard
unhooked the wings and let them drop into the water. The men
argued over what to throw off next, finally deciding on the bag of
mail. But the balloon was still flying too low. Then went the bottle of brandy they were saving for the landing. Still too low. Then,
much to Jeffries' dismay, went his thermometer, his barometer, and
his telescope. *Still* too low. So Blanchard stripped off his clothes—
his heavy overcoat, his pants and shirt, then everything else, and
he urged Jeffries to do the same. But the doctor was too dignified
to land in France *completely* naked, and only stripped down to his
undergarments. And they were still dangerously close to the water.

The first presidential armored car, used by Franklin Roosevelt, originally belonged to Al Capone.

I'M AMERICAN, AND EUROPEAN

Jeffries had an idea: They'd had a lot to drink with breakfast, and neither had gone to the bathroom before they left. "We were able to obtain, I verily believe, between five and six pounds of urine," Jeffries later wrote, "which circumstance, however trivial or ludicrous it may seem, I have reason to believe, was of real utility to us." Perhaps he was right—peeing into the Channel probably saved them from crashing into the Channel, but the fact remained that they were still flying too low. When the bottom of the carriage actually *touched* the water, Jeffries panicked and started climbing up the ropes. Blanchard yelled for him to come down; he was making it even more unstable. Jeffries climbed down; the two men put on their cork life jackets. They braced for impact.

Then, just as they saw the French coast ahead in the distance, a sudden updraft pushed the balloon up into the January sky. "From the height which we were now at," recalled Jeffries, "and from the loss of our clothes, we were almost benumbed with cold." But the cold was the least of their troubles—all of Blanchard's steering equipment and anchors had been thrown overboard, leaving him no way to control the craft. They could only watch in horror as the balloon got caught in a downdraft and headed straight for Felmores Forest. Luckily, just above the canopy, they leveled out and Jeffries was somehow able to grab hold of the top of a tall tree and slow them down. The carriage unceremoniously flopped into a clearing, with the silk balloon still caught in the branches. Some farmers gave them clothes and a ride to the town of Calais, where another crowd had gathered to witness the historic landing.

EPILOGUE

• Jeffries had kept one letter—in his underwear—from the jettisoned mailbag. It was addressed to Benjamin Franklin (serving as American Ambassador to France) from Franklin's son. That was the first airmail-delivered letter in history.

• Blanchard went on to become the first man to fly a balloon in several countries, including the U.S., where George Washington and two future presidents were in attendance. In 1809, at 56 years old, Blanchard was ballooning over the Netherlands when he suffered a heart attack and fell 50 feet to the ground. Though he never recovered, he'd met his end doing what he loved.

HIS LOUSY HIGHNESS

Throughout history, many leaders were given lofty nicknames—
Catherine the Great or Richard the Lionhearted, for example.
But not everyone could be Great or Magnificent. Some
rulers got strange, and strangely specific, nicknames.

ALFONSO THE SLOBBERER: King Alfonso IX ruled
Leon (now part of France) from 1188 to 1230. He was
prone to fits of rage, and anytime he got especially angry,
especially while in battle, he drooled uncontrollably, sometimes to
the point of foaming at the mouth.

PIERO THE GOUTY: Heir to the powerful Medici family,
which ruled Florence, Italy, in the 1500s, Piero suffered from gout,
a form of arthritis commonly characterized by a large, painful sac
of uric acid that forms somewhere inside the body. In Piero's case,
it was in his big toe.

HARALD THE LOUSY: At the age of 12, Harald vowed to
found a kingdom for the Norwegian people. He also vowed not to
cut his hair until he achieved that goal. By 872, he'd founded the
kingdom, but in the 10 years since he'd made his vow, Harald's
hair had grown extremely dirty and was riddled with lice. This
earned him the nickname "the Lousy," meaning "full of lice," not
"inadequate." (Oh, that's better.)

IVAR THE BONELESS: Historians believe that the ninth-
century Danish Viking chieftain suffered from *osteogenesis imper-
fecta,* or extremely brittle bones. That, however, didn't stop him
from becoming a Viking warlord and leading successful invasions
into northern England.

IVAN I DANILOVICH, MONEYBAGS: In the 14th century,
Ivan was the grand prince of Muscovy, now part of Russia. He
earned his nickname not only from his wealth but also because he
was a tax collector for the Tatar Empire, which required him to
haul around big bags of money.

A freshly laid chicken's egg won't start growing into a chick until it reaches 86°F.

CONSTANTINE THE DUNG-NAMED: Eighth-century Byzantine Emperor Constantine V got his nickname from political opponents, who started a rumor that as a baby, he had pooped in a baptismal font. (He might have—he *was* a baby, after all.)

PTOLEMY VI THE MOTHER-LOVER: Ptolemy was the king of Egypt in the second century B.C. He ascended to the throne at age six and ruled jointly with his mother, the queen— Cleopatra I. Since kings and queens are generally married to each other, Ptolemy became know as "the mother-lover." But he didn't really *love* his mother. (He did, however, marry his sister.)

ETHELRED THE UNREADY: Although Ethelred was just 10 years old when he became king of England in 978 C.E., that's not where the nickname originates. "Unready" comes from an Anglo-Saxon word that meant "ill-advised," which reflects the unpopular decisions made by his advisors.

ERIC THE PRIESTHATER: King Eric II of Norway (1280–99) earned his nickname from his (successful) efforts to keep the Catholic Church from garnering special favors and obtaining land from the Norwegian government.

LONGSHANKS: Edward I of England (reigned from 1272 to 1307) had very long "shanks," or legs. Standing at more than 6', he was extremely tall for that era.

BOLESLAW THE WRY-MOUTHED: A Duke of Poland in the 12th century, Boleslaw III was a scheming dictator who assumed power after forcing out his brother. "Wry" means "cleverly humorous" as well as "physically crooked," and by historical accounts, Boleslaw possessed both kinds of wry mouth.

IVAILO THE CABBAGE: A rebel leader and briefly the emperor of Bulgaria in the 1270s, Ivailo probably got the name because, before becoming a politician, he was a peasant farmer. According to some translations, Ivailo was also known as "Radish" and "Lettuce."

I'M GOING TO COUNT TO 10

Twenty years ago on a trip to Oktoberfest, Uncle John learned how to count to 10 in German—and he still remembers how to do it. Here's how the speakers of some languages count to 10.

JAPANESE

一	ee-chee	大	roh-koo
二	nee	七	nah-nah
三	san	八	ha-chee
四	yohn *or* shee	九	q *or* koo
五	goh	十	joo

ARABIC

١	wa-Had	٦	sit-ah
٢	ith-nain	٧	sub-ah
٣	thah-lath-ah	٨	tha-man-ee-ah
٤	ar-bah	٩	tiss-ah
٥	kham-sah	١٠	ash-ra

TURKISH

1	bir	6	alti
2	iki	7	yeddi
3	ooch	8	sakkiz
4	doord	9	dokkuz
5	besh	10	on

MANDARIN CHINESE

一	eee	大	leo
二	are	七	chee
三	sawn	八	baw
四	soo	九	joe
五	ooh	十	sure

HEBREW

א	aleph	ו	vav
ב	bet	ז	zayin
ג	gimel	ח	het
ד	dalet	ט	tet
ה	hei	י	yud

POLISH

1	ye-den	6	shesh-ch
2	dva	7	shedem
3	t-r-sh-ih	8	osh-em
4	ch-teri	9	jev-yench
5	p-yench	10	je-shench

THAI

๑	neung	๖	hok
๒	song	๗	jed
๓	sam	๘	bad
๔	see	๙	gao
๕	har	๑๐	sib

HINDI

एक	ek	छः	cheh
दो	dho	सात	saath
तीन	theen	आठ	aath
चार	chaar	नौ	nau
पाँच	paanch	दस	das

While most of it lies in Africa, a small part of Egypt—the Sinai Peninsula—is located in Asia.

SPUN-OUT SPIN-OFFS

Many successful TV series were "spin-offs" of other shows—Cheers begat Frasier, Dallas gave us Knot's Landing, and Grey's Anatomy spawned Private Practice, for just three examples. Some spin-offs, however, never even make it to air, even when an entire episode of the parent series is used to introduce the new show.

ORIGINAL SERIES: *The Cosby Show*
SPIN-OFF: *Mr. Quiet* (1985)
STORY: *The Cosby Show* was a surprise hit for NBC in 1984 and is even credited with lifting the network from third to first place. Show star/creator Bill Cosby had free rein at the network, and in 1985 he produced an episode of his show to serve as a pilot to star his friend, singer Tony Orlando, for whom he'd opened concerts in the 1970s. On that episode, the Huxtable family volunteered at an inner-city community center run by Orlando's character. Despite Cosby's pull, the pilot was never made into a series because, according to Orlando, his own performance "stunk."

ORIGINAL SERIES: *The Office*
SPIN-OFF: "Untitled *Office* Spin-Off" (2009)
STORY: In 2008 NBC executives asked producers of the hit comedy *The Office* to create a spin-off. They didn't want to split up the original show's ensemble, so the producers planned to introduce a new character to *The Office*, to be played by *Saturday Night Live*'s Amy Poehler, and then base a new, office-based show around her. NBC announced that the untitled show would debut in the plum, post-Super Bowl time slot in February 2009, but the show's writers were having a hard time creating a show that was different enough from *The Office*. So they scrapped the idea of the spin-off and made a show called *Parks and Recreation* "inspired by" *The Office* instead—shot in the same dry documentary style but this time set in the world of local politics. The show was a modest hit when it finally debuted in April 2009, and it was renewed for a second season.

Charles Richter, who developed the Richter scale (for measuring earthquakes), was a nudist.

ORIGINAL SERIES: *Emergency!*
SPIN-OFF: *905-Wild* (1975)
STORY: Writer/actor Jack Webb created the cop show *Dragnet* in the 1950s and revived it in the late 1960s. The new show then spun off another police drama called *Adam-12*, which in turn begat *Emergency!* (1972–79), about a pair of paramedics/firefighters. And a 1975 episode of *Emergency!* served as a pilot for yet another rung on the ladder of *Dragnet*-derived shows. *905-Wild*, as the show was to be titled (based on police code for "wild animal, loose and threatening"), followed a Los Angeles animal control worker (portrayed by Mark Harmon in one of his first roles). The *Emergency!* cast showed up briefly, but the rest of the episode showed Harmon fighting off a tiger in a grocery store and saving dogs caught in a brush fire. Apparently the *Dragnet* magic didn't transfer to the animal kingdom—NBC passed on *905-Wild*.

ORIGINAL SERIES: *Buffy the Vampire Slayer*
SPIN-OFF: *Buffy the Animated Series* (2002)
STORY: *Buffy* has a rich backstory and mythology, but with the exception of the spin-off *Angel*, none of the many other proposed offshoots of the teenaged monster-hunter show ever made it to air. One of these was a Saturday morning cartoon version for kids, commissioned by the Fox Network in 2001. A four-minute, fully animated teaser video (with most of the original cast providing their voices) was produced, and Fox gave *Buffy* creator Joss Whedon the go-ahead to make 13 full episodes. But just a few weeks later, in early 2002, Fox shut down its Saturday morning cartoon division. Whedon shopped the animated *Buffy* to other networks, but nobody was interested—it was too dark for kids and too kiddie for adults.

ORIGINAL SERIES: *Welcome Back, Kotter*
SPIN-OFF: *The Horshacks* (1977)
STORY: Next to John Travolta's Vinnie Barbarino, the most popular of the teenage delinquent Sweathogs on *Welcome Back, Kotter* was the scrawny, nerdy, and weird Arnold Horshack (Ron Pallilo). A two-part episode made during *Kotter*'s second season, "There Goes Number 5," was intended as a spin-off, focusing on Horshack and his equally weird family. When Horshack's fourth stepfather

dies, he has to take a job with his uncle to feed his brothers and sisters. The episode was among the lowest-rated *Kotters* of the year, proving that a little Horshack goes a long way.

ORIGINAL SERIES: *The Brady Bunch*
SPIN-OFF: *Kelly's Kids* (1974)
STORY: By the end of the show's fifth season in 1974, the Brady kids were getting older and not quite so cute, and chances that the show would be renewed for a sixth season by ABC were slim. So *Brady* creator Sherwood Schwartz devised another show about a nontraditional family with a bunch of adorable youngsters. The pilot was aired as an episode of *The Brady Bunch*—the Bradys are visited briefly by their good friend (although he'd never been mentioned before) Ken Kelly (portrayed by Ken Berry of *F Troop*), who has just adopted three orphans: one white, one Asian, and one African-American. ABC passed on the pilot, and *The Brady Bunch* was canceled a few weeks later. The "Kelly's Kids" episode ties in so little with *The Brady Bunch*, in fact, that it's almost never seen in the perpetual reruns of the show.

ORIGINAL SERIES: *Heroes*
SPIN-OFF: *Heroes: Origins* (2008)
STORY: It was devised to run in spring 2008, between the second and third seasons of the cult science-fiction show about modern-day superheroes. Each episode of *Heroes: Origins* was supposed to explain how one of the parent show's many characters obtained or discovered their special powers. Major filmmakers like Kevin Smith (*Clerks*) and Eli Roth (*Hostel*) were signed to direct episodes. So why did it die? *Heroes: Origins* was a casualty of the Writer's Guild of America strike in 2007–08, which halted production on all scripted TV shows for three months. By the time Hollywood got back to work, the TV season was nearly over, and there was no time to make *Origins*.

* * *

"The phrase 'sort of' doesn't really mean anything. But after certain things, it means everything. Like after 'I love you,' or 'You're going to live,' or 'It's a boy!'"
—**Demetri Martin**

DOUGH NUTS

For the person who has more money than they know what to do with.

LUXURY ITEM: "I Am Rich" iPhone App
DESCRIPTION: Apple iPhone users have access to thousands of applications, or "Apps." Most cost around $2 and serve a purpose—weather forecasts, movie times, GPS locators, etc. The "I Am Rich" App went on sale in 2008. What does it do? Not much. It fills the iPhone screen with a picture of a ruby, supposedly to indicate to passersby that the iPhone user is rich.
COST: $999.99. Who would buy one? Eight people did—including a man who thought it was a joke...until he got his credit card statement. When he complained to Apple, they refunded his money and pulled "I Am Rich" from their online store.

LUXURY ITEM: Chanel Segway
EXPLANATION: If a no-frills Segway isn't expensive enough (around $5,000), now you can get a super-deluxe Chanel Edition Segway. It's the same as a regular Segway, but with quilted leather mudflaps and a Chanel handbag mounted on the front.
COST: $12,000

LUXURY ITEM: Crystal-covered paintball gun
EXPLANATION: The Aurora Nexus Ego is adorned with thousands of tiny crystals, and until recently was the world's most expensive paintball gun at a cost of $5,000. But in 2009, Planet Eclipse came out with the Argyle Eg09, which is decorated with more than 11,000 much fancier *Swarovski* crystals.
Cost: $5,001

LUXURY ITEM: Diamond-encrusted USB thumb drives
EXPLANATION: Thumb drives are popular. They're also cheap—you can get 2GB of data storage for about $10. So if you lose one, who cares...unless it's a White Lake USB Stick, which is 14-carat gold-plated and covered in diamonds.
Cost: $3,500. (If you're on a budget, you can get it without the diamonds for just $2,800.)

Can you find them all? There are 4 cars and 11 light posts on a $10 bill.

A ROYAL MESS

Have you always dreamed of being a princess or a king? Be careful what you wish for—you might end up like one of these folks.

ALL IN THE FAMILY

For the past thousand years, the royal families of Europe have routinely intermarried. Why? They did it to create dynasties and to keep the royal wealth within their families. The problem: Over time it can create a genetic nightmare. The poster family for royal inbreeding is the House of Hapsburg. Since the 15th century, the Hapsburgs have intermarried with royal relatives in Spain, Austria, England, Hungary, Bohemia, Greece, Portugal, and Mexico. Somewhere along the line it created a genetic deformity called the "Hapsburg lip," which then spread through the family tree. This condition, known as *mandibular prognathism,* causes the lower jaw to protrude in front of the upper teeth like a bulldog. Other common Hapsburg traits due to inbreeding: a large misshapen nose, sagging lower eyelids, stunted bodies, and *hydrocephalus.* This genetic disorder, known more commonly as "water on the brain," makes fluid accumulate in the skull, putting pressure on the brain. It causes mental disabilities, convulsions, and death—symptoms the Hapsburg royals had in abundance.

ROYAL DISASTERS

Two extreme examples:

• In 1793 Emperor Franz II married his double first cousin (they had the same four grandparents) Marie-Therese. Their son, Ferdinand I (1793–1875), was born with a hydrocephalic head, shrunken body and epilepsy. He had the Hapsburg jaw, a tongue too large for his mouth, and only marginal intelligence. One of his favorite pastimes was to wedge his bottom in a wastebasket and roll around the floor in it. Despite that, he reigned as emperor for 18 years.

• In 1649 King Philip IV of Spain married Mariana of Austria... his niece. Their son Charles II (1661–1700) had maladies like those of Ferdinand I except that his tongue was so huge he could hardly eat or talk. He was also impotent, which ended the Hapsburg's reign in Spain.

Geography fact: Chicago is closer to Moscow than it is to Rio de Janeiro.

MAD MEN

The Hapsburgs weren't the only royal house muddying the gene pool. In 1802, as British essayist Walter Bagehot noted, "every hereditary monarch in Europe was insane."

• George III of England (1738–1820) was taken to Kew Palace in a straitjacket in 1801 and never seen in public again.

• Queen Maria I of Portugal (1734–1816), whose half-wit husband was also her uncle, liked to dress like a little girl and throw temper tantrums.

• Christian VII of Denmark (1749–1808) ran around the palace smashing furniture and banging his head until it bled.

• Russian Emperor Paul I (1754–1801) may have been a paranoid schizophrenic, and was given to unpredictable behavior: In 1797 he banned shoes with laces, then sent troops into the streets of St. Petersburg with orders to kill anyone violating his edict.

• Ludwig I of Bavaria (1786–1868) was prone to wander the city of Munich in rags carrying a tattered umbrella.

VICTORIA'S SECRET

By all accounts Queen Victoria of England (1819–1901) and her husband (and cousin) Prince Albert (1819–1861) had a happy marriage. Together they produced nine children and married them into every royal family in Europe. Unfortunately, one son and two of their five daughters carried a deadly gift from their mother in their genes—*hemophilia*. Hemophiliacs lack the protein that clots blood, making the smallest cut a potential killer. Victoria's children who carried this defective chromosome passed it on through their children, some of whom passed it onto their children. The disease is believed to be extinct among the remaining European monarchies, but since female descendants can carry the gene without knowing it, it's possible it's still out there somewhere.

THE WACKY WINDSORS

The current ruling dynasty of England, the House of Windsor, is carrying on the breeding habits of their ancestors. Queen Elizabeth II (1926–) is married to Prince Philip, her second cousin once removed through King Christian IX of Denmark, and her third cousin through Queen Victoria. The beat goes on...

SCAT-R-US

Some bathroom-related toys and products (mostly) for kids.

THE TURDS. Each of these English action figures (basically a plastic poo that wears clothes) comes with its own "log book and bowlography." Some popular characters: "Bravefart," "Turdinator Poo," "Julius Squeezer," and "Dries Hard."

PEE & POO. A pair of stuffed plush dolls. One is a brown mound (Poo); the other is shaped like a yellow water droplet (Pee). Both have cute little feet and eyes and "work just as well at potty-training inspiration as they do a cuddly companion."

TOILET MONSTER. The hands of this rubber toy have suction cups that attach to the inside of the toilet lid, while its gruesome leering face remains in the bowl. "The moment some unsuspecting guest lifts the lid," says the description, "the toilet monster explodes to scare them out of their wits. Be sure they will think twice before doing their business in your home ever again!" Also available: the motion-activated Toilet Screamer.

STINKOR. Introduced into the *He-Man* universe in 1985, this humanoid-skunk action figure was designed to smell bad (he attacks his foes with foul smells). Though they were made more than 20 years ago, the original Stinkors still stink. Why? When making the molds, the manufacturers added a strong, long-lasting, musky fragrance called patchouli oil, popular with hippies of the 1960s and '70s (and believed to be an effective insect repellent).

THE SPONGEBOB RECTAL THERMOMETER. One end is shaped like the cartoon character, and the other end…isn't. It's designed to add a little fun to an otherwise not-fun activity. It even plays the *SpongeBob SquarePants* theme song.

BABY ALIVE LEARNS TO POTTY. Your toilet-training toddler feeds this animatronic baby doll "green beans," "banana chunks," and "juice." But then Baby Alive must get to her "potty" fast, or she'll have an "accident" (really) and announce: "I made a stinky!" (A warning on the box reads: "May stain some surfaces.")

WATER WORDS

What's the difference between a lake and a pond? You may be surprised.

Channel: a narrow body of water that connects two other, larger waterways. Example: The English Channel connects the North Sea to the Atlantic Ocean.

Gully: an indentation in the land, such as a valley or ravine, worn down by thousands of years of flowing water. They often serve as natural drainage areas after heavy rains.

Arroyo: a gully that flows with water only during the rainy season. Otherwise, it's dry, and called a gulch.

Inlet: a narrow water passage between two pieces of land.

Sound: a wide inlet from a sea or ocean that runs parallel to a coastline.

Fjord: an inlet (or sound) bordered by tall, steep cliffs.

Bay: a body of water that is surrounded mostly by land and leads out into another, larger body of water.

Cove: a horseshoe-shaped bay.

Estuary: the place where a river flows into an ocean.

Lakes and Ponds: Standing bodies of water that feed rivers and creeks, respectively. Lakes are bigger than ponds, but there's no standard measurement for determining the size difference between the two. Many geographers set the area limit of a pond at about 12 acres; anything larger is considered a lake. Depth is also a factor—ponds are usually shallow enough for light to penetrate to the bottom.

Sea: a large lake (fresh or saltwater) that connects to an ocean via an inlet or river.

Ocean: the single body of saltwater that encircles the continents. It is split up into five geographical divisions— the Atlantic, Pacific, Indian, Arctic, and Antarctic.

Gulf: a portion of ocean partially enclosed by land. For example, the Gulf of Mexico is part of the Atlantic Ocean, but it is surrounded by parts of Mexico and the U.S.

River: a wide, moving body of fresh (non-salty) water that flows into an ocean or other large waterway.

Less than a third of stolen artwork worth more than $1 million is ever recovered.

DUMB JOCKS

Some are dumb, some are clever, and all are funny.

"I can play in the center, on the right, and occasionally on the left side."
—David Beckham, when asked if he was "volatile"

"I have two weapons: my legs, my arm, and my brains."
—Michael Vick

"We've got a good squad and we're going to cut our cloth accordingly. But I think the cloth we've got could make some good soup, if that makes any sense."
—Ian Holloway, soccer coach

"We're starting to show spurts of consistency."
—Jamaal Magloire, NBA player

"Don't say I don't get along with my teammates. I just don't get along with some of the guys on the team."
—Terrell Owens

"Chemistry is a class you take in high school or college, where you figure out two plus two is ten, or something."
—Dennis Rodman

"Soccer is like chess but without dice."
—Lukas Podolski, soccer player

"It's a humbling thing being humble."
—Maurice Clarett, football player

"I found a delivery in my flaw."
—Dan Quisenberry, pitcher

"I'm the Rocky of Philadelphia."
—Bernard Hopkins, boxer

"I feel like I'm the best, but you're not going to get me to say that."
—Jerry Rice

"The pain is very painful."
—Ze Maria, soccer player

"When a fielder gets the pitcher into trouble, the pitcher has to pitch himself out of the slump he isn't in."
—Casey Stengel

"Strength is my biggest weakness."
—Mark Snow, college basketball player

Disneyland has a regulation-size basketball court for employees...inside the Matterhorn.

FOUNDING FATHERS

You already know the names—here are the people behind them.

JOSEPH PILATES

In his youth, Pilates (pronounced pa-lah-dees) suffered from asthma, rickets, and arthritis. He wanted to be fit, so he took up a regime of bodybuilding, gymnastics, yoga, calisthenics, and weight training. In 1912 the 32-year-old German moved to England, where he worked as a physical trainer for Scotland Yard, and later refined his exercise program, calling it *Contrology*. He focused on strengthening the "core muscles," mostly the abdomen, through slowly stretching and holding muscles in place while sitting on a mat. Pilates realized that most people weren't strong enough to do that, so he developed machines that worked the core muscles through resistance training—weights on pull cords. He opened a studio in New York City in 1925, attracting famous dancers such as George Balanchine and Martha Graham as clients. When Pilates died at age 87 in 1967, a handful of his students opened their own studios specializing in what they now called *pilates*. Ron Fletcher's Beverly Hills studio led directly to the current popularity of pilates. Today, more than 10 million Americans are adherents.

ROBERT MONDAVI

After graduating from Stanford University in 1937, Mondavi settled in the nearby Napa Valley. Convinced that the region was the future of winemaking, he talked his father, who owned a fruit packing company, into buying the struggling Charles Krug Winery. Mondavi turned it around and ran it at a profit for nearly 30 years. In 1965 he and his brother Peter got into an argument about the direction of the business. It escalated into a fist fight, and Robert was forced out of the company. So he started his own winery a few miles down the road in Oakville, California, where he created wines popular with average consumers and critics alike. As Mondavi's winemaking empire grew, he introduced both high-end brands and affordable ones, such as Woodbridge. Other contributions: He introduced the concept of naming wines by their grape, such as Zinfandel or Sauvignon Blanc, into the United

States, and he promoted the California wine industry, helping to turn it from a group of small businesses into a billion-dollar industry that could compete in quality with European winemakers...or even surpass them. In 1997 Grand European Jury Wine Tasting (the most prestigious wine contest in the world) a panel of judges blind-tasted 27 Chardonnays, most of them from France. The winner: Mondavi's Chardonnay Reserve, the first American wine ever to win the Grand European.

AH BING

In his Milwaukie, Oregon, orchard, Seth Lewelling specialized in cross-breeding cherry trees. In 1875 he grafted branches from several different cherry trees onto a Black Republican cherry, one of the first dark cherry trees ever developed. (Today the Black Republican is used to flavor most black-cherry-flavored foods.) The resulting fruit was dark red, firm...and twice the size of regular cherries. He named the new fruit Bing cherries, after his orchard foreman Ah Bing, a Chinese laborer who'd cared for the new plants. When Lewelling exhibited Bing cherries in 1876 at the Centennial Exposition in Philadelphia, they were so big that fairgoers thought they were crabapples. Lewelling made a fortune shipping Bings on ice via railroad to the East Coast, where they sold for 3 cents each—the equivalent of 60 cents today.

RUDOLPH HASS

In 1928 Whittier, California, mailman Rudolph Hass bought a dozen avocado-tree saplings and planted them in his backyard. He thought he was getting all Lyon trees, but one of them bore black, bumpy avocados, not the smooth, green fruit of the Lyon. Hass wanted to chop down the odd tree, but his children begged him not to—they thought the fruit was smoother and richer than the Lyon avocados. So Hass took out a patent on the plant in 1935 (and named it after himself). Then he hired a local nursery owner named Harold Brokaw to market it to grocers. It was an easy sell—the Hass tree yields more fruit than the Lyon, and does so year-round. Today, 80 percent of the seven billion pounds of avocados sold worldwide each year are Hass.

*　　*　　*

The best answer to anger is silence. —**German proverb**

A REAL-LIFE GHOST STORY, PART I

Are you scared of the dark? Do you sleep with the light on? Do you hear noises in other parts of the house when you know you're alone? You're about to read a ghostly tale with an incredible twist: It really happened!

DOCTOR WHO?
William Wilmer, an ophthalmologist who practiced in Washington, D.C. in the early 1900s, was one of the most distinguished eye doctors of his era. Among his patients were eight different presidents, from William McKinley to Franklin Roosevelt. He also treated Charles Lindbergh, the famous aviator; Joseph Pulitzer, the New York newspaper tycoon and creator of the Pulitzer Prize; and countless other prominent Americans. But perhaps his most unusual claim to fame is the fact that in 1921 he managed to talk a prestigious medical journal, *The American Journal of Ophthalmology*, into printing a ghost story.

The story had been recounted to Dr. Wilmer by one of his patients, whom he identified only as "Mrs. H" to protect her privacy. The strange occurrences she and her family experienced began in 1912, shortly after she, her husband, and their children moved into a large, run-down old house that hadn't been lived in for about a decade. The house didn't have electricity—it was lit with gaslights and heated by an old furnace in the basement.

THIS OLD HOUSE

The gloomy old house soon began to exert a strange influence on its new occupants, as Mrs. H recounted in Dr. Wilmer's article. "Mr. H and I had not been in the house more than a couple of days when we felt very depressed," she wrote. The floors were covered with thick carpets that absorbed all sound of the family's servants going about their tasks, and Mrs. H found the quiet a little overpowering. But even more disturbing than the silent footsteps of the people who were in the house were the noisy footsteps of people who *weren't* there...or at least could not be seen with the naked eye. "One morning, I heard footsteps in the room over my head," Mrs. H recounted. "I hurried up the stairs. To my surprise, the room was empty. I passed into the next room, and then into all the rooms on that floor, and then to the floor above, to find that I was the only person in that part of the house."

YOU ARE BEING WATCHED

The house's strange power seemed to grow over time. Soon the entire family began to suffer from headaches and exhaustion, yet whenever family members took to their beds to regain their strength, the headaches and fatigue only grew worse. The children were affected most of all: They were pale much of the time, often felt tired and ill, and had poor appetites.

No part of the house offered refuge: When Mr. H sat in the dining room, he was so overcome by the sense of an unseen presence standing *right behind him* that he began turning his chair to face the hallway so that he would see anyone who tried to sneak up. The children developed an aversion to spending time in their playroom on the top floor of the house, Mrs. H. remembered: "In spite of their rocking horse and toys being there, they begged to be allowed to play in their bedroom."

RING RING

By December Mrs. H and the children were so worn out that she decided to take them on a short vacation while Mr. H remained at home. The break worked wonders for Mrs. H and the kids, but poor Mr. H was more tormented than ever. Strange and unexplained noises disturbed his sleep at night, making it impossible for him to get any rest. "Several times he was awakened by a bell ringing, but on going to the front and back doors, he could find no one at either," Mrs. H said. "Also several times he was awakened by what he thought was the telephone bell. One night he was roused by hearing the fire department dashing up the street and coming to a stop nearby. He hurried to the window and found the street quiet and deserted."

In early January, Mrs. H and the children returned home, but no sooner were they back inside the house that the trouble started again. The children came down with colds—which normally would necessitate remaining indoors, especially in the winter. But their symptoms seem to *lessen* when they went outside, only to recur when they came back into the house. Soon Mrs. H, like her husband, was awakened at night by strange noises—the sounds of doors slamming, pots and pans being thrown around the kitchen, and heavy footsteps climbing a staircase behind the wall in her bedroom. "There was no staircase behind the wall," Mrs. H. wrote.

The live-in servants weren't spared the house's torments, either. During the day they had the feeling that someone—or something—was following right behind them, on the verge of reaching out and grabbing them as they went about their duties. At night they, too, were awakened by strange noises: tinkling and rattling china, heavy footsteps walking on the upstairs floors, and furniture being dragged across floors and shoved up against doors.

Then came the apparitions.

Who (or what) was responsible for the H family's horror? Turn to page 354 to find out.

*　　*　　*

IF AT FIRST YOU DON'T SUCCEED, TRY TRY TRY TRY TRY TRY TRY TRY TRY TRY TRY TRY TRY TRY TRY TRY TRY TRY TRY TRY TRY TRY TRY AGAIN

All that Ramchandra Katuwal wanted was a happy marriage. But his first wife, whom he married in 1985, left him for another man. So Katuwal, whose job is to carry heavy loads for people across the steep Nepalese terrain, found another woman and married her. "My second wife also ran away," he said, "and the third one, too." He tried again...and again...and again...and by 2001 he'd been married 24 times in 16 years, give or take a wife or two (Katuwal says he's lost count). He believes that they all left him because he's poor and his job pays very little, so he finally gave up and declared that he would never marry again. But he couldn't even keep *that* vow, and soon after married a 23-year-old woman named Sharada—her first, his 25th. "A house is not a house without a wife!" said a proud Katuwal.

RICE IS NICE

More than three billion people eat it every day.

RICE TO SEE YOU
What is rice? It's a grain, technically a member of the grass family, of which there are more than 100,000 varieties. It's also *the* staple food for about half of the world's population.

Carbon-dated evidence shows that a wild variety of rice was being cultivated on the banks of the Yangtze River in China as far back as 8,000—and possibly even 11,000—years ago. Around the year 5,000 BCE, as settled communities began to appear in Asia, rice was developed into a domestic crop. Scientists think that rice cultivation occurred simultaneously across various parts of central and southeast Asia, eventually extending to China, Thailand, Cambodia, Vietnam, India, Korea, Japan, Myanmar, Pakistan, Sri Lanka, the Philippines, and Indonesia.

By 800 BCE, rice was grown in the Middle East, by 700 CE in Spain, and by the 1400s in Italy and France. In 1694 rice was successfully cultivated in the New World in what is now South Carolina, a few decades after the Spaniards brought it to South America. Today it's grown in 110 countries, on every continent except Antarctica, in a variety of climates and conditions.

HOW DOES RICE GROW?

Rice can be grown on dry uplands, on land fed only by rainfall, or in flood-prone fields of deep water, but 75 percent of the world's rice is grown in *paddies*—level land covered with a shallow layer of water. In most of Asia, where farming is generally not mechanized, it's a labor-intensive crop cultivated by hand. The seeds are germinated, and 30 to 50 days later the seedlings are transplanted—one at a time—into the paddies. Weeds are pulled by hand; fertilizer is spread by hand. After three more months, the rice is mature, and the fields are drained to let the ground dry out before the grain is harvested (by hand). The grasslike stalks are cut and then threshed to separate the grains from the stalks, and the grains are dried. Each dry grain is still covered with a hard husk that protects the kernel inside; these grains are called "paddy rice" or "rough rice." In the final step of the harvesting process, the paddy rice is milled to remove the husks.

KNOW YOUR RICE

• **Brown rice.** Any variety of rice can be "brown," because brown rice is simply rice with only the outer husk removed. It's more nutritious than white rice because it still has the bran layers that contain minerals and vitamins, especially the B-complex vitamins, but very little brown rice is eaten worldwide. Brown rice is perishable because of the high oil content in the bran and the germ. Maximum shelf life: only about six months.

• **White rice** is any rice that's been milled to remove both the outer husk and the brown bran layer. (That's what makes it white.) It cooks in half the time of brown rice.

• **Parboiled (or converted) rice** has been put through a process of soaking, steaming, and drying before it's milled. When cooked, the kernels fluff up, but they're firmer and less sticky and retain more vitamins than ordinary white rice. Parboiled rice can be overcooked without losing its shape or getting mushy, which makes it well suited for restaurant use.

• **Instant rice** is precooked and then dried so that it can be reconstituted in as little as three minutes. Unfortunately the texture suffers, compared to ordinary white rice (which takes 15 minutes to cook) or parboiled rice (which takes about 18 minutes).

RICE FACTS

• The world's top five rice producers *and* consumers: 1) China; 2) India; 3) Indonesia; 4) Bangladesh; and 5) Vietnam.

• Irrigated rice can be grown on the same land year after year and can produce two or three harvests each year.

• Rice is cholesterol-free, nearly fat-free, high in fiber (especially brown rice), and a good source of B-vitamins. It's a complex carbohydrate (for a slow, steady source of energy) and is relatively low in calories: 205 calories per cup of cooked white rice, compared to a large potato at 270 calories.

• Ever wonder if Rice Krispies are actually made of rice? Yes, they're "crisped rice"—grains of white rice that have been steamed, and then toasted. It's a process similar to popping popcorn.

UNCLE JOHN'S PAGE OF LISTS

Some random bits from the BRI's bottomless trivia files.

5 NAMES THAT ONCE DENOTED PROFESSIONS
1. Carter (wagon driver)
2. Clark (clerk)
3. Barker (leather tanner)
4. Webster (weaver)
5. Fletcher (arrow maker)

4 ORIGINAL LUCKY CHARMS MARSHMALLOWS (1964)
1. Yellow moons
2. Green clovers
3. Orange stars
4. Pink hearts

3 BESTSELLING ISSUES OF PEOPLE
1. Selena in memoriam (1995)
2. Princess Diana in memoriam (1997)
3. John F. Kennedy, Jr. in memoriam (1999)

5 DEFUNCT RESTAURANT CHAINS
1. Burger Chef
2. Druther's
3. Sambo's
4. Howard Johnson's
5. Pup 'N' Taco

4 TITLES CONSIDERED FOR *THE GREAT GATSBY*
1. *Trimalchio's Banquet*
2. *The High-Bouncing Lover*
3. *Gold-Hatted Gatsby*
4. *Incident at West Egg*

6 NAMES OF COUNTRIES IN THEIR NATIVE LANGUAGE
1. Zhongguó (China)
2. Suomi (Finland)
3. Misr (Egypt)
4. Hellas (Greece)
5. Norge (Norway)
6. Bharat (India)

5 METHODS OF EXECUTION LEGAL IN THE U.S.
1. Lethal injection (35 states)
2. Electric chair (9)
3. Gas chamber (5)
4. Hanging (2)
5. Firing squad (2)

7 FOOTBALL PLAYERS WHO HAVE HOSTED *SATURDAY NIGHT LIVE*
1. Fran Tarkenton
2. Joe Montana
3. Walter Payton
4. Deion Sanders
5. Tom Brady
6. Peyton Manning
7. O. J. Simpson

4 COUNTRIES WITH NO MILITARY
1. Costa Rica
2. Grenada
3. Haiti
4. Vatican City

The IRS admits that 1 in 5 people who call their help line get the wrong answer to their question.

THE WALK OF LIFE

In recent years, the word "pedestrian" has come to mean something ordinary. But these pedestrians were extraordinary.

JOHN STEWART (1747–1822)

Stewart was an English philosopher and writer who got off to a bad start in life. In school he was labeled a dunce, and his frustrated father sent him to work as a clerk for the East India Company in Madras, India, when he was just 17 years old. Sometime around 1765, Stewart left that job...and started walking. Over the next 25 years he walked across India, Persia, Arabia, parts of Africa, through all of Europe, and finally back to Britain. Even when he could have used a horse or carriage, he walked. Then he went to the American colonies and walked some more. "Walking" Stewart, as he became known, went on to become a celebrated character around London. Nobody knows exactly how many miles he walked during his lifetime—but it's probably in the hundreds of thousands.

WILLIAM WORDSWORTH (1770–1850)

One of the English Romantic Era's greatest poets, Wordsworth, at the age of 20, went on a walking tour of France and Switzerland, during which he walked about 1,000 miles in just a few months. After that he walked for at least a couple of hours nearly every day for the rest of his life. (He was actually a friend of Walking Stewart and was greatly influenced by him.) And that was just his outdoor walking—in addition, he composed his poetry while walking back and forth on his home's terrace for hours every day. His friend, the poet Thomas de Quincey, estimated that Wordsworth walked some 170,000 miles in his lifetime.

CAPTAIN BARCLAY (1779–1854)

Captain Robert Barclay Allardice of Stonehaven, Scotland, was known as "The Celebrated Pedestrian." He regularly wagered with people that he could complete some preposterous feat of walking...and then did it. His most impressive feat: In 1809 he bet 1,000 guineas (more than $55,000 in modern value) that he could walk one mile every hour...for 1,000 hours. He started on June 1 in the town of Newmarket, England, walking back and forth between two half-mile-apart marks, taking about 15 minutes per hour for each mile and grabbing naps when he could. Crowds grew as Barclay marched on and on, and 42 days later thousands watched as he walked his 1,000th mile in the 1,000th hour, a feat that many people have tried to break since, without success. Barclay's walking bouts were legendary in the U.K., and kicked off what became known as the "Age of Pedestrianism," during which many people in Europe and the U.S. became professional walkers.

PHYLLIS PEARSALL (1906–1996)

In 1935 Pearsall, a 29-year-old painter from London, tried to use a map to get to a party in the city one evening, but got lost. So she decided that a better map of London was needed—and that she'd make it herself. The next day she got up at 5:00 a.m. and started walking London's streets, keeping a record of every street as she did. Pearsall walked nearly every day, 18 hours a day, and over the course of the next year walked all 23,000 streets of London— about 3,000 miles. She got a draughtsman to help turn her information into a map booklet, published it, and started the A-Z Map Company. Pearsall ran A-Z until she died at the age of 89, in 1996. It's still one of the largest map companies in the U.K.

PLENNIE L. WINGO (1895–1993)

In 1931 Wingo, a restaurateur from Abilene, Texas, lost his restaurant in the financial stress of the Great Depression. After hearing about people who'd dealt with the difficulties by doing stunts— pole-sitting was a craze at the time—Wingo decided to pull one of his own. He got some sponsors and started walking east from Fort Worth, Texas…backward. The stunt became bigger news the farther he went; crowds and headlines awaited him in every town he entered. And that was just the start: Wingo walked all the way to New York, then walked backward up a ship's gangplank, sailed to Europe, and continued walking (backward) from there, eventually reaching the Pacific Ocean. He sailed to Santa Monica, California, and then walked (backward, still) home to Texas. It took him 18 months to complete his round-the-world walk, and by the end he was an international celebrity. In 1976, at the age of 81, Wingo completed a shortened version of the feat to celebrate the nation's bicentennial, walking backward from San Francisco to Santa Monica (and then appeared on *The Tonight Show Starring Johnny Carson*).

There is a British TV show called *Watching Paint Dry*. It shows paint drying.

FLUBBED HEADLINES

Whether naughty, obvious, or just plain bizarre—they're all real.

**Rally Against Apathy
Draws Small Crowd**

Blind kids on the brink of
being shown the door

INSTITUTE WILL IMMERSE
STUDENTS IN VOLCANO

**World Bank Says Poor
Need More Money**

*Community Rallies to
Help Massacre Survivors*

Viagra Doesn't See
Growth It Expected

Cuts hurt patients, nurses say

*Crack Found
in Man's Buttocks*

Delay in switch
to digital TV is delayed

ONE-ARMED MAN APPLAUDS
THE KINDNESS OF STRANGERS

*The Fresno Nutritional Home
Served Sick Children*

*Obama: Gays Will Be Pleased
by End of My Administration*

The solution to hunting's
woes? Setting sights
on women

WIMBLEDON: FEDERER
STILL RIDING HIGH ON GRASS

**Brawl Erupts at
Peace Ceremony**

*Poison Control Center
Reminds Everyone
Not To Take Poison*

**Scientists Warn Male
Infertility Can Be Passed On**

**Royals To Get A Taste
Of Angels' Colon**

ARMY SUICIDES
EXPECTED TO JUMP

**Hooker named Lay Person
of the Year**

MOUSTACHIOED HORSE
EVADES BARBERS

Count 'em: A Boeing 767 airliner is made of 3,100,000 separate parts.

NATURAL GAS REPORT

*"Breaking wind," as the English so politely call it, is a natural
and inevitable part of life. So it's not surprising that
farts occasionally make it into the news.*

POLICE LOG

• In November 2008, a 13-year-old student at Spectrum Junior-Senior High School in Stuart, Florida, was arrested by the campus law enforcement officer for "continually disrupting his classroom environment by intentionally breaking wind." After his arrest, the young man, who was not named in police reports, was released into the custody of his mother. (No word on whether he'll have to do time in the *can*.)

• In a similar story, 34-year-old Jose Cruz of Charleston, West Virginia, was charged with battery after he farted in a police station and fanned the fumes in the direction of a police officer. Cruz, who was originally stopped by traffic cops for driving without headlights, had been taken to the police department for a breathalyzer test after failing a field sobriety test. (In his defense, Cruz says he only farted because his request to use the men's room was denied, and he insists he never fanned his gas at the cops.) At last report, the fart-and-battery charge had been dropped, but Cruz still had to answer for the DUI charge.

IN A GALAXY FART, FART AWAY

In January 2009, NASA announced that huge plumes of methane gas had been discovered in the atmosphere of Mars in three different locations. On Earth, 90% of all methane is produced by living things, and that leads scientists to speculate that the methane detected on Mars may also have been created by living things—Martian farts! The most likely form of life on Mars is simple bacteria, living deep underground. And even if the bacteria died off millions of years ago, the gas may only now be rising to the Martian surface. The other 10% of the methane in Earth's atmosphere is caused by geological activity not related to any living things, so it's also possible that lifeless geological processes are causing the plumes. Still, says NASA researcher Michael Mumma, "Nothing else has done as much to increase the chances of finding life."

On average, more Americans die during the first week of a month than the last.

A WASTED PAGE

For Uncle John's Legendary Lost Bathroom Reader, *we compiled a
list of old-time slang words that all mean "drunk"—looped, bombed,
blotto, etc. Well, that was a few years ago, and we've had a few
drinks since then, so here's a whole new list. (Hiccup!)*

Whipcat (1590s)

Soused (1600s)

Fuddled (1690s)

Pickled (1700s)

Muddled (1700s)

Whisky-frisky (1790s)

Afloat (1810s)

Groggy (1840s)

Stewed (1850s)

Flush (1860s)

Malted (1880s)

Under the table (1880s)

Decks awash (1880s)

Sozzled (1890

Moist around the edges
(1900s)

Loaded (1900s)

Bleary-eyed (1910s)

Lit (1910s)

Corkscrewed (1910s)

Polluted (1910s)

Stinko (1920s)

Pie-eyed (1920s)

Jugged (1920s)

Slopped-up (1920s)

Dithered (1920s)

Plootered (1920s)

Impixlocated (1930s)

Hooched (1930s)

Sodden (1930s)

Plotzed (1930s)

Sauced (1940s)

Smashed (1940s)

Wiped-out (1940s)

Twisted (1950s)

Hammered (1950s)

Tore up from the floor up
(1950s)

Blitzed (1960s)

Schnockered (1970s)

Dipso (1970s)

Comboozelated (1970s)

Stuccoed (1980s)

Obliterated (1980s)

STRANGE LAWSUITS

These days it seems that people will sue each other over practically anything. Here are some real-life examples of unusual legal battles.

The Plaintiff: Batman, Turkey

The Defendants: Warner Bros., producer of the Batman films, and Christopher Nolan, director of two Batman films

The Lawsuit: Batman is a city in southeastern Turkey, named after the nearby Bati Raman Mountains, and it was founded in the 1920s, before the first appearance of the superhero Batman in DC Comics in 1939. But in November 2008—around the same time that Warner's Batman movie *The Dark Knight* was accumulating $1 billion in worldwide ticket sales, the Turkish Batman threatened to sue the American Batman makers for monetary damages. Huseyin Kalkan, Batman's mayor, claimed that the psychological impact over the city losing its "identity" to a superhero was to blame for its high number of unsolved murders. Further, he said that residents living abroad should be able to name their businesses after their hometown—they currently cannot due to trademark law.

The Verdict: As of 2009, Batman (the city) was still preparing its paperwork, but the case probably won't go very far. Since Batman (the character) has been around since 1939, the statute of limitations has likely run out on suing for trademark infringement.

The Plaintiff: Scott Gomez Jr.

The Defendant: Pueblo County Jail, Colorado

The Lawsuit: In 2007 Gomez was serving time as an inmate at the Pueblo County Jail when he tried to escape. He melted the ceiling tiles of his cell with a homemade candle, climbed out, got to the roof, and attempted to scale down the outside wall of the prison. Instead, he fell 40 feet to the pavement below and was severely injured. Gomez sued the jail, arguing that prison guards were responsible for his injuries because they should have done more to stop him from escaping. Specifically, they "failed to provide ceiling tiles that could not be removed by melting them with a homemade candle" and ignored his "propensity to escape" (he'd tried to escape twice before).

The Verdict: Lawyers for the prison pointed out a Colorado state law that prevented citizens from suing for damages sustained while committing a felony...such as escaping from prison. Case dismissed.

The Plaintiff: Jeb Corliss, daredevil
The Defendant: W&H Properties, owner of the Empire State Building
The Lawsuit: In 2006 the 31-year-old Corliss went to the 102nd-floor observation deck of the Empire State Building in New York City. And then...he tried to jump off, with a parachute. (Why? Why not?) But before he could get around the many safety barriers and into the air, he was tackled and restrained by security guards. Corliss was arrested and charged with reckless endangerment, and was later convicted of the lesser charge of second-degree endangerment, for which he received probation. But then W&H Properties sued Corliss for $12 million, after which he countersued *them* for $30 million for defamation of his character—claiming that there is no law against jumping off skyscrapers, and W&H's attempt to have him arrested damaged his reputation.
The Verdict: Pending.

The Plaintiff: Paul Sanchez, a 67-year-old golfer
The Defendant: Candia Woods Golf Links outside of Manchester, New Hampshire
The Lawsuit: Sanchez drove his ball down the fairway during a round of golf at Candida in 2006. The ball hit a yardage marker, ricocheted back, and hit Sanchez hard in the right eye. It all happened in under a second. Sanchez's right supraorbital ridge was shattered and his vision was severely impaired—he is temporarily (and possibly permanently) blind in one eye, and his remaining vision is blurred. In 2008 he sued Candia for negligence in designing the course (the markers, he says, shouldn't be right on the fairway) and for failing to warn him of the dangers of yardage markers.
The Verdict: Pending, but Sanchez probably won't win. In a similar case in Hawaii, the state ruled against a golfer trying to sue another golfer for accidentally hitting him in the eye with a ball because "hitting a golf ball at a high rate of speed involved the very real possibility that the ball will take flight in an unintended direction."

NAME THAT FABRIC

Uncle John couldn't help but wonder this morning as he was putting on his corduroy vest over his gingham shirt and spandex pants, where did all these fabrics get their names?

TWEED

Description: A coarse woolen fabric traditionally used to make suits and sport coats. It can have a plain weave or a "twill" weave that creates a pattern of diagonal lines or herringbone across the fabric.

How It Got Its Name: Tweed owes its name to a mistake made in the 1830s. In those days, fabric woven with a twill weave was called *tweel* in Scotland. But when a London merchant unfamiliar with that name received a letter from a textile firm in the Scottish town of Hawick, he mistook the handwritten word "tweel" to be "Tweed," the name of a river that flows near Hawick. The merchant assumed that the textile firms in the area had named their fabric after the river to differentiate it from fabrics woven in other parts of Scotland. Acting on this false assumption, the merchant advertised the fabric as "tweed." Both the plain and twill weaves of the fabric have been called that ever since.

GINGHAM

Description: A cotton fabric that almost always has a checkerboard pattern.

How It Got Its Name: Gingham originally came from Indonesia, where it had a striped pattern. The Indonesian or Malayan word for the fabric was *genggang*, which meant "striped." When genggang entered the Dutch language in the early 17th century, it became *gingang*, which in turn became *gingham* in English.

POLYESTER

Description: A synthetic fabric used to make everything from clothing to bedsheets to the seatbelts in your car. When used to make clothing, polyester is often blended with natural fibers like cotton to create fabrics that feel natural but offer improved wrinkle resistance and other desirable qualities of artificial fabrics.

How It Got Its Name: Developed by British chemists in the early 1940s, it's made of *polymers*—large molecules that are created by linking smaller molecules together into long chains. These smaller molecules are linked to one another with *esters*, a class of oily or fatty substances that are created when acids react chemically with alcohols: *Poly-ester.*

RAYON

Description: A fine, soft, smooth fabric that feels artificial but is actually made from *cellulose*—fibers from wood pulp or cotton. The fibers are dissolved down to a liquidy goo, and then the goo is re-spun to make new fibers—that's why it feels so artificial. Hawaiian shirts are often made with rayon fabric.

How It Got Its Name: Created by a French inventor named Hilairede Chardonnet in 1889, rayon was known as "artificial silk" until 1924, when it was first marketed under the name *rayon*—"ray," to call attention to its satiny sheen, and "on," to show that it was similar to cot*ton* fabric.

CORDUROY

Description: This fabric is woven in a way that creates a pattern of raised ribs that run across it.

How It Got Its Name: If what you learned in high school French class led you to conclude that corduroy is "the King's cord," you're mistaken…but don't feel too bad. People have been making that same mistake for centuries, and it still pops up in reference books today. Actually, corduroy has never been known as *corde du roi* in France. The name actually refers to *duroy* or *deroy*, a type of woolen fabric once made in western England. Duroy woven with raised ribs or *cords* was known as *corduroy.*

SPANDEX

Description: Invented by DuPont chemist Joseph Shivers in 1959, spandex is a highly elastic, synthetic fabric used to make swimsuits, bicycling shorts, ski pants, and other body-hugging garments. Spandex is often sold under the brand name "Lycra."

How It Got Its Name: In most of the world, spandex is known as *elastane.* But in the United States, it's *spandex*, an anagram of the word "expands."

THE FUTURE...
ACCORDING TO
SCI-FI MOVIES

What will the future be like? Pretty grim, if these dystopian science-fiction movies are to be believed. On the other hand, some of them aren't so far-fetched. (Is there one about $25-per-gallon gas?)

2008...according to *Split Second* (1992). Global warming will leave the Earth at a perpetually toasty 170°F. The polar ice caps will melt, cities will be knee-deep in water, and a giant mutant will go around killing people and eating their hearts.

2008...according to *Terminal Justice* (1995). Police officers will be equipped with computerized eyes that can see in the dark and across town. Also, human cloning will be perfected, but the technology will be used largely to make illegal clones of celebrities for use as prostitutes by the Mafia. (Bada-bing!)

2009...according to *I Am Legend* (2007). A cancer vaccination will backfire, killing the entire human population...except for one scientist and a clan of mutant vampires.

2013...according to *The Postman* (1997). A nuclear war (and the violent, paranoid survivalists left in its wake) will destroy civilization, kill billions, and wreak havoc on the climate, turning America into a desert wasteland run by a power-mad militia.

2015...according to *Robocop* (1987). Detroit will turn into a crime-infested wasteland in which no one is safe. The shambles of the city government will contract with the massive Omni Consumer Products Corporation to privatize the police department and introduce an experimental, criminal-killing cyborg that is half-robot, and half-deceased cop.

2017...according to *The Running Man* (1987). The American economy will collapse, and the country will be run as a police

---

Eggplants contain no fat and almost no calories. (And no eggs.)

state. To keep people calm and distracted, the government will air live gladiatorial game shows that feature criminals being forced to defend their lives in sadistic human-hunting games. The most violent (and most popular) game show will be *Running Man*, shot in a burned-out section of Los Angeles that was destroyed in the great earthquake of 1997.

2019...according to *The Island* (2005). Those with the financial means will get a clone of themselves made, and it will serve as a bank of spare parts should the original human part ever be lost to disease or injury.

2022...according to *Soylent Green* (1973). Overpopulation will lead to a worldwide food shortage. Most people will subsist on the processed food products of the Soylent Corporation. Soylents Red and Yellow are made from vegetables, but the source of the newly introduced delicious, protein-rich, meatlike Soylent Green is a mystery. (It's dead people.)

2022...according to *Tank Girl* (1995). A comet will strike the Earth with such force that it will alter the atmosphere—it will stop raining everywhere. Water will become scarce and expensive, and a fascistic global water company will control its distribution. The employees will be frequently attacked by Rippers, failed genetic experiments that are half-man/half-kangaroo. It will finally rain again...in 2033.

2027...according to *Children of Men* (2006). Humans will be infertile from 2009 on—we will be a dying race. With little future, society will slowly collapse, governments will descend into anarchy, and doctor-assisted suicide as well as acts of terrorism will be on the rise. But when a teenage refugee becomes pregnant, she will offer the world a glimmer of hope.

2054...according to *Minority Report* (2002). By 2048 Washington, D.C. will have a murder rate of zero. How? The police will use the visions of three psychic mutants to predict—and prevent—crimes. It will be an extremely effective law-enforcement technique until one cop discovers that some of their bleak predictions of the future...could be wrong.

DIRTY AIR & BRAIN BUCKETS

If you've ever watched a NASCAR race and had no idea what the announcers were talking about, use this handy guide to help you decipher the lingo of this complex sport.

AIR DAM. Part of the car's body, under the front grille. It reaches very close to the ground, causing air pressure to push down on the car, which improves handling.

APRON. The innermost paved part of an oval stock-car track. It separates the track from the unpaved infield.

BACK MARKER. Derogatory term for a driver who regularly places very far back.

BANK. All NASCAR tracks are bowl-shaped, meaning the tracks are inclined upward from the infield out. This helps the drivers take the corners at high speed. On some tracks, the "bank" can be as steep as 36 degrees.

BLUE OVAL. Nickname for Ford vehicles, taken from their blue oval logo.

BOW TIE. Nickname for Chevrolet, from their logo.

BRAIN BUCKET. Helmet.

DIRTY AIR. The turbulent air that comes off the car in front of another. Some cars run well in dirty air, others do better out in the open, in "clean air."

DOWNFORCE. The downward pressure created by air traveling over a moving car. Race teams try to find a balance between the benefits of downforce (increased grip on corners) and the detriments (increased drag and slower straightaway speeds).

DRAFTING. When several cars run very close together, single file, sometimes nearly touching (at 185 mph!), it results in less drag on all the cars, making them capable of higher speeds than one car alone. That's called "drafting."

GROOVE. The quickest and most efficient path around a particular race course. Sometimes it's the "high groove" along the outside of the track near the outer wall, and sometimes it's the "low groove" around the inside of the track near the apron.

HAPPY HOUR. The last official practice session before starting the race.

LOOSE. When a car's rear end tends to slide out of control while cornering, it's said to be "loose." A loose car is generally faster than a "tight" car, but harder to handle.

MARBLES. Debris that builds up on the track, mostly made up of rubber from tires.

PITS. Parking spots just off the inside of the track, where "pit crews" quickly service the cars—change tires, clean windows, fill gas tanks, etc.—during "pit stops."

POLE POSITION. A term originally used in horse racing, it's the location of the driver who is first when the race starts.

PUSH. A car is said to have "push" when the front tires lose grip during a turn and the car is *pushed* up the face of the track toward the outer wall.

QUALIFYING. The position at which drivers start a race is determined by driving "qualifying" rounds beforehand, during which each driver takes a few laps alone and as fast as possible. The driver with the fastest single round starts the race in the "pole position."

RESTRICTOR PLATE. An aluminum plate with four holes in it, placed between the carburetor and the intake manifold, reducing air flowing into the combustion chambers. They were implemented to slow cars down after driver Bobby Allison's horrific 1987 crash at Talladega Superspeedway, which tore out a section of fence meant to protect spectators, injuring several fans in the process. They're required only at Talladega (in Alabama) and Daytona (in Florida), the two fastest tracks on the circuit. Many drivers say restrictor plates actually are *more* dangerous because they equalize the cars' speeds, causing them to bunch together during races, thereby causing crashes that involve multiple cars.

ROAD COURSE. A long race course with turns to the left and right, as opposed to an oval track. (NASCAR runs two road-course races per year.)

For more NASCAR terminology, drive over to page 296.

OLD MAN RIVERS

Because early peoples depended on rivers for survival, they were among the first geological features to receive official names. Many of the origins are so old, in fact, that they're lost to history. Here's what we do know.

MISSISSIPPI
Description: The U.S.'s second-longest river (after the Missouri) begins at Lake Itasca in Minnesota and travels 2,340 miles south, all the way to the Gulf of Mexico.
Origin: The name is believed to be a combination of two Indian words, though experts aren't certain which ones. It may have been the Ottawa *mici* ("great") and *zibi* ("river"), or the Algonquian *misi* ("father") and *sipi* ("water"). What is certain is that in 1666 French explorers in the Great Lakes region recorded it as *Messipi*. As they traveled south, that name supplanted all of the other names in use. In 1798 U.S. Congress officially named the new territory after the Algonquin version, "Mississippi."

THAMES
Description: Pronounced "tems," it flows through several cities in southern England, most notably London.
Origin: The first known reference comes from the Celtic *Tamïssa*, meaning "dark river." In Latin it became *Tamesis* and then in Middle English, *Temese*. The "h" was added during the Renaissance, possibly as an homage to the Thyamis River in Greece, but the pronunciation of the hard "T" remained.

NILE
Description: The Nile is actually two rivers—the White Nile and the Blue Nile—that join up in Sudan before flowing north across Egypt and into the Mediterranean. In all, the world's longest river system travels 4,100 miles through ten African nations.
Origin: Because many different cultures have lived along the Nile's banks for at least 5,000 years, this river has gone by many names: *Iteru* ("River of Life"), *Ar* ("Black," due to the black sediment left behind after the annual floods), and *Nahal* ("Valley"). When the

Hydronymy is the study of how bodies of water receive their names.

ancient Greeks traveled to the region, they called it *Nelios*, meaning "River Valley." It is from this word that we get "Nile."

YANGTZE

Description: Originating from a glacier on the Tibetan plateau, the Yangtze flows 3,915 miles before emptying into the East China Sea. It's China's principal shipping route and Earth's third-longest river (only the Nile and the Amazon are longer).

Origin: Yet another river of many names, it was referred to by Western explorers as both "Yangtze," Chinese for "ocean child," and "Chang," for "river." Those two names are still used interchangeably by the rest of the world. In China, however, the river is called *Chang Jiang*, which means "Long River" and dates back to the Sui Dynasty (A.D. 581–618).

AMAZON

Description: Flowing from Peru to Brazil and into the Atlantic Ocean, the Amazon is the world's highest-volume river.

Origin: The most commonly cited story says that in the 16th century, tribal warriors waiting on the banks attacked Spanish explorers sailing upriver. Because some of these warriors were women, the explorers believed they were Amazons, the female army from Greek mythology—hence the name. Another theory: It's a derivation of *Amassona*, meaning "boat destroyer." It was called that by indigenous people because of the Amazon's tidal bores, or swells, known locally as *pororoca*. These bores occur during the high spring tides, which creates devastating waves that can travel several miles upriver.

DANUBE

Description: The second-longest river in Europe (after the Volga), the Danube begins in Germany and flows 1,771 miles east through ten countries before emptying into the Black Sea.

Origin: Ancient Greeks called this river *Ister*. It was also called *Danu* by the Celts after the goddess Danu, a motherly protector of the Indo-European world. When Roman fleets patrolled it roughly 2,000 years ago, they Latinized the Celtic name to *Danuvius*. In 1066, when the Normans conquered Europe, the river took on the French version of the Latin name, *Danube*.

Sign of the times: Times Square's National Debt Clock ran out of digits on September 30, 2008.

QUIT WHILE YOU'RE AHEAD

Sometimes the people who get all the glory are the ones who never give up and keep going and eventually win. Here's our tribute to people who were at the top of their game...and walked away.

ARTHUR RIMBAUD

Career: In the early 1870s, Rimbaud was the rising star of the Paris poetry scene in the midst of its "Decadent movement." Rimbaud fit perfectly. He drank too much, took drugs, was exceptionally rude (even to his friends), was prone to violence, and almost never bathed. And he wrote what is still considered among the most inspired, imaginative, and visionary poetry in history. And although it didn't do much for him during his lifetime, after his death Rimbaud became one of the best-known poets in history, even to this day. With works such as *Le Bateau ivre* (*The Drunken Boat*) and *Une Saison en Enfer* (*A Season in Hell*), Rimbaud influenced hundreds of modern poets, novelists, and songwriters, including T. S. Eliot, Dylan Thomas, Henry Miller, Jack Kerouac, Bob Dylan, and John Lennon, to name just a few.

Bye-bye: Rimbaud quit writing poetry...at the age of 20. He had done most of his writing as a teenager. In fact, the piece "Ophélie," considered one of his best poems, was written when he was just 15. Rimbaud spent the remainder of his life traveling in Europe, Africa, and Asia, trying to make money. He spent his last 10 years as a merchant in Ethiopia, at one point becoming an arms dealer in a war between rivals for the Ethiopian crown. He died in 1891 after having a leg amputated due to tumors, at the age of 37.

JIM BROWN

Career: Brown was drafted by the NFL's Cleveland Browns in 1956 after a stellar college career that included baseball, basketball, lacrosse, and track in addition to football. He went on to have one of the most successful careers in any sport in history, breaking dozens of NFL records, including most rushing yards in both a season and a career, most rushing touchdowns, and most seasons leading the league in all-purpose yards, and he is still the only player to average more than 100 yards a game for an entire career.

Bye-bye: One of the most amazing things about Brown's record-smashing career is that he completed it in just nine years. He retired in 1965, at the age of only 29, to pursue an acting career and to work on improving race relations in the United States and around the world. He has since made dozens of films, most notably *The Dirty Dozen* (1967), and founded and worked with numerous social organizations, including the Negro Industrial Economic Union and the Amer-I-Can program. He has still not retired from from either of his "secondary" careers.

KIM NOVAK

Career: In the late 1950s, Novak was Hollywood's premier starlet and one of its top box-office draws, with hits like *Picnic* (1955), *The Man with the Golden Arm* (1955), and Alfred Hitchcock's *Vertigo* (1958). She could literally be in any film she chose, with whatever co-stars she chose.

Bye-bye: Novak was never comfortable with her "sexpot" image or with stardom in general. In 1966, when she was just 33, she went into semiretirement and became a recluse of sorts. She made just 10 more films over the next 27 years, and in 1991 retired altogether. Today she lives with her veterinarian husband and several animals on a ranch in Oregon. And she still gets offers to do films: In a rare interview in 2004 with Larry King, she said she still had an agent, and he was still bugging her about film roles. She said she may still do another film someday.

TOM LEHRER

Career: Lehrer was a classically trained pianist who wrote satirical songs for fun, and in the 1950s he started selling recordings of his music to people at Harvard, where he was studying mathematics. Songs like "Fight Fiercely, Harvard," "The Wiener Schnitzel Waltz," and "We All Go Together When We Go," a darkly humorous song about the "benefits" of all-out nuclear war, became underground hits, and by the end of the 1950s Lehrer was touring the country to sold-out shows. In the early 1960s, he became a songwriter for the American version of the BBC news-satire television show *That Was the Week That Was* and got a record deal with Reprise Records.

Bye-bye: Lehrer chose to become a mathematics professor rather than a star, and performed only rarely after the 1960s. Why? In a 2001 interview, Lehrer said he hated performing. "I didn't relish the prospect of doing the same show night after night," he said, "any more than a novelist would enjoy reading his book aloud every night." In 2000 Rhino Records released a box set of all of Lehrer's songs (there are only 37), titled *The Remains of Tom Lehrer*. He still has a large cult following all over the world.

ART BELL

Career: Radio host Bell landed a five-hour, middle-of-the-night, political talk radio show in Las Vegas in 1989. In 1993 it went national under the name *Coast to Coast AM*, and soon thereafter switched to its now-famous "all things weird" format, with Bell and his callers talking about UFOs, paranormal events, government corruption, and every conspiracy theory imaginable. By the late 1990s, the show was on more than 500 stations with an audience of more than 15 million listeners.

Bye-bye, Part 1: On October 13, 1998, Bell abruptly announced that he was retiring from broadcasting for good—effective immediately. Two weeks later he was back on the air, again without explanation. (He later said it had to do with threats to his family.)

Bye-bye, Part 2: Citing family problems, in April 2000 Bell retired from broadcasting again, leaving the show to radio host Mike Siegel. Ten months later Bell returned, saying Siegel had taken the show in the "wrong direction."

Bye-bye, Part 3: Apparently Bell is the retiring type, because he retired again in late 2002, citing chronic back pain due to a fall from a telephone pole as a kid. (Note to kids: Don't climb telephone poles.) George Noory took over as host, but Bell still owned the show...and in late 2003 he unretired again, returning to host on weekends.

Bye-bye, Part 4: In July 2007, Bell, age 62, retired for the very last time. (Really. No kidding.) But stay tuned, because strange things often happen in the middle of the night...

2008 newspaper study: 36% of recent Atlanta Police Academy graduates have a criminal record.

IT A GRIL!

Here's something funny that landed in our in-box the other day—photos of real cakes that people ordered that went very, very wrong. What happened? Maybe a telephone order was taken too literally, or English wasn't the decorator's first language. But whatever the reason, it ruined the cake...and made it better at the same time.

Write "Welcome" on it

❄

Congradelations!

❄

Happy Brian Day!

❄

Best Wishes Susan
Under Neat That
We Will Miss You!

❄

Welcome Little Swetty

❄

I Think Your Sweet

❄

It a Gril!

❄

Congratulations
Three Times

Welcome Baby In Pink

❄

Happy Birfday!

❄

Congradulations!
60 miles you did!

❄

Happe Holidaye's

❄

Merrychrist Mas

❄

Let It's Snow!

❄

OH OH OH

❄

We Love Freymoto
Put heart in place of love

Brian: Find a cake fact for this page. Don't screw it up! –U.J.

Farewel 6th Grades

God Luck, Don!

Happy Patricks Jamie

Vote OBMOA 08!

Wee Your 3!

I Want Sprinkles

Go Steelrs!

Happy Fater's Doty!

Congratulations on
your weeding

Happy Bitrdhay!

My eyes cry to see you.
My lips to kiss you.
My arms to huge you.

Happy Sping!

1# Dad

Contragulations Ian

Last Daz of School

FAST FOOD

In 2008 the Tehran (Iran) Women's Committee set out to beat the record for building the world's largest sandwich. The previous record was 1,378 meters, set in Italy. The Iranian women brought together more than 1,000 cooks with a goal of building a 1,500-meter sandwich—about 5,000 feet long. The event drew a crowd, but even with 1,000 cooks, the sandwich took several hours to make. Finally, the crowd got too hungry wait, stormed passed the cooks, and ate the sandwich before the cooks could finish assembling it.

A SPORTS CAR IS BORN

One measure of the desirability of a sports car is whether or not it has teenagers drooling over it before they're even old enough to drive. Here's the story of one of the most drool-worthy cars in auto history. (See how long it takes you to guess which car we're talking about.)

THINKING SMALL

In the early 1950s, Harley Earl, the legendary head of General Motors' Styling department, began to notice an uptick in interest in small, imported sports cars. The soldiers who fought in World War II had taken a liking to the Fiats, Triumphs, Jaguars, Morgans, and other convertible roadsters they had seen in Europe, and they'd been buying modest numbers of them from import auto dealers ever since. When Earl went to auto races, he was struck by the affection that drivers had for their little sports cars, and now even his own employees were beginning to drive them to work.

Earl had devoted his entire working life to making GM's cars ever longer, wider, lower, more powerful, more streamlined, and more fanciful, as his automobile designs drew inspiration from everything from locomotives to bombers to rocket ships. He'd worked on plenty of cars that might be considered sporty, but he'd never really designed a *sports car*, at least not one that had found its way into dealer showrooms. Sports cars may have looked pretty and been fun to drive, but they didn't sell very well. Of the more than 4.6 million vehicles sold in the U.S. in 1952, barely 11,000 of them were sports cars. That's less than $\frac{1}{4}$ of one percent.

BUY AMERICAN

It had been years since any of the major American auto companies bothered to make *any* kind of a two-seater, let alone a sports car, and this was undoubtedly one of the things that crossed Earl's mind. How can consumers be expected to buy many roadsters if there aren't any on the market? Remember, the auto industry was a lot different in the 1950s: Together, GM's five automobile divisions (Chevrolet, Pontiac, Oldsmobile, Buick, and Cadillac) manufactured roughly half of all the automobiles sold in the United States each year. Ford, Chrysler, and a handful of other small U.S.

companies sold nearly all the rest. Few Americans had ever owned a foreign-made car or would have considered making such a purchase—the image and perceived superiority of the American automakers was that dominant in those days. But with no domestic sports cars available, customers who wanted to buy one had to get it from a foreign automaker or go without.

Earl didn't know if sports cars would ever be a major segment of the U.S. auto industry, but he did understand that they had a great deal of appeal with young people. GM was a big company and made big profits year after year. Why not spend a tiny fraction of that money on an *American* sports car that would appeal to the kids who bought MGs and Triumphs? Once they were in the GM fold, Earl figured, when the time came for them to trade up to a four-seater, they'd be much more likely to buy it from GM.

TOP SECRET

Harley Earl's innovative design work played a major role in GM's postwar dominance, and the company's other executives knew it. So when he hired a young engineer named Bob McLean, paired him with another young stylist named Duane Bohnstedt, and hid the two of them on the third floor of an obscure old GM building with instructions to work on something called "Project Opel," few executives had the gall to ask what Project Opel was all about.

What it was all about, of course, was a two-seater convertible sports car. Working from Earl's rough outline, McLean and Bohnstedt came up with a design for the car's body that appears to have been inspired by an Italian roadster called the Cisitalia 202. In those days, most sports cars had long engine compartments that narrowed almost to a point at the front end of the car, with broad, flowing fenders that were a separate and quite distinct element of the car's design. Not so with the new GM roadster: Like the Cisitalia 202, it was a low, flat, wide, almost square box with fenders that were integrated into the rest of the body. Today the integrated-fender look is standard—it's so common that it's difficult to even remember what cars looked like when their fenders were separate from the rest of the engine compartment. But to see that look on a roadster in the 1950s was not only novel, it was stunning.

THE ROADSTER FINDS A HOME...

When McLean and Bohnstedt were finished with their design, they made a full-size model out of clay, and then Earl invited executives from GM's five different divisions to take a look at it and see if they wanted it for their division. Cadillac passed. So did Buick and Oldsmobile. Pontiac wasn't interested, either.

The story might have ended right there, were it not for the fact that Chevrolet, GM's high-volume, low-cost, no-frills division, was having a bad year. As recently as 1950, it had sold more cars than Ford, but its sales had slipped considerably since then. Tom Keating, Chevrolet's general manager, and Ed Cole, its chief engineer, were looking for ways to freshen up the division's dowdy image. A V-8 engine was in the works to replace Chevy's lackluster six-cylinder motor, but it was still a couple of years off. Harley Earl's secret roadster seemed like just the ticket to excite interest in Chevrolet right away. Even if the car didn't sell in great numbers, its sporty image would give the entire division a lift. And who knows? Maybe people who came to Chevy dealers to gawk at the roadster might stick around to buy a car.

...AND A NAME

But what should the roadster be called? Chevrolet executives got together with the company's advertising agency and mulled over a list of more than 300 names, none of which seemed to really fit the car. It wasn't until after the meeting that an assistant advertising manager named Myron Scott—whose other claim to fame is founding the American Soap Box Derby—suggested naming it after a class of small, highly maneuverable warships that had been used on coastal patrols and to escort convoys of merchant ships across the North Atlantic during World War II.

In a sense, then, credit for giving the roadster its name can be indirectly attributed to British Prime Minister Winston Churchill. For when a British naval designer named William Reed drew up plans for this new class of small warships in the late 1930s, it was Churchill, then First Lord of the Admiralty, who suggested naming them after a type of small sailing ship that had served a similar purpose during the Age of Sail. The name: *Corvette*.

Did you guess correctly? Part II of our story is on page 329.

WHAT A DOLL!

Barbie is one of the most popular—and versatile—toys ever made. More than 2,000 different Barbies have been released since 1959, most of them special editions for collectors. Here are some odd but real Barbie dolls you probably won't find at Toys "R" Us.

Alfred Hitchcock's *The Birds* Barbie (2008). Dressed in a green skirt-suit like Tippi Hedren in the movie, the doll has three black birds attached, posed in perpetual attack.

Pooper Scooper Barbie (2008). This Barbie comes with a golden retriever doll named Tanner, who eats dog biscuits and then ejects them out the other end. (Really.) Barbie has a shovel and pail to clean them up.

Barbie Loves McDonald's (1982). How did Barbie get the money for all those Dream Houses and pink convertibles? She earned it by working the McDonald's drive-through. This doll wears a red and yellow McDonald's uniform and includes a headset.

Marie Antoinette Barbie (2003). She comes in an elaborate 18th-century gown. (Unfortunately, the head is not detachable.)

Cabaret Dancer Barbie (2007). While not specifically from the movie *Cabaret*, this Barbie in a see-through body stocking and fishnet tights would still fit in there.

***I Love Lucy's* Santa Barbie** (2006). Based on a 1956 episode of *I Love Lucy*, Barbie is dressed as Ethel Mertz (Vivian Vance), dressed as Santa Claus.

Lingerie Barbie (2000). It sounds scandalous (and it was briefly debated on Fox News in 2007), but this Barbie is fairly modest in her choice of underwear—large, full-coverage underwear and a matching half-slip. The Goldie Hawn Barbie has fewer clothes.

George Washington Barbie (1997). Shouldn't they have dressed Ken as George? No— Barbie is far more powerful. Here she's depicted as the father of her country...if his Revolutionary War uniform had been hot pink.

On average, 40% of all American hotel rooms are empty on any given night.

NBA Barbie (1996). This doll was available wearing the uniform of most NBA teams, including the Pistons, Lakers, Celtics, and Bulls. Curiously, there's never been a WNBA Barbie.

X Files Barbie (1998). Along with a Ken doll dressed as David Duchovny's *X Files* character Fox Mulder, Barbie is dressed in a pantsuit, as Gillian Anderson's character Dana Scully, the skeptical investigator of mysterious phenomena.

Goldie Hawn Barbie (2009). Which of Goldie's many roles is memorialized by Barbie? The bikini-clad go-go-dancer Hawn played on the 1960s series *Laugh-In*.

Harley-Davidson Barbie (1998). Barbie as a biker chick, in head-to-toe leather.

Other real Barbies:
- Civil War Nurse Barbie
- Gay Parisienne Barbie
- French Maid Barbie
- Lady of the Unicorns Barbie
- Urban Hipster Barbie
- Flintstones Barbie
- John Deere Barbie
- *Star Trek*'s Lt. Uhura Barbie
- *Titanic* Barbie
- NASCAR Barbie
- Bowling Champ Barbie
- Queen Elizabeth I Barbie
- Barbie and Ken as *The Munsters*
- Pepsi Barbie and Coca-Cola Barbie

*　　*　　*

A LAUGHING MATTER

Veteran stand-up comic Buddy Hackett once told film critic Roger Ebert one of the secrets of show business. "Buddy was a student of the science of comedy," recalled Ebert. "His favorite Las Vegas stage was at the Sahara. 'I was offered twice the dough to move to a certain hotel,' he told me, 'but nothing doing. Comics who work that room always flop. There's a physical reason for that. The stage is above the eye lines of too much of the audience. At the Sahara, the seats are banked and most of the audience is looking down at the stage. Everybody in the business knows: Up for singers, down for comics. The people want to idealize a singer. They want to feel superior to a comic. You're trying to make them laugh. They can't laugh at someone they're looking up to.'"

French writer Michel Thaler's novel, *Le train de nulle part*, is 233 pages long. It has no verbs.

FADS

*Here's a look at the origins of some of the most
popular obsessions from days gone by.*

BUTTON BEANIES
Also known as palookaville caps, Whoopee caps, club-house hats, and kingpins, these were worn by young men in the 1920s, '30s, and '40s. Guys would take an old felt fedora, cut off the brim, turn up the edge to fit, and cut a zigzag crownlike pattern around the edge. Then they'd decorate the hat with pins, buttons, and bottle caps. The beanie was especially common among mechanics and factory workers, who wore them for mild protection. In the movies and on TV, a button beanie instantly characterized someone as a street tough (such as Leo Gorcey in the Bowery Boys films) or a harmless rube (Goober on *The Andy Griffith Show*). You might also recognize this 1940s relic as part of another 1940s relic: on the head of cheeseburger-loving Jughead in the Archie comics.

MEDLEYS
In late-1970s discos, it was common for DJs to string several songs together to create one long piece of music. Then a thumping beat was added to make it perfect for people to dance to. In 1980 Dutch music publisher Willem Van Kooten heard a bootleg of a medley of Beatles songs and Frankie Avalon's "Venus" (for which he owned the copyright). That inspired him to create a legitimate version with studio musicians billed as Stars on 45. Because of copyright law, the names of all 10 of the songs he used had to be listed in the title, so it was called "Intro"/"Venus"/"Sugar, Sugar"/"No Reply"/"I'll Be Back"/"Drive My Car"/"Do You Want to Know a Secret"/"We Can Work It Out"/"I Should Have Known Better"/"Nowhere Man"/ "You're Going to Lose That Girl"/"Stars on 45." Fueled by Beatles nostalgia after John Lennon's death in 1980, the medley went to #1 in the U.S. and in Europe. Stars on 45 released dozens of other dance medleys featuring the songs of ABBA, the Rolling Stones, and Stevie Wonder. Between 1981 and 1983, more anonymous studio projects churned out medleys of Rod

---

Villanova University's 2004 commencement speaker: Caroll Spinney (*Sesame Street's* Big Bird).

Stewart, Bee Gees, and Beach Boys songs. Big-time musicians got in on the craze, too, as record labels rushed to craft medleys from *their* artists (the Hollies and the Supremes, for example). Even the Royal Philharmonic Orchestra's Beethoven and Tchaikovsky-based "Hooked on Classics" was a Top-10 hit. By 1983 the concept had oversaturated pop music, and the need for nonstop disco dance medleys was fading, as disco itself had gone out of style.

HYPERCOLOR

In February 1991, Seattle-based Generra Sportswear introduced the Hypercolor T-shirt into stores across the United States. The shirts were very simple: a solid neon color, like red, yellow, purple, pink, or green, with "Hypercolor" written on the front. But the shirts were heat-sensitive; wherever you touched it, the fabric would change color for a few hours. A purple shirt could suddenly have a pink handprint, or a green shirt could have yellow spots. Even though they cost more than $20 each (a lot for a T-shirt in 1991), more than four million were sold in four months. They were *the* fashion fad of the year, more so after they were worn by characters on *the* teen show of the day, *Beverly Hills, 90210*. But like many fashion fads, this one was short-lived. By fall 1992, the shirts were passé, and Generra filed for bankruptcy.

ZIMA

Introduced by Coors in 1993, this clear, citrus-flavored malt beverage bridged the end of one beverage fad, fruity wine coolers of the 1980s, and the beginning of another—clear drinks, such as Crystal Pepsi and Clearly Canadian, of the mid-1990s. Zima (it means "winter" in several Eastern European languages) was malty like beer but sweet like soda pop. After a $50 million marketing campaign touting it as a beer alternative for women, Zima became wildly popular in 1994, with more than 80 million six-packs sold. Half of all American alcohol drinkers bought Zima at some point in 1994. The problem: They didn't buy it *again*. Sales dropped year after year as comedians (David Letterman) and TV shows (*The Simpsons* and *Saturday Night Live*) frequently mocked the drink for being unmanly or for not tasting very good. The final blow: In 2000 Smirnoff introduced a clear/fruity/fizzy beer alternative called Ice, which sold well and forced Zima out of business.

Kosher? New York City drinking water contains microorganisms that are technically shellfish.

THE OBITS

*These real death notices weren't written by journalists,
but by the witty families of the dearly departed.*

James Robert "Beef" Ward, 39, will be sadly and sorely missed by his loving family. Jimmy, who his family affectionately called "Pork" or "Bubba," was preceded in death by his mother, Barbara Jean "Buffalo Butt" Ward. Survived by his fiancée, Annie "Red" Callahan; father, J. Richard "Old Fart" Ward; sisters, Cathy "Funny Face" Graf, Karen "Turtle" Ward, and "Hamburger" Patty Ward.

—*Columbus Dispatch*

Edward "Bruce" Merritt. Born April 3, 1951 in North Carolina. His older sisters regularly beat him up, put him in dresses, and then forced him to walk to the drugstore to buy their cigarettes. Bruce never met a stranger, and in many ways was stranger than most. He is survived by one daughter, two grandchildren, two ex-wives, unpaid taxes, and many loyal loving friends.

—*Dallas Morning News*

Chuck P. Dimmick passed away suddenly on April 18, 2009 while attending a NASCAR race to watch his favorite driver, Jeff Gordon. Chuck was the Director of Marketing for the Lund Cadillac Group. We are sure he would still want all to know that 0.9% financing is still available on all new 2008 Hummer H2's.

—*Arizona Republic*

Theodore Roosevelt Heller, 88, was discharged from the U.S. Army during WWII due to service-related injuries, and then forced his way back into the Illinois National Guard insisting no one tells him when to serve his country. In lieu of flowers, please send acerbic letters to Republicans.

—*Chicago Tribune*

Arthur (Fred) Clark, who had tired of reading obituaries noting others' courageous battles with this or that disease, wanted it known that he lost his battle as a result of an automobile accident on June 18, 2006. During his life he excelled at mediocrity. He had lifelong love affairs with bacon, butter, cigars, and bourbon. His sons said of Fred, "He was often wrong, but never in doubt." When his family was asked what they remembered about Fred, they fondly recalled how Fred never peed in the shower—on purpose.

—*Richmond Times Dispatch*

Ruth E. Rencevicz, born on August 28, 1927, passed away on September 7, 2008, due to complications resulting from her children making her old before her time. Ruth served her country as a covert spy for the CIA, where during the Cold War she was largely responsible for the breakup of the Soviet Union. At least, that's the way she told it. Ruth was also very active as a volunteer known to selflessly give of her time by standing on her balcony yelling at kids for "playing that rap music" at all hours of the day and night.

—*Akron Beacon Journal*

Louis J. Casimir Jr. bought the farm Thursday, Feb. 5, 2004, having lived more than twice as long as he had expected and probably three or four times as long as he deserved. Although he was born into an impecunious family, in a backward and benighted part of the country

at the beginning of the Great Depression, he never in his life suffered any real hardships. For more than six decades, he smoked, drank, and ate lots of animal fat, but never had a serious illness or injury. His last wish was that everyone could be as lucky as he had been, even though his demise was probably iatrogenic. Lou was a daredevil: his last words were "Watch this!"

—*The Daily Item* **(Pa.)**

Jack Balmer. As this is my auto-obituary, I'd like to write it in my own fashion! I was born in Vancouver on All Saints day, 1931. Apart from practicing dentistry for 30 years, I have also at one time or another been fairly adept as a skier, private pilot, race car driver, vintner, mechanic, model builder, marine aquarist, carpenter, photographer, plumber, scuba diver, writer, boat builder, Olympic team member (coach for a bronze medal), and a Canadian Coast Guard Auxiliary member. Since I've had a ball in life, with no regrets and nothing left still undone, and since our world seems to be quickly deteriorating, it's a good time for me to cash in. Goodbye, and good luck!

—*Vancouver Sun*

TAIWAN'S #2 RESTAURANT

When Uncle John read about this Taiwanese restaurant chain, he laughed a little, recoiled a little, and then wondered, "Why didn't I think of that?" (Then again, it's probably better that he didn't.)

POO-BOT

You've probably never heard of the Japanese comic-book character *Arale Norimaki*. She's a purple-haired robot teenager whose favorite hobby is "poking poop with a stick." Arale Norimaki has a huge following not just in Japan, but in other parts of Asia as well, including Taiwan. That's where, in 2004, a 26-year-old banker named Wang Zi-wei was inspired by Norimaki's poop-poking example to go into the soft-serve ice cream business.

(If you're at all squeamish, you should probably stop reading *right now* and turn to another page.)

GENIUS AT WORK

Somehow, Wang came to the conclusion that if people liked watching cartoon robots poking at poop, they'd probably love eating soft-serve ice cream that looks like poop, served in paper dishes that look like tiny toilets.

What's even stranger than the way Wang's mind works is the fact that his business instincts were dead-on. His human-waste ice cream stand was a big hit—customers not only lapped up all the "diarrhea with dried droppings" (chocolate ice cream with chocolate sprinkles), "bloody poop" (strawberry ice cream), and "green dysentery" (kiwi ice cream) he served, they pestered him to come up with more similarly themed treats.

After four months of working in the bank by day and selling his frozen fecal confections by night, Wang decided to expand. "The success with 'toilet ice cream' was a leap of faith for me to quit the stable, but boring, banking job and start my business, despite strong objections from my family," Wang says. In May 2004, he opened what would become the first location in the Modern Toilet restaurant chain.

After an accident, a deployed airbag adds as much as $2,000 to the cost of repairing a car.

LOOKS FAMILIAR

If you've never had an opportunity to dine in a Modern Toilet, it's pretty easy to conjure up a mental image of what one looks like. Picture a large public restroom, say one at an airport or a shopping mall. See all those bathroom stalls? Take the *stalls* out...but leave the toilets, and then keep adding more toilets until you have about 100. Now arrange them tastefully around bathtubs and sinks that have been covered with glass tabletops. Now hang some showerheads and shower curtains from the ceiling, and install some urinals on the tiled walls to serve as light fixtures. Need a napkin? Help yourself to the toilet paper dispenser on your bathtub/table. That's pretty much what Modern Toilet restaurants look like—and as of early 2009, there were seven of them in Taiwan, an eighth in Hong Kong, and many more planned for cities in Macao, Malaysia, and mainland China.

IT GETS WORSE

"Go Pee-Pee or Go Poo-Poo?" That's the Modern Toilet way of directing you to the beverage (Pee-Pee) and food (Poo-Poo) sections of the menu. There are plenty of entrées to choose from; if Modern Toilet Beef Curry (served in a toilet-shaped bowl) doesn't strike your fancy, there's always the Japanese Milk Hot Pot, the Texan Chicken, or the No. 2 Double Surprise Banquet Combo (Korean beef and German smoked chicken with cream sauce), also served in little toilets. Appetizers, such as the Fun Platter (California potato fries, onion rings, and popcorn chicken), are served in tiny bathtubs.

BODILY FLUIDS

Wash your meal down with your choice of 18 different tea drinks, including Ice Cream Black Tea, Pudding Milk Tea, or Coffee Jelly Milk Tea, plus plenty of non-tea beverages, including Plum-and-Cola and Honey Lemon Juice. If you're feeling homesick (as opposed to just plain sick), Modern Toilet also serves Ovaltine.

If you prefer your beverage hot, it will be served in a plain mug. Too boring? Order your drink cold, and it will be served in your choice of either a plastic "urinal bottle" similar to those used by bedridden hospital patients, or in a miniature plastic urinal that looks disturbingly like the porcelain fixtures in the Modern Toilet men's room. Bonus: When you're finished with your meal, the urinal (or the urinal bottle) is yours to keep!

Did you manage to keep your dinner down? Is there still room for dessert? The dessert menu has been expanded from soft-serve ice cream to include a dozen varieties of shaved ice.

Yes, they even serve yellow snow.

A WORD OF ADVICE

As with any well-designed restaurant, the restrooms at Modern Toilet are clearly marked. But since the entire restaurant looks like a restroom, if nature calls be sure to ask for directions to the restroom and listen *very carefully* when they are given. If you have any doubts as to whether you really are in the restroom, as a courtesy to other diners, please confirm that you are where you think you are before using the toilet for its intended purpose.

*　　*　　*

TWO PHRASE ORIGINS

MY BAD
Meaning: It's my mistake; it's my fault.
Origin: "This slang term originated in about 1970. The first citation in print is the 1986 book *Back-in-Your-Face Guide to Pick-up Basketball*: 'My bad: an expression of contrition uttered after making a bad pass or missing an opponent.' It came into widespread popularity thanks to the 1995 movie *Clueless*." (From "The Phrase Finder" at *phrases.org.uk*, by Gary Martin)

IF IT LOOKS LIKE A DUCK, WALKS LIKE A DUCK, AND QUACKS LIKE A DUCK, IT'S PROBABLY A DUCK
Meaning: Don't look beyond the obvious when trying to determine someone's true nature.
Origin: "Usually ascribed to Walter Reuther, the American labor leader during the McCarthy witch hunts of the 1950s. He came up with it as a test of whether someone was a Communist." (From *The Phrase That Launched 1,000 Ships*, by Nigel Rees)

"MAKE MY DAY"

Fifty years in film have taught Clint Eastwood a thing or two about real life.

"Everybody wishes they had the ability to say, 'Go ahead, make my day' at the perfect time. But most people don't. The boss gives them a lot of crap and they go out and they say, 'Why didn't I tell him to such and such and so and so.'"

"Whenever a congressman wants a little publicity, he goes on a tirade about the movies."

"Eighty is just a number. A lot of people are old at 40."
—on turning 80 in 2010

Q: "Do you consider yourself an artist?"
A: "Isn't there an art to everything? There's an art to a plumber fixing a sink, or a mechanic working on cars. There's an art to it if you know how to do it and you do it well. A good bartender could be an artist. A bad one is not."

"What men want from women is pretty much what women want from men: respect."

"Life is a constant class, and once you think you know it all, you're due to decay."

"Respect your efforts, respect yourself. Self-respect leads to self-discipline. When you have both firmly under your belt, that's real power."

"I don't believe in pessimism. If something doesn't come up the way you want, forge ahead. If you think it's going to rain, it will."

"We boil at different degrees."

"My father used to say to me, 'Show 'em what you can do, and don't worry about what you're gonna get. Say you'll work for free and make yourself invaluable.'"

"You're never in total control. But you have to have ambitions to set the agenda and fate does the rest."

"Without sounding like a pseudointellectual dipsh*t, it's my responsibility to be true to myself. If it works for me, it's right."

"Smaller details are less important. Let's get on with the important stuff."

Odds that a burglary in the United States will be solved: 1 in 7.

LOST AND FOUND: THE CLOUD PEOPLE OF PERU

How much can we really know about a long-lost civilization when our only information about them comes from their conquerors? Not a lot. But thanks to some recent discoveries, we're starting to find out more.

ILLUMINATING DISCOVERY

Five centuries ago, deep in the mountainous jungles of what is now Peru, the Spanish conqueror Pedro Cieza de León encountered a tribe of people who were different from the ruling Incas. "They are the whitest and most handsome of all the people that I have seen," he wrote, "and their wives were so beautiful that because of their gentleness, many of them deserved to be the Incas' wives and to also be taken to the Sun Temple." In addition to being lighter-skinned than the Incas, these people were said to be much taller—and they had blond hair and blue eyes.

What they called themselves has been lost to history; the Incas called them the *Chachapoyas*, which anthropologists think meant "People of the Clouds." They lived in the dense forests that rise above the Marañón and Huallaga Rivers, a remote region of the Andes Mountains on the northern edge of the Amazon Rain Forest—so high above sea level that they're literally in the clouds. And because the area is still very remote, most of the Chachapoyas' secrets have remained hidden in the forests.

DISAPPEARING ACT

A century before the Spaniards arrived in the 1500s, the Inca Empire spread throughout South America, conquering the hundreds of tribes that inhabited the region. The Cloud People, however, proved to be fierce adversaries. In order to keep them subjugated, Inca liaisons lived in the Chachapoya villages. When civil war broke out between different factions of the Incas, the Chachapoyas found themselves caught in the middle. That's why they so readily sided with the Spanish *Conquistadores* in their subjugation of the Incas. Unfortunately, that proved to be the Cloud People's undoing. Although the Spanish freed them from Inca rule, they introduced small pox and other European diseases. Less than 200 years later, the Chachapoyan culture was gone. What physical evidence remained was quickly enveloped by the densest jungles on Earth.

Up until the 1840s, the outside world had little proof that the Chachapoyas even existed. And then the fortress of Kuelap was discovered. Located on top of a mountain at nearly 10,000 feet, Kuelap once had 400 circular stone huts and buildings surrounded by a 60-foot-high wall. Built between A.D. 600 and 800, Kuelap protected the Cloud People from other warring tribes for more than six centuries before the Incas conquered them. When word of Kuelap spread, scientists, profiteers, and thrill seekers went in and removed most of the artifacts. Today, only a portion of the wall and a few structures remain.

RAIDERS OF THE LOST PEOPLES

Throughout the 20th century, the Chachapoyan culture was one of the great mysteries of archaeology. But in 2006 a Peruvian farmer was exploring a cave in the Utcubamba province deep in the northern Amazon jungle. About 820 feet below the surface, he discovered five mummified bodies surrounded by an array of artifacts and textiles. The farmer led a team of archaeologists to the cave—this time with a much improved knowledge of how to preserve and protect such a site. "This is a discovery of transcendental importance," said lead archaeologist Herman Crobera. "It is the first time any kind of underground burial site this size has been found belonging to the Chachapoyas."

Then in 2007 a group of hikers found themselves in a jungle so thick that they had to hack their way through it with machetes. Following the sound of rushing water, they emerged into a breathtaking area: A huge waterfall plunging down a 1,500-foot cliff. Bright blankets of flowers covered the ground. And on a nearby rock wall overlooking the valley far below were some buildings carved into the stone. As the hikers searched the area, they came upon a small village overgrown by the jungle. The round buildings were all intact; the artifacts were all still there.

When archaeologists were brought to the 12-acre site, they compared the artifacts to those from the cave. It was finally possible to start putting together a picture of how the Cloud People lived.

- Like other indigenous peoples, they were very religious and very much interested in making art. On the walls of their huts and meeting places were depictions of gods, birds, and couples dancing. (It's unknown whether the dancing was ceremonial or for fun.)
- Wooden platforms found in the village were most likely used for grinding up plants for food and medicine. The pottery, though not as advanced as lower-land peoples such as the Mochica or Nazca, was skillfully made and decorated with ornate patterns.
- The Chachapoyas revered the color red. Nearly all of their clothes were red; even the bones of the dead were painted red.

THE SKINNY

But the big question: Did the Chachapoyas really have light skin? Based on the Spanish accounts, it was definitely *lighter* than the other Native American peoples, but there's no proof that they were pale like Caucasians. There are two fascinating theories.

- **Adaptive Indians.** Before retreating to the highlands, the Chachapoyas had dark complexions. But over the centuries, the isolated population evolved lighter skin and taller stature due to the darker conditions and cooler climate. That still doesn't explain the blond hair and blue eyes—neither of which are evident on the 500-year-old mummies.
- **Jungle Vikings.** Unlike just about every other dark-skinned native culture in the Americas—who crossed the Bering Strait from Asia thousands of years before—these people may have come from Europe. This gives credence to an Inca legend that says the Cloud People arrived on ships from the east. To the east is the Atlantic Ocean. So perhaps, during Europe's Dark Ages, Nordic tribes traversed the Atlantic and landed somewhere near the mouth of the Amazon River. Then, finding the temperature too hot and muggy, they migrated hundreds of miles into the mountains before settling in the cooler cloud forests.

So far, there's no conclusive DNA evidence to support either theory. But answers may be coming soon, so stay tuned for new insights into a culture whose legacy was once thought to be gone forever. Until then, if you want to see a remnant of the Cloud People, take a look at the beginning of *Raiders of the Lost Ark:* The idol that Indiana Jones attempts to "collect" is Chachapoyan.

MUSIC...WITHOUT THE MUSIC INDUSTRY

*The music business used to be simple: Singer makes an album, record company
makes the CD and sends it to stores, people buy it, singer gets a royalty.
But it's much more complicated in the era of digital music. Here are
some musicians who found new ways to get their music to their fans.*

Artist: Radiohead
Method: Download, and pay what you want
Story: Radiohead was one of the world's most popular
bands in the 2000s, but in 2007, having fulfilled a contract with
EMI, they didn't have a record deal and didn't really want one.
They started recording, and on October 1, guitarist Jonny Green-
wood announced online that the new album, *In Rainbows*, was
done. Not only that, it would be available in just 10 days, and
only via digital download directly from the band. But the most
surprising part: Fans could pay whatever they felt like paying—the
$15 they would normally pay for a CD, or $5, or $100...or even
nothing. In the first week *In Rainbows* was available, it was down-
loaded 1.2 million times with buyers paying an average of about
$6 each. The standard royalty rate per copy sold via a record label
is about $1. But because Radiohead didn't have to pay a record
company to manufacture or distribute *In Rainbows*, the band got
all the money—approximately $7.2 million.

Artist: Danger Mouse
Method: Buy a blank CD, fill it with a "pirated" version of the
album
Story: Danger Mouse, a DJ who is part of the popular duo Gnarls
Barkley, collaborated with the singer Sparklehorse on the 2009
album *Dark Night of the Soul*. The record's scheduled May release
was delayed indefinitely due to a legal dispute between Danger
Mouse and his record label, EMI (the details of the problem were
not made public). So Danger Mouse figured out a way to get the
album out while still making money for himself (and, subsequent-

---

Eeeew! 45% of people admit that they pee in the shower.

ly, for EMI). Fans could buy a CD case labeled *Dark Night of the Soul* with a blank, recordable CD inside. The album had been "leaked" to several illegal online music piracy sites, so Danger Mouse just encouraged fans to download the music and copy it to the CD. (Who leaked the album to the Internet? Danger Mouse.)

Artist: Jill Sobule

Method: Defray recording costs with fan contributions

Story: Other than a single radio hit in 1995, "I Kissed a Girl," singer-songwriter Jill Sobule has never had much commercial success or much luck with record labels—two big ones dropped her for low sales, and two small ones went out of business. So she decided to record, release, and promote her eighth album, *California Years*, completely independently, with no involvement from the music industry. She set up a Web site where fans could donate money to help her make the album, with special rewards for especially large gifts. *Dancing With the Stars* host Tom Bergeron donated $1,000, for which Sobule wrote him a James Bond-style "personal theme song." A British woman gave $10,000, entitling her to sing a duet with Sobule on the album. Exceeding her expectations, Sobule raised the necessary $75,000 in just six weeks. *California Years* was released in May 2009, to the best reviews and the best sales of Sobule's career.

Artist: Prince

Method: Give away the CD to promote concerts

Story: Most artists go on concert tours to promote their CDs, but by the mid-2000s, long past his 1980s prime, Prince was making more money from concerts than from album sales. So to him, it made more sense to use albums to promote his concerts. In 2004 Prince played more than 90 shows in the United States and Canada, and anybody who bought a ticket—about 1.5 million people—got a free copy of his latest album, *Musicology*. And because the cost of the CD was included in the price of the ticket, *Musicology* made it to the *Billboard* Top 10, despite little radio exposure. The promotion worked—most concerts sold out. Prince did it again in 2007, but this time, fans only had to buy a newspaper to get Prince's *Planet Earth*. The July 15, 2007, edition of the British *Mail on Sunday* came with a free copy of the CD as a publicity stunt to promote Prince's upcoming European tour.

Tall tree: The Peruvian quenal tree grows at an altitude of 16,000 feet.

KALASHNIKOV PAT & THE HELICOPTER JAILBREAKS

Since 1986 there have been 11 helicopter-assisted jailbreaks from French prisons. Three of them involved the same man.

BACKGROUND: Pascal Payet, a.k.a. "Kalashnikov Pat," is one of France's most notorious criminals. In 1997 he was arrested for armed robbery and murder after an attack on an armored truck, during which he shot a guard 14 times. Payet was sent to Luynes Prison in southeast France to await trial.

ESCAPE! On October 12, 2001, a helicopter appeared above the prison exercise yard. A rope ladder was lowered, Pascal and one on other inmate climbed it, and the chopper flew off. The daring escape shocked French authorities and made headlines worldwide.

ESCAPE II! In May 2003, Payet was still on the loose when he and some associates decided to go *back* to Luynes Prison (in a hijacked helicopter) to pick up a few friends. Two of the men belayed commando-style down to the steel net that had been put over the exercise yard after Payet's previous escape, sawed a hole in it and dropped a ladder through, and three inmates, all cohorts of Payet, climbed up. The helicopter landed in a nearby sports stadium, and the men left in a waiting car. The three friends were recaptured a week later; Payet, some months later. In 2005 he was sentenced to 30 years in Grasse Prison in southeast France.

ESCAPE III! On July 14, 2007, Payet escaped again—and again it was with a helicopter. This one was hijacked in the nearby seaside resort town of Cannes; it landed on the roof of a building at Grasse Prison half an hour later. Three armed men jumped out and overtook the guards, went straight to Payet's cell, took him back to the chopper, and flew away. The chopper eventually landed at a local hospital's heliport, and the men all disappeared. Payet was arrested in Spain two months later and is currently serving a lengthy sentence in a French prison. Where is the prison? Cautious French authorities refuse to disclose its location.

George Washington spent about 7% of his annual salary on liquor.

BELLE GUNNESS: THE TERROR OF LA PORTE

A dark tale from our "Dustbin of Gruesome History" files.

THE DISCOVERY

On the night of April 28, 1908, Joe Maxson, a hired hand on a farm outside of La Porte, Indiana, awoke in his upstairs bedroom to the smell of smoke. The house was on fire. He called out to the farm's owner, Belle Gunness, and her three children. Getting no answer, he jumped from a second-story window, narrowly escaping the flames, and ran for help. But it was too late; the house was destroyed. A search through the wreckage resulted in a grisly discovery: four dead bodies in the basement. Three were Gunness's children, aged 5, 9, and 11. The fourth was a woman, assumed to be Gunness herself, but identification was difficult—the body's head was missing. An investigation ensued, and Ray Lamphere, a recently fired employee, was arrested for arson and murder. Before Lamphere's trial was over, he would be little more than a sidebar in what is still one of the most most horrible crime stories in American history…and an unsolved mystery.

BACKGROUND

Belle Gunness was born Brynhild Paulsdatter Storseth in Selbu, Norway, in 1859. At the age of 22 she emigrated to America and moved in with her older sister in Chicago, where she changed her name to "Belle." In 1884 the 25-year-old married another Norwegian immigrant, Mads Sorenson, and the couple opened a candy shop. A year later the store burned down, the first of what would be several suspicious fires in Belle's life. The couple collected an insurance payout and used the money to buy a house in the Chicago suburbs. Fifteen years later, in 1898, *that* house burned down, and another insurance payment allowed the couple to buy another house. On July 30, 1900, yet another insurance policy was brought into play, but this time it was life insurance: Mads Sorenson had died. A doctor's autopsy said he was murdered, probably by strychnine poisoning, so an inquest was ordered. The coroner's

investigation eventually deemed the death to be "of natural causes," and Belle collected $8,000, becoming, for 1900, a wealthy
woman. (The average yearly income in 1900 was less than $500.)
She used part of the money to buy the farm in La Porte. But there
was a lot more death—and insurance money—to come.

MORE SUSPICIONS

In April 1902, Belle married a local butcher named Peter Gunness
and became Belle Gunness. One week later, Peter Gunness's infant
daughter died while left alone with Belle...and yet another insurance policy was collected on. Just eight months after that, Peter
Gunness was dead: He was found in his shed with his skull crushed.
Belle, who was 5'8", weighed well over 200 pounds, and was known
to be very strong, told the police that a meat grinder had fallen
from a high shelf and landed on her husband's head. The coroner
said otherwise, ruling the cause of death to be murder. On top of
that, a witness claimed to have overheard Belle's 14-year-old
daughter, Jennie, saying to a classmate, "My mama killed my papa.
She hit him with a meat cleaver and he died."

Belle and Jennie were brought before a coroner's jury and questioned. Jennie denied making the statement; Belle denied killing
her husband. The jury found Belle innocent—and she collected
another $3,000 in life insurance money. And she was just getting
started.

NOT WELL SUITED

Not long after Peter Gunness's death, Belle started putting ads in
newspapers around the Midwest. One read:

> Comely widow who owns a large farm in one of the finest districts
> in La Porte County, Indiana, desires to make the acquaintance of a
> gentleman equally well provided, with view of joining fortunes. No
> replies by letter considered unless sender is willing to follow answer
> with personal visit. Triflers need not apply.

The ads worked, and suitors began to show up at the farm with
visions of "joining fortunes" in mind. John Moo arrived from Minnesota in late 1902 with his life savings of $1,000 in hand. He
stayed at the farm for about a week...and disappeared. Over the
years several more met the same fate: Henry Gurholdt from Wisconsin, who had brought $1,500; Ole B. Budsburg, also from

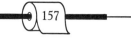

Wisconsin, who brought the deed to his property, worth thousands, and was last seen in a La Porte bank in April 1907; and Andrew Hegelein, from South Dakota, also last seen in the bank, in January 1908.

Andrew Hegelein turned out to be the last of the disappearing suitors, because a few weeks after his disappearance, his brother, A.K. Hegelein, wrote to Gunness to inquire about him. She replied that he'd gone to Norway. Hegelein didn't believe her—and threatened to come to La Porte to find out what had happened to him.

LAMPHERE

We said at the start of the story that when the Gunness home burnt to the ground, killing the three children and, presumably, Belle Gunness, former employee Ray Lamphere was arrested. The reason: Lamphere had been hired in 1907 and, by all accounts, had fallen in love with Gunness. The seemingly constant coming and going of suitors enraged him, and he and Gunness fought about it. In February 1908, around the time of Hegelein's disappearance, Gunness fired Lamphere. Not only that—she went to the local sheriff and told him that Lamphere was making threats against her. The day before the house fire, she went to a lawyer and made out a will, telling the lawyer that Lamphere had threatened to kill her and her children...and to burn her house down. Under the circumstances, the sheriff *had* to arrest Lamphere—but the focus of the investigation would soon turn elsewhere.

THE WOMAN IN THE BASEMENT

Lamphere denied any involvement with either the arson or the murders. Few people believed him...but there were serious questions about the body of Belle Gunness. Doctors who inspected the remains said they belonged to a woman about 5'3" (they had to account for the missing head, of course) who weighed about 150 pounds. Gunness was much larger than that. And several neighbors who knew Gunness well viewed the remains—and said it wasn't her. Then A. K. Hegelein showed up looking for his brother. He told the police his story and insisted that a search be made of Gunness's property. The search began on May 3. Two days later, five bodies, carefully dismembered and wrapped in oilcloth, were discovered buried around the farm.

BUT WAIT! THERE'S MORE!

The first body was determined to be that of Gunness's daughter Jennie, who, according to Belle, had been in school in California since 1906. The second body was Andrew Hegelein. The third was an unidentified man; the fourth and fifth were unidentified eight-year-old girls.

Neighbors told investigators that they had often seen Gunness digging in her hog pen, so they dug up that area—and found body after body after body. Included in the group: suitors John Moo, Ole Budsburg, and Henry Gurhold. In the end the remains of more than 25 bodies (some reports say as many as 49) were found, many of them unidentifiable.

Belle Gunness had obviously lured the men to her farm and killed them for their money. People in La Porte began to believe that if she could do that, she could fake her own death, and that the body found after the fire was yet another of her victims. It was beginning to look like A. K. Hegelein's threat to come look for his brother made Gunness panic and come up with her bloody plan. But then a problem arose: On May 16 a part of a jawbone and a section of dentures were found in the ruins of the house. Gunness's dentist, Ira Norton, inspected them—and said the dental work on the teeth belonged to Belle Gunness.

THE AFTERMATH

After a long investigation the body of the woman in the fire was officially declared to be that of Belle Gunness, and was buried as such. Ray Lamphere was tried for arson and murder—but because of all the lingering questions surrounding the case, he was convicted only of arson. He received a 20-year prison sentence and died less than a year later of tuberculosis. While in prison he reportedly confessed to a prison minister that he had helped Gunness bury some of her victims—and that the woman in the basement was *not* her. Gunness had hired a woman from Chicago as a housekeeper just days before the fire, he said, and drugged her, killed her, decapitated her, dressed her in Belle's clothes, and put her in the basement. He helped Gunness start the fire, he said, and was then supposed to escape with her, but she double-crossed him and left on her own. However, none of his story could be substantiated.

People reported seeing Belle Gunness at dozens of locations across the U.S. over the following decades. None of those sightings were ever confirmed. Then, in 1931, a woman named Esther Carlson was arrested for the poisoning murder of her husband in Los Angeles...and she reportedly looked a lot like Belle Gunness. Carlson died awaiting trial, but some La Porte residents made the trip to the Los Angeles morgue and viewed the body. They said that they believed it was Gunness.

UPDATE

In 2008 Andrea Simmons, an attorney and graduate student at the University of Indianapolis in Indiana, led a team of forensic biologists to the graveyard where Belle Gunness was buried. With permission from Gunness's descendants, they dug up the grave with the intent of extracting DNA from the corpse and comparing it to the DNA of living relatives. Results were hoped for by April 28, 2008, the 100th anniversary of the fire at the Gunness farm, but they were, unfortunately, inconclusive. Attempts are ongoing, and someday, possibly soon, the mystery of Belle Gunness, one of the most diabolical serial killers in history, might finally be solved.

*   *   *

TWO ILLEGAL WORD ORIGINS

• In 1849 a man named William Thompson would walk up to strangers in New York City and, after making friends with them, ask, "Have you confidence in me to trust me with your watch until tomorrow?" If they said yes, Thompson would gratefully borrow the watch...and then keep it. When he was caught, the prosecutors referred to him as a "confidence man." That didn't fit on headlines, so newspapers shortened it to "con man."

• Another trickster in 1840s New York was Alec Hoag. He used prostitutes to lure men into hotel rooms. When the men's clothes were on the floor, Hoag lifted money from the pockets via a hole in the wall. He was known for his ability to stay one step ahead of the police...and brag about it all over the city. The nickname the cops gave to Hoag survives as a slang term used to describe an intelligent, cocky person: "smart alec."

Pilgrims ate popcorn at the first Thanksgiving dinner.

HOW TO DO THINGS

Because there are certain things everyone should know how to do.

HOW TO PICK A GOOD COMPUTER PASSWORD
1) Don't use any part of your name, your spouse's name, your parents' names, your children's names, or your pets' names. Don't use any part of your phone number, Social Security number, birthdate, driver's license number, address, or a pattern (like "12456"). Don't use any of them reversed or doubled, either. Don't use anything that would be easy to guess by someone watching you type. Never write it down or share it with anyone.
2) Use upper- and lower-case letters, plus numbers and symbols (if the site allows symbols). Use a mnemonic device, with abbreviations that include multiple words. Example: Uj$t#1w0rx ("Uncle John says this one works.")
3) Change it every three months.

HOW TO JUMP-START A CAR
1) Turn off the engines of both cars. As an extra precaution, engage the emergency brakes too.
2) Open the hoods of both cars and remove the plastic protective caps on the battery connections.
3) After you've untangled the jumper cables from your trunk, clamp the red cable onto the positive (+) connection of the dead battery.
4) Clamp the other end of the red cable to the positive (+) connection of the working car.
5) Clamp the black cable to the negative (–) connection on the working car.
6) Do *not* attach the other black end to the dead battery. Instead, "ground" it by clamping it to the metal frame of the car.
7) Start the engine of the working car and gently rev the engine.
8) After about 30 seconds, turn the key on the dead car.
9) Once both cars are running, remove the cables in reverse order: the grounded black clamp first, then the other black clamp, the red on the car that provided the jump, and the last red clamp.

HOW TO BOIL AN EGG

1) Place an egg in a pot.

2) Run cold water into the pot, enough to cover the eggs.

3) Bring the water to a boil on the stove.

4) Once it reaches boiling, turn the burner down so that the water is simmering.

5) For soft-boiled eggs, remove them after they've simmered for three minutes. For hard-boiled, remove after 10 minutes.

HOW TO WRITE A THANK-YOU NOTE

1) It doesn't have to be long—that's why you use a small card. Always handwrite it.

2) Start with a direct "Thank you."

3) Add a few sentences that put acceptance of the gift on a personal level to show that you really like it: why you like the gift, what it means to you, and what you plan to do with it.

4) Finish this section by tying the gift—and your relationship with the person—into a larger context, like a stated goal. For example, "I hope our families can spend more time together."

5) Reiterate your thanks.

6) End with "Love" or "Sincerely" and your name.

HOW TO TELL IF A STEAK IS COOKED

1) Touch the meat with your fingertip.

2) Compare it to the meatiest part of your hand, on your palm right under the thumb. If the meat feels like that, it's rare.

3) Touch your index finger to the thumb of the same hand, forming an "O." Press the meaty part of your palm right under the thumb again. If the steak feels like this, it's medium-rare.

4) Touch your middle finger to the thumb of the same hand, again forming an "O," and touch that same place under your thumb. If your steak feels like that, it's medium.

5) Touch your ring finger to your thumb, and poke the meaty part of your palm again. That's medium-well.

6) Touch your pinky to your thumb. If the steak feels like that, it's well-done.

ANTARCTIC JARGON

Living as a research scientist at the McMurdo Station in Antarctica must be a unique experience. And it has its own lingo.

Boomerang: An outgoing airplane flight that has to return immediately after takeoff due to bad weather.

CHC: Pronounced "Cheech," it stands for Christchurch, New Zealand, the closest major city to Antarctica.

Green Brain: A small green notebook issued to all researchers.

Ivan: Short for "ice van," it's the large, iceworthy bus that transfers researchers from one building to another.

Apples: Warming huts—red, fiberglass, domed igloos.

Polie: Research workers (as in "South Polies").

Oden: Named after the powerful Norse god Odin, it's a huge icebreaking vessel used on the water channels where the supply ships enter.

Gerbil Gym: The workout room, which consists almost entirely of treadmills.

Freshies: The weekly food delivery from New Zealand.

Southern: There are two bars for the scientists off duty. The Southern (short for Southern Exposure) allows smoking; the other bar, Gallagher's, doesn't.

FNG: Pronounced "fingee," it means a new person on the Station. (NG stands for "new guy." You'll have to guess what the F stands for.)

WinFly: The day-long switchover from the winter crew (Feb.–Oct.) to the summer crew (Oct.–Feb.). It's short for "winter fly-in."

Yak Tracks: Traction-providing grips that go on the bottom of boots.

Big Red and Bunny Boots: The two main pieces of standard issue ECW, or "extreme cold weather" gear. Big Red is a big puffy coat; Bunny Boots are white rubber boots.

Uppercase: The three-story dormitory researchers live in.

The Ice: Antarctica itself.

Frosty Boy: Soft-serve ice cream, which is surprisingly popular in Antarctica.

Aerosmith has made more money from Guitar Hero than from the sales of any of their albums.

INDIANA BASKETBALL: THE "MILAN MIRACLE"

Hoosiers is one of the most popular sports movies ever made. Here's the true story that inspired the movie—and an even better story about how one team changed the game of basketball.

THE CHURCH OF BASKETBALL

Indiana's love of basketball goes all the way back to 1893, when the state hosted the first game ever played outside of Massachusetts, where it was founded. By the 1950s, the game was so integral to Indiana's culture, wrote sportswriter David Halberstam, that "there was church and there was basketball." Every town with a high school had a basketball team, even towns too small to put together a football or baseball team. And on Friday nights, gyms across the state were filled with hundreds—even thousands—of fans.

For all of those young teams, the holy grail was winning the Indiana High School State Basketball Championship. And amazingly enough, every team had that chance. In most states, high school sports are divided into three or four classes, based on the school's size and location. But Indiana had one big winner-take-all tournament, where small schools played large schools, inner-city schools played rural schools, and, by the 1950s, all-white schools played all-black schools.

THE MIRACLE

One result of Indiana's state tournament program was the 1954 "Milan Miracle," when a tiny rural school won the state championship, an event immortalized in the 1986 movie *Hoosiers*. In the film, all-white "Hickory High" won the State Championship by defeating an all-black inner-city team that was dominated by one super-talented player. But that isn't exactly how it happened. In real life, small-town Milan (pronounced "MY-lin") High School beat Muncie Central, an integrated team with three black players. The super-talented black player that the character in *Hoosiers* was modeled on—future NBA Hall-of-Famer Oscar Robertson—

didn't play for Muncie; he played for Crispus Attucks High School in Indianapolis, which didn't make it to the finals. And that year Robertson was only starting out as a player.

But the David-and-Goliath aspect of the story is true. Robertson later described the players from Milan as "a bunch of farm boys who were unfamiliar with stoplights, let alone neon." Milan High School had a total of 161 students; Muncie Central had 1,500. Even so, the Milan Indians were a seasoned, well-coached team that had made it all the way to the Finals the previous year. The 1954 squad was dominated by seniors, particularly their star guard, Bobby Plump. As small as the town of Milan was, Plump was from even smaller Pierceville (population: 45).

CAT AND MOUSE

The Indians were famous for a four-corners offense called the "cat and mouse." "It was an extremely successful offensive weapon, a slow-down game," said Plump. The guard—in this case, Bobby—would stand at the top of the "key" (at the foul line), while the other players went to four corners, forming a square. They'd then pass the ball back and forth at least four times until an opening in the defense showed and someone would take a jump shot.

But the "cat and mouse" didn't really work against powerhouse Muncie Central in the championship game, and Plump had a bad night shooting. With Muncie ahead 28–26 in the fourth quarter, Plump held the ball on his hip…for four minutes. How is that possible? There was no 30-second shot clock in those days, so Plump could hold it as long as he wanted. After a couple of scores by both teams, they were tied 30–30 with less than a minute to go. Plump held the ball for another half a minute, and then with the clock running down, he sank a 15-foot jump shot to win the game, 32–30.

STAR QUALITY

By today's standards, the Milan victory may not sound very exciting, but that night all 15,000 spectators at Butler Fieldhouse in Indianapolis were on their feet, and all of Indiana went crazy over the spectacular win. To this day, Bobby Plump is still one of the most famous basketball players in Indiana. (He owns a popular Indianapolis restaurant called Plump's Last Shot.)

World's smallest winged insect: the Tanzanian parasitic wasp. It's smaller…

WAITING IN THE WINGS

Milan *did* play Oscar Robertson's team that year, but not in the Finals. The two teams met in the Regional Finals, known as the "Semi-states." Robertson was just a sophomore playing in the tournament for the first time. (Even so, he had 22 points in that game.) Bobby Plump was the dominant player, leading all scorers with 28 points, and Milan won 65–52. But the Milan coach, Marvin Wood, recognized that the grace and power of Oscar Robertson had only been held in check by the age and experience of his own squad. Bobby Plump agreed: "I'm glad we got him when he was a sophomore and not a senior." Only a footnote in Milan's David and Goliath story, Oscar Robertson's team—the Crispus Attucks Tigers—would make their own history over the next two years.

For Part II of the story, turn to page 284.

* * *

11 ACTUAL EXCUSES FOR BEING LATE FOR WORK

- "My heat was shut off so I had to stay home to keep my snake warm."
- "I had to go to bingo."
- "I got locked in my trunk by my son."
- "My husband thinks it's funny to hide my car keys before he goes to work."
- "I walked into a spider web on the way out the door and couldn't find the spider, so I had to go inside and shower again."
- "A gurney fell out of an ambulance and delayed traffic."
- "I was attacked by a raccoon, so I had to stop by the hospital to make sure it wasn't rabid."
- "A groundhog bit my bike tire and made it flat."
- "My driveway washed away in the rain last night."
- "I feel like I'm in everyone's way if I show up on time."
- "My left turn signal was out so I had to make all right turns to get to work."

THE KING OF AUCTIONS

A few months before his death in 2009, more than 2,000 items belonging to Michael Jackson were put up for sale at a Los Angeles auction house to help pay the financially troubled singer's debts. But just before the items could go on the block, Jackson sued to stop the auction. Here's a sampling of some of the bizarre stuff that was to be sold.

Item: A classical-style oil painting of Jackson dressed as a 16th century king, à la Henry VIII.
Auction estimate: $4,000 to $6,000

Item: An orange glove covered with hundreds of tiny, orange crystals. It's similar to the rhinestone-covered white glove Jackson frequently wore in the mid-1980s, except that it's orange and it's covered with expensive Swarovski crystals instead of rhinestones.
Auction estimate: $1,000 to $5,000

Item: An electric golf cart. Painted on the hood is an airbrushed image of Jackson as Peter Pan, surrounded by golden fairy dust and flying pirate ships.
Auction estimate: $4,000 to $6,000

Item: A silver robotic head—a prop from the 1988 film *Moonwalker*, in which Jackson transforms into a robot in order to defeat the villain. Each face part juts out at the push of a button.
Auction estimate: $2,000 to $3,000

Item: A mural of Jackson wearing a sparkly white glove and sunglasses, surrounded by images of George Washington, the Mona Lisa, Albert Einstein, Abraham Lincoln, and E.T., all of whom are also wearing a single white glove and sunglasses.
Auction estimate: $1,000 to $2,000

Item: A framed letter from President Ronald Reagan to Jackson. It's a "get well soon" letter dated February 1, 1984, sent after Jackson was injured when his hair caught fire during the filming of a Pepsi commercial. "I was pleased to learn that you were not seri-

ously hurt in your recent accident. I know from experience that these things can happen on the set."
Auction estimate: $400 to $600

Item: An 8'-tall "welcome" sign from Jackson's former home at Neverland Ranch. It depicts a Norman Rockwell-esque image of an African-American boy scout talking to a wood nymph, who is playing the flute in front of a full moon.
Auction estimate: $300 to $500

Item: A 5'-by-8' black marble tablet etched with the original Jackson poem, "Children of the World." An excerpt:
Children of the world, we'll do it
With song and dance and innocent bliss
And the soft caress of a loving kiss
We'll do it
While traders trade and haggle their price
And politicians try so hard to be nice
We'll meet on endless shores and floating our boats
We'll do it
Auction estimate: $600 to $800

Item: The sparkly socks Jackson wore when he performed the Moonwalk for the first time on the 1983 Motown 25th-Anniversary TV special. The uppers (the calf-covering portion) are covered in rhinestones, but they are sewn onto regular old white athletic socks.
Auction estimate: $600 to $800

Item: A 13"-tall statuette of Jackson as a California Raisin. Custom-made by Will Vinton Studios (creators of the California Raisins), Jackson is purple, wrinkly, and wearing a white glove.
Auction estimate: $100 to $150'

*　　*　　*

BIZARRE (BUT REAL) JELLY BEAN FLAVORS
Buttered Toast • Cheese Pizza • Ear Wax
Garlic • Pencil Shavings • Moldy Cheese

THE POTTY POLLS

You'd be surprised how many surveys of bathroom behavior there are, not just in the U.S., but all over the world. So next time you're in the bathroom, remember…your opinion counts!

GOING OUT

- 99% of Americans say they are willing to use public restrooms if and when the need arises, according to a 2009 poll. (No word on what the other 1% do.) Of these, 30% say they will use public restrooms only in an emergency.

- 19% of men and 13% of women say they've stopped whatever it was they were doing and gone home to use the bathroom rather than use a public restroom that was deficient in some way (too dirty, no toilet paper, etc.). Half said that if the restroom were in a restaurant, they'd warn friends and neighbors not to dine there.

- 56% of women and 51% of men say they've "snuck" into a restaurant, store, or other business establishment to use the restroom, even though they had no intention of buying anything.

- According to 2007 survey by Dyson, a manufacturer of restroom hand dryers, 42% of Americans say they use toilet paper or paper towels to avoid touching restroom surfaces. And 90% of Americans say they perform "bathroom gymnastics"—turning on the hand dryer with an elbow, flushing the toilet with their shoe, etc.—to avoid touching surfaces in public restrooms.

ELECTRIC COMPANY

According to an online poll conducted in 2008 for Ideal Standard International, a Belgian manufacturer of plumbing fixtures, 80% of respondents around the world say they've used at least one electronic device in the bathroom.

- Most popular for men: personal data assistants (PDAs), computer games, DVD players, and devices that provide Internet access.

- Most popular for women: telephones or cell phones, bathroom scales, and portable music players.

- 60% of all respondents said they'd spend more time in the bathroom if more electronic products were available in there.

By the time it's a year old, the average mockingbird already knows 25 to 30 songs.

YOU'VE GOT B-MAIL

• 59% of Americans say they check e-mail while going to the bathroom, according to a 2008 survey by American Standard, a manufacturer of plumbing fixtures. Top three benefits cited for taking care of business while taking care of business: 1) It saves time (53–56%); 2) It increases availability (25–29%); 3) The bathroom provides privacy (19–22%).

POT PEEVES

• In the same survey, American Standard asked respondents what annoyed them most about their toilets. Top four complaints: 1) More than one flush needed for the toilet to flush all the way; 2) Unattractive appearance; 3) You have to jiggle the handle to stop the water from running; and 4) Not a model that conserves water.

• As annoying as these problems are, only about a third of Americans say they're willing to tackle a plumbing problem that requires anything more than a plunger. 17% of respondents call their plumber so often that they know them on a first name basis.

CREATURE COMFORTS

• 47% of Americans who own pets say they bathe them in the bathroom, according to a survey by Moen International, a faucet manufacturer. Another 22% of pet owners bathe them in the driveway or the yard. 6% take their pets to a professional groomer.

• One third of pet bathers bathe their pets at least once a month, and 21% bathe them at least once a week.

• Fewer than 5% of pet owners say they have ever bathed a bird, guinea pig, rabbit, lizard, or snake, and fewer than 1% have ever bathed a ferret, turtle, pig, or horse. (Horses are almost never bathed in the bathroom.)

CUBISM

• 25% of Americans who work in offices say their office is the "germiest" place they visit all day, according to a 2007 study by the polling company Booth Research. That's more than the 19% who said that public restrooms are the germiest places they visit.

• In another survey, nearly 50% of cubicle workers say their cubicle is smaller than their bathroom at home.

For more Potty Polls, turn to page 325.

BUSINESS SHORTS

Flops, flubs, and foibles from Corporate Land.

OPEN WIDE. Claiming trademark infringement, in 2009 the Austria-based PEZ Candy Company ordered Gary Doss, who runs the PEZ Museum in Burlingame, California, to destroy "The World's Largest PEZ Dispenser," an eight-foot-tall replica he built. "It's just a piece of art that draws people into our store so we can sell PEZ!" argued Doss. Not only that, even though he's provided PEZ with sales and free advertising for 14 years, the company wants Doss to turn over all profits from the museum.

AN OFFER THEY SHOULD HAVE REFUSED. In 2009 video-game company Electronic Arts sent out promotional materials for their "The Godfather Part II" game to journalists and reviewers. Included in the promo pack: brass knuckles. But then EA learned that brass knuckles are illegal in most of the states they'd been shipped to, so they had to send out requests for the weapons to be sent back. That created another problem: It turns out that it's not only illegal to *own* brass knuckles, it's also illegal to *ship* them. So EA sent out one more notice requesting that anyone who received the illegal brass knuckles please "dispose of them immediately."

GOING GREEN THE HARD WAY. Toronto's Better Buildings Partnership (BBP) issued a one-page press release in 2009 about incentives for builders who utilize eco-friendly practices. Proving they're green themselves, the one-page release was printed on recycled paper. But it came inside a nonrecycled paper envelope that included plastic bubble wrap, a cardboard box, nonrecycled tissue paper, a plastic building made of green LEGOs, and a color photo of the LEGO building. "Maybe the packaging could have been a little bit better," said a BBP spokesperson.

THE AGONY OF DEFEATS. The Detroit Lions ran a banner-ad campaign on several football Web sites in summer 2009 inviting fans to "Relive the exciting '08 season!" by watching streamed videos of all 16 games. The campaign was widely criticized, however, because the Lions had lost every one of their games.

WEIRD CANADA

Ah, Canada—home of Mounties, billboards in two languages, excellent doughnuts, Anne Murray…and some really odd news stories.

THE PUNCH WAS TOO PUNCHY

A 58-year-old man went out to dinner at a St. John's, Newfoundland, steakhouse in February 2009, but when his meal arrived, he was unhappy with what was on the plate. The man complained to his waiter that his steak was "too meaty." The waiter and restaurant manager tried to figure out exactly what the man meant, or how a piece of meat could have too much meat on it, but the man would not elaborate, and he only got angrier. The man paid his bill, and as he left he pushed his waiter, then punched him in the face. The man faces assault charges.

POT HEAD

In early 2007, Antonio Batista, 75, got fed up with the many pot-holes in his home town of Mississauga, Ontario. So he wrote a letter to his city councilmember, Pat Saito. Batista never received a response, so he kept writing letters—no response to those, either. In frustration about the lack of action, he wrote a protest poem called "Parked Cars and Pot Holes" and posted it on telephone poles and bulletin boards around town. One part reads,

six feet long and three feet wide
and five feet deep to hide
her body and God will take care
of Her Soul, but We cannot
Forgive her for doing nothing.

For seeming to suggest the live burial of Saito, Batista was arrested for making a death threat. The conviction was overturned on appeal in November 2008 on the grounds that the poem was not a stated intent to murder, but "literary expression."

AN ANGRY LITTLE BOOGAARD

Derek Boogaard plays in the National Hockey League. His position is left wing, but he's primarily an "enforcer," which in hockey is a player who responds to aggressive or violent action by the opposite team by slamming the offending party into the boards or starting a fight. (Boogaard once hit an opponent so hard he required reconstructive facial surgery.) In 2007 Boogaard teamed up with his brother Aaron to put his distinct abilities to use—they opened the Derek and Aaron Boogaard Fighting Camp in Saskatchewan, the only training facility in the world that exists specifically to teach teenage hockey players how to fight properly.

JUST FOR KICKS
Jarrett Loft was one of the most notorious—and strangest—criminals on the loose in Guelph, Ontario. At least seven times, the 28-year-old approached women on the street and politely asked them to kick him in the groin. Every time, fearing attack if they refused, the women complied, kicking him repeatedly in the groin. Loft would then thank the woman and ride away on his bicycle. Arrested and sentenced to 60 days in jail in March 2008, Loft said he did it because he was "curious."

IT USUALLY TASTES BETTER
Elanie Larabie of Ottawa was trying to get her terrier, Missy, to eat some dog food, but Missy just wouldn't touch it. So Larabie thought the dog might learn by example—Larabie nibbled a mouthful of the kibble. It worked. Missy finished off the bowl. The next day, Larabie and Missy were in a hospital and veterinarian's office (respectively) with stomach pain, vomiting, and foaming at the mouth. Doctors believe that both dog and master ate food that was tainted with rat poison.

A VERY EXPENSIVE PENNY
In 2007 the city government of Toronto launched a campaign urging voters to approve a 1-cent tax increase to pay for civic and municipal projects, such as buildings and roads. The bill passed, but the money didn't go to funding any projects right away. Instead, it had to be diverted to pay a licensing bill sent by the Royal Canadian Mint. Posters and Web sites created to promote the tax campaign used a photograph of a Canadian penny and the words "one cent," which the mint says are registered trademarks. Total bill: $47,000.

PRANKSTERS

*We love a good prank here at the BRI, and these are
some of the cleverest ones we've heard about.*

FAKE PROPOSAL

In September 2007, Amir Blumenfeld learned that his friend Streeter Seidell was going to attend a New York Yankees game with his girlfriend, Sharon. So Blumenfeld called Yankee Stadium and paid $500 for a marriage proposal to be displayed on the stadium's Jumbotron—Seidell's proposal to Sharon. In the middle of the fifth inning, this message appeared on the huge screen in front of 57,000 people: "Dear Sharon, I love you forever. Will you marry me? Streety Bird." Sharon immediately burst into happy tears and jumped to her feet, shouting, "Yes!" Seidell, however, went into a panic. He denied he'd actually proposed, insisting it was a hoax. And when he said, "I don't wanna f***ing marry you," Sharon slapped him across the face and stormed out of the game. Blumenfeld, meanwhile, had enlisted some friends to sit near Seidell to videotape the proposal and its aftermath, and that video wound up being viewed by hundreds of thousands of people...because Blumenfeld and Seidell both worked for the Internet comedy site CollegeHumor.com.

FAKE RESTAURANT

Robin Goldstein is a wine critic and food writer. He's dined at many restaurants whose menus boasted the Award of Excellence from *Wine Spectator* magazine, despite having wine lists that Goldstein knew were populated with mediocre wines. Suspicious, he decided to try an experiment. In 2009 he invented a restaurant called Osteria l'Intrepido (Italian for "the fearless tavern") and typed up a menu of ordinary Italian dishes. Goldstein also included a wine list—the lowest-rated wines from the last 20 years of *Wine Spectator* magazine. Then he submitted his menu, along with the $250 fee, to *Wine Spectator* to apply for their Award of Excellence. Despite a list of wines *Wine Spectator* itself said were terrible, and despite the fact that his restaurant wasn't real, Osteria l'Intrepido was awarded the *Wine Spectator* Award of Excellence. Goldstein posted the story on his Web site, published it in a magazine, and shared it with the attendees of a wine conference. (And *Wine Spectator*'s reputation will never be the same.)

FAKE BEST BUY

A New York-based group called Improv Everywhere stages good-natured pranks with hundreds of volunteer operatives. Past pranks include a book signing at a Barnes and Noble with Russian playwright Anton Chekov (who died in 1904), a morning subway commute in which hundreds of people didn't wear pants, and another subway prank in which eight sets of twins rode around and performed every action in perfect unison. In April 2006, IE staged "Operation Best Buy." Eighty volunteers simultaneously entered a Best Buy electronics store, all wearing the same outfit—blue polo shirt and khaki pants. The goal: to look like Best Buy employees, who wear the same clothes (only with nametags and company logos). IE instructed the pranksters to be kind and even help customers find what they were looking for. The only motive behind the prank was silly amusement—to create, if only for an hour, a comically overstaffed electronics store.

FAKE TORCH

The 1956 Olympics were held in Melbourne, Australia. Nine University of Sydney students thought it was appalling that the Olympic torch relay—created by the Nazis for the 1936 Berlin Games—was elevating the torch to the level of a religious icon, with thousands of Australians lining the streets of Sydney wherever the relay passed through. So they devised a plan to protest the torch with a phony relay. In the real relay, cross-country athlete Harry Dillon was supposed to run through downtown Sydney and hand the torch to mayor Pat Hills, who would then make a speech and give the torch to another runner. Moments before Dillon was to arrive, however, one of the protesters began running in the streets with a "torch"—a silver-painted chair leg topped with a flaming pair of underpants. The crowd laughed at the prank, but then the underwear fell off and the runner panicked and ran away. Another student took up the torch with a relit pair of underpants and continued to run the route...and police thought he was the real deal. They escorted him all the way to town hall, where he presented the flaming underpants to Mayor Hills.

CHILDREN'S BOOKS

Walk into any bookstore today and you'll find walls full of books written specifically for kids. But a few hundred years ago it wasn't like that—there were actually very few. Here are the first children's books ever written.

THE COLLOQUY

Possibly the earliest example of literature made specifically for children, *The Colloquy* was written and distributed in England around A.D. 1005 by a Benedictine monk named Aelfric. At the time, the Benedictines were trying to use education to help Europe emerge from centuries of social decline, and this playful textbook was meant to teach kids about both careers and Latin grammar. The book is written in the form of dialogue between a teacher and several pupils (*colloquy* means "dialogue" in Latin), the pupils taking on the roles of several professions. An example:

> **Teacher:** How did you dare to cut the boar's throat?
> **Hunter:** My dogs drove him towards me, and I stood against him and suddenly slew him.
> **Teacher:** You must have been very brave indeed.
> **Hunter:** A hunter must be very brave, since all kinds of beasts lurk in the woods.

THE DISTICHS OF CATO

This collection of witty proverbs for adults was written in Rome by Dionysius Cato around A.D. 300. Rediscovered in Europe in the 1200s, it was translated into many languages and used to teach children grammar and morals. *Distich* means "couplet," which was the form of the writing. Example: "Be stupid when the time or situation demands / To fake stupidity is at times the highest prudence." *The Distichs of Cato* remained one of the most popular Latin textbooks for several centuries—and even made its way to the American colonies, where it was published by Benjamin Franklin in 1735.

THE BOOK OF THE KNIGHT OF THE TOWER

In 1371 French aristocrat Geoffroy IV de la Tour Landry wrote this collection of fables to teach his two daughters proper behavior in royal society. The moral of one story: Do not have sex with a knight, because you might get pregnant, and then your father

---

2008 study: If you smell roses while you're sleeping, you're more likely to have pleasant dreams.

would have to drown you in a well in the dark and the knight would be "flayed alive." *The Book of the Knight of the Tower* was translated into German and English and was very popular for two decades.

A TOKEN FOR CHILDREN

The 1600s were the height of the extremely conservative and religious Puritan movement in England. How did adults teach kids to fear hell? Pastor James Janeway's *A Token for Children: An Exact Account of the Conversion, Holy and Exemplary Lives and Joyful Deaths of Several Young Children*, published in 1671. It's a collection of stories about kids (some as young as two) who commit sins, see the error of their ways, become pious, and then die. But because they repented, their deaths are accompanied by beautiful lights and the singing of angels. For the next two centuries, *A Token for Children* was one of the most popular children's books in England and the American colonies.

TOMMY THUMB'S PRETTY SONG BOOK

By the mid-1700s, attitudes toward children were changing—they were allowed to be what we think of as kids for the first time. *Tommy Thumb's Pretty Song Book*, written by "M. Cooper" in 1744, was an early fun book, and is said to be the first published collection of nursery rhymes, many of them still familiar, including "Sing a Song of Sixpence," "Baa Baa Black Sheep," and "Hickory Dickory Dock." Only one copy of *Tommy Thumb's Pretty Song Book* exists today—in the British Museum in London.

A LITTLE PRETTY POCKET BOOK

First released in 1744, English author and publisher John Newbery's *A Pretty Little Pocket Book: Intended for the Instruction and Amusement of Little Master Tommy and Pretty Miss Polly* consisted of illustrations, rhymes, and instructions for various games. An example, titled "Base-Ball": "The Ball once struck off / Away flies the Boy / To the next destin'd Post / And then Home with Joy." Newberry was the first publisher to market literature just for kids, emphasizing education through entertainment. To honor Newbery for essentially creating modern children's literature, the American Library Association's award for the best children's book of the year is named the Newbery Medal.

NAME GAME

The famous people listed below are better know by their initials.
Can you identify them all? (Answers on page 536.)

1) Reclusive novelist Jerome David...

2) Architect Ieoh Ming...

3) Fantasy author John Roland Reuel...

4) Author Clive Staples...

5) Circus impresario Phineas Taylor...

6) Poet Thomas Stearns...

7) Canadian country singer Kathryn Dawn...

8) Poet Wystan Hugh...

9) Illustrator Maurits Cornelis...

10) Horror writer Howard Phillips...

11) Psychologist Burrhus Frederic...

12) Race car driver Anthony Joseph...

13) TV star of *The Defenders* Everett Grunz...

14) Fictional *A-Team* mercenary Bosco Albert...

15) Science-fiction author Herbert George...

16) Tycoon John Pierpont...

17) Baseball pitcher Carsten Charles...

18) *Grey's Anatomy* co-star Theodore Raymond...

19) Stand-up comedian Darryl Lynn...

20) Tobacco baron Richard Joshua...

21) Poet Edward Estlin...

22) *Dallas* main character John Ross...

23) Silent film director David Wark...

24) *Winnie the Pooh* creator Alan Alexander...

25) Real name of the Big Bopper, Jiles Perry...

26) American pundit Henry Louis...

27) Political satirist Patrick Jake...

28) *Peter Pan* author James Matthew...

29) 1980s TV cop Thomas Jefferson...

Fidgeting can burn up to 350 calories a day.

A SHAGGY DOG STORY

Wanna hear a joke?

A "shaggy dog story" is a classic style of joke—one that goes on for a long time and escalates in detail and scope before ultimately ending in a short, ironic punchline or pun. It gets its name from a joke that dates to the early 1940s—and it was actually about a shaggy dog. By increasing the level of detail, the storyteller can easily stretch it out 5 or 10 minutes (or longer), but be prepared: Your audience may think you're the funniest person on Earth...or they may want to hurt you. Today, comedians still tell long, meandering "shaggy dog stories" about a number of topics. One famous example was the basis for the 2005 movie *The Aristocrats*. We can't print that one (it's X-rated), but here's a brief version of the original shaggy dog story.

• • •

A wealthy man lost his beloved, valuable pet dog, an incredibly shaggy dog, maybe the shaggiest in the world. The man took out a newspaper advertisement that read, "Lost: World's Shaggiest Dog. Large Cash Reward." A young boy saw the ad and wanted the reward, so he decided he'd find the world's shaggiest dog and return it. The boy combed his town, and the next town over, and the one after that, looking for shaggy dogs. He found some in pet stores and dog pounds, and they were shaggy...but not shaggy enough.

Finally, at the 30th dog pound he visited, the boy found an incredibly shaggy dog. The dog was so shaggy that he tripped over his own fur, because it covered both his paws and his eyes. When it barked, you couldn't even hear the sound because it got lost in the dog's layers of fur. It was the shaggiest dog the boy had ever seen in his life, and there was no way a dog could ever be shaggier.

So, the boy bought the dog and carried it all the way to the home of the wealthy man who'd placed the ad for the lost shaggy dog. (He had to carry it because the dog was so shaggy it couldn't see or walk properly.) The boy went to the rich man's home and rang the doorbell. The man answered the door, glanced at the dog, and then said to the boy, "Not *that* shaggy."

AMERICAN CHEESES

*No, not orange, plastic-wrapped, processed stuff that
makes cheese snobs groan. These are world-class
cheeses invented and produced in the U.S.A.*

TILLAMOOK CHEDDAR

Tillamook County is a fertile valley on the coast of Oregon that's home to 150 dairy farms and more than 26,000 cows. The county was already an important milk-producing center in 1894 when T. S. Townsend opened the first Tillamook cheese factory, hiring a Canadian cheesemaker named Peter McIntosh to create high-quality cheddar. McIntosh, known as the "Cheese King of the Coast," was so skillful that his cheddar won a national prize at the 1904 St. Louis World's Fair. Local dairy farmers saw how profitable it might be to produce great cheese, which could be transported to market fairly easily and wasn't as perishable as milk. And in 1909 ten of them started the cooperative Tillamook County Creamery Association; by 1968 all of the county's cheese factories had united under the same roof.

What makes Tillamook cheese taste different? They use a proprietary process called "heat shocking," which doesn't heat the milk for as long or to as high a temperature as pasteurization. The process preserves the crucial enzymes in the milk, while cheesemakers who use pasteurization may have to add those enzymes back in.

Today the TCCA comprises about 110 family-owned dairy farms. The Tillamook cheese factories produce more than 78 million pounds of cheese annually. Their cheddar still routinely wins prizes at the National Milk Producers Federation annual cheese contest, and in 2005 Tillamook was named dairy Processor of the Year by *Dairy Foods* magazine.

MONTEREY JACK

Europeans first saw Monterey Bay, located on the California coast between San Francisco and Los Angeles, when Spanish explorers sailed into it in 1542. In 1770 Father Junípero Serra built California's first cathedral, San Carlos Borromeo, in Monterey. The city was the Spanish (and then Mexican) capital of Alta California. Sometime in the 1700s, Franciscan monks started making a mild cow's-milk cheese that was called *queso de país*—"country cheese." Local farmers continued to make it after the missionaries were gone, but it wasn't until a sharp-eyed Scottish immigrant named David Jack recognized its commercial potential that the cheese's popularity spread farther. In 1882 he began shipping his version of *queso de país* to other parts of California. The cheese was labeled "Jack's Monterey," which evolved into "Jack Monterey," and in a final, unaccountable twist people began to call it "Monterey Jack." The FDA made the name official in 1955, and today you'll find it in every supermarket in the country. Variations: horseradish jack, pepper jack, salsa jack, Colby jack, cheddar jack, skim milk jack, dry jack, and even a jack from Vermont (it's called Vermont Jack.)

MAYTAG BLUE

When the Maytag Dairy Farms herd of Holstein cows began winning prizes in the 1930s, Maytag, Inc., was already famous for making washing machines. The Newton, Iowa, dairy was just a hobby for E. H. Maytag, son of the company's founder; he only sold the milk and cream locally. But when his son, 29-year-old Fred Maytag II, took over the appliance operation in 1940, he began scouting around for a more profitable way to use the dairy's high-quality milk. A year later, Fred and his brother Robert heard that two Iowa State University microbiologists had been working on a new process for making blue cheese. The scientists were trying to come up with a Roquefort-style blue-veined cheese that could be made with cow's milk instead of the traditional sheep's milk—and a recipe that would cut down on the long time it took to develop the flavor and color. They succeeded by using more rennet, which coagulates milk and turns it into the curds and whey needed for cheese-making. Result: a new kind of blue cheese that was consistent in color and quality, with a tangy flavor and a firm but crumbly texture. By agreement with the university, the Maytags began to produce the new cheese at their dairy. The Maytag corporation has changed hands, but Maytag Dairy Farms is still a family-owned, family-run business.

A Weddell seal can travel underwater for seven miles without surfacing for air.

LIEDERKRANZ

Emil Frey was a Swiss immigrant who started working as a cheese-maker for the Monroe Cheese Company in Monroe, New York, in 1888. Adolphe Tode, one of the owners, asked Frey to create a new cheese that tasted like Bismarck Schlosskäse (a Limburger-like cheese he imported), which often spoiled on the long trip from Germany. In 1891 Frey came up with something so good—a soft cheese with an edible crust and a very pungent flavor—that Tode told him to forget Bismarck and concentrate on making the new cheese. They named it "Liederkranz" after one of Tode's most prestigious customers—a German-American men's choral society called the Liederkranz of New York City (*liederkranz* means "wreath of songs"), and their endorsement helped the cheese become hugely popular.

Frey (who also invented Velveeta) kept close watch on the production of Liederkranz after the company was sold to Borden in 1929, and remained as general manager (and Liederkranz supervisor) of the plant in Van Wert, Ohio, until 1938. He died in 1951. Borden sold the factory to the Fisher Cheese Company in 1982, and Fisher expected to go on making Liederkranz forever. Unfortunately, in 1985 several of Fisher's cheeses, including the Liederkranz, somehow suffered bacterial contamination...and that was the end of Liederkranz. The name and bacterial culture were sold off (it's unknown whether the culture still exists), and the original Liederkranz cheese was never made again.

* * *

BEFORE THEY WERE FAMOUS

• In 1979, when Simon Cowell was 20 years old, he worked at Elstree Film Studios in England. One of his jobs was to polish the ax that Jack Nicholson used to break down a door in *The Shining*.

• The still-standing record for most field goals kicked in a season by a member of University High School's varsity football team in Irvine, California, was set in 1986 by Will Ferrell.

• On July 1, 1967, as part of Canada's 100th birthday celebration, the nation honored the first child born in Canada's second century. That "Centennial Baby" grew up to be Pamela Anderson.

SOCIAL NOTWORK

"Social networking" Internet sites like Facebook and Twitter invite two-way communication, and many companies now use them to generate buzz about their products. Turns out this can go wrong very fast.

• **THAT'S SO SWEET.** In March 2009, Skittles candy launched a new Web site built around Twitter, the blogging service in which all entries are 140 characters or less. Anytime anybody anywhere wrote about Skittles on their personal Twitter page, it went into a feed, which then displayed it on the front page of Skittles.com. Within hours, thousands of Skittles-related "tweets" were posted, the majority of them negative and humorous, such as "Skittles causes cancer" and "Skittles killed my brother." Mars, Skittles' parent company, quickly removed the feature from Skittles.com.

• **BUS FARE.** To precede an image overhaul, the Jack in the Box fast-food chain launched an ad campaign in which Jack, the company's mascot, gets hit by a bus. His "recovery" was updated on www.hangintherejack.com, and visitors were urged to post comments, such as "We love you, Jack" or "Get well soon." But negative comments (some serious, some in jest) overwhelmed the posts. Examples: "Jack in the Box killed people with poor sanitary habits and spread disease across the nation" and "Defeat death, Jack! We would have sex with a mullhawk gorilla under the sewer for you." The company let most comments stay, deleting only the most profane or offensive ones.

• **JAVA JIVE.** On May 19, 2009, Starbucks created a Twitter page to interact with its customers. On the same day, filmmaker Robert Greenwald premiered his latest project on YouTube: *What Do Starbucks and Wal-Mart Have in Common?* In the film, Greenwald alleges that Starbucks aggressively prevents its workforce from unionizing. From his own Web site, Greenwald encouraged viewers to photograph themselves outside of their local Starbucks, holding signs protesting Starbucks or in support of union labor, and then post the pictures to Starbucks' Twitter page. Within a couple of days, the Starbucks Twitter site was riddled with photos of the protests. (Starbucks removed them all.)

OBSCURE MONSTERS

*You've heard of Bigfoot, Nessie, and the Abominable
Snowman. Here are a few of their more obscure
(but just as fascinating) cousins.*

MONSTER: Sciopod
WHERE IT LIVED: Ethiopia
LEGEND: Latin for "shade foot," these relatively
peaceful creatures were first recorded in around A.D. 77 by the
Roman historian Pliny the Elder. They were said to live in the
wilds of what is now Ethiopia and were described as small, pale,
humanlike creatures—but with only one leg and a giant foot.
They hopped around on that giant foot, but they also used it as a
sun shade: Sciopods reportedly spent several hours a day lying on
their backs with their giant feet in the air to block the harsh
North African sun. Sciopods were extremely powerful, too. They
could kill a large animal (or a human) with a single jumping kick.
But never fear—the strange creatures didn't eat meat. Or plants.
Or anything. They existed solely on the aroma of living fruit,
which they always carried with them. Sciopods are mentioned in
numerous writings over several centuries, ending sometime in
the Middle Ages.

MONSTER: Gowrow
WHERE IT LIVED: Arkansas
LEGEND: This monster was first heard of in the 1880s, when
Arkansas farmers reported being terrorized by a huge lizard. In
1897 Fred Allsopp, a reporter for the *Arkansas Gazette*, wrote
about an encounter with the beast. The monster, which Allsopp
named a "gowrow" after the sound it made, had been eating
livestock in the Ozark Mountains in the northwest of the state.
A local businessman named William Miller formed a posse to
hunt and kill it. They found its lair, which was littered with animal (and human) bones, and waited for it. It surprised them by
emerging from a nearby lake and attacking them—but they were
able to kill it with several gunshots. Miller described the

Texas is the only state that permits residents to cast absentee ballots from space.

gowrow as being 20 feet long, with huge tusks, webbed and clawed feet, a row of horns along its spine, and a knifelike end to its long tail. He said he sent the body to the Smithsonian Institute—but it mysteriously never made it. Allsopp finished the article by saying he believed it was a "great fake," but sightings of a similar lizardlike creature were reported in the Ozarks for many years.

MONSTER: Encantado
WHERE IT LIVES: The Amazon River
LEGEND: *Encantado* means "enchanted one" in Portuguese and refers to a special kind of *boto*, or long-beaked river dolphin native to the Amazon—that can take human form. Encantados are curious about humans and are especially attracted to big, noisy festivals, which they often attend as musicians, staying in human form for years. How can you recognize one? Look under its hat: They always have bald spots that are actually disguised blowholes. Encantados are usually friendly, but they occasionally hypnotize and kidnap young women and take them back to the *Encante*, their underground city. Sometimes the women escape and return…pregnant with an Encantado baby.

MONSTER: Kappa
WHERE IT LIVES: Japan
LEGEND: Kappas are said to inhabit lakes and rivers throughout the Japanese islands. They look like frogs, but with tortoise-like shells on their backs. They can leave the water—carrying their shells with them—because they have shallow depressions in their heads in which they keep a bit of water that not only allows them to walk around on land but also makes them incredibly strong. If you encounter one, bow to it. They're very polite, so they'll have to bow back to you…and the water will spill out of their head-bowls, weakening them. Their favorite food: the blood of small children. Their second-favorite: cucumbers. That's why you can still see people in Japan throwing fresh cucumbers into lakes and rivers—with the names of their children carved into them. This, the legend says, will protect their little ones from the kappa's clutches.

AFTER THE OLYMPICS

Cities spend billions in civic improvements and new sports facilities to host the Olympics, hoping that afterward they can be converted to other uses and lure tourists. Sometimes it works out; sometimes it doesn't. Here are some stories of what happened to Olympic host cities.

ATHENS (2004). The Greek government paid $9 billion to make its capital city Olympics-ready, with new roads, airport and public-transit improvements, and the construction of 22 new sports venues. Despite the fact that some of them had been under construction since the early 1990s (Athens incorrectly assumed that it was a lock to host the centennial 1996 games), several facilities were finished just hours before the 2004 opening ceremonies. But five years after the Olympics, 21 of those 22 buildings are unused and abandoned or have been vandalized, largely because they were placed in poorer neighborhoods in an effort to revitalize those areas of the city. Two large outdoor stadiums are completely closed, the tae kwon do and volleyball complex is now a homeless camp, and a sports field that was supposed to be converted into an ecological education park became a garbage dump, because that's where thousands of residents started throwing their household trash. On the bright side, the city did get a new airport and pedestrian walkways that link ancient Greek historical sites, a project that had been planned for more than 150 years and finally was built to coincide with the Olympics. But Athens will be paying off the Games for a long time—the debt amounts to $500,000 per household.

MONTREAL (1976). The main facility, Olympic Stadium, was a futuristic-looking building with a curved 556-foot tower that was meant to be a lasting symbol of the Games. And it is—it's come to symbolize the financial disaster of the Montreal Olympics. The games were mostly paid for by the provincial government of Quebec, and at the time Montreal mayor Jean Drapeau assured residents that the revenues generated by the sports events would offset the expense of holding them. "The Montreal Olympics can no more have a deficit than a man can have a baby," Drapeau boasted. When Montreal won the bid in 1970, organizers said the games would cost $310 million. But cost overruns and frequent labor strikes pushed up the final cost to just under $2 billion. Most of that money was connected to building Olympic Stadium, designed by French architect Roger Taillibert. Initially projected to cost $150 million, it had a final price of $800 million...and the tower and retractable roof weren't even finished on time. (The roof wasn't finished until 1987, more than a decade later.) Taillibert also designed the bicycling velodrome, which cost $59 million—five times the original estimate. After the Games, the velodrome was converted into a biosphere, and the Montreal Expos baseball team moved into Olympic Stadium. But in 1986, a mysterious explosion in the tower caused it to burst into flames (it was later repaired), and in the late 1980s, roof tiles began dropping onto the playing field. The province of Quebec did eventually pay off its Olympic debt through a tobacco tax. The last payment was made in October 2006—30 years after the closing ceremonies.

LOS ANGELES (1984). The long-lasting effect of the Olympics on the infrastructure of the southern California megalopolis? Other than a welcome infusion of cash into the local economy, not much. Shortly after the financial disaster of the 1976 Olympics, the International Olympic Committee took bids from cities wishing to host the 1984 event, and Los Angeles was the only one seriously interested. The organizing committee had a plan to prevent another Montreal: Do it on the cheap, with very few new costs to the city or taxpayers. They'd accomplish that in two ways: 1) use pre-existing facilities, and 2) get corporate sponsors to foot the rest of the bill. Only two new venues were constructed: a velodrome, paid by (and named for) 7-Eleven, and an aquatic sports building, paid by (and named for) McDonald's. Result: After the games, there were only two buildings to convert or worry about instead of two dozen. The Los Angeles games actually made $200 million, the most profitable Olympics ever.

SEOUL (1988). Although the Olympics brought crushing debt to some countries, the attention given to South Korea in the years leading up to the 1988 Games brought the country democracy. In 1979, two weeks after South Korea bid for the 1988 games, dictator Park Chung-hee was assassinated by the pro-democracy leader of the country's major intelligence agency. Pro-democracy demonstrations were on the rise around the country, but a new dictatorial regime took power anyway, a military government led by Major General Chun Doo-hawn. Chun declared martial law and used the military to violently snuff out the democratic rallies. In one such instance in the city of Kwangju, 191 people were killed and 850 were wounded. But despite objections from human rights groups, in 1982 Seoul was awarded the 1988 Summer Olympics... because no other city had put in a serious bid. The Chun regime prepared for the Olympics the way it dealt with political rallies: with brutal violence. Government security forces terrorized more than 750,000 Seoul residents—they raped women, beat up men, and burned down homes to get people to leave the areas to be razed for Olympic venues. And in June 1987, a Seoul University pro-democracy protester was arrested, tortured, and killed by Chun's death squads. Then another student was killed by a police tear gas bomb at a protest. The two deaths led to a resurrection of widespread pro-democracy demonstrations, as well as the formation of a political group called the Resistance of June, whose goal was to remove Chun from power. And it was successful. On June 29, 1987, Chun changed the constitution to allow for direct presidential elections—in other words, democracy. He then stepped down. Today, Seoul is a high-tech, skyscraper-filled city and the centerpiece of South Korea, which is now one of the wealthiest and most politically stable countries on the planet.

* * *

ODDLY NAMED RESTAURANT FOOD
Quesadilla Explosion Salad (Chili's)
Chicken Parmesan Tanglers (Applebee's)
Chocolate Thunder From Down Under (Outback Steakhouse)
Weight Management Chicken Salad
(The Cheesecake Factory)
Super Sizzlin' Sausage Sunrise (Friendly's)
Feesh Neeblers (White Castle)
Moons Over My Hammy (Denny's)
Rooty Tooty Fresh N' Fruity (IHOP)

FACTS THAT CUT THE...

...mustard. (What'd you think we were going to say?)

• The recipe for yellow mustard: ground mustard seed, water, vinegar, and turmeric.

• Yellow mustard gets its color from the spice turmeric, not from the mustard seed. This addition was the idea of food manufacturer George French in 1904 to market his (still best-selling) French's Mustard.

• Mustard seed was first cultivated in India in about 3000 B.C. Romans brought it west to Britain, where it was used as a pickling agent.

• Ground mustard seed alone is not spicy. When it's mixed with a liquid, such as the water or vinegar in yellow mustard, an enzyme is released that provides the tangy flavor.

• The ancient Greek philosopher Pythagoras believed mustard could cure a scorpion bite.

• 700 million pounds of mustard are consumed worldwide annually, which is enough to top about 67 billion hot dogs.

• 90% of the world's mustard seed is grown in Canada.

• Folk remedy: putting mustard flour (ground mustard seed) in your socks is said to prevent frostbite.

• Pope John XXII, who was French, loved mustard so much that he created the office of *grand moutardier du pape*, or "mustard maker to the pope."

• The Mount Horeb Mustard Museum in Wisconsin houses the world's largest mustard collection: 4,400 varieties.

• "Mustard" comes from the Latin *mustum ardens*, for "burning wine." The Romans used fermented grape juice—called *must*—as a liquid base, into which they mixed crushed mustard seeds.

• There are hundreds of different kinds of prepared mustard (brown mustard, hot mustard, honey mustard, etc.), but Americans call the familiar yellow mustard "mustard." The rest of the world calls yellow mustard "American mustard."

• What's Dijon mustard? Regular, prepared mustard with a dash of white wine. (It originated in Dijon, France.)

LIFE IMITATES ART

Real-life events that are eerily similar to TV or film plots.

ON THE SCREEN: It's a famous TV moment: the 1973 episode of *The Brady Bunch* in which Peter throws a football and hits Marcia (Maureen McCormick) in the face, severely damaging her nose and ruining her school dance plans.

IN REAL LIFE: On February 9, 1973, the night the episode aired, McCormick left the Burbank, California, studio where *The Brady Bunch* taped. On her way home, she got into a car accident; on impact, McCormick smashed her nose into the steering wheel.

ON THE SCREEN: The last season of *The West Wing* (2005–06) followed a fictional presidential election. Despite predictions that the established candidate, Bob Russell (Gary Cole), would win the Democratic nomination, he's edged out by upstart Mexican-American Matt Santos (Jimmy Smits). The Republican nominee is decided early: prickly Senator Arnold Vinick (Alan Alda) appeases his party by choosing the staunch conservative governor of a small state (West Virginia) as his running mate.

IN REAL LIFE: In the 2008 presidential campaign, Hillary Clinton was assumed to be the Democratic nominee until African-American Barack Obama beat her in the final days of the primary. Republican John McCain, labeled a "maverick" for often breaking with his party, locked up the nomination early. His running mate: Sarah Palin, the conservative governor of a small state (Alaska).

ON THE SCREEN: The scheme used by Gus Gorman (Richard Pryor) in 1983's *Superman III* to steal thousands of dollars in tiny increments was based on the real-life "salimi technique" of embezzling. In the 1999 comedy *Office Space*, the main characters attempt the same kind of scheme, even referencing *Superman III*.

IN REAL LIFE: In 2007 Michael Largent, 22, created thousands of fake accounts with E-trade, which sends each new account a "micro amount" of a few cents. He'd made $50,000 before the FBI captured him, tipped off because he used cartoon names—including "Hank Hill," created by Mike Judge, who wrote *Office Space*.

About 80% of all marijuana grown outdoors in the United States is on state or federal land.

RANDOM BITS
ON '80s HITS

Pop songs are short, catchy, and memorable—just like these facts.

• **"9 to 5," by Dolly Parton.** The song is about working in an office...so the song's rhythm was provided by typewriter noises. (Parton came up with the idea when she was tapping her acrylic fingernails on a table and thought it sounded like a typewriter.)

• **"Sailing," by Christopher Cross.** With this song, Cross became the only performer to ever win all four major Grammy awards: best new artist, album of the year, record of the year, and song of the year.

• **"Start Me Up," by the Rolling Stones.** When they initially recorded it as a reggae song in 1975, the Stones hated it. They decided to rework it as a straight-ahead rock song in 1981, and it became the band's last smash hit, peaking at #2.

• **"I Can't Go For That (No Can Do)," by Hall and Oates.** One of the first pop songs (and the first #1 pop hit) to use a drum machine. Michael Jackson later thanked Daryl Hall for allowing him to steal the song's drum-and-bass hook for his hit "Billie Jean."

• **"Eye of the Tiger," by Survivor.** It was used as the theme to *Rocky III*. Director/star Sylvester Stallone wanted to use Queen's "Another One Bites the Dust" but couldn't get the rights, so he commissioned Survivor to write this one.

• **"Holiday," by Madonna.** Her first hit single. It was originally written for ex-Supreme Mary Wilson, who turned it down.

• **"Beat It," by Michael Jackson.** Eddie Van Halen is widely credited with performing the guitar part. He just performs the solo; the rest was done by Steve Lukather of Toto.

• **"Stand Back," by Stevie Nicks.** Nicks wrote this song right after hearing Prince's "Little Red Corvette." When she told Prince about it, he agreed to play synthesizer on "Stand Back."

- **"Born in the USA," by Bruce Springsteen.** It's not a patriotic anthem—the ironic chorus follows verses about the poor treatment of Vietnam veterans. Nevertheless, President Ronald Reagan wanted to use it at rallies, and Chrysler offered Springsteen $12 million to use it in commercials. (Springsteen refused both.)

- **"Caribbean Queen," by Billy Ocean.** Different versions were recorded for release to different parts of the world, including "European Queen" and "African Queen."

- **"Uptown Girl," by Billy Joel.** His girlfriend and future wife Christie Brinkley appeared in the video, but actually Joel wrote the song before they met. It was about how strange he felt going from a married nobody to a newly divorced pop star who could attract models, including 6'0" Elle MacPherson. (Joel is 5'5 ½".)

- **"We Are the World," by USA For Africa.** Prince was scheduled to participate in the all-star charity record but didn't show up. He later offered to add a guitar solo, but producer Quincy Jones turned him down. The lines Prince was supposed to sing solo were performed by Huey Lewis.

- **"Footloose," by Kenny Loggins.** Ironically, Loggins wrote this song about moving when he couldn't—he was laid up in a hotel room recovering from broken ribs suffered in a fall from a stage.

- **"Summer of '69," by Bryan Adams.** It's about nostalgia; Adams himself was 10 years old in 1969.

- **"Rock Me Amadeus," by Falco.** The only German-language song to hit #1 in the United States (although the three-word chorus is in English).

- **"Faith," by George Michael.** The opening organ line is a version of "Freedom," a 1984 hit by Michael's group Wham!

- **"La Bamba," by Los Lobos.** This cover of the 1958 Ritchie Valens song (for the soundtrack of the 1987 Valens biographical movie *La Bamba*) was the first—and to date, only—song sung in Spanish to go to #1. (It's also the only chart hit for Los Lobos.)

- **"Foolish Beat," by Debbie Gibson.** With this song, the 16-year-old Gibson became the youngest person to ever write, produce, and perform a #1 hit.

Last instrumental song to hit #1: Jan Hammer's *"Miami Vice Theme"* (1985).

EVERYDAY HEROES

More proof that not all superheroes are in the comics.

NEITHER RAIN, NOR SLEET, NOR...FIRE!
In March 2009, Indianapolis postal carrier Jackie Jefferson was substituting on another carrier's route. Having been on the job for only a few months, Jefferson approached a house and heard a fire alarm beeping from inside. Then she heard someone calling for help. "It was instinctive," she said. "I wasn't thinking. I puffed up my nerves and did it. I can't believe it happened." What did she do? Jefferson dropped her mailbag, ran in to the burning living room, found an 80-year-old woman sitting in a wheelchair, and pushed her outside. Seconds later, flames started billowing out the front door. The victim was treated at a hospital, and Jefferson went on to finish her daily rounds.

BUS DRIVER BOY
Eleven-year-old David Murphy's school bus was stopped at a Cleveland, Ohio, gas station one day in 2008. The bus driver was in the restroom—he'd left the 27 grade-school students unattended, left the engine running, and neglected to put on the parking brake. While the kids waited, the bus began to roll out of the parking lot, picking up speed as it headed downhill on a crowded two-lane road. Kids were screaming, and some even jumped out of the moving bus. But David jumped into the driver's seat...only to see a grim situation: A semitruck, horn blaring, was coming straight for them. There was no room to veer left, and ahead on the right were four concrete bridge supports. Beyond the underpass, there was nothing to stop the bus except for the Cuyahoga River, at the bottom of a very long hill. David grabbed the wheel and steered to the right, barely avoiding the semi. He then steered the bus toward the last bridge support and dove behind the driver's seat just before impact. The bus hit the barrier hard, and a lot of students were shaken up—including David—but there were no serious injuries. The bus driver was fired and charged with several offenses. A shy kid, David later admitted that he didn't tell anyone what he did at first because he was afraid he'd get into trouble for driving the bus.

READ YOUR MOLE-O-SCOPE

Nowadays the only thing the moles on your skin can predict is skin cancer, but that wasn't always the case—fortune-tellers used to "read" people's moles like they were horoscopes. What do your moles reveal about you?

LOCATION, LOCATION, LOCATION

According to one school of fortune-telling, the mole's position on your body is the most important thing—not its color, shape, or texture. Some moles portend good luck, happiness, and a long life. Some others…well, be sure to read *all* of your moles, so that the lucky ones offset the unlucky ones to give you a fuller sense of what life has in store for you. Here are the mole basics.

YOUR FACE

• **On the right side of the forehead:** You're active, hard-working, and passionate. You'll have a successful life, marry happily, and at least one of your children will go far in the world.

• **On the right eyebrow:** You're courageous, gallant, and persevering and will succeed in love, war, business, and anything else you set your mind to. You'll marry well, have children who love you, and die of old age. The only catch: You'll die far from home.

• **On the left forehead or eyebrow:** You're moody, lazy, and prone to alcoholism and debauchery. You're also a coward who will probably spend time in jail and experience extreme poverty. Just about everything you attempt in life will end in failure, including your miserable marriage (to a foul-tempered spouse) and your relationship with your irresponsible, ungrateful children.

• **On the outside corner of either eye:** You're sober, honest, and steady, and have a fulfilling love life. You will experience many ups and downs in your life, and though you will keep poverty at bay, you'll die a violent, painful death.

• **On either cheek:** You're sober, hard-working, generous, and courageous. You'll have a rewarding love life and will be moderately successful careerwise, avoiding poverty but never accumulating much wealth either. Your marriage will be a happy one and produce two children, both of whom will eclipse your success.

• **On your nose:** You're loyal and passionate to a fault, strong, honest, and courageous. You'll win the respect of your community, marry well, have a happy family life, and travel widely, especially by water. Your biggest fault: You drink too much.

• **On your lips:** You're sober and restrained, except where love is concerned. You will have great financial and romantic success and will rise above your present station in life. Not everything will come easily, but if you strive, you will prevail.

• **On your chin:** You're calm and happy and have a bright future ahead of you. You'll be rich in money and friends and will have a happy marriage and children who love you. But you'll also suffer losses at home, at sea, and in foreign countries. So beware!

YOUR BODY

• **On your left shoulder:** You're an argumentative person who gets in a lot of fights. You lose your temper often and over the slightest little things. But on the other hand, you're a passionate person and faithful to your mate. You won't have lots of highs in life, but you won't have a lot of lows either. You'll have lots of children. One more thing: Avoid travel over water.

• **On your right shoulder:** You're prudent, wise, and trustworthy. You're also a little sneaky, and though you work hard, you lack passion. You're likely to find great wealth and power in your career, and you'll have lots of friends. Expect to take a long trip to a foreign country in your mid-thirties or early forties.

• **On your torso:** You have an even temper, but you also have a cowardly streak. You're passionate but unfaithful; whatever health and wealth you accumulate in life will slip away in later years. And your kids are going to drive you nuts.

• **On your loins:** You may be very successful in business, but don't lend out your money! For all the wealth you accumulate in life, you stand to lose much of it by lending it to fair-weather friends who are out to take advantage of you.

Don't see your mole here? Turn to page 396 for more.

HORSE MYSTERIES

*In 2009 twenty-one of the world's finest polo horses suddenly died
before a match in Florida. The cause: an error that occurred during
the manufacture of a common dietary supplement. We wondered
if similar tragedies had ever occurred. Sadly, they had.*

THE CASE OF THE BRISBANE BATS

In 1994 several horses on the farm of Vic Rail, a celebrated
trainer in Brisbane, Australia, stopped eating and became
ill. A few days later, 13 of the stable's 23 horses were dead. Then
Rail, whose work to save the horses included force-feeding them by
pushing food down their throats, got sick. Within a week he was
dead. News that he'd died of the same illness that had killed the
horses sent a panic through Brisbane's horse-racing community
(not to mention the medical community). It took a year to find out
what had happened, but a virus related to canine distemper and
human measles—and unknown to science at the time—was finally
identified as the cause. Carried by fruit bats, which aren't harmed
by it, the virus becomes deadly in larger animals. It's known as the
Hendra virus today, named after the Brisbane suburb where Rail's
farm was located. There have been eight more outbreaks since
then, all in Australia, killing 12 more horses and one more human.

THE CASE OF THE SUDDEN SWELLING

On the morning of June 28, 2003, Wild-Eyed & Wicked, an 11-
year-old American Saddlebred and two-time World Grand Champion, was found in his stall at Kentucky's Double D Ranch with a
severely swollen left foreleg. His trainer, Dena Lopez, who had ridden the horse to both his championships, thought it was a virus.
Then his stablemate, Meet Prince Charming, became sick—with a
swollen left foreleg. Then three more horses at the ranch developed the same symptoms. A veterinarian was called…and he told
Lopez to call the police; the left front forelegs of all the horses had
been injected with a toxin. The horses' conditions worsened over
the following weeks, and on July 17, Wild-Eyed & Wicked was
euthanized. Meet Prince Charming and one of the other victims,
Kiss Me, were euthanized the next day. The other two horses

It takes a newborn horse about an hour to begin walking. It takes a zebra only 20 minutes.

recovered. Wild-Eyed & Wicked is buried near the Hall of Champions in the Kentucky Horse Park in Lexington. Despite a lengthy investigation, the culprit was never found.

THE CASE OF THE FALLEN FOALS

In April 2001, mares in Kentucky started having miscarriages, and foals started dying. Within a month, more than 500 cases were reported, severely damaging Kentucky's world-famous horse-breeding business. At first, poisonous mushrooms were thought to be the cause, but there weren't enough of them to support that theory. Scientists then made a correlation between the affected farms and black cherry trees, which produce naturally occurring cyanide in their leaves. How did the cyanide get from the trees to the horses? Researchers at the University of Kentucky solved the mystery: A very warm spring, followed by a frost, they reported, resulted in high concentrations of cyanide. Then an unusually heavy infestation of Eastern tent caterpillars arrived. The voracious bugs nested in black cherry trees and fed off their leaves—leaving abnormally large amounts of cyanide-laden feces in the area around the trees. Grazing horses consumed the toxic poop, which wasn't enough to kill full-grown horses, but it was too much for foals or fetuses. If similar conditions ever converge again, the researchers noted, horse owners will now know what to look out for.

THE CASE OF THE EL PASO PUNCTURES

On October 11, 2005, Ned Sixkiller found six of his horses and one burro dead on his ranch in El Paso County, Colorado. The cause of death was originally ruled to be gunshot wounds, as punctures were found in the animals' hides. But a closer examination found every puncture to be about ¾ " deep, and no bullet fragments were found. Cause of the puncture marks: unknown. Less than two weeks later, 16 horses were found dead on William DeWitt's ranch, about a mile from Sixkiller's. No exact cause of those deaths was found, but the veterinarian on the case said that the cause was probably a lightning strike—all the horses' eyeballs had exploded, and in the three days they laid on the ground, no scavengers had eaten them, which is common for lightning-struck animals. That didn't satisfy many of the people in El Paso County, who for years have reported seeing strange lights in the sky, as well as "black helicopters." Many in the area believe the deaths were the work of UFOs.

THE GARBAGE PROJECT

What does our garbage reveal about us? A University of Arizona professor and his students spent 30 years looking into it.

TRASHAEOLOGY

It's been said that archaeology is really the study of garbage. All those thousand-year-old pot shards and spearheads in dusty museums are just discards from ancient civilizations that give us a peek into the habits and behaviors of the people who lived in those times. So what would we learn about ourselves if we studied our own garbage today? Well, someone's already done it. Spanning 30 years and 30,000 pounds of trash, The Garbage Project has sifted and sorted its way through the modern waste stream, from trash cans to landfills, collecting information and dispelling myths not only about the garbage itself, but about human behavior.

The project got its start in 1972 when some University of Arizona archaeology students compared fresh garbage from a low-income household and an upper-income household. Professor William Rathje was so intrigued by the concept of learning about people's habits by monitoring their trash that he started teaching a Garbage Studies—or *Garbology*—class that grew into the Garbage Project. From 1973 to 2005, more than 1,000 students donned protective clothes (and got tetanus shots) to sort out household trash and landfill contents.

DIGGING IN

Their first project: studying the trash of 60 Arizona households in 1973. Students went door to door asking permission to go through garbage cans and, remarkably, people said yes. Garbage was then collected from the participating households and brought to the university, where pairs of students sorted it according to assigned codes. Some of the nearly 200 codes that were used: Beef–001; Other meat (not bacon)–002; Tissue containers–135; Crustaceans and mollusks–006; Peanut butter–017; Tortillas–029; Potato peels–044; Illicit drugs–105; Pet toys–156; Jewelry–164; Health foods–066; and TV dinners (including potpies)–094.

What they found the most of surprised them: wasted food.

There are more than 900,000 known ant species in the world.

They classified food waste as "edible or once-edible food." That doesn't include things like pits, rinds, bones, or peels—only food that someone could have eaten. Before the Garbage Project, there was no way to know how much food people actually wasted, but it turned out to be a lot. After more than 10 years and 6,000 households, the Garbage Project concluded that Americans wasted 10–15% of the food they bought, almost half of it fresh fruits and vegetables that rotted before they could be used.

What they found at the bottom of almost every garbage bag or container was something they called *slops* (sorting code: 069), a gooey mixture of coffee grounds, cigarette butts, bits of food, and unidentifiable gunk. A detailed analysis showed slops to be 28% cereal; 36% vegetables; 8% meat, poultry, and seafood; 8% fruit; 6% cheese and milk products; and 5% oils and fats.

THE GARBAGE SYNDROME

Previous garbage studies had relied solely on interviews and questionnaires where people "self-reported" their habits. But when the Garbage Project compared answers on questionnaires to actual discards, they discovered many differences between what people *said* they did and what their garbage *showed* they did. The Project named some of the most common reasons:

1. The Good Provider Syndrome. Heads of households who purchased and prepared the family meals regularly exaggerated the total amount of food their families ate by 10–30%.

2. The Lean Cuisine Syndrome. People usually underreported how much junk food they bought and overreported how much fruit or "healthy" foods they bought. In one Tucson neighborhood, people underestimated their intake of potato chips by 81% and overestimated their intake of cottage cheese by 311%. People also consistently underreported their alcohol consumption by 40–60%. But watch out for teetotalers: Nondrinkers accurately reported how much alcohol drinkers in the household consumed.

3. The Rationality Principle. People weren't necessarily lying when they self-reported—they may have exaggerated somewhat, but they also just may not have remembered, or may have estimated incorrectly. There's a disconnect between what people do and what they think they do. The Rationality Principle also applies to things like recycling and other "good" behaviors.

The rich *are* different: A Garbage Project study in Marin County, CA, found...

4. First Principle of Food Waste: "The more repetitive your diet, the less food you waste." People who ate the same foods regularly threw out the least amount of food. For example, only 5–10% of everyday sliced bread was thrown away, while 35–50% of specialty breads like muffins, or hot dog and hamburger buns, were discarded.

FIRST PRINCIPLE...OF WEIRD BEHAVIOR

The Garbage Project also uncovered some odd behaviors.

• When a food shortage was reported in the news, people would actually buy *more*—and waste more—of the scarce product. During a 1970s beef shortage, for example, investigators found the rate of discarded meat, often still in its original packaging, was 9%. Once the "crisis" was over, the rate went down to 3%.

• In 1986, after news reports that fat from red meat was a cancer risk, the Garbage Report found a decrease in overall red meat consumption, as well as an increase in the amount of fat from red meat that was cut off and discarded. Sounds like a reasonable response to a health scare...until they also recorded a spike in deli meat, hot dogs, and sausage, which actually have much more harmful fat than red meat does. People who thought they were acting responsibly were actually hurting themselves more.

ALL THE NEWS THAT'S FIT TO PRINT

In 1987 Rathje expanded the Garbage Project to include landfills. Over the next dozen or so years, the archaeologist and his students dug up, cataloged, and studied the contents of 22 landfills across the United States and Canada. Again, the results were surprising.

For example, it was always assumed that things like food and paper would *biodegrade*, or break down, in landfills. The Garbage Project discovered just the opposite. They found well-preserved food in all of their landfill excavations, including a 15-year-old hot dog in Staten Island and a 16-year-old T-bone steak in Illinois that Professor Rathje described as "still in damn good condition. I've had steaks in my own refrigerator that looked worse." They found a 25-year-old bowl of guacamole, so well preserved that it could be identified by sight. How did they know it was 25 years old? It was next to an old newspaper on which you could still read the date—it hadn't biodegraded either.

In fact, they found even more well-preserved paper than food.

Paper in a landfill didn't biodegrade so much as it *mummified*. Rathje estimated that paper, especially newspapers and telephone books, accounted for half the garbage in modern landfills. (Construction debris and yard waste came in second and third.) According to Rathje, finding so much well-preserved old food and paper proved that landfill biodegradation was "the biggest myth since Santa Claus." Biodegradation does take place, he said, but at a much slower rate than people think. As a result, today there's a major effort underway to keep organic material like food and paper out of landfills.

GARBAGE: THE FINAL FRONTIER

The University of Arizona no longer has a Garbage Project class, and Rathje now teaches at Stanford University. But though the Garbage Project itself is inactive, Garbology goes on. Programs at schools around the country teach kids the science of garbage and educate them on reducing waste and recycling more. With co-author Cullen Murphy, Rathje also wrote a bestselling book on the subject called *Rubbish! The Archaeology of Garbage* and co-authored another, *Use Less Stuff: Environmental Solutions for Who We Really Are*, which spawned a Web site and newsletter. These days Rathje is interested in *exo-garbology*—the study of space junk. As an archaeologist, he wonders what will happen to all of the refuse from satellites and space stations left in orbit, and how (and when) all that garbage will return to Earth.

*　　*　　*

THE GOOD OLD DAYS

In the late 19th century, horses posed two significant municipal waste-disposal problems.

• **Dead:** New York City "disposed" of as many as 15,000 dead horses a year by dumping them in the rivers and bays (the bodies would sometimes wash up on area beaches) or sending them to rendering firms that would remove the "useful" parts for glue and fertilizer before boiling the rest down in giant vats.

• **Alive:** A horse of the time produced an average of 22 pounds of manure and a quart of urine per day which, since there were no "pooper-scooper" laws, was just "deposited"…on the streets.

Results of a 2-year FBI "study": The lyrics to the song "Louie Louie" are unintelligible.

SMELLS FUNNY

Perfume is a huge industry, from famous brands like Chanel No. 5
and White Diamonds to some truly bizarre concoctions.
But who wouldn't want to smell like a burger?

WHAT'S THAT SMELL? Flame
BACKGROUND: During the 2008 Christmas season,
Burger King sold a novelty cologne for men called
Flame—designed to mimic the smell of flame-broiled beef patties.
Flame was available only in limited quantities through Burger
King's Web site and at a single cosmetics boutique in New York
called Ricky's. Despite its scarcity and poor reviews (one critic
likened the scent to "a Burger King when it's burning down in a
horrible grease fire"), within a week the entire stock had sold out.
It originally cost $3.99, but bottles of the smelly beef water were
soon selling for $70 on eBay. Demand was so high that Burger
King relaunched the cologne in the summer of 2009 with a series
of print ads featuring *America's Got Talent* judge Piers Morgan,
photographed nearly naked, next to the tagline "The scent of
seduction with a hint of flame-grilled meat."

WHAT'S THAT SMELL? *Star Trek* cologne and perfume
BACKGROUND: Three separate scents were marketed in 2009
as tie-ins with the reboot of the *Star Trek* movie series.
• **Tiberius.** Named after the captain of the Starship *Enterprise,*
James Tiberius Kirk, and the (over)actor who played him, William
Shatner. So does it smell like ham? No, it smells like vanilla and
sandalwood. According to the manufacturer, the scent is for men
who, like Kirk, are "casual, yet commanding."
• **Red Shirt.** This one pays homage to an in-joke among Trekkies.
In many 1960s *Star Trek* episodes, the main crew explores a mysterious planet and one anonymous crew member—known as a "red
shirt"—gets killed by hostile alien natives. Red Shirt, the cologne,
is a "daring scent for those brave enough to place no trust in
tomorrow."
• **Pon Farr.** A fragrance for women, this one is named after (and
could theoretically trigger) the Vulcan mating ritual.

WHAT'S THAT SMELL? Politics

BACKGROUND: During the hoopla surrounding the 2008 U.S. presidential election, a company called Nature's Garden created three different scents designed to allow consumers to display their political affiliation via their personal odor. *Republican* smells like "love of country and a strong family unit" (and apples), *Democrat* exudes "a love for mankind" (and clover), and *Independent* evokes "the desire to preserve the quality of our environment" (it smells like daffodils).

WHAT'S THAT SMELL? Virtue

BACKGROUND: According to California perfumers IBI, if you wear Virtue, you can actually smell like Jesus. Using the Bible as a guide to what kind of plants were used as perfumes in the Holy Land when Jesus walked the Earth, IBI scientists claim that Virtue is a close approximation of what Christ and his followers would have smelled like. It's a sweet blend consisting mostly of apricot, with a dash of frankincense and myrrh, which were given to Jesus at birth by the three wise men.

WHAT'S THAT SMELL? Play-Doh

BACKGROUND: One of the most memorable parts of playing with Play-Doh was the musky, almost candylike odor of the clay when it's soft and fresh out of the can. Turns out that the scent comes largely from wheat flour, so it's pretty easy to reproduce. In 2006 Demeter Fragrance did just that, creating a Play-Doh perfume in honor of the toy's 50th anniversary. It smells exactly like Play-Doh. (Demeter makes many other perfumes that evoke nostalgia for childhood, including crayon, jelly bean, and Tootsie Roll.)

*　　*　　*

BUT WOULD YOU WANT TO LIVE THERE?

"In January 2007, a foreigner who wanted to visit England's North Country was denied entry after tourism officials claimed it was 'not credible' for anyone to want to spend a week in Gateshead."

—*Telegraph* (London)

COOKING WITH JULIA

*Julia Child was America's first celebrity chef. She ate all
the butter she wanted...and still lived to be 91.*

"In spite of food fads, fitness programs, and health concerns, we must never lose sight of a beautifully conceived meal."

"The best way to execute French cooking is to get good and loaded and whack the hell out of a chicken."

"If you're afraid of butter, just use cream."

"The only real stumbling block is fear of failure. In cooking, you've got to have a 'what the hell' attitude."

"Gin."
        —*when asked what her
        favorite wine was*

"I don't think about whether people will remember me or not. I've been an okay person. I've learned a lot. I've taught people a thing or two. That's what's important."

"A baked potato is one of the safest things to eat. Even in a hospital, where the food is pretty bad, they can usually do a baked potato perfectly well."

"Meals don't need to be anything elaborate, just something simple to share with your family."

"Small helpings. No seconds. A little bit of everything. And have a good time."
        —*her philosophy of eating*

"If you're alone in the kitchen and you drop the lamb, you can always just pick it up. Who's going to know?"

"How can a nation be called great if its bread tastes like Kleenex?"

"I was always hungry. My feeling was the more you ate, the better. And that lasted until the age of about 42, when I discovered that too many calories did something."

"I enjoy cooking with wine. Sometimes I even put it in the food."

"It makes no difference how long it takes or how difficult it is. If the final product is marvelous, it's worth the effort."

In support of animal rights, Rome has banned goldfish bowls and ordered mandatory dog walking.

THE DIGITAL CAMERA REVOLUTION, PART II

In Part I (page 91), we saw the rise of digital camera technology. Now watch as it takes over.

TEAMING UP

According to tech industry experts, 1995 marked the beginning of the consumer digital photography era. Among other advances, that year saw the introduction of the Kodak DC40—the first digital camera with a *liquid crystal display*, or LCD monitor. This gave photographers an opportunity never before available: to view the image on the back of the camera just seconds after it was taken. A few months later, Microsoft and Kodak formed a partnership to outfit Kinko's copy stores with kiosks that allowed customers to make photo CDs and send images over the Internet, which was still in its infancy. Around the same time, Hewlett-Packard released the first inkjet printers designed to print out images taken on digital cameras.

All of this technology coming together simultaneously highlights an important aspect of the digital camera: It's just one part of greater revolution that involves the Internet, home computing, scanning, and printing. Technological innovations in each field spurred the others to keep up, which helped spur innovations in those fields as well. And by this point, major advances in the cameras themselves were occurring at such a fast pace that new models were outdated shortly after they hit the market.

IT'S A SNAP

But even through 2000, film cameras were still selling well. Why? Despite the advances, a digital camera *still* couldn't render as sharp an image as a film camera in the same price range. That changed in 2003 when Canon released the Digital Rebel 300D. Not only could the Rebel's CCD technology record an image finally on par with film, it was the first digital SLR (a camera with interchangeable lenses that can be focused manually) to sell for under $1,000. Digital cameras have outsold film cameras ever since.

FROM THE FIELD

The first profession to truly embrace the advantages of digital was photojournalism. No longer did a photographer on a field assignment have to overnight the negatives to the newsroom: Digital images could be sent instantly. In a highly competitive, deadline-driven field, news photographers had no choice if they wanted to be the first to deliver the scoop.

Photojournalism also played a big part in propelling technological innovations that have since been embraced by the rest of the picture-taking world. Roving photographers complained that the bulky battery packs required to power early digital cameras were too heavy to lug around, so in 1994 the Associated Press partnered with Kodak to create the NC2000—a groundbreaking camera that required a much smaller battery pack, could use standard lenses from film cameras, and had the ability to take hundreds of exposures on a single memory card. By the late '90s, only half of professional photojournalists were using digital technology. Just a few years later, nearly all of them were.

JUMPING SHIP

After most photojournalists made the switch, it took a few years for the pros who shoot products, architecture, fashion, landscapes, wildlife, and weddings to follow suit.

• One of the first big names to go digital was acclaimed *National Geographic* nature photographer Jim Brandenburg, who did so in in 2003. "Remember when vinyl records and tapes were up against CDs?" he asked in his defense (many purists thought he'd sold out). "Now you can hardly find a turntable or a tape player. Some people still prefer the sound of analog, and it will be the same with film. I predict that four years from now, you're going to see one-hour photo shops closing."

• One of the last high-profile film holdouts was British celebrity photographer Brian Aris. When he shot the Queen Mother's 70th birthday party in 2006, he admitted that it would most likely be the last major royal event ever captured with traditional film. When asked what he thought about digital, Aris begrudgingly said, "We've all got to embrace it."

GOING, GOING, GONE

Jim Brandenburg's prediction was off by one year: Most one-hour photo shops were gone by 2006. As for the rest of the industry, it was either switch to digital or go out of business. The choice was clear...film had become an endangered species.

• In 2006 Nikon announced that it was going to keep only two film cameras on the market and convert the company's focus to digital.

• In 2008 Polaroid put an end to its line of of analog instant film.

• In 2009 Kodak halted production of Kodachrome slide film, ending an era that began in 1936. "It was certainly a difficult decision to retire it, given its rich history," said Mary Jane Hellyar, President of Kodak's Film, Photofinishing and Entertainment Group. "However, the majority of today's photographers have voiced their preference to capture images with newer technology."

TOPSY-TURVY

In a little over a decade, the entire field of photography was turned upside down: What had been viewed as an interesting novelty—digital—is now the industry standard. And film—which reigned supreme for more than 150 years—has become a novelty product used only by purists and a few fine-art photographers.

However, the digital camera's true impact on society wasn't because the pros switched over—it was because the rest of us did.

For Part III, turn to page 382.

*   *   *

WHAT'S YOURS IS...

During a Major League Baseball game in 2004, Alex Rodriguez of the Yankees was on second base when his teammate hit a pop fly to the infield. Toronto Blue Jays third baseman Howie Clark ran over to catch the ball, but backed off when he heard someone yell, "Mine!" Who yelled it? Rodriguez, who ran to third base after Clark missed the catch.

JUST PLANE WEIRD

If you're reading this book on an airplane, you might want to skip this section until you're safely back on the ground.

NUDE ATTITUDE

Air New Zealand came up with a novel way to make passengers actually pay attention to the pre-flight safety announcements: nude flight attendants. Well…sort of. In 2009 the airline produced a video called "The Bare Essentials of Safety," starring three real Air New Zealand flight attendants and a pilot demonstrating the oxygen mask, seat belts, and flotation devices while dressed only in body paint designed to look like their flight uniforms. To make sure they didn't offend anyone, the oxygen mask, seatbelt, and flotation device were "strategically placed" in the video.

GOOD LUCK!

As part of their wedding celebration in a park in Suvereto, Italy, a couple chartered a small plane to "throw the bouquet" in the traditional gesture to the single women in attendance. A 44-year-old man named Isidoro Pensieri was tasked with tossing the flowers to the ground below. They never made it. The bouquet was sucked into the plane's engine, it ignited, and the engine exploded, causing the plane to crash nearby. The only casualty was Pensieri, who suffered some broken bones.

SHE'LL HAVE THE RIBS

When a 62-year-old woman en route to Italy passed through a security checkpoint at the Munich airport in 2008, technicians noticed something odd in her suitcase: a complete human skeleton, disassembled, and stuffed in a sealed plastic bag. The woman was immediately ushered into a room where security guards questioned her. Turns out she wasn't a murderer—she was returning home from Brazil, where she had picked up the remains of her brother, who'd died 11 years earlier in São Paulo. Once she produced documentation from the Brazilian government indicating why she was carrying a skeleton, she and her brother caught their flight.

10% of Italian women, 30% of U.S. women, and 57% of British women wear D-cup bras.

NO MEALS, NO PEANUTS, AND YOU HAVE TO PUSH
A September 2008 flight on the Chinese airline Shangdong landed safely and normally on the runway in Zhengzhou. But just as it touched down, the engine died, leaving the plane stuck on the edge of the runway. One big problem: Other flights were scheduled to come in, and the runway was now blocked, creating a hazard. Seeing no other option, the captain asked all able-bodied people on board to get out…and push. And they did—about 70 passengers helped the crew push the stranded plane to the terminal.

DON'T MAKE ME TURN THIS PLANE AROUND
In December 2008, a Flybe Airlines flight from Cardiff, Wales, was approaching Charles de Gaulle airport in Paris. Just as the plane was about to begin its descent, the pilot announced to passengers that they would be returning to Wales. The reason: It was foggy, and the pilot had not yet received his certification for flying in foggy conditions, so he had no choice but to turn back. Amazingly, the man has been a pilot for 30 years.

OUTTA HERE
A 2008 Delta Airlines flight from New York landed in Georgetown, Guyana. When economy, or "coach," passengers were allowed to exit the plane first, one first-class passenger was so angry at having to wait that he pried open the emergency exit. This instantly inflated the emergency chute, and the man slid down it to the tarmac. He wasn't quite free, however—he was arrested for interfering with a flight crew.

CABIN PRESSURE
Maria Castillo was on a United Airlines flight from Puerto Rico to Chicago. She'd had a few drinks before the flight and had another on the plane, and when she started behaving aggressively, flight attendants refused to serve her any more. Castillo came unglued. She allegedly spanked a flight attendant and intentionally fell onto a blind passenger's head and pulled her hair. Flight attendants restrained Castillo to her seat, legally, with ankle cuffs. But Castillo kept slipping them off, leaving the flight crew no choice but to secure her to her seat with duct tape. A lawsuit is pending.

DON'T HAVE A COW

Uncle John: We need a two-page article about animals—anything but cows.
Jay: How about some random stories, facts, and tidbits about cows?
Uncle John: Pigs, llamas, blowfish—anything but cows!
Jay: All right then, cows it is!

ROAD TRIPPING

Joseph P. Ford was driving along Route 146 in Massachusetts during rush hour traffic in 2009 when he spotted two calves running in and out of traffic. Determined to catch them before they got hit or caused an accident, Ford parked his SUV in the road, blocking traffic, got out, and gave chase. He corralled one of the calves and carried it back to his truck; he put his belt around the little bull's neck and then attached the other end to his tailgate before running off to get the other calf. A veterinarian who witnessed the incident took the calves to her vet. Ford was called a hero by police. When a reporter asked him if he had any experience capturing animals, he replied, "Well, I do have two children."

PEE-PSI COLA

In 2009 a Hindu nationalist group in India announced it would be releasing a soft drink made with cow urine. Om Prakash, chief of India's Cow Protection Department, reassured reporters that medicinal herbs would be added to the soda, and all toxins would be removed. "It won't smell like urine and will be tasty, too," he said. The main purpose of the soda is to give Hindus a "healthy alternative" to Coke and Pepsi.

BIG, OLD, BUSY BERTHA

The average life span of a cow is 15 years. But the Guinness World Record for the oldest cow ever was Big Bertha. She reached 48 years old before heading to greener pastures in 1993. Bertha also holds another record: She produced 39 calves.

MOOOVE OVER

A woman was riding her bicycle on a trail in Boulder, Colorado, in 2009 when a cow ran up to her, knocked her down, and stepped on her legs. Then the cow ran off. The woman was lucky—both she and her bike escaped without serious injury. Boulder Mountain Bike Alliance vice president Jason Vogel described the cow attack as "odd, rare, and random."

MAGNETIC PERSONALITIES

In 2009 a team of biologists were studying satellite images of cow herds on Google Earth and noticed something interesting: Cows usually stand pointing along a north-south axis. But not always. When they stand near power lines, something disrupts their "magnetic cow sense" and they stand any which way.

HOLY COW

In August 2009, Cambodian villagers held a three-day memorial ceremony for a calf that only lived for two days. "The cow looked strange," said village chief Sok Mim. "Its legs have signs like carved arts, and its skin is like a crocodile's skin. Some people used the spit from the cow's mouth to cure their toothache and other illness." They knew the calf was special because just after it was born, the village—suffering from drought—received its first significant rainfall in years.

FAIR THEE WELL

A pregnant cow was being delivered to the "Miracle of Birth" exhibit at the 2009 Kalamazoo County Fair in Michigan, so spectators could see what it looks like when a calf is born. But the cow had other ideas: As she was being walked off her trailer, she escaped from her handlers, bolted through a fence, and barreled into the fairgrounds. For the next 45 minutes, the expectant Holstein ran around and even knocked a few people down. She was finally captured after staffers used a calf to lure her into a corner near the grandstands. Then fairgoers created a wall with their bodies and several trucks. The cow was herded back onto her trailer and taken home, where she was allowed to give birth in private.

❋ ❋ ❋

"Look at cows and remember that the greatest scientists in the world have never discovered how to make grass into milk."

—**Michael Pupin**

FORGOTTEN FIRSTS

*Just because we've forgotten their names, that doesn't
take away their claim to fame: They did it first.*

Claimant: Lieutenant John B. Macready of the U.S. Army
Air Service
Claim to Fame: The first crop "duster"
Story: In 1921 Macready, then the holder of the world altitude
record, participated in a test conducted by the Ohio Agricultural
Experimental Station. A six-acre grove of catalpa trees near Troy,
Ohio, was infested with leaf caterpillars and the station wanted to
see if the bugs could be killed from the air. It had never been done
before, but on August 3, 1921, Macready flew his Curtiss JN-4
"Jenny" repeatedly over the grove at a height of about 30 feet, dispensing 175 pounds of lead arsenate pesticide from a special container attached to the fuselage of the plane. It took six passes of
less than nine seconds each to spray the nearly 5,000 trees in the
orchard. Two days later 99 percent of the caterpillars were dead.
Crops have been dusted from airplanes ever since.

Claimant: A collie named Blair
Claim to Fame: The first canine movie star
Story: In 1905 Blair starred in "Rescued by Rover," a six-minute
British silent film about a dog who rescues a baby after a gypsy
beggar woman snatches it from its stroller. (Rover crosses a river
and searches house-to-house through a slum until he finds the
baby, then races home and leads the father to it.) Six minutes may
not sound like much, but motion pictures had been around for less
than a decade and feature-length films were still many years off.
Rescued by Rover played to so many packed movie houses that the
film had to be remade three times to replace the negatives as they
wore out from overuse.

Claimant: Dr. Miller Reese Hutchinson
Claim to Fame: The world's first electric hearing aid
Story: Hutchinson was on the staff of the Thomas Edison Labs
when he invented the Acousticon. It was a box about the size of a

hardcover book that contained a microphone and batteries. An earpiece was attached to it with a cord and was held to the user's ear whenever they wanted to hear what someone was saying.

Footnote: One of Hutchinson's other inventions was the Klaxon, an extremely loud horn that makes an "AH–OOOH–GAH!" sound. Originally used on autos and bicycles, the Klaxon found greater fame as the dive alarm on submarines. Mark Twain reportedly joked that Hutchinson invented the Klaxon to deafen the public so that they would buy more Acousticons.

Claimant: Mary Dyer (1611–60)
Claim to Fame: First woman in American history ever hanged
Story: In 1658 Dyer, a Quaker, entered the (Puritan) Massachusetts Bay Colony to protest a law that banned Quakers from the colony. She was arrested and thrown out of Massachusetts, only to return a second time and then a third, after which she and two other Quakers, both men, were tried, convicted, and sentenced to death. The two men were hanged; Dyer was spared at the very last minute—literally as the noose was being placed around her neck —and banished from the colony for the third time. When she returned a *fourth* time in 1660, a judge ordered that the earlier death sentence be carried out. The following morning, June 1, 1660, on Boston Common, Dyer was given one last chance to renounce her Quaker faith. She refused, whereupon she was hanged…for the crime of being a Quaker in Massachusetts.

Claimants: Joshua Pusey and Charles Bowman
Claim to Fame: Inventors of the first matchbook
Story: Pusey was a cigar-smoking patent attorney who hated carrying around a bulky box of wooden matches everywhere he went. In 1889 he came up with something more compact: two rows of cardboard matches (which Pusey called "flexibles") attached to a paper wrapper "adapted to be opened and closed as the covers of a book." A *match-book*. The name survives, but Pusey's book cover design does not—in 1893 a Pennsylvania inventor named Charles Bowman patented the version we use today. (Bowman also patented a "safe" match that would not ignite when chewed by rats.)

Herbivores eat plants. *Folivores* eat just the leaves. *Granivores* eat the seeds.

SODA POPPED

Coke and Pepsi pretty much rule the marketplace, so it's hard for a new brand to find success. Soda companies have tried new flavors, old flavors, brighter colors, no colors, more caffeine, less caffeine, bigger bottles, smaller cans, and even retro-sugar. Here are some pops that fizzled.

Soda: C2
Year: 2004
Story: In 2004 Coca-Cola's market research indicated that more men wanted to buy low-calorie "diet" drinks but were reluctant to do so because they thought diet drinks were too feminine. So Coke created C2, which was a regular/diet hybrid—half the sugar (and calories) were replaced with sugar-free sweeteners. Despite promising market research, the product bombed, capturing less than 1% of the soda market. What happened? People (men and women alike) who wanted Coke with no sugar preferred to buy Diet Coke, and those who didn't mind the sugar bought regular Coke.

Soda: Hubba Bubba
Year: 1986
Story: A. J. Canfield was a small company whose specialty was making soda in unusual flavors, such as chocolate fudge, cherry chocolate fudge, and Swiss creme. In 1986, on a license from the Wrigley Company, Canfield manufactured Hubba Bubba—bubble-gum-flavored soda. It was hard to find in the '80s, and didn't last long. To date it is the only soda ever based on bubble gum.

Soda: Pepsi Blue
Year: 2002
Story: Inspired by its successful launch of Mountain Dew Code Red (cherry-flavored, red Mountain Dew) in 2001, Pepsi unveiled Pepsi Blue the following year. Would you drink a soda that looked like window cleaner? Pepsi apparently thought millions would, despite the fact that it didn't taste like Pepsi (it tasted more like cotton candy) and it was dyed with Blue No. 1, a coloring agent banned outside the United States years earlier because of fears that it may cause cancer. Pepsi Blue lasted about a year in stores.

Soda: 7-Up Gold
Year: 1988
Story: The Dr Pepper Company was working on a light-colored, caffeinated, extra-spicy ginger ale in 1988, when the company merged with 7-Up. Since the soda resembled 7-Up more than it did Dr Pepper, the new bosses released the ginger ale drink as a new 7-Up flavor called 7-Up Gold. Marketing experts think 7-Up Gold sold poorly because of 7-Up's famous "never had it, never will" slogan—referring to caffeine—and 7-Up Gold had a lot of caffeine. Others say it's because 7-Up Gold tasted weird. Either way, it went off the market in 1990.

Soda: dnL
Year: 2002
Story: Not learning from the failure of 7-Up Gold, 7-Up once again tried to infuse its product with caffeine. Meant to compete with the caffeine-loaded energy drinks that were gaining popularity at the time (Red Bull, Rockstar, and Monster), dnL tasted exactly like 7-Up...it just had caffeine in it. The product was marketed as "7-Up, turned upside-down," and "dnL" is actually "7-Up" upside-down. Despite the clever name, it didn't work, and dnL was gone by 2003.

Soda: Coke Blak
Year: 2006
Story: By 2005 gourmet-coffee culture had evolved from a fad into a part of the American mainstream. Coca-Cola didn't want to lose any more business to Starbucks—which had partnered with Pepsi to bottle its own drinks and sell them in supermarkets—so it entered the coffee-drink business in 2006. Its entry: Coke Blak. The recipe: one part Coca-Cola, one part cold coffee, and one part sweet cream (so it wasn't even *black* coffee, like the name implies). It was pulled from American store shelves in 2007...but it continues to sell very well in France.

*　　*　　*

"We learn from history that man can never learn anything from history."
—**George Bernard Shaw**

The Chihuahua in the Taco Bell commercials was named Gidget.

I LOST ON *JEOPARDY!*

*Recently, one of our writers auditioned for and made it on
to the TV game show* Jeopardy! *Here's his report of how
a game show is made, what it's really like, and why
he couldn't tell us if he won. (He didn't.)*

• **Getting an audition is fairly difficult.** Each January, *Jeopardy!*
offers an online contestant test: 50 general-knowledge questions
in 10 minutes. If you pass (reportedly you have to get at least 48
correct), a contestant coordinator sends you an e-mail a few
weeks later and invites you to one of the auditions, held in hotel
ballrooms in several major cities around the country.

• **The audition is a grueling test of you, your smarts, and your
personality.** It's a three-hour ordeal that gauges about 20 potential contestants' knowledge, personality, and ability to play the
game. Part one: another 50-question quiz. Part two: auditioners
participate in a mock game of *Jeopardy!* with a computerized game
board and buzzers. Scores aren't kept—it's a test to see if you
speak clearly, phrase your responses in the form of a question, and
keep the game moving along briskly. Part three: a personality
interview. Three contestant coordinators simply ask you about
yourself and what you would do with all that prize money. If you
passed the written test and impressed the panel with your
sparkling personality, several months later the coordinator calls
with congratulations and a show taping date.

• **Multiple shows are taped in one day.** Most game shows, *Jeopardy!* included, film five episodes—a week's worth of shows—in
one day. Taping occurs on Tuesday and Wednesday. Because of
this, contestants are told to bring three outfits with them in case
they win a game and come back as the next episode's "returning
champion." The different clothes create the illusion for home
viewers watching the next day that it's the next day.

• **There are no "fabulous parting gifts."** That may have been a
game show standard in the 1960s and '70s, but it's no longer true.
Gone are the cases of Turtle Wax, Rice-a-Roni, and the board-
game version. Contestants receive a *Jeopardy!* tote bag and a silver

picture frame with *Jeopardy!* written on it. (It's for the photograph they get of themselves with host Alex Trebek.)

• **...but you do get money...** The player who comes in first gets to keep whatever money they win. Second- and third-place contestants get a flat fee: $2,000 for second place, $1,000 for third.

• **...which covers your expenses.** *Jeopardy!* tapes in Culver City, California. You have to pay for your own travel and hotel. However, if you are a returning champion and win enough to return for the next week's taping, *Jeopardy!* pays your airfare.

• **It's a long day.** Each day's contestants (about 15 people) stay at the same hotel (which offers a special contestant discount), and at 7:00 a.m. they all gather in the lobby to board the *Jeopardy!* Bus, a shuttle that takes them to the Sony Pictures Studio. *Jeopardy!* is one of the many productions filmed there—*Wheel of Fortune* is made on the set next door to *Jeopardy!* Once they reach the studio, contestants are ushered into a "green room" with couches and bottled water, where they get an orientation ("speak clearly, don't be nervous, phrase your answers in the form of a question").

• **You have to rehearse.** After a mic fitting and a few minutes in the makeup chair, the contestants get to check out the *Jeopardy!* set. Each player gets to test the "clicker" or "answering device" and play a rehearsal game for a few minutes. At about 10:00 a.m., the studio audience is let in and the contestants head back to the green room. The order of who gets to play in each of the five episodes is chosen at random—names are placed on notecards, face down on a table. Until their names are picked, contestants may watch from the studio audience.

• **Alex Trebek is kept far, far away.** Since the 1950s quiz-show cheating scandals, FCC rules prohibit the host from interacting with contestants, as he may have prior knowledge of the day's questions. So contestants do not meet or even see Trebek until the taping begins and he saunters out on stage.

• **It's shot in real time.** The commercial breaks on TV last about two minutes, and they do in taping as well. If Trebek flubbed a question (or "answer") during the game, he rerecords it during the break. The time can also be used for the judges (an independent accountant and one of the show's writers) to deliberate on any disputed answers. If there are no problems to fix, Trebek takes questions from the studio audience. Most commonly asked question: "How many of the answers do you know?" Trebek's standard response: "All of them, because I have them in front of me."

- **You have to wait.** There's a three-month lead time between filming and airing. A show shot in January, for example, won't air until April, although at the time of taping, they tell you exactly what day it will air so you can tell your family and set your TiVo. You also have to wait for your prize money. Whether it's first-place winnings or the runner-up fee, the check comes three months after the episode airs.

- **You can't tell anyone how you did.** They want to keep the element of surprise, both to discourage betting and for good TV. Producers begrudgingly allow contestants to tell their family how they did, but they'd prefer you didn't.

*   *   *

A WINNING PHRASE ORIGIN

In November 1986, Disney CEO Michael Eisner and his wife, Jane, were dining with famed pilots Dick Rutan and Jeana Yeager, who had just flown a plane around the world nonstop. Jane Eisner asked what they were doing next, and they said, "We're going to Disneyland." The Eisners thought that would make an excellent slogan. So Disney rushed to create an ad around it, and about two months later the first ad was aired. After Super Bowl XXI on January 25, 1987, an unseen reporter asked New York Giants quarterback Phil Simms, "Now that you've just won the Super Bowl, what are you going to do next?" Simms's scripted reply, shot on field amid the postgame chaos: "I'm going to Disneyland!" The ad has been repeated after almost every Super Bowl since and extended to other sports...and beyond. Stars who have appeared include Magic Johnson, Miss America Gretchen Carlson, Joe Montana, Michael Jordan, Nancy Kerrigan, Mark McGwire (after breaking the single-season home run record), Tom Brady, Curt Schilling, and *American Idol* winner David Cook.

OOPS!

Everyone enjoys reading about someone else's blunders.
So go ahead and feel superior for a few moments.

WHEN IS A DEATHBED NOT A DEATHBED?

In 2009, 58-year-old Michael Anderson of Shawnee, Oklahoma, suffered a stroke. Barely holding on to life in the hospital, he decided it was time to come clean about something that had haunted him for decades. He summoned police to his bed and told them his name was really James Brewer. In 1977, he said, he shot and killed a man in Tennessee named Jimmy Carroll, who he thought was having an affair with his wife. He was arrested but jumped bail, changed his name to Michael Anderson, and settled in Oklahoma. His conscience clean, Brewer could now die in peace. Except he didn't: A few weeks later, he made a full recovery from the stroke, and police arrested him for murder.

WHEN IS AN APOSTLE NOT AN APOSTLE?

In an April 2009 issue of the *Daily Universe*, the student newspaper at Brigham Young University—which is owned by the Mormon Church—a story referred to the Mormon leadership council as the Quorum of the Twelve Apostates. What's wrong with that? It should have been the Quorum of the Twelve *Apostles*. An apostle is a faithful religious follower; an apostate is someone who has bitterly abandoned their religion. All 18,000 copies of the *Daily Universe* were recalled and shredded.

I'M NOT DEAD YET

Milo Bogisic of Montenegro decided to end it all in 2009. But he wanted the aftermath of his suicide to be clean and easy, so he took his gun to a funeral home, where he bought a coffin (he paid in cash). Then he asked the undertaker to wait a moment while he wrote out his own obituary. Finally, Bogisic got into the casket, put the gun to his head, and pulled the trigger. But he didn't die: The bullet went through his chin and nose and missed his brain—a serious wound, but not fatal. Despite repeated requests, Palma will not give Bogisic a refund on the casket.

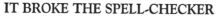

IT BROKE THE SPELL-CHECKER

The longest place name in the United States is Lake Chargogga-goggmanchauggagoggchaubunagungamaugg in Webster, Massachusetts (most residents just call it "Webster Lake"). But the local *Worcester Telegram & Gazette* recently discovered that the name is actually misspelled on signs, in guidebooks, and in official documents. It turns out that there are more than 20 spelling variants stretching back hundreds of years, and somehow along the line, the lake took on the name Lake Chargoggagoggmanchaoggagog-gchaubunaguhgamaugg, instead of the properly spelled Lake Char-goggagoggmanchauggagoggchaubunagungamaugg. All signs will be corrected at taxpayer expense.

GRAM CRACKERS

In 2005 Ohio resident Calvin Wells was convicted of possessing 100 grams of cocaine, which carried a mandatory 10-year prison term. But the bailiff goofed—the verdict form (signed by the jury) had a typo: It listed Wells's crime as possession of "ten one hundred (100) grams." An appeals court later ruled that the wording could be interpreted as 10/100th grams—or $\frac{1}{10}$ of a gram—of cocaine, a misdemeanor whose punishment of four years Wells had already served. So he had to be set free. Or did he? The media attention generated by the case reached court officials in New Jersey, where Wells was wanted on a parole violation from 2000. Before he was released from an Ohio jail, he was extradited to New Jersey, where he faces a 10-year prison term.

BLACK (HUMOR) FOREST

In May 2009, a woman living near a forest in Elmstein, Germany, heard loud screams coming from the woods. Alarmed, she dialed 999 (the German equivalent of 911) to summon police—she was convinced a person was being tortured. Elmstein police dispatched several heavily armed officers—and a rescue helicopter—to the site. Over a loudspeaker, police ordered the perpetrator to release the victim and turn himself in. Roland Hoffman of Elmstein slowly emerged from the forest. He had gone in there to read a book, and was laughing so loud at it that the woman mistook it for tormented screams. "We realize that people think the sound of Germans laughing is unusual, but we're sure the caller meant well," one officer told reporters.

BIG VIDEO TREASURES

Great films to watch when you feel like living large.

THE BIG COUNTRY (1958) *Western*
Starring: Gregory Peck, Jean Simmons, Charlton Heston
Review: "A sweeping Western epic about two families feuding over water rights. Staggering vistas and a grandiose story make this an emblematic Western, and some critics believed that it was an allegory about the Cold War." (*All Movie Guide*)

BIG DEAL ON MADONNA STREET (1958) *Comedy/Foreign*
Starring: Marcello Mastroianni, Vittorio Gassman
Review: "A charming comedy. A robbery meticulously planned (by a sadsack mix of desperate unemployed and washed-up pros) in which everything goes hilariously wrong." (*TimeOut Film Guide*)

BIG WEDNESDAY (1978) *Drama/Comedy*
Starring: Jan-Michael Vincent, Gary Busey, William Katt
Review: "The years have been kind to director John Milius's gorgeously shot surfing epic about 12 years in the life of hotheaded hero Mattt and his two Malibu pals. Milius, a former lifeguard and surfer, based it on his heated feelings on men, guns, sex, surfboards, and war." (*Peter Travers' 1,000 Best Movies on DVD*)

BIG NIGHT (1996) *Comedy*
Starring: Stanley Tucci, Tony Shalhoub, Allison Janney
Review: "This gem tells the beautiful and touching story of two brothers trying to make it as restaurateurs, straight off the boat from Italy. A warm, funny, and heartbreaking look at one night in the company of some truly interesting people." (*FilmCritic.com*)

BIG FISH (2003) *Comedy/Fantasy*
Starring: Ewan McGregor, Albert Finney, Billy Crudup
Review: "This Tim Burton movie is about a grown son's exasperated search for the truth behind his father's larger-than-life stories. Think of the Arabian Nights meets Grimm's Fairy Tales, with just a touch of *Forrest Gump* and *The Wizard of Oz*." (*Film Threat*)

Most of the clothes that actor Jeff Bridges wore in *The Big Lebowski* were his own.

LITTLE VIDEO TREASURES

Great films to watch when you need a little pick-me-up.

LITTLE BIG MAN (1970) *Adventure/Western*
Starring: Dustin Hoffman, Faye Dunaway
Review: "121-year-old Jack Crabb spins a series of yarns about how he tried his hand at a gaggle of professions: gunman, gambler, alcoholic, and businessman, alternating between life in town and on an Indian reservation. One of the most entertaining (and overlooked) Westerns of the early 1970s." (eFilmCritic)

LITTLE NEMO (1992) *U.S./Japanese/Animation*
Review: "Nemo is a youngster whose dreams have transported him, his flying squirrel, and his bed to Slumberland, where he's tricked by a con man into unlocking a forbidden door. An entertaining animated feature for older children." (*Video's Best*)

LITTLE VOICE (1998) *British/Comedy/Drama*
Starring: Brenda Blethyn, Michael Caine, Jane Horrocks
Review: "Laura never speaks above a squeak—unless she's listening to the records of Judy Garland or Shirley Bassey. In those moments, she can perfectly imitate each singer. When her mother hooks up with an unscrupulous talent agent, they try to exploit her for their own gain. A miraculous performance." (*Boxoffice Magazine*)

LITTLE CAESAR (1931) *Crime/Drama*
Starring: Edward G. Robinson, Douglas Fairbanks Jr.
Review: "Small-time hood becomes underworld big-shot; Robinson as Caesar Enrico Bandello gives star-making performance in classic gangster film, still exciting." (*Leonard Maltin's Movie Guide*)

LITTLE MAN TATE (1991) *Drama/Family*
Starring: Jodie Foster, Dianne Wiest
Review: "A dramatization of the struggle between a working-class mother and a wealthy educator for custody of a gifted child. It isn't often that a family film is both heartwarming and thought-provoking, but this little gem is the exception." (*DVD & Video Guide*)

Highest-grossing movie-musical of the '80s: *The Best Little Whorehouse in Texas.*

THE GREAT MOON HOAX

No, not the one about the Hollywood
studio and all that—the other one.

A WALK ON THE MOON

On August 25, 1835, the first of a series of front-page articles was published in the *Sun*, a two-year-old newspaper in New York City. The subject was Sir John Frederick William Herschel, one of the most respected scientists of his day, especially in the field of astronomy. He'd already identified and named seven moons of Saturn and four of Uranus, and had received numerous awards for his work, including a British knighthood. The information for the article came from the *Edinburgh Journal of Science* and a Dr. Andrew Grant, who had recently accompanied Herschel to South Africa, where they were mapping the skies of the Southern Hemisphere. To do the job properly, Herschel had built a massive telescope—the lens was 24 feet in diameter—that operated "on an entirely new principle." It was all very scientific and complicated.

The first article didn't reveal much, but over the next six days readers received some amazing news. In the course of his investigations with the new device, Herschel had aimed his new telescope at the moon. The scope was so powerful that looking through it was almost like standing on the lunar surface, enabling Herschel to make an astonishing discovery: The moon was teeming with life. And not just plants—there were animals running all over the place.

EXPERTS AGREE

Extraterrestrial life was a hot topic in the early 1800s. Telescopes were getting larger, and astronomers were discovering more and more stars, moons, planets, comets, nebulae, etc. Along with these discoveries came claims—sometimes from respected astronomers—that it was only a matter of time before life was discovered on other planets. One especially popular book at the time was *The Christian Philosopher, or the Connexion of Science and Philosophy with Religion*, by Scottish scientist and minister Thomas Dick, first pub-

---

When Neil Armstrong walked on the moon, he took his first step with his left foot.

lished in 1823. In it Dick estimated (somehow) that there were roughly *21 trillion* inhabitants in our solar system—*4 million of whom lived on our moon!*

MOON BATS

Over the six days, the *Sun's* readers learned even more new information about the moon. A few examples: The lunar surface is covered in forests, lakes, rivers, and seas, inhabited by spherical creatures that roll across the beautiful beaches, blue unicorns that wander the mountains, and two-legged beavers that live in huts and use fire. But there was one even more outlandish claim: There are intelligent humanoids on the moon—about four feet tall, largely covered in hair, with faces that are "a slight improvement upon that of the large orangutan." And they have wings. They spend their time flying around, eating fruit, bathing, and talking with each other. Herschel gave them the scientific name *Vespertilio-homo,* or "man-bat," and said they were actually civilized:

> They seemed eminently happy, and even polite, for we saw, in many instances, individuals sitting nearest these piles of fruit select the largest and brightest specimens, and throw them archwise across the circle to some opposite friend or associate who extracted the nutriment from those scattered around him, and which were frequently not a few.

The articles caused a sensation. Newspapers across America reprinted them without raising any questions (the *New York Times* called the information they contained "probable and possible"), and the *Sun* instantly became the biggest-selling paper in the country. To further cash in on the "moon fever" they had started, the *Sun* even reprinted the story in pamphlet form, along with sketches of the newly discovered moon species, and sold thousands of them, too.

BACK TO EARTH

Over the next few weeks, the story spread to Europe, where it enjoyed the same success it had in America. But doubts about the story were growing, too. Eventually it got to South Africa...and to Sir John Herschel. He, of course, denied the claims immediately. And it turned out that the *Edinburgh Journal of Science* had ceased to exist years earlier and there was no such person as Dr. Andrew Grant. "The Great Moon Hoax," as it became known, was over.

The truth of the hoax's origin remains a mystery. Most accounts say the story was written by the *Sun's* Cambridge-educated reporter Richard Adams Locke, and that he did it as a satire to mock the gullible public and "scientists" like Thomas Dick, who made wild claims based on nothing but speculation. (Locke never publicly admitted to writing the articles, although there are some credible accounts of him later confessing to their authorship in private.)

Herschel later said he thought the hoax was hilarious…at first. But he grew annoyed at having to answer questions about the "moon people," which continued for years afterward. The *Sun* never issued a retraction for the story, and never admitted that it was a hoax. By 1836 the *Sun* had a circulation of 20,000—and was the largest newspaper in the world.

EPILOGUE

• Richard Adams Locke left the *Sun* in August 1836 and started his own paper, *The New Era.* There he published another hoax, "The Lost Manuscript of Mungo Park," the purported diaries of a famed Scottish adventurer in Africa. It failed to catch the public's imagination, as too many people knew that Locke was the author.

• Thomas Dick, who was probably overjoyed about the articles when he first heard of them, was much less happy when he found out they were hoaxes, saying that "such attempts to deceive are violations of the laws of the Creator."

• An American preacher who heard about the story took up a collection in the hopes of sending Bibles to the man-bats on the moon. (Just how he proposed to do that is unknown.)

• In April 1844, the *Sun* published the story of a European aerial-ist named Monck Mason, who had just completed the first cross-ing of the Atlantic Ocean in a hot-air balloon…in three days. The "Balloon Hoax" is the second-most famous of the *Sun's* hoax stories—and it was written by Edgar Allan Poe.

CHEATING DEATH

By all measures, these people should have died. Yet somehow, some way, miraculously…they survived.

HELLO, I MUST BE GOING

On August 6, 1945, Tsutomu Yamaguchi was in the worst possible place at the worst possible time: He was in Hiroshima, Japan, on a business trip. That day, the United States dropped an atomic bomb on the city, eventually killing 140,000 people. But Yamaguchi survived, suffering just some burns to his upper body. He returned to his hometown…of Nagasaki, Japan. Three days later, on August 9, the United States dropped an atomic bomb on *that* city. As of 2009, 93-year-old Yamaguchi was still alive, the only person to have witnessed and survived both atomic bombings.

FATHER KNOWS BEST

Joseph Rabadue, 17, was sitting on the floor of his Bangor Township, Michigan, living room watching TV in March 2009. His father told him to "get off the floor and sit on the couch." Good timing. A few minutes after Joseph moved to the couch, a pickup truck smashed into the house, tossing the family's TV across the room and onto the spot on the floor where Joseph had been sitting. Had he not moved, he'd probably have been killed.

THE HITS JUST KEEP COMIN'

The 1997 Macy's Thanksgiving Day Parade in New York City was plagued by high winds. The Cat in the Hat balloon came loose from a float and, carried by the strong winds, knocked down a lamppost. The post struck Kathleen Caronna, who was knocked unconscious and remained in a coma for a month, but recovered completely. Nine years later, New York Yankees pitcher Cory Lidle was flying his private airplane over New York City when he lost control and crashed into the Belaire Apartments in Manhattan. Lidle died, but a resident of the Belaire cheated death for the second time: Kathleen Caronna, who avoided death and injury because she wasn't home.

HEAD CASE

After a domestic-violence conviction in April 2009, Donald Sexton was ordered to stay away from his wife, Tammy, for six months. But a week into the restraining order, he went to her rural Mississippi home in the middle of the night, intending to murder her. As Tammy Sexton lay in bed, Donald shot her in the head, and then went outside and shot himself. He died instantly; Tammy Sexton, however, did not. When police arrived, she had a rag around her head and was drinking a cup of tea. A medical examination at the University of Alabama revealed that the .380-caliber bullet had somehow entered Tammy's forehead and exited through the back of her head, passing through the lobes of her brain without leaving any damage whatsoever.

PLANE AMAZING

In January 1972, Vesna Vulovic was working as a flight attendant for Yugoslav Airlines. An hour into a flight from Denmark to Yugoslavia, an engine suddenly exploded, ripping the plane apart and sending 27 people plunging more than 33,000 feet to their deaths. But not Vulovic. The explosion thrust her into part of the fuselage, which crashed into a snow-covered hill. Somehow, Vulovic survived—she fell into a coma when she crashed, but awoke three days later in a hospital. In less than a year, she had fully recovered and become a national hero in Yugoslavia. She still gets noticed in public, especially when she flies. "People always want to sit next to me," Vulovic says.

*   *   *

MOVIE TRIVIA

In 2009 the average movie ticket costs $9.00. Where does all the money go? According to *Money* magazine,

- $.61 goes to pay the actors.
- $.90 covers distribution, such as prints and shipping the movie reels to theaters.
- $1.54 goes to the studio that made the movie.
- $1.90 goes to cover marketing costs (previews, advertising, etc.).
- $4.05 goes to the movie theater itself.

THE WRONG MEANING

Language is a constantly evolving system. Over time, the meanings of words can change dramatically, leaving their original or "true" definitions behind. Here are some examples of words that, technically, most of us misuse every day.

PERUSE
How We Use It: To skim or browse written material quickly to get the gist
What It Really Means: The opposite—to read it thoroughly and carefully

BLATANT
How We Use It: Extremely obvious or unabashedly conspicuous
What It Really Means: Offensively loud or noisy

DISINTERESTED
How We Use It: Indifferent
What It Really Means: Impartial (as in lacking a conflict of interest)

PLUS
How We Use It: And
What It Really Means: It's a subtle difference, but "plus" means "added to" or "increased by," not "another"

PRESENTLY
How We Use It: Now
What It Really Means: Soon

RETICENT
How We Use It: Reluctant
What It Really Means: Inclination to be quiet

FORTUITOUS
How We Use It: A lucky happenstance for the good
What It Really Means: Any chance action, good or bad

ANXIOUS
How We Use It: Eagerly looking forward to an upcoming event
What It Really Means: Full of anxiety; dreading an upcoming event

PRISTINE
How We Use It: Very clean, perfectly spotless
What It Really Means: Unchanged from its original state

DAWN
How We Use It: The beginning of the day—sunrise
What It Really Means: The twilight just *before* sunrise

FOOL'S GOLD

*Everybody is familiar with the phrase, "If it looks too good
to be true, it probably is." We know better, yet we're
still susceptible to promises of getting something for
nothing. So why do we keep falling for them?*

IT REALLY SUCKS!

One day in late 1896, the Reverend Prescott F. Jernegan
approached Arthur P. Ryan, a jeweler in Middletown, Connecticut. He told Ryan that he was quitting the preaching business and entering a new field of work: God had come to him in a
vision, he said, and told him how to build a device that could
extract gold from seawater. He had been working on the device for
years, he said, and had finally perfected it. And he wanted Ryan
to verify that it worked.

Jernegan was a member of an old and respected New England
family, not to mention a respected local preacher, and it *had* been
discovered a few years earlier that there are indeed trace amounts
of gold in seawater. Ryan trusted Jernegan, so he agreed to test the
device.

TESTING, TESTING...

Jernegan's "Gold Accumulator," as he called it, was a wooden
box whose interior was lined with zinc. It had holes cut into its
sides, which allowed water to enter it. Inside the box was a battery connected to a metal pan. If you put mercury into the pan,
along with a "secret ingredient," Jernegan explained to Ryan,
and then lowered the box into seawater, the electrified mercury-
and-secret-ingredient mix would absorb the gold out of the
water.

Ryan and several colleagues took the Gold Accumulator to
the coastal town of Providence, Rhode Island. Jernegan refused to
go along—to assure them that he wouldn't be able to somehow
falsify or influence the results of the test. Ryan and the others
lowered the device off a pier into the water and spent the night
in a nearby shed to make sure nobody interfered with it. In the
morning, they pulled it back up and opened it. What did they

All the gold ever mined would fit in two large swimming pools.

find? Flakes of gold in the pan. There was only a little gold—maybe a couple of dollars' worth—but Jernegan's plan was to build a seaside factory with more than 1,000 accumulators. Ryan and the others believed they'd be rich and quickly signed on to invest in the project.

GOLD FEVER

Over the following few months, Jernegan built several more accumulators and, along with his longtime friend and assistant, Charles E. Fisher, founded the Electrolytic Marine Salts Company, based in Boston, Massachusetts. In the fall of 1897, they signed an agreement with Ryan and several prominent Boston investors to take the company public, with Jernegan and Fisher getting 40 percent of the proceeds from the stock sale. Share price: $1. More than 350,000 shares sold in three days. An elaborate factory was built in the remote town of North Lubec, Maine, and within weeks the accumulators were taking $150 worth of gold from the sea every day. Newspapers all over the country wrote about the success of the company, and in the months that followed, the number of shares sold climbed to more than a million. Jernegan, Fisher, Ryan and the others were all becoming very rich men. And it looked like they were just getting started.

But then, in July 1898, Fisher disappeared. And, strangely, the gold accumulators stopped working.

YOUR GOLD SMELLS FISHY

What was wrong with the accumulators? Fisher wasn't there to seed them anymore. He was a trained deep sea diver, and right from the start he'd been diving down to the accumulators at night and seeding them with gold that he and Jernegan had purchased earlier. When investors went to Jernegan to find out what was wrong, he told them he'd get to the bottom of it…and fled to France with his family. He was found there but disappeared again before he could be arrested. (He eventually ended up in the Philippines, where he became a teacher.) Fisher was never seen again, though some reports say he went to Australia. The scam made the men in the neighborhood of $200,000 each…millions in today's money. It remains one of the most successful financial hoaxes in U.S. history.

CREATIVE SENTENCING

Prisons are overcrowded. Diversion or "anti-recidivism" programs
don't always work, so some judges are getting a little more
inventive with the sentences they hand down.

TURNING THE PAGE

In 2002 in Warren County, Ohio, Judge Mark Wiest introduced a unique program to discourage repeat offenses by low-level criminals: a book club. People convicted of misdemeanors and minor felonies (for which the sentence is 100 hours of community service) have to read six books in 12 weeks and attend discussion sessions. If they do, Wiest knocks 60 hours off the sentence. "Usually we're telling them when they're on probation, 'Don't do this, don't do that.' This just gives them something more positive." The reading list includes Stephen King's *The Green Mile* and John Steinbeck's *Of Mice and Men*.

NOT SO CROSS

Houston man James Lee Cross was convicted on a domestic abuse charge in 2004 for slapping his wife. Judge Larry Standley sentenced Cross to a year of probation, anger management training…and a yoga class once a week for a year. Standley said that anger leads to a lack of control, which leads to violence, and that the yoga could give Cross that control. "For people who are into it," Standley said, "it really calms them down."

PUTTING THE "PAIN" IN PAINESVILLE

In 2007 in Painesville, Ohio, Judge Michael Cicconetti introduced a new punishment for men convicted of soliciting prostitutes. Rather than go to jail, offenders spend three hours walking up and down a busy street…in a chicken suit. They also have to hold a sign that reads, "No Chicken Ranch in Our City / *No Gallinero En Nuestro Ciudad*." The Chicken Ranch is a famous Nevada brothel; the sign is bilingual because many people in the area speak only Spanish and Cicconetti doesn't think anyone should miss out on the convict's humiliation. Cicconetti frequently issues bizarre punishments:

- He ordered teens who painted graffiti on the baby Jesus statue in a church nativity scene to dress up as Mary and Joseph and walk around town with a donkey, carrying a sign that read, "Sorry for the Jackass Offense."
- He sentenced two teenagers who shot paintball pellets at a neighbor's house to shoot paintball pellets at their own cars and then clean them up.
- He forced a man who called a policeman a "pig" to stand next to a live pig with a sign that read, "This Is Not a Police Officer."

HURRICAN'T

Like thousands of others, Kim Horn fled New Orleans when Hurricane Katrina tore through the city in 2005. She moved to Mason, Michigan, where, after telling her landlord her situation, she got free rent. Only problem: Horn wasn't a refugee. She wasn't even from New Orleans. In June 2006, after Horn was convicted on fraud charges, Judge Beverly Nettles-Nickerson sentenced her to six months of cleaning the house she'd lived in rent-free.

BACKSEAT HURLER

A 17-year-old boy in Olathe, Kansas, told his friends that he was planning to play a major prank on David Young, the teacher of the Spanish class he was failing. On the last day of school in June 2005, he walked up to Young...and vomited on him. Johnson County Judge Michael Farley found the teen (he's a minor, so his name was withheld from the media) guilty of battery and sentenced him to four months of cleaning up the vomit of people who throw up in police cars.

HOW MANILOW CAN YOU GO?

If you're driving through Fort Lupton, Colorado, keep the hard rock, rap, or other abrasive music turned down. Otherwise, Judge Paul Sacco may convict you of violating the town's noise ordinance. The punishment: an hour of easy listening. Sacco has been doling out the sentence for more than 15 years. His favorite "punishments": Barry Manilow, Carpenters, and Dolly Parton's "I Will Always Love You."

At its current pace, hurricane-devastated New Orleans won't be completely rebuilt until 2028.

PEOPLE STUFF FOR DOGS

Anthropologists theorize that early humans and wild dogs became such close companions because of the canine's ability to mimic people's emotions. Humans encouraged it. Judging by these actual products, we still do.

PAWLISH ($11.95). Give your dog a "pet-icure" with this line of nontoxic, quick-drying nail polish for dogs. Choose from Poodle Pink, Bow Wow Green, Mutt's New Purple, Fire Hydrant Red, Yuppy Puppy Silver, and Doghouse Blues. (Ironically, "Pawlish is tested on people, not animals.")

SONGS TO MAKE DOGS HAPPY ($15.98). This CD is the brainchild of two Los Angeles-based musicians, Skip Haynes and Dana Walden. With the help of an "animal communicator" named Dr. Kim Ogden, they test-marketed different sets of lyrics and musical styles at L.A.-area animal shelters. All of the tracks are upbeat, and none include the word "no" or any sudden noises.

PENTHOUSE DOG POTTY ($319). It's a big, fancy litter box, but instead of litter, it's covered with artificial grass. Underneath is a drainage system (basically a bucket) to dispose of #1. For the other "duty," you do the same thing you'd do outside—scoop it up.

DIAMOND BONE PENDANT ($2,900). From Bark Avenue Jewelers, this pricey bling is supposed to be worn on your dog's collar. It features 30 diamonds set in 14-karat gold. (Also available in platinum.)

SLAVE LEIA DOG COSTUME ($14.99). StarWarsShop.com offers the Princess Leia Slave Girl Dog Costume so you and your pooch can recreate Jabba the Hutt's palace scene from *Return of the Jedi*. Or, if you'd prefer that your dog teach you how to use the Force, you can get him the official Yoda Dog Costume.

NEUTICLES. These are silicon implants designed to replace neutered dogs' missing "bits." According to Gregg Miller, who invented Neuticles in 1993, they're not just for vanity, but they control pet overpopulation "by encouraging thousands of caring pet owners to neuter that simply would not have before." Cost: $170 per set (neutering and implantation not included).

Pigging out: Humans eat more pork than any other kind of meat.

WHEN HARRY MET BESSIE

And other stories of presidential romance.

When Georgie Met Martha: In 1758 Martha Dandridge Curtis was 27 and recently widowed, and a very wealthy woman. That year George Washington, also **27** and already a colonel in the Virginia militia—and not at all wealthy—met Martha via the Virginia high-society social scene and proceeded to court her. Courtship was quick, and they were married in January 1759, in what at the time was viewed as a marriage of convenience. They were, however, happily married for **41** years. (Note: The marriage took place at the plantation that Martha owned, in what was called the "White House.")

When Johnny Met Louisa: Louisa Catherine Johnson, who was born in London, met John Quincy Adams at her home in Nantes, France, in 1779. She was 4; he was 12. Adams was traveling with his father, John Adams, who was on a diplomatic mission in Europe. The two met again in 1795 in London, when John was a minister to the Netherlands. He courted her, all the while telling her she'd have to improve herself if she was going to live up to his family's standards (his father was vice president at the time). She married him anyway, in 1797—and his family made it no secret that they disapproved of the "foreigner" in their family. Nevertheless, they were married until John Quincy Adams's death in 1848. Louisa remains the only foreign-born First Lady in U.S. history.

When Jimmy Met Ann: In the summer of 1819, James Buchanan, 28, became engaged to Ann Coleman, 23, the daughter of a wealthy iron magnate in Lancaster, Pennsylvania. He spent very little time with her during the first months of the engagement, being extremely busy at his law office, and rumors swirled that he was seeing other women and was only marrying her for her money. The rumors are believed to be untrue, but Ann took them to heart, and in November, after several distraught weeks, she wrote to him that the engagement was off. On December 9 she died of an overdose of laudanum, possibly in a suicide. Buchanan was devastated, and even more so when her family refused to allow him to see Ann's body or attend her funeral. He disappeared for some time but eventually returned to his work in Lancaster. After Ann's death, Buchanan vowed that he would never marry. He didn't...and remains the only bachelor president in American history.

When Gracie Met Calvin: One day in 1903, Grace Anna Goodhue was watering flowers outside the Clarke School for the Deaf in Northampton, Massachusetts, where she taught. At some point, she looked up and saw a man through the open window of a boarding house across the street. He was shaving, his face covered with lather, and dressed in his long johns. He was also wearing a hat. Grace burst out laughing, and the man turned to look at her. That was the first meeting of Grace and Calvin Coolidge. They were married two years later.

When Harry Met Bessie: Harry Truman met Bess Wallace in 1890, at the Baptist Church in Independence, Missouri. They were there for Sunday school—he was six; she was five. Truman later wrote of their first meeting: "We made a number of new acquaintances, and I became interested in one in particular. She had golden curls and has, to this day, the most beautiful blue eyes. We went to Sunday school, public school from the fifth grade through high school, graduated in the same class, and marched down life's road together. For me she still has the blue eyes and golden hair of yesteryear." Bess and Harry were married in 1919.

When Lyndie Met Lady: Lyndon Baines Johnson met Claudia "Lady Bird" Taylor in 1934, a few weeks after she'd graduated from the University of Texas. Johnson was a 26-year-old aide to Texas congressman Richard Kleberg, and was in Austin, Texas, on business. They went on a single breakfast date, at the end of which Johnson proposed marriage. She said she'd think about it. He returned to Washington, and sent her letters and telegrams every day until he returned to Austin 10 weeks later, when she accepted. "Sometimes," she later wrote about her husband, "Lyndon simply takes your breath away."

When Richie Met Pattie: Thelma "Pat" Ryan graduated from the University of Southern California in 1937 at the age of 25. She got a job as a high school teacher in Whittier, a small town near Los Angeles, and became a member of the amateur theatrical group the Whittier Community Players. In 1938 Richard Nixon, a 26-year-old lawyer who had just opened a firm in nearby La Habra, joined the theater group, thinking that acquiring acting skills would help him in the courtroom. In their first performance, Nixon was cast opposite Ryan. He asked her out—and asked her to marry him on their first date. They were married three years later.

When Ronnie Met Nancy: Ronald Reagan wrote in his autobiography that he first met Nancy Davis when she came to him for help. He was president of the Screen Actors Guild, and she couldn't get a job acting in movies because another Nancy Davis's name had shown up on the Hollywood blacklist of alleged communists. Nancy. But according to Jon Weiner's book *Professors, Politics, and Pop*, SAG records show that Nancy's blacklist problem occurred in 1953—a year after the Reagans were married. So how did they meet? Reagan biographer Anne Edwards says that in 1949 Nancy, who had just become an MGM contract player, told a friend of Reagan's that she wanted to meet him. The friend invited the two to a small dinner party, and the rest is history.

When Georgie Met Laura: Joe and Jan O'Neill lived in Midland, Texas, and were childhood friends of Laura Welch. In 1975 another childhood friend, George W. Bush, came back to Midland after being away for a few years. The O'Neills bugged Laura to go out with George, but she didn't want to. She later said that the O'Neills were only trying to get them together "because we were the only two people from that era in Midland who were still single." She finally agreed to meet him at a backyard barbecue in 1977, when she was 30 and he was 31. George was smitten; Laura was, too. They were married three months later.

When Barry Met Michelle. In 1989 Michelle Robinson was working at a Chicago law firm when she was assigned to mentor a summer associate from Harvard with a "strange name"—Barack Obama. Not long after, Barack, 27, asked Michelle, 25, on a date. She later said she was reluctant to date one of the few black men at the large firm because it seemed "tacky." She finally relented and after dating for several months, she suggested they get married. He wasn't interested. One night in 1991, during dinner at a Chicago restaurant, she brought it up again. Again he said no. But when dessert showed up, there was an engagement ring in a box on one of the plates. They were married in 1992.

Average fashion model: 5'11" and 117 lbs. Average American woman: 5'4" and 140 lbs.

GO, ARTICHOKES!

Calling them Lions, Tigers, or Warriors might make your college sports team sound intimidating, but everyone does that. Want to really stand out? Try one of these unintimidating college sports team nicknames.

School: Webster University Gorloks
Story: *Gorlok?* There's no such thing as a "gorlok." The word was invented by Webster staff and students in a name-the-team contest. According to the school, the gorlok has "the paws of a speeding cheetah, the horns of a fierce buffalo, and the face of a dependable St. Bernard."

School: Whittier College Poets
Story: The college was founded by the American poet John Greenleaf Whittier.

School: Presbyterian College Blue Hose
Story: Blue hose are the socks traditionally worn by some Scottish clans with their kilts. Really, it's no different from, say, the Red Sox (although "sox" is more intimidating than "hose").

School: Scottsdale Community College Fighting Artichokes
Story: When the school opened in 1970, a student-written school constitution put a limit on how much money could be spent on athletics. The administration diverted funds to sports anyway and asked the student body to propose a mascot. In protest, the student government came up with the Artichokes.

School: Amherst College Lord Jeffs (and Lady Jeffs)
Story: Named after Lord Jeffrey Amherst, a British army officer best known for giving smallpox blankets to Native Americans during the French and Indian War in the 1760s.

School: Rhode Island School of Design Nads
Story: The prestigious art school plays some semiformal hockey games against other art schools. Obviously it doesn't take its mascot name too seriously—"nads" is a slang term for male genitalia. (The basketball team has a different name. They're called the Balls.)

FABULOUS FLOP: THE GYROJET

Flying cars, food replicators, and other bits of sci-fi technology have been "just around the corner" since the 1950s...and yet they never seem to get here. In the 1960s, however, one company did manage to bring a futuristic weapon to market. Here's the story.

THINKING SMALL

In the 1960s, as NASA was preparing to send astronauts to the moon aboard giant Saturn V rockets, two inventors in San Ramon, California, were hard at work trying to prove that tiny rockets, small enough to fit in the palm of your hand, could do big things, too. Robert Mainhardt and Art Biehl were partners in a company called MB Associates that worked mostly on classified military projects. But in 1965, they patented a product intended for sale to the public as well as the military: the "Gyrojet," a handgun that fired rockets instead of bullets.

The Gyrojet looked a lot like an ordinary handgun: At first glance the only obvious difference was the holes that were drilled down the length of the left and right sides of the barrel—vents for the rocket exhaust. But the gun's performance was nothing like that of an ordinary pistol.

BULLET BASICS

A typical round of ammunition—what is commonly called a "bullet"—has several parts: the actual bullet (the projectile), a metal casing, the gunpowder inside the casing, and a primer. The bullet is attached to the casing at one end, and the primer is at the opposite end. When you pull the trigger of a handgun, the hammer—the part you cock when you're getting ready to shoot—strikes the primer, causing it to explode. The exploding primer ignites the gunpowder, which also explodes. The rapidly expanding gases given off by the exploding gunpowder are what separate the bullet from the cartridge and propel it out the barrel of the gun.

Gyrojet rocket rounds, by comparison, were not filled with loose gunpowder. They contained a carefully shaped piece of solid rocket fuel. The rocket fuel was ignited by a primer, just like ordinary ammunition, but that's where the similarity ended. The rocket fuel *burned* for a short period of time instead of exploding in an instant, and expelled the resulting hot gas through four tiny holes in the base of the rocket. These holes, which served the same purpose as rocket nozzles, were slightly angled so that the escaping gases would cause the rocket to spin rapidly enough to keep it on a straight course as it blasted out of the gun barrel.

ROCKET SCIENCE

So why even bother with rocket guns when ordinary handguns were perfectly good for the task? One of the limitations of a traditional handgun is that the bullet stops accelerating the instant it leaves the barrel, and loses speed and power from then on. Not so with the Gyrojet—each rocket burned for 1/10th of a second. That may not sound like much, but in that short time the rocket could travel a full 60 feet, gaining speed and power all the while. It was as if the gun barrel was 60 feet long instead of just a few inches. At a distance of 70 yards, a rocket round fired from a Gyrojet gun struck the target at greater speed and more than twice as much force as an ordinary .45 caliber bullet. Bonus: The Gyrojet could be fired underwater…or in outer space.

THE GUN OF THE FUTURE

The Gyrojet had plenty of other advantages, too. It takes a pretty big explosion of gunpowder to send an ordinary bullet on its way, so handguns have to be built out of very strong, very durable, and very heavy materials in order to contain those explosions. Since Gyrojet rocket fuel burned instead of exploding, and the burning did not need to be contained within the gun, the Gyrojet handgun could be built with almost any lightweight material, including aluminum and even plastic. And with no empty cartridges to expel from the gun after firing, Gyrojets were also mechanically simpler than most typical handguns, which further reduced their weight, complexity, and cost of manufacture.

Another drawback of ordinary handguns is that they have a powerful "kick" or *recoil* when you shoot them—a by-product of the powerful explosion. The kick causes the gun to jerk sharply after each shot, and you have to re-aim the gun before you can

fire again. With no explosion, the Gyrojet had almost no kick—
you could fire one shot after another in rapid sequence, until
all six of the rockets contained in the gun's magazine were
launched.

AND NOW THE FINE PRINT

So why didn't the Gyrojet banish the ordinary handgun into
oblivion like the musket and the blunderbuss before it? Because
even though the Gyrojet offered the *promise* of a science-fiction
weapon of the future, what it actually delivered was something
more akin to a gun in a Saturday morning cartoon.

Sure, the Gyrojet had a lot of power at a distance of 70 yards,
but at point-blank range it was useless. The rocket had so little
power before it got up to speed that if you shot it at someone
standing right in front of you, there was a very good chance that
the rocket would bounce right off their chest. And not that anyone was ever foolish enough to try it, but the Gyrojet was probably the first gun in history that really did allow you to defend
yourself against it by sticking your finger in the barrel to block the
rocket…just like cartoon characters do.

MORE BAD NEWS

From the prototype onward, poor design and poor quality control
also meant that as many as 20 percent of the early rocket rounds
had flaws. Some never ignited; others launched only after you
cocked and fired the gun twice. If a rocket did fail to ignite on the
second try, there was no way of telling whether it was genuinely
dead…or a slow-burner that would suddenly ignite as you tried to
remove it from the gun. The company's own literature advised
Gyrojet owners to remove dud rockets from the gun only "after a
10-second waiting period" if it didn't launch on the second attempt.
Wait 10 seconds before clearing and reloading your weapon? In a
combat situation? When other people are *shooting at you?*

Even when the rocket round did ignite properly, there was no
guarantee that it would even build up enough thrust to exit the
barrel of the gun. Many rockets jammed in the barrel and flamed
out. Of those that did manage to exit, some had flawed nozzles
that caused them to travel in a circular, corkscrew path instead of
flying straight to the target.

WHAT A LOAD

Any one of these flaws by itself could have meant the difference between life and death in a firefight. And the problem was made worse by the fact that the Gyrojet was both time-consuming and cumbersome to load. Most semiautomatic handguns have a clip that allows you to load eight or more bullets at the same time. Revolvers can be reloaded quickly using a device called a speed loader. The Gyrojet, on the other hand, required the user to feed individual bullets into the spring-loaded magazine one at a time, all the while taking care to keep a thumb pressed down on top of the inserted bullets. If the user's thumb happened to slip, the spring popped the rockets up and out of the gun, almost like toast out of a toaster—another huge disadvantage in combat.

Even the Gyrojet's strongest selling points, its high speed and power at great distances, worked against it. The Gyrojet rockets were designed to exceed the speed of sound, but as an accelerating object approaches the speed of sound, there is a great deal of turbulence that can deflect it from its course. This often caused Gyrojet rockets to miss distant targets entirely. In other words, the gun was too weak to be effective at close range and too inaccurate to be effective at long range.

THANKS, BUT...

When the Gyrojet hit store shelves in the mid-1960s, gun owners who were used to the heft of ordinary handguns thought it felt (and looked) like a toy gun. That didn't stop MB Associates from charging $100 for it—as much as an ordinary revolver. And the rockets themselves sold for about $1.35 apiece, far more than ordinary bullets. The Gyrojet quickly developed a reputation as a gun that everyone wanted to shoot, just out of curiosity...but nobody wanted to own. Collectors with money to burn bought them for their novelty value, but shooters never took them seriously, and by the early 1970s they were gone.

If you were one of the few to buy a Gyrojet in the 1960s, you made a good investment: Today they range in value from $1,500 for the most common handgun models to $5,000 or more for the rarer carbine and rifle models. And if you still have some of the rockets lying around, think twice before you shoot them off— today those tiny $1.35 rockets are worth more than $100 *each*.

Studies show: Drinkers are likely to rate someone as 25% more attractive after 2 pints of beer.

GOODBYE, HOLLYWOOD

Sometimes your job—no matter how successful you are or how fulfilling it once was—just doesn't do it for you anymore and you've got to quit and do something else. It can happen to anyone, even actors.

GRACE KELLY

One of the most glamorous actresses of Hollywood's Golden Age, Kelly was a movie star for just four years: from 1952 to 1956. In that time, she appeared in such classics as *High Noon*, *Dial M For Murder*, *To Catch a Thief*, *High Society*, and *The Country Girl*, for which she won an Oscar. But in 1956, she married Prince Rainier of Monaco, the tiny but wealthy principality in the South of France, and became Princess Grace. Rainier thought appearing in movies was beneath a princess, so Kelly gave up her acting career. She never left the limelight, however, and remained a tabloid fixture until her death in a car accident in 1982.

KAL PENN

Penn is best known for his starring roles in the two cult *Harold and Kumar* movies, and in 2007 he joined the cast of the popular TV medical drama *House*. But in an April 2009 episode, Penn's character shocked audiences when he killed himself. The reason: Penn had decided to leave the show (and acting) for politics. He'd accepted a job in the Obama administration as associate director of the White House Office of Public Engagement, where he became the president's liaison to Asian, Pacific Islander, and arts groups.

GLENDA JACKSON

This British actress was one of the most acclaimed movie stars of the late 1960s and early 1970s, starring in controversial films (*Sunday Bloody Sunday*), comedies (*A Touch of Class*), and dramas (*Women in Love*). She even won two Oscars for best actress. In the late 1980s, Jackson became concerned about the direction in which conservative prime minister Margaret Thatcher was taking the country. So in 1992, Jackson gave up acting and ran for a seat in the House of Commons...and won. In Parliament she focused on transportation issues, earning an appointment as junior minister of transportation in 1997. After unsuccessfully running for mayor of London in 2000, Jackson returned to the House of Commons, where she continues to serve as a member of Parliament.

BOBBY SHERMAN

Sherman became a teen idol with his role as an 1870s logger on the 1968–70 TV series *Here Come the Brides*. He parlayed the role into a successful singing career and earned six gold records for songs like "Easy Come, Easy Go" and "Little Woman." But it was while filming an episode of the 1970s medical drama *Emergency!* in 1974 that Sherman realized what he really wanted to do: real-life emergency response. Since leaving acting, Sherman has been a volunteer Los Angeles police officer, a first-aid class instructor, a paramedic, and a deputy sheriff in San Bernardino County, California.

ANDREA THOMPSON

As a character actress, Thompson co-starred on several television dramas in the 1980s and 1990s, including *Falcon Crest*, *Babylon 5*, and *JAG*. In 1997 she landed a leading role as Detective Jill Kirkendall on the hit series *NYPD Blue*. Then suddenly, at the end of her third season on the show in 2000, Thompson quit to follow a new career: TV journalism. And she did it the hard way, working her way up. She took a job as a reporter at a local Albuquerque, New Mexico, television station before moving on to *CNN Headline News* in 2001 and to Court TV in 2002.

DOLORES HART

Hart made her first film appearance in the 1956 Elvis Presley movie *Loving You*. It made her a star, and she appeared with Presley again the following year in *King Creole*. After starring in *The Pleasure of His Company* on Broadway in 1959, Hart returned to movies, making the teen hit *Where the Boys Are*, followed by *Come Fly With Me*. And that was it. In 1963, finding Hollywood "needlessly competitive and negative," the 24-year-old Hart joined the Regina Laudis Abbey in Bethelehem, Connecticut, and became a nun. She eventually became the prioress (person in charge) of the convent. Bonus: Still a member of the Academy of Motion Picture Arts and Sciences, Hart gets to vote for the Oscars each year. (She is the only member of AMPAS who is a nun.)

WORST TEAMS EVER

On page 37, we told you about some of the most dominating performances in sports history. Here's the other side of the story: the teams who suffered the most miserable seasons in the history of their sports.

WORST HOCKEY TEAM

It's not just, "Who had the most losses in a single season?" National Hockey League standings are calculated by points—two for a win, one for a tie, zero for a loss. So the season's worst team is the one that racks up the fewest points. The all-time worst was the 1974–75 Washington Capitals, with 21 points. Their record: 8 wins, 5 ties, and 67 losses. Only once in NHL history has another team come close: the 1980–81 Winnipeg Jets, who won 9 games and lost 57 (but racked up a relatively impressive 14 ties).

WORST FOOTBALL TEAM

In the 1970s, the NFL played a 14-game season. In 1976, its first year in existence, the Tampa Bay Buccaneers went 0-14 and became the first team ever to lose every game of the season. The next season, they weren't much better at 2–12. The following year the NFL went to a 16-game schedule, and it took 30 more years for a team to lose every single one of them: the Detroit Lions, who achieved a "perfect" 0–16 record in 2008.

WORST BASKETBALL TEAM

Only once in a full NBA season has a team won fewer than 10 games—the 1972–73 Philadelphia 76ers, who finished the season with a 9–73 record. That dismal year included three of the longest losing streaks in NBA history. The Sixers opened the year with a 14-game losing streak, had a 20-game losing streak midseason (a record at the time), and ended the season by losing 13 consecutive games.

WORST COLLEGE FOOTBALL TEAM

Prairie View A&M University's football team, the Panthers, won five national titles in the 1950s and '60s. But between 1990 and

'98, they lost 80 straight games, the worst losing streak ever for a college team. And the worst year of the streak was 1991, in which the Panthers' opponents scored an average of 56 points per game, while PVAMU scored 48 points...for the entire season. PVAMU did win the final game of the 1998 season, and the following season they doubled their wins—finishing with a record of 2-9.

WORST MODERN BASEBALL TEAM

The New York Mets joined the National League in 1962. While first-year teams normally don't do well, the rookie Mets set a new standard: 40–122. They finished more than 60 games behind the pennant-winning San Francisco Giants. The record was nearly toppled in 2003 when the Detroit Tigers amassed a 43–119 record.

WORST COLLEGE BASKETBALL TEAM

Generally speaking, the more academically prestigious a college is, the worse its sports teams are. (Alumni contributions go to research labs, not football arenas.) Case in point: the well-funded CalTech (California Institute of Technology). The CalTech Beavers men's basketball team plays in the NCAA's Division III, and over 11 years from 1996 to 2007, they didn't win a single game. That's a 207-game losing streak, the longest in North American history in any sport, collegiate or otherwise.

WORST OVERALL PRO SPORTS TEAM

Comparing every NFL, NHL, NBA, and MLB team, the one with the worst overall lifetime record is the NBA's Los Angeles Clippers. Including their previous incarnations as the Buffalo Braves (1970–78) and the San Diego Clippers (1978–84), there are only 3 seasons out of 40 in which they have won more games than they lost. The Clippers' all-time record: 1,146 wins and 2,020 losses, for a won-lost percentage of .362. No other pro team even dips below .400.

*   *   *

Luck never gives; it only lends.
—Swedish proverb

MUSHROOM READER

The study of mushrooms is called mycology. *Here's more mushy trivia.*

• Mushrooms reproduce by launching microscopic "spores"—airborne seedlike structures—into the air. There are probably 10,000 spores in the air around you right now, many of which will land in wet dirt and grow into mushrooms.

• Mushrooms eat by extending tiny tubes called *hyphae* into their food (like dead wood). This injects an acid into the food that dissolves it into a soup, which then travels back up the hyphae to the mushroom.

• 90% of mushrooms purchased in the U.S. are white, or "button," mushrooms.

• Mushroom Capital of the World: Kennett Square, Pennsylvania. Farms and businesses in and around the town produce half of all American mushrooms.

• September is National Mushroom Month.

• Every year about 40 people in the United States die from eating wild mushrooms they didn't think were poisonous.

• MSG, the flavor-enhancing chemical often added to Chinese food, is a synthetic form of glutamic acid, found naturally in mushrooms.

• Of the 10,000 known species of mushrooms, only 250 are edible.

• Wild mushrooms were eaten in ancient Egypt and ancient Rome, but mushrooms weren't cultivated until the 1600s, in France. Mushrooms weren't cultivated in the United States until around 1890.

• Most expensive mushroom: truffles—they cost hundreds of dollars per pound. A fungus of oak and hazel trees, they grow only underground. Truffle hunters have to use trained pigs or dogs, usually Dachshunds, to sniff them out. Pigs, however, tend to eat the truffles when they find them.

• Murder by mushroom: Czar Alexander I of Russia, King Charles V of France, and Pope Clement VII were all killed when they ate poison mushrooms.

YOU CALL THAT ART?

If dogs can play poker, then why can't trees paint pictures?

ARTIST: Michael Fernandes

THIS IS ART? Fernandes placed a banana on the windowsill of an art gallery in Halifax, Nova Scotia, and titled it *Banana*. Each night during July 2008, Fernandes replaced the banana with a slightly greener one to represent the "reversing of the aging process." Two collectors put holds on the work. "You do realize it's a banana, don't you?" gallery owner Victoria Page asked them. Instead of actual fruit, however, the winning bidder received photographs of the bananas. Price: $2,500.

ARTIST'S STATEMENT: "Like bananas, we humans are also temporal, but we live as if we are not."

ARTIST: Tim Knowles

THIS IS ART? Although Knowles props up the canvas and attaches the pens to the tips of the branches, it's the willow trees that do the work…and the oaks, sycamores, and so on. Guided by the wind, the trees paint delicate patterns that, to the unsophisticated eye, look like random scribbles on a canvas. The British artist has sold his works for thousands of dollars in galleries all over the world.

ARTIST'S STATEMENT: "The work attempts to make visible the invisible."

ARTIST: Paul McCarthy

THIS IS ART? McCarthy is a 63-year-old American artist who gained fame in the 1960s for using his body as a paint brush and then using some of his bodily fluids as paint. His latest piece of "shocking" art is a house-sized balloon shaped like a giant pile of dog doo. (The work made headlines in 2008 when it came loose from its moorings outside of a Swiss art museum and flew 200 yards before landing on the grounds of a children's home, where it broke a window.)

ARTIST'S STATEMENT: "To put an unrefined, clumsy-appearing object into art is a political act."

ARTIST: Tracey Emin

THIS IS ART? Emin created shockwaves with her controversial piece *My Bed* when it was displayed at London's Tate Gallery in 1999. It was just that—her messy bed, with crumpled bed sheets and dirty clothes on the floor next to it. But what shocked the public the most was her inclusion of used condoms and women's underwear. Although the installation was described as "crass" and "vulgar," Emin was nominated for the prestigious Turner Prize. She didn't win, but her dirty bed sold for £150,000 ($211,000).

ARTIST'S STATEMENT: "When I got the phrase 'media whore' thrown in my face, I thought, oh my god, if you only knew."

ARTIST: Aelita Andre

THIS IS ART? This artist's abstract paintings were very well received at the Brunswick Street Gallery in Melbourne, Australia, in 2009. Renowned art critic Robert Nelson described them as "heavily reliant on figure/ground relations." They were priced between $250 and $1,400. It was later revealed, however, that Aelita was only 22 months old when she painted them. The doodles were submitted by her mother, Russian photographer Nikka Kalashnikova, who kept the artist's age to herself until after the work was approved.

ARTIST'S STATEMENT: "Baba! Mama! (spittle)."

ARTIST: Deborah Grumet

THIS IS ART? Titled *Studies in Digestion*, Grumet's 18" x 24" colored-pencil drawing is separated into four quadrants, each depicting the human digestive system in the style of a famous artist: Keith Haring's graffiti, Georges Seurat's pointillism, René Magritte's surrealism, and Pablo Picasso's single-line drawings. Grumet couldn't get a gallery to display the work (it was actually rejected by the Museum of Bad Art in Dedham, Massachusetts, as "too commercial"), so she auctioned it online, offering the proceeds to the struggling art museum at Brandeis University. No bidders chose the "Buy It Now" option for $10,000, but the gutsy painting did sell...for $152.53.

ARTIST'S STATEMENT: "If you scroll way, way, down towards the bottom of the Wikipedia article about the Museum of Bad Art, you will see that my *Studies in Digestion* drawing is mentioned. This could be my proudest moment ever!" (Until she finds out that she made it into an *Uncle John's Bathroom Reader*.)

A wig worn by artist Andy Warhol (with tape still inside it) sold at auction for $10,800.

ODD BOOKS

We like to include a wide variety of topics in our Bathroom Readers.
Here are some real books that have a much more limited focus.

Baboon Metaphysics

Curbside Consultation
of the Colon

The Large Sieve
and Its Applications

Strip and Knit with Style

Bombproof Your Horse

How to Write a
How-to-Write Book

Camping Among Cannibals

The Care of Rawhide
Drop Box Loom Pickers

Octogenarian Teetotalers

Practical Candle Burning

Jaws and Teeth of
Ancient Hawaiians

Short-term Visual
Information Forgetting

Who's Who in Barbed Wire

How to Save a Big Ship From
Sinking, Even Though Torpedoed

What to Say When You
Talk to Yourself

The Romance of Rayon

Selected Themes and
Icons from Spanish
Literature: Of Beards, Shoes,
Cucumbers, and Leprosy

The Toothbrush: Its Use
and Abuse

A Do-It-Yourself
Submachine Gun

Correct Mispronunciations of
Some South Carolina Names

Defensive Tactics with
Flashlights

How to Write While You Sleep

Fancy Coffins to Make Yourself

The Encyclopedia of Suicide

Yoga for Cats

The Fun and Exciting
World of Roots

Extraordinary Chickens

A chipmunk can store about a teaspoon's worth of nuts in each cheek.

A TURKEY IN BOSTON

With more tame people and more wild animals living next door to each other (page 481), some bizarre encounters are bound to occur.

AN ALLIGATOR IN THE GARAGE

Anna Labita was standing in the kitchen of her Pinellas Park, Florida, home in 2009 when she heard a noise coming from her garage. She slowly opened the door, and there, only a few feet away, was an 8-foot-long alligator leaning up against the wall. It was staring right at her—at eye level. Labita slowly *closed* the door and called 911. A reptile control officer came out (they get a lot of work during the spring mating season) and taped the hungry gator's mouth shut before hauling it off.

A BEAR IN THE MEDIAN

Several drivers traveling Interstate 5 just south of Stanwood, Washington, in 2008 reported seeing a 250-pound black bear that seemed to be living in a small stand of trees between four lanes of 65-mph traffic. Officials were worried: Either a driver would slow down to gawk at the bear and cause an accident, or worse yet, the bear would try to cross the road and cause an accident. When game wardens realized that the bear had been living in the median for almost a year, they knew there was little chance he'd leave on his own. So they baited a trap with pickled herring, bacon grease, honey, and doughnuts. It worked…and the bear was introduced into a new habitat in the foothills of the Cascade mountain range.

A TURKEY IN BOSTON

In 2007 a wild turkey chased Kettly Jean-Felix down a sidewalk, across Beacon Street, and into an optometrist's office—pecking at her bottom the whole way. "It was so scary!" she said. It turns out this turkey wasn't alone. Boston police had been receiving *hundreds* of calls from people who were harassed by the ornery birds. Interestingly, wild turkeys flourished in eastern Massachusetts until the 1850s. But by the 20th century, overhunting had driven them nearly to extinction. Efforts to revitalize the population in rural areas began in the 1970s and were extremely successful. One

---

U.S. president who vetoed the most bills: Franklin Roosevelt (635). Least: George W. Bush (12).

thing that officials never anticipated, though, was that thousands of the birds would end up invading the cities and suburbs.

A BIRD ON THE HEAD
In June 2008, Chicago resident Holly Grosso was walking down the sidewalk on West Grand Avenue talking on her mobile phone when, "Something just came down, pecked me in the head, pulled out my hair, and then flew away. It was so bizarre. It was a little bird." That little bird was actually a red-winged blackbird, and during nesting season, they're very territorial, having been known to take on much larger vultures and ospreys. Grosso's attacker pursued many victims that summer, earning it the nickname "Hitchcock" (after the man who directed the 1963 horror film *The Birds*).

A BOAR IN THE BACKYARD
When Cassandra Frank of St. Petersburg, Florida, awoke on a spring morning in 2009, she heard strange noises coming from her backyard. Still groggy, she went to investigate. All of a sudden, she saw a black, 200-pound sow charging her. It happened so fast that Frank had no chance of getting out of the way. The animal pierced her left leg with one tusk and pinned her up against a tree, squealing the entire time (the pig, not Frank). Then the sow ran off and terrorized a few other people in the neighborhood. It took nine men from animal control to capture it. Frank was fortunate— she escaped with minor injuries and only had to get a tetanus shot. Officials aren't sure how such a big wild pig—normally found in the forests—made it so far into the suburbs.

A FISH IN THE WIRES
At 7:10 a.m. on April 29, 2009, employees at a Salem, Oregon, aerospace manufacturing plant suddenly heard a loud POP! Then all of the lights and all of the machines shut down. Upon investigating the outage, one of the workers found the culprit: a large fish, burned to a crisp, lying on the ground beneath some nearby power lines. The electric company concluded that the fish was accidentally dropped onto the line by an osprey (they nest in the area). "This is the first instance we've heard of a fish causing a power outage," said Bob Valdez of the Oregon Public Utility Commission, adding, "Cooked squirrel is pretty common, though."

IT'S PHOSPHORIFIC!

In the days when smoking was a bigger part of American culture, matches were everywhere. Hotels and restaurants gave matchbooks away; people carried them in their pockets and purses. Well, you'll never believe where the stuff in the match head came from.

MELLOW YELLOW

Ever heard of *alchemy*? It was a medieval "science" and philosophy, and one of its goals was to find a way to turn base metals into gold through a process called *transmutation*. Scientists now know that this is impossible, but in the 1600s, it was a viable—and potentially lucrative—form of research.

An alchemist from Hamburg, Germany, named Hennig Brand believed the way to create gold was by chemically altering a very common substance: urine. At the time, it made sense. A prevailing theory of the day was that because urine and gold were both yellow, some advanced form of alchemy might be able to turn one into the other.

With this in mind, Brand spent months collecting urine. When he'd accumulated 50 buckets of the stuff—mostly donated by local soldiers—he went to the second phase of his plan: He put them in his basement to "age," or allow the water to evaporate out and concentrate the urine.

BLUE GENIE

One day in 1669, Brand was experimenting with his bucketloads of concentrated soldier pee and came up with something interesting. Scientists later figured out that this is what he did: First, he boiled the urine until it was what chefs call a "reduction"—a thick, condensed syrup with most of the water evaporated out of it. The bright yellow reduction was then heated until it coalesced into three separate substances (which we now know were mostly made up of *phosphates*): a reddish oil, a porous black material, and a salty residue.

Brand discarded the salt, then mixed the red oil back into the spongy black stuff, which he then heated for the better part of a day, probably about 16 hours. At this point, the mixture started breaking down into the various chemicals of which it was com-

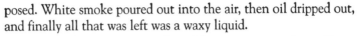

posed. White smoke poured out into the air, then oil dripped out, and finally all that was left was a waxy liquid.

Brand had never seen anything like it—it was a vibrant blue-green and appeared to glow, both in the light and in the dark. Brand tested the ominous goo by placing it in a jar of cold water. Not only did the substance hold together, it hardened and cooled and became icy to the touch. Although Brand had absolutely no idea what he'd just discovered (or created), he knew he was on to something. But after six years of experimenting on the greenish stuff (and hundreds more buckets of urine), he still hadn't struck gold. He hadn't even figured out how to make a second batch.

KRAFT'S WORK

Another German alchemist, Daniel Kraft, had heard about the results of Brand's experiments, and in 1675 he went to Hamburg to either buy a load of the blue-green extract or at least learn how to make it. Brand was desperate for money (six years of fruitless experimentation while living off his wife's inheritance had left him nearly broke), so he decided to sell what remained of the blue goo to Kraft...since he didn't know how to re-create it.

It didn't matter, because Kraft wasn't concerned with the science behind the substance, or even with the potential of turning it into gold—he wanted to use it to make money *now*. How'd he do it? He travelled around and made a fortune showing it off to royalty and other wealthy Europeans. Kraft's act was basically magic tricks: He'd light candles with the stuff, throw it into gunpowder to make explosions, and write glowing blue-green words with it. He'd pass it around the room to show that it was cold to the touch. And Kraft always told audiences that he'd discovered the substance himself.

FINALLY...

It wouldn't be until 100 years later that the blue-green substance that Brand had discovered would be named: phosphorus. Thanks to Brand's experiments, it was the first element to be synthesized in pure form and one of the first to be identified as a chemical element. Today, phosphorus is abundant in manufacturing, commonly used in products such as soda, fertilizer, matches, flares, and fireworks. (And they don't have to get it from urine.)

GOVERN-MENTAL

Elected officials often do the strangest things.

LOOK BEFORE YOU LEAP

In 2009 Arizona State Senator Linda Gray (R-Phoenix) received an error-ridden e-mail from a ninth-grader complaining about the lack of state funds for education. The Senator's response was harsh: "Why didn't you take to (sic) time to write an e-mail with the proper punctuation? Your example tells me that all the money we have spent on your education shows a lack of learning on your part." Only after the letter found its way into the press did Gray find out that the student had special needs. "I wrote harsh words to her," admitted the Senator, who apologized profusely. "I don't know what got into me."

STOP—IN THE NAME OF THE LAW

For years, residents of the Chicago suburb of Oak Lawn have been complaining that motorists don't come to a complete stop at stop signs. So in 2007 mayor Dave Heilmann came up with a creative solution: He added a second, smaller octagonal sign below 50 of the town's stop signs so, for example, drivers would see:

STOP

and smell the roses

Other signs read "STOP right there, pilgrim," "STOP billion dollar fine," and "STOP in the naaaame of love." The Illinois Department of Transportation deemed the signs violations of the Federal Uniform Traffic Control Act, and threatened to withhold funds for road projects if the signs weren't removed. Heilmann complied, but complained, "I think government needs to take itself less seriously."

THE YOLK'S ON HIM

Jiří Paroubek, a Czech politician running for a seat in the European Union Parliament, was the victim of several egg attacks in 2009. At first, only a few were thrown at him. But at each subsequent event, more egg throwers showed up. Every time, Paroubek continued speaking even though his head was covered with shells

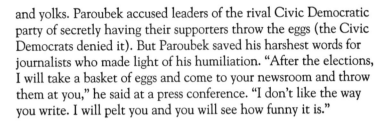

and yolks. Paroubek accused leaders of the rival Civic Democratic party of secretly having their supporters throw the eggs (the Civic Democrats denied it). But Paroubek saved his harshest words for journalists who made light of his humiliation. "After the elections, I will take a basket of eggs and come to your newsroom and throw them at you," he said at a press conference. "I don't like the way you write. I will pelt you and you will see how funny it is."

PELOSI-ROLL'D

In 2009 Speaker of the House Nancy Pelosi (D-CA) posted a short video on the new Congressional YouTube Channel. It began with her two cats running around her office at the U.S. Capitol. At the 37-second mark, Pelosi pulled a popular prank called "Rickrolling": The footage suddenly cut to singer Rick Astley's 1987 music video for "Never Gonna Give You Up." Many pundits derided the fact that the person second in line for the presidency was engaging in such "juvenile" behavior, but *Time* magazine wrote, "It reflects a relatively sophisticated understanding of how the modern Internet works for an elected public official."

SPACE WAR

A coveted parking space right next to the side entrance of City Hall in Oakland, California, opened up in 2008 when a councilman retired. Who would get the space? It was narrowed down to two councilwomen: Desley Brooks and Jean Quan. Their colleagues suggested they flip a coin. Quan agreed, but Brooks claimed seniority and demanded that Council President Jane Brunner make the decision. After deliberating, Brunner ruled that since both women started in 2002, both had equal seniority; they should just flip a coin. Brooks disagreed and ordered City Attorney John Russo to decide. Finally, after the dispute had gone on for three months (during which time the parking space went to whoever got there first), Russo issued a five-page written opinion, concluding that the women were equally entitled to the space. His solution: Flip a coin. (Brooks won.)

*   *   *

"Politicians are the same all over. They promise to build a bridge even where there is no river."
　　　　　　　　　　　　　　　　　　　—Nikita Khrushchev

Only 7% of homes in Afghanistan have a flush toilet. 19% have a television.

YOU MUST BE DREAMING

Uncle John had a dream about balloons, a coffin, and a laughing white rabbit at a picnic on a deserted island. What does it all mean? Here are some dream interpretations we found in a fortune-telling book from the 1920s. Read them, and all will be revealed.

Beggars: If you refused a beggar, your life will be miserable; if you gave freely to a beggar, you will have a long and happy life.

Coffins: You will soon marry and have a house of your own.

Gambling: If you won, a friend will die. If you lost, you will move to a new residence.

Falling snow: There will be obstacles in your path.

Umbrella: Good luck is near.

Watching a ball game: Money will soon come to you.

Sleeping dog: Relax—you have nothing to worry about.

Police officer: Beware of false friends!

Saving a drowning woman: You will marry someone famous.

Climbing a ladder: If you're climbing *up* the ladder, wealth is coming your way. If you're climbing *down*, you're headed for the poorhouse.

Killing a spider: Bad luck.

Warts: If it's summertime, you'll have good luck. If you dream of warts in the winter, you'll have bad luck.

You, hiding in the forest: You are in danger.

You, on a deserted island: A friend will turn against you.

Pigeons: Good news is coming your way.

Running, barking dog: Pay attention to your personal affairs; someone could be taking advantage of you.

The gallows: You will soon have an opportunity to make lots of money.

Balloons: Something you're planning for the future may seem likely to succeed, but like a balloon, it will burst into nothing.

Mirror: Someone will betray you.

Riding a train: You and your mate will soon separate.

Slow down! Under 37 mph, most bugs bounce off the windshield. Above that speed, they splatter.

A large building: You'll meet someone who will become an intimate acquaintance.

An angel approaching: Good news is coming your way. But if the angel is avoiding you, watch out! Your life is on the wrong track—change your ways before it's too late!

Laughter: You will soon be in tears.

Sweeping: If you're sweeping your own room, you'll have good luck in business. If you're sweeping out the cellar, you're headed for misfortune.

White rabbit: Success is in your future.

Black rabbit: Watch out! You'll soon have an accident.

Rabbit meat for dinner: You will have good health.

A storm: For a rich person, it's a sign that things will get worse. For a poor person, it's a sign that things will get better.

You, at a picnic: You will fall in love with a vain person and it will end badly.

Blood: The sight of blood means you will inherit an estate, provided that it's someone else's blood. If it's *your* blood, disappointment and sorrow will soon be upon you.

Eating a salad: Sickness is coming your way.

Jewels: If the jewels belong to you, you will lose something of value. Tempted to steal someone else's jewels? You're at risk of disgracing yourself.

A naked lady: A relative of yours will die soon.

Riding on the back of a lion: Someone powerful is protecting you.

Medicine: If you're taking medicine, you will soon know poverty. If you're dispensing the medicine, you will come into some money.

Thirst: Represents ambition. If you quench your thirst, your ambition will be realized.

A bell: Can you hear the bell ringing? Bad luck's in store for whom the bell tolls.

*　　*　　*

SUIT UP

The town of Dunedin, New Zealand, holds a "Nude Rugby Invitational" every two years. During a match in 2009, play was briefly interrupted when a fully clothed streaker ran out onto the field.

Until rubber erasers were invented, people often used bread crumbs to erase pencil marks.

TWUNGE TISTERS

Er, ting twusters. No, twing testers. Oh, you know what me wean.

I wish to wash my Irish wristwatch.

If Stu chews shoes, should Stu choose his shoes?

The soldiers shouldered shooters on their shoulders.

A skunk sat on a stump and thunk the stump stunk.

Plague-bearing prairie dogs.

Let's listen to the local yokel yodel.

Six sick hicks pick six slick bricks.

Betty bought some bitter butter and it made
her batter bitter, so Betty bought some better
butter to make her bitter batter better.

Sheena leads, Sheila needs.

Knapsack strap.

I'm not the fig plucker, nor the fig plucker's son,
but I'll pluck figs till the fig plucker comes.

Cows graze in groves on grass that grows in grooves.

She sits in her slip and sips Schlitz.

A black bug bled blue blood.

An anesthetist's nurse unearthed a nest.

No need to light a night-light on a light night like tonight.

The quick-witted cricket critic cried quietly.

THE INVENTIONS OF PROFESSOR LUCIFER GORGONZOLA BUTTS

Who? That's the name cartoonist Rube Goldberg gave to a character who came up with crazy contraptions that took simple jobs (like fishing an olive out of a jar) and made them as complicated as possible.

A MAN CALLED RUBE

From 1907 to 1964, Rube Goldberg regularly drew cartoons and comic strips for newspapers. He'd started out with an engineering degree from the University of California, but his first job—designing sewer systems for the city of San Francisco—depressed him so much that he quit after a few months. Drawing was what he really loved, but in 1904, where could he make a living by drawing? At a newspaper, doing cartoons. It took Goldberg a couple of years to establish himself as a cartoonist in San Francisco, and then he moved to New York and hit his stride, drawing daily and Sunday strips for several newspapers. By 1915 his work went into syndication and became nationally known.

THE GOLDBERG VARIATIONS

His most famous comic strips were *Mike and Ike (They Look Alike)*, *Boob McNutt*, and *Lala Palooza*, but his most enduring creations are the outlandish machines invented by a character called Professor Lucifer Gorgonzola Butts. These cartoon machines did everything from lighting a cigar (Goldberg was a cigar smoker) to putting toothpaste on a toothbrush, and each machine accomplished its task by means of an absurd chain reaction. Goldberg used wheels, pulleys, springs, pipes, weights, bells, household items, and usually an animal or two to "build" the machines, although he never actually built a single one of them. The machines were so complicated and distinctive that the phrase "Rube Goldberg device" entered the American vocabulary: If you call something a "Rube Goldberg," you're talking about a contraption that is weird-looking, made up of unlikely components, precariously constructed, and guaranteed to turn a simple task into a needlessly and hopelessly complicated one. Here are a few examples:

THE "AUTOMATIC" BACK-SCRATCHER

1. The sequence starts with a small kerosene lamp placed beside a curtained window.

2. The flame from the lamp catches on the window curtain.

3. The fire department sends a stream of water through the window to douse the flame.

4. The stream of water lands on the head of a bearded man.

5. The bearded man thinks it's raining and reaches for an umbrella, which is attached to a string looped over a pair of pulleys.

6. When the bearded man grabs the umbrella, the string lifts the end of a small platform.

7. An iron ball on the end of the platform rolls off, pulling another string, which is attached to a hammer.

8. The hammer hits a glass plate.

9. The sound of breaking glass wakes a puppy sleeping in a cradle that has a back-scratcher attached to one of its rockers.

10. As the puppy's mother rocks the cradle to quiet the puppy, the back-scratcher moves up and down against a man's back.

GETTING AN OLIVE OUT OF A BOTTLE

1. The sequence starts with a clock attached high on a wall with a cylindrical weight hanging from it.

2. At 6:30, as the clock's hands are both pointing down, the weight drops onto the head of a man sitting in a chair, smoking a cigar.

3. The man yells in pain and the cigar drops from his mouth.

4. The cigar falls onto a pile of paper, setting it on fire.

5. The heat from the fire enrages the man's wife, who's sitting in a chair suspended above the pile of paper.

6. The angry wife sharpens a knife on a grindstone, which sits on a small platform before her.

7. The grindstone is attached to a wheel. When the grindstone turns, the wheel also starts to turn.

8. A handle on the wheel has a string tied to it, and the string is looped over a pulley. The other end of the string is tied to a spoon, which dangles at the mouth of a tall jar of olives. When the wheel turns, the spoon descends into the jar and fishes out an olive.

9. If the spoon can't grab an olive, 15 minutes later another clock (on the floor) automatically runs a glass cutter against the jar and breaks out a piece of glass large enough to accommodate a finger.

SHARPENING A PENCIL

1. The sequence starts at a window. A pulley is attached to the windowsill; the string of a kite is looped around the pulley.

2. The window is opened and the kite flies outside.

3. When the kite is aloft, the string—which runs under one pulley and over two pulleys attached to the ceiling—becomes taut and raises a small door in a cage sitting on top of a pole.

4. Moths escape from the cage and eat a flannel shirt hanging from the end of another string looped over another pair of pulleys.

5. As the shirt gets lighter (from being eaten), a shoe that's dangling from the other end of that string drops and steps on a switch.

6. The switch turns on an electric iron that's resting flat on a pair of pants on an ironing board. The iron burns a hole in the pants.

7. The smoke from the pants funnels through a tube into the trunk of a hollow tree and smokes out an opossum living in the tree.

8. The opossum jumps out of the tree into a basket hanging from one of the branches. A string attached to the basket is looped over the branch and tied to the top of a birdcage.

9. When the opossum lands in the basket, the string lifts the cover of the birdcage and a woodpecker inside the cage leans forward and chews the end of a pencil attached to short clamp. The pencil is sharpened. (If the opossum or the woodpecker gets sick and can't do his job, there's an emergency penknife nearby.)

*   *   *

GOLDBERG VARIATIONS

Purdue University holds an annual Rube Goldberg Machine Contest where teams of college students build Rube Goldberg-style contraptions no larger than 5' high, 6' wide, and 6' deep. The devices must complete simple tasks like replacing a light bulb, making a hamburger, or screwing a lid on a jar in 20 or more separate steps.

Only English word with three consecutive sets of double letters: Bookkeeper.

UNHEARD ALBUMS

These albums were announced, promised, started, and at least partially—if not completely—finished. And while some have been leaked or bootlegged, for whatever reason, they've never officially been released to the public.

MC HAMMER, TOO TIGHT

MC Hammer presented rap music in a way that made it accessible to mainstream pop audiences with hits like "U Can't Touch This" and "2 Legit 2 Quit." But just five years later, rap had evolved into hard-edged, profanity- and violence-laden "gangsta rap." Result: MC Hammer, with his smiling face, Saturday morning cartoon show, and shiny parachute pants, was passé. So he decided to make a gangsta rap album. In 1995 he signed with Death Row Records—the biggest rap label of the day and home to 2Pac, Dr. Dre, and Snoop Dogg—and recorded *Too Tight*, with contributions from Death Row staff writers and a cameo from 2Pac. When 2Pac was murdered in 1996 (possibly by people connected to a rival rap label), MC Hammer realized that his new label was a dangerous place to be. He left Death Row and shortly after filed for bankruptcy. He became a minister, which inspired a series of reflective, spiritually based albums. Death Row has since gone out of business, and gangsta rap itself is now becoming passé, so *Too Tight* will probably never see the light of day.

PRINCE & THE REVOLUTION, *DREAM FACTORY*

Prince is well known for being a prolific songwriter and recording artist who supposedly has a vault full of thousands of unreleased songs. *Dream Factory* was a planned project that was completed but never released. On breaks from his 1985 Hit & Run Tour, Prince popped into recording studios around the world to record the *Dream Factory* tracks, which included an instrumental piano piece, a 10-minute hard-rocking anti-war song, a song built around train sound effects, and a 1930s-style jazz number (Prince even sang it through a megaphone). It was the most avant-garde album Prince had recorded to that point. By June 1986, he had a polished 18-track double LP, containing some songs recorded with his band, the Revolution, and others recorded solo. But in October, the temperamental star suddenly fired the Revolution and removed the band members' contributions from *Dream Factory*. Combining his solo tracks with songs from a half-finished project called *Camille*, in which he sang like a woman with the aid of voice software, Prince assembled an even longer *triple* album called *Crystal Ball*. Prince's label, Warner Bros., balked at an experimental triple LP and refused to release it. So, he dropped a third of the songs and called it *Sign 'O' the Times*, a double album that went on to critical and commercial success.

NEIL YOUNG, *HOMEGROWN*

In 1973, Young recorded *Tonight's the Night*, a sad, mournful album recorded in reaction to the drug-overdose deaths of two friends. His label, RCA, refused to release it, claiming it was "uncommercial." Young made and released *On the Beach* instead before delving into another dark, highly personal album called *Homegrown*, about the breakup of his relationship with actress Carrie Snodgress. He then held a listening party for *Homegrown* and found a copy of *Tonight's the Night* on the same reel. Young's guests were ambivalent about *Homegrown* but loved *Tonight's the Night*. Young agreed. (Apparently the album about drug overdoses was less depressing than the one about the end of the love affair.) So, he convinced RCA to shelve *Homegrown*—even though a cover had already been designed and printed—and release *Tonight's the Night* instead. Many of the songs on *Homegrown* turned up on later Young albums, but the album in whole form remains locked away.

BEASTIE BOYS, *WHITE HOUSE*

For rabid fans of the rap/rock group, this shelved dance-music album is their most coveted and controversial recording. In 1988 the Beastie Boys left their longtime label Def Jam Records for Capitol Records, where they recorded the hit album *Paul's Boutique*. Def Jam president Russell Simmons was furious at the band for jumping ship. So he hired Public Enemy rapper/producer Chuck D to craft a new Beastie Boys album to compete with *Paul's Boutique*...without the Beastie Boys. Simmons gave Chuck D unused vocal outtakes from old Beastie Boys sessions with instructions to set them to dance beats. When Chuck D found out that *White House* was being done against the band's wishes, he backed out, and the nearly completed project was abandoned.

When playing *Monopoly*, John Lennon always stood up to roll the dice.

CRUNCHY LOGGS

*Breakfast cereals are as much a part of pop culture as
movies, video games, or TV. And like those products,
the cereal industry has had its share of bizarre ideas.*

GREEN SLIME. In the 1980s, Nickelodeon aired a show
called *You Can't Do That on Television* in which cast members got "slimed"—dumped with buckets of green slime.
Cashing in on the fad, General Mills came out with Green Slime
Cereal, chunky, green-colored "slime-shaped" cornmeal puffs
(almost as bad as slime) that consisted of a whopping 47% sugar.

EAT MY SHORTS. What's less appetizing than green slime?
Used underwear. Based on the catchphrase made famous by Bart
Simpson, with this underwear-shaped cereal, produced in 2003,
you could literally eat Bart's (sugar and cornmeal) shorts.

OJ's. Orange and milk flavors go together nicely in a Creamsicle,
but evidently not in a breakfast cereal. Orange-flavored OJ's were
released in 1984 and gone by the end of the year.

ADDAMS FAMILY CEREAL. Ralston-Purina released this as
a tie-in for the *Addams Family* movie in 1991. Ads called it "the
weird part of a complete breakfast," and it was: The cereal and
marshmallow bits were shaped like skulls and severed hands.

CRUNCHY LOGGS. Possibly the most aptly named—and least
appetizing—breakfast food ever produced. The 1978 cereal was
little brown "logs" made out of corn and oats. And they were
crunchy. (Although little brown "logs" makes Uncle John think
of something besides cereal.)

BIGG MIXX. It seems as if Kellogg's took whatever Corn Flakes,
Raisin Bran, Rice Krispies, and other cereals were left at the end
of the day, mixed them up, and threw them in a single box. The
advertising character concocted to match the cereal was "Bigg
Mixx," a weird, mutated combination of a chicken, a wolf, a
moose, and a pig. The cereal was released with a huge advertising
campaign in 1990…and quickly disappeared into obscurity.

USED COWS FOR SALE

Actual signs from roadsides, stores, and restaurants.

STOP
No Stopping Anytime

**Slow Children
No Hunting**

*LODGING NEXT EXIT
STATE PRISON*

NO SOCCER—May Only Be
Played On Archery Range

MIDNIGHT BOWLING
SATURDAY AT 9 P.M.

Village of Crestwood
ENGLISH IS OUR
LANGUAGE
NO EXECTIONS
LEARN IT

**POO PING
Chinese and Thai Cuisine**

HO-MADE SOUPS

Anyone Caught Collecting
Golf Balls Will Have
Their Balls Removed

**PUSH BUTTON TO OPEN
AUTOMATIC DOOR**

*Accidents Are Prohibited
On This Road*

Seafood brought in by
customers will not
be entertained.

0% Off Select Items

USED COWS FOR SALE

4th Anal Chili Cook-off

Cruise Ships Use Airport Exit

**Do Not Molest
Trees and Shrubs**

Evacuation Instructions:
Alternate exit to the left
then right then left then
right then left to exit

TOILET Please Stay In Car

WATCH YOUR HEAD
Clearance 8'6"

**Ladie Faints At
Unbelievable Prices!**

Diesel Fried Chicken

TOUCHING WIRES
CAUSES INSTANT DEATH
$200 fine

Please do not sit on crocodile

The average baby cries at 90 decibels...only 15 decibels less than a power mower.

Q&A: ASK THE EXPERTS

Everyone's got a question they'd like answered, like, "Why is the sky blue?" Here are a few of those questions, with answers provided by the nation's leading trivia experts.

WRONG TURN AT ALBUQUERQUE?

Q: *When flying south for the winter, how do birds know which way to go?*

A: "They can check the stars. Scientists say that birds probably use constellations like the Big Dipper to determine directions like north and south, just as we humans do. Since most birds migrate mainly at night, they have learned to be very good astronomers. Of course, some nights are cloudy. What's a traveling bird to do? The Earth is a giant magnet, with magnetic field lines looping out from near the North and South Poles. Birds can sense or even see this force field, and make sure they are travelling in the right direction." (From *How Come? Planet Earth*, by Kathy Wollard.)

FOR LOVE OF THE GAME

Q: *Why is tennis scored so strangely? Why "Love"-15-30-40-win instead 0-1-2-3-4?*

A: "Tennis scoring has its origin in medieval numerology. The number 60 was considered to be a 'good' or 'complete' number back then, in about the same way 100 is today. The medieval version of tennis, therefore, was based on 60—the four points were 15, 30, 45 (which we abbreviate to 40) and 60, or game. The equally puzzling 'love' comes from the idea of playing for love rather than money—the implication being that one who scores zero consistently can only be motivated by a true love for the game." (From *The Straight Dope*, by Cecil Adams)

THE YELLOW RIVER GOT ITS NAME FROM I.P. FREELY

Q: *How did the Yellow, Black, and Red Seas get their names?*

A: "Whenever floods occur, yellow mud is carried into the sea, giving it a yellow color. That is how the Yellow Sea got its name. The Black Sea has no outlet, and because it is entirely landlocked, its deficiency in oxygen at a depth of 200 meters gives it a high concentration of hydrogen sulfide. This comes from the decomposed bacteria that drift down from above, resulting in a black color. The Red Sea got its name because there is an ever-recurring bloom of small algae that gives the sea its permanent look of red." (From *How Does a Bee Make Honey? And Other Curious Facts*, by Martin M. Goldwyn)

HAIR IT IS

Q: *Why do fabrics, paper, and hair appear darker when they get wet?*
A: "Porous objects become darker when they are wet because the many tiny reflecting surfaces that cover their surface become filled in by the water and cease to reflect specular light back to the observer. This makes the object appear darker." (From *The Last Word 2*, edited by Mick O'Hare)

HAIR IT ISN'T

Q: *What makes men go bald?*
A: "Testosterone comes into contact with an enzyme found in the hair follicles. The testosterone is converted to *dihydrotestosterone* (DHT), a more potent androgen that has the ability to bind to receptors in follicles. This binding, in turn, can trigger a change in the genetic activity of the cells, which initiates the gradual process of hair loss. Some people inherit a tendency for certain hair follicles, in the presence of DHT, to become progressively smaller over time. This causes the growing cycle of the follicle to shorten, more hairs to be shed, and the existing hair to become thinner and thinner." (From *How It Happens*, by Barbara Ann Kipfer)

CHECK IT OUT

Q: *Why do stores often refuse out-of-state checks?*
A: "The discrimination against out-of-state checks probably stems from Regulation CC, a federal law which determines how long banks can hold funds from checks. A bank is allowed to retain money longer for out-of-state checks than for local ones. So if you are a merchant in Sarasota, Florida, who receives a check from Urbandale, Iowa, your bank is entitled to withhold the funds for days longer, a killer to cash flow for the retailer." (From *What Are Hyenas Laughing At, Anyway?*, by David Feldman)

IT'S A WEIRD, WEIRD WORLD

Proof that truth really is stranger than fiction.

WON'T GIVE YOU THE TIME OF DAY

Yvan Arpa, CEO of the Swiss wristwatch company Romain Jerome, claims that two-thirds of wealthy people don't even use their watches for the intended purpose. "Anyone can buy a watch that tells time," Arpa explains, "but it takes a truly discerning customer to buy one that doesn't." That's the strange idea behind the company's "Day & Night" watch. It's intended to be more a status symbol than a time piece, because it doesn't give the wearer the hour or even the minute—only whether it is currently daytime or nighttime. Cost: $300,000.

WITH FRIENDS LIKE THESE...

In 2008 a health spa in Zneleznovodsk, Russia, dedicated a statue to an important member of its team: the enema. "We administer enemas nearly every day," said spa administrator Alexander Kharchenko. "So I thought, why not give it a monument?" They commissioned local artist Svetlana Avakina to create the work. She drew inspiration from 15th-century Renaissance painter Sandro Botticelli's *Venus and Mars*, which depicts three cherubs stealing a sword from the God of War. Avakina replaced the sword with an enema syringe. The bronze statue stands 5' tall and cost $42,000. "An enema is an unpleasant procedure, as many of us may know," said Avakina. "But when cherubs do it, it's all right."

AT LEAST HE CAN'T COMPLAIN ABOUT THE NOISE

A Japanese man (name not released to the press) who lives alone noticed that little bits of food kept disappearing from his refrigerator. So he installed a security camera in his kitchen and set it up so he could watch from his mobile phone. The next day, while he was away, he saw the culprit: an old woman. He called the police and met them at his house, where they discovered that all the doors and windows were locked from the inside. She was still in there. After an intensive search, they finally found her hiding on the upper shelf of a closet. When questioned, the 58-year-old homeless woman told them that she'd snuck into the house through an unlocked door a year ago, and had been secretly living there ever since. How'd she go undetected? By being very quiet and only leaving the closet to eat, use the bathroom, and take showers. She hadn't left his house even once.

GET YOUR GOAT

In a bid to help struggling New Zealand farmers—in the midst of both a recession and a drought—in 2009 Mitsubishi Motors announced a new promotion: Anyone who purchased a Triton pickup truck would receive a free goat. "Like our Tritons, goats are hardy, versatile units which will integrate directly into existing farm operations," said company spokesman Peter Wilkins. (If the purchaser didn't want the goat, they were offered a five-year warranty instead.)

END OF THE ROAD

In 2009 the residents of a neighborhood in Conisbrough, England, lobbied the town council to have the name of their street changed, even though it had gone by that name for centuries. The neighbors were tired of tourists stopping to take pictures of the street sign. "We've even had people flashing their bottoms for photographs," said Paul Allot. On top of that, residents weren't getting some of their mail because delivery drivers didn't believe it was a real road. The council agreed and changed the street to Archer Way. However, an Internet petition has since sprung up in an effort to change it back to its original name, which comes from an old English term for a communal rain barrel—"water butt." What was the name of the street? Butt Hole Road.

*   *   *

MULTITASKING

According to an American Standard poll, the most popular extracurricular activities performed in the john in three major U.S. cities are: reading magazines or the mail (Boston), listening to the radio (Atlanta), and talking on the phone (Miami).

THE GREAT RACE, PART II

Reality TV show? No, reality—in 1908. (Part I starts on page 44.)

GENTLEMEN, RESTART YOUR ENGINES
Once they docked in Japan, the remaining competitors had to get their cars to the port of Vladivostok, Russia, where the race would officially resume. The Germans and Italians took another ship; the Americans and the French drove across Japan and took a ferry. It was too much for the De Dion-Bouton. After 7,332 miles, the French team threw in the towel, and only three cars were left: the German Protos, the Italian Zust, and the American Thomas Flyer. After another rousing send-off from a roaring crowd of spectators, the cars zoomed out of Vladivostok…and into the mud. The spring thaw had turned the Siberian tundra into a quagmire.

Only a few miles out of Vladivostok, the American team came upon the German Protos stuck in deep mud. George Schuster carefully nudged his car past the Germans onto firmer ground a few hundred yards ahead. With him were mechanic George Miller, assistant Hans Hansen, and *New York Times* reporter George Macadam. When Hansen suggested they help the Germans out, the others agreed. The stunned Germans were so grateful that their driver, Lt. Hans Koeppen, uncorked a bottle of champagne he'd been saving for the victory celebration in Paris, declaring the American gesture "a gallant and comradely act." The two teams raised a glass together, reporter Macadam recorded the moment for his paper, and the subsequent photograph appeared in papers around the globe and became the most enduring image of the race.

HUMAN OBSTACLES

Road conditions in Siberia were even worse than they'd been in the western United States. Once again the cars took to the rails—this time on the tracks of the Trans-Siberian Railway. An attempt by Schuster to use a railroad tunnel could have been a scene from a silent-movie comedy, as the American car frantically backed out of the tunnel ahead of an oncoming train. There were other obstacles, too. At one point the American team was charged by a band

The see-no-evil, hear-no-evil, and speak-no-evil monkeys have names: Mizaru, Mikazaru, Mazaru.

of horsemen brandishing rifles. The Americans burst into laughter and drove right through the herd of riders, leaving the bandits in the dust.

Driving around the clock created other problems: The relief driver often fell out of the open car while sleeping, so the team fashioned a buckle and strap to hold him in—the world's first seat belt. The length and rigor of the race took its toll as well, and tempers flared. At one point an exasperated Schuster threatened to throw Hansen out of the car and off the team. Hansen responded by pulling his pistol and snarling, "Do that and I will put a bullet in you." Mechanic George Miller drew *his* gun and snapped, "If any shooting is done, you will not be the only one." Finally both sides agreed to holster their weapons and press on.

ITALIAN TRAGEDY

By May the cars had been racing around the world for four months. The quicker German Protos had pulled ahead of the American Thomas Flyer, while the underpowered Italian Zust fell farther and farther behind but pressed on, convinced that they'd catch up. Then disaster struck. Outside Tauroggen, a Russian frontier town, a horse drawing a cart was startled by the sound of the passing Zust and bolted out of control. A child playing near the road was trampled and killed. The Italians drove into Tauroggen to report the accident and were promptly thrown in jail, where they remained for three days, unable to communicate with anyone outside. Finally, the local police determined the driver of the cart was at fault for losing control of his horse, and released them. They continued on toward Paris in a somber mood.

AND THE WINNER IS...

On July 30, 1908—169 days after the race's start—the Thomas Flyer arrived on the outskirts of Paris, smelling victory. The Protos had actually gotten to Paris four days earlier, but because of the Americans' 15-day bonus and the Germans' 15-day penalty, everyone knew the American team had an insurmountable margin of victory. Or did they? Before the Americans could enter the city, a *gendarme* stopped them. French law required automobiles to have two working headlights. The Flyer had only one; the other had been broken back in Russia (by a bird). A crowd gathered.

Q: What's the shortest English word to contain the letters A, B, C, D, E and F? A: Feedback.

Parisians, like thousands of others around the world, had been following the progress of the Great Race for months in the papers. They were anxious to welcome the victors at the finish line on the Champs-Elysées.

Schuster's crew pleaded with the gendarme, but he wouldn't budge. No headlight, no entry. A frustrated Schuster was about to set off an international incident by attacking the gendarme when a bicyclist offered the Americans the headlamp from his bike. Mechanic Miller tried to unbolt the light but couldn't pry it off. The solution: They lifted the bike onto the hood of the car and held it in place by hand. The gendarme shrugged his shoulders and waved them on. A few hours later they crossed the finish line. Victory at last!

A NEW ERA BEGINS

The celebrations lasted for weeks, long enough for the Italian team, weary but unbowed, to roll into Paris on September 17 and take third place. The Great Race was officially over. The drivers and their crews became national heroes in their home countries. When the Americans got back to New York, they were given a ticker-tape parade down Fifth Avenue and invited by President Theodore Roosevelt (the first U.S. president to drive a car) to a special reception at his summer house on Long Island. Today the Thomas Flyer is on display in Harrah's Automobile Collection in Reno, Nevada. Munich's Deutsches Museum has the German Protos. The Italian Zust was destroyed in a fire only months after the race, but the ultimate fates of the cars involved didn't matter. All three finishers had proved that a car could reliably and safely go anywhere in the world at any time, and under any conditions. No other form of transport could make the same claim. With the conclusion of the Great Race, the Automobile Age had officially arrived. That same year, Henry Ford put the Model T into full production on the assembly line, and the world has been car-crazy ever since.

POSTSCRIPT

In all the hoopla after the race, the race sponsors "neglected" to hand over the $1,000 prize money to the Thomas Flyer team. It wasn't until 60 years later, in 1968, that the *New York Times* awarded the prize money to George Schuster. By then, he was the only member of his team still alive.

About once a year, a house in the United States is hit by sewage falling from a plane.

"ALWAYS"...OR "NEVER"?

Can you figure out which is which? (Answers are on page 537.)

1. "_____ play fairly when one has the winning cards."
—Oscar Wilde

2. "_____ eat spinach just before going on the air."
—Dan Rather

3. "_____ take hold of things by the smooth handle."
—Thomas Jefferson

4. "_____ do whatever's next."
—George Carlin

5. "_____ mind your happiness; do your duty."
—Peter Drucker

6. "_____ read something that will make you look good if you die in the middle of it."
—P. J. O'Rourke

7. "_____ do what you are afraid to do."
—Ralph Waldo Emerson

8. "_____ go to other people's funerals; otherwise, they won't come to yours."
—Yogi Berra

9. "_____ hold discussions with the monkey when the organ grinder is in the room."
—Winston Churchill

10. "_____ think of the future; it comes soon enough."
—Albert Einstein

11. "_____ put off till tomorrow what you can do the day after tomorrow."
—Mark Twain

12. "_____ contract friendship with a man that is not better than thyself."
—Confucius

13. "_____ be nice to people on the way up; because you'll meet the same people on the way down."
—Wilson Mizner

14. "_____ bet on baseball."
—Pete Rose

15. "_____ bend your head. _____ hold it high. Look the world straight in the eye."
—Helen Keller

HOBBS STRIKES OUT

For many reasons—poor test audience response, studio interference, a director's whim—the original ending of a movie is sometimes replaced, usually with a happier one. Here are the ways some movies were "supposed" to end.

THE NATURAL (1984)

Plot: Roy Hobbs (Robert Redford) is a baseball star whose career is presumed over when he is shot and nearly killed by a female serial killer. Nearly two decades later, he triumphantly returns to the big leagues.

Familiar Ending: In the last game of the season, injured and with his special bat broken, Hobbs steps up to the plate and hits a home run that shatters a stadium light. Hobbs is showered with sparks as, in slow motion, he rounds the bases to win the pennant.

Original Ending: In the original Bernard Malamud novel, Hobbs strikes out…on purpose. Game over, no pennant. A little boy later confronts him and accuses him of throwing the game. Hobbs weeps, indicating that the rumor is true. Producers changed the ending because they wanted to make an *uplifting* baseball movie, not Malamud's depressing story about a broken man.

PRETTY WOMAN (1990)

Plot: Wealthy businessman Edward (Richard Gere) hires Vivian, a hooker with a heart of gold (Julia Roberts), to spend a week with him. They fall in love.

Familiar Ending: They have a fight, and Vivian leaves. But Edward finds her apartment and serenades her with a recording of an opera they'd attended together. They kiss, make up, and live happily ever after.

Original Ending: In the first draft of the script, Vivian has a drug problem and agrees to kick it as part of the weeklong deal. They fall in love, but Vivian doesn't give up the drugs. Edward throws her out of his car. No reunion. Director Garry Marshall liked J. F. Lawton's script, but thought audiences might not. So he had Lawton change it to a more traditional love story—one with no drug problem and a happy ending.

In Death Valley, the ground can be up to 40% hotter than the air.

CLERKS (1994)

Plot: Convenience-store clerk Dante (Brian O'Halloran) endures idiotic customers, a fine for selling cigarettes to a minor, and a dead man in the bathroom during the course of his day on the job, when all he wants to do is play a hockey game on the roof.

Familiar Ending: Dante closes up shop after a long, crazy day that he wasn't even scheduled to work and goes off to enjoy the night with his best friend and fellow clerk, Randall.

Original Ending: This was director Kevin Smith's first movie, and he says that he didn't know how to end it. His first attempt: As Dante is locking up the store for the night, a man enters the store, empties the cash register, and shoots Dante, who bleeds to death.

FIRST BLOOD (1982)

Plot: The Vietnam War is long over, but it left veteran John Rambo (Sylvester Stallone) emotionally disturbed. Homeless and hitchhiking, he gets hassled by a small-town sheriff. He escapes into the forest and starts waging a guerrilla-style war on the town.

Familiar Ending: Rambo surrenders to his old commanding officer, Colonel Trautman (Richard Crenna).

Original Ending: As in David Morrell's original novel, Rambo is cornered by Trautman and, emotionally devastated, begs for his murder to avoid capture. Trautman refuses; Rambo shoots himself. Stallone saw it at a screening and hated it. He threatened to block the movie's release if the hero died, and had enough clout to force the filmmakers to change the ending. Rambo lived.

THERE'S SOMETHING ABOUT MARY (1998)

Plot: Ted (Ben Stiller) tracks down his high-school prom date, Mary (Cameron Diaz), with whom he is still in love, enduring humiliating and painful tribulations along the way.

Familiar Ending: Ted and Mary fall in love, despite challenges from Mary's stalker as well as her other ex-boyfriend.

Original Ending: Ted and Mary fall in love. Immediately after, Ted gets hit by a bus. He lives, but a bystander finds his severed foot in a storm drain. Directors Peter and Bobby Farrelly felt they'd already pushed the gross humor as far as it could go and took a more commercial way out: a happy ending.

TOILET TECH: BABY EDITION

Here at the BRI, we never get tired of reading about new bathroom inventions. But it turns out that they're not all yucky fart-and-odor-related appliances (although those are pretty funny). Some are actually kind of cute...like these.

THE BABYKEEPER

Inventors: Sisters Tonja King and Elisa Johnson of Woodinville, Washington, who sell the product through their company, Mommyssentials

Product: A baby carrier—that's especially useful in public restrooms

How It Works: The Babykeeper is a wearable device designed for carrying babies 6 to 18 months old. It's worn over one shoulder, with the baby sitting in a harness on the wearer's hip. But the amazing part about it is that if Mom has to use a public restroom toilet, the device comes off and—using the two straps ending in hooks—it can be hung from the top of the restroom partition wall. So the baby just hangs there while mom does her business. Cost: $39.99.

THE TUMMYTUB

Inventor: Childcare providers in the Netherlands

Product: A small clear container on a colorful stand

How It Works: The TummyTub is simply a small, bucket-sized tub on a short stand that purports to mimic the conditions inside the womb, thereby making the transition from womb to the outside world easier. The baby is placed into a few gallons of warm water up to his or her shoulders, making it feel, according to the TummyTub Web site, "warm, reassured, and secure." (Of course you have to keep the baby's head out of the water so he or she doesn't drown.) And the tubs are see-through—so it's like seeing inside your tummy! TummyTub is currently used in maternity hospitals all over the U.K. Cost: about $50.

Game over? At least 50 American colleges offer courses in video-game study.

THE NITE TRAIN'R

Inventor: Koregon Enterprises, Beaverton, Oregon

Product: A moisture-activated alarm system

How It Works: This is designed for kids with bedwetting issues. It consists of a washable plastic pad that is worn inside the child's underwear or pajamas at night. It's connected by wires to a small plastic box that attaches to the child's pajama top or t-shirt. If the sensors come into contact with just a few drops of urine…it gives the kid a shock! Just kidding—the plastic box actually beeps out an alarm, hopefully waking the child and allowing him or her to high-tail it to the bathroom. The manufacturer promises that your child can never be electrocuted by the Nite Train'R, because it's powered by harmless 9-volt batteries (not included). Cost: $69.99.

THE WEEBLOCK

Inventor: Sozo, a baby products company based in Unionville, Connecticut

Product: A colored sponge shaped like a men's athletic "cup," but it's for babies—*boy* babies

How It Works: If you're a parent of a boy, or if you've ever had to babysit for very young boys and had to change their diapers, then you're probably familiar with what one might call the "Sudden Geyser Effect." Weeblocks were invented with that in mind. They're colorful, cuplike, vinyl-covered sponges that you place over your baby boy's geyser-spouter while you're changing his diaper. They really work, they're machine washable—and they come with cute sayings on them like "Whiz Kid," "Li'l Squirt," and "Captain Blast Off!" Cost: $10.

*   *   *

OLD NEWS

In 2009 the state of Iowa changed the name of its Department of Elder Affairs to the Department of Aging. Though the new wording is more politically correct ("elder" or "elderly" is now considered inappropriate), the state is thinking about changing it again due to protests over the acronym formed by the new name: D.O.A.

Taipei 101, the world's tallest skyscraper, has 67 elevators.

3-D TV

All you need to see in three dimensions are two slightly different images, one for each eye. Simple, right? Yet getting uncomplicated, inexpensive, and realistic 3-D TV into our homes has turned out to be a lot harder than it looked.

HELP ME, OBI-WAN!

Since the invention of television, there have been countless claims about promising new technologies. Amazing new improvements!...but always sometime in the future. Many of the predictions have come true—color TV, video players, HDTV—but many more have not. The prime example: three-dimensional TV. Over the years, engineers and marketers have periodically announced impending breakthroughs to give depth to our TV screens. Almost invariably, though, the methods proved unwieldy, unworkable, expensive, or unsatisfactory—good for a novelty broadcast or two, and then, having been found lacking, put back on the back burner again. Here are some of the most promising failures, near misses, and almost-rans...so far.

STEREOSCOPE 3-D

• **The Possibility:** One of the ways 3-D TV could work would be to send separate images to each eye using two tiny TV screens. It's not a new idea. Using two still images to create a 3-D effect has been around since Sir Charles Wheatstone invented the stereoscope in the 1840s, a technique that used side-by-side cameras to take nearly identical photographs, which the viewer would then look at through a binocular apparatus. These viewers were a huge hit over the next few decades, allowing people to see 3-D images of distant places and historic events. Disaster photos from Civil War battles and the 1906 San Francisco earthquake were especially popular.

It didn't take long after the invention of movies for somebody to try a cinematic version of Wheatstone's invention. British film pioneer William Friese-Greene, who filed the first 3-D movie patent in 1890, designed a modified stereoscope with two reels of film that had to be perfectly synchronized in order for the effect to work properly. In a fate that would be shared by many 3-D

In 150 years, only one hurricane has made landfall in South America.

schemes, there is no evidence that Friese-Greene's idea ever actually made it to the production stage.

ViewMaster 3-D viewers, which appeared as children's toys in the 1940s, used the same idea as Wheatstone's invention. So why not adapt it for video?

• **The Problem:** To adapt it for TV, each viewer would require two tiny television screens showing two separate, synchronized video signals. Watching a movie or football game as a group experience would be difficult; the headgear would be uncomfortable and expensive.

• **The Result:** Something like this has actually been tried successfully in a few arcade video games, including *Sub-Roc*, a 1983 submarine game by Sega in which you look into a "periscope." But rather than two TVs, there was a high-speed shutter that quickly alternated the correct image to one eye and then the other. In other words, if the video speed were 30 frames per second, each eye's shutter would open and close 15 times per second, alternating so that the correct 15 frames would go to each eye. Still, the technology is expensive and clunky and will probably never make it to home television.

RED-GREEN ANAGLYPH

• **The Possibility:** This method predates television. In 1915 Edwin S. Porter presented a public demonstration of short depth-enhanced movies of actress Marie Doro, belly dancers, and Niagara Falls using the red-green anaglyph method. He was 40 years ahead of his time. 3-D movies wouldn't become a commercial success in theaters until the mid-1950s. And then it became the first "successful" method of getting 3-D on television. As long as viewers had a color TV and those red-and-green glasses, it was possible to broadcast the 3-D movies that had been prepared for movie theaters.

• **The Problem:** Viewers had to have a color TV at a time when television was broadcast in black and white, and many people complained that the red-green glasses gave them headaches. And, when seen through the glasses, the 3-D image appeared black and white (or red and green), not in true color.

• **The Result:** The 3-D movies of the 1950s turned out to be a short-lived fad. By the time color TV became common, viewers weren't much interested in watching black-and-white movies, whether in 3-D or not. Although later attempts allowed something like color TV, the limited spectrum was unsatisfying.

POLARIZED-LENS 3-D

• **The Possibility:** When Edwin Land invented polarized lenses in 1936, he saw the possibility for using them to view 3-D movies. The lenses let in light vibrating in only one direction and blocked out the rest. He figured out that if he projected two different images on the same screen using polarized lenses at different angles, glasses with the similar alignment could route a separate image to each eye. The system worked, and because it allowed full-color images, it became the most popular method of presenting 3-D in theaters.

• **The Problem:** TV is another matter. There's no known way to send polarized images through a TV screen.

• **The Result:** Nothing.

PULFRICH-EFFECT 3-D

• **The Possibility:** For this one, credit German physicist Carl Pulfrich in 1922. He discovered that low light makes your eyes see things a split second slower than bright light. So if you cover one eye with a dark lens and look at a 2-D video, the darkened eye will always be a split second behind its brightly lit partner.

The Pulfrich effect allows a 3-D method that depends on an interesting optical illusion. It can be rendered easily on existing TV technology and in full color. It has produced convincing 3-D images for a Rolling Stones concert special, some commercials, a shark documentary on the Discovery Channel, and special episodes of *Doctor Who* and *3rd Rock from the Sun*. Although broadcasters have sometimes provided decoder glasses, all you really have to do is put a dark sunglasses lens over one eye.

• **The Problem:** The objects on the screen must be constantly moving sideways in the correct direction and at the right speed. If you watch something made for Pulfrich viewing, you'll quickly notice that the subject or the camera is always moving sideways. (The movement can cause motion sickness in some viewers.)

• **The Result:** It's had very limited usage. Producers have learned that Pulfrich 3-D is best used in small doses—for example, in one song in the Rolling Stones concert, or short dream sequences in *3rd Rock From the Sun*.

Still, you can get the effect right now with football games, nature shows, car races, or any program that provides predictable sideways movement across the screen. If it's moving left across the screen, darkening your left eye will make it see the object slightly to the right of what your right eye sees. This discrepancy tricks your mind into interpreting the object as if were popping out from the 2-D screen. Done right, the effect can be pretty impressive.

COLORCODE (AMBER-BLUE ANAGLYPH)

• **The Possibility:** ColorCode, a brand name owned by a Danish company, uses the same idea as red-green anaglyph. The difference is in the color of the lenses: ColorCode uses amber and dark blue instead of red and green. This system was first used on TV in a highly publicized 2009 Super Bowl commercial for *Monsters vs. Aliens* in 3-D, and in an episode of *Chuck*. What's striking is how different the images in each eye are: The amber lens lets in the yellows, reds, and greens, while the blue lens darkens everything into twilight shades of blue. Still, despite the contrasting images, your eyes and brain somehow make it work. The amber allows a wider range of colors than red-green anaglyph, so the effect is full-color. Viewed without glasses, the image looks almost like a normal 2-D video, with just a fuzzy yellow-blue halo around objects on the screen.

• **The Problem:** ColorCode still requires glasses. The difference between what's seen by each eye is pretty extreme, which could be a recipe for eyestrain or headaches for some people.

• **The Result:** If you have to wear glasses, it's not bad. In fact, it's the best, most practical method for 3-D TV so far. And since it's the method used for recent 3-D cartoons released by major movie studios, its future on DVD is guaranteed.

3-D TV WITHOUT GLASSES?

• **The Possibility:** Convinced that few people actually *like* wearing 3-D glasses, several manufacturers have been working to create a practical 3-D TV system that will stand alone. The methods of directing a different picture to each eye include *lenticular* lenses that angle two different images from the same screen (used in the

3-D illustrations you sometimes see attached to magazine covers and DVD cases) and *parallax barriers* (a fancy name for a slitted material that allows each eye to see only half of the pixels on a screen). Other systems use eye-tracking systems that automatically follow a viewer's eyes.

• **The Problem:** It's insanely expensive, and most of the systems require you to sit with your head in exactly the right place, without moving. There's no reason to believe that Hollywood is going to release content formatted to play on systems for the few people willing to spend $25,000 or more for an eyeglass-free 3-D system.

• **The Result:** These expensive systems are probably suitable only for novelty advertising displays that show films customized for that one specific use. (Ironically, an equally practical, inexpensive, glasses-free 3-D system could be accomplished by projecting two images side-by-side on a wide-screen TV and having viewers cross their eyes until the two images overlap.)

HOLOGRAPHIC TV

While we're dreaming, let's go to the next step. Forget flat-screen 3-D; the holy grail of TV technology is 360-degree holographic images in the round—just like in *Star Wars*—that you can watch from any side. Impossible? Never say never. Many futurists predict holographic TV will be a reality by 2018. With most such predictions, the future is always "just around the corner," yet it seldom seems to come. But who knows? If we keep predicting that we'll have holographic TV within 10 years, one of these decades there's a decent chance we'll be right.

*　　*　　*

MAKE YOUR OWN 3-D VIDEO

1. What you need: a video camera and one lens from a pair of sunglasses.

2. Sit on the right side of a bus, train, or car and aim your camera at the window.

3. Watch the video on a TV, holding the lens from the sunglasses over your right eye.

4. Voilà! Amazing 3-D!

UNCLE JOHN HELPS OUT AROUND THE HOUSE

Some tips and tricks from the BRI's "Home & Garden" section.
(Disclaimer: We haven't tried every single one of these.)

• To determine whether you have mice, put some flour on the floor near holes in the walls. If you have mice, they'll leave little footprints.

• Water won't remove grease stains from a deck, so cover them with cat litter and then grind it in with your heel. Leave it for a day, and then sweep it up.

• If you're going to spend the day painting, rub some petroleum jelly onto your hands before you start; the paint will wash out more easily at the end of the day.

• Steam loosens dirt and grime, so clean your bathroom after taking a hot shower.

• The easiest way to dust a ceiling fan: Put an old sock over your hand and dust away.

• Coat your dustpan's surface with a bit of furniture polish—that will help keep the dirt in the pan.

• Want to deter a line of ants? Put catnip in their path. They hate it. Other flavors they don't like: salt, pepper, curry powder, and powdered laundry detergent.

• Next time you have a fire in your fireplace, throw in a handful of salt—it will help keep your chimney clean.

• What do a bar of soap, a candle, Chapstick, and the graphite from a pencil tip have in common? They can get a stuck zipper unstuck.

• Before putting your leftover spaghetti sauce in a plastic container, spray the container with non-stick cooking spray so it won't stain orange.

• If your hands smell like fish, garlic, or even garbage, pour a teaspoon of sugar on them, then add a few drops of water, and rub it in. Then rinse in warm water with a little lemon juice and—voilà! Stink-free hands.

- Can't get the grime out from under your fingernails? Try using toothpaste.

- Don't use a knife to cut pizza into slices; use scissors.

- You've just moved a couch, and it left indentations on the carpet. Place an ice cube on each dent. When the ice melts, the dents will be gone.

- Do you have a vase that's impossible to clean with a brush? Add water, then drop in some AlkaSeltzer. (It also makes a great toilet cleaner.)

- Soaking a new shower curtain in saltwater will inhibit the buildup of mildew.

- You've tried vacuuming, you've tried using packing tape, but nothing gets pet hair off of furniture. Try this: Put on some latex gloves, wet them, and rub the upholstery with your hands.

- To repel deer, place bars of deodorant soap in glasses and position them around your tastiest garden items. (Irish Spring is especially effective.)

- Are there mice in your basement or garage? Put some *used* cat litter in cups and place them near the walls. The mice will think there's a cat and vacate the premises.

- Rub a fabric softener sheet on your TV screen to keep dust from accumulating.

- Believe it or not, peanut butter can be effective for getting bubble gum out of hair.

- A pencil eraser can be used to get crayon off a wall. But what about ink? Try scrubbing it with rubbing alcohol.

- If you have to mow wet grass, spray the blades with cooking oil so the grass won't stick to them.

*   *   *

FEATHER-BRAINED POLITICS

Jaime Negot, mayor of Guayaquil, Ecuador, had received so many "undesirable questions" from reporters at press conferences in 2003 that he appointed a parrot as his official spokes...bird. "Some people only talk nonsense to me," he said, "So the parrot will answer back in the same way. I need to use my time for work."

INDIANA BASKETBALL: THE CRISPUS ATTUCKS TIGERS

On page 163, we told the story of the Milan Indians, the small-town basketball team that inspired the film Hoosiers. *But a few miles northwest of Milan, another Indiana team was about to make history of their own—and change the face of basketball.*

COLOR LINE

In the United States of the 1920s, the Ku Klux Klan was a fact of life. The racist organization was at its zenith, with nearly five million members nationwide, and Klan-backed politicians rose to power in many states, particularly in the Midwest. Nowhere were they more politically powerful than in Indiana, where the governor, the mayor of Indianapolis, and a majority of members in the state legislature had Klan ties. In this atmosphere, the city of Indianapolis decided to build a segregated all-black high school—the only one in the city—in 1927. In defiance of its racist origins, the school's first administration named it Crispus Attucks, after an African-American sailor and runaway slave who is said to be the first American killed in the Revolutionary War.

Racism was so prevalent in the school's early days that it was barred from the Indiana High School Athletic Association, and its basketball team had to travel out of state to find teams who would play them. Even after they were allowed to play in Indiana (starting in 1943), they played mostly small rural schools, where team members were often subjected to racial slurs. The rest of the state avoided them—bigger schools didn't want to compete with (or get beaten by) an all-black school.

BEST BEHAVIOR

Taking a "don't rock the boat" approach, Crispus Attucks's principal, Russell Lane, thought of sports as a way to show the black community in a positive light. To that end, he recruited players

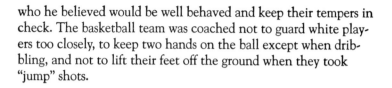

who he believed would be well behaved and keep their tempers in check. The basketball team was coached not to guard white players too closely, to keep two hands on the ball except when dribbling, and not to lift their feet off the ground when they took "jump" shots.

NEW ATTITUDE

But when Ray Crowe took over as coach in 1950, things changed. Crowe agreed that sports and sportsmanship were a way of breaking down barriers between the races, but he also believed that everyone—black and white—respected excellence and competition.

Crowe coached a more aggressive offense, with more emphasis on speed and ball-handling, and utilized a man-to-man defense instead of the traditional zone defense. He emphasized fundamentally sound basketball, but he wasn't opposed to a little flash too, though it took him a few years to fully embrace it. Under Coach Crowe, the Attucks scored more points than most high-school teams did, and they ran up and down the floor more. He also recruited bigger, more athletic players than most high schools did. The result was a new kind of basketball.

THE BIG TIME

In the early 1950s, Coach Crowe, like Principal Lane and many others in the African-American community, worried how white Indianapolis would react to an all-black winning team. They soon found out.

In 1951 the Crispus Attucks Tigers made it all the way to the Regional Finals, where they played all-white Anderson High School at the 15,000-seat Butler Fieldhouse. The game was sold out—black fans rooted for Attucks, white fans for Anderson—and the event was broadcast on radio and fledgling TV stations across the state. Before the game, Principal Lane gathered the team in the locker room and delivered a lecture on the "importance of good sportsmanship" (code for "don't play too aggressively"), much to the players' and Coach Crowe's dismay.

The game lived up to all the hype. Down by 10 points with less than four minutes to go, the Tigers' Willie Gardener and Hallie Bryant stepped up their offense, repeatedly stealing the ball and scoring easy fast-break baskets. With 11 seconds left, the score was 80–79 Anderson. Crispus Attucks had the ball, and Coach Crowe set up a play for Bryant. At the last minute, he also put in sophomore Bailey "Flap" Robertson. The inbounds pass was deflected to Gardener, who quickly passed it to Robertson in the far corner. Robertson jumped and let the ball fly—and Attucks won the game, 81–80. It was the greatest win in school history, making Attucks the first all-black basketball team ever to advance to the State Championship Final Four.

But then something happened: In the Semifinals, Coach Crowe backed off, sounding less like himself and more like Principal Lane. He lectured the team on good sportsmanship, or what he saw as "the relationship between the players' attitudes and the morale of the community." Flap Robertson wasn't even called on to play in the game, perhaps because he was only a sophomore but perhaps because his style of play was a little too flashy and he was known to "talk trash" to other players and even to referees.

NEVER AGAIN

Crispus Attucks lost in the Semifinals to Evansville Reitz, 66–59. Afterward, Coach Crowe took responsibility for the loss. He knew he hadn't let the team play all out, and that had been a mistake. He never coached that way again. "We were not ready," he said later. "And that was my fault. I made up my mind right then that we would be back, and the next time we would be ready."

But though the Tigers lost, they'd made it farther than any Attucks team ever had, and became the first Indianapolis team— black or white—to make it to the state Final Four. Their success inspired the black community and gained them new respect in the press…and even among some white fans. But one fan was probably more inspired than any other by the team's win. That night, Flap Robertson's 13-year-old brother, Oscar, went to sleep thinking of the glory the Tigers had achieved and dreaming of his own future.

For Part III of the story, turn to page 424.

THE FAKE NEWS NETWORK

Is objective TV news dying? Details at 11:00.

BROADCAST BLUES
Do you tune in to your local news on television each night? Every year, fewer people do. In some U.S. markets, the viewership for local news has declined by more than 50 percent since the 1980s. And as more people get their news from cable and the Internet, advertisers aren't willing to pay the same money to sponsor local newscasts as they once did. The only way for the stations to get that vital ad revenue back is to get those viewers back. To do that, the local newscast has been revamped significantly over the last couple of decades.

The most obvious change: the weather report. Local weather is the reason most viewers tune in, so that segment has become much longer, taking up to 20 percent of the entire broadcast; the most expensive ad slots come prior to and after it. But that still leaves about 17 minutes of news to fill up with the top local stories, a segment sent directly from the network covering the day's national stories, plus sports, traffic, and a "puff piece" at the end.

To fill up those 17 minutes, the stations get news stories from wire services or online services. But sitting alongside actual stories from legitimate outlets such as Reuters or the Associated Press are well-produced news reports that aren't really news at all.

FROM THE WIRE

They're called *video news releases*, or VNRs, paid for by corporations and produced by public relations companies. "A VNR is a short clip of marketing propaganda produced in the language and style of real news," explains tech journalist Farhad Manjoo in his book *True Enough: Learning to Live in a Post-Fact Society*. "Public relations firms send news stations thousands of such videos every year, the most sophisticated of which are virtually indistinguishable from honest news, featuring interviews with (paid) experts

First political slogan on a T-shirt: "Do It With Dewey" (for 1948 pres. candidate Thomas Dewey).

and voice-overs by (fake) reporters who subtly pitch products during their narratives."

MONEY FOR NOTHIN'

Another benefit: VNRs give stations provocative stories they can use in promos to "tease" viewers into watching. So not only does the station get a news story for free, they get one that can increase ratings...and ad revenue. Perhaps you saw one of these VNRs:

• *What you don't know about flu season might kill you!* This two-minute VNR began with the results of a "national flu survey" that stated that people don't take flu season seriously enough. A "family doctor" warns of the risks of dehydration and even heart failure. Then the narrator says, "But there's a new product on the market which simultaneously treats multiple flu symptoms: Zicam flu medicine." The only edit that most stations made before running the segment was to remove the corporate logo at the end.

• *Is your child's iPod a portable pornography machine?* This VNR, which ran during the 2005 holiday shopping season, reported that the Apple iPod Nano is capable of video, and because it can connect to the Internet, kids could easily access what the narrator referred to as "iPorn." Newscasters teased it as "the scariest gift of the season." (It turns out that the VNR was made by a firm hired by Apple's competition—Panasonic, Namco, and Techno Source.)

• *Coming up: Do you have that Latina Glow?* This VNR about strong Hispanic role models aired on the E! network, VH1, and some Spanish language stations. It centered around Jennifer Lopez's accomplishments, including launching her own line of perfume, "Glow." The story's main purpose: to sell the perfume.

• *Tomorrow begins National Pancake Week!* In March 2006, several stations ran a 75-second VNR that talked about the benefits of "heart smart" pancakes. The segment made multiple mentions of Bisquick and Betty Crocker products, both of which are owned by General Mills, who paid for the VNR.

IS THIS EVEN LEGAL?

Consumer advocacy groups such as the Center for Media and Democracy (CMD) have been lobbying the federal government to crack down on commercialized news. But it isn't that simple because, technically, the practice is legal. If the companies paid the stations to run VNRs, *that* would be illegal. But because no money changes hands, no "payola" (or pay-for-play) laws apply. What is illegal, however, is news stations failing to inform viewers that they're watching an ad. The CMD did a 10-month study of stations all over the United States and found that 77 had tried to pass off fake news stories as real. On the heels of that report, the FCC fined each of the stations approximately $4,000 per violation.

But the fines have done little to slow down the practice. And the FCC never addressed the VNRs that were paid for by the federal government. In 2005 the *New York Times* reported that PR firms hired by the Bush administration provided local stations with VNRs that showed the president's policies—mainly the wars in Iraq and Afghanistan—in a positive light. From the report:

> The federal government has aggressively used a well-established tool of public relations: the ready-to-serve news report that major corporations have long distributed to TV stations to pitch everything from headache remedies to auto insurance. At least 20 federal agencies have made and distributed television news segments in the past four years. Many were subsequently broadcast on local stations across the country without any acknowledgement of the government's role.

As alarming as the implications are—the government controlling the flow of news (as is the case in China)—the practice, so far, has been quite limited compared to the staggering number of corporate VNRs that are continually fed to local newsrooms.

THE NEWS-VERTISING AGE

As long as news organizations need money, it looks as if they will remain open to new options. For example, in 2009 a PR firm representing McDonald's made a deal with a local Las Vegas morning news show to place the restaurant's new iced coffee drinks on the table in front of the newscasters during the "Lifestyle" segment. When asked what the newscasters would do if they had to report a story that showed McDonald's in a negative light, the station manager explained, "We'd remove the cups before reading the story."

The lesson: Take all of your news with a grain of salt...but not just any salt—make sure it's pure Morton's Salt!

Man's best friend: In 2004 Americans spent $10 billion more on dog food than on baby food.

URBAN LEGENDS

If a story sounds true, but sounds too perfect (and too bizarre) to be true, then it's probably an urban legend.

THE LEGEND: In a scene in the 1987 film *Three Men and a Baby*, Jack (Ted Danson) and his mother (Celeste Holm) walk through the rooms of Jack's apartment carrying the baby that was left on his doorstep. In the rear of the scene you can see a mysterious human figure standing behind curtains in a doorway. About the size of a child, it's wearing a white shirt and black pants and carrying a long black object that appears to be a gun. Who is it? It's a ghost. No one really noticed it until the movie came out on home video in 1988. That's when the filmmakers researched it and found there was no one on set at the time who matched the description of the "ghost." More research revealed that the ghostly image looked exactly like a nine-year-old boy who had accidentally shot himself in the apartment where the movie was filmed.

HOW IT SPREAD: This is one of the most famous movie-related urban legends of all time, but it's unclear how it spread. One theory: The *Three Men and a Baby* ghost started appearing in newspapers and on TV magazine shows in 1990, right around the time the sequel, *Three Men and a Little Lady*, was hitting theaters. The suggestion is that Universal Studios, the production company behind the movies, invented the legend as a publicity stunt.

THE TRUTH: There *is* a figure in the scene in question. But it's not a ghost. It's a standee—a lifesize cardboard cutout—of Ted Danson. His character, a famous actor, has a lot of old movie promotional materials lying around the house. The cutout depicts Danson in a black tuxedo jacket, matching pants, and a white shirt. The curtains obscure the jacket, with the visible part forming what sort of looks like a gun. The standee reappears throughout the movie in the background. And no boy shot himself in the apartment where the movie was filmed, because it was filmed on a soundstage in Toronto.

THE LEGEND: There's a secret underground network of people who produce, collect, and enjoy "snuff films"—films that depict actual murders.

HOW IT SPREAD: In 1969 Charles Manson and his "family" were terrorizing Los Angeles with bloody murders and other violent crimes. At one point, they stole an NBC news truck and were known to be in possession of a few Super-8 cameras. In the 1971 documentary *The Family*, filmmaker Ed Sanders claims that Manson's followers used the equipment to make "brutality films" of their victims. Ever since, rumors of various serial killers recording their crimes, as well as police discovering these tapes, have surfaced.

THE TRUTH: No law enforcement agency in the United States, Europe, or Asia, has ever actually discovered a genuine snuff film. Very convincing fakes have been reported and turned over to authorities (in 1991 actor Charlie Sheen saw a Japanese movie called *Flower of Flesh and Blood* that was so convincing that he thought it was real and gave it to the FBI). But a real one has yet to surface. As for the Manson tapes, those are a legend, too. The Super-8 cameras and the NBC equipment was later recovered; there were no films of murders.

THE LEGEND: The name of the band is KISS, not Kiss. It's in all capital letters because it's an acronym for "Knights In Satan's Service"—in other words, the band worships the devil. And it's all there in their stage show: bassist Gene Simmons spitting fire, spewing blood, and dressing up as a character called "The Demon."

HOW IT SPREAD: In 1974, shortly after the release of KISS's debut album, Simmons did an interview with *Circus* magazine. He jokingly said he wanted to know what human flesh tasted like. This, Simmons believes, is what started the devil-worship rumors. But Simmons is probably just as responsible—whenever he was asked outright if he worshiped the devil, he was noncommittal because he thought it was good publicity and made the band seem more dangerous and interesting.

THE TRUTH: KISS singer Paul Stanley thought up the name. He thought it summed up early '70s glam rock pretty well, and was good for marketing because it was a simple word that was understood worldwide. It was in all capitals to look good on stage, rendered in giant lights—it's not an acronym for anything. And Simmons, who has a degree in theology and was an elementary school teacher before he started KISS, isn't a Satan worshipper.

In 2009 astronomers discovered a star made of a 10-billion-trillion-trillion-carat diamond.

GARDY LOO!

Uncle John found a book called Slang and Euphemism, *by Richard Spears, with strange (and risqué) expressions from all over the world, some dating back centuries. Here are a few that we can print.*

Eruct: To belch

Gug: An unpleasant person

Have a jag on: Intoxicated

Woozle water: Whiskey

Tirliry-puffkin: A flighty woman

Fribble: A silly oaf

Ignatz: An ignoramus

Scrower: A drunkard

Wowser: A prudish person

Gaw-gaw: An oafish sailor

Yackum: Cow dung

Prep chapel: A toilet

Ethel: An effeminate male

Gooey: A gob of phlegm

Arse ropes: The intestines (Eww!)

Frogsch! Nonsense!

Bat house: An insane asylum

Dustman: A corpse

Joe-wad: Toilet paper

Rib-roast: A scolding from one's wife

Ubble-gubble: Utter nonsense

Wretchcock: A puny or worthless person

Drain the bilge: To vomit

Tiger sweat: A strong alcoholic drink

Snow: Underwear

Tattle water: Tea (because people gossip at tea parties)

Assteriors: Buttocks

Gardy loo! What a chambermaid yelled before dumping a chamber pot out of a window

Timber-headed: Stupid

Grubber: An unclean person

Alley apple: Horse manure

Pull a cluck: To die

Bingoed: Drunk

Hickus: A gadget

Make faces: Have children

Earth-bath: A grave

WOULD YOU BELIEVE...

For years we've done "Dustbin of History" stories about people who were famous in their time but are now forgotten. Here's a variation on that theme: theories that were once widely believed, but that modern science has since discredited.

CONCEPT: Phrenology (Medicine)
WHAT IT MEANT: Developed by 18th-century Austrian anatomist Franz Joseph Gall, phrenology was a pseudoscience that held that 1) different personality traits were located in different areas in the brain, and 2) the shape of an individual's skull was influenced by the size and shape of these areas of the brain. By carefully measuring different parts of the skull, especially the bumps, phrenologists believed it was possible to gain insight into an individual's personality traits, even to the point of evaluating their fitness for a particular occupation, suitability as a potential mate, and potential for criminal behavior. Though it was never taken seriously by the scientific community, phrenology remained popular throughout the 19th century and still has a handful of adherents today.

CONCEPT: Blending Inheritance (Biology)
WHAT IT MEANT: The hereditary characteristics of the father and mother are averaged or "blended" in their offspring. For example, if a tall man has children with a short woman, the children will be of medium height. The problem with this theory is that if it were true, in relatively few generations the features that distinguish one person from another would fade away, and everyone would be the same. Yet over the thousands of years that humans have been on Earth, it hasn't happened. The theory of Blending Inheritance fell out of favor as botanist Gregor Mendel's theory of dominant and recessive genes gained acceptance at the turn of the 20th century.

CONCEPT: Humorism (Medicine)
WHAT IT MEANT: A person's health and personality are determined by the proportions of four basic substances—blood, phlegm,

yellow bile, and black bile—in the body. When the four humors were in balance, the person was healthy; when they were out of balance, the person was sick. Diet and physical activity of various kinds affected the balance and could make it better or worse; treatments such as bloodletting, inducing vomiting, and purging the bowels were administered to sick people to restore proper balance of the humors. Humorism dates back to 400 B.C. and persisted well into the 1800s, when advances in medical research led to a more accurate understanding of human physical and mental health.

CONCEPT: Diluvialism (Geology)
WHAT IT MEANT: Many geological features—such as fossils of sea creatures found on mountain tops and deposits of boulders, sand, and clay found in the valley floors of many parts of Europe—can be attributed to the great Flood or Deluge described in the Bible. Diluvialism was popular in the 18th and 19th centuries but was displaced by the theory of Uniformitarianism, which held that rock formations could be explained by *natural* forces such as erosion and volcanic activity rather than *super*natural forces like Biblical floods. (Science may have discarded Diluvialism, but some religious groups still accept it as true.)

CONCEPT: The King's Touch (Medicine)
WHAT IT MEANT: A sort of royalist equivalent of faith healing, this was the belief that the touch of a king or queen, who ruled by divine right, could actually cure diseases. The theory dates back to the 1200s in Europe and persisted for more than 600 years. The royal touch was thought to be especially effective in curing *scrofula*, a form of tuberculosis that causes swelling of the lymph nodes in the neck. Scrofula sores can disappear without treatment, which likely explains why the King's Touch was thought to be so effective with this particular ailment.

*   *   *

"The universe is full of magical things, patiently waiting for our wits to grow sharper."

—Eden Phillpotts

UNCLE JOHN'S PAGE OF LISTS

A few miscellaneous bits of information we've picked up here and there.

6 Items Banned from eBay
1. Used cosmetics
2. Stun guns
3. Alcohol
4. Contact lenses
5. Body parts
6. Live animals

The 4 Items on Franklin D. Roosevelt's 1945 Inauguration Luncheon Menu
1. Chicken salad
2. Rolls (no butter)
3. Pound cake (no frosting)
4. Coffee

5 Lesser-Known Constellations
1. Boötes, the Wagoner
2. Noah's Dove
3. Bernice's Hair
4. Tucana, the Toucan
5. Grus, the Crane

3 Public Figures with Unusual Middle Names
1. Jimmy Riddle Hoffa
2. Nelson Rolihlahla ("Troublemaker") Mandela
3. Thelonius Sphere Monk

7 Oddly Named Popes
1. Cletus
2. Fabian
3. Hyginus
4. Innocent
5. Linus
6. Urban
7. Zosimus

3 Passengers on the World's First Hot-Air Balloon Ride in 1783
1. A duck
2. A rooster
3. A sheep

3 Memorable Zip Codes
1. Arlington, Virginia: 22222
2. Newton Falls, Ohio: 44444
3. Young America, Minnesota: 55555

4 People Honored *Twice* with New York City Ticker-Tape Parades
1. Charles DeGaulle
2. Dwight D. Eisenhower
3. John Glenn
4. Haile Selassie (ruler of Ethiopia)

4 Pet Life Spans
1. Indoor cat: 12–18 years
2. Outdoor cat: 4–5 years
3. Parakeet: 8–10 years
4. Tarantula: 20–30 years

Only person honored with *three* NYC ticker-tape parades: Polar explorer Richard Byrd.

TRADING PAINT & SPRING RUBBER

More NASCAR terminology to frighten your friends with on your next drive around town. (Part I is on page 127.)

ROOF FLAPS. Plates on the a race car's roof that pop up if the car spins and ends up going backward. They cause air pressure to push down, helping prevent the car from flipping.

SILLY SEASON. The weeks leading up to the end of the NASCAR season (it runs from February to November), during which teams may make drastic changes such as hiring and firing people, changing sponsors, etc.

SPLASH-N-GO. A very quick pit stop during which the car is only given gas.

SHORT TRACK. A track less than one mile long. (The shortest NASCAR track, Martinsville Speedway in Virginia, is .526 miles long.)

SPOTTER. A member of a driver's crew who sits high in the grandstand and speaks to the driver via radio, providing information about positions of other cars, accidents, etc.

SPRING RUBBER. Curved pieces of hard rubber that are inserted between a car's springs to "stiffen" its suspension and feel.

STAGGERING. To stagger a car means to put different-size tires on opposite sides to improve its performance around corners.

STICKER TIRES. Brand-new tires, often with the sticker still visible on the side.

STOCK CAR: When NASCAR was founded in 1948, it stipulated that the cars used had to be "stock"; that is, passenger models made for the public, or from parts available to the public, and not modified in any way from their original form. The idea was that they were street cars, not souped-up race cars. Over the years, that's changed for safety reasons (roll bars, fire extinguishers, etc.), and for higher speeds and horsepower. Today's stock cars have bodies that *resemble* stock models, but just about everything else in them is custom made.

SUPERSPEEDWAY. A racetrack more than one mile long. (The longest: Talladega, Florida, at 2.66 miles.)

TEAR-OFFS. Sheets of very thin, clear Mylar that adhere to a race car's windshield and can be torn off after they get dirty during a race. Cars average six tear-offs per race.

THRESHOLD BRAKING. To brake the car hard, but just below the point where the wheels lock up.

TIGHT. When a car's front tires lose traction before the rear tires, it becomes hard to steer and is said to be "tight."

TRACK BAR. During a race you often hear announcers refer to adjustments to the "track bar." What is it? A long steel tube that runs from the left side of the rear axle to the frame on the right side of the car. Purpose: to prevent the axle from moving side to side. Many trucks and cars have them, but on NASCAR cars they're adjustable. Because of the effect it has on the car's suspension, lowering it makes the car more "tight," raising it makes it more "loose." (Also referred to as a "Panhard bar.")

TRADING PAINT. The term used when cars bump side-to-side during the race, usually causing scrapes and paint loss to both cars.

WIRE TO WIRE. To win a race "wire to wire" is to have the pole position in a race, lead in every lap...and win.

VICTORY LANE. Last (but certainly not least), this is where the winning driver goes to climb out of his car, receive the winner's award, and thank his sponsors 15 times during the post-race interview. Yee-ha!

*   *   *

SOMETHING TO REMEMBER ME BY

LEGO pays for its employees' business cards. Big deal. Most companies do that, right? But the Danish company's business cards are special: They're little LEGO people, with the employee's name and contact info on the little LEGO person's shirt. And the figures are designed to look like the person they represent.

BEHIND THE (MOB) HITS

*A fancy hotel, a homey Italian restaurant, a local bar and grill.
What do these seemingly innocent places have in common? Each
was the scene of the assassination of a ruthless gangster.*

ARNOLD "THE BRAIN" ROTHSTEIN

Background: Rothstein was one of the earliest leaders of
American organized crime. He wasn't a gun-toting mobster, though—he was a planner, bankroller, and political fixer.
Instead of muscle, he used brains to forge alliances among underworld factions and crooked politicians. He kept a low profile as he
financed the bootlegging activities of Dutch Schultz and other
gangsters. But Rothstein was also a compulsive gambler. In September 1928, he bought into a high-stakes poker game run by a
man named George McManus. The game lasted two days; Rothstein lost $320,000. Claiming the game was fixed, he refused to
pay up.

The Place: On November 4, Rothstein received an urgent phone
call from McManus to meet him at the Park Central Hotel. The
Park Central was (and still is) located across the street from
Carnegie Hall. Opened in 1927, this ritzy hotel quickly became
one of Manhattan's most popular spots. Ben Pollack's orchestra
(featuring Benny Goodman) packed them in nightly at the hotel's
Florentine Grill. It was a public place with lots of people around—
a place where Rothstein would have felt safe.

The Hit: Hotel employees later found him in the stairwell holding his abdomen—he'd been shot. Was it because of the debt, or
had one of his rivals simply found a viable excuse to eliminate
him? No one knows for sure, because in the one day that Rothstein lived, every time police asked him who shot him, he
answered, "Me mudder did it."

ARTHUR "DUTCH SCHULTZ" FLEGENHEIMER

Background: Only 33 when he died, Schultz was the FBI's Public
Enemy #1, and one of the best-known criminals of his day. During
Prohibition, "The Dutchman" bootlegged beer, ran an illegal
saloon in the Bronx, and forced rival saloons to buy beer from

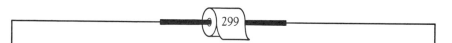

him…and *only* from him. He was an extortionist who also ran illegal gambling and slot machines, and didn't hesitate to murder anyone who interfered with "business."

Schultz's activities got a lot of attention from the Feds. In 1933 he was indicted on charges of income tax evasion, but he beat the rap. When he did, New York Mayor Fiorello LaGuardia was furious. He banned Schultz from New York City and ordered special prosecutor Thomas E. Dewey to investigate the Dutchman's rackets. Now Schultz was furious—he asked the "National Crime Syndicate" for permission to take Dewey out. They said no (it would have brought the full force of the Feds down on all of them). After Schulz stormed out, the other bosses decided that *he* needed to go.

The Place: The Palace Chophouse on E. 12th Street in Newark, New Jersey, was no palace—just a dark, narrow bar and diner. But since Schultz was no longer allowed to operate in New York, he used a room in the back of the Newark restaurant as his office. And that's where he was on the night of October 23, 1935.

The Hit: At 10:15 p.m., two gunmen walked into the Palace. They found Schultz in the men's room and shot him in the chest, and then gunned down three of his cronies in the restaurant's back room. Schulz died two days later in the hospital, but never said who shot him.

"JOE THE BOSS" MASSERIA

Background: Masseria was an old-line Sicilian mob boss whose ultimate goal was to become head of the Mafia in New York. Not sharing Masseria's dream, though, were younger "family" members Lucky Luciano and Vito Genovese. They wanted him out of the picture, as did powerful mobsters Lepke Buchalter and Owney Madden. When another rival mafioso, Salvatore Maranzano, began to encroach on Masseria's businesses, Joe the Boss fought back. That was the beginning a power struggle that came to be known as the Castellammarese War, during which more than 60 men (on both sides) were killed. Luciano and Genovese secretly contacted Maranzano and offered him a deal: If he'd end the bloodshed, they'd whack Masseria. Maranzano agreed.

The Place: On April 15, 1931, Luciano invited Joe the Boss to a

---

Giraffe meat is certified kosher (and really hard to find in supermarkets).

meeting at the Nuova Villa Tammaro Restaurant, a cheap "spaghetti house" in the Coney Island section of Brooklyn. They ate, played some cards, and then Luciano went to the bathroom.

The Hit: According to eyewitnesses, while Luciano was in the bathroom, two unknown men strolled into the restaurant, fired 20 shots at Masseria, and strolled out again. Luciano took over Masseria's crime family. The Nuova Villa Tammaro's owner, an Italian immigrant named Gerardo Scarpato, shut down the restaurant and moved back to Italy. Six months later he returned to New York and was murdered. No one was ever convicted.

JOSEPH "CRAZY JOEY" GALLO

Background: After Gallo and his two brothers split off from the Profaci Family in 1950s, they were involved in several high-profile mafia battles in New York City. The wars were put on hold in 1961 when Gallo was convicted of extortion and sent up the river. (In prison, he reportedly amused himself by trying to poison his fellow convicts with strychnine-laced Italian food.) When he got out in 1971, Gallo resumed his war against Joe Colombo, whom he had never forgiven for murdering one of his men. After Colombo was gunned down that June as he was walking to the podium to deliver a speech at the Italian-American Civil Rights League's Italian Unity Day, the heads of the Five Families surmised that it was Gallo who had ordered the hit, even though they had no proof. They put out a contract on Gallo's life.

The Place: In the wee hours of the morning of April 7, 1972, Gallo was winding down after celebrating his 43rd birthday at the Copa Cabana (Don Rickles was performing). He and his friends wanted something to eat. They went to Chinatown, but everything was closed, so they went to nearby Little Italy. The only place that was open: Umberto's Clam House—the newest restaurant in the "old neighborhood," owned by another mobster, "Matty the Horse" Ianniello.

The Hit: Two (or possibly more) gunmen were waiting at Umberto's. They opened fire. Gallo was hit five times and still managed to stagger out into the street, where he collapsed and died. No one was ever charged with Crazy Joey's murder.

LITTLE THINGS MEAN A LOT

"The devil's in the details," says an old proverb. It's true—one seemingly tiny goof can cause major headaches down the road.

ONE INCH

New York City Metropolitan Transit Authority officials were left red-faced in January 2009 when the opening of a new subway station had to be postponed. Reason: The gap between the platform and the train car was four inches wide. Although that distance wouldn't pose a danger to most abled people, it violates the Americans With Disabilities Act, which specifies that the gap can be no longer than *three* inches. The goof was blamed on engineers, who failed to take into account the slight curve of the platform. Cost of the extra inch: a two-month delay in opening the station and $200,000 to extend the platform.

A DATA-ENTRY ERROR

In late 2007, two Maryland state assessment workers, both new to the job, were entering data into all of the counties' proposed budgets for 2008. At one point, one of them accidentally entered the *estimated* taxable real estate for Montgomery County in 2008, instead of the *actual* 2007 numbers. That single incorrect number created a domino effect that threw off several other county budget estimates. Once officials realized something was wrong, it took eight months and a small army of number-crunchers to find the error. In all, it threw off budget estimates by $16 billion and cost taxpayers more than $31 million to correct.

A MOIST SENSOR

In February 2008, a ground crew was preparing a B2 Stealth Bomber for takeoff at a U.S. Air Force base in Guam. They noticed odd readings coming from three sensors that relay information to the flight computer. Unfortunately, this particular crew hadn't heard about an "unofficial fix" to send a blast of hot air through the system to evaporate any moisture on the sensors.

While she was serving time in prison in 2005, Martha Stewart became a billionaire.

Instead, they recalibrated the sensors and cleared the plane for takeoff. But as it sped down the runway, the moisture evaporated. Result: The sensors sent incorrect data to the computer. "The pressure differences were miniscule," said Maj. Gen. Floyd Carpenter, "but they were enough to confuse the flight control system." As the plane lifted off, the pilots thought they were traveling at 158 knots but were actually only going about 124 knots. The plane immediately stalled; the pilots ejected as the left wing dragged against the ground…right before the $1.4 billion bomber erupted into a huge fireball. (Update: Removing moisture from the sensors pre-takeoff is now an *official* fix.)

A SOFTWARE GLITCH

In 2001 Marguerite Nunn intended to donate a $130 check to Zoo To You, a nonprofit wildlife education program. But due to what was later deemed a "software error" on her computer, her zip code was entered into the amount box on the check. Result: She donated $93,447. When Nunn, an innkeeper from Paso Robles, California, realized the error two weeks later, she asked for Zoo To You to return her money. But they'd already spent more than half of it (the check had cleared the bank because Nunn and her husband Tom had recently sold some property). The nonprofit paid back $30,000, and then a little more over the next few years, but nothing came after 2006. Seeing no other choice, the Nunns sued. In 2009, eight years after the initial goof, they were awarded a settlement reported as "somewhere in the middle." When all was said and done, the error cost the couple tens of thousands of dollars.

A KEY AND A PAIR OF BINOCULARS

David Blair, the original second officer of the *Titanic*, was relieved of duty shortly before the ship set off for New York on April 10, 1912. In Blair's haste to leave, he forgot to turn over all of his equipment to his replacement. One of the forgotten items was the key to the crow's nest telephone. Blair had also left the crow's nest binoculars in his cabin. According to crew survivor testimony, if the lookouts had been given the binoculars, they would have seen the iceberg sooner. And if they'd had access to the phone, they could have alerted the bridge sooner. Either scenario might well have given the *Titanic* enough time to get out of the way.

DYING WORDS

Help Uncle John save them from the brink of exuviation!

USE IT OR LOSE IT

The English language is like a living organism—always growing in some areas while shrinking in others. Those in charge of tracking this change are called *lexicographers*. Their mission: To scour new books, articles, and other media to determine which new words are taking hold and which old ones are being used less and less. Then, about every 10 years or so, they update official dictionaries such as *Merriam-Webster's* and *The Oxford English Dictionary*. So, as "rightsize" and "phat" nudge their way into the *lexicon* (the vocabulary of a language), archaic words like "oppugnant" and "pantdress" find themselves on the chopping block. If you, like us, are sad to see "oppugnant" go, then start working it into your daily conversation, along with the rest of these little-used words...before they're gone forever.

THE CADUCITY LIST

Caducity: Transitory; the state of being impermanent or perishable

Embrangle: To confuse; make more complicated

Mansuetude: Gentleness of manner

Compossible: Able to exist with another thing; consistent

Agrestic: Rural; rustic

Hither: To this place

Long play: A phonograph record that plays at 33 ⅓ revolutions per second

Muliebrity: The condition of being a woman

Retirant: Retiree

Exuviate: To shed; cast off

Impudicity: Immodesty; shamelessness

Olid: Foul-smelling

Abstergent: Cleansing

Frutescent: Resembling or assuming the form of a shrub

Ten-cent store: A shop for low-cost items

Caliginosity: Dim; misty; dark

Fatidical: Prophetic

Snollygoster: A shrewd, unprincipled person, especially a politician

Skedaddle: To leave a place suddenly

Vaticinate: To prophesize or foretell

Nigh: Nearly; almost

Skirr: A whirring sound, as of the wings of birds in flight

Mimeograph: A duplicating printer that presses ink through a stencil

Vilipend: To vilify; treat with contempt

Oppugnant: Combative; opposing; antagonistic

Roborant: Tending to fortify

Recrement: Waste material

Vitamin G: It is now known as riboflavin

Malison: A curse

Pantdress: A one-piece ladies' garment, where the lower part is pants instead of a skirt

Griseous: Having a light grayish color

Apodeictic: Unquestionably true by virtue of demonstration

Periapt: An amulet

Nitid: Bright with a steady but subdued shining

Fubsy: Chubby or squat

Hootenanny: An informal gathering featuring folk singing and often dancing

Zounds: An exclamation of anger or wonder (a contraction of "God's wounds")

*　　*　　*

KID TALK

In 2009 the editors of the *Oxford Junior Dictionary* decided to remove a few hundred words from their newest edition to make room for new ones. Out: "bishop," "disciple," "pew," "devil," "cheetah," "porcupine," "almond," and "fern." In: "blog," "MP3 player," "endangered," "tolerant," and "negotiate." Conservation groups and religious advocates, not to mention linguists, were upset by the replacements. Defending the changes, Vineeta Gupta, the head of children's dictionaries at Oxford University Press, said, "We are limited by how big the dictionary can be. Little hands must be able to handle it." He also maintained that the kids' dictionaries must reflect the lexicon of the times. "The decision to remove nature words is due to the reduced presence of nature in children's lives," he said. And the religious omissions? "People don't go to church as often as before."

A camel drinks water at a rate of 50 cups per minute.

BATHROOM NEWS

The latest from the news stream.

SEAT-SEEKING MISSILE

In 2009 a man was hunting for geese outside the Swedish village of Hökerum and took aim at one a few dozen yards away. He shot and missed, but the bullet kept going. And going. And going. It traveled nearly a mile, over a lake, into a cottage, past the three people who lived in the cottage, and into the outhouse, where it struck and destroyed the toilet seat. The angry homeowners called police, who arrested the hunter on charges of "endangering human life."

DEARLY DE-POTTED

A man was pulling up his pants after using the toilet at a Centerville, Utah, Carl's Jr. restaurant when the gun he was carrying fell out of its holster and hit the floor. The gun went off, which instantly shattered the toilet (no one was harmed). Criminal charges weren't filed, but the Carl's Jr. staff decided to hold a mock funeral for the toilet, which they named "John." Bottles of John's favorite toilet cleanser (Kaboom Bowl Blaster) were given away to mourners. "He was survived by the men's urinal and wash sink," restaurant manager Christian Martinez said.

RING AROUND THE DRAIN

In 2009 Allison Berry was flushing the toilet in the Black Bear Diner in Phoenix, Arizona, when her seven-carat $70,000 wedding ring slipped off her finger, fell into the bowl, and went down the drain. The diner called the city, who sent workers to open a sewer line outside the restaurant. They flushed the toilet continuously, hoping the ring would be forced out. It didn't work, so they called Mr. Rooter, a local plumbing service. Mr. Rooter's Mike Roberts snaked a miniature video camera with an attached infrared light into the pipe, where he found the ring in the plumbing system just a few feet below the bathroom. After five hours of searching, and then 90 minutes of jackhammering and pipe removal—at a cost of $6,500—Berry was finally reunited with her ring.

There is no one in the Marshall Tucker Band named Marshall Tucker.

TASTELESS TOYS

Some playthings that make us ask, "What were they thinking?"

THE TITANIC SLIDE. Measuring 33' high and 50' long, this inflatable slide (available for party rentals) depicts the doomed ship's aft end sticking up out of the water. Just like the passengers who slid to their deaths, kids can slide into...fun. From the description: "Adding to the realism are the famed triple-screw propellers and rudder. One could almost believe the ship is sinking! Who will survive the slide down?"

DALLAS COWBOYS CHEERLEADER BARBIE. Named "Worst Toy of the Year" in 2009 by the Boston consumer advocacy group Campaign for a Commercial-Free Childhood. Their reason: Even though this Barbie doll was rated for children as young as six years old, "She comes with the shortest of short shorts, stiletto boots, and a revealing halter top."

GOD*JESUS. A plastic robot from Japan in the 1980s. It had glowing red eyes and held up a big cross. But was it a religious toy? Not exactly—the robot was more of a fortune-teller: It answered yes-or-no questions just like a Magic 8-Ball.

THE *SWEENEY TODD* RAZOR. "Your friends will think you're really sharp when you flash this authentic prop replica of the murderous singing barber's straight razor! Fashioned from real metal, the realistic reproduction is intricately detailed and arrives in a red-velour, drawstring pouch, ready for more musical mayhem in your hands!"

A SCARY THING HAPPENED. This coloring book, designed to help kids deal with disasters, used to be available for download on the Federal Emergency Management Agency's Web site but was removed in 2009. Why? Because parents complained about the disturbing drawings—tornadoes ripping houses apart, planes crashing into burning buildings—as well as the morbid instructions, such as, "Draw a picture of yourself before the disaster."

TAP, TAP, TAP!

As a kid, Uncle John spent many a Sunday morning watching old movies, many of which featured tap dancing. Even then, he wondered—where'd that dancing come from?

BACKGROUND

Tap dance is one of the true American art forms. It combines elements of the Irish jig and English clog dances with the step dancing and rhythmic drumming of West Africans, brought to the American colonies as slaves. Here are the elements that led to the development of tap dancing as we know it today.

• **Drumming.** It was actually a form of direct communication (like Morse code), which amounted to secret messages sent among slaves—and a way to subjugate authority. Result: Most plantation owners had banned drumming by the 1750s, forcing the slaves to turn to other forms of percussion, such as beating out rhythms with hands, feet, and even bones. Over generations the "language" of drumming was lost, and the rhythmic beating grew to be more about music and entertainment—both for the slaves and for the plantation owners, who taught the slaves clog dances and jigs to go along with the percussion.

• **Buck-and-Wing.** The most popular form of entertainment in the U.S. in the 1840s was the minstrel show. White performers in "blackface" makeup sang songs, performed comedy sketches, and spoke in "Negro" dialects, all in a crude parody of black people. Parodying black dance was also included, especially one called "buck-and-wing"—a slow, shuffling dance in which balance is shifted from the heel to the tip of the foot, which is emphatically and loudly tapped on the ground. After the Civil War, as black performers joined minstrel shows, buck-and-wing was developed into a precise, lightning-fast dance, with the best dancers tapping their toes and heels many times a second. Also gaining popularity in minstrel shows: challenge dances, in which two performers tried to outdo each other with faster steps and more-intricate moves.

• **Soft Shoe.** By the early 1900s, "vaudeville" variety shows were the dominant entertainment across the United States, and dance was part of it. In addition to buck-and-wing, performed in wooden-soled shoes, a slower, smoother style called "soft shoe" developed, performed in shoes with leather soles. Eventually the two styles blended, and to make the tapping sound more prominent, around 1920 dancers started to nail blocks of cheap metal to the heels of their shoes, marking the invention of metal taps and the birth of modern tap dancing. Perhaps the best challenge dancer of all was Bill "Bojangles" Robinson, who never lost a face-off on the black vaudeville circuit. (He wouldn't get to perform before a white audience until he was 50 years old, in the film *Blackbirds of 1928*.)

• **Flash.** As jazz music took hold in the 1920s, jazz tap dance grew with it. The footwork was fast and worked with the complex syncopated rhythms of jazz. Broadway shows began to incorporate chorus lines doing complicated tap routines, and a style of acrobatic tap dancing called "flash" became popular. Most notable "flash" dancers: the Nicholas Brothers, who jumped from platforms, leaped into the air, slid down ramps, and just kept tapping.

• **Tap in the movies.** During the Great Depression of the 1930s, tap reached its widest audience yet. Director Busby Berkeley's lavish musicals (such as *42nd Street* and *Footlight Parade*) featured hordes of showgirls tap dancing in complicated patterns. Fred Astaire and Ginger Rogers brought another kind of tap dance to audiences with films like *Top Hat*, *Swing Time*, and *Shall We Dance*. They had glamour, grace, and an elegance that made them the most popular dancing pair in movie history. Secret weapon: a stationary camera filming each dance number in a (usually) single unbroken shot while keeping the dancers in full view in the frame. This made it possible for fans to focus on the perfection of the dancing.

• **Decline...and comeback.** By the 1960s, tap's popularity had waned, and many well-known dancers left it entirely. But it found a new audience with the release of the documentary film *No Maps on My Taps* (1979), followed by the hit Broadway musical *Sophisticated Ladies* (1981), which starred the best-known modern tap dancer (and tap advocate), 35-year-old Gregory Hines. Other tap films: *The Cotton Club* (1984), *A Chorus Line* (1985), and *Tap* (1989), starring Hines, Sammy Davis Jr., and 16-year-old Savion Glover, who fused tap with urban dance forms. He became a sensation with the 1996 Broadway musical *Bring in da Noise, Bring in da Funk*. Hines called him not just a good tap dancer but the *best* tap dancer who's ever lived.

First video game based on a movie: *Raiders of the Lost Ark* (Atari, 1982).

GRIP

Bathroom readers take note: You can find inspiration in the oddest places.

On the third floor of the Philadelphia Free Library is a glass case displaying a stuffed crow. It's a raven, to be precise—the very bird considered by many scholars to have been the inspiration for Edgar Allan Poe's classic poem "The Raven." How this stuffed bird came to inspire Poe's poetry lies in the life and work of another great 19th century writer. Charles Dickens had a talking raven named Grip as a pet. The bird delighted his family and friends with pronouncements like, "Keep up your spirit!" "Never say die!" and "Polly, put the kettle on, we'll all have tea!" Grip died in 1841 after eating lead paint off a wall, an event Dickens recounted in a letter to a friend: "On the clock striking twelve he appeared slightly agitated, but soon recovered, stopped to bark, staggered, exclaimed, 'Halloa, old girl!' and died."

Dickens had the bird stuffed and set in a glass case. His novel *Barnaby Rudge*, published later that year, featured a talking raven named Grip. When the bird first appears in the book, someone asks, "What was that tapping at the door?" Someone else answers, "'Tis someone knocking softly at the shutter." Poe was working as a reviewer for *Graham's Magazine* when *Barnaby Rudge* was printed in the United States. His review was favorable, except for one major flaw: the talking raven. Poe felt it could have been more "prophetically heard in the course of the drama." Four years later Poe published his famous poem, with its lines "Suddenly there came a tapping...at my chamber door," and "Quoth the Raven, 'Nevermore.'" The poem was an immediate success and secured Poe's lasting reputation in American literature.

As for Grip, after Dickens' death the bird and case were sold at auction (the bird went for $210; the letter describing its death for $385), eventually ending up in the collection of Col. Richard Gimbel, the world's foremost collector of Poe memorabilia. By then Grip's association with Poe's poem had been well established by scholars. In 1971 Gimbel's entire collection, including the bird, was donated to the Philadelphia Library, where you can still see it today in the Rare Book department.

Author Norman Mailer claimed to have invented thumb wrestling.

SPOKESTHINGIES

Why spend big bucks on an unpredictable, real-life celebrity to endorse your products when you can make one up from scratch?

MAVIS BEACON
If you used a computer program to learn to type in the past 20 years, you probably used *Mavis Beacon Teaches Typing*. It's one of the bestselling instructional software titles ever, with more than five million copies sold since 1987. But the professorial-looking woman who appears on the box, it turns out, isn't typing wizard Mavis Beacon. Beacon isn't even a real person. The attractive woman in the photo is former fashion model Renee Lesperance. In 1985 Les Crane, chairman of Software Toolworks, the educational software company behind the program, spotted Lesperance in a store in Beverly Hills and hired her to "be" Mavis Beacon. The marketing department created the name—Mavis, in honor of singer Mavis Staples, and Beacon, as in a guiding light.

THE GEICO CAVEMEN
In 2004 GEICO insurance hired the Martin Agency, which had created the GEICO Gecko, to come up with a new ad campaign to direct customers to its Web site. The agency's writers built on the idea that the Web site was so user-friendly, "even a caveman can do it." The first ad depicted a TV-commercial shoot: An actor says the catchphrase, then the boom microphone operator—an actual caveman—storms off the set, shouting, "Not cool!" In the second ad, a GEICO rep takes two cavemen out to dinner to apologize. The cavemen are dressed in tennis whites and ordering "roast duck with mango salsa," the joke being that they aren't dumb and primitive, they're Yuppies. By 2007 dozens of Caveman commercials had aired and were so popular that ABC turned the concept into a sitcom called *Cavemen*. The show wasn't as popular—it lasted only six episodes.

THE NAUGA
In the late 1960s, the industrial chemical giant Uniroyal created a synthetic leather substitute out of plastic and vinyl. It was devel-

oped in its Naugatuck, Connecticut, plant, so they called it
naugahyde. But the company still had to convince consumers that
naugahyde was a viable material for products like car seats and
sofas, and that it was different from cheap, hard plastic surfaces—
more like a soft animal hide. Solution: Invent an "animal" to be
the source of naugahyde. Uniroyal launched a tongue-in-cheek ad
campaign that claimed naugahyde was the (shed) skin of a magical animal called the Nauga. Uniroyal's artists designed a short,
smiling brown creature, reminiscent of the Tasmanian Devil from
the old Warner Bros. cartoons, and writers created an elaborate
backstory: They are native to Sumatra and, in the 18th century,
came to America, where they gladly donated their skins to make
uniforms for George Washington's Continental Army. The campaign worked—by the end of the 1970s, naugahyde was the most
commonly used synthetic leather in the U.S.

JACK
In the 1970s, fast food chain Jack in the Box used a simple graphic
of a clown head as their logo—a white ball with two blue dots for
eyes, a red smile, and a little yellow hat. They stopped using the
logo in 1980, when the restaurant chain wanted a more adult-
friendly image. But they brought it back in 1995, when the clown
head was turned into an advertising mascot: Jack, the company's
eccentric CEO. From the shoulders down, Jack was a man in a
business suit. From the shoulders up, he was a gigantic version of
the clown logo. Cheeky ad campaigns provided Jack's backstory—
he loves hamburgers because he grew up on a Colorado cattle
ranch, he's married to a normal-headed human woman, and he
has a son who shares his "genetic" condition. The character was
the brainchild of the chain's marketing executive Dick Sittig, who
also provides the voice for Jack. Since the introduction of CEO
Jack, the chain's sales have tripled.

*　　　*　　　*

"I have always believed that writing advertisements is the second
most profitable form of writing. The first, of course, is ransom
notes."

—**Philip Dusenberry**

At least two original copies of the Declaration of Independence have been discovered at flea markets.

MEET HITLER'S DOCTOR

Was der Führer felled by foolish fart pharmacology?
Here's Part II of the foul tale. (Part I is on page 77.)

STRANGE BEDFELLOWS

By the mid-1930s, the Nazis had already begun destroying what before their rise had been one of the most advanced medical communities in the world. At the same time that they undermined the scientific underpinnings of the German medical establishment with their loony racial theories and crackpot pseudo-science, the Nazis were driving German Jews out of the profession, along with any "Aryan" Germans who opposed Nazism. And yet for all the damage the Nazis did to German medicine, there were still plenty of skilled, capable doctors from whom Hitler could choose his personal physician. So it's all the more remarkable that he chose someone as peculiar and incompetent as Dr. Theodor Morell.

DOC MEDIOC–RITY

Morell's resume left a lot to be desired. A onetime ship's doctor who served as an army physician during World War I, he opened a general practice on the fashionable Kurfürstendamm street in Berlin after the war and counted a lot of society figures—politicians, actors, artists, nightclub singers—among his patients. With the exception of occasional cases of bad skin, impotence, or venereal disease, Morell shied away from treating people who were gen-uinely ill, referring these cases to other doctors while he built up a clientele of fashionable, big-spending patients whose largely psy-chosomatic illnesses responded well to his close attention, flattery, and ineffective quack treatments.

Morell's skill at coddling his patients was masterful, but his abilities as a physician were clearly deficient, to the point of put-ting their health at risk. "In practice he was occasionally careless," biographer John Toland writes in *Adolf Hitler*. "He was known to have wrapped a patient's arm with a bandage he had just used to wipe a table, and to inject the same needle without sterilization into two patients."

Hitler had a bowling alley in his home in southern Germany.

"MADE" IN BULGARIA

In addition to overseeing his practice, Morell served on the board of Hageda, a pharmaceutical company that manufactured a strange medication called Mutaflor, whose active ingredient was live bacteria cultured from the fecal matter of "a Bulgarian peasant of the most vigorous stock."

Mutaflor was intended to treat digestive disorders—the theory being that digestive problems were caused when healthy bacteria, which lived in the intestinal tract and were essential to good digestion, were killed off or crowded out by unhealthy bacteria. Ingesting the cultured dung of a vigorous, clean-living Bulgarian peasant, the theory went, would reintroduce beneficial bacteria into an unhealthy digestive tract and restore proper function.

That was the theory, and while it *sounded* pretty good, in truth it was literally a load of crap, and good German doctors knew it. Not so Dr. Morell—and because he had a financial interest in the company that made Mutaflor, he prescribed the pills to virtually all his patients, whether they suffered from digestive complaints or not. Hitler *did* suffer from digestive complaints, of course, and Morell soon had the Führer taking regular doses of Mutaflor …plus two tablets of Dr. Koester's Anti-Gas Pills at every meal.

PRIMARY PHYSICIAN

Hitler's intestinal ailments were intermittent and, as had been the case during his childhood, still had a considerable psychological component: He suffered from attacks of cramps and farting during times of stress, then when things calmed down his symptoms abated. After he placed himself under Morell's care, it was just a matter of time before his condition improved, and when relief finally came a few months later—at about the same time his eczema began to clear up—Hitler naturally attributed his deliverance to Morell.

The "cure" was only temporary, but no matter—the Führer had finally found a doctor he could believe in. "Nobody has ever before told me so clearly and precisely what is wrong with me," Hitler told his chief architect, Albert Speer. "His method of cure is so logical that I have the greatest confidence in him. I shall follow his prescription to the letter." Morell would remain by Hitler's side until almost the very end.

HEAVEN SCENT

Hitler took to Morell immediately, but the Führer's inner circle despised the doctor from the start, and not just because he was an obvious quack—he was also an extremely unpleasant person to be around. The morbidly obese Morell did not bathe regularly: His skin and hair were greasy, his fingernails often filthy, and when his powerful body odor and bad breath weren't enough to clear the room, his propensity for belching and farting in polite company usually did the trick. "He has an appetite as big as his belly and gives not only visual but audible expression of it," Speer observed.

Even Eva Braun found Morell repulsive, but Hitler didn't care. When she and others complained about his offensive body odor, the Führer brushed them off. "I do not employ him for his fragrance, but to look after my health," he'd say. (Who knows? Maybe Hitler liked having another farter in the room, so that no one who "smelt it" could tell for sure who'd "dealt it.")

TAKE THIS...AND THIS...AND THIS

In those early days, Morell's influence on Hitler was fairly benign; the stinky doctor limited himself to giving diet tips and, of course, prescribing Mutaflor and Dr. Koester's Anti-Gas Pills. But over time he became more controlling over what Hitler was allowed to eat, and the number and strength of the medications he prescribed increased dramatically. In the years to come he would prescribe enzymes, liver extracts, stimulants, hormones, painkillers, sedatives, tranquilizers, muscle relaxants, morphine derivatives (to induce constipation), laxatives (to relieve it), and other drugs by the dozen.

According to one estimate, by the early 1940s Hitler was taking 92 different kinds of drugs, including 63 different pills and skin lotions. Some medicines were taken only when specific complaints arose, but others were taken every day. By the summer of 1941, Hitler was popping between 120 and 150 pills a week on average. And on top of all the pills, Morell also administered injections—as many as 10 a day, sometimes more. So many, in fact, that even Herman Goering, Hitler's heir apparent and himself a morphine addict, was startled by their frequency and took to calling Morell the "Reich Injection Master."

Nobody knew for sure what Morell was giving Hitler. There were other physicians in the Führer's service—two surgeons, Dr.

Karl Brandt and Dr. Hans Karl von Hasselbach, traveled with Hitler in case he ever needed emergency surgery, and other specialists, such as visiting ear, nose, and throat doctor Erwin Giesing, were called on from time to time to treat specific complaints. But none knew what Morell was really up to. Any physician worth his salt would have been alarmed by all the injections Morell was administering. But whenever Brandt or anyone else asked him what was in the shots or why Hitler needed so many, he shrugged them off as vitamin or glucose (sugar) injections, or answered cryptically, "I give him what he needs."

THE ONE-TWO PUNCH

Considering all the medications that Morell was administering to Hitler, why was it Dr. Koester's Anti-Gas Pills that finally prompted the other physicians to act? It may have been the simple fact that they came in a tin. Most of the pills and shots that Hitler took were unidentified and mysterious, but Dr. Koester's Anti-Gas Pills came in a little metal container (like Altoids breath mints or Sucrets throat lozenges) that identified them by name and even listed the active ingredients: gentian, belladonna, and an extract of something called *nux vomica*.

The gentian was harmless enough. But the presence of the other two ingredients in the pills, plus the revelation that Hitler, on top of all his other medications, was popping as many as 20 of the anti-gas pills a day, was startling. Even if Dr. Morell *had* read the label on the tin, he might not have known that *nux vomica* is a seed that contains large amounts of *strychnine*, commonly used as the active ingredient in rat poison. Belladonna, also known as deadly nightshade, contains *atropine*, a toxic substance that can cause excitement, confusion, hallucinations, coma, and death if taken in large quantities.

That's what alarmed Dr. Giesing when he saw the six black pills sitting on Hitler's breakfast tray that morning in July 1944: Without even realizing it, Hitler's own personal physician had exposed him on a daily basis to significant doses of not one, but *two* deadly poisons.

DER GUINEA PIG

By then it was obvious to everyone around him that Hitler's physical and mental state were deteriorating. His tremor had become quite pronounced, his memory was slipping, he was having trouble following conversations, and his mood swings were intensifying. Giesing wondered if the rat poison in the fart pills was the cause of some or all of these symptoms. He popped a few tablets himself...and when he began to experience some of the same symptoms, including irritability and abdominal cramps, he shared his theory with Hitler's surgeons, Dr. Brandt and Dr. von Hasselbach.

THE PLOT THICKENS

Brandt and von Hasselbach had never liked Dr. Morell and had no faith in his abilities, and like Dr. Giesing they were concerned for the state of Hitler's health. Now, they thought, they had an opportunity to get rid of Morell once and for all and give the Führer the proper medical care he clearly needed. But if they thought getting rid of Morell would be easy once his incompetence was exposed, they soon learned how mistaken they were. When Brandt told Hitler what was in the pills he was popping like candy, he not only took Morell's side, he *fired* Brandt and von Hasselbach for daring to interfere with Morell, and he told the visiting Dr. Giesing that his services were no longer needed.

Even though Morell was as stunned as everyone else to learn that he'd been medicating the Führer with rat poison, Hitler himself didn't seem to mind. "I myself always thought they were just charcoal tablets for soaking up my intestinal gases, and I always felt rather pleasant after taking them," he explained.

And though it was Morell's responsibility to keep track of how many of the pills Hitler was taking, Hitler himself had ignored Morell's instruction to take only two at a time and had begun popping six or more before each meal. The dictator didn't blame the pills for his stomach cramps, either, since those dated back to his childhood.

Now that Hitler understood that the fart pills were potentially dangerous, he stopped taking so many...but his health did not improve. His physical and mental decline not only continued, it accelerated.

So what was the true cause of his collapse?

Part III of the story is on page 441.

70% of wallets lost in the United States are eventually returned to their owners.

VERY QUIZ-LIKE

*Latin words that end in "ine" describe the characteristics of particular animals
—canine, for example, means doglike. Can you match the other "ines"
to what animal they refer to in English? (Answers on page 537.)*

1. Bear		**a)** Porcine
2. Dove		**b)** Acrine
3. Fox		**c)** Ursine
4. Horse		**d)** Butine
5. Squirrel		**e)** Feline
6. Cat		**f)** Ovine
7. Pig		**g)** Spermophine
8. Dolphin		**h)** Bovine
9. Wolf		**i)** Cavine
10. Yak		**j)** Bosine
11. Cow		**k)** Cervine
12. Sheep		**l)** Rhombomine
13. Elephant		**m)** Equine
14. Orangutan		**n)** Lupine
15. Turtle		**o)** Terrapine
16. Hare		**p)** Vulpine
17. Deer		**q)** Macropodine
18. Gerbil		**r)** Lapine
19. Frog		**s)** Proboscine
20. Killer whale		**t)** Columbine
21. Hawk		**u)** Orcine
22. Guinea pig		**v)** Delphine
23. Gila monster		**w)** Bubaline
24. Kangaroo		**x)** Pongine
25. Water buffalo		**y)** Helodine

Say what? Your central nervous system filters out 99% of what your senses register.

THE PROVERBIAL TRUTH

*You know that "all that glitters isn't gold," but there are countless
other proverbs that you may never have heard. Here are
some of the BRI's favorites from around the world.*

If everyone gave one
thread, the poor man
would have a shirt.
Russian

If begging should
unfortunately be thy
lot, knock at the
large gates only.
Arabian

No one is rich
enough to do with-
out a neighbor.
Danish

Worry often gives a
small thing a big
shadow.
Swedish

When you're thirsty
it's too late to think
about digging a well.
Japanese

To request timidly is
to invite refusal.
Latin

Slander slays three
persons: the speaker,
the spoken to, and
the spoken of.
Hebrew

To take revenge is
to sacrifice oneself.
Congolese

Who does not disci-
pline his child will
later punish himself.
Persian

A half-truth is a
whole lie.
Yiddish

He who marries
might be sorry. He
who does not *will* be
sorry.
Czech

Beware the man
who does not talk
and the dog that
does not bark.
Portuguese

To you your religion;
to me my religion.
Muslim

Those who give
have all things;
those who withhold
have nothing.
Hindu

Who gossips to you
will gossip of you.
Turkish

A wise man changes
his mind, a fool
never does.
Spanish

Who accepts noth-
ing has nothing to
return.
German

The tongue is but
three inches long,
yet it can injure a
man six feet high.
Japanese

He who has not yet
reached the opposite
shore should not
make fun of him
who is drowning.
West African

What is true by
lamplight is not
always true by sun-
light.
French

He who laughs, lasts.
Norwegian

Spit-shine: Art restorers often use saliva to clean old oil paintings.

IT (PROBABLY) WON'T KILL YOU TO EAT…

All sorts of "natural" stuff you would never want to eat is consumable by humans. You shouldn't actually do it (you really, really, shouldn't), but, technically, all of these things are edible.

…Leather. It's made from the skin of a cow, so it's actually beef—very, very chewy beef. But don't think you can just feast on that old motorcycle jacket in the back of the closet—most leather has been treated with dyes and chemicals to make it durable.

…Raw meat. People all over the world eat it every day. Steak tartare, for example, is a European gourmet dish that consists of spiced raw ground beef. (Lamb tartare is a British version.) And don't forget Japanese sushi, which often contains raw fish.

…Sand. You probably eat sand already. Finely ground common *silica*, or beach sand, is an ingredient in anti-caking agents used in many packaged foods, such as sugar and flour. But it's a *very* small amount—too much can scratch your teeth.

…Paper. As it passes through the body, fiber attracts cholesterol and other unwelcome substances. Fiber exits your body largely intact—in other words, it is not digestible. Most paper is made of wood cellulose, which is fiber. But the bleach that makes paper white, the dye that colors it, and the ink that printers print it with are all toxic to humans.

…Packing peanuts. *Some*—but not all—brands are made of highly processed, molded cornstarch. Not only does that make them biodegradable, but technically it makes them edible, too. Chemicals are added, which aren't good for you, but if you had to eat a mouthful, they would probably taste like a rice cake.

…Flowers. Botanically speaking, many common vegetables, such as broccoli and cauliflower, are flowers. Other safe-to-eats: dandelions (they're sweet like honey), carnations (also sweet), mums (tangy), marigolds (like saffron), and sunflowers (like artichokes).

First U.S. President to be protected by the Secret Service: Grover Cleveland (1893–97).

IRONIC, ISN'T IT?

*There's nothing like a good dose of irony to put the
problems of day-to-day life into proper perspective.*

DE-PROGRAMMED

In July 2008, California didn't have enough money to pay
all state employees, so Governor Arnold Schwarzenegger
laid off 10,000 workers. A week later, state controller John Chiang
discovered that the money-saving expenditures couldn't be applied
to state payroll records because the system was written in an old
computer language called COBOL...and the only state employees
who knew how to use it were the ones who had just been fired.

WIPING THE SLATE CLEAN

Slate Rock Park in Providence, Rhode Island, commemorates
the spot where the state's founder, Roger Williams, first arrived
in 1636. Williams stepped off a boat on the Seekonk River and
onto a slate ledge, which was marked with a plaque. In 1877
workers were attempting to expose more of the underground
slate to create a larger monument to Williams. They accidentally
dynamited the entire piece of slate...and now there's no slate in
Slate Park.

FAMILY ISSUES

Attendees of a May 2008 New York concert by the band Ellis
Unit got a gift with their $20 admission: a free one-year subscrip-
tion to the music magazine *Blender*. The lead singer and guitarist
for Ellis Unit is Gus Wenner, son of Jann Wenner, publisher of
Blender's chief rival, *Rolling Stone*.

STONE COLD DEAD

A 77-year-old man went to visit the graves of his parents in the
St. Gregoire Cemetery in Buckingham, Quebec, in 2008. For some
reason, he decided to rearrange some ornamental rocks around
one of the tombstones. Bad idea: The rocks were holding the
tombstone in place, and as the man was digging around in the
dirt, the tombstone fell, struck him on the head, and killed him.

KURBY AND KRYSTAL GO TO WHITE CASTLE

After a year of dating, Kurby and Krystal of London, Kentucky, were married in March 2009. They met when both were employed by the local White Castle fast food restaurant, so they decided to make their wedding White Castle-themed—it was held at "their" White Castle and the cake was shaped like a hamburger. Congratulations to Kurby and Krystal...McDonald.

SWEET IRONY

In 2008 a semi-truck overturned at the intersection of Highways 6 and 59 in Texas. Its cargo: sticky-sweet molasses. More than 5,000 gallons of the sugary stuff leaked onto the road, causing road closures and traffic delays into the nearby city of Sugar Land.

CUTTING REMARK

Though it's a very common practice in the United States, some parents choose not to circumcise their newborn boys. In 2009 a co-director of newborn nurseries at Massachusetts General Hospital in Boston came out in favor of the procedure in an interview with *Men's Health* magazine, saying that its sanitary benefits outweigh fears of surgical complications. His name: Dr. Wang.

HAMBURGLAR

In 2008 McDonald's went on social networking sites such as Facebook and MySpace to solicit amateur musicians' takes on hip-hop updates of its Big Mac "two all-beef patties, special sauce, lettuce, cheese" jingle. One of the finalists—Tamien Bain, who'd finished in fourth place—was disqualified because he'd recently served 12 years in prison...for robbing a McDonald's restaurant at gunpoint.

*   *   *

IT'S USUALLY THAT

"In January 2007, a rotten-egg smell descended on Manhattan for hours, causing several buildings to be evacuated and frightened throngs to wonder if terrorists were attacking the city with gas. Officials later blamed swamp gas from New Jersey."

—*The Week*

According to one 2002 study, counting sheep doesn't help you get to sleep any faster.

ADVENTUROUS SPIRITS

Every culture, advanced or primitive, makes some type of alcoholic beverage. What they make depends on what ingredients are available…which might account for these.

VINE SNAKE WHISKEY. Mescal is traditionally bottled with a worm inside. This concoction goes a step further. The whiskey, made in Thailand, is flavored with a coiled vine snake right inside the bottle. Good news: It's only mildly venomous.

CYNAR. Liqueurs are heavily sweetened alcoholic drinks flavored with fruit, nuts, or spices. Cynar is an *artichoke*-flavored liqueur. It is the same greenish color as a pan of water in which you've just cooked your artichokes, and it's very popular in Italy, its country of origin.

GRAPPA. It's a kind of *pomace*, which is a brandy (distilled grape juice) made from the leftovers of winemaking— grape seeds, grape skins, and stalks.

FERNET. This liqueur is used as medicine in Italy, but in Argentina they drink shots of it. It's made from many different fruits and herbs, including myrrh, aloe, rhubarb, saffron, and grapes. It's described as tasting like minty charcoal.

AGWA. The manufacturers promise an "energy boost" with this liqueur, which makes sense because it's made with coca leaf, which is also what cocaine is made from. But it doesn't actually contain any cocaine…it's just flavored to taste like it does.

PELINKOVAC. Many spirits, such as anisette or Jagermeister, taste like licorice. This Balkan liqueur does, too, only there's no sugar added, so it tastes like bitter licorice, supposedly like chewing on licorice root.

ADVOCAAT. Popular in the Netherlands, this is a creamy drink that tastes like pudding and has the consistency of pancake batter. That's because, like pancake batter, it contains raw egg yolks.

DUMB CROOKS: SILLY WEAPONS UNIT

"Give me all your cash or I'll shoot you with this flip-flop!"

Crook: Michael Reed of Fort Worth, Texas
Weapon: A tree branch
Story: In December 2008, Reed stormed into Eddie's Fried Chicken, waving the tree branch around, and demanded all the money in the register. But the 50-year-old robber's branch was no match for a 56-year-old employee's broom. After a brief battle, Reed was de-branched and ran away empty-handed. He hid in a nearby dumpster and was captured by police a short time later.

Crook: Karen Lee Joachimi of Lake City, Florida
Weapon: An electric chain saw
Story: In 1996 the 20-year-old attempted to rob a Howard Johnson's. Her chances of success would have been better had she plugged in her chain saw first. She was easily apprehended.

Crook: A 22-year-old man (unnamed) from Fresno, California
Weapon: A kielbasa
Story: The man entered a home in the middle of the night in September 2008 and stole some cash while the residents were asleep. Then for some reason the intruder took a piece of sausage out of the refrigerator, went into the bedroom, and began hitting the sleeping couple with it. They awoke and chased him out of the house. He was easy to find because he'd left his wallet behind.

Crook: Gelando Olivieri of Deland, Florida
Weapons: A palm frond and a pair of flip-flops
Story: In 2009 Olivieri pulled his T-shirt up over his head and entered V and F Discount Beverage. He waved the pointy end of a palm frond at the clerk and repeatedly said, "Give me 50 dollars!" while he tapped the palm frond on the counter and occasionally slapped the clerk's hand with it. According to witnesses, Olivieri

was also brandishing a pair of flip-flops. The robbery was thwarted by another odd weapon when a customer picked up a bar stool and pointed it at Olivieri, who then ran out of the store. He was quickly apprehended.

Crook: William McMiller of Indianapolis, Indiana
Weapon: A screwdriver
Story: In 2006 McMiller walked into a Kentucky Fried Chicken, waited in line, ordered some food, and then told the cashier, "Give me the money before I shoot you." He reached into his back pocket, as if he were going for a gun, but all he had was a screwdriver. Another customer *did* have a gun...and pointed it at McMiller until police arrived and took away the screwdriver (and McMiller).

Crook: An unidentified man from Colorado Springs, Colorado
Weapon: A Klingon *Bat'leth*
Story: In February 2009, the masked man robbed two 7-Eleven stores in one night with a replica of the sword used by the alien race on *Star Trek: The Next Generation*. Neither clerk was injured because neither tried to fight back, possibly because of the imposing appearance of the curved implement with two sharp blades on each end. Bucking the "dumb crooks" trend, this thief was never caught; police still aren't sure if his "weapon" was made of metal or plastic.

Crook: Michael Kaminski of Akron, Ohio
Weapon: Cheap cologne
Story: In 2008 Kaminski attempted to rob two men in the parking lot of a video store using a gun-shaped cologne dispenser. Bad move: One of the "victims" was a martial arts expert who easily pinned Kaminski to the ground. Adding insult to injury, the cologne bottle broke and spilled all over Kaminski, who spent a fragrant night in jail.

*　　*　　*

"A lot of people think kids say the darnedest things, but so would you if you had no education."

—Eugene Mirman

THE POTTY POLLS, PT. II

More information on bathroom habits collected by pollsters in the
United States and around the world. (Part I is on page 168.)

YOUR TOOTHBRUSH AND YOU

• 54% of Americans polled in a 2007 survey commissioned by Phillips Sonicare, a brand of electric toothbrushes, said they'd continue to use their toothbrush after dropping it on the bathroom floor. 9% of American men say they've reused a toothbrush after dropping it in *the toilet.*

• 44% of Americans say they'd be willing to share their toothbrush with their spouse in a pinch; 8% say they'd share with a friend.

CLEANLINESS IS NEXT TO...IMPOSSIBLE

• 47% of Americans say they clean the bathroom once a week, and 88% say they at least replace the hand towels that often, according to a 2008 study of bathroom habits.

• Cleaning the toilet is—understandably—one of the least-popular bathroom jobs. According to a 2008 study by S.C. Johnson & Son, makers of Scrubbing Bubbles, 28% of Americans say they'd rather pay bills than clean the toilet, and a third of Americans polled say they put off cleaning it until it starts to *look* dirty.

IN THE SHOWER

• 14% of Americans and Canadians surveyed in 2007 by Grohe, a manufacturer of bathroom products, say they clean the bathtub or shower every time they use it. 20% of Americans and 24% of Canadians say that they clean the shower *while taking* a shower.

• 28% of people who sing in the shower say they sing rock 'n' roll tunes; 19% sing country tunes.

• Five most popular songs sung in the shower: 1) "Singin' in the Rain," 2) "Amazing Grace," 3) "Splish Splash," 4) "Hey Jude," 5) songs the bather makes up. (Uncle John sings "Rubber Duckie.")

• 22% of Americans say they've showered with another person for amorous purposes. This includes 26% of American men...and only

18% of American women. With Canadians the roles are reversed: 24% of women and only 19% of men.

• If you could take a shower with anyone in the world, who would it be? Top three shower-worthy female celebrities: 1) Angelina Jolie, 2) Jessica Alba, and 3) Pamela Anderson. Top three males: 1) Brad Pitt, 2) George Clooney, and 3) Johnny Depp. (In Canada, Depp is tied with Mel Gibson.)

• One third of all Scots surveyed in a 2008 poll said they'd consider sharing a shower or bath with another person "in order to save money."

GOING GREEN

• 91% of Americans say they have modified their bathroom behavior to save water, according to the 2008 survey. Most popular method of conservation: not running the water while brushing teeth—71% of Americans surveyed say they keep the water off.

• In the same survey, nearly half of respondents say they've cut back the amount of time they spend in the shower, and just under a third say they take fewer showers and baths. A similar number said they flush the toilet less often than they used to.

AROUND THE WORLD

• 60% of Australians say they feel perfectly comfortable "relieving themselves in front of their partners," according to a 2007 survey conducted by the New Zealand *Herald*.

• Only 20% of Canadians say they'd fish their cell phone out of the toilet if it fell in, according to a 2007 survey by Microsoft.

• Nearly 1 in 3 South Koreans polled in 2008 say they have a TV in the bathroom; 65% say they talk on the phone. (No word on how many watch TV while talking on the phone.)

• Top five reasons British women give for ending relationships with men, according to a survey by the dating Web site Cupid-bay.com: 1) He doesn't wash his hands after using the bathroom; 2) He farts too much; 3) His feet smell; 4) He leaves toothpaste in the sink; 5) He doesn't clean the bathtub after using it.

• Top five reasons British men give for ending relationships with women: 1) Her friends are annoying; 2) She talks too much; 3) She shops too much; 4) Her new (short) haircut looks terrible; 5) She hates pets/would never buy his mates a round.

ROCK 'N' ROLL DIARY

Gossip and trivia from pop music.

RADIOHEAD. Bucking the tradition of rock groups trashing hotel rooms, Radiohead actually does the opposite. Not only do they clean up their own rooms, but they once snuck back into a hotel after checking out to clean up a room that their opening band had trashed.

THE WHITE STRIPES. Before he was a rock star, Jack White repaired furniture. At 21 years old, he even started his own business, called Third Man Upholstery. (His slogan: "Your furniture's not dead.") Although White enjoyed the work, he wasn't into the business aspect of it, which began to suffer when his clients stopped taking him seriously. Why? According to White, he'd write poetry inside their furniture and write his invoices in crayon.

HAWKWIND. The '70s progressive-rock band was playing an outdoor concert during a rainstorm. As part of their theatrical act, singer Nik Turner dressed up in a frog costume and ran onto the stage. On this particular day, however, the stage was muddy and Turner slid all the way across, over the edge, and into a muddy puddle on the ground (just like a real frog).

JOHN & YOKO. In 1969 Lennon and Ono released the avant-garde *Wedding Album*. Side 1 featured 22 minutes of the couple yelling each others' names. Side 2 featured recordings of the couple on their honeymoon. According to the book *Rock Bottom*, "The album caused great hilarity when it was reviewed by a London journalist who was sent an advance copy, in the form of two single-sided discs. Sadly, he didn't realize that some record companies distribute test pressings in this form, and commented that he preferred the two sides which contained an electronic hum."

THE COMMODORES. How did they get their name? In 1968 keyboardist William King put on a blindfold, opened up a dictionary, and placed his finger on a random word. "We lucked out," King recalled. "We almost became the Commodes!"

CLASS ACTS

To balance out heavy classes like advanced calculus, medieval literature, and organic chemistry, many schools offer a few oddball courses like these.

Zombies in Popular Culture. "The history, significance, and representation of the zombie in horror and fantasy texts. Final projects foster thoughtful connections between students and the zombie." (Columbia College, Chicago)

Whiteness: The Other Side of Racism. "While racism disadvantages people of color, it provides benefits to whites. By examining the other side of racism—whiteness—we can see the advantages in education, health care, and employment that white people continually accrue." (Mount Holyoke College, MA)

Learning From YouTube. "What can YouTube teach us, and is this how, what, and all we'd like to learn?" (Pitzer College, CA)

Popular "Logic" on TV Judge Shows. "The seminar will be concerned with identifying logical fallacies on *Judge Judy* and *The People's Court* and why such strategies are so widespread. It is *not* a course about law or 'legal reasoning.'" (U. C. Berkeley)

Tightwaddery. "On a theoretical level, we will consider how living frugally benefits your mind, your body, your relationships, your community, and the environment. On a practical level, we will sharpen haggling skills." (Alfred University, NY)

The Science of Superheroes. "Have you ever wondered if Superman could really bend steel bars? Would a gamma ray accident turn you into the Hulk? In this seminar, we discuss the science (or lack of science) behind many famous superheroes." (U. C. Irvine)

Far Side Entomology. "The course is designed to introduce you to the humanistic side of entomology by utilizing the humor of Gary Larson as paradigms of human-insect interactions. The 'cartoon' format normally provides an anthropomorphic view of insects. This can be an incredibly rich venue as an introduction to the more serious aspects of insects and their relevance to human activities." (Oregon State University)

THE CORVETTE HITS THE ROAD

On page 136, we told you how Chevrolet got the Corvette and how the Corvette got its name. Here's how the first models made it into the hands of consumers…and how they very nearly became the last Corvettes ever built.

THE PARTS BIN SPECIAL

The full-size clay model of the Corvette was, in terms of style, ahead of its time and a sight to behold. But it was still a two-seater sports car, and there was a limit to the amount of money GM was willing to spend on a class of vehicle that made up less than a quarter of one percent of all auto sales in the United States. Bob McLean had the unenviable task of building the Corvette using as many existing Chevrolet parts as possible—in other words, he had to build a sports car out of non-sports-car parts. Using preexisting parts did, however, offer one advantage: Chevy could bring the car to market much more quickly than if it had been engineered from scratch.

Harley Earl had a lot of muscle at GM, but even *he* couldn't pry a V-8 out of Cadillac, Buick, or Oldsmobile, so jealously did the executives of those higher-end divisions guard their turf. The Corvette would have to settle for Chevrolet's standard six-cylinder engine, the 150-horsepower Blue Flame, also known as the "Stovebolt Six."

The Corvette was a very low car for its day, with the roofline a good foot lower than that of other cars. This made it too low to use Chevy's three-speed manual transmission, so the two-speed Powerglide automatic transmission was used instead. They used standard Chevrolet drum brakes and suspension, and a chassis that had been modified from an ordinary sedan. Power steering was out—instead, the Corvette got a large, 17" steering wheel that was easy to turn at slow speeds.

BELLE OF THE BALL

In those days, GM previewed its designs for new cars in a traveling car show called Motorama. Before a new model was put into production, a single concept car was built by hand and displayed at the show. Then, if the car was well received by the public, GM would gear up to manufacture it for sale. To save time and money, the body panels of the hand-built Corvette show car were made of fiberglass—literally plastic reinforced with glass fibers—instead of steel.

READY OR NOT

Chevrolet had a sense that the Corvette would be a hit when it made its debut at Motorama in January 1953, but the public reaction to the show car surpassed even their expectations. When was the last time you wrote a letter to an auto company? A *complimentary* letter? More than 7,000 people who saw the Corvette at Motorama wrote Chevrolet to tell the company that they would buy a Corvette if the company ever offered them for sale—and this was at a time when the entire U.S. market for sports cars was just over 11,000 cars a year. In fact, the response was so enthusiastic that Chevrolet rushed the Corvette into production to ensure that at least a few hundred of the cars would make it onto showroom floors before the year was out.

Initially the plan had been to manufacture the cars' body panels out of steel, not fiberglass, just like every other car made by the big domestic automakers in the 1950s. But supply disruptions caused by the Korean War prompted GM to gamble on fiberglass and begin manufacturing what would become the first-ever high-volume, mass-produced car with an all-fiberglass body.

START YOUR ENGINES

Three hundred cars were manufactured for the 1953 model year. Because the fiberglass body panels proved to be so different from the steel the autoworkers were accustomed to, all 300 had to be assembled by hand, just like the Motorama show car. And like the Motorama car, they were beautiful—bright red interiors, bodies painted "Polo White," stylish wraparound windshields, headlights covered with chromed metal mesh to protect against stones, wide oval grilles with 13 chrome "teeth," and a convertible top hidden beneath a rear deck lid so that the exquisite, flowing lines of the car weren't disrupted by the clutter of the folded top.

For publicity purposes, Chevrolet set aside all 300 of the 1953

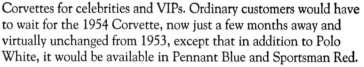

Corvettes for celebrities and VIPs. Ordinary customers would have to wait for the 1954 Corvette, now just a few months away and virtually unchanged from 1953, except that in addition to Polo White, it would be available in Pennant Blue and Sportsman Red.

If you were lucky enough to buy one of those '53 Corvettes (sticker price: $3,498), *and* you managed to hold onto the car all these years, you must be very glad that you did. As the first of what would become the most successful line of sports cars in automotive history, those 1953 Corvettes have soared in value over the years. Today one in good condition can sell for more than $300,000 at auction—more than three times the price of a new Corvette. (The 1954s can fetch as much as $130,000.)

CORVETTE EMPTOR

Those 1953–54 Corvettes are still a joy to look at, and considering how much they're worth, it's hard to believe how disappointing they were to the thousands of fans who'd waited months to buy one. They were beautiful, to be sure—especially if you stood back far enough—but the cars had so many problems that almost everyone found something to hate about them, including the automotive press. "The amazing thing about the Corvette is that it comes so close to being a really interesting, worthwhile and genuine sports car, yet misses the mark almost entirely," *Road & Track* magazine wrote.

Sports car enthusiasts were turned off by the underpowered six-cylinder engine, and they *despised* the automatic transmission, which not only offered poor performance but also denied roadster drivers their God-given right to a stick shift. The suspension that had been borrowed from an ordinary sedan *felt* like it had been borrowed from an ordinary sedan, and so did the brakes.

NO LOCKOUTS

Ordinary drivers who might not have been bothered by poor performance still found plenty about the 1953–54 Corvettes to scare them away from showrooms. For one thing, the cars were surprisingly lacking in standard amenities. No power steering? People were used to that. But no *roll-down windows?* The Corvette had "side curtains"—clumsy plastic panels that had to be removed and stored in bags in the trunk when not in use.

The 1953–54 Corvettes didn't even have exterior door handles—you had to reach into the car and open the door using the inside handle. That was fine when the top was down, but when the top was up and the side curtains were in place, such as, say, during a rain storm—when you had to get into the car *right now*—getting the door open was a hassle. It also meant that the car couldn't be locked securely if it was parked outside.

(FIBER)GLASS HOUSES

But the biggest problem of all was the fiberglass body panels—62 in all—that Chevrolet had gambled on without knowing what it was getting into. Fiberglass was a relatively new material in the 1950s and had never been used on a mass-produced car before. And as Chevy learned (to its dismay), fiberglass still had plenty of bugs that had to be worked out.

Chevrolet and its subcontractors had yet to figure out a way to manufacture the panels to a standard, uniform thickness. As a result, the pieces fit together terribly. The doors, hood, trunk, and rear deck lid could be out of alignment by as much as half an inch, and when they stuck out that far they not only spoiled the car's flowing lines, they created huge gaps that were impossible to seal against rain and water on the road.

Painting the fiberglass was another nightmare. There were air bubbles in the fiberglass panels and in the material used to bond them together. When the cars were painted and placed in giant ovens to dry, the bubbles expanded and popped, ruining the paint job. Each popped bubble had to be sanded down and repainted, with no guarantee that the problem wouldn't happen again. Some cars that were painted multiple times never did get a decent, unblemished coat of paint. After several failed attempts, they were just shipped to Chevy dealers the way they were.

THANKS...BUT NO THANKS

Soon word of mouth surrounding the Corvette was so bad that the company couldn't even find 300 VIPs willing to buy one. Then, when the 1954s became available, so many buyers complained about the poor quality of their Corvettes that some Chevy dealers stopped taking orders for the cars. More than a thousand unsold 1954s piled up on the Corvette factory grounds, prompting

Chevrolet to delay production on the 1955 Corvette until all the 1954s were sold. Result: Only 700 Corvettes were manufactured for the 1955 model year.

THUNDERSTRUCK

By now the Corvette was such a disaster that GM was seriously considering killing the whole program. So what saved it? The 1955 Thunderbird, Ford's answer to the Corvette. Ford had been secretly working on its own two-seater convertible since 1952, when Franklin Q. Hershey, Ford's head of styling, saw a picture of the Corvette show car at a dinner party and ordered his employees to come up with some kind of a response. Ford higher-ups killed the project in late 1952, but when the Corvette show car made its huge splash at Motorama in January 1953, the Thunderbird was revived—in other words, the car that saved the Corvette was itself saved by the Corvette.

Introduced to the public in September 1954, the 1955 T-Bird was everything the Corvette wasn't: It was powerful, with a V-8 engine instead of an underpowered six-cylinder engine, and it offered buyers a choice of either a three-speed manual transmission or a three-speed automatic. It had roll-up windows, exterior door handles and locks, and it was made of *steel*, not fiberglass. It wasn't really a sports car—Ford called it a "Personal Luxury Car"—but it was beautiful and a lot of fun to drive.

Ford set out to sell 10,000 T-Birds in 1955 and ended up selling more than 16,000. It probably would have sold a lot more than that, had the factory been able to build them fast enough.

CAN'T QUIT NOW

The Thunderbird proved that a two-seater convertible could be successful, *if* it was built correctly. Its strong sales were a big blow to Chevrolet's pride. Now that the T-Bird was a success, dumping the Corvette was out of the question. Killing it would be an admission of defeat, an acknowledgement that Ford knew how to make a two-seater and GM, the world's largest automaker, did not.

The Corvette was safe...for the time being.

Part III of the story is on page 429.

Part III of the story is on page 429.

Leopards and tigers can both swim, but only tigers do it for pleasure.

RUSSELL'S RUMINATIONS

Some cynical words of wisdom from Bertrand Russell (1872–1970),
a philosopher, mathematician, and Nobel Prize-winning author.

"I would never die for my beliefs because I might be wrong."

"It has been said that man is a rational animal. All my life I have been searching for evidence to support this."

"We still tend to think that a stupid man is more likely to be honest than a clever man."

"Science may set limits to knowledge, but should not set limits to imagination."

"The universe may have a purpose, but nothing we know suggests that, if so, this purpose has any similarity to ours."

"A life without adventure is likely to be unsatisfying, but a life in which adventure is allowed to take whatever form it will is sure to be short."

"Every man is encompassed by a cloud of comforting convictions, which move with him like flies on a summer day."

"Anything you're good at contributes to happiness."

"Fear is the main source of superstition, and one of the main sources of cruelty. To conquer fear is the beginning of wisdom."

"To fear love is to fear life, and those who fear life are already three parts dead."

"Freedom is the absence of obstacles to the realization of desires."

"If all our happiness is bound up entirely in our personal circumstances, it is difficult not to demand of life more than it has to give."

"It is preoccupation with possessions, more than anything else, that prevents men from living freely and nobly."

"I think we ought always to entertain our opinions with some measure of doubt. I shouldn't wish people dogmatically to believe any philosophy, not even mine."

Schlimazel: Yiddish for someone who has very bad luck.

SAME CO.

*For whatever reason—a changing marketplace, a negative image,
a lawsuit—well-known, long-established companies sometimes
change their names. (By the way, the* Bathroom
Reader *is now called* LooRead.)

WORLD WRESTLING FEDERATION

Story: The World Wrestling Federation was a "sports entertainment" business founded in the U.S. in 1979. The World Wildlife Fund is an environmental preservation group established in Switzerland in 1961. For 20 years, the two organizations were able to share use of the abbreviation "WWF," probably because one was a business and the other was a charity. But in 2000, the nature WWF sued the wrestling WWF for unfair trade practices, claiming the wrestling WWF had used the WWF abbreviation internationally, which, under a 1994 agreement, was the charity's domain.

New Name: A British court ruled in favor of the charity, forcing the wrestling organization to change its name (and abbreviation) to World Wrestling Entertainment (WWE).

BLACKWATER WORLDWIDE

Story: Established in 1997, Blackwater Worldwide was a private security and military service. During the war in Iraq, the U.S. government contracted with the firm to provide private troops and security. (Essentially, its troops are mercenaries.) But between 2006 and 2008, Blackwater became the subject of a number of controversial charges, including opening fire on civilians (killing 12), smuggling weapons, and helping a jailed Iraqi politician escape prison and the country. In February 2009, Blackwater was expelled from the country by the Iraqi government. And its contract was not renewed by the Obama administration.

New Name: To disassociate itself from all of its Iraq-related problems, Blackwater rebranded itself Xe (pronounced "zee").

PHILLIP MORRIS

Story: By the early 2000s, the Phillip Morris company was a $30-

---

The *Flintstones* movie (1994) had 32 screenwriters, a record for a Hollywood film.

billion corporation that had diversified beyond its original core business of tobacco. No longer just the manufacturer of Marlboro, Virginia Slims, and Chesterfield cigarettes, it also made Kool-Aid, pudding, Cool Whip, instant coffee, mayonnaise, and cheese—the company owned an 84 percent stake in Kraft Foods. After losing several wrongful death lawsuits because of the cigarettes they manufactured, the company wanted the public to focus on its wholesome foods divisions, not the tobacco.

New Name: In 2003, Phillip Morris became Altria. The word is a derivative of *altus,* the Latin word for "high."

DIEBOLD

Story: Diebold is an American company that today is best known for making electronic voting machines—the ones that didn't work properly during the 2004 national election. The company's primary business is selling safes and automated teller machines; voting machines were produced by an individual division within the company called Diebold Election Systems. In 2007 the main corporation sought to distance itself from the troublesome voting machines and the segment of the company that made them. By selling off the division? No—they just changed its name.

New Name: Premier Election Solutions

GMAC FINANCIAL SERVICES

Story: In 1919 General Motors created its own financing branch, General Motors Acceptance Corporation, in order to help World War I veterans buy their first cars. Over the past 90 years, GMAC expanded to offer not only car loans, but also mortgages and insurance. Technically, it wasn't a bank; it was a loan agency. But in the 2008 financial meltdown, GMAC struggled with the same problems that banks had—they were hemorrhaging money because consumers weren't keeping up with their car loans or mortgage payments. So in December 2008, GMAC converted to a bank, entitling it to receive part of the $700 billion federal bailout money. It got about $6 billion.

New Name: In order to disassociate itself from its past problems—and its parent company's current ones—in May 2009, GMAC "rebranded" as Ally Bank.

THE HISTORY OF JUDO

In the late 1870s, a short, skinny kid started taking jujitsu classes in Tokyo. Martial arts would never be the same. (Right down to their fancy, colored belts.)

NINETY-POUND WEAKLING

In 1878 Jigoro Kano, the 17-year-old son of a sake maker, moved from the island of Honshu to Tokyo to attend Tokyo Imperial University. Shortly after arriving he started taking lessons in the Japanese martial art *jujitsu*. Kano was small, just over five feet tall, and weighed only about 90 pounds, but he was incredibly focused, and in just a few years became a master in the *Tenjin-Shinyo-Ryu*, or "Divine True Willow," school of jujitsu. Then he started studying other techniques—including western wrestling styles—and began developing his own moves, primarily takedowns. In 1882 Kano opened his own school, beginning with just 12 students. At the time he felt he was still teaching a form of jujitsu, but in 1884, at the age of just 24, he founded a new school of martial arts—*judo*, meaning "the gentle way."

JU-JISTORY

Jujitsu had been the dominant martial art in Japan for centuries. The name, which means "the art of softness," was first used in the 1500s, and referred to a wide variety of combat techniques which had been developed by Japan's warrior class, the *samurai*, since at least the 12th century.

During its formative years jujitsu involved the use of weapons, such as swords and spears, and was used on battlefields by heavily armored samurai. In the 1600s, that all changed when the Tokugawa Shogunate conquered the entire country. Over the following 250 relatively peaceful years, jujitsu naturally evolved, reflecting those more peaceful times. Rather than fighting with weapons and in full armor, combatants studied and developed unarmed fighting techniques in schools. This is known as the "Golden Age" of jujitsu, when literally thousands of different schools and styles flourished.

Then in the mid-1800s, everything changed again: The

Tokugawas lost power and the country emerged from its primitive, feudal framework, ended its policy of complete isolation, and embraced the West and the modern, industrialized world. As a result, old Japanese traditions became very unpopular—and that included jujitsu. The storied martial art was in danger of dying out completely…but then Kano showed up.

I GENTLE YOU TO DEATH!

Jujitsu may mean "the art of softness," but that's deceiving: It includes the use of foot and hand strikes, and can be brutal. To make the art more appealing—to people who didn't want broken bones on a regular basis—Kano removed the strikes, making judo truly more "gentle," relying instead on throws, holds, and choking submission techniques.

But the most important aspect of judo, according to Kano, was *kuzushi*, or "off-balancing," which referred to moves designed to put an opponent off balance, making it easier to take them to the ground. It was nothing new, but it had never been a central theme in a martial art before—and it was very effective. Within months, Kano began beating one of his former jujitsu teachers, something that he had never done before. That immediately brought judo a lot of notice.

Two years later, because of Kano's growing success, the Tokyo Metropolitan Police organized a contest between Kano's judo students and students of the most popular jujitsu school in the city. Tokyo police officers—who normally studied jujitsu, pledged that if Kano's school won—they'd switch to judo. Kano sent his 15 best students. Out of their 15 matches they won 12. Judo soon became popular all over Japan, and Kano certainly couldn't have known it at the time, but it would eventually have enormous influence on martial arts all over the world.

RANK AND RE-FILE

One of Kano's biggest influences on other martial arts was the student ranking system he chose. Instead of using jujitsu's *menkyo*, or "license" system, which awarded students certificates based on skill level—and which was not used uniformly around the country— Kano adopted a straightforward system that virtually all Japanese people were already familiar with: It was from the ancient Chinese

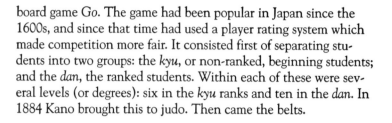

board game *Go*. The game had been popular in Japan since the 1600s, and since that time had used a player rating system which made competition more fair. It consisted first of separating students into two groups: the *kyu*, or non-ranked, beginning students; and the *dan*, the ranked students. Within each of these were several levels (or degrees): six in the *kyu* ranks and ten in the *dan*. In 1884 Kano brought this to judo. Then came the belts.

BELT HIM!

In 1885 two of Kano's students became the first to reach the first *dan* level. At the time all students of Japanese martial arts wore simple kimonos with a white sash around their waists. To give his two *dan* students a visual sign of their achievement, Kano had them wear black sashes—and invented the colored belt ranking system that is probably the most recognizable aspect of any martial art in the world today. By 1895 virtually all of Japan's hand-to-hand martial arts schools were using Kano's ranking system, belts included. And when new martial art schools later appeared, such as modern karate and aikido, they did, too.

Kano was an especially adept teacher, businessman, and diplomat, and over the following decades he and his students traveled the world promoting the martial art he founded, often at the invitation of world leaders. By the 1920s there were judo schools, or *dojos*, in most European countries, and several in the U.S.

Jigoro Kano died in 1938 at the age of 77, before his dream of seeing judo competition in the Olympics. It finally made it in 1964, when Tokyo became the first Asian city to host the summer games. The host country gets to add a sport of their choosing—and Japan chose Kano's judo. It was the first Asian martial art to become an Olympic sport, and judo is still one of the most popular martial arts in the world today.

Extra: In 1935 one of Kano's students, Mikonosuke Kawaishi, opened a dojo in Paris. To give Westerners more incentive to stay in school, he tried an innovation: he started awarding different colored belts—white, yellow, orange, green, blue, and brown—to the six levels of beginner *kyu* students, who would normally wear only white. It was a hit, and quickly spread to other European schools, and over the years to many other martial arts, and finally all over the world.

Worth the wait: It can take a puppy two months before it starts wagging its tail.

POLI-TALKS

Public officials suffering from foot-in-mouth disease.

"If crime went down 100 percent, it would still be 50 times higher than it should be."
—**John Bowman, Washington, D.C., Councilman**

"I'm probably one of the four or five best-known Americans in the world."
—**Rudy Giuliani, to British reporters**

"On this Memorial Day, our nation honors its fallen heroes, and I see many of them in the audience here today."
—**President Barack Obama**

"*Saturday Night Live* could use a good Obama impersonator like you."
—**Rep. Ileana Ros-Lehtinen, thinking it was a prank when Barack Obama called her on the phone**

"I'm sure a lot of you have tripped out on alcohol. It's actually a lot safer to do it on marijuana."
—**Sen. Mike Gravel, to high school students**

"Every week we don't pass a stimulus package, 500 million Americans lose their jobs."
—**Nancy Pelosi, Speaker of the House**

"It is perfectly American to be wrong."
—**Newt Gingrich**

Impeached Illinois Gov. Rod Blagojevich: I've wanted to be on your show in the worst way for the longest time.
David Letterman: Well, you're on in the worst way, believe me.

"President Washington, President Lincoln, and President Roosevelt have all authorized electronic surveillance on a far broader scale."
—**Alberto Gonzalez, Attorney General, testifying to Congress**

"You had some good points. It was kind of long, so I forgot some of them."
—**Sen. Diana Bajoie, during a debate**

Tastes better? Pirates who sailed the Great Lakes plundered whiskey and venison instead of gold.

"I'm the former chairman of the Ethics Committee. I know what's ethical and what isn't, and there's nothing unethical about this."

—Sen. Ted Stevens,
on appearing in a TV ad
for a military contractor

"Now, the only thing that remains unsolved is the resolution of the problem."

—Thomas Wells, Ontario
Minister of Education

"I talked to the White House this morning—I mean, you can't talk to a building, but I talked to some people *in* the White House this morning."

—George Stephanopoulos

"I am running for President of the United States to enable the Goddess of Peace to encircle within her arms all the children of this country and all the children of the world."

—Rep. Dennis Kucinich

*   *   *

REAL REDNECK RECIPES

Hillbilly Hash: Heat up an iron skillet and melt two teaspoons of butter. Add a cup of ground beef and ½ cup of finely chopped possum meat. When it sizzles, add in a cup of boiling water. Brown the meat and add two cups of diced, boiled tomatoes (2 ½ cups if the possum meat is extra greasy). Let cook for about 10 minutes, and add a dash of moonshine whisky. Serve with fried eggs.

Vinegar Pie: Combine 1 ¼ cups sugar, ¼ cup of flour, and a tablespoon of lemon zest, and blend together in a heated saucepan. Stir in two cups of water and ½ cup of apple cider vinegar. Bring to a boil, remove from heat, and combine with a mixture of three beaten eggs. Pour into a pie crust and bake.

Black Stew: Fry two cups of chicken gizzards, chicken livers, or possum in a skillet until crispy. Add in a whole chopped onion and fry for a few minutes. Dump it all into a large pot and add six cups of boiling water. Throw in five cups of collard greens, two cups of wild mushrooms, a cup of pinto beans, a chopped potato, and anything else you've got lying around that might be good in a stew. Just before serving, add in a spoonful of butter and ½ cup of bacon grease.

RANDOM ORIGINS

Once again, Uncle John answers the question:
Where does all this stuff come from?

LICENSE PLATES

The first license plates for automobiles appeared in France in 1893. In the United States, the first state to require them was New York in 1901. Two years later, Massachusetts became the first state to issue them. But these early plates were inconsistent. Some were issued by towns or states, others were homemade, and they could be made of wood, clay, porcelain, or metal. More inconsistencies: some plates displayed the owner's initials, some displayed the owner's registration number, and others were numbered sequentially according to when the cars were purchased. How long did it take for license plates become the 6 x 12-inch metal rectangles we know today? Half a century. In 1957 Congress finally passed national standards for what are technically called "vehicle registration plates."

THE INFINITY SYMBOL

John Wallis, a mathematics professor at Oxford University, was creating a text book called *Arithmetica Infinitorum* in 1655, and needed a symbol to represent a number so high that it could not be counted. He came up with this: ∞. Most historians believe that Wallis simply altered the Roman numeral M (1,000), which was sometimes used to mean "many."

THE PERIODIC TABLE OF ELEMENTS

In 1868 Russian chemist Dmitri Mendeleev, a professor at the University of St. Petersburg, set out to categorize the 60 known elements. Although scientists didn't know what atoms were made of, they knew that elements were different kinds of atoms, each with its own unique atomic weight. Mendeleev made a little card for each element, complete with all of its physical and chemical properties. Then he laid them all out on a table and tried different ways of arranging them. He noticed that when he started with the lightest weight, a pattern emerged: Basically, certain types of elements would always follow each other based on their reactivity. Although Mendeleev had only 60 of what we now know to be 110 elements—and much of what was assumed about them was wrong—he was able to predict most of the ones that had yet to be discovered, and as such, his periodic table is still in use today.

THE TAPE MEASURE
In Sheffield, England, in the late 1820s, James Chesterman manufactured long steel bands that were rolled into continuous loops for use as frames in hoop skirts. But when the hoop skirt fashion fell out of favor, Chesterman was left with a lot of light-weight, bendable steel bands. Solution: He put notches into them at incremental distances and sold them to surveyors as "Steel Band Measuring Chains." He even built a special casing with a spring inside that would roll up the band. In New Haven, Connecticut, in 1868, Alvin Fellows improved on Chesterman's design by adding a clip that locked the tape in any desired position. Tape measures have changed little since then.

SUDOKU
In 1783 Swiss mathematician Leonhard Euler devised what he called a "Latin Square," a 9 x 9-square grid in which every number appears once in each row and column. In the late 1970s, a U.S. puzzle maker named Howard Garnes turned Euler's squares into a game by removing some of the numbers from the grid. Called "Number Squares," they first appeared in a Dell puzzle magazine. The game caught the eye of Maki Kaji, president of the Japanese puzzle company, Nikoli, Inc., and in the mid-1980s, he altered it—making it more difficult by restricting the amount of given numbers to 30 and making each pattern symmetrical. Maki also thought the game should have a more Japanese-sounding name, so he combined the words *Su*, meaning "number," and *Doku*, meaning "single." In 1997 a New Zealander named Wayne Gould discovered Sudoku in Japan, and set out to create a computer program that could generate new puzzles. Seven years later, in 2004, Gould's puzzles began appearing in London's *The Times*, and were so popular that soon other newspapers in Europe and the United States started running them. Today, Sudoku books outsell all other puzzle books combined by 10 to 1.

A cat goes to its food dish an average of 36 times a day.

PSEUDOCIDAL TENDENCIES

On page 75, we told the stories of some people who didn't want to go on living their lives, but didn't want to die— so they faked their own deaths. Here are some more.

GRAHAM CARDWELL. In 1998 the belongings of 46-year-old Cardwell, an assistant dockmaster, were found on the mud flats near Immingham, England. Air and sea search teams did all they could to find him, but his wife and three children had to give him up for dead, assuming he'd drowned in the nearby Humber Estuary. But he hadn't drowned—he had begun a new life 200 miles away in the West Midlands of England as a bachelor with a new name, new job, and new apartment. After his secret was found out, Cardwell claimed he took off because he was depressed, convinced he was dying of cancer, and didn't want to distress his family. The police declined to prosecute, and his family declined to have anything more to do with him.

ALLEN KIRK WOLFORD. In 2006 Wolford, a Colorado funeral director, tried to forge his own death certificate, hoping it would get him out of paying $42,000 in overdue child support and $7,000 in student loans. But before the certificate was officially registered at the state Department of Public Health, authorities pegged it as fake. Wolford's first mistake: He listed the Evergreen Funeral Home, his workplace, as his home address—which looked odd to state officials. Second mistake: He listed the Nolan Funeral Home as the facility that cremated his body. When officials called to check with owner Neva Nolan, she said she'd never heard of him. Wolford was arrested and convicted of fraud, but he skipped out on his court date. He surfaced in New Zealand in 2007— applying for a job as a funeral director.

KARL HACKETT. In 1987 Hackett, an Englishman, served a one-year prison sentence for assault. When he got out of prison, he assumed the name of a dead friend, Lee Simm, who had committed suicide. For more than a decade, the new "Lee Simm" lived

---

The Chinese equivalent to "Once upon a time..." is "Before a very long very long time..."

a perfectly respectable life as a computer consultant with a (false) driver's license and (false) passport to prove his (false) identity. Then, in 1999, came London's infamous Paddington train crash, which killed 31 people and injured 520. It seemed to "Simm" that this was the ideal opportunity to kill off his real identity. On the day of the crash, he called the police to report his concern that his "lodger," Karl Hackett, was missing and might have been on the train. A day later, the police got another call, this time from someone claiming to be Hackett's brother, confirming that Hackett was on the train. Hackett's father and sister got the news and attended a memorial service for the Paddington victims, assuming that Karl, whom they hadn't seen in years, was among the dead. But suspicious police took one of Hackett's relatives to "Simm's" house...and the jig was up. In England it's not illegal to disappear and adopt a new identity, but it is illegal to waste police time: The local magistrate gave Hackett/Simm a suspended sentence and urged him to get help for his "psychological problems."

JOHN DARWIN. On March 21, 2002, Darwin took his canoe out onto the calm North Sea, half a mile from his home on the east coast of England. Later, the smashed-up remains of the canoe washed onto shore, and the 57-year-old ex-teacher was presumed drowned. His wife, Anne, watched the massive search operations from the window of their five-story home and accepted the condolences of friends and family. "All I want is to bury my husband," she said. After the inquest, a death certificate was issued and the life insurance money—a whopping £250,000 ($400,000) —was paid to the grieving widow. She also collected death benefits and a widow's pension. The real story? Less than a year after his "death," Darwin showed up at Anne's door and quietly moved back into their home. They also owned the house next door, and for the next three years, whenever friends came calling he'd slip through the interior door that connected the two residences and hide until they left. In 2006 Anne sold the two houses for nearly £500,000, and she and John moved to Panama. But a few weeks later, John started complaining that he didn't want to live in hiding for the rest of his life. On December 1, 2007, he walked into a London police station, looking tanned and healthy, and claimed he'd had amnesia for the past five years. Both Darwins were arrested for insurance fraud. (They didn't even bother asking their friends for bail money.)

The amount of heat your body gives off each day is enough to boil 8 gallons of freezing water.

DECENT PROPOSALS

These three guys really went the extra mile for love.

The Setup: Texan Kyle Sandoval told his girlfriend, Shannon McCarthy, that they were going to San Diego to see his brother and maybe visit the San Diego Natural History Museum. But Sandoval had more planned. He arranged with the museum to place an engagement ring inside one of the exhibits. **The Proposal:** As they browsed the museum's rocks and gems exhibit, McCarthy noticed something unusual among the samples of calcite and gypsum: a diamond ring. Next to it was a small sign that read "Shannon's diamond, on loan from the Sandoval collection." (She said yes.)

The Setup: Aaron Weisinger and Erica Breder had bonded over the fact that both had great-grandparents who'd come to America via the immigrant processing center at Ellis Island, New York, and the Statue of Liberty had deep personal meaning for both of them. So when the monument was scheduled to reopen for the first time after 9/11 on July 4, 2009, Weisinger entered a lottery for the 240 available tickets. He won, and he and Breder flew from their home in San Francisco to New York City. **The Proposal:** They climbed the 354 steps up the steep, spiral case to the statue's crown. That's where Weisinger got down on one knee and presented a ring. (She said yes.)

The Setup: One of the biggest hit songs of 2009 was Beyoncé's "Single Ladies (Put a Ring On It)," advising men to marry their girlfriends before they lose them, or else "if you like it, then you should've put a ring on it." **The Proposal:** During a show in Florida in June 2009, halfway through "Single Ladies," the music stopped and the lights went out. A single spotlight came on. "Lindell has something he wants to say," said Beyoncé, as she handed her microphone to a man in the front row. "Beyoncé told me if I like it, I need to put a ring on it," Lindell said as he got down on one knee and proposed to his girlfriend. It's unclear exactly how he contacted Beyoncé and got her to agree to pause her concert...but his girlfriend said yes.

THE SOCIETY FOR THE COALITION OF ORGANIZATIONS AND ASSOCIATIONS

Since 1988, the Bathroom Readers' Institute has stood up for those who like to sit down and read in the bathroom. In the spirit of camaraderie, we thought we'd showcase a few other societies of people who band together for a specific cause. Because if they didn't, who would?

Society for Barefoot Living. "We are a group of people who love going barefoot pretty much **everywhere**." (They also love bolding certain **words** on their Web site.) Founded in 1994, the SBL's mission is to remind the shoe-wearing public that it's a lot healthier and more fun to let your soles touch the ground than to keep them covered up. They also dispel the myths about going bare-footed, such as the likelihood of catching athlete's foot (it's less than with shoes); that it's illegal to walk into a restaurant without shoes (it isn't); and that it's gross to go into a public restroom in bare feet ("Urine is **not** a toxic waste product and this has been scientifically **proven!**").

National Coalition for the Advancement of Baton Twirling. Don't think spinning around a metal stick is a sport? The NCABT says, "Try it." Not only is baton twirling a sport, but a very difficult one to master, and therefore should get the respect it deserves. The NCABT, formed by a group of coaches, is lobbying the NCAA to make it an officially sanctioned college sport. Meanwhile, another organization, the U.S. Twirling Association, is working tirelessly to make baton twirling an Olympic event.

Society for Creative Anachronism. If you don't feel at all weird referring to your friends as "Milord" and "Milady," then you may be stout-hearted enough to join the SCA. Formed in 1966 by a group of history buffs in Berkeley, California, members dress up as

Medieval knights, damsels, royalty, and villains. The SCA has 30,000 members all over the world, which they've broken up into 19 "kingdoms," such as "Calontir" (the U.S. Midwest) and "Drachenwald" (Europe, Africa, the Middle East). SCA members hold local events and attend renaissance fairs, where they compete in tournaments of jousting, archery, and axe-throwing. After the last foe has been waylaid, they feast merrily and pay tribute to the guy who's dressed up as the king.

The Skeptics Society: Do you believe in ghosts, aliens, Bigfoot, or ESP? Then this isn't the organization for you. "Some people think we are a bunch of grumpy curmudgeons unwilling to accept any claim that challenges the status quo, but this is not so," says scientist Michael Shermer, who founded the Society in 1992. Its 55,000 members simply maintain that "seeing is believing." And for the kids, they offer the Junior Skeptic Club. Their hero: Scooby-Doo. Why? Because at the end of every cartoon, the dog (and those meddling kids) prove that the ghost isn't real.

National Coalition for Men. Is today's man still supposed to open a door for a woman? Is it okay for guys to talk about their feelings? What specifically *is* the role of the male in this increasingly complex society? The NCFM—born in 1977 at the height of the Women's Liberation Movement—aims to help "emotionally adrift" men. They hold workshops and conduct support groups in an effort to help guys gain their freedom from male stereotyping, conditioned competitiveness, fear of sharing their feelings, getting their sense of identity from their jobs, thinking that violence is manly, having distant emotional relationships with their children, and a host of other issues. (And it's still okay to open the door for a woman.)

The Society for the Scientific Study of Sexuality. Founded in 1957, this nonprofit organization consists of more than 1,000 educators, doctors, psychologists, anthropologists, sociologists, and biologists who share theories and findings with each other. They operate under the assumption that science illuminates sexuality, and sexuality enhances the quality of our lives. The 2009 SSSS Annual Congress was held at a spa in Puerto Vallarta, Mexico.

MOMENTS OF CANDOR

On page 26, we shared some shallow "Confessions" from stars. This page is kind of like that but...deeper. These celebrities really do open up.

"The trouble with being me is that at this point, nobody gives a damn what my problem is. I could literally have a tumor on the side of my head and they'd be like, 'Yeah, big deal. I'd eat a tumor every morning for the kind of money you're pulling down.'"

—Jim Carrey

"With my sunglasses on, I'm Jack Nicholson. Without them, I'm fat and 60."

—Jack Nicholson

"I have a lust for diamonds, almost like a disease."

—Elizabeth Taylor

"I used to make appearances at cocktail parties in Florida, pretending that I was an old friend of the host."

—Mickey Rooney

"I feel cheated never knowing what it's like to get pregnant, carry a baby, and breast-feed."

—Dustin Hoffman

"It's pretty sad when a person has to lose weight to play Babe Ruth."

—John Goodman

"Fame can be just so annoying because people are always so critical of you. You can't just say, 'Hi.' You say hi and people whisper, 'Man, did you see the way she said hi? What an attitude.'"

—Juliette Lewis

"I could be the poster boy for bad judgement."

—Rob Lowe

"My biggest nightmare is I'm driving home and get sick and go to the hospital. 'Please help me,' I ask. And they say: 'Hey, you look like...' And I'm dying while they're wondering whether or not I'm Barbra Streisand."

—Barbra Streisand

"I had my first childhood depression at eight. It was severe, intense, hole-in-the-soul loneliness. No one noticed."

—Ashley Judd

"Life is like a B-picture script! It is that corny. If I had my life story offered to me to film, I'd probably turn it down."

—Kirk Douglas

Originally, "007" was the number on James Bond's license to kill, not his agent number.

(NOT) COMING TO A THEATER NEAR YOU

*Here's one of our regular features about movies that were
planned, but never saw the light of day (so far).*

BATMAN: YEAR ONE (2003)

Christopher Nolan's *Batman Begins* and *The Dark Knight*
are dark, gritty reimaginings of Batman's origins, but they
could have been even darker and grittier. In 2001 Warner Bros.
executives' first choice to create a new Batman series was
writer/director Darren Aronofsky (*Pi, Requiem for a Dream, The
Wrestler*). Aronofsky's script was a complete overhaul of Batman—
Bruce Wayne was an orphaned, homeless teenager who uses an
abandoned subway station as a "batcave," installs a bus engine in
an old Lincoln for his "batmobile," and randomly and brutally
murders street thugs. The idea of Batman as a mentally ill, violent,
homeless psychopath was too much for Warner Bros. They let
Aronofsky go and hired Nolan.

AMERICAN IDIOT (2006)

The popular '90s band Green Day enjoyed a comeback in 2004
with *American Idiot*, a concept album about the coming-of-age of a
weirdo named Jesus of Suburbia who lived in a boring, anonymous
suburb. It sold 14 million copies and told a complete story, so the
idea to turn it into a movie à la the Who's *Tommy* or Pink Floyd's
The Wall seemed like a no-brainer. The band talked to numerous
directors and screenwriters throughout 2005 before lead singer Billie Joe Armstrong decided to write the script himself. Just a few
months later, though, putting together a big-budget movie-musical
proved to be too much work. So Armstrong adapted his script into
a stage musical, and *American Idiot: The Musical* premiered at the
Berkeley Rep, a major West Coast theater, in 2009.

KING KONG VS. FRANKENSTEIN (1962)

Willis O'Brien was an animation pioneer who made the stop-
motion segments of the giant ape (and the dinosaurs) in the

According to dog breeders, Afghan Hounds are the dumbest dogs; Border Collies are the smartest.

original *King Kong* (1933). In 1961, with the availability of color film, he set about making a sequel to *Kong*. His idea: Kong would fight a 20-foot-tall Frankenstein monster in downtown San Francisco. Almost immediately, O'Brien changed his idea because he thought securing the rights to Frankenstein from Universal Studios would be too difficult. (In reality, Universal owned only the rights to the look of the monster as characterized by Boris Karloff—green skin and neck bolts.) He changed the title to *King Kong vs. Prometheus* (a reference to Mary Shelley's original novel, *Frankenstein, or the Modern Prometheus*). But by then, producer John Beck, to whom O'Brien had shown his screenplay and concept art, had sold the idea to Toho Studios of Japan, who used it to make *King Kong vs. Godzilla*. O'Brien only found out about it when that film was released in 1962. He died just a few months later.

STRAWBERRY FIELDS FOREVER (1987)

In 1985, shortly after he'd purchased the rights to dozens of Beatles songs, Michael Jackson licensed some of them to animation producer Don Bluth (*The Secret of N.I.M.H.*) for use in a new Beatles-based cartoon called *Strawberry Fields Forever*, to be done in the style of the 1967 animated film *Yellow Submarine*. It wasn't going to be a sequel, though. It was going to be more like *Fantasia*: a series of vignettes, each based on and scored by a different Beatles song. Bluth planned to computer-animate the entire movie, which would have been a first. He hired a computer animator named Hank Grebe, who drew sketches and prepared 10 minutes of test footage in which he completely revamped the project as Beatles "characters" (Mean Mr. Mustard, the Walrus, Mr. Kite, etc.) in a 1940s gangster movie. *Strawberry Fields* died when none of the surviving Beatles would allow their (animated) images to be used in the film.

*   *   *

OLD-TIMEY INSULTS YOU CAN USE

dodunk • muttonhead • hunky • shuttle-wit • dumbsocks Boobus Americanus • clinchpoop • yuckel • droob • slangrill lorg • flapdoodle • gazook • jobbernoll • ning-nong • sonky zib • slubberdegullion • oofus • wooden spoon • peagoose

Clean getaway: Almost 600,000 towels are stolen from Holiday Inns each year.

THE 50TH STATE

What does it take to become a state? Judging by Hawaii's history, a lot.

BACKGROUND

With the Hawaiian Islands united as a kingdom since 1810, King Kalakaua ascended to the throne in 1874. The following year, he signed the Reciprocity Treaty with the United States. Hawaii won the right to sell sugar to the U.S. duty- and tax-free; the U.S. won the right to build the Pearl Harbor naval base on Oahu. Here's the rest of Hawaii's timeline to statehood.

• **1887:** The Honolulu Rifles, an armed militia of mostly American and European sugar-plantation owners, force King Kalakaua to sign the Constitution of the Kingdom of Hawaii. It strips the king of most of his power, turning Hawaii into a constitutional monarchy. Voting rights are restricted to males over 20 who own property and are not of Asian descent. This disenfranchises almost all natives.

• **1891:** Upon the death of Kalakaua, his sister Liliuokalani takes over the monarchy. Resentful that non-natives have taken over, she nullifies the Constitution. This angers the ruling whites, as does the McKinley Tariff, passed by Congress, which repeals the tax-free trade of sugar. The whites seek annexation to the U.S. to reacquire duty-free status.

• **1893:** The pro-annexation Committee of Public Safety, led by American Ambassador John L. Stevens, calls in 200 troops to intimidate Liliuokalani. It works; she relinquishes all control. On February 1, Hawaii becomes a protectorate of the United States.

• **1898:** Under the direct order of President William McKinley (the same McKinley of the McKinley Tariff), the U.S. annexes Hawaii and the white aristocracy runs it as a dependent republic.

• **1900:** Congress passes the Hawaii Organic Act, reclassifying the protectorate as a territory. Citizenship—and the right to vote for a local legislature—is given to all adult males. Hawaii gets a nonvoting delegate to the U.S. House of Representatives.

• **1903:** The Hawaii legislature passes a resolution to petition

Congress for the right to draw up a state constitution, the first step to statehood. Congress denies the request.

- **1919:** Congressional delegate Prince Kalanianaole (son of King Kalakaua) introduces the first of many statehood bills. All fail when members of Congress express fear that the islands might fall under the control of the increasingly imperialistic Japanese.

- **1934:** In a move to boost the mainland sugar industry in the middle of the Depression, Congress passes the Jones-Costigan Act, which severely limits foreign sugar imports. Hawaii is classified as a foreign importer, crippling the sugar trade there. White plantation owners quickly form a statehood exploratory committee.

- **1937:** Congress holds statehood hearings in Hawaii and recommends that it be put to a local vote. Hawaiians approve the referendum in 1940 by a two-to-one margin.

- **1941:** The naval base at Pearl Harbor is bombed by the Japanese, and the U.S. enters World War II. The drive for statehood is postponed; Hawaii is placed under martial law until 1944.

- **1947:** Based on the pre-war statehood vote, statehood is put to a vote on the House floor. It passes, 196 to 133.

- **1948:** Sen. Hugh Butler, chairman of the Rules Committee, which oversees new statehood proposals, kills a Hawaii statehood bill in committee because he believes the Hawaiian Democratic Party has been infiltrated by Communists.

- **1949:** To demonstrate to Congress that it is ready for democracy (and is not Communist), the territorial legislature writes a state constitution, hoping to lead Congress into granting statehood.

- **1953:** Hawaii delegate Joseph Farrington proposes another statehood bill. It passes the House. The Senate approves it in 1954 but joins it to a pending Alaskan statehood bill. Back to the House for approval, it dies there, as Speaker Joseph Martin favors statehood for Hawaii alone and not Alaska.

- **1959:** Shortly after Alaska is admitted as the 49th state, the Senate passes the Hawaii Statehood Bill. More than 94 percent of Hawaiian voters approve. On August 21, President Dwight Eisenhower signs a proclamation making Hawaii the 50th state.

A REAL-LIFE GHOST STORY, PART II

How many ghost stories get written up in medical journals? This one made it into the American Journal of Ophthalmology *in 1921. Read on...if you dare. (Part I starts on page 110.)*

WHO'S THERE?
According to Dr. William Wilmer's account, everyone in the H family had heard unexplainable noises and sensed eerie presences, but no one had actually *seen* any ghosts... until January 1913. Mrs. H saw them first: "On one occasion, in the middle of the morning, as I passed from the drawing room into the dining room, I was surprised to see at the further end of the drawing room, coming towards me, a strange woman, dark haired and dressed in black. As I walked steadily on into the dining room to meet her, she disappeared," she wrote. "This happened three different times." Another night one of the servants awoke to see an old man and a young woman sitting at the foot of her bed, staring at her. She lay in bed paralyzed until an unseen hand tapped her shoulder and she was suddenly able to sit up. But as she did so, the man and woman vanished.

One night Mr. and Mrs. H went to the opera, leaving their children in the care of the servants. That evening at about 8:30, the H's young son was awakened by the ghost of a "big, fat man" that sent him screaming from his room. The boy spent the rest of the night sleeping fitfully in the nanny's room, and when he awoke the following morning he complained that someone or something heavy—perhaps the fat man?—had sat on his chest the entire night, making it difficult for him to breathe.

FROM BED TO WORSE

Mr. and Mrs. H fared no better: After they returned home from the opera and went to bed, Mr. H was awakened by the sensation of ghostly fingers grabbing his throat and trying to strangle him. He still heard ringing bells at night, and now they were complemented by the sounds of people moving through the house. He assumed the noises were made by burglars, but every time he got up to confront the intruders, they were nowhere to be seen. And, Mrs. H wrote, "it was about this time my houseplants died."

YOU ARE NOT ALONE

If only one person had seen or heard unusual things in the house, they could easily have been dismissed as the figments of an over-active imagination. But *everyone* in the house was now seeing, hearing, and even feeling things. And besides: You can't kill houseplants with figments of someone's imagination.

Whatever was happening in the house, it was very real. When they contacted the home's previous residents, the H's learned that the bizarre events had been going on for many years. "The last occupants we found had exactly the same experiences as our-selves," Mrs. H wrote, "with the exception that some of them had seen visions clad in purple and white crawling around their beds. Going back still further, we learned that almost everyone had felt ill and had been under the doctor's care, although nothing very definite had been found the matter with them."

SOMETHING IN THE AIR

The first hint of what might really be happening came in late January, after Mr. H described the terrifying goings-on to his brother. Brother H remembered an article he'd read years before, describ-ing a family that had been tormented by the same kinds of sounds and visions that his brother described. Brother H suggested that perhaps Mr. H and his family were being poisoned.

Poisoned? Now, on top of everything else, the ghosts were poi-soning them? No, Brother H explained: The article he'd read said the family in question had had a faulty heater that released large quantities of carbon monoxide gas into the home, and that all of the symptoms the family experienced—depression, fatigue, illness, strange noises and visions, the feeling of being watched and even touched by unseen people, even dead houseplants—were entirely consistent with carbon monoxide poisoning. Brother H suggested they contact a doctor.

In those days doctors still made house calls, so the following day when the physician came by to examine the H family, he also took a look around their home. As soon as he examined the old furnace in the basement, his suspicions—and those of Brother H—were confirmed. "He found the furnace in very bad condition, the combustion being imperfect, the fumes, instead of going up the chimney, were pouring gases of carbon monoxide into our rooms," Mrs. H reported. "He advised us not to let the children sleep in the house another night. If they did, he said we might find in the morning that some of them would never wake again."

WHAT'S UP, DOC?

Unlike most ghost stories, this one ends with the family living happily ever after. Mr. and Mrs. H took the doctor's advice and moved out of the house until the furnace could be repaired. When they moved back in, the eerie sights and sounds...were gone.

A lot has changed since 1912, but one thing hasn't: Carbon monoxide poisoning is still the leading cause of accidental poisoning deaths in North America. The reason it's so deadly is that carbon monoxide is odorless and tasteless, and it doesn't irritate your airways when you breathe it. That makes it very difficult to detect, and a concentration of as little as 400 parts per million can be fatal. Often the first sign that something is wrong with the air is when someone loses consciousness.

The good news: Hardware stores now sell carbon monoxide detectors (similar to smoke detectors) for about $40. If you have a gas furnace, clothes dryer, or other appliance, or if you have a fireplace or a wood-burning stove, investing in a carbon monoxide detector can mean the difference between life and death...or ghosts and no ghosts.

DÉJÀ VIEW

From time to time, modern carbon monoxide ghost stories still find their way into print. An article in a 2005 issue of the *American Journal of Emergency Medicine*, for example, describes the case of a 23-year-old woman who collapsed while taking a shower after she saw what she thought was a ghost. The problem was traced to a new gas water heater, which had not been properly installed and was leaking carbon monoxide into her home.

The average American spends $100 more per year on footwear than they do on vegetables.

THE FIRST AMERICAN...

Everyone knows George Washington was the first American President. Here are a few less-familiar firsts.

PENITENTIARY

Jails and prisons have been around since early colonial times. But there were no such things as penitentiaries—prisons designed to *reform* people convicted of major crimes, not just punish them—until the first one opened in Philadelphia in 1790. The concept of long-term confinement for rehabilitation originated with Quakers in Pennsylvania in the late 1700s. The first actual penitentiary was a small building with rows of cells built at the Walnut Street Jail in Philadelphia in 1790, the original idea being to keep prisoners in solitary confinement so they could be reformed through spiritual contemplation.

NATIVE-BORN GORILLA

In early 1956, Millie and Baron Macombo, a pair of western lowland gorillas at the Columbus Zoo in Ohio, successfully mated, and on December 22 Millie gave birth to a baby girl, who was named Colo. She was the first gorilla of any species to be born in the U.S. and the first born in captivity anywhere, even Africa. Colo has since given birth to three infants herself and still lives at the Columbus Zoo, making her the oldest captive gorilla in the world. (And in 2003 she became a great-great-grandmother.)

BOOK

Around 1638 Stephen Daye and his family emigrated from London to the the newly founded town of Cambridge in Massachusetts Bay Colony. He was under contract to the Reverend Joseph Glover, who was also on the journey and who had paid for the Daye family's passage. To repay that debt, Daye was to set up a printing press, which had been brought along on the ocean voyage and would be the first press in the colonies. Glover died during the voyage, but Daye still owed the work to Glover's widow, so he set up the press in her house. In 1639 he published America's first broadsheet—a single sheet of paper meant for public posting. Then he printed the first almanac, written by celebrated colonial sea captain William Pierce. And in 1640, he printed 1,700 copies of *The Bay Psalm Book*, a new version of the Book of Psalms translated directly from Hebrew by several local ministers. The book, the first published in North America, became very popular—it went through numerous editions and was even distributed back in Britain.

Extra: Most historians believe that Stephen Daye may have had some printing experience, but that he was actually a locksmith by trade. His works were riddled with spelling and punctuation errors, leading one colonial historian to call him "an exceedingly illiterate printer."

CRICKET MATCH

Cricket was invented in southern England in the 1500s and was spread across the world by British colonists. The earliest recorded match in the United States was played in 1751 between teams called New York and London XI in the area of Manhattan that later became the Fulton Fish Market. The game took a long time to catch on in the states, but actually became quite popular in the mid-1800s...until it was eclipsed by baseball.

BABY BOOM

In 2005 Jean-Pierre Bocquet-Appel, an anthropologist at the National Center for Scientific Research in Paris, studied 62 prehistoric burial grounds located in various regions of North America. He discovered that for a period of about 700 years, beginning 2,800 years ago, progressively more and more young people were being buried. Why? Bocquet-Appel says it had a lot to do with a baby boom. The era coincides with the shift from hunting and gathering to farming in North America. That resulted, as it did at different times in different locations all over the world, in permanent dwellings being built, and food supplies becoming more secure, which resulted in a rapid increase in population—and more people, paradoxically, meant more people dying young.

WINE

The oldest continuously inhabited city in the continental United States is St. Augustine, Florida, founded by the Spanish in 1565. When those settlers arrived, they were pleased to discover wild *muscadine* grapes, which they used to create the first wine ever made in North America. (Native Americans didn't make wine.) Sometime over the next few decades, the first cultivation of grapes began, resulting in several varieties, the best known being the *Scuppernong*, or Big White Grape, still found in the Southeast today. Scuppernongs were used to make some of the most popular wines in the United States in the 19th and early 20th centuries, and they're making a comeback today. According to the USDA's Agricultural Research Service, muscadine grapes contain more *resveratrol*—a natural compound that lowers cholesterol levels—than other grapes.

KOREAN

Seo Jae-pil was born in Korea in 1864. While still a teenager, he joined a reform movement working for equality, and in 1884 he took part in the Kapsin Coup, a bloody attempt to take over the country. Seo's entire family was killed in the three-day melee, but Seo escaped and fled to Japan, where, in 1885, he boarded a ship for San Francisco, changing his name to Philip Jaisohn along the way. In 1890 he became a naturalized American citizen—the very first Korean to do so. He was also the first Korean to receive a college degree in the United States (a medical degree from George Washington University in 1892); founded *The Independent*, the first Korean newspaper in America; and in 1945 became the first Korean-born American to receive a medal from Congress, for his service as a physician during World War II. He died at his home in Norristown, Pennsylvania, in 1951. A statue of Jaisohn stands in front of the South Korean embassy in Washington, D.C.

PUBLICLY FUNDED ART PROJECT

Swedish-American painter Gustavus Hesselius (1682–1755) was one of the New World's first professional (and first widely acclaimed) portrait painters. On September 21, 1721, he received a £17 commission from St. Barnabas Church in Prince George's County, Maryland, for a painting of "our Beloved Saviour and ye Twelve Apostles at ye last supper."

Hesselius's *The Last Supper* is the first known instance of a public art commission in American history. The painting was lost when the church was rebuilt in 1773 and wasn't rediscovered until

1914. Since then it has been displayed at various museums, but today is back at St. Barnabas, where it hangs in the choir gallery.

...CAR RACE

In 1895 Herman H. Kohlsaat, editor of the *Chicago Times-Herald*, heard about an 1894 "horseless carriage" race from Paris to Rouen, France. It had been sponsored by the newspaper *Le Petit Journal*, so Kohlsaat decided to sponsor a similar race. He placed an ad promising $2,000 to the winner, and at 8:55 a.m. on a snowy Thanksgiving Day in 1895, six automobiles left Jackson Park in downtown Chicago on a 54-mile race to the town of Evanston and back. Three were Benz automobiles imported from Germany, and three were American-made, two of them electric-powered. The winner: J. Frank Duryea, who with his brother Charles had founded the first American company formed for the sole purpose of making cars: the Duryea Motor Wagon Company of Springfield, Massachusetts. Duryea covered the distance in 7 hours 53 minutes, averaging a rip-roaring 7.3 mph along the way. The win was a boon for the company, which sold 13 vehicles the next year. The Duryea brothers went their separate ways some years later, and although Charles continued to form car companies, he had only limited success, and the Duryeas ended up a footnote in automotive history, disappearing in the shadow of the juggernaut that was the Ford Motor Company. (But at least they'll always be known as the winners of America's first automobile race.)

*   *   *

ALWAYS CHECK YOUR LINKS

In 2009 a political battle took place in Minnesota between the Democratic Party and Republican Governor Tim Pawlenty. After the governor made a speech criticizing President Obama, the Democrats sent out an online press release denouncing the remarks. At the bottom of the release was a link that was supposed to have gone to a YouTube video of Pawlenty's speech, but instead went to one called "Chinese Grandma Learns English," which featured a kid tricking his grandmother into saying several swear words. The Democrats blamed the goof on an "outside researcher" and promised to double-check their press releases in the future.

The average American company loses about 6% of its revenue to fraud each year.

WHY ARE THEY CALLED "GREENHORNS"?

On page 21 you can find the origin of the word "tank."
(Tanks!) Here are a few more interesting word
and phrase origins. (You're welcome!)

TERM: Match

MEANING: A small piece of wood or cardboard used to light a fire

ORIGIN: From the Greek word *myxa*, which meant "lamp wick"—and also meant "mucus." The idea was that an oily wick sticking out of a lamp's spout or nozzle resembled snot dangling from someone's nose. (Really.) Myxa became *micca* in Latin, then *meiche* in Old French, and finally the English *match* in the 1330s. The term wasn't applied to what we think of as a match until 1831, a few years after its invention by English chemist John Walker. (And matches were also called "lucifers" for many years.)

TERM: Greenhorn

MEANING: Novice

ORIGIN: It goes all the way back to England in the 1400s, when it referred to a young ox with immature, or "green," horns. (The horns weren't actually green; the reference was probably taken from unripe, or "green," fruit.) Around 1650 *greenhorn* became a nickname for young, recently enlisted soldiers, and by the 1680s it was being used for novices in any field.

TERM: March Madness

MEANING: Nickname for the NCAA's basketball championship tournament

ORIGIN: In 1939 Henry V. Porter, an athletic administrator for the Illinois High School Association (IHSA), wrote an article entitled "March Madness" for the organization's newsletter. It was about the enthusiasm of the fans of Illinois high-school basketball, which held its yearly championship tournament in the month of

---

Ptooey! The spitting spider spits out gobs of sticky, venomous fluid to capture its prey.

March. The phrase was associated solely with Illinois high-school basketball until 1982. That year CBS announcer Brent Musburger, who began his career as a sportswriter in Chicago and had undoubtedly heard the term before, used it to refer to the NCAA college tournament, which also takes place in March. It caught on, and in 1996 the IHSA sued the NCAA for using the phrase on their official merchandise. The NCAA won in court, but the two groups agreed to form the "March Madness Athletic Association," giving the IHSA control of the name on the high-school level, while the NCAA owns it for college.

TERM: Digs

MEANING: Home, or rented rooms

ORIGIN: "Digs" is a shortened version of "diggings," first used by gold prospectors in the 1820s Georgia Gold Rush, the first gold rush in the United States. Prospectors would go into the wilderness, set up camp, and "dig" for gold, and the area around their mines and camps became known as "diggings." By the 1830s, the term was being used in reference to the rooms in the boarding houses that sprang up near successful mines. "Diggings" spread around the English-speaking world as a nickname for any rented rooms. Decades later, in the 1890s, it first appeared in its shortened version, *digs*—in England. And even then, the word had the same casual, hip feel to it that it has today, as shown in this 1893 publication by English bicycle enthusiast John Augustus Lunt, writing about a tour of North Wales:

> Arrived Betws-y-coed [a village in Wales] 2.35pm. Grand little place down the hollow hemmed in with trees & woods. Dropped on splendid digs—Mrs Williams Pont-y-Pair House just by bridge over R Conway. Sitting room we had all to ourselves.

"Digs" is most commonly used today in the expression "Nice digs!"

*　　*　　*

DUMB CROOKS

"In 2009 five people were arrested in Maine and charged with arson after police viewed a YouTube video they made describing their crime, complete with theme music and cast credits."

—*News of the Weird*

Underworld? There are more than 9 acres of tunnels hidden under Disney World.

PORTA-NEWS

When outdoor portable toilets make headlines.

TANGLED UP IN EWW!

In summer 2008, Bob Dylan's neighbors in Malibu, California, started complaining about the stench emanating from a porta potty located on the singer's property. "It's a scandal!" said David Emminger, whose house sits downwind of Dylan's. "'Mr. Civil Rights' is killing our civil rights!" Emminger claims the fumes have sickened his family, forcing them to install high-powered fans in their yard in the hopes of blowing the stench back toward Dylan's. Malibu officials are looking into the matter, and each side has hired lawyers. But as of summer 2009, the outhouse is still standing, and its aromas are still blowin' in the wind.

SHOW SOME RESPECT

When presidential candidate Barack Obama appeared at a rally in Portland, Oregon, in May 2008, he unknowingly angered the entire police force. How? An Obama staffer set up a row of porta potties on top of a concrete memorial that honored fallen officers. "There was plenty of room elsewhere, so space wasn't an issue," said officer Thomas Brennan. "So someone used some really poor judgement. I mean, it's hallowed ground!" (Flags were still being flown at half-mast from a service that had taken place earlier that week.) All that the police wanted, they said, was an apology to the families of the fallen officers, and perhaps an explanation. Both eventually came from Obama's staff. The explanation: The spot was chosen because of a "safety issue for wheelchair access."

NOWHERE TO RUN, NOWHERE TO HIDE

In 2008, in a shopping mall parking lot in Tampa, Florida, a man witnessed someone breaking into his pickup truck. So he and a friend chased the burglar, Lorenzo Earl Knight, into a nearby construction site. Knight ducked into a porta potty, hoping that his pursuers hadn't seen him. They had. And they tipped over the toilet, causing the unit's "holding tank" to empty all over Knight. Police arrived and took him into custody.

THE MAN WHO WOULD NOT DIE

*Here's a real-life crime story that reads like something
out of a cartoon. Warning: It's pretty gruesome
...but it's also pretty fascinating.*

THE NEFARIOUS SCHEME

During the waning days of Prohibition, Tony Marino's speakeasy served illegal liquor in the Bronx, New York. Marino and his bartender, Joe "Red" Murphy, did some additional business on the side: They'd take out insurance policies in the names of vagrants and then feed them so much booze that they'd die. By December 1932, after having pulled off the scheme successfully a couple of times, Marino and Murphy set their sights on one of their regular customers, a 60-year-old Irish immigrant named Michael Malloy. A firefighter in his younger days, Malloy was now just another old drunk with no money, no home, and no family.

With three insurance policies secretly taken out in Malloy's name, the two conspirators offered him an open tab and a cot in the back in exchange for sweeping out the bar each morning. The men stood to collect $3,500 (nearly $60,000 in today's money), but only if Malloy's death was accidental. But no matter how much hooch he put down (reportedly more than enough to kill any other man), he'd just sleep it off and then ask for more. Not only that, but Malloy's health was actually *improving*—forcing Marino and Murphy to take their plan to the next level.

A TOUGH CONSTITUTION

• Murphy, a former chemist, mixed antifreeze with whiskey and told Malloy it was "new stuff." After drinking it down, Malloy said, "That was smooth!" Then he fell unconscious to the floor. The men dragged him into the back room and left him to die. But he didn't.

• The next morning, they found Malloy cheerfully sweeping the bar. So over the next few days, Malloy's drinks were spiked with

---

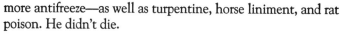

more antifreeze—as well as turpentine, horse liniment, and rat poison. He didn't die.

• Murphy gave Malloy a potentially lethal sandwich. The ingredients: sardines that had been left to spoil in an open tin for a week, along with some metal shavings and carpet tacks. Malloy happily ate the sandwich. He didn't die.

• Then they gave Malloy another rotten sandwich, this one containing oysters that had been soaked in a batch of whiskey and wood alcohol—a poison that, if it didn't kill you, would blind you. Malloy didn't go blind. And he didn't die.

• January brought a cold snap. One night, when the temperature was −14°F, the men fed Malloy so much hooch that he passed out. They then took him to a park, stripped off his shirt, and threw him onto a snowbank. Then they poured a few gallons of cold water over him for good measure. He didn't die.

• Then the men paid a cab driver named Hershey Green $50 to run over Malloy. Another accomplice, "Tough Tony" Bastone, held up Malloy's unconscious body in the road. Just before the cab hit Malloy at 45 mph, Bastone jumped out of the way. They left Malloy's mangled body in the road, believing he was finally dead.

HE LIVES!

Over the next few days, the gang scanned the obituaries and police reports for news of Malloy's death. It didn't come. And then, three weeks later, Malloy walked back into Marino's speakeasy, ordered a shot of rotgut, and explained to the astonished men, "I must have really tied one on, because I woke up in the hospital with a cracked skull and a busted shoulder!"

The men were at their wits' end. Bastone, a part-time hit man, offered to "fill the bum full of lead" for $500. Marino refused. He had another plan: He hired a fruit dealer named Daniel Kriesberg to rent a room, take Malloy there, and give him all the gin (mixed with wood alcohol) that he could drink. After Malloy passed out, Murphy brought in a length of rubber hose. He put one end in Malloy's mouth and the other into a gas jet, and then he turned it on. On February 22, 1933, Michael Malloy was finally dead.

That night, Marino paid a crooked doctor $50 to sign a death certificate listing Malloy's cause of death as "lobar pneumonia, with alcoholism as a contributing cause." Then another member of the gang, an undertaker named Frank Pasqua, buried Malloy in a $12 coffin without even embalming him. The next day, Murphy, posing as the deceased's brother, collected $800 from Metropolitan Life. One policy down, two to go.

CAUGHT!

But then the scheme began to unravel as the conspirators squabbled over who should get a bigger cut. Bastone even threatened to go public. The next day, two Prudential agents came to the speakeasy looking for Murphy but were told he was down at the police station being questioned about Bastone...who had mysteriously turned up dead the night before. The agents became suspicious and told the cops that it looked like a case of insurance fraud. Police exhumed Malloy's body and concluded that he was indeed gassed to death.

In a headline-grabbing trial, the Bronx's "Murder Trust" captured the attention of the public. In his opening statement, Bronx District Attorney Samuel J. Foley referred to the scheme as "the most grotesque chain of events in New York criminal history." While on the witness stand, each gang member tried to pin the whole thing on Bastone, testifying that he had forced them to kill Malloy. The jury didn't buy it. The verdict: Guilty. Green, the cab driver, turned state's evidence and was given a lesser sentence—life in prison. Marino, Murphy, Pasqua, and Kriesberg were each put to death in the electric chair at Sing Sing Prison in the summer of 1934.

And to this day, doctors still have no idea how Malloy could have possibly survived all of those murder attempts.

* * *

A RANDOM ORIGIN

Ralph Teetor (1890–1982) was a prolific inventor who developed many car improvements. Ironically, he was sight-impaired and unable to drive, so his lawyer frequently offered to chauffeur him. The lawyer was a bad driver, though, prone to jerky starts and stops, which annoyed Teetor...and inspired him to invent a way to regulate the car's speed at a consistent level: cruise control. (It was invented in 1945, but first offered as an option on 1958 Chryslers.)

OOPS!

More tales of outrageous blunders.

THE TWEETER AND THE BRANCH

While jogging to work one morning in early 2009, 23-year-old James Coleman of Bristol, England, decided to post an update on his Twitter account. So he took out his BlackBerry (while jogging) and started typing. Bad idea: He ran headfirst into a low-hanging tree branch, which sent him tumbling down to the pavement. The resulting bruise on Coleman's face forced his left eye to stay closed for several days. "I feel a twit," said the tweeter.

GET A GRIP

In June 2009, 22-year-old Eugene Scott Duncan, an amateur mountaineer from West Virginia, decided, for some reason, to try rappelling down a power line tower near his house. (This was one of those very high towers with a metal frame and three sets of high-voltage power lines.) Duncan made it the first part of the way down without incident, but when his foot hit one of the live power lines, the shock caused him to let go of his rope and plunge the rest of the way down, all the way to the ground. He was treated for severe injuries, but survived. Police charged him with trespassing.

ARREST ME, WILL YOU? BWA HA HA HA!

Late one night in November 2008, police in Hackney, England, saw some suspicious activity through the window of a building: men wearing white lab coats, flashing colored lights, and strange fluids gurgling in glass bottles and tubes. The police raided the room and arrested the leader, 29-year-old Richard Watson, on charges of terrorism. The cops then evacuated the entire area and called in the bomb squad. "There were a ridiculous amount of police there," Watson later said. Why ridiculous? As he'd tried to explain (while he was being arrested and for the hour he was handcuffed to a van), he was simply having a "Mad Scientist" theme party. The equipment was fake and the chemicals were just food coloring, bicarbonate of soda, and vinegar. Watson was freed without charges.

Red-green color-blind people can see more shades of khaki than people with normal vision can.

CELLO WHAT?

"Fiddler's neck" is a real ailment suffered by people who play the violin; "flautist's chin" is a real ailment suffered by flute players. Here's the strange story of two more strange musical maladies.

LETTER TO THE EDITOR

In April 1974, the *British Medical Journal* published a letter from a physician in southern England:

> SIR,
>
> I have recently seen three patients with traumatic *mastitis* [inflammation] of one breast. These were all girls between 8 and 10 and the mastitis consisted of a slightly inflamed cystic swelling about the base of the nipple. Questioning revealed that all three were learning to play the classical guitar, which requires close attention to the position of the instrument in relation to the body. In each case a full-sized guitar was used and the edge of the soundbox pressed against the nipple. Two of the patients were right-handed and consequently had a right-sided mastitis while the third was left-handed with a left-sided mastitis. When the guitar-playing was stopped the mastitis subsided spontaneously.
>
> I would be interested to know whether any other doctors have come across this condition.
>
> I am, etc.,
> P. Curtis,
> Winchester

Clearly, Dr. Curtis believed that the pressure of the guitar against the children's chests caused an irritation that cleared up as soon as they stopped playing the guitar. As was common practice at the time, the *British Medical Journal* printed the letter as a courtesy to see if any other doctors had seen such an ailment. The letter did attract responses from a number of physicians, but none had ever seen a case of "guitar nipple," as it came to be called.

Light-headed: Thinking for one hour burns about 1/15 of a gram of fat.

Some doctors did, however, write in with helpful suggestions for the original sufferers: One wondered if the problem was caused by left-handed children playing guitars intended for right-handed adults, or vice versa. Another doctor suggested that if the irritation persisted, the children should get another guitar instructor.

HEADING SOUTH

But the most interesting response of all came from a J. M. Murphy, who had this to say:

> SIR,
> Though I have not come across "guitar nipple" as reported by Dr. P. Curtis, I did once come across a case of "cello scrotum" caused by irritation from the body of the cello. The patient in question was a professional musician and played in rehearsal, practice, or concert for several hours each day.
> I am, etc.,
> J. M. Murphy

As had been the case with "guitar nipple," "cello scrotum" attracted some interest from physicians, but no cases of other patients suffering from the condition were ever reported.

Instrument-induced ailments are not uncommon, especially among professional musicians who play their instruments day after day for hours on end. Overuse can cause injury all by itself, and the nickel, chromium, brass, and other materials used to make musical instruments can also cause irritation to sensitive skin. So not much notice was taken of "guitar nipple" and "cello scrotum" when they surfaced; they were just added to the list of music-related maladies that get written up in medical journals from time to time. Years passed before much thought was given to them again.

BODY OF EVIDENCE

Then in 1991 a Connecticut doctor named Philip Shapiro read about "cello scrotum" in the *Journal of the American Academy of Dermatology*. Shapiro knew from personal experience (he played the cello) that the intimate parts of the male anatomy never come in contact with the instrument—the large size of the cello and the position in which it must be held to be played made it almost impossible. The musician's crotch is at least six inches away from the cello at all times, and besides, most men play the cello while *wearing pants.*

Dr. Shapiro stated his case in a letter to the journal and included a photograph of himself playing the cello (with his crotch nowhere near the instrument) as supporting evidence. Even if some cellists do experience irritation in the aforementioned area, he argued, the *cellist,* not the cello, would be at fault: "Just as people sometimes scratch their heads repetitively, some also scratch their genitals," he wrote. The journal published Dr. Shapiro's letter; from then on whenever "cello scrotum" was mentioned in medical journals, it was accompanied with a caveat that the ailment's existence had been questioned on the grounds that getting it "would require an extremely awkward playing position."

OH, NUTS

Then in 2009, after "cello scrotum" was mentioned in yet another *British Medical Journal* article, Dr. Elaine Murphy, a former medical school professor serving in the British House of Lords, came forward and admitted that the ailment was a hoax. Dr. Murphy and her husband, John M. Murphy—the J. M. Murphy who signed the original letter—had gotten such a laugh out of Dr. P. Curtis's original "guitar nipple" letter in 1974 that they decided to try and top it. "Somewhat to our astonishment, our letter was published," she wrote. "Anyone who has ever watched a cello being played would realize the physical impossibility of our claim."

That clears up "cello scrotum"…but what about "guitar nipple"? After all, it's been written up in many prestigious publications, including the *British Medical Journal* (and *Uncle John's Fast-Acting Long-Lasting Bathroom Reader*). So, if you play the guitar, should you still be on guard against it? Probably not—Dr. Murphy says she and her husband had suspected back in 1974 that it, too, was a hoax. "The following Christmas we sent a card to Dr. Curtis of 'guitar nipple' fame, only to discover that he knew nothing about it," Dr. Murphy wrote. "Another joke, we suspect."

LIFE IMITATES ART

Typically, fiction is based on real-life events. But some things first appear in fiction...only to be repeated later in reality.

ON THE SCREEN: In the 1984 "mockumentary" film *This Is Spinal Tap*, the fictitious band orders their prop maker to build them a 12-foot-tall statue of Stonehenge. But there's a miscommunication. Result: When the statue is lowered to the stage during a live performance, it's only 12 *inches* tall.

IN REAL LIFE: Wayne Coyne, lead singer of the Flaming Lips, told this story to London's *The Times*: "Back in 1999, we were supposed to be using a giant gong on stage that was about five feet high, and I would slam it dramatically. But at one show in Barcelona, someone screwed up: The gong was more like one of those pathetic little dinner gongs that a Chinese restaurant would use to tell everyone dessert was being served. I don't know how much closer to *Spinal Tap* you could get."

ON THE SCREEN: In 1929 German film director Fritz Lang made one of the first science fiction movies, *Frau im Mond* (*The Lady in the Moon*). In the scene where the rocket launches, Lang wanted to add more dramatic tension. So instead of using the standard method of counting up to a predetermined number (1-2-3-launch), Lang used a countdown: 10-9-8-7-6-5-4-3-2-1.

IN REAL LIFE: Three decades later when NASA began sending rockets into space, it adopted the countdown popularized by Lang.

ON THE SCREEN: In Robert Bloch's 1959 novel *Psycho* (and in the 1960 Alfred Hitchcock film that starred Anthony Perkins), innkeeper Norman Bates impersonates his dead mother and blames "her" for the crimes he commits.

IN REAL LIFE: In 2003 Thomas Parkin of New York City pretended to be his deceased mother so he could collect her Social Security and benefits. He even wore a wig, sunglasses, and painted nails when he went to the DMV to renew "her" license. In 2009 when police arrested Parkin, he said, "I held my mother when she was dying and breathed in her last breath, so I am my mother."

ON THE SCREEN: On a February 2009 episode of the comedy show *Flight of the Conchords*, the prime minister of New Zealand attempts to arrange a meeting with America's new president, Barack Obama. He's denied, though, because the U.S. "doesn't recognize New Zealand as a country."

IN REAL LIFE: A few weeks later, New Zealand's real prime minister, John Key, attempted to arrange a meeting with Obama, but was denied. "I'm a bit of the view that he's got so many things to deal with and, on a relative basis, we are a pretty small country," said Key.

ON THE SCREEN: In the *Friday the 13th* movies, a deranged man named Jason dons a hockey mask and attacks his victims with an axe. Some of his victims fight back.

IN REAL LIFE: At a party for the premiere of 2009's *Friday the 13th* remake, an actor who played Jason in a previous movie jumped onto the stage with the trademark axe and hockey mask. A nearby woman must have thought it was real, because she wrestled the axe away from him, severely slashing his hand. "It was straight out of a horror movie," said a witness, "Lingerie-clad models were screaming, as a blood-soaked Jason ran off the runway to get to a hospital."

ON THE SCREEN: In the 1988 movie *Naked Gun*, Lt. Frank Drebin (Leslie Nielsen) leaves a press conference to go to the restroom...forgetting that his lapel microphone is still on. Outside, everyone can hear him peeing while he sings to himself.

IN REAL LIFE: In 2006 CNN was covering President Bush's speech on the one-year anniversary of Hurricane Katrina. But in addition to the president's plans to rebuild New Orleans, viewers heard CNN anchor Kyra Phillips go to the restroom, where she complained to a coworker about how hard it is to find a compassionate man. Then a loud zip was heard. (That's when CNN finally turned off her microphone.)

MORE REAL LIFE: In 2009 the cast of the sitcom *How I Met Your Mother* was doing a Q&A session with fans when Neil Patrick Harris got up to go to the bathroom...with his mic still on. His publicist could hear the shuffling sounds and ran in to tell Harris to turn it off, but not before everyone in the room heard the actor unzip and say to himself, "Wake up!"

Poll result: 41% of Americans say they've considered attacking their computers. 7% have done it.

ENGLAND'S ROSWELL

Most Americans are familiar with the legend of the UFO landing near Roswell,
New Mexico in 1947. But what about the "Incident at Rendlesham" that took
place near Ipswich, England, the day after Christmas in 1980? It's been cited
by UFO buffs as one of the most credible sightings of the 20th century.

NOT-SO-SILENT NIGHT

Just before 3:00 a.m. on the morning of December 26, 1980, a bright light was seen racing across the night sky over Rendlesham Forest, which separates two Royal Air Force bases: RAF Bentwaters to the north, and RAF Woodbridge, which juts out of the forest's western edge. The strange light made no noise, but the sight was so startling that the airmen who saw the light thought that an aircraft might have crashed in the forest. They asked for permission to investigate.

Three U.S. Air Force airmen who were patrolling Woodbridge —Staff-Sergeant Jim Penniston, Airman Edward Cabansag, and Airman First Class John Burroughs—were dispatched into the forest to take a look. Nearly 30 years later, they still can't agree on what they saw among the trees—except for one thing: They all saw a lot of lights. Big lights. Little lights. Colored lights. "Blue, red, white, and yellow," Cabansag wrote in a report several days later.

(SOMEWHAT) CLOSE ENCOUNTER

In his report, Penniston stated that he thought they had come within 50 yards of the source of the flashing lights. "It was definitely mechanical in nature. This is the closest point that I was near the object at any point. We then proceeded after it." They moved closer to where they thought the object was, but they never seemed to get any closer to it—it appeared to move farther away as they approached. "It moved in a zig-zagging manner back through the wood and then [we] lost sight of it," he wrote.

Even creepier than the unexplained lights were the *noises*. "Strange noises," Burroughs wrote in his statement, "like a woman screaming. Also the woods lit up and you could hear the farm animals making a lot of noises, and there was a lot of movement in the woods."

The airmen were in the forest for about an hour before it became clear that whatever they were seeing and hearing, it wasn't the result of an airplane crash. They were ordered back to base.

At 4:11 a.m., an airman named Chris Armold called the local police, the Suffolk Constabulary, and asked if they'd received any reports of a downed aircraft. They hadn't, but they sent two officers out to examine the scene anyway. The officers saw nothing unusual. A short time later, Armold accompanied Burroughs on a second trip into the forest. "We could see lights in the distance, and it appeared unusual as it was a sweeping light," Armold recalled in a 1997 interview. "We also saw some strange colored lights in the distance but were unable to see what they were."

MAKING AN IMPRESSION

Then after daybreak, more airmen went into the same part of the forest. They found three small indentations in the ground, each one roughly 1 ½" deep and 7" in diameter, laid out on the ground in a triangular pattern. Were they made by the landing gear of a UFO? The airmen also noticed some strange marks in the surrounding trees: The bark had been removed and the sap had crystallized in the wound. Were they burn or scrape marks made when the UFO lifted off?

A second call to the Suffolk Constabulary brought another officer to the scene…but he didn't note anything particularly unusual about the marks on the ground or in the trees.

DÉJÀ VIEW

That might have been the end of the "Incident at Rendlesham" were it not for the fact that on the following night (December 27), airmen on guard duty at the back gate of RAF Woodbridge, which faced Rendlesham Forest, again saw strange lights coming from the forest. When word of the sighting reached the deputy base commander, Lieutenant Colonel Charles Halt, he organized another team of airmen and sometime after midnight led them into the forest to investigate. This time the party brought a Geiger counter and a tape recorder, into which Halt recorded nearly 18 minutes of live observations as the group examined the site over the next four hours.

Halt's tape recording makes for compelling listening: He and the search team examined the impressions in the ground and the marks on the trees, carefully taking radiation readings as they went. The strongest reading was from one of the indentations, which gave a reading of 0.07 millirems per hour. The men also noticed small branches that had been freshly broken off nearby trees about 15' to 20' off the ground, and reported hearing strange animal noises just like the first team had the night before.

WITH THEIR OWN EYES

Then, around 13 minutes into the 18-minute tape, Halt and the men suddenly saw a strange, flashing yellowish-red light in the forest. "It's coming this way. It's definitely coming this way! Pieces of it are shooting off," Halt says into the tape recorder. "There is no doubt about it. This is weird!"

Halt and his team followed the strange light out of the forest, through a field, and past a farmer's house into another field. "Now we have multiple sightings of up to five lights with a similar shape and all," he says on the tape, "but they seem to be steady now rather than a pulsating or glow with a red flash."

They crossed a creek as they pursued the lights, which were now considerably farther away. "Made sighting again about 110°," Halt says. "This looks like it's clear off to the coast. It's right on the horizon. Moves about a bit, and flashes from time to time. Still steady or red in color." The men saw strobe-light flashes, and then two "strange objects...with colored lights on 'em" to the north, and a similar object to the south, about 10 degrees off the horizon. "Hey, here he comes from the south, he's coming toward us now," Halt says. "Now we're observing what appears to be a beam coming down to the ground. This is unreal!"

Halt and his men watched the strange lights for another 15 minutes, until 3:30 a.m., then headed back to base. At 4:00 a.m., Halt ends the tape by reporting, "One object still hovering over Woodbridge base at about 5 to 10 degrees off the horizon, still moving erratic and similar lights and beaming down as earlier."

ON PAPER

In the days that followed, Halt had several of the witnesses to the events of December 26 submit written statements describing what they saw and experienced. He used these statements, along with his own recollections from the night of December 27, to write a one-page official memo titled "Unexplained Lights." In it he describes the object that some witnesses claimed to have seen as "a strange glowing object…metallic in appearance and triangular in shape, approximately two to three meters across the base and approximately two meters high."

EXTRAORDINARY

Two separate sightings in the same place two days apart, each witnessed by numerous credible witnesses. Written statements describing what was seen, backed by police logs that confirm the dates and times. An official Air Force memo written by the deputy commander of the military base where the events took place. Physical evidence, in the form of indentations in the ground and marks on nearby trees. An actual *tape recording* of the second encounter as it unfolds. That's *a lot* of evidence. Rarely—if ever—has a reported UFO encounter been documented as thoroughly as the Incident at Rendlesham.

So what really happened in the woods those two nights?
Part II of the story is on page 499.

Part II of the story is on page 499.

*　　*　　*

NOW THAT'S A CLOSE ENCOUNTER

"Alleged victims of UFO abductions occasionally claim to have had sexual relationships with the occupants of extraterrestrial spaceships. Such an incident is referred to by some writers as a *Close Encounter of the Fourth Kind* (CE-IV), although others use the term to denote only an abduction in which no sexual activity has occurred. Mating between earthlings and extraterrestrials is a theme encountered in the arguments of supporters of the Ancient Astronauts hypothesis. Many of them believe that the human race was actually the result of the interbreeding of extraterrestrials and some advanced species of animal on Earth, such as Bigfoot."

—*The UFO Encyclopedia*

PRIMETIME PROVERBS

Some "wisdom" from the flickering oracle in your living room.

ON TRUTH
"The truth ain't like puppies, a bunch of them running around, you pick your favorite. There's one truth, and it has come a knockin'."
—**Emerson,** *Pushing Daisies*

"Lies are like children—they're hard work, but it's worth it because the future depends on them."
—**Dr. House,** *House, M.D.*

ON ADVERTISING
"What you call love was invented by guys like me to sell nylons."
—**Don Draper,** *Mad Men*

ON CHURCH
"I love it here, man. You can sing as loud as you want. That dude wails away on the organ. That dude up there tells stories. It's almost a religious experience!"
—**Leo,** *That '70s Show*

ON DISAPPOINTMENT
"I didn't think it was physically possible, but this both sucks and blows."
—**Bart,** *The Simpsons*

ON PAIN
"I'm no VIP, I'm not even an IP; I'm just a lonely little P sitting out here in the gutter."
—**Robin,** *How I Met Your Mother*

"Maybe we like the pain. Because without it, maybe we just wouldn't feel real. What's that saying: 'Why do I keep hitting myself with a hammer? Because it feels so good when I stop.'"
—**Meredith,** *Gray's Anatomy*

ON BEING YOURSELF
Jack: I don't believe in destiny.
Locke: Yes you do; you just don't know it yet.
—*Lost*

Frank: I tried nice once. Didn't care for it.
Marie: Is that what happened to smart?
—*Everybody Loves Raymond*

ON ART
"Sometimes for an artist, the only difference between insanity and genius is success."
—**Reid,** *Criminal Minds*

Originally, Fonzie was named Arthur "Mash" Marsciarelli.

ON INTELLIGENCE

Sanders: I'm like a sponge: I just absorb information.
Grissom: I thought that was *my* line.
Sanders: Yes, and I absorbed it.
—*CSI*

"I learned a valuable lesson that night. If you're going to try to fly a bicycle, you'd better make sure E.T. is sittin' in your basket instead of a twelve-pack of beer."
—Earl, *My Name Is Earl*

Dan: You're 19 feet tall! Why are you wearing heels?
Sally: Are you feeling diminutive?
Dan: No, but now I have to go look up that word.
—*Sports Night*

ON TELEVISION

"I do not like television. Notice how I didn't say 'TV,' for 'TV' is a nickname, and nicknames are reserved for friends, and television is no friend of mine."
—David, *Mr. Show with Bob & David*

ON GOING TO WORK

"When I tell people that I work at Dunder Mifflin, they think that we sell mufflers or muffins or mittens…and frankly, all of those sound better than paper so I let it slide."
—Jim, *The Office*

ON CRIMINAL JUSTICE

"Criminals are the vomit of society, and we cops are the sawdust."
—Deputy Garcia, *Reno 911*

ON EGO

"The only person more self-centered than me is Carlos; he's so self-centered, he doesn't even know how self-centered I am."
—Gabrielle, *Desperate Housewives*

ON BELIEF

"I believe that the moon does not exist. I believe that vampires are the world's greatest golfers but their curse is they never get a chance to prove it. I believe that there are 31 letters in the *white* alphabet. Wait…what was the question?"
—Tracy, *30 Rock*

* * *

"Television is the triumph of machine over people."
—Fred Allen

OLD TWO-TOES

Here's a story that clawed its way out of our "Man vs. Animal" files.

BEAR THIS IN MIND
While much is made of the ferocity of bears, there are, on average, only 10 to 20 bear attacks in North America each year, with fewer than half of one percent of those resulting in deaths. Bears are exceptionally shy creatures and typically will attack a human being only if they're surprised or if their food or cubs are in danger. And it's even rarer still for an individual bear to become an infamous man-eater. But that's exactly what happened a century ago in the case of one particularly ferocious grizzly known as "Old Two-Toes," who earned both his name and his fearsome reputation all on the same day.

GRAHAM CRACKER

In early May of 1912, near Crevice Mountain, Montana, a 63-year-old prospector named Johnny Graham found tracks belonging to "the biggest bear I ever seen." Suspecting that it was headed to feed on the carcass of a pack horse that Graham had recently put down, he decided to trap and kill the giant "grizz." He set a 60-pound Newhouse Bear Trap (which featured large steel teeth) near the dead horse, went home, and waited. Two days later, Graham went to check the heavy trap...and it was gone. He followed the trail 200 yards down the hill and found the enormous bear—still in the trap—struggling to free itself from between two fallen logs where the trap had become wedged. Graham raised his rifle, took careful aim, and put two bullets in the bear's chest.

The grizzly lay still as Graham leaned his rifle against a tree and prepared to skin the massive beast. Bad idea: It wasn't dead, just stunned. The bear suddenly lurched upward and freed itself from the steel jaws, losing three toes (complete with four-inch claws) in the process. Then it ripped into Johnny Graham.

Old Two-Toes, as the bear was called from then on, fled the scene, leaving the wounded prospector behind. A passerby came upon Graham and heard his harrowing tale. He promised to get help. When news of the vicious grizzly spread, a heavily armed posse tracked him down. They were closing in on him, but he escaped by crossing a river and fleeing into Yellowstone National Park—where no hunting was allowed. The men, knowing they'd face stiff fines and the confiscation of their weapons if caught, grudgingly gave up the chase. By the time help reached Graham, he was dead. Old Two-Toes, however, was just getting started.

WELSH RAREBIT

Four years later, two men were hauling supplies across Yellowstone when they paused at Soda Butte Creek to camp for the evening. In the middle of the night, one of the men, 61-year-old Pat Welsh, was awakened by the unmistakable sounds of a bear tearing into his stocks of cured ham and bacon. Scrambling from his bedroll, Welsh tried to scare the animal away by banging on pots and pans. Bad idea #2: The bear turned on Welsh, who grabbed a hand axe and swung it wildly. The grizzly casually swatted the axe away, knocked Welsh to the ground, and mauled him. Welsh's partner frightened the giant grizzly off with Roman candles, but it was too late for Welsh, who died of his wounds a few days later. Tracks later found at the scene confirmed that Old Two-Toes had claimed his second victim.

FRENCH FRY

It was nearly six years before Old Two-Toes struck again. On June 12, 1922, notorious prospector and poacher Joseph "Frenchy" Duret found a gargantuan grizzly caught in one of the many traps he'd set along Slough Creek near Yellowstone's border. Duret hurried home to grab his Winchester 45-70 rifle, informed his wife of the find, and told her he'd be home before nightfall. Bad idea #3: Frenchy's mangled body was found two days later, nearly a mile and a half from where he'd battled with the bear. His rifle was found at the scene, its barrel deeply scarred and the stock chewed in half. There was a single empty cartridge on the ground.

It's unknown whether Duret's bullet had hit its mark, but one thing was certain: The mark got away. Old Two-Toes had claimed another victim and escaped again, this time carrying the 60-pound trap with him—its severed chain trailing behind as he lumbered away. The empty trap was found a year later; Old Two-Toes, on the other hand, was never heard from again...so watch out!

Suggested alternate title for *Back to the Future: Spaceman from Pluto.*

EXERCISE YOUR BRAIN

Given a little time and a modicum of strength, you should be able to solve these. (But in case you can't, the answers are on page 536.)

1. Only two states in the United States have names that begin with two consonants. What are they?

2. Rearrange these letters to make four different six-letter words: **B E L S T U**

3. If today is Saturday, and you have to clean your bathroom two days after the day before the day after tomorrow, when do you have to clean your bathroom?

4. What do these seven little clues suggest to you?
mean, stupid, allergic, tired, timid, healing, content

5. Riddle time: Which one of the Osmonds likes books but not libraries, letters but not words, mirrors but not windows, kittens but not cats, and puppies but not dogs?

6. How can you use half a dozen ones to make a dozen?

7. What do the following words have in common?
BROW HORSE BALL WAY

8. If a pilot flies 200 miles due north and then 100 miles due south, what's the closest distance he can be from his starting point? What's the farthest?

9. Can you think of a triumphant adjective that contains double C, double S, and double L? Now think of a second one that is the opposite.

10. These famous quotations are missing their vowels. Once you figure out the theme, you should be able to get them all.

SHWMTHMNY
HSTLVSTBBY
MYTHFRCBWTHY
WRNTNKNSSNYMR
DNTCLLMSHRLY

11. How is it possible to add 4 to 9 and come up with 1?

12. You have $63 cash in your pocket. But you have no $1 bills, and no coins. What do you have?

13. Another riddle: God never sees one; kings rarely see one; you and I see them every day. What?

THE DIGITAL CAMERA REVOLUTION, PART III

*Now we get to see what develops when nearly every person
alive is armed with a camera. (Part II is on page 204.)*

JUST POINT...AND SHOOT!

By the early 2000s, most of the advancements in digital camera technology had been with 35mm SLRs. But these larger cameras and their interchangeable lenses are primarily used by serious hobbyists and professionals. Most people use their cameras for a much simpler reason: taking snapshots.

The first compact digital point-and-shoots were released in the late 1990s, but it wasn't until 2002 that the first models under $100 became available. In 2003 the first *single-use* digital cameras became available for less than $20. Similar to disposable film cameras, you just snap away until the camera's built-in memory card is full (anywhere from 25 to 50 shots) and take it back to the store to receive a set of prints along with a CD of your files. Both of these new cameras caused digital sales to skyrocket. Canon, for example, released its first compact digital in 2000; in 2008 the company celebrated the sale of its *100 millionth* compact digital. But even that feat would be dwarfed by another product of the digital era...a product you probably have with you right now.

PROUD PAPA

While point-and-shoot digitals make it easier than ever to take and share pictures, they still require people to actually have their cameras on hand when the picture-taking moment arrives. Few people take their camera *everywhere* they go, but these days nearly everyone has another item with them—a cell phone. Putting the two together has altered the way we view our world.

The cell phone camera was invented by Philippe Kahn in 1997. Kahn, a software developer, was sitting in a hospital waiting room in Santa Cruz, California, while his wife was preparing to give birth. He wanted to photograph the new arrival and send the pictures to his friends and family...immediately. So he wrote a crude program on his laptop computer and sent an assistant to get a soldering iron. After some tinkering, Khan took pictures of the delivery and then used his cell phone to send them out via e-mail. Needless to say, his friends were amazed to receive pictures of an event that had occurred only moments earlier—and from a *phone*.

After that, it took three years of development before cell phone cameras became available, first in Japan in 2000, and in the U.S. in 2002. Now, nearly every cell phone comes standard with the ability to shoot digital images and even videos. It's projected that by 2011, more than a billion cell phone cameras will have been sold.

A WORLD OF PAPARAZZI

A camera now sits in nearly every pocket and purse in the developed world. It's turned everyday people into photojournalists—and has had nearly as big an effect at deterring crime as security cameras. "We've been under surveillance under these big black-and-white cameras on buildings and at 7-Eleven stores," said Fred Turner, an assistant professor of communications at Stanford University. But thanks to cell phones, "the candid camera is wielded by individuals now." Cell phone cameras have allowed people to capture incidents that might have otherwise gone unrecorded: the prisoner abuse at Abu Ghraib in Iraq in 2004, Britain's Prince Harry wearing a Nazi uniform at a party in 2005, the shooting spree at Virginia Tech in 2007, and countless other accounts of "citizen paparazzi."

And now, instead of just calling the police on your cell phone after you've been mugged or carjacked, you can send pictures of the perpetrators and their getaway car. A typical example of a crime-fighting cell-phone camera took place in 2009 in Cape Coral, Florida. A woman was walking her dog when she saw a man breaking into a vacant house. She snapped some pictures on her phone and then called 911. The suspect was quickly captured.

But even more than the news-making moments, it's the cell phone camera's ability to capture the everyday moments that has made it so popular; it's even replaced the wallet as the preferred place to keep baby pictures. "Cell phone cameras have had such a massive impact because they're just so convenient," said Philippe Kahn. "There's always a way to capture memories and share them.

You go to a restaurant, and there's a birthday and suddenly everyone is getting their camera phones out. It's amazing."

OVERSATURATION

The cell phone camera phenomenon has become so widespread, in fact, that it's significantly cutting into to the sales of regular digital cameras. And for the first time, the sales of point-and-shoots—which have been steadily climbing—may soon be on the decline. "The manufacturers were rewarded with market growth, but once they filled that bucket, there wasn't any other bucket to fill," said Chris Chute, a digital imaging analyst for the research firm International Data Corporation (IDC).

Why the sudden decline? First, because of aggressive marketing, every time a new camera was released with a slightly higher megapixel capacity, the average consumer's camera became outdated—they *had* to have the new one. But cameras' capacity and reliability have both increased so much since 2005 that only cutting-edge professionals need to update every year or so. Result: In 2006 the IDC concluded that "the digital camera market will peak prematurely, missing the opportunity to replace film cameras as the predominant method of taking photos. Instead the market will be made up of a more diverse range of digital devices with photo capturing abilities, such as cell phones and other combination devices." They predict that 2011 will be the first year that digital camera sales will decrease from the previous year.

EYES OF THE WORLD

But even if there *is* a decline in sales, between cell phones, point-and-shoots, SLRs, and closed-circuit security cameras, there are *a lot* of digital cameras in the world today. How many? It's tough to say, but there are billions—at least one camera for every person in the world. And according to the International Imaging Industry Association, roughly six billion digital pictures are taken each year. That works out to about 190,000 photos taken around the world every second.

So there's no question that this influx has profoundly affected society—the question is how. Turns out that the digital photography revolution has a downside (a few, actually).

For Part IV, go to page 518.

No reporters or photographers have ever been allowed inside the Slinky factory.

THEME CRUISE

It's a modern vacation concept: an ocean cruise with all the aspects of a regular cruise, from free buffets to spinning classes, but with a twist—special activities designed around a common theme. Here are a few examples.

WEST COAST GROOVE CRUISE

Details: It's advertised as "the #1 party cruise in America, for those who love dance music and live by the mantra to work hard and play harder." So it's a crazy, wild week of debauchery at sea, right? Wrong. The cruise is popular with religious groups; participants must sign an agreement that prohibits the use of alcohol, illegal substances, weapons, pets, non-PG-rated music, costume parties, toga parties, and "lingerie modeling."

SEPTEMBER MORN CRUISE

Details: Named for a Neil Diamond song, the cruise is dedicated to the music and life of Neil Diamond. Shipboard entertainment includes the cover band Hot August Nights performing the songs of Neil Diamond, a Neil Diamond karaoke contest, and a meet-and-greet with members of Neil Diamond's touring band. Not appearing on the cruise: Neil Diamond.

CLOTHING-OPTIONAL HOMECOMING CRUISE

Details: It's just like a typical cruise: There's sunbathing, swimming, disco dancing, a casino, shuffleboard...except that everybody is naked. There are special naked-themed activities, such as a workshop called Sensual Awakening, nude drawing classes, and couples massage. The only place where cruisers are required to wear clothes is the formal dining room.

FRIENDS OF ABBOTT AND COSTELLO

Details: Officially, this 2009 cruise was for fans of the classic comedy duo of Bud Abbott and Lou Costello. But more specifically, it was for fans of the movie *Abbott and Costello Meet Frankenstein*. Since the two stars are long dead, they didn't appear on the cruise, but two of Costello's children were aboard, as was

Abbott's niece and the niece of Glenn Strange, the actor who played Frankenstein.

SPYCRUISE

Details: A cruise for Cold War and espionage buffs, Spycruise offers lectures and discussions with former CIA, MI-6, and even KGB agents. While cruising the Black Sea around eastern Europe to formerly Soviet-controlled areas (Ukraine, Bulgaria, Romania), daily lectures are given on topics such as spy life, spy history, and "clandestine equipment," or spy gear.

MOTORCYCLE CRUISE

Details: This voyage allows travelers to take their bikes—Harleys, Hondas, and choppers—aboard the ship, where they show them off to fellow enthusiasts en route to "party destinations" such as rocker Sammy Hagar's Cabo Wabo resort in Mexico. It's not as much fun as it could be: Participants are expressly forbidden from starting or riding their motorcycles on board. (They must walk them off the ship before starting them up.)

THE BEST OF PUBLIC BROADCASTING CRUISE

Details: Among the classic elements of a vacation are sun, sand, and...PBS? On the 2009 Public Television at Sea cruise, vacationers discussed current events with Gwen Ifill, moderator and managing editor of the PBS news series *Washington Week*, and David Fanning, the executive producer of *Frontline*.

STAR TREK ADVENTURE CRUISE

Details: There have been quite a few *Star Trek*–themed cruises in the past, but this 2009 expedition was different—it was part sailing *Star Trek* convention and part "whodunnit" game. After vacationers got autographs from an array of supporting and minor players from recent *Trek* TV shows, they participated in a *Trek*-themed murder-mystery game. (We're going to venture a guess that the murderer was Khaaaaaaaaaaaaaaaaan!)

*   *   *

"You couldn't get me on Mars if it were the last place on Earth."

—Erma Cohen

BEHIND THE HITS

*Ever wonder what inspired your favorite songs? Here are
a few inside stories about some legendary hit tunes.*

The Artist: LL Cool J
The Song: "Mama Said Knock You Out" (1991)
The Story: LL Cool J (real name: James Smith) was suffering from a street-cred problem. After releasing the sensitive ballad
"I Need Love," the talk in the rap world was that he'd "gone soft."
Unsure how to respond in song when recording his fourth album
in 1990, Smith thought of his grandmother (not his mama), who
often told him, "If a task is once begun, never leave it 'til it's
done." He called his grandmother and told her about his problem.
She told him to simply "knock out" the competition…but to keep
his lyrics profanity-free. Smith listened and then crafted "Mama
Said Knock You Out," an aggressive rap song that addresses his
critics. It went to #1, the biggest hit of LL Cool J's career.

The Artist: Counting Crows
The Song: "Mr. Jones" (1994)
The Story: One night in 1993, Crows lead singer Adam Duritz
went out to a bar in San Francisco with his friend (and former
bandmate) Marty Jones to see Jones's father, a Spanish flamenco
guitarist, perform. They got drunk, hoping it would give them
courage to talk to some girls, but they still lacked the nerve. They
did talk (to each other) about how they'd *definitely* have the nerve
to flirt if they were big stars. That conversation inspired Duritz to
write "Mr. Jones" about the near-universal desire to be a rock star.
Released in 1994, the song went to #5 and, ironically, launched
the band to fame. (Duritz made good on his wish—after becoming
famous, he dated Jennifer Aniston and Courteney Cox.)

The Artist: The Bellamy Brothers
The Song: "Let Your Love Flow" (1976)
The Story: Phil Gernhard was a top producer in the 1960s and
'70s, and he routinely used members of Neil Diamond's touring band
as session musicians. One day in 1975, Diamond's drummer brought
him a demo tape of a country/rock song written and performed by a

Diamond roadie named Larry Williams. Gernhard had an ear for hits—he'd produced many, such as "Stay" by Maurice Williams and the Zodiacs (1960) and "Me and You and a Dog Named Boo" by Lobo (1971). He knew the song had potential, but felt that Williams had the wrong voice for it. But a year later, he heard another roadie, Howard Bellamy, singing to himself backstage at a concert and immediately thought of Williams's demo. The song written by a roadie would be perfect if it were sung by *this* roadie. As it turned out, Bellamy (and his brother, David) had a band called the Bellamy Brothers. Sung by Howard Bellamy and produced by Gernhard, Williams's song, "Let Your Love Flow," went to #1 in 1976.

The Artist: Cyndi Lauper
The Song: "Time After Time" (1984)
The Story: Toward the end of recording Lauper's debut *She's So Unusual,* producer Rich Chertoff thought the record was *too* unusual—mostly silly, upbeat pop songs—and needed a ballad to show off Lauper's voice. Lauper demanded she be allowed to cowrite it and began looking for inspiration around the studio. She started riffing on phrases picked out of a *TV Guide,* and the one that stuck was the title of a 1979 movie, *Time After Time.* She created a melody while cowriter Rob Hyman wrote the verses about breaking up with his long-term girlfriend. Cobbled together only three days before the album's deadline, "Time After Time" ultimately became *She's So Unusual*'s second single and hit #1.

The Artist: Stevie Wonder
The Song: "Higher Ground" (1973)
The Story: Wonder was inspired by an eerie feeling of doom. "It was almost as if I had to get it done," he said years later. "I felt *something* was going to happen. I didn't know what or when, but I felt something." Consumed by the idea that his life was somehow about to move to a different level, he wrote and recorded "Higher Ground" in three hours, playing all of the instruments on the reincarnation-themed song himself. It was included on *Innervisions,* released in June 1973. On August 6th, Wonder was severely injured in a car accident in North Carolina. He was in a coma for four days and nearly died. The prescient singer/songwriter recovered, and "Higher Ground" went to #4.

THE NEW INDIAN WARS

When we think of the term "Indian Wars," we generally think of the Wild West of the 1800s. But it's not just an old-time phenomenon.

RESURGENCE
On December 29, 1890, 500 soldiers of the U.S. 7th Cavalry surrounded 350 Lakota Sioux near Wounded Knee Creek in South Dakota. While the soldiers attempted to confiscate rifles from the Indians, who had surrendered, a firearm discharged. Historical records are unclear as to how the gun went off, and whether it was accidental or not. In any event, the soldiers then opened fire on the Sioux with rifles and howitzer-like Hotchkiss guns, and in less than an hour more than 150 Indians—according to some reports, as many as 300—were dead, most of them unarmed women and children.

The Wounded Knee Massacre, as it's now known, has come to be regarded as the last major clash between North American Indians and white settlers. For the next 70 years, Indians in the U.S. were relegated to reservations and suffered cultural and economic hardships whose repercussions are still felt to this day. But there were no more major armed conflicts—until the 1960s. By then, inspired by the American civil rights movement, American Indian rights organizations such as AIM (American Indian Movement) began forming across North America, not unlike the Black Panthers and other militant African-American groups. Here are a few of the major milestones in the still-ongoing "Red Power Movement."

Alcatraz (1969). On November 20, Mohawk activist Richard Oakes led about 100 "Indians of All Tribes" in the occupation of Alcatraz Island in San Francisco Bay. Their reason: They were invoking a clause in an 1868 treaty stipulating that any U.S. territory abandoned by the federal government reverted back to Indian ownership. Alcatraz was abandoned, so they were taking it back, and they demanded the deed to the island and funding to establish an Indian university, cultural center, and museum there. The U.S. government refused and ordered the Indians to leave within 24 hours. Meanwhile, Coast Guard ships surrounded the island.

Average life span of a retiree after retirement in 1900: 1.2 years. In 2000: 20 years.

Not only did the Indians not comply, they occupied the island for nearly 18 months, with the help of supplies they ferried in from San Francisco. Initially, the Indians' cause enjoyed strong public support, but it eroded as infighting increased among the protesters, especially after a fire destroyed four historic buildings on Alcatraz in June 1971. Most of the remaining occupiers left after the fire, and on June 11 federal agents peaceably removed the last 15 men, women, and children from the island. None of their demands were met, but Indians viewed the occupation of Alcatraz as a remarkable success, as it brought their issues to headlines all over the country—and the world—for the first time in modern history. It was also instrumental in spurring Congress to pass a series of laws in the 1970s that expanded the policy of self-rule on reservations and greatly improved conditions there.

Wounded Knee II (1973). In February 1973, elders on the Pine Ridge Indian Reservation in South Dakota called on the leaders of AIM to help them in their fight against mistreatment by federal agents on the reservation and corruption among their own government-backed leaders. The response: On February 27, more than 200 armed AIM members entered the reservation town of Wounded Knee and took over the trading post, several homes, and a church—and took 11 white hostages. What followed was the largest miliary conflict on U.S. soil since the Civil War, as hundreds of heavily armed tribal police officers and government agents surrounded the town and cut off all roads in and out. Over the following weeks, two Indians were shot and killed, and a U.S. Marshal and an FBI agent were wounded. The Indians held the town for 71 tense days before a peaceful end was finally negotiated, and on May 8, the last of the occupiers left the town and were arrested. Nearly all of the hundreds of charges filed against them were later dismissed.

The Oglala Shootout (1975). On June 26, FBI Special Agents Jack Coler and Ronald Williams were in the Pine Ridge Reservation searching for an Oglala Sioux man named Jimmy Eagle, a suspect in an assault and robbery case, when someone opened fire on their unmarked cars. Both Coler and Williams were later found dead—shot at close range, execution-style. A massive nationwide manhunt followed. Two suspects, Darelle "Dino" Butler and Bob Robideau, were arrested in September; another, Leonard Peltier, was arrested in Canada in February 1976. All of them were AIM members. Robideau and Butler pled not guilty by reason of self-defense, and both were acquitted. Peltier might have been acquitted, too, if he'd been part of that trial. But he chose to stay in Canada and fight extradition—a battle that he lost. He ended up being tried alone and, in what many observers believe was an unfair trial, was convicted on two counts of first-degree murder. His sentence: two consecutive life terms in prison. Peltier's case has been the source of much controversy ever since, and remains a *cause célèbre* for many Native Americans, as well as for celebrity activists around the world. Among those who have publicly called for his release (or retrial) are Robert Redford, Bono, Johnny Depp, Archbishop Desmond Tutu of South Africa, Coretta Scott King, the Dalai Lama, and Pope John Paul II.

The Oka Crisis (1989). In 1989 the mayor of Oka, a small town on the Ottawa River in southwestern Quebec, announced that a 9-hole golf course owned by the city was going to be expanded into an 18-hole course, and that 60 condominiums were going to be built nearby. The land was once Mohawk territory and contained a sacred pine forest and a burial ground. In March 1990, armed members of the Mohawk Warrior Society took over the land and blockaded all roads leading to it. After three months of unsuccessful negotiations, the situation exploded: In the early morning hours of July 11, more than 100 members of Quebec's Provincial Police stormed the blockades, firing tear gas and concussion grenades. A battle ensued, and an officer was killed. That was followed by a 78-day standoff, during which Indian groups across Canada blockaded roads and bridges in solidarity, creating enormous traffic jams and escalating tensions. By August the situation was so bad that the Canadian army was called in and troops stormed the barricades, forcing the Mohawks into a tiny section of the forest. They held out until September 26, when the last 50 or so dismantled their weapons, walked out of the woods, and surrendered. Thirty-four were arrested, but not a single one was convicted. A commission looking into the event found that the July 11 attack by Provincial Police was one of the chief reasons the incident escalated as it did. The Oka golf course still has just nine holes.

The Seneca Cigarette Wars (1992). The most recent incidents involving American Indians have their roots in 1985, when the

Seneca Nation in southwestern New York started selling cigarettes and gasoline—tax-free—on their three reservations. The enterprise was a huge success, and gave the Senecas their first substantial source of income after two centuries of poverty. But business owners outside the reservations cried foul, and the state began trying to impose taxes on the Senecas. That led to a number of confrontations that continue today.

• In July 1992, a New York court ruled that the state could tax the tribe's sales of gas and cigarettes to nonnatives—which was the majority of their business. A week later, more than 100 Senecas set fire to piles of car tires on the three-mile stretch of Interstate 90 that runs through one of their reservations, closing down the highway for 11 hours. A week of violent clashes with New York State Police followed. Result: The state stopped enforcing the taxes.

• By 1997 Seneca businesses were selling cigarettes online—and making hundreds of millions of dollars a year. Again the state tried to tax them, which led to more violent clashes and another blockade of the highway. Again New York stopped trying to tax the Senecas.

• In 2006 New York Attorney General Eliot Spitzer announced that the state would begin enforcing the taxes. The Senecas responded in June 2007 by sending the state a bill for $2.1 million. What for? A toll of $1 on each car that drove through Seneca reservation land on Interstate 90—and that bill only covered the previous couple of months' worth of cars. It was never paid.

• In December 2008, Governor David Paterson signed a bill that would tax the businesses that supplied the Senecas with cigarettes, a move that would severely cripple the tribe's economy. In response, Seneca Nation President Barry Snyder announced that the I-90 toll would now be raised to $2 per vehicle. And if the state didn't pay, the Senecas would build tollbooths and collect the money themselves.

*　　*　　*

"The foolish man seeks happiness in the distance. The wise man grows it under his feet."

—James Oppenheim

BLIND SPEED DEMONS

*Does the idea of a blind person driving a car seem preposterous? It turns
out that some blind people are not only operating motor vehicles,
they're setting speed records. How do they do it? Read on...*

KEN MOSS (Automobile—solo)
A former police officer, Moss lost his sight in 1992 when his
patrol car was involved in a crash during a high-speed chase.
Speed Record: In October 1999, he set the world blind land speed
record when he drove an MG sports car 131 mph down a two-
mile-long runway on a Ministry of Defense airbase near Salisbury
in southern England. (Virtually all blind speed record attempts are
made on runways—they're the only stretches of pavement that are
long enough, wide enough, and well-enough maintained for blind
people to drive safely at such high speeds.)
How He Did It: Moss steered his MG with the aid of a guidance
system developed for jet fighter missiles: When gyroscopic instruments detected that the car was veering from a straight course, a
signal was sent to Moss via earphones. A beep in the left ear
meant he needed to steer left; a beep in the right meant steer
right. A tone in both ears meant the car was perfectly straight.

MIKE NEWMAN (Automobile—solo)
Newman, a 47-year-old bank manager, developed glaucoma as a
child and has been blind since age eight. He made his attempt at
breaking Moss's record to raise money for a charity that provides
guide dogs for the blind.
Speed Record: In August 2003, Newman reached 144.7 mph
driving a Jaguar XRJ down a runway near York, England.
How He Did It: Newman was closely followed by another car
driven by his stepfather (a driving instructor), who kept an eye on
the road and communicated with Newman by radio. In 2005 he
set another record when he drove a BMW 166 mph.

LUC COSTERMANS (Automobile)
Costermans, 43, was blinded in an accident in 2004.
Speed Record: The Belgian smashed Mike Newman's 2005 record

when he drove 193 mph down the runway of a French Air Force base near Marseille in October 2008.

How He Did It: Costermans was accompanied by a sighted "co-pilot," Guillaume Roman.

STEVE CUNNINGHAM (Speedboat)

Cunningham developed glaucoma at age eight and was totally blind by age 12. He made his attempt to raise money for the charity group Dogs for the Disabled.

Record Attempt: In September 2000, Cunningham set the world blind speedboat record when his V-8 powered monohull "Bat Boat" reached 66 mph off the coast of Dorset in southern England.

How He Did It: Cunningham was accompanied by a powerboat racer named Mike Mantle, who sat in the passenger seat and kept an eye out for waves. The Bat Boat was also equipped with a GPS system developed by the British Army Special Air Service to steer boats at night without using lights. When the system detected that the Bat Boat was straying from a straight course, it activated vibrating pads attached to Cunningham's wrists. The system was similar to the one in Ken Moss's MG: When the left wrist vibrated, Cunningham needed to turn left, and vice versa.

BILLY "THE WHIZZ" BAXTER (Motorcycle—solo)

Baxter lost his eyesight in 1997 when he contracted a viral infection while serving with the British Army in Serbia.

Record Attempt: Baxter, 39, set the blind solo world land speed record of 165.85 mph on a Kawasaki Ninja ZX-12R in August 2003. He made the attempt on a Royal Air Force runway in southern England. At the time he set his record, he was the fastest blind man on land—car or motorcycle.

How He Did It: Baxter was accompanied by two sighted riders who rode their motorcycles on either side of his and called out his his speed and other information to him over a two-way radio. (Because Guinness World Records lists *blindfolded* motorcycle speed records, not *blind* speed records, Baxter wore a blindfold during his attempt, even though he is completely blind.)

For Baxter, who has ridden motorcycles most of his life, the most challenging part was riding at speeds *under* 60 mph, when the motorcycle was less stable and he had a harder time sensing how fast it was moving, or indeed whether it moving at all. (If Baxter were to put his feet on the ground while the motorcycle was still moving, he could be thrown off.) "The guys had to count me down so that when I lowered my legs, the ground had stopped moving," he says. Another trick: Baxter wore thong underwear. Why? His fear of emergency-room doctors seeing him in thong underwear made him that much more determined not to crash.

GRAHAM "G-FORCE" HICKS (All-Terrain Vehicle)

Hicks, a bicycle mechanic, is deaf *and* blind—he has been deaf since age three and blind since age six; he uses his record-breaking attempts to raise money for deaf-blind charities.

Speed Record: Hicks set the world ATV speed record of 99.26 mph in 2001, then topped it in 2002 with a 104-mph run. That wasn't the blind-deaf world record, either—it was the *world* record: No one, sighted or not, had ever ridden faster than Hicks on an ATV. "I'm just not interested in trying for disabled records," he says. In August 2004 he smashed his own record when he drove his ATV at 130.78 mph. (In 2002 he set the record for the fastest Jet-Ski trip from the U.K. to the Netherlands. He made the 127-mile crossing in just under six hours.)

How He Does It: Hicks is accompanied by a second person who sits behind him and serves as his eyes and ears. For his 2004 ATV run, he brought along policeman Brian Sharman, who communicated with Hicks by touch. "If I want him to speed up, I squeeze him with my knees," Sharman explained to the London *Times*. "If I want him to slow down I tap his chest with both hands. It's not just a matter of the odd tap here and there—every run is a constant series of taps and pulls, from start to finish."

Update: As late as 2009, the 48-year-old Hicks was still raising money for blind-deaf charities with appearances at auto races and other events, popping wheelies on his ATV and making speed runs for the crowds. But that came to a halt when his insurer raised his premium to £250 *a day*, or about $450. Until he can find another insurer, Hicks will have to settle for more sedate fund-raising activities. In August 2009, for example, he and a sighted cousin rode a tandem bicycle 203 miles from London's Tower Bridge to the Eiffel Tower in Paris. How long would it take *you* to make that trip? Hicks did it in three days.

READ YOUR MOLE-O-SCOPE

Having your fortune told, like reading your horoscope in the newspaper, is fun even if you don't take it seriously. Here's more of what your moles may reveal about what fate has in store for you. (Part I is on page 193.)

YOUR LEGS AND FEET

• **On either hip:** You're hard-working, content, and full of passion. You're also abstemious and trustworthy. Yet for all your desirable traits, you will enjoy only moderate success in your business life. Your many children will suffer hardships in life, but they will prevail in the end and be the wiser for it.

• **On your right thigh:** Do not have this mole removed! You're pleasant-natured, passionate, and courageous. You'll be successful in your career, come into even more money by marriage, and have lots of children, the majority of whom will be girls.

• **On your left thigh:** You're happy and generous. And you're a hard worker. But none of this counts for much. Your love life will be a snooze, and you'll experience poverty, misery, and betrayal by "friends," one of whom will tell a lie that gets you arrested.

• **On your left knee:** You're passionate, but too quick for your own good. You're not particularly honest, either, and your generosity is often offset by insensitivity. You're likely to be successful in your own right and marry into a wealthy family on top of it. Despite your inclination toward debauchery, the odds are against you having more than a single child.

• **On the right knee:** Another keeper—you're honest, even-tempered, and passionate. You'll work hard in life and love, and experience great fortune in both. Your few sorrows will be more than offset by the love of your children and the loyalty of your friends.

• **On either leg:** You're thoughtless, lazy, corrupt, and overindulgent. These and other failings will cause great trouble, and yet somehow, you will overcome your problems...only to end up in prison at an early age. You'll marry an agreeable person (no word

Tip: If you don't like the fortune a particular mole gives you, pretend it's a freckle.

on whether that's in or out of prison), and they will outlive you. You'll have four children (two will die young).

• **On either ankle:** You're a slave to fashion and a snazzy dresser. If you're a man, you're a coward; if you're a woman, you're clever and brave. Both genders will have great success in love and life.

• **On either foot:** You're sad. And you're lazy, which only adds to your sadness. You lead a sedentary life and read lots of books (some of them in the bathroom). For you, life will always be a bumpy road, with at least one bad marriage made worse by troubled, ungrateful children.

YOUR HANDS AND ARMS

• **On your wrist or hand:** You're an intelligent, serious person. You're reliable, have a strong work ethic, and are in the habit of saving your money and resources rather than frittering them away on whims and passing fancies. You'll likely marry well and have a happy family life, but you will hit a string of bad luck at about age 30 that could last for years. A man with a mole on his wrist or hand will marry twice in his lifetime; a woman, only once, and she will outlive her husband.

• **Between your elbow and your wrist:** You have a peaceful, cheerful personality, and you love hard work almost as much as you love to read a good book. Your life may start out a little rough —including even an arrest or a major lawsuit of some kind—but as you reach middle age your past trials and tribulations will enable you to appreciate life that much more. If you have a son, he will go far in the world and marry a wealthy widow.

• **Near either elbow:** You are restless and unreliable. If you're in a relationship, it's an unhappy one. If you have children, they're likely to cause you a lot of problems, too. You enjoy traveling and passing time idly, but your idleness can get in the way of travel. Getting off the couch has always been an unnatural act for you.

• **On either arm:** You're strong, courageous, resolute, hard-working, and faithful to your friends. You'll face plenty of battles in life but will prevail over adversity. If you're male, you'll be a widower by 40; if you're female, your husband will outlive you. Either way, the good things will outweigh the bad, and your life will be happy and prosperous.

In 2005 the average CEO earned more in 1 workday than the average worker earned all year.

THE PANTS SUIT

*It all started simply enough: A man goes to his dry cleaner
for a $10 alteration…and ends up suing for $54 million.*

SUITING UP

In May 2005, Roy Pearson, a 55-year-old Washington, D.C.
lawyer, landed a job as an administrative law judge. Pearson
wanted to wear his nicest suit, but his pants needed to be let out,
so he took them to his neighborhood dry cleaner, Custom Cleaners. When he returned two days later, the pants weren't ready. Soo
Chung, one of the owners, apologized and said she'd have them
finished the next morning. But when Pearson returned, the pants
couldn't be found. Angry, he pointed to two signs on the wall—
"Same-Day Service" and "Satisfaction Guaranteed"—and then
stormed out. A few days later, Chung told Pearson she'd found his
pants. He claimed they weren't his. Chung insisted they were; his
receipt was still attached. Pearson didn't believe her and demanded $1,150 for a new suit. The Chungs offered to give him his
pants back. "Those are not my pants!" Pearson reiterated. He
threatened legal action and left.

A PRESSING MATTER

Soo and Jim Nam Chung, who owned Custom Cleaners as well as
another dry cleaner, hired attorney Chris Manning to help them.
He advised them to offer Pearson $3,000 to settle the whole mat-
ter. Pearson declined, as he did subsequent offers of $4,600 and
$12,000. Pearson had been poring through law books and building
a case, and ended up suing the Chungs for "mental suffering,
inconvenience, and discomfort"—both for the loss of his pants
and for the two signs in the shop, which he claimed were false
advertising. The amount he wanted: $67 million.

Why so high? Pearson was taking advantage of a vaguely worded consumer protection law that provides for damages of $1,500
per violation per day. Pearson counted 12 violations taking place
over 1,200 days, multiplied by three—one for each of the two
owners and their son, who also worked there. Why so many days?
Pearson didn't own a car and claimed he'd have to rent one every

week for the next four years to drive to the next closest dry cleaner. Having to do this, he concluded, was a violation of his rights. Pearson also sought damages for the time he would log as his own lawyer (at his regular rate).

CLASSLESS ACTION

The lawsuit made international headlines: On one side there was Pearson, a well-dressed African-American lawyer with a flair for the dramatic. And then there were the humble Chungs, Korean immigrants who spoke so little English that they needed an interpreter. The legal community took notice as well, concerned that Pearson was giving trial lawyers an even worse name. In fact, the American Tort Reform Association, whose goal is to end frivolous lawsuits, and the American Trial Lawyers Association—their sworn enemy—came to a rare agreement that Pearson had crossed the line. The Tort Reform Association even offered to buy "Judge Fancy Pants," as some were calling him, a new suit if he dropped the case.

Instead, Pearson put up flyers in his neighborhood denouncing the Chungs and calling for other dissatisfied customers to join him in a class-action lawsuit. That case was dismissed when Pearson failed to gather enough signatures…so he pressed on with his civil suit. Meanwhile, business at Custom Cleaners had dropped off considerably after the flyers went up. But outside the neighborhood, public support helped the Chungs raise nearly $100,000 to pay (most of) their legal bills.

ALL RISE

The bench trial (one in which there is no jury) went before D.C. Judge Judith Bartnoff in June 2007. In his bizarre opening statement, Pearson spoke so softly that the fans had to be turned off so that everyone could hear him (and there was no air-conditioning). After spending a half-hour describing his childhood, he was interrupted by Judge Bartnoff, who said, "Why don't we get to why we're here?" When Pearson finally did, he explained that the case wasn't really about the pants—it was about the sign that falsely advertised "Satisfaction Guaranteed." (He also reduced his request from $67 million to $54 million.)

Pearson kept using the term "we," because in his mind, he was speaking for everyone who'd ever been taken advantage of by

---

There are 6,469,952 black spots in *101 Dalmatians*.

shady business tactics. Judge Bartnoff told him to stop it: "Mr.
Pearson, you are not 'we'. You are an 'I.'" That was one of several
exchanges that drew laughs from the spectators. At one point, a
teary Pearson sobbed, "Never before in recorded history has a
group of defendants engaged in such misleading and unfair business practices," and then rushed out of the courtroom.

JUDGING THE JUDGE

When it was defense attorney Manning's turn to speak, he painted
Pearson as a "bitter man" who was still reeling from a divorce.
Manning spoke of earlier disputes between Pearson and the
Chungs. Three times he had been banned from their shop for
being rude and had to beg them to let him back in. Manning also
told the court that Pearson was desperate for money. Although he
made $100,000 per year, he'd maxed out his credit cards in order
to pay for legal fees from a previous lawsuit against his ex-wife
(which was dismissed for being frivolous). "This case is very simple," said Manning. "It's about one sign and the plaintiff's outlandish interpretation."

Pearson called several witnesses to the stand who said they'd
also had trouble at the Chungs' laundromat. He even called a fellow administrative law judge, who testified that it is indeed important for a judge to wear a nice suit to work. When Pearson took
the stand himself to be cross-examined by Manning, he started
crying. "What if this had been...?" He never even finished the
sentence and ran out of the courtroom. "This case shocks me on a
daily basis," Manning told reporters that night.

The next day, Soo Chung cried on the stand—twice—when
describing the ordeal. And while many in the press made light of
the proceedings, the Chungs weren't laughing, "It's not humorous,
not funny, and nobody would have thought that something like
this would have ever happened," said Soo, who added that they
were thinking about moving back to Korea.

THE VERDICT

Pearson lost. Judge Bartnoff wrote in her ruling, "I have significant
concerns that the plaintiff is acting in bad faith because of the
breathtaking magnitude of the expansion he seeks." Pearson was
ordered to pay the Chungs' court costs, but not their legal fees.

He filed an appeal based on the assumption that the judge had made a "fundamental legal error" because she failed to comprehend the true nature of "Satisfaction Guaranteed." The second judge dismissed the appeal. So Pearson filed *another* one. The third judge threw it out, ruling that Judge Bartnoff's original decision showed "basic common sense."

AFTERMATH

In 2008, after being denied reinstatement as a judge (thanks in part to the negative press he brought upon himself and his profession), Pearson sued the D.C. government for $1 million for wrongful termination. He lost. Pearson threatened to take his case all the way to the U.S. Supreme Court, but the statute of limitations ran out before he had the chance. At last report, Pearson was still unemployed…but still has an active license to practice law.

Although the Chungs "won," the three-year-long lawsuit put Custom Cleaners out of business. Today, they are focusing their attention on their original shop, Happy Cleaners. And there's no sign on the wall that promises "Satisfaction Guaranteed."

*   *   *

OUR SUGGESTIONS FOR
10 HONEST MOVIE TITLES

Not-So-Goodfellas

Sort of Dirty Dancing

Gone With the War

The Neverending Story That's About 90 Minutes Long

Mission: Possible

Indiana Jones and the Second-to-Last Crusade

Home Alone, but Not Really Because There Are Burglars

Kill Lots of People, Then Bill

~~*Planet of the Apes*~~ *Earth*

(Trying Not to) Die (Is) Hard

Your brain will generate more electrical impulses today than all the telephones in the world will.

CAUTION:
SLOW CHILDREN

*Kids just "act"—they often don't know any better. Sometimes
this can lead to trouble...for the rest of us.*

SHE'S GOT GAME

In 2009 two-year-old Natalie Jasmer was playing hide-and-seek with her two older siblings at their Greenville, Pennsylvania, home. And it turns out that Natalie is *really* good at the game—her family looked and looked, but couldn't find her. They called police and friends, and for an hour, a crowd of people searched all over town for her, fearing the worst. Natalie was eventually found—safe and sound—by the family dog. She'd hidden in a drawer underneath the washing machine in the laundry room and then fallen asleep. "I'm sorry," said Natalie.

ON A ROLL

A four-year-old girl was visiting her father at the oil refinery in Baden-Württemberg, Germany, where he worked. While he was briefly distracted with a work matter, the little girl climbed onto a forklift and released the brake, which started the machine rolling. It went only about 20 feet...because it was stopped by a 400-gallon tank of heating oil. The forklift rammed the oil tank with such force that it punctured the hull, spilling about 130 gallons of heating oil onto the ground and into a sewer. "We're still not sure how the little girl released the brake. Four-year-olds don't have the kind of strength it takes to do that on a forklift," said a police spokesman.

WATERING HOLE

In May 2009, four-year-old Daniel Blair of London decided that his one-week-old Cocker Spaniel puppy needed his first bath. So he put the dog into the smallest pool of water he could find—the toilet. Once Daniel washed all the mud off the dog, he flushed the toilet...with the puppy still in it. Daniel immediately told his mother what he'd done, and she called a plumber who was able to locate the dog in an underground pipe 20 yards from the house. Amazingly, the dog survived.

MO MONEY, MO PROBLEMS

Madeline Hill runs a pub attached to her house in Sittingbourne, England. One night she was sitting in her kitchen counting up the night's cash earnings when she heard a knock at the door. She went to answer it, but first did what she always does with her cash if she's interrupted while counting it—she put it in the microwave. While Hill was out of the room, her 20-month-old son, Jordan, toddled into the room and pressed a bunch of buttons on the microwave, turning it on. The money, about $1,500, was burned to a crisp. (Hill doesn't put her money in the microwave anymore.)

*   *   *

AN AMAZING FIND

In 2008 Bill Waters of Tulsa, Oklahoma, was traveling through Texas and stopped at an antique store in the small town of Shamrock. Underneath a wooden crate full of old medicine bottles, Waters found an old leather-bound ledger that looked like it must have been 100 years old. On the front, in fading letters, was written "Castles Formulas." Waters paid $200 for the book, intending to sell it for at least that on eBay. But when he began preparing it for sale, he starting thumbing through it and found prescription sheets from "W.B. Morrison & Co. Old Corner Drug Store, Waco, Texas." He did some research and found out that a man named John Castles was a pharmacist at Morrison's in the 1880s. The formulas were for things like piano polish, hair restorer, cough syrup, and a stomach-pain remedy...called D Peppers Pepsin Bitters. More research revealed that Morrison's is where, in 1885, pharmacist Charles Alderton invented Dr Pepper, based on Castles's D Peppers Pepsin Bitters. In other words, Waters had discovered the original recipe for Dr Pepper. (Today, the company that makes the soda is secretive about its flavor blend, but if they're still using Castles's instructions, the secret ingredient is mandrake root.) Waters plans to sell the book at auction, where it's expected to fetch as much as $75,000.

Scientific studies have shown that chimpanzees have a better short-term memory than humans.

THE WORLD'S WORST ACCIDENT

The International Atomic Energy Agency ranks nuclear accidents on a scale of 1 to 7. So far only one accident has received the worst classification, Level 7: the 1986 nuclear meltdown at Chernobyl.

RADIOACTIVE WIND

On April 26, 1986, a safety test gone terribly wrong destroyed one of the four nuclear reactors at the Chernobyl power station in the former Soviet Republic of Ukraine. Notoriously secretive—particularly where issues of nuclear technology were involved—the Soviet government instituted a news blackout and tried to prevent any information about the accident from leaving the country. It didn't work. A large plume of radioactive debris entered the atmosphere and crossed Soviet borders, where it set off radiation detectors at several European nuclear power plants. By studying weather patterns and satellite photographs, western countries were able to determine the approximate source of the nuclear fallout.

Under international pressure, Soviet officials eventually admitted that there had been an accident. But that's about all they said. As radiation continued to spew from the damaged reactor, scientists in the West could only speculate about the extent of the damage—and the danger it posed to the rest of the world.

DON'T PANIC!

As the cloud of radioactive debris spread across Europe, western governments scrambled to implement safety measures. Many banned food imports from all points east. Polish officials prohibited the sale of milk from grass-fed cows, and Sweden warned its citizens not to drink water from open wells. West Germans were advised to stay inside and out of the rain. Most of these governments distributed iodine tablets, which were taken to prevent the thyroid gland from absorbing radiation from contaminated food.

The fallout affected North America, too. One week after the accident, Chernobyl radiation was detected at ground level in the

---

National nuclear warhead stockpiles: United States: 5,236. Russia: 3,400. France: 350...

United States—first on the West Coast and later throughout the country. Though the EPA was quick to say that the increased radiation levels were too small to pose any real danger, drugstores reported a run on iodine tablets.

The world had to wait four months for Soviet scientists to release any details about the damaged reactor. Even then, experts disagreed on what the health effects would be. For the most part, advocates of nuclear energy downplayed the risks; opponents exaggerated them. Though debate over the long-term health and environmental effects of Chernobyl continues today, the story of how the accident came to happen has been fairly well established.

NUCLEAR POWER 101

A nuclear power plant is not unlike a conventional coal or oil-fired plant. They all boil water to produce steam; the steam drives big, electricity-generating turbines. The difference is in how they heat the water. The heat source in a nuclear plant is *fission*—the splitting of atoms—in a controlled chain reaction.

For those of us who weren't paying attention in science class, here's a recap of how it works: Atoms are made up of protons, neutrons, and electrons. When a single atom of nuclear fuel (Uranium-235) splits, it sends two or three neutrons flying off into space. When these neutrons run into other U-235 atoms, it causes *those* atoms to split—sending more neutrons flying, causing still more atoms to split, in ever-increasing numbers. And each time one of these atoms splits, it releases energy. This is the chain reaction that's at the heart of nuclear power.

In a nuclear power plant, this released energy is absorbed by water as *thermal*, or heat, energy, and used to create the steam that drives the steam turbines. The faster the chain reaction is allowed to happen, the more energy it releases. This translates into greater heat and more steam—spinning the turbines faster to generate more electricity.

CONTROL FREAKS

Plant operators are able to regulate this chain reaction by inserting *control rods* into the reactor. Control rods are made of a substance (such as cadmium or boron) that absorbs neutrons. Should the chain reaction become too "hot," plant operators can insert more control rods, thereby reducing the number of neutrons flying around inside the reactor. This causes the rate of the nuclear chain reaction to slow and reduces the amount of energy being released.

In addition to control rods, nuclear reactors need something called a *moderator*. It turns out that when all those U-235 atoms split, the neutrons are moving too fast to be absorbed by other U-235 atoms in great enough numbers for the chain reaction to take place. A moderator is simply a substance that slows, or moderates, those flying neutrons to enable them to run into and split other fuel atoms in sufficient numbers to cause the fission chain reaction.

Any number of substances could be used to moderate neutrons. The safest and most common is water. Water-moderated reactors are ideal because the water doubles as both moderator and coolant. The nuclear chain reaction produces such extreme temperatures that the reactor must have coolant constantly circulating through it to prevent the whole system from breaking down. And a water-moderated reactor has a basic built-in safety feature: Any sudden loss of coolant is also a sudden loss of the moderator—and without a moderator the chain reaction stops.

Chernobyl, however, did not use water as the moderator—it used giant blocks of solid graphite. Within the graphite blocks were channels containing nuclear fuel and water-circulating systems that both cooled the reactor and provided steam to turn the electricity-generating turbines. In such a reactor, a sudden loss of coolant wouldn't stop the fission reaction, and it *could* lead to the worst-case scenario in a nuclear power plant: a core meltdown.

THE CHINA SYNDROME

A core meltdown is what can happen if plant operators lose control of the nuclear chain reaction. With nothing to regulate the extreme heat produced by the fission process, the reactor fuel actually melts. The phrase "China Syndrome" was coined in the 1970s to describe the idea that a runaway core meltdown could burn through the floor of the reactor and on down through the Earth until it came out the other side—in China.

While the "China Syndrome" may be far-fetched, a molten reactor core certainly could breach whatever containment structure was beneath it and release significant quantities of radioactive

Discovered in 2006, the ghost slug is a carnivore. It hunts earthworms.

debris into the environment. Redundant safety mechanisms are typically built into nuclear power plants to prevent the possibility of a meltdown. Ironically, the disaster at Chernobyl began with a test of one such safety mechanism.

COOL IT

The Chernobyl reactors had an emergency cooling system specifically designed to regulate the reactor core temperature in case of an accident. It depended on electric-powered water pumps to maintain circulation. And during an emergency shutdown of the plant, diesel generators were supposed to provide the electricity needed to run the pumps. But the problem with relying on generators is that they take time to power up—as much as 60 to 75 seconds. In the event of an emergency reactor shutdown, the Soviet plants were designed to use the momentum of the steam turbines as they ran *down* to deliver electricity to the water pumps until the diesel generators could take over.

Problems started when the ill-fated test of this emergency rundown power system had to be postponed for almost 10 hours, and the night shift was working in the control room rather than the day shift. Why is that a problem? Because the day shift workers were familiar with the test procedures; the night shift hadn't been prepared for it.

The plan was to reduce reactor power to a relatively low level and then cut off the steam supply to the turbines so that engineers could measure the amount of electricity generated as they powered down. Unfortunately, plant operators accidentally brought the reactor power down too low. Result: The turbines were spinning slower than they ever would be during normal plant operation. If the engineers wanted to complete their test, they had to get the turbines back up to speed.

WHAT NOT TO DO

This may sound obvious, but because nuclear fuel and the by-products of the controlled chain reaction are so volatile, it is dangerous to fiddle around too much with a nuclear reactor. A Soviet report later issued to the International Atomic Energy Agency concluded that the operators should have aborted the test and shut down the reactor when the power output became too low.

Instead, determined to continue the test, the operators tried to increase power by removing most of the control rods. The computer system ordinarily would not have allowed this, but the automatic emergency shutdown systems had been disabled for the test. At 1:23 a.m. on April 26, 1986, with the reactor controls at inherently unstable settings, engineers began their test by shutting off the flow of steam to the turbines—and the cooling system overheated.

UH-OH...

Realizing that the reactor was overheating and that too many of the control rods had been removed for them to manage the chain reaction, plant operators pushed a panic button to shut down the entire reactor just 36 seconds after closing the steam valves...but it was already too late. The graphite reactor core had become so hot that it began breaking apart. The fuel and control rod channels in the broken graphite became blocked, preventing the control rods from being inserted all the way. There was no way to stop the chain reaction. Twenty seconds after the panic button was pushed, a steam explosion blew apart the plumbing system that carried coolant into the core. A few seconds later another, larger explosion—this one caused by excess hydrogen that was most likely created by the chemical reaction of hot graphite and steam—blew the roof off of the building.

This second explosion sent burning graphite and nuclear fuel flying into the air. The debris started fires on the roofs of several adjacent buildings. It also let oxygen into what was left of the reactor core, which ignited the graphite. As this was going on, nuclear fuel within the burning core continued the runaway fission chain reaction. The core turned molten and began burning through the floor, creating a huge crater.

THE BATTLE OF CHERNOBYL

Local fire crews arrived quickly and began fighting the many fires. Amazingly, these emergency workers had no special equipment to protect themselves from the massive doses of radiation to which they were exposed. (Survivors later reported that smoldering chunks of graphite and fuel from the core were strewn all around the grounds of the plant.) One crew even went into the remains of the reactor hall and tried to pour water into the crater where what was left of the reactor core continued to melt down. Most of the men who went into the damaged reactor building died of acute radiation sickness within weeks. All told, 31 people died containing the meltdown, including two plant workers killed in the initial blast.

Within four hours of the explosions, the fires surrounding the destroyed reactor were contained, but the reactor core itself was still burning—and the nuclear fuel inside *continued* to melt down. Over the next six days, Soviet helicopters dropped more than 5,000 tons of sand, clay, lead, and fission-inhibiting boron into the crater to put out the graphite fire and stop the runaway nuclear reaction.

Hundreds of thousands of emergency workers—many of them military personnel—were involved in the containment and cleanup of the disaster. Crews pumped liquid nitrogen into the ground beneath the reactor to freeze it solid in an effort to cool the molten core. Remote-control bulldozers were used to bury radioactive debris. And eventually, the entire reactor site was encased in a gigantic concrete and steel sarcophagus.

THE PEACEFUL ATOM?

Years later, it is clear that one design flaw above all others made the accident worse than it needed to be. The Soviet reactors at Chernobyl lacked something that almost every other reactor in the world has: a sealed, concrete containment structure designed to prevent radiation from reaching the outside environment in the event of an accident. Following on the heels of the 1979 near-disaster at the Three Mile Island plant in Pennsylvania (in which a containment structure prevented most of the radiation from a partial core meltdown from entering the atmosphere), Chernobyl added momentum to the anti-nuclear power movement.

In general, pro-nuclear groups blame the dysfunctional Soviet system for the accident, while anti-nuclear groups contend that it could happen anywhere. Perhaps the only thing they do agree on: It is nearly impossible to calculate the full cost and long-term impact of the Chernobyl disaster.

What's happening in Chernobyl today? Turn to page 489.

LOST CONTINENT

*Atlantis is one of the longest-lasting—and most easily disproved—
myths in world history. Yet people just keep looking for it.*

PLATO'S RETREAT

According to the ancient Greek philosopher Plato, Atlantis
was a continent larger than Asia and Africa combined, sitting on the western edge of the Mediterranean Sea. Its capital city
was built in a perfect circle, composed of alternating bands of
earth and water. At its center was a temple to the Greek god
Poseidon, surrounded by walls of solid gold and coated in silver.
The city was equipped with canals, tunnels, racetracks, and a
prodigious merchant fleet, all remarkable achievements for more
than 12,000 years ago and more than 9,000 years before the gold-
en age of ancient Greece.

And then…it vanished. As the Atlantian army attempted to
conquer the known world, having already enslaved much of
Asia, Africa, and Europe, it was defeated by an early incarnation
of Greece. In what the Greeks believed to be an act of divine
intervention, the continent of Atlantis was destroyed in 24
hours by violent earthquakes and floods, sending it to the bottom
of the sea.

There's just one big problem with this story: It's just a story.
Everything "known" about Atlantis was laid out in two of Plato's
dialogues: *Timaeus* and *Critias*. The story may have been based on
real events, such as the volcanic eruption on the Greek island of
Thera. It may also have been inspired by older mythical tales such
as the Trojan War. Or it may have been purely an invention of
Plato's imagination. We may never know for sure. No evidence of
any civilization matching Plato's description has ever been discovered, but his descriptions are so vivid that for centuries many have
believed Atlantis to be real.

BANANA FLOAT

Plato may have started the legend, but it was popularized (and
expanded on) in modern times by late 19th century Minnesota
congressman, academic, and eccentric Ignatius Donnelly. He dab-

A snowflake can be 50 times as wide as it is thick.

bled in astronomy, geology, botany, religion, law, and science fiction, all in order to help him prove that Atlantis was real. Donnelly had two major pieces of "evidence."

• The first was the Biblical story of the Great Flood and similar flood tales from around the world. That would explain how Atlantis sank and disappeared: It was the same flood that prompted Noah to build his ark.

• The second piece of proof: the banana. Since it's seedless, Donnelly believed its propagation would require humans to plant the fruit as they migrated from one part of the world to the next. And since the banana is native to Africa, Asia, and South America, there would have to be some sort of land bridge that banana planters would have used. The land bridge: Atlantis, of course.

Based on Plato's writings, Donnelly pinpointed Atlantis's original location as just outside the Mediterranean Sea. The Azores Islands, west of Spain, would be the exposed portion of the highest peaks of the sunken continent. Donnelly's addition to the myth: He proposed that Atlantians were technologically advanced, inventing the compass and gunpowder thousands of years before the rest of the world invented written language.

STEINER'S WAY
Rudolf Steiner, a 20th-century German philosopher, added more to the theory of Atlantis, suggesting it was the place where the actual physics of life on Earth developed. According to Steiner, millions of years ago on Atlantis, solid objects behaved more like liquids, liquids behaved more like gases, and humans had not yet split into two separate genders. The technologically advanced humanoids on Atlantis, located off the coast of India, drove flying cars, which they powered with "spiritual energy" and the life force found in plant seeds. And where did Steiner discover this? In his book *Cosmic Memory*, he claimed that he "was not at liberty to disclose" his sources, but his number-one source was clearly his own vivid imagination.

MUCKING ABOUT
In the 1940s, German researcher Otto Muck joined Donnelly's "theories" with a sprinkling of actual science. Muck theorized that a cataclysmic volcanic explosion, triggered by a hammering of

meteors, is what ultimately destroyed the Atlantian empire. Like Donnelly, Muck hunted down parallel tales of a big flood in many world mythologies. Unlike Donnelly's, Muck's description and dating of the event is much more exact. Using a calendar system inspired by the ancient Mayans (who Muck believed were colonists from Atlantis), he claimed to have calculated the destruction of Atlantis down to the hour: about noon on June 6, 8498 B.C.

While Donnelly looked to bananas, Muck's preferred theory involved eels. In his book *The Secret of Atlantis*, he discusses the European eel, which hatches in an area of the mid-Atlantic Ocean called the Sargasso Sea, and migrates to freshwater streams all over Europe. Muck's explanation: The eels used to migrate to Atlantis. When it disappeared, they had nowhere else to go, so they started migrating to Europe.

SO, WHERE IS IT?

Modern geology and oceanography simply do not allow for the existence of a continent the size of Atlantis anywhere in the Atlantic Ocean. Bananas and eels notwithstanding, the thousands of years spent searching for evidence that proves the existence of Atlantis have yielded exactly...nothing. But that hasn't stopped the true believers. Atlantis hunters like to get creative with Plato's data, theorizing that he somehow fudged the location, which means that Atlantis could be *anywhere*. Theories have placed the lost continent near Ireland, near Bolivia, in the South China Sea, and in the Bahamas.

Or maybe Atlantis is right in front of us. In February 2009, British newspapers reported that Atlantis was visible on the Google Earth satellite imaging service. A look at the Atlantic Ocean off the coast of Morocco indeed yields a strange series of lines and angles. Google says the discrepancy is the result of an error in processing the satellite image. But this happens to be near Spain and the Mediterranean Sea—the exact spot where Plato said Atlantis was.

* * *

"It's not true that life is one damn thing after another; it's one damn thing over and over."

—Edna St. Vincent Millay

THE NATURAL GAS REPORT

More breaking news from people—and animals—who break wind.

BOMBED OUT
In December 2007, a retired bus driver named Maurice Fox was *rip*-rimanded by the Kirkham Street Sports and Social Club in Paignton, England, for farting too noisily and too often inside the club. Fox, 77, wasn't stripped of his membership, but he did receive a sternly worded letter from Club secretary George Shepherd asking him to *please* step outside whenever an attack was imminent. Fox denies any deliberate malice: "Sometimes it takes me by surprise and just pops out," he told *The Guardian* newspaper. Shepherd disagrees: "We've had so many complaints over Maurice deliberately lifting himself up off the seat and letting fly," he says. "The last straw came when he fired off as three ladies came through the front door for a darts match. They were disgusted. We had to act."

AIR APPARENT

It may sound silly, but the issue is no laughing matter: The burps and farts given off by livestock around the world are thought to produce as much as 25 percent of all methane emissions. That's pretty serious, because methane is a greenhouse gas that is *25 times* as harmful to the environment as the carbon dioxide given off when fossil fuels are burned. A single cow can emit as much as four tons of methane per year, which is as polluting as driving a midsize car 12,000 miles. Some cattle ranchers in the United States, the U.K., New Zealand, and other countries fear that punitive "fart taxes" are already in the works, though most governments deny it.

In the meantime, the race is on to find ways to minimize the impact that burping, farting livestock have on the environment. Adding fish oil to animal feed has been shown to reduce emissions by up to 21 percent; adding beneficial bacteria to the feed cuts them by up to 70 percent. Another promising idea: *kangaroo farts*. Kangaroos don't emit any methane when they burp or fart, thanks to bac-

---

The US Patent Office is so backlogged that, in 2009, Apple was still waiting for its iPod patent.

teria found in their digestive tracts. Scientists are trying to isolate the bacteria and develop ways to transfer it to cattle, sheep, and other livestock, but that could take several years. Why wait? Some environmentalists argue that people should eat kangaroo in place of other meats. "It's low in fat, it's got high protein levels, and it's very clean in the sense that it's the ultimate free-range animal," says Peter Ampt of Australia's Institute of Environmental Studies.

A FINE EXAMPLE

In 2008 43-year-old Theresa Bailey sued her former employer, the direct–marketing firm Selectabase, demanding compensation for the abuse she suffered at the hands of her boss, David Nye. Bailey, who worked at Selectabase for three months in 2007, claimed that Nye regularly farted in her direction just for laughs. "The number of times he would lift up his bottom off the chair and fart and think it's funny is unreal," she says. In addition to the gas attacks, Bailey says she was ordered to wear a badge that read "I'm simple," after she asked for instructions on how to log phone calls into her computer, and had a beach ball thrown at her head when she took offense at sexist jokes. Bailey won; Selectabase had to pay her £5,146 (about $10,000) but still denied that any of its employees acted in "an inappropriate, unfair, or discriminatory way."

LAW AND ODOR

In March 2009, the Air-O-Matic company of Florida, makers of "Pull My Finger"—a fart-noise generator that was the second-most popular iPhone application sold in the Apple iPhone App Store—threatened legal action against a Colorado company called Info-Media. They're the makers of the #1-selling application—the iFart, which is also a fart-noise generator. Air-O-Matic claims that "Pull My Finger" is a protected trademark, and wants InfoMedia to stop using the expression in its marketing materials. InfoMedia argues that the expression is in the *public domain*—no one owns it, so anyone is free to use it. InfoMedia is seeking a declaratory judgement to that effect against Air-O-Matic, which, if granted, would guarantee its right to say "pull my finger" anytime it wants. Air-O-Matic co-founder Sam Magdalein says he hopes that the dispute can be resolved amicably. "Believe it or not, I'm really uncomfortable with bathroom humor. It would be pretty ridiculous to have this end up in court," he said.

AMAZING COINCIDENCES

Do you like reading in the bathroom? So do we! Wow.

• **On Christmas Eve** 1994, two cars collided near Flitcham, England. The drivers were twin sisters who were delivering presents to each other. Their names: Lorraine and Levinia Christmas.

• **On June 6, 2009,** two men in China picked the same winning seven-digit lottery number. Though they were hundreds of miles away from each other, they bought their tickets at the exact same time, down to the second.

• **A hot-air balloon** crashed into a power line in Ruthwell, Scotland, interrupting the movie being shown on local television: *Around the World in 80 Days*...about a voyage in a hot-air balloon.

• **American journalist** Irv Kupcinet was in a London hotel room in 1953 when he found a few items that belonged to a friend of his, basketball star Harry Hannin. Two days later, Kupcinet received a letter from Hannin—he'd found a tie with Kupcinet's name on it in a Paris hotel room.

• **A blurry photo** of a man stealing a wallet in a store ran on the bottom of the front page of the December 14, 2007, edition of Idaho's *Lewiston Tribune*. Above it was an unrelated photo of a man painting a business. Readers noticed both men were wearing the same clothes...and could be the same man. He was, leading to his arrest.

• **In 1972 a taxi driver** from Bermuda accidentally struck and killed a man who was riding a moped. One year later, the taxi driver accidentally struck and killed the man's brother—who was riding the exact same moped on the exact same stretch of road.

• **In 1911 three men—** named Green, Berry, and Hill—were convicted of a murder. They were hanged at London's Greenberry Hill.

• **On June 24, 2005,** veteran actor Paul Winchell died at age 82. He voiced the character of Tigger in Disney's *Winnie the Pooh* films. The next day, John Fiedler died at age 80. He was the voice of Piglet.

Did you notice? The year 2008 was exactly one second longer than the year 2007.

CELEBRITY GOSSIP

Here's the latest edition of our cheesy tabloid section.

ALEC BALDWIN
In 2009 Baldwin joked on the *Late Show with David Letterman* that he was "thinking about getting a Filipino mail-order bride." The comment created an uproar in the Philippines, where the practice of mail-order brides is illegal. The government not only banned Baldwin from the country but issued a vague threat. Said Senator (and former action movie star) Ramon "Bong" Revilla Jr.: "Let him try to come here, and he'll see mayhem."

BOB DYLAN
According to *American Idol* judge Paula Abdul, Dylan snuck in to a taping of the hit show...twice. "He had a beard and tried to be in disguise," said Abdul, "but I knew it was him."

JENNIFER ANISTON
Although she says she likes the "natural look" when it comes to her appearance, in 2008 Aniston brought her personal hairdresser to the U.K. premier of her film *Marley & Me*. According to *Daily Mail*, the actress paid for the hairdresser's first-class flights, his plush hotel room, and daily expenses for a week, plus the daily fee for his cosmetological duties. Total cost: $59,000. And what did Aniston get for all that? A hair straightening.

SARAH JESSICA PARKER
One night in 2009, the *Sex and the City* star was pulled over by a police officer for driving without her headlights on. Parker explained that she had recently purchased the Mercedes luxury minivan and hadn't yet figured out how to work the headlights. The cop showed her how and let her off with a warning. "The officer was very patient," said Parker's representative.

MICK JAGGER
While attending a party in the late 1990s, the aging rock star was

introduced to one of his idols, British jazz singer George Melly. "I didn't expect you to have so many wrinkles," said Melly. "They're not wrinkles. They're laugh lines," Jagger replied. To which Melly said, "Surely nothing could be *that* funny."

KEVIN BACON

Whenever he attends a wedding reception, Bacon bribes the DJ $20 to *not* play Kenny Loggins's title song from the 1984 movie *Footloose*, in which Bacon starred. Reason: If the song comes on, guests form a circle around the actor and expect him to dance.

KATHARINE HEPBURN

Hepburn had a phobia of dirty hair and reportedly sniffed the heads of her cast and crew and told them if they needed to wash it. (Another piece of Hepburn gossip: She went through a phase when she was 10 years old—she cut her hair short, wore boys' clothes, and called herself "Jimmy.")

LINDSAY LOHAN

In September 2008, Lohan announced that she wanted to hold a fund-raiser for presidential candidate Barack Obama. But Obama's campaign asked her not to, fearing that Lohan's former reputation as a "wild party girl" might send the wrong message to undecided voters.

BRAD PITT

Before becoming an actor in the late 1980s, Pitt had a job driving strippers to and from parties. "It was not a wholesome atmosphere, and it got very depressing," he says. So Pitt decided to quit, but his boss convinced him to do one last gig. There, he talked to a girl who urged him to take the acting class she was in. "It really set me on the path to where I am now," he says. "Strippers changed my life."

ALEX TREBEK

When the *Jeopardy!* host was saying his vows at his wedding ceremony in 1990, the officiant asked if he would "take this woman as his lawfully wedded wife." Trebek replied, "The answer is...Yes!"

GREED: THE LOST MASTERPIECE

For film director Erich von Stroheim, bringing his favorite novel to the big screen was a work of passion, but it would nearly undo his career. The story is as epic as any classic movie, even if the final product itself is lost to history.

TRINA AND McTEAGUE

Loosely based on a real-life San Francisco murder, Frank Norris's 1899 novel *McTeague* was all about the destructive power of greed. The main plot: Marcus is engaged to Trina, a German immigrant. One day, Trina falls off a swing and chips a tooth, so Marcus takes her to see his friend McTeague, an unlicensed dentist. Despite Marcus's objections to gambling (because he can't afford to play), Trina wins a massive fortune in an underground lottery. They fight, and Trina leaves Marcus for McTeague. But she hoards her money, lives like a pauper, and turns into a hag. Out of jealousy, Marcus gets McTeague's dental practice shut down. McTeague has no way of making a living, but Trina still won't share with him, either. So McTeague kills her.

The nearly 500-page novel takes place over two decades, features dozens of other characters and subplots, recurring motifs, and lengthy physical descriptions of the characters and the seedy San Francisco neighborhoods in which they live. The many subtle touches and countless details would make it a hard book to turn into a movie, but silent film director Erich von Stroheim knew he could do it.

THE GERMAN INVASION

Von Stroheim emigrated from Vienna to the United States in 1909 at age 24, and after a few years of odd jobs found work as a crewman on the 1914 silent film epic *The Birth of a Nation*. He parlayed that job into a stint as an actor in World War I-era films, playing loathsome German military captains. Von Stroheim's portrayals of evil Germans were so popular that his films were marketed as "Starring Erich von Stroheim, the man you love to hate." In *The Heart of Humanity*, for example, von Stroheim's character

---

Take a cab? Just one sneeze on a crowded subway can give 150 passengers a cold.

tears off a nurse's uniform with his teeth and throws a crying baby out of a window.

But by 1916 the jingoism he'd helped spread backfired on him—Germans were so hated in the United States during and immediately after World War I that von Stroheim couldn't get work anymore (even though he wasn't really German—he was Austrian). With no acting work being offered to him, the former movie star was reduced to renting a room in a boarding house in New York City. In his room, he found an old, beat-up copy of *McTeague* left by the previous tenant. The book struck a nerve, especially in how McTeague had suddenly lost his means of employment when others turned on him. Von Stroheim vowed to himself that he'd make a movie out the book someday.

A few months later, he got a break: D. W. Griffith, director of *The Birth of a Nation,* asked him to co-star in his latest movie, *Intolerance.* So von Stroheim headed for the world's emerging film capital—Hollywood, California.

ARTISTIC VISION

Intolerance was von Stroheim's ticket back into the movie business. The anti-German sentiment died down enough to where he acted in a dozen more silent movies. They were commercial hits, so in 1919 Universal Pictures allowed him to direct a script he'd written, called *Blind Husbands.* It, too, performed well at the box office, so Universal let him direct more movies. But von Stroheim was a self-styled artist who refused to compromise his artistic vision. Shoots ran long, dozens of takes were required—von Stroheim would do whatever it took to get exactly what he wanted. Result: his movies went *way* over budget.

To rein him in, Universal hired a new studio head—21-year-old Irving Thalberg. For their first film together, *Foolish Wives,* Thalberg gave von Stroheim a $250,000 budget. Despite Thalberg's attempts to penny-pinch, von Stroheim managed to spend $1.25 million. Halfway through production of von Stroheim's next film, 1923's *Merry-Go-Round,* Thalberg decided that he was still spending too much money, so he fired him. Von Stroheim signed with rival studio Metro-Goldwyn.

Thalberg's method at Universal was to make cheap, profitable movies, period. At Metro-Goldwyn, executives believed they could make commercial movies and turn a profit while allowing directors to make the movies they wanted to make (as long as they stayed under budget). So, seven years after he'd first discovered the book, von Stroheim pitched his idea of adapting *McTeague* to the studio bosses. They gave him the go-ahead with only one condition: He had to retitle it *Greed*.

Hoping to make the most of his artistic freedom, but also hoping to avoid pushing his bosses at Metro-Goldwyn too far, von Stroheim had to make sure he had enough money to make the *Greed* he wanted, so he supplemented the movie's budget with his own personal funds. To get the money, he took out a second mortgage on his house and sold his car. To further lower costs, he took a pay cut. Although contracted to write, direct, and edit the picture, he accepted only a small fee for editing—two weeks' scale salary.

KEEPING IT REAL

Have you ever watched the movie version of a novel you read, and found yourself disappointed because too much had been left out? That's pretty much a necessity—a book contains far more material than can be included in a two-hour film. Von Stroheim didn't want that to be the case with *Greed*. He wanted to include *everything*—every subplot, every line of dialogue, every piece of furniture and physical trait present in the novel. That would be an extremely ambitious concept today, but this was 1923—color film, special effects, and even sound were not yet available.

So in striving for realism and staying absolutely faithful to the book, von Stroheim had to innovate: He filmed on location, which was seldom done in 1923. (*Greed* was the first feature film ever made without any sets or soundstages.) The bulk of the action takes place in and around McTeague's apartment in San Francisco, so von Stroheim rented a dilapidated house there and furnished it with run-down furniture exactly as Norris's book described. To get a better sense of their characters, von Stroheim even made his actors *live* in the house. He also insisted that the scenes that took place in Death Valley, the hottest place in North America, be shot there. During filming, the temperature reached a blazing 142°F. Jean Hersholt, who portrayed Marcus, was hospitalized for internal bleeding triggered by dehydration.

A VERY LONG ENGAGEMENT

It took von Stroheim nine months and $500,000 to make *Greed*—18 times longer and five times more expensive than most movies of the time. But it was worth it to von Stroheim: Every miniscule detail of all 496 pages of *McTeague* was present in *Greed*. As a final touch, to emphasize the recurring themes of wealth and greed, von Stroheim hand-painted the actual film, using gold paint to color every gold object in the movie.

The director had made his masterpiece, but there was one big problem: It was more than *nine hours* long. No movie studio in Hollywood would release a movie that long, not even one that let directors do what they wanted. Von Stroheim realized he'd have to abandon his original vision of *McTeague*...and chop it down to a more manageable length.

But first he held a private screening of the complete, "true" *Greed* for his friends, family, and a few reporters. Exactly 12 people saw the nine-hour film in its first showing. It was also the *only* screening ever made of the full film. Those 12 people are the only ones who ever saw von Stroheim's masterpiece the way he intended it to be seen. And they loved it.

BIG BUSINESS

But in April 1924, there were big changes at Metro-Goldwyn Studios. Lowe's Theatres bought the company. They also bought Mayer-Schulberg Studios, and merged them into Metro-Goldwyn-Mayer. Former Mayer-Schulberg chief Louis B. Mayer was appointed head of production, and he did not share Metro-Goldwyn's "the director rules" approach. He shared Thalberg's philosophy: Make a movie fast and cheap with a producer overseeing expenses. In fact, Mayer hired Thalberg—von Stroheim's nemesis at Universal—to enforce these new rules.

Von Stroheim, meanwhile, still had a movie to finish. He carefully edited *Greed*, somehow getting the running time down to four hours with most of the plot, subplots, and themes intact. He sent the four-hour cut to his friend, editor Rex Ingram, asking if he could recommend anything else to delete. Ingram removed an hour, then sent the film back to von Stroheim with a note reading, "If you cut one more foot I shall never speak to you again."

CUT IT OUT

Von Stroheim presented the three-hour version to Mayer…who didn't even watch it. Instead, he passed it off to a staff editor with instructions to cut it to an even 120 minutes. The two-hour *Greed* was a completely different movie from the nine-hour, the four-hour, or even the three-hour *Greed*. According to *Film Monthly* magazine, it "turned a tragedy rich with telling detail into a bare outline."

The two-hour *Greed* concentrates exclusively on McTeague (Gibson Gowland), Trina (ZaSu Pitts), and Marcus. Most of the many subplots and characters were eliminated. Here's a taste of some elements that were in Norris' novel and filmed by von Stroheim, but completely removed from the final film:

• McTeague's backstory, showing his early life, growing up in mining towns, and how he learned dentistry.

• Two old people who live in an apartment near McTeague's. They fall in love over the course of the film—a counterpoint to the slow destruction of McTeague and Trina's relationship.

• A subplot concerning Maria, a greedy junk collector who sells Trina the fateful lottery ticket. Her boyfriend, Zerkow, marries her because he believes she has a secret stash of gold dishes worth a fortune. When Zerkow discovers they are made of tin, he kills Maria and then kills himself by jumping into San Francisco Bay. (The actor playing Zerkow actually jumped into the San Francisco Bay during filming and contracted pneumonia.)

REEL TRAGEDY

Contractually obligated to screen it *somewhere*, Mayer debuted the film in a single New York theater during the Christmas season of 1924. A blunt tragedy about the dark side of humanity is not the kind of movie people want to see at Christmas and, predictably, *Greed* bombed at the box office. For tax purposes, MGM wrote off the production costs—$500,000—as a total loss.

But was the full nine-hour *Greed* ever smuggled out of MGM? Later in his life, von Stroheim claimed that he'd screened it personally in Argentina during World War II, and that he'd given a print to Italian dictator Benito Mussolini. And there's a rumor that David Shepard of the American Film Institute supposedly found it in a garage several decades later, but it's untrue—the uncut *Greed* is on the AFI's list of most wanted lost films.

Benito Mussolini was given an honorary British knighthood in 1923. (It was withdrawn in 1940.)

As for von Stroheim, he made an interesting comeback. In the 1930s, after the *Greed* debacle and a few more box-office bombs, he moved to France, where he starred in Jean Renoir's 1937 classic, *La Grande Illusion*. Then, in 1950, director Billy Wilder cast him in *Sunset Boulevard*, which reflects on the broken careers of giants of the silent film era. Von Stroheim portrayed Max von Mayerling, one of "the three great silent film directors" next to Cecil B. DeMille and D. W. Griffith, now reduced to working as the butler for his ex-wife, silent film star Norma Desmond. He received an Academy Award nomination for Best Supporting Actor for his work in *Sunset Boulevard*, and appeared in seven more films before he died in 1957 at the age of 72.

IN PIECES

As far as anyone knows, the nine-hour *Greed*—more specifically, the seven hours of cut footage—really is gone. Irving Thalberg later told reporters that the missing footage was melted down for its valuable silver content (photographic film contains tiny silver salt crystals). There probably was only one print of the full version—von Stroheim's working copy. MGM certainly wouldn't have paid for duplicates if Mayer had no intention of ever using them.

Von Stroheim's masterpiece did eventually see the light of day...sort of. In 1999 film preservationist Rick Schmidlin set out to restore and recreate *Greed* as much as possible. Taking the existing footage and 650 surviving production stills, with von Stroheim's screenplay as a guide, Schmidlin constructed a four-hour version believed to be, based on Stroheim's production and editing notes, very close to the director's four-hour cut. It aired on Turner Classic Movies in December 1999. If you didn't see it then, you may never see it. Jut as the nine-hour and four-hour versions are lost forever, Schmidlin's take is not available on DVD.

*   *   *

AN EPITAPH
Here lies a man named Zeke,
Second-fastest draw in Cripple Creek.

INDIANA BASKETBALL: OSCAR ROBERTSON

The Crispus Attucks Tigers had become the first all-black team to reach the Indiana High School Basketball Finals. What could they do for an encore? Change the entire look of basketball—with the help of one phenomenal player. (Part II starts on page 284.)

THE CHANGING OF THE GUARD

When Oscar Robertson first started playing basketball in his hometown of Indianapolis, he was known as "Li'l Flap," after his big brother, Bailey "Flap" Robertson (named for how his wrist turned after a shot). Oscar honed his skills playing against older, taller Crispus Attucks stars like Flap and Hallie Bryant, and he practiced constantly, perfecting a one-handed jump shot, behind-the-back passes, and "fakes"—moving one way and then the other to put the defender off guard. He was quick and agile, and by the time he made the varsity squad at Crispus Attucks as a sophomore in 1953, he was 6'2". When he scored 15 points as a substitute in the team's first game (a win), Coach Ray Crowe made him a starter. And after he almost single-handedly won a game against Shortridge High in double overtime, people stopped calling him Li'l Flap.

It's not an understatement to say that, between Coach Crowe's aggressive game plan and Robertson's size and talent, they revolutionized high school basketball. Instead of scoring 50 or 60 points a game, the Attucks team scored 80 or 90. Robertson didn't have to rely on holding the ball for minutes at a time or passing from corner to corner, hoping for an opening. Because he was bigger and faster than most players, he could dribble past his defender and either shoot a basket or pass it to a teammate who had a wide-open shot because the other defenders had moved to cover Robertson. As Willie Merriweather, who played forward with Robertson, put it, "Their team would be in disarray, and then we would start to run."

THAT CHAMPIONSHIP SEASON

In 1955, with an older, taller Oscar Robertson (he'd grown to 6'4" since losing to Milan the previous year), the Tigers were practically unstoppable. The city of Indianapolis had never won a State Championship, and everyone—black and white—started rooting for them. Ticket demand was so high that many of their home games were moved to the 15,000-seat Butler Fieldhouse (the basketball arena of nearby Butler University). The team went 21–1 in the regular season. Their only loss that year was in the dead of winter to a small-town team whose gym floor was laid over a frozen swimming pool...and that was the last time an Attucks team with Oscar Robertson would *ever* lose a game.

ROLLING THUNDER

Having beaten their playoff opponents by an average of 28 points, they cruised to the 1955 State Championship Final game in front of 15,000 fans at the now-familiar Butler Fieldhouse. Their opponent: Gary Roosevelt High, another all-black segregated school. That made it the first time in Indiana history that two all-black schools faced off in the State Final. Gary Roosevelt had an excellent team, including a 6'6" center named Jake Eison, who was named Indiana's "Mr. Basketball" that year, and Dick Barnett, a future NBA star. But Attucks ran away with the game, winning 97–74.

Crispus Attucks's first State Championship, the first Championship for an all-black school in Indiana or anywhere else in the United States, was also the long-awaited first Championship for the city of Indianapolis. Fans both black and white celebrated. Robertson later said, "I remember that night they called us Indianapolis Attucks, not Crispus Attucks. To me, that meant we'd arrived. They just wanted you to win; they didn't care what color you were."

THE REAL HOOSIERS

In 1956, led by Oscar Robertson as a senior, the Crispus Attucks Tigers had their best season yet. Robertson broke the city scoring record twice, once with 45 points, then later with 62 points—still an Indianapolis record—and the Attucks team drew huge crowds wherever they played, at home or on the road.

They rolled through the 1956 regular season and playoffs, and other teams seemed to stand still as the Tigers ran past them. Lafayette Jefferson High School, the team they faced in the 1956

Championship Finals, played an old-fashioned game, similar to Milan's—they held the ball and controlled the pace of the game with multiple passes. They even shot their free throws underhand. Needless to say, they were overmatched. Robertson scored 39 points despite being double- and triple-teamed all night, and Crispus Attucks won 79–57. With that win, they became Indiana's first undefeated State Basketball Champions.

The build-up to that moment had been remarkable. The Tigers had gone 30–1 back in 1955 and 31–0 in 1956, setting a state record with 45 consecutive wins over two seasons. And over the course of just two years, they had changed everything—not just the way the game of Indiana basketball was played, but its color, too. The 1954 Championship Game had three black players; the next year, the Championship Game was contested by two all-black high schools. Now, in 1956, an all-black team was the best that had ever been—the state's first undefeated state championship team. Over the next few years, high schools in Indianapolis and around the state started recruiting black students who once would have been segregated in schools like Crispus Attucks and Gary Roosevelt.

OVERTIME

The renowned winner-take-all Indiana High School State Championship Tournament no longer exists; the state went to a four-class system in 1998. Crispus Attucks itself was integrated in 1970 under court-ordered desegregation. Because of declining enrollment, it was converted to a junior high school in 1986 and then later to a middle school. In 2006 it became a high school again—a magnet school for students preparing to become medical professionals. And in 2008, more than 50 years after they won their first State Championship, the Crispus Attucks Tigers returned to playing varsity basketball.

❋   ❋   ❋

SMALL-TOWN NEWS

"Police responded to a report of two dogs running loose and attacking ducks last Sunday. The officer cited a resident for the loose dogs. The ducks refused medical treatment and left the area, according to police."

—*Ashland (Oregon) Daily Tidings*

The color green was once considered unlucky in Ireland. (It was thought to anger the fairies.)

GOURMET FOOD: HUMBLE ORIGINS

*Most people's first encounters with fancy foods make them say "Eww."
Corn fungus, pickled cactus, weird mushrooms, and the like actually
do seem pretty unappetizing, even if they taste good. Turns out
that many were first consumed out of hardship and necessity.*

LOBSTER

Lobster may taste like shellfish (crab, shrimp), but it looks like an insect. And technically, it's an arthropod—more closely related to spiders than to anything from the sea. Lobsters are abundant off the coast of New England, and from the colonial era until the 19th century, they were treated like insects; fisherman considered them pests that took up room in nets meant for more desirable fish. But fishermen caught them in large quantities and were reluctant to throw them back, especially since they were edible and could be sold (cheaply) for other uses. Those uses: ground up and used as high-protein plant fertilizer or as food for slaves, indentured servants, and prisoners. In fact, during the American Revolution, some British prisoners revolted over being served lobster too often. When the railroads made mass transport of goods possible in the late 1800s, East Coast fisheries realized that they could ship lobster west...where nobody knew it wasn't an expensive delicacy. In other words, they decided they could make a buck by *calling* lobster a delicacy. They did, and it worked.

FOIE GRAS

Pronounced "fwah-grah," it's the extra-fatty, rich-tasting liver of a goose that was force-fed until its liver grew to 10 times normal size. Today, the food is banned in many places because force-feeding the goose is considered by some to be an act of cruelty. Goose liver was a favorite dish of rulers in ancient Egypt. But its popularity died out over time, until Jewish people in the Middle Ages discovered that the fatty liver of the common wild goose was delicious. Not just that, but geese are *kosher*, meaning they pass the rigorous Jewish dietary guidelines. By the Renaissance, most of the Jewish population of Rome was confined to ghettos. Word got out to the ruling elite that the Jewish dish of fatty goose liver was pretty good, so the wealthy went into butcher shops in the Jewish ghettos to buy it. Suddenly, fattened goose liver was a fancy food. And as the Roman Empire's cultural influence spread throughout Europe, the dish became especially popular in what is now France. (*Foie gras* is French for "fat liver.")

OYSTERS

It's amazing that anybody ever discovered that oysters are edible. They securely affix themselves to shoreline rock clusters, and they themselves *look* like rocks—they're encased in thick, hard-to-crack shells. And then, once you've got one open, the edible portion is a slimy, misshapen, gelatinous glob. (Never eat oysters that were open when you found them—they'll give you a "gut-wrenching" experience.) But people do have to eat, and the lower the income bracket, the more creative the food sources sometimes have to be. The late-19th-century immigration boom created a population explosion, particularly on the east coast of North America, where oysters were abundant at the time. They became a cheap favorite of the working and lower classes. By the 1920s, oysters were overconsumed to the point of scarcity. And things that are scarce tend to become more expensive...and more desirable.

SNAILS

They've been eaten all around the world for thousands of years, but we know snails, or *escargots*, as a French dish. Poor French peasants ate snails at least as far back as the 1600s. The most commonly consumed variety: vineyard snails, which are easily caught and found in abundance in (obviously) vineyards. Snails remained a rustic French country dish until the early 20th century. That's when restaurants became common in the United States and, as is partly still true today, the fanciest restaurants were the French ones. And because French food was considered exotic, American diners didn't know that when they ordered expensive plates of *escargot*, they were actually ordering slimy creatures from the yard cooked in the same way they were in the 1600s: baked with inexpensive, easily obtained ingredients—butter, garlic, and parsley.

Chinese philosopher Confucius has more than three million living descendants.

THE MARK OF ZORA

*The Corvette may be the quintessential American sports car, but
the man who made it great was a European immigrant with
a thick accent and an exotic last name. Here's Part III
of our story. (Part II is on page 329.)*

SKIN DEEP

In January of 1953, a Belgian-born, Russian-Jewish immigrant named Zora Arkus-Duntov paid a visit to the General Motors Motorama auto show at the Waldorf-Astoria Hotel in New York City. There the first Chevrolet Corvette was unveiled to the public, and like so many other people who got their first look at the car, Duntov was struck by its beauty.

Unlike most of the spectators, Duntov was an automotive engineer who'd spent years working on and around race cars. As he studied the Corvette's motor and other components, he realized that it would not be able to deliver on the promise of performance that its sporty good looks implied. "Mechanically, it stunk, with its six-cylinder engine and two-speed automatic transmission," he remembered. "But visually, it was superb."

DREAM JOB

Duntov had been looking for a job with one of the major American automakers for several months. Before Motorama, he wasn't too particular about which company he went to work for, but after seeing the Corvette, he knew he wanted a job at Chevrolet. *This* was a car he could work on—this was a car that needed his help. Luckily for Duntov (and for *you*, if you're a Corvette fan), Ed Cole, Chevrolet's chief engineer, was impressed with his credentials and gave him a job. In May 1953, Duntov started as an assistant staff engineer in Chevrolet's Research & Development department.

If Duntov thought he was going to be assigned full-time to the Corvette, he was probably disappointed—the car was so new and sold at such low volumes that *no* employees were assigned to it full-time. People worked on the car on temporary assignment and only when their work on other, more important projects permitted.

In 2008 Doritos chips broadcast an ad to Ursa Major, 42 light years from Earth.

A TOUGH FIT

Duntov had run his own businesses before, but he'd never worked for a big corporation, and he had a tough time adjusting to life at GM, then the world's largest. Just a few weeks after landing his job at Chevrolet, he nearly lost it when he insisted on taking a leave of absence to honor a prior commitment and go to France to race at Le Mans, a grueling 24-hour road race. Result: When he (reluctantly) returned to Detroit, he was demoted and reassigned to work on GM trucks and schoolbuses. In December 1953, however, he worked his way back into the good graces of his superiors by drafting a memo titled, "Thoughts Pertaining to Youth, Hot-Rodders and Chevrolet."

In his memo, Duntov observed that the hobby of fixing up cars and turning them into hot rods was a rapidly growing fad with young men. Currently Fords were the cars of choice for hot-rodders, and Duntov speculated that when these young men outgrew their street racers, they were likely to continue buying Fords. In the Corvette, Duntov saw an opportunity to win some of this business for Chevrolet. But the performance of the standard Corvette had to be improved considerably, and on top of that, Chevy had to begin offering a full line of optional high-performance parts for buyers who wanted their Corvettes to be able to take on all those souped-up Fords.

THE RIGHT MAN FOR THE JOB

The 1953 Corvette aside, Chevrolet had a reputation for selling low-priced, underpowered, and unexciting cars to buyers who didn't have the money to buy the cars they really wanted—hardly the car of choice for hot-rodders. The division's bargain-basement image had cost it a lot of business in recent years, and that was one of the reasons Cole had wanted the Corvette for Chevrolet. It was also one of the reasons he wanted *Duntov* for Chevrolet, even after he'd run off to Europe to play with race cars. Duntov may well have been the only engineer at GM who would have known *how* to play with race cars, and he was certainly one of the few with the insight to write his famous memo about Chevrolet and hot-rodders.

Remember that, though Chevrolet had been founded by a race car driver, Louis Chevrolet, in 1911, it had been decades since

Chevy or any other GM division had built anything resembling a race car (or a sports car). And paradoxically, GM could be a tough place to work for people who were interested in cars. A typical career path for a GM engineer was to start out working on designs for one small part of the car—say, the latch mechanism for the hood—then eventually move on to another, such as engine mounts or trunk lid hinges. A job at GM was steady, high-paying work for people willing to endure years of tedium as they paid their dues, but serious "car guys" who were passionate about hot rods and racing stayed away. Duntov was one of the few who was willing to take a chance at GM. And that was why Cole only banished him to work on trucks and schoolbuses instead of firing him outright.

Duntov's hot-rod memo laid out a strategy for Chevrolet to become a dominant force in auto racing, just the kind of thing the division needed to change its image. Cole agreed with many of Duntov's observations and set to work implementing them. Soon, for example, a full line of high-performance parts became available from every Chevy dealer in the country.

ONE STEP AT A TIME

As soon as Cole felt that Duntov had been punished enough, he pulled him off of trucks and schoolbuses and assigned him to the team that was developing fuel injection for the 195-horsepower V-8 engine that would soon be replacing the Corvette's six-cylinder Stovebolt Six. The V-8 was ready in time for the 1955 model year; all but 6 of the 700 Corvettes manufactured that year had them. (Fuel injection, which increased the engine's power to as high as 283 hp, didn't become available until 1957.)

Bit by bit, Duntov and the other engineers and stylists who worked on the Corvette chipped away at the long list of things that were so annoying about the early cars. A three-speed manual transmission was made available as an option in 1955; the following year, it became standard equipment.

1956 was also the year that the Corvette's body received a bumper-to-bumper cosmetic restyling. In the process, many of the amenities that had been left out of the 1953–55 Corvettes—roll-up windows and exterior door handles and locks, to name three—were put in. By now GM had also solved many of the technical challenges associated with working with fiberglass body panels, so there was no talk of going back to steel. Corvettes kept their fiberglass bodies for more than 50 years, until they were finally replaced with a new composite material in 2005.

A RACY REPUTATION

As the Corvette made steady improvement from one year to the next, Duntov also worked to raise Chevrolet's racing profile. In 1955 he entered a 1956 Chevy Bel-Air in the annual race to the top of Pike's Peak in Colorado. He drove the car himself to a record-breaking first-place finish, shaving a full two minutes off the old record, which had been set by a Ford. Then in January 1956, Duntov took a modified 1957 Corvette to Daytona Beach, Florida, and set a 150-mph speed record there.

Chevrolet wouldn't be directly involved in racing for very long. The sport's image took a beating after a 1955 car crash at the Grand Prix race in Le Mans, France, killed 80 spectators. In mid-1957, GM, citing safety concerns, joined with the other big U.S. automakers and got out of auto racing altogether. Auto racers would continue to race American cars, of course, but the automakers no longer fielded their own teams or race cars. By then, however, Chevrolet's reputation as a manufacturer of fast, exciting cars was secure.

1957 was also the year that Duntov was appointed to the newly created position of Chevrolet's Director of High Performance. For the first time in his career, he had an official title to go with his growing public persona as the "Father of the Corvette."

Corvettes had improved dramatically, but the best was still to come. For Part IV of the story, turn to page 458.

*   *   *

MYTH-CONCEPTION

Myth: Napoleon Bonaparte was very short—about 5'2".
Truth: His body was measured at that height when he died in 1821. At the time, France used a slightly different system of measurement. In today's universally agreed-upon measurements, that height corresponds to about 5' 6 ½ "—short, but not that short.

The verb "to google" was added to *Merriam-Webster's Collegiate Dictionary* in 2006.

THE "OLD GLORY" STORY

People seem to like to give things nicknames. It's not just your house, it's "The Ponderosa." It's not just your car, it's "Big Blue." A lot of Americans refer to the U.S. flag as "Old Glory," unaware that it started out as the nickname of one specific flag. And that flag still exists.

YOUNG GLORY

William Driver was just 13 years old when he left his Salem, Massachusetts, home in 1816 to work as a cabin boy on a sailing ship. By the age of 21, he was a seasoned enough sailor to earn a captain's license. To celebrate the occasion, his mother and family friends presented him with a gift they'd made: a 10'-by-17' American flag, with 24 stars (the number of states at the time), to fly from his first ship. After gazing on it for the first time, the story goes, Driver dubbed the flag "Old Glory." It flew from Driver's ships for the rest of his career—twice circling the globe on whaling ships—before he retired in 1837.

Shortly after that, Driver's wife died, and he moved his three children to Nashville, Tennessee, where his two brothers lived. He became a salesman, married again, had nine more children, and over the years became a well-known man around town. His flag became well known, too: On every national holiday (and on March 17—his own birthday), Old Glory flew from the peak of the Driver house on what is now Nashville's Fifth Avenue.

FLAG OF OUR ENEMIES

In 1861 Driver's daughters gave the flag an update, removing the 24 stars and replacing them with 34 new ones (10 states had joined the union since he'd received the flag in 1824) and adding a small white anchor to the lower right corner of the blue field in honor of their seafaring father. By then, the flag was beloved by the townspeople, but within a few short months that would change dramatically.

In April 1861, the Civil War began. Driver, originally from Massachusetts, was pro-Union, but he lived in the capital of a state that had joined the Confederacy—and suddenly his cherished flag became a symbol of an enemy country. On two occasions, mobs of

Confederates showed up at the house, one directed by the Tennessee governor himself, and demanded the flag, vowing to burn it. In a letter to one of his daughters, Driver wrote:

> The Texan Rangers had been told I had a flag and intended to hoist it, and they swore to burn me in my house if I did not give it up: but a bunch of Union friends, and many of our city watch, saved my house and flag.

After that, the flag disappeared until February 1862, when Nashville became the first Confederate capital to fall to the North. Members of the 6th Regiment of the Ohio Volunteer Infantry, who helped take the city, hoisted their military flag to the top of the recaptured Capitol building...but Driver, who was at the scene, would have none of it.

OLD BLANKETY

Escorted back to his home by soldiers, Driver went up to his bedroom took a quilt out from under his bed—and cut it open. He'd gotten a neighbor to sew the flag into it months earlier, hiding its location even from his family. Driver marched back to the Capitol, climbed the stairs to the top of the tower—and hoisted the flag up the pole himself. From that same letter:

> I always hoped, although against hope, that this hour would come. With my own hand, in the presence of thousands, I hoisted that flag where it now floats, on the staff which has trembled with the fluttering of treason's banner.

Old Glory was eventually returned to Driver, but it never flew again. In 1873 he gave it to one of his daughters, telling her, "Mary Jane, this is my ship's flag, 'Old Glory.' It has been my constant companion. I love it as a mother loves her child. Cherish it as I have cherished it."

Driver died in 1886 and was buried in the Nashville City Cemetery. His daughter kept the flag for nearly 50 years until 1922, when she presented it to President Warren G. Harding. Being in too delicate a condition to display, it was stored away in the Smithsonian Institute. There it sat for 60 years until it was restored in 1982 and put in a special glass case in the National Museum of American History, right alongside another large flag—the 30'-by-34' "Star Spangled Banner" that inspired America's national anthem—where it remains today.

FAKE-LORE

Most folktales are part of an oral tradition passed down over generations, and are often based on real people or events. Some, however, are not. "Fakelore" is a term invented in 1950 by folklorist Richard Dorson to describe these tales that seem like they're old, with stories that developed naturally, but are actually much newer and completely made up by writers or ad agencies. Examples: Paul Bunyan and Rudolph the Red-Nosed Reindeer. Here are some others.

Legendary Hero: Pecos Bill

The Tale: Bill was born in Texas, but fell out of a covered wagon when he was a baby and was raised by coyotes. He grew up to be the most powerful cowboy in the Old West. He used a rattlesnake as a lasso, could ride a tornado like a rodeo bull, and personally dug out the Rio Grande River.

The Truth: *The Century* magazine writer Edward O'Reilly began publishing Pecos Bill stories in 1916, claiming that they were part of a cowboy oral tradition. They weren't. O'Reilly made them all up.

Legendary Hero: Astrild

The Tale: In the 900-year-old pantheon of Norse gods (which also includes Odin and Thor), Astrild, whose name means "love fire," was the god of love—like Cupid.

The Truth: Astrild was a popular subject for romantic poets in the 18th and 19th centuries, but he was never actually worshiped by ancient Scandinavians. That's because he was the invention of Swedish poet Georg Stiernhielm in the mid-1600s.

Legendary Hero: Joe Magarac

The Tale: A folk hero in the steel-making towns of Pennsylvania, Magarac was the greatest steelworker who ever lived. He was made of steel and worked every moment of every day. Not only that, but he would show up just in the nick of time to save steelworkers from danger.

The Truth: The story spread when it was mentioned in a 1931

Scribner's Magazine article by Owen Francis, who heard the story from steelworkers. However, according to historians, the men who told Francis the Joe Magarac story probably made it up on the spot. They were eastern European, and "magarac" means "jackass" in several Slavic languages.

Legendary Heroes: Wesley and Princess Buttercup
The Tale: The classic 1987 movie *The Princess Bride* is based on a 1973 novel by William Goldman. But Goldman's book, as stated in the introduction, is an abridged version of a 200-year-old folk-tale that he took from a much longer book of the same name by a reclusive writer named S. Morgenstern. *The Princess Bride* is, in fact, one of the most beloved stories of Morgenstern's home country of Florin (where the book takes place).
The Truth: There's no such place as Florin, and no such writer as S. Morgenstern. Goldman wrote the book, and the idea that he abridged it from an older novel was used as a "literary device."

* * *

MORE COMMONLY MISUSED WORDS

DILEMMA
How We Use It: A problem
What It Really Means: Specifically, a problem in which one must choose between two or more unsavory choices

TERRIFIC
How We Use It: Something that's pleasingly fantastic
What It Really Means: Something that causes terror

PLETHORA
How We Use It: A lot of something
What It Really Means: Too much of something

ENORMITY
How We Use It: Enormous
What It Really Means: Evil

RANDOM BITS ON '90s HITS

Pop songs are short, catchy, and memorable, just like these facts.

- **"Ice Ice Baby,"** by Vanilla Ice. The first rap song to ever reach #1 on the *Billboard* chart.

- **"Losing My Religion,"** by R.E.M. Their first (and only) top-5 hit, it's one of only two hit songs ever to feature a mandolin prominently. (The other is Rod Stewart's "Maggie May.")

- **"I Love Your Smile,"** by Shanice. This teen pop song by an 18-year-old former child star (at age 8, Shanice appeared in a KFC commercial with Ella Fitzgerald) features a sax solo by jazz star Branford Marsalis.

- **"Achy Breaky Heart,"** by Billy Ray Cyrus. The first country song to sell a million copies since Dolly Parton and Kenny Rogers' "Islands in the Stream" in 1983. The song and its accompanying dance, the "Achy Breaky," spawned 1992's country line-dance fad.

- **"November Rain,"** by Guns N' Roses. At 8 minutes, 59 seconds, it's the longest top-10 hit of all time.

- **"Dreamlover,"** by Mariah Carey. The first of three Carey singles to sample the 1982 Tom Tom Club hit "Genius of Love." Like the other two ("Heartbreaker" and "Fantasy"), it was a #1 hit.

- **"Stay (I Missed You),"** by Lisa Loeb and Nine Stories. Loeb got this song on the *Reality Bites* soundtrack because her neighbor was the film's star, Ethan Hawke. It went all the way to #1, making her the only artist ever to score a #1 hit without a record deal.

- **"Waterfalls,"** by TLC. The song is about the dangers of ignoring consequences. Group member Lisa Lopes had to record her mid-song rap from a prison cell...where she was being held for ignoring the consequences of setting her boyfriend's house on fire.

- **"You Were Meant For Me,"** by Jewel. First released in 1995 as a more up-tempo country rock song with prominent electric gui-

---

The average unwanted can of food sits in the cupboard for 2.7 years before it's thrown away.

tar, the song bombed. Jewel re-recorded it as an acoustic ballad, and it went to #2 on the pop chart.

• **"Scream," by Michael Jackson and Janet Jackson.** The video was the most expensive ever, at $7 million (nine times what it cost to make Jackson's "Thriller").

• **"One Sweet Day," by Boyz II Men and Mariah Carey.** The fourth song ever to debut at #1, it holds the record for the longest time spent at the top of the chart: 16 weeks in 1995–96.

• **"Don't Speak," by No Doubt.** Original band member Eric Stefani wrote it as an upbeat love song. In 1995, just months before the band scored a string of major hits, Stefani left the band to work as an animator on *The Simpsons*. Also around that time, bassist Tony Kanal broke up with the band's singer, Gwen Stefani, prompting her to re-write "Don't Speak" as a breakup ballad.

• **"Bitch," by Meredith Brooks.** The FCC allows the word "bitch" to be broadcast on the airwaves when it's sung in songs, but not when it's spoken. So, when DJs introduced this song, they had to call it "a song by Meredith Brooks."

• **"How Do I Live," by LeAnn Rimes.** Rimes was denied the chance to sing this song for the *Con-Air* soundtrack; producers opted for Trisha Yearwood instead. Rimes recorded and released the song anyway...and it was the far bigger hit of the two versions.

• **"Doo Wop (That Thing)," by Lauryn Hill.** Half sung and half rapped (and written, arranged, and produced entirely by Hill), every single line rhymes.

• **"Believe," by Cher.** This set a record for largest gap between #1 hits—25 years. Cher's previous #1 was "Dark Lady" in 1974.

• **"Livin' La Vida Loca," by Ricky Martin.** Writers Desmond Child and Robi Rosa (Martin's former bandmate in the group Menudo) claim that they were *trying* to write a bad song—"the Millennium party song from Hell." (No comment.)

* * *

"How young can you be and still die of old age?"
—Steven Wright

THE PORTMANTEAU MOVIE QUIZ

A portmanteau is a word that results from two other words being combined. So, here's a wordplay game we came up with: We took two movies and made "portmanteaus" of their titles. Can you guess the movies, and their combined titles, based on these wacky combined plots? Answers are on page 537.

1. After humanity has covered the planet in garbage and abandoned it, a robot spends his days collecting and compacting trash. He is painfully lonely, until one day he's visited by a big-eyed, telepathic alien with a glowing finger and pulsing red heart. The robot gives the alien Reese's Pieces; the alien takes the robot on a magical flying bicycle ride.

2. A small-town sheriff (Josh Brolin) finds a bag of money at a murder scene. The bag belongs to a dangerous criminal (Javier Bardem), who is actually an evil alien bent on dominating the universe. He is defeated by two sassy secret government agents (Will Smith and Tommy Lee Jones).

3. A newspaper editor (Cary Grant) will do anything to stop his top reporter (Rosalind Russell)—his ex-wife, with whom he's still in love—from remarrying and quitting her job. And that includes donning a hockey mask and terrorizing a summer camp.

4. An Australian woman (Meryl Streep) goes camping in the Outback. Her baby is killed, and she's put on trial for murder, despite her insistence that dingoes ate her baby. Proving her innocence is up to her attorney, who's distraught over the murders of his parents. His name: Batman (Christian Bale).

5. A man (Sidney Poitier) helps a group of German nuns build a church in the Arizona desert. Why? A mysterious voice told him to "build it and they will come." Ghosts of old baseball players appear and play catch with the nuns.

6. The lion Scar (voice of Jeremy Irons) kills the lion Mufasa (voice of James Earl Jones) to become king of the jungle animals. After years of tyranny, the true king returns to claim his throne—and he's a crass, beer-drinking, overweight lounge singer (John Goodman).

7. As he attempts to write the play that ultimately becomes *Romeo and Juliet*, young William Shakespeare (Joseph Fiennes) meets his muse, a young woman (Ali MacGraw) that he can't have...because she's suddenly dying.

8. Professor Higgins (Rex Harrison) bets his colleague (Wilfrid Hyde-White) that he can turn Eliza, a Cockney street peddler (Audrey Hepburn), into a proper lady. Higgins falls in love with her, but so does another suitor: a scruffy dog from the wrong side of the tracks.

9. A bumbling klutz (Charlie Chaplin) goes to the wilds of Alaska to mine for gold with his partner, a Chinese police detective (Jackie Chan) who speaks little English but knows a lot of martial arts. Despite the language barrier—and the fact that the gold miner is completely silent—they manage to save a kidnapped girl from drug lords.

10. In the middle of a four-day bender, an alcoholic (Ray Milland) whose life is in shambles discovers the dead body of his boss (Terry Kiser), which he props up and parades around, pretending that his boss is alive so as not to frighten the pretty girls who are coming over to party.

11. While making one of the first "talkies," a silent movie star (Gene Kelly) falls in love with a young actress (Debbie Reynolds) brought in to dub the voice of another silent film star (Dustin Hoffman) whose voice is unsuitable for the movies—all he can say is "K-Mart sucks," and "15 minutes to Judge Wapner."

12. Despite losing his hand in a light-saber fight with the most brutal leader in the universe (voice of James Earl Jones), who, he just found out, is his father, a young intergalactic warrior (Mark Hamill) must travel back in time in his crazy inventor friend's (Christopher Lloyd) DeLorean-based time machine and make sure his parents meet, fall in love, and marry.

All the lawns in America, put together, would be about the size of Mississippi.

DER FARTENFÜHRER, PT. III

What was to blame for the rapid decline in Hitler's physical and mental health in the last years of his life? Here's the final installment of the story. (Part II is on page 312.)

BACK TO THE DRAWING BOARD
All doubts about the safety of Dr. Koester's Anti-Gas Pills were resolved when some of them were sent to a lab for analysis. The fart pills were found to contain small enough doses of strychnine and atropine that Hitler would have had to have consumed 30 pills or more—all in one sitting—for them to pose a threat to his health. He never took more than 6 at a time, and never more than 20 over the course of a day. Strychnine is quickly neutralized by the human body and does not accumulate in body tissues; because of this, nonlethal doses such as those contained in Dr. Koester's anti-gas pills can be taken for years on end with little or no ill effect. (Still, don't try it at home!)

Neither the rat poison nor the peasant poop had done Hitler much good…but they hadn't done him much harm, either. But the intravenous injections that Morell administered to Hitler beginning in the late 1930s were a different story. Morell was very secretive about what was in the Führer's regular daily shots; in his surviving medical records he never suggests that they contain anything other than vitamins or glucose. Some of the injections undoubtedly did contain these relatively innocuous ingredients, but not *all* of them. There's considerable evidence to suggest that many of the shots Morell administered contained something much more powerful—and that they, not the Mutaflor or Dr. Koester's Anti-Gas Pills, were responsible for the collapse in Hitler's health at the end of his life.

GOOOOOOOOOD MORNING!

Some of the most convincing pieces of evidence are the eyewitness accounts of how Hitler responded to the intravenous injections. In the late 1930s, the shots were administered infrequently, usually just before an important meeting or a major speech, when Hitler wanted a quick boost. But by late 1941, they were being

administered every morning, before Hitler had even gotten out of
bed, as part of his daily routine. Hitler's valets, secretaries, and
other close aides occasionally witnessed the shots being administered, and after the war they all described how the sleepy and at
times completely exhausted Führer responded to the injections
instantly, sometimes even while the needle was *still in his arm*: One
moment he was groggy and noncommunicative, and the very next
he was fully alert and sitting up in bed, contentedly chatting away
with whoever was in the room. Ordinary vitamins and glucose
don't produce the instant surge of energy that Hitler experienced,
even when injected directly into the veins.

THANK YOU SIR, MAY I HAVE ANOTHER

By 1943 Hitler was receiving two shots a day, more if the news
from the front was especially bad. As the years progressed—and
the tide of the war turned against Germany—Hitler called on
Morell more and more frequently to give him the injections. By
late 1944, the doctor was administering so many shots that he was
having trouble finding fresh areas in Hitler's needle-pocked arms
to give new injections.

And as Morell confided to an assistant, Hitler's tolerance for
whatever was in the shots had increased so dramatically over time
that Morell had had to increase the dosage from 2 cubic centimeters
per injection to 4, then 10, and eventually to 16 cc—an increase of
700 percent—for the injections to have the desired effect.

As Dr. Leonard Heston and Renate Heston point out in their
book *The Medical Casebook of Adolf Hitler*, human tolerance for
vitamins and glucose does not change over time. The fact that
Hitler was building up a tolerance for the injections is further
evidence that they contained a drug of some kind.

THE DRUG CULTURE

When you compare this evidence to the eyewitness accounts of
Hitler's instant response to the drug, a likely candidate for *which*
drug he was taking begins to emerge. "The effects described," the
Hestons write, "are characteristic of an injection of a stimulant
drug of the amphetamine group or cocaine, and are not compatible with any other drug." Of the two possibilities, "amphetamine
…is a much more probable because its injectable form was readily

available, while injectable cocaine was an illegal drug....Also, the effects of amphetamine last two or three hours, while the action of cocaine is much more rapidly terminated. The effects on Hitler were relatively long-lasting."

SIDE EFFECTS
Amphetamines give the user a surge in energy and an improvement in mood, just as the witnesses to Hitler's injections described. But they are now illegal for very good reasons: They're terribly addictive and they have numerous debilitating negative side effects that more than outweigh the handful of desirable effects.

When taken even in moderate amounts, amphetamines can cause insomnia—which Hitler suffered from—and loss of appetite. As dosages increase, so do the number and intensity of the side effects. Psychological side effects associated with amphetamine toxicity include euphoria, irritability, paranoia, impulsiveness, loss of emotional control, and rigid thinking that is often marked by an obsession with minor, unimportant details at the expense of the larger picture. Because these symptoms impair the user's ability to perceive events and the surrounding environment rationally, decision making also suffers.

NO SURRENDER
Hitler suffered from all of these symptoms and, at least as far as his generals were concerned, his thinking did indeed become impaired, especially his ability to make intelligent, rational decisions. A number of the generals assigned to Hitler's headquarters were convinced he was losing his mind.

One of the reasons the war in Europe ended in the spring of 1945 and not many months or even years later is that even as the tide of the war turned against Germany, Hitler irrationally demanded that his battlefield commanders hold every inch of ground they had conquered, even when their situations became hopeless. In late 1942, for example, General Friedrich von Paulus, commander of the Sixth Army, requested permission to withdraw his troops from the Russian city of Stalingrad to avoid being surrounded by a superior force of Russian troops. Hitler, who by now was receiving shots every day, responded with the lunatic reply that the Sixth Army could withdraw from Stalingrad, "provided that it could still hold Stalingrad." Unable to think of a way to abandon a position *and* hang onto it at the same time, von Paulus dutifully remained in the city. Stalingrad was surrounded a few weeks later, and in January 1943, the Sixth Army surrendered. As many as 800,000 Axis troops died in the Battle of Stalingrad, and when it ended, the 90,000 soldiers who survived it were marched off to Siberia. All but 6,000 perished.

Had Hitler allowed von Paulus to withdraw to a defensive position when requested, hundreds of thousands of German soldiers would have lived to fight another day, and the war might have dragged on for years. Instead, Stalingrad marked the turning point of the war and the beginning of the end for Nazi Germany. Who knows? We may have Dr. Morell and his amphetamines to thank for the war ending when it did.

MIND...AND BODY

In addition to the psychological side effects of amphetamine abuse, there are physical side effects, among them twitching, tremors, and what are called "stereotypes": compulsive behaviors, such as repeated picking at or biting of one's own skin. Hitler was twitchy, his head jerked uncontrollably, and he had tremors in spades—the shaking that began in his left hand soon spread down his left leg and then to his right hand. He also exhibited at least two types of stereotypical behavior: compulsively biting the skin around the fingernails of his thumbs, index fingers, and middle fingers, and picking and scratching at the skin on the back of his neck until it became infected.

The trembling in Hitler's left leg impaired his ability to walk normally, but there may be another explanation for the slow, foot-dragging shuffle and loss of motor function that he displayed at the end of his life. Chronic amphetamine abuse takes a terrible toll on the cardiovascular system and can cause both heart attacks and strokes. Electrocardiographs taken of Hitler's heart in July 1941 and again in September 1943 show a deterioration in heart function between the two dates that is consistent with a heart attack. And among Dr. Morell's surviving medical records is an article torn from a June 1943 medical journal that may provide another clue. Topic of the article: How to treat a heart attack.

Then, in February 1945, the Hestons write, "Hitler suffered at least one small stroke; but he may have had several, and, indeed, his rapid decline from this time onward suggests widespread vascular disease." The odds of a healthy 56-year-old man suffering both a heart attack *and* one or more strokes are "distinctly improbable," say the Hestons: "The most parsimonious explanation, given the lack of conclusive evidence, is to attribute both vascular events to the injection of intravenous amphetamine." By April 1945, Hitler was so close to death that had he not killed himself, it may have been just a matter of time before he dropped dead from amphetamine-induced "natural" causes.

SO LONG

Morell remained by Hitler's side until almost the very end...but not quite. Ironically, the cause of Hitler's falling-out with his beloved quack was an *injection*: Hitler had resigned himself to remaining in Berlin and committing suicide before the city fell to the Russians. Many in the Führer's inner circle wanted him to escape to the mountains of southern Germany, where it might have been possible for remnants of the military, led by Hitler, to hold out indefinitely. Hitler would hear none of it. He was determined to die in his capital, but he feared that his subordinates would drug him and take him out of Berlin against his will. And who better to administer the drugs than Morell? When the doctor came to Hitler on April 21 with yet another syringe filled with who-knows-what (probably just more amphetamines), the raging, paranoid Führer fired him on the spot. Not that Morell minded— by then the bombs were dropping on the führerbunker 24 hours a day, and he was desperate for an excuse to escape.

LAST GASP

Morell did make it out of Berlin, and he survived the war, but not by much. A few days after fleeing the city, he checked into a hospital complaining of heart problems. On July 17, 1945, he was arrested by the Americans and imprisoned. After investigators determined he wasn't guilty of any war crimes, he was released. Morell's health continued to deteriorate, and by June 1947 he was back in the hospital, where he remained bedridden until May 1948, when he died shortly after suffering a stroke.

PHRASE ORIGINS

We've heard these expressions before and perhaps even used them in conversation, but how many of us know where they come from?

DRAWING ROOM

It's a familiar scene in period films: After a party or banquet held in the home of a wealthy person, the ladies retreat into the drawing room, leaving the gentlemen behind to enjoy brandy and cigars. If you're like Uncle John, you've probably wondered why nobody ever *draws* in the drawing room. It turns out the name has nothing to do with drawing: It dates back to the days when large English country houses contained entire suites of rooms set aside for visiting royalty and other important guests, along with the servants and staff that accompanied them on such visits. Included in the suite were one or more "withdrawing rooms," parlors or living rooms that these guests could withdraw to for more privacy. Over time the name was shortened to *drawing* room.

JERKWATER TOWN

This term for a remote or unimportant town dates back to the days when towns were further apart than trains could travel without having to stop to take on fresh water for the boilers. When a train low on water came upon a pond or a creek running alongside the track, it stopped and the train crew hauled, or "jerked," buckets of water back to the train. (In some places water towers were set up and the boilerman swung a spigot arm over the train's water tender, then "jerked" on a chain to start the water flowing.) Small settlements often grew up in places where the trains were known to stop. These towns—in the middle of nowhere—came to be know as *jerkwater* towns.

BEAR HUG

Bears walk on all fours, but rear up on their hind legs when they lunge at other bears; two bears fighting can look like they're wrestling or even dancing. For centuries, people believed that they killed their prey and each other with giant, crushing hugs. (Hunters unlucky enough to find out how bears really killed their prey probably would have preferred a hug.)

IT'S A WEIRD, WEIRD CRIME

*In the history of the BRI, we've written about smart crooks,
dumb crooks, and even nice crooks. But these crimes were
committed by crooks of an entirely different breed.*

IF CONVICTED, HE WILL A-PEEL

In 2007 a man walked into a 7-Eleven in Monrovia, Maryland,
just past midnight and attempted a holdup. The unidentified
man didn't have a gun or any kind of weapon at all—he merely
demanded that the clerk give him money. The clerk refused, so
the man started picking up items off the counter to use as
weapons. After repeatedly hitting the clerk with a banana, the
attacker fled (empty-handed) before police arrived.

BED RIDDEN

Police in Ferrol, Spain, charged Antonio Navarro with driving
while intoxicated on a highway. He was only going 12 mph, and
he wasn't driving a car. Navarro is a quadriplegic, and police busted him driving his motorized bed on the freeway. Where did he
need to go in such a hurry? Navarro was on his way to a local
brothel.

SMALL CRIMES DIVISION

Swedish police are trying to bust a ring of thieves who steal
valuables from bus travelers' luggage. Criminal teams work in
twos: The first person rides inside the bus; the second, who by
the crime's nature must be a "little person," hides inside a suitcase. The suitcase is placed in the bus's baggage compartment…
and the weird (but clever) robbery begins. As soon as the baggage compartment door is closed, the little person comes out of
his suitcase and begins to rifle through other people's bags and
suitcases, looking for valuables. He pockets whatever he finds,
and then returns to his own suitcase before arrival at the destination. Police are looking at crime records to identify "criminals
of limited stature."

KIDNEY REMOVAL

In 2007 the Seattle Museum hosted "Bodies...The Exhibition," an educational display of preserved corpses and internal organs. One of the display kidneys was stolen. Police are still searching for the culprit, but do not fear the kidney will turn up on the black market, because even though the kidney is real, it's not "usable," as it's been filled and covered with plastic resin.

GETTING TANKED

Grand theft auto is a common crime; grand theft tank is not. At about 4:00 one morning in February 2009, an 18-year-old British army soldier stationed in northern Germany decided to steal one of his squadron's tanks. The unnamed serviceman, who had never driven one before, broke into the eight-ton Scimitar tank and made it about a third of a mile outside of his camp before the vehicle ran off the road and got stuck. So he returned to base and stole *another* tank. This time, British military police followed him. They blocked the soldier's path, forcing him to swerve and crash into a tree.

STOOL SAMPLE

Police in Newark, Ohio, arrested 28-year-old Kile Wygle for drunk driving in March 2009. But Wygle wasn't driving a car—he was driving a motorized bar stool, which he had built himself. (It's powered by a lawn mower engine.) Adding insult to injury was the fact that Wygle was the one who called police. He was riding his stool—drunk—at 20 mph. He lost control, fell off, and called 911 for medical assistance. Instead of paramedics, police arrived.

*   *   *

THE BRIDE WILL KEEP HER LAST NAME

In February 2009, a 20-year-old Florida woman named Kelly Hildebrandt did a search on the Internet for anybody with the same name as hers and found just one: a 20-year-old man in Lubbock, Texas. So she wrote him a note, and then he wrote back. After three weeks of increasingly flirtatious e-mails, he went to Coral Springs, Florida, to meet her in person. And in October 2009...Kelly Hildebrandt married Kelly Hildebrandt.

Swedish children dress up as witches and walk around neighborhoods collecting candy...on Easter.

SEE YOU LATER, NAVIGATOR

In the summer of 1972, the U.S. Air Force was in full crisis mode.
The enemy had made significant technological advances,
threatening all they had been fighting for. Russia?
China? No, the "enemy" was the Navy.

BATTLE FOR POSITION

Rivalries within the military can help boost morale. But they can also waste a lot of money as each branch of the service competes for funding to support its own weapons systems, its own airplanes, and its own way of doing things. That was the case in 1972 with the U.S. Air Force and the U.S. Navy.

A Naval Research Laboratory team headed by physicist Roger Easton had been making huge strides toward a satellite-based navigation system that would cover the entire world, making it possible to navigate ships with incredible accuracy, land a missile within a few feet of its target, and, as one engineer put it, "drop five bombs into the same hole."

Even before the Russians launched *Sputnik*, the first man-made satellite, in 1957, Easton had been working on a system in which dozens of satellites would broadcast time signals to Earth below. By comparing nanosecond differences in the arrival times of the satellites' signals, a ground receiver could decipher exactly where it was, within a few feet. Combining the words "time" and "navigation," Easton called his system "Timation."

LOST AND FOUND

Timation's benefits to the Navy were obvious. Although the military already had 43 different navigation systems, they were largely incompatible. Furthermore, there were entire expanses of ocean worldwide that weren't covered by *any* of the systems, making it hard for the Navy to accurately navigate, track ships and airplanes, or find lost and shipwrecked sailors. By the early 1970s, the Navy had launched four satellites to test Easton's ideas.

Average SAT score of an American millionaire: 1,190 out of 1,600.

As far as Air Force commanders were concerned, this would not do. They were, after all, the *Air* Force, and they jealously laid claim to anything that flew, hovered, or orbited. A challenge like this could not be left unanswered.

COUNTERATTACK

An Air Force response was already in the making. Months earlier they had convened a team of their own engineers, and then got in touch with a Raytheon engineer named Ivan Getting. For years, Getting had been telling anybody who'd listen about how an array of satellites could be used for navigation. One of the Air Force engineers remembered seeing Getting's cocktail-napkin sketches of satellites beaming signals to receivers on the ground, so they brought him in to help them beat the Navy. They came up with a navigation concept they called the "621B System," and in November 1972, the Air Force appointed a reluctant colonel and engineer named Bradford Parkinson to manage the program.

By the following summer, the Air Force had a basic concept that seemed feasible, at least on paper. They had to get their system approved by the Department of Defense to have any hope of moving ahead of the more developed Navy plan. Parkinson managed to arrange a meeting with a key DOD committee to pitch it. The committee, knowing of the Navy's program, voted no.

REGROUP AND TRY AGAIN

After the rejection, Parkinson was given a new task: Come up with a joint proposal *with* the Navy, and get the Army involved as well. He approached the task by first reviewing the plans in great detail over three months. His superiors pressured him to give preference to their 621B system, which made things difficult because it became clear that the Navy's was a much better plan—it was more accurate, more likely to work over the entire globe, more stable even if a few satellites went bad, less vulnerable to attack, and less expensive. Suddenly, his job had become more political than technical. How was he going to get the Air Force and the Army to accept the Navy plan?

Over the three-day Labor Day weekend, deliberately hosted in the empty Pentagon motel to get away from Air Force pressure, Parkinson's committee made a few (mostly cosmetic) changes to

Timation: They would solicit the Army's input on the system and perform tests on Army bases to get that branch's buy-in, and they would change the satellite's signal format to the one proposed by the Air Force in the belief that it was marginally harder to jam by hostile forces. (That turned out to be true, but the Air Force format also turned out to be weaker, resulting in a loss of signal inside buildings, in forests, and under heavy cloud cover.) The Air Force would also administer the program. In truth, however, the heart of the system was still the Navy's technology. In December of that year, the Department of Defense approved implementation of the program, and the renamed NAVSTAR Global Positioning System (GPS) would soon become a reality.

SORE WINNERS

Despite being given responsibility for the program, many of the Air Force brass were angry about the fact that development costs were going to come out of its budget, even though it would benefit all military branches and even civilians. But what really stuck in their collective craw was that their rival's plan had won.

The problem with engineers is that they're often not very good at politics. While Easton focused on making the system work, he lost control of his brainchild, and then he lost recognition for it as well. Despite the fact that the United States Patent Office issued him patents for the systems he invented, the Air Force began writing him out of the history of the GPS, giving the credit to Parkinson, who did deserve credit for his management skills, and Ivan Getting, who didn't deserve credit for anything except, as one account put it, "incubating GPS in his mind."

Sadly, the disinformation campaign worked. Throughout the 1970s and '80s, Easton rarely appeared in the histories of GPS, and when he did, it was as in an "also contributed" footnote. Parkinson and Getting got the press, the awards, and the places in the National Inventors' Hall of Fame; Easton continued quietly working in the Naval Research Lab.

More than two decades passed before Easton started to get belated public recognition. In 1997 the American Philosophical Society jointly awarded its prestigious Magellanic Premium to Parkinson and Easton (no mention of Getting). Easton was presented with the 2004 National Medal of Technology, with President George W. Bush citing "his extensive pioneering achievements in spacecraft tracking, navigation, and timing technology that led to the development of the NAVSTAR Global Positioning System (GPS)."

Despite that, many sources still slight Easton, citing Getting and Parkinson as the inventors of the GPS. So it's not surprising that in his acceptance of the Magellanic Premium, Easton revealed a touch of hurt feelings, saying, "On the Labor Day weekend, 1973, the Air Force accepted the Navy technology for satellite positioning, and here I salute Dr. Parkinson for knowing a good technology when he sees it."

* * *

THEY'RE HEIRLESS

Two of history's most important men have no direct descendants.

- **William Shakespeare** and his wife, Anne Hathaway, had three children: Susanna, born in 1583, and twins—a boy named Hamnet and a girl named Judith, born in 1585. Hamnet died of bubonic plague in 1596 at age 11. Judith married in 1616. She and her husband, winemaker Thomas Quiney, had three boys: Shakespeare Quiney, who died in infancy, and Richard and Thomas, who died at ages 21 and 20, respectively, having fathered no children. The line carried on only with Susanna, who married Dr. John Hall in 1607. Their only daughter, Elizabeth Hall, married but had no children. She, and the Shakespeare lineage, died in 1670.

- **Abraham Lincoln** and his wife, Mary Todd Lincoln, had four boys, but three died in childhood—Edward at age 4, Willie at 11, and Tad at 18. The only one to survive into adulthood was Robert Todd Lincoln (1843–1926), who served as secretary of war in the 1880s. He married Mary Harlan, daughter of an Iowa senator, in 1868, and they had three children: daughters Mary "Mamie" (b. 1869) and Jessie (b. 1875), and a son, Abraham II, nicknamed Jack (b. 1873). Abraham II died at age 16. Mamie married and had a son named Lincoln Isham in 1892. A musician, farmer, and socialite, he died in 1971, childless. Jessie married athlete Warren Beckwith in 1897. They had a daughter, Mary, and a son, Robert, neither of whom had any children. Robert Beckwith, the last direct descendant of Abraham Lincoln, died at age 71 in 1985.

THE NEW DEAL

A massive government effort to get people back to work and restart the economy, the New Deal had its detractors, then and now. But it remains one of the most popular and effective government programs in American history.

CRASH AND BURN

In October 1929, during the first year of Herbert Hoover's presidency, the U.S. stock market crashed. By 1933 unemployment had climbed from 4 percent to 25 percent, plunging the nation into the Great Depression. Hoover, a Republican, took a lot of the blame for it and was beaten by a landslide in his 1932 reelection bid by the Democratic candidate, former New York governor Franklin D. Roosevelt. FDR promised Americans a "New Deal"—sweeping government intervention to revive the economy, and new laws to make sure the collapse was never repeated. His legislation was quickly passed through Democrat-controlled Congress.

Although heavily criticized at the time as socialism or even communism, the New Deal put millions of Americans back to work, provided security to senior citizens, and in the process helped to stabilize the American economy. Most importantly, it gave Americans hope. Here's a look at some of the many agencies created in the New Deal to institute Roosevelt's reforms.

Federal Emergency Relief Administration. The first relief agency of the New Deal, it provided emergency welfare and aid. More than $3 billion was allocated to states and cities for homeless shelters, soup kitchens, and vaccinations, as well as literacy training and free childcare for job-seeking parents. FERA also provided temporary work for as many as 20 million people—construction and maintenance jobs, such as repairing public buildings, laying sewer pipe, and raking leaves for $15 per week. The agency was terminated in 1935, and its projects were absorbed into other programs.

National Recovery Administration. The aim of the NRA was to stimulate economic recovery by asking businesses to set a 40-

cents-per-hour minimum wage and standardizing the work week at 40 hours for white-collar jobs and 36 for blue-collar. More than 23 million people worked under NRA-abiding companies, but violations of the code were common. Also, participation by firms was voluntary, so the agency really didn't have a lot of authority. In 1935 the Supreme Court declared the NRA unconstitutional because the federal government had overstepped state labor laws. Nevertheless, minimum-wage and work-hour laws were later passed by Congress.

Civilian Conservation Corps. Not only did the CCC raise awareness of the importance of preserving natural resources, but in doing so it created 250,000 conservation, forestry, and land improvement jobs in 2,600 locations. Nicknamed by workers "Roosevelt's Tree Army," CCC workers planted more than three billion trees from 1933 to 1942, accounting for half of all organized planting in American history. But "conservation" meant a lot of things for the CCC—workers constructed fire towers, built 100,000 miles of fire roads, fought and prevented wildfires, preserved wildlife habitats, controlled floods, and prevented soil erosion. One clever element of the CCC was how it reallocated labor surpluses to areas where there were labor shortages. American cities had far too many needy workers, so the CCC moved them to sparsely populated rural areas, where there was work to be done and few to do it.

Public Works Administration. In one of the first New Deal programs enacted in 1933, the government allocated $4 billion for the construction of what was ultimately 34,000 projects, including airports, highways, aircraft carriers, bridges (including San Francisco's Golden Gate Bridge), hospitals, and schools. By June 1934, the PWA had planned all of its projects and allocated all of its money. So in 1935, Congress created a new agency called the Works Progress Administration to develop more civic construction and job creation programs in the same vein.

Works Progress Administration. Picking up where the PWA left off, the WPA employed 8.5 million people between 1935 and '43 at an average wage of $2 per day for civic construction projects, such as roads (650,000 miles), bridges (78,000), buildings (125,000), and 700 miles of airport runways. The WPA was the nation's largest "employer" at the time, and the largest New Deal agency—it spent $11 billion over its life span. Some WPA projects still in existence: Dealey Plaza in Dallas (where John F. Kennedy was shot in 1963), LaGuardia Airport in New York, Timberline Lodge in Oregon, and the presidential retreat Camp David (which was initially a resort for all federal employees). One notable branch of the agency was the Arts Program, which hired thousands of artists, musicians, actors, photographers, and writers to use their talents for public works. For example, future major authors Saul Bellow and Ralph Ellison wrote state guidebooks, and painter Jackson Pollock produced murals.

Federal Deposit Insurance Corporation. During the Depression, consumers lost faith in banks. Many had failed and closed suddenly, and their customers' money was irretrievably lost. But banks are an important part of the financial system—no modern economy can function without them. Created by the Glass-Steagall Banking Reform Act of 1933, the FDIC restored faith in banks with a government-backed insurance policy on deposits. If a bank failed, a consumer's account was insured up to $5,000. (Today, the guarantee is $250,000.)

Agricultural Adjustment Administration. In order to increase the market price of crops and livestock, and thereby make farms financially stable again, there had to be either a greater demand or less supply. The AAA paid farmers a subsidy to grow less. The AAA opened in May 1933, by which point the year's crops were already planted. Since it was too late to pay farmers not to plant, the agency destroyed existing stockpiles and reduced the size of livestock herds. Twenty-five percent of the nation's cotton fields were razed, and six million piglets and 220,000 pregnant cows were slaughtered. Destroying crops while so many Americans struggled to put food on the table made the AAA very controversial. Besides, it didn't work—large farms benefited most; they simply evicted tenant farmers and sharecroppers, let the land go fallow, then collected a fee from the government. And by 1937, wholesale food prices hadn't changed much from before the AAA went into effect.

Federal Housing Administration. During the Depression, home mortgages were mostly short-term—about 3 to 5 years, as opposed to the 30-year standard of today. The FHA, born out of the National Housing Act of 1934, regulated interest rates and mortgage terms so home ownership was more within reach for middle- and low-income families. The agency also helped to ensure that enough affordable housing existed for purchase by offering loans for home-building companies, which had suffered greatly in the economic downturn.

Securities and Exchange Commission. Fraud, deception, and insider trading contributed to the stock market crash, so in an attempt to make sure it never happened again, Congress passed the Securities Exchange Act in 1934. In addition to requiring disclosure of a company's financial information and dealings to investors, it made securities (stock) fraud a crime and established the Securities and Exchange Commission. Its five commissioners are appointed by the president to police the financial world.

National Labor Relations Board. Created by the National Labor Relations Act of 1935, the board's purpose was to protect and enhance the rights of workers to organize into unions and collectively bargain for better wages and better working conditions.

Farm Security Administration. Formed by the Resettlement Administration Act of 1935, this agency delivered aid to the nearly one million farm families who'd fled the Dust Bowl agricultural disaster in Arkansas and Oklahoma for California, as well as those evicted by farm bosses after AAA subsidies. The FSA purchased ruined farms from victims of the Dust Bowl and relocated the farmers to 34 government-owned group farms, where they grew food for themselves while learning modern techniques from agriculture scientists. The FSA also set up refugee camps for farmers and provided educational grants to farm families. But the most famous project of the FSA was its photography branch—it sent out photographers, most notably Gordon Parks and Dorothea Lange, to document the plight of the Depression-era farmers.

Social Security Administration. The SSA provided financial assistance for single mothers, a free food program for children of low-income families, and unemployment insurance. But most famously, the SSA created and managed a federal pension system for retired people. Not only did it allow aging citizens to retire from the workforce (without starving), it also opened up their jobs to new workers. Social Security payments were financed by a payroll tax, and they still are: It remains in effect today, covering 40 million people and accounting for a quarter of the federal budget.

*　　*　　*

PRESIDENTIAL GAFFES

• When Indian Prime Minister Rajiv Gandhi was in the U.S. on an official visit in 1985, President Ronald Reagan held a 30-minute one-on-one talk with him. "They really hit it off," one White House official reported. "It was a warm, cordial session." The gaffe? At the end of the meeting Gandhi tactfully pointed out that none of the points the president had made had anything to do with India. Reagan had in fact studied and repeated notes that related to the King of Jordan.

• In 1977 President Jimmy Carter was riding in an elevator with chief of protocol Shirley Temple Black. When the elevator stopped, Black stepped aside and said, "After you, Mr. President." That was correct protocol, but Carter felt it was ungentlemanly for him to leave the elevator before Black. After the two argued about it for a while, an aide finally pushed them both off the elevator at the same time.

• While on a 12-day trip through the western Pacific in 1992, President George H. W. Bush came down with an intestinal flu. He carried on with his schedule anyway, but he still wasn't feeling well at a state dinner in the home of Japanese Prime Minister Kiichi Miyazawa...and threw up all over himself. The prime minister held Bush's head in his lap until the president had recovered sufficiently to walk to his limo for a speedy return to the guest suite at Akasaka Palace. For the short walk, Mr. Bush wore a green overcoat given to him by a Secret Service agent to cover up the unsightly mess on his suit. The incident inspired the birth of a new Japanese verb: *bushusuru*—to do a Bush, or "to commit an instance of embarrassing public vomiting."

STING OF THE STING RAY

Zora Arkus-Duntov may be the "Father of the Corvette," but as the years progressed, the car diverged further and further from his vision of what it should be. Here's Part IV of our story; Part III is on page 429.

BORN AGAIN
For all the improvements that had been made in the Corvette over the years from 1953 to 1962, the car's chassis and suspension hadn't changed much from the 1953 model, which borrowed its components from ordinary Chevy sedans. A mechanical redesign was long overdue, and for the 1963 model year the Corvette got one, along with a styling makeover, both inside the car and out. So many changes were made to the 1963 model, in fact, that it is considered the beginning of the "second generation" of Corvettes, not just an improved version of the original car.

Duntov replaced the existing chassis with one that was much stiffer, to give it better handling. He also upgraded the front suspension and replaced the rear "solid-axle" suspension entirely, giving the 1963 Corvette its first independent rear suspension, which produced another huge improvement in handling.

HIGH WATERMARK

Many purists consider the 1963 Corvette to be the best model in the car's history of 50+ years, and much of this is due to Duntov's work under the hood. But it's also due to the Corvette's change in body style, which was breathtaking. Dubbed the Sting Ray, the new Corvette had a look partially inspired by a Mako Shark that Bill Mitchell, Harley Earl's successor as the head of GM's styling department, had caught while deep-sea fishing off the island of Bimini.

The Sting Ray was available as a convertible or—for the first time—as a 2-door coupe. And what a coupe! The car's most distinguishing features were its "fastback" roofline that tapered almost to a point at the rear of the car, and a split rear window (abandoned the following year) that made the 1963 coupe arguably the most collectible Corvette of all. That model was also the first to feature concealed pop-up headlights, which would remain a 'Vette trademark for the next 41 years.

Premature infants are five times more likely to be left-handed.

HARLEY'S GHOST

The '63 Corvette was the first one that could give European sports cars like Jaguars and even Ferraris a real run for their money, and it had a beautiful look that was all its own. Publicly, Duntov was proud of the new car. "For the first time, I now have a Corvette that I can be proud to drive in Europe," he told reporters at the car's debut. But privately, he was frustrated at having lost so many battles over the car's design. The Sting Ray's exciting new body style was the work of stylist Larry Shinoda, not Duntov.

In a sense, Duntov wasn't too concerned about what the cars he worked on looked like. He valued performance over everything else. If a styling feature improved a car's operation or enhanced the driver's ability to operate the vehicle, he was for it. If it didn't, he was indifferent at best and vehemently opposed at worst. A sports car inspired by a *shark*? What for? The coupe's split rear window in particular drove him to distraction. Dividing the window in two with a vertical bar may have looked cool, but it obstructed the driver's ability to see behind the car, which was what the rear window was there for in the first place.

But the designers in the Styling department had the final say on the car's appearance, and they were in the dreamboat business—they made cars that people lusted for, cars that people had to have *right now*. If splitting the rear window in two and adding fake scoops and air vents was what it took to get the kids drooling, Bill Mitchell had the power to make it happen, no matter how loudly Duntov objected.

MIDDLEMAN

If Duntov had ever risen high enough at Chevrolet to dictate the design of the Corvette, it would have eventually become a mid-engined car (with the motor behind the seats), because he believed that a mid-engine configuration was the next logical step in improving the Corvette's performance. He proposed the idea in 1963 and again in 1968, and he even managed to get a few mid-engined concept cars built. But his political skills were never the match of his engineering skills, and he never did gain enough clout at GM to realize his dream.

When work began on the third-generation Corvette in the late 1960s, Duntov became increasingly upset by the direction this new car was taking. Mechanically it had little that was new or improved. And stylistically, thanks again to Larry Shinoda's skill as a designer, it looked even more like a shark than before, complete with gill-shaped vents on the left and right front fenders. Duntov complained so frequently about the new car that he was "promoted" to a new role as a Corvette public relations figurehead (he was the Father of the Corvette, after all), which effectively cut him off from any further say in the design of the car.

FROM A LEMON, LEMONADE

The only thing that saved Duntov from permanent exile was the fact that the all-new 1968 Corvette was an even bigger disaster than the first Corvette had been in 1953. For one thing, the new body style interfered with the cooling system, causing the engine to overheat. And the roofline was so low that the seat backs had to be tilted back from 25° to an uncomfortable 33°, an angle akin to a living-room recliner, which caused the occupants to continually slide forward in their seats while the car was in motion.

Quality control was another big problem. When *Car & Driver* received a Corvette to test-drive, it was in such bad shape that they refused to accept it. "The car was unfit for a road test," the magazine complained. "No amount of envious gawking by the spectators could make up for the disappointment we felt at the car's shocking lack of quality control. With less than 2,000 miles on it, the Corvette was falling apart." The magazine's scathing review not only got Duntov his old job back, it got him a new title to go with it: Chief Engineer of the Corvette.

SHARK ATTACK

As disappointing as the 1968 Corvette was to Duntov and the automotive press, the car's exciting new look struck a chord with the buying public. They snapped up more than 28,000 that year—a new record. *Car & Driver* may not have liked it, but the magazine's readers voted it the "Best All-Around Car in the World." Sales of the new Corvette remained impressive for the rest of the decade, even as quality control continued to be a problem, and the phasing in of new federal emissions regulations caused the car to lose horsepower from one year to the next.

LOSING ITS STING

Duntov hit GM's mandatory retirement age of 65 in December 1974. Professionally speaking, it wasn't a bad time for him to go. GM was so busy grappling with the energy crisis and changing federal emissions and fuel economy standards that it didn't have money to spare for developing the next generation of Corvette. The car's horsepower sank to 165 hp in 1975, down from 270 in 1971, and remained low for the rest of the decade. That didn't hurt the car's popularity, though: Sales passed the 40,000 mark for the first time in 1978 and hit an all-time high of 53,807 cars the following year. For all its problems, the Sting Ray became the longest-running, bestselling series of Corvettes ever, lasting from 1968 through the 1982 model year.

Duntov lived to see the Corvette regain much of the performance it had lost during the 1970s. Thanks to advances in automotive technology, the horsepower in the fourth-generation Corvette, introduced in 1983, began to climb again, reaching 230 hp by 1985 and 300 by 1992. And Duntov lived to see work completed on the fifth generation, 345-hp Corvettes, introduced in 1997, as well. He died in April 1996 at the age of 86, just months before the models began arriving on showroom floors. (The sixth-generation, 400-hp Corvette made its debut in 2005.)

DROP IN FOR A VISIT SOMETIME

At Duntov's request, his ashes were interred at the National Corvette Museum in Bowling Green, Kentucky, which is also home to the auto plant where Corvettes have been manufactured since 1981. The ashes are part of an exhibit that commemorates Duntov's life and work. Look for them near the display that showcases a copy of his memo, "Thoughts Pertaining to Youth, Hot-Rodders and Chevrolet."

*   *   *

POP QUIZ

Q: How long does it take to completely digest a meal?
A: About 12 hours.

Q. What was the TV character MacGuyver's first name?
A. Angus.

...would cost $15.6 septillion to build—roughly a trillion times the amount of money in the world.

TALES FROM THE MORGUE

*A few short pieces about death and dying
to remind you that it's good to be alive.*

WHERE'S HEDVIGA? Hedviga Golik of Zagreb, Croatia, was reported missing in 1966—her neighbors hadn't seen her for a few days and assumed she had moved away. The police finally found her…in 2008. She was at home, sitting in a chair in front of the television. Now a skeleton, Golik had been dead since 1966, when she had first been reported missing. (Authorities can't explain why she wasn't discovered sooner.)

IT WORKED TOO WELL. In 2004 the University Medical Center in Leiden, the Netherlands, made a public plea to Dutch citizens: Donate your body to the center so medical students could use it as a hands-on learning tool. Four years later, the University Medical Center asked Dutch citizens to *stop* donating their bodies—so many had been donated that there were now more bodies than students. Two out of every three bodies donated were used; the third had to be discarded.

THE LATEST THING. There are only so many ways to dispose of a dead body—interment (above- or below-ground), cremation, and now, according to *Funeral Industry Insider*, dissolving it in caustic chemicals. Technically called *alkaline hydrolysis*, the process involves an undertaker placing a body in a steel drum, filling it with lye, and then heating and pressurizing it until the remains condense into a brown fluid similar in consistency to motor oil. It's sterile, so it can simply be poured down the drain. The small amount of bone residue is returned to the family in an urn.

BRING OUT YOUR DEAD. Great Britain isn't very large, and it's been inhabited for millennia. Result: The British are running out of burial space. So in 2007 the government announced that the dead would have to start sharing burial plots. Caskets buried for more than 100 years will be exhumed so that their holes can be dug deeper. The caskets will then be returned to the ground so when the time comes, there's space for a new "upstairs neighbor."

It figures: Hugh Hefner owns the burial crypt next to Marilyn Monroe's.

SURF'S UP!

From the warm-water beaches in South America to the frigid waters off the North Coast of Scotland, if it can be surfed it probably has been. But it wasn't too long ago that the sport was unknown outside of Hawaii.

HE'E NALU

For at least 3,000 years, seafaring Polynesians who settled the many island chains in the Pacific Ocean have been surfing. The Hawaiian Islands were among the last that the settlers reached, sometime around 400 A.D. These pioneers depended on the ocean for their livelihood and were skilled at navigating the white water that surrounded their island homes. Their surfing skills were a byproduct of their canoeing skills—the ability to pilot a canoe through heavy surf onto an unprotected beach was key to their survival. Early Hawaiians called the sport *he'e nalu*, or "wave sliding," and rode two different types of boards: *Olo* boards were 16 to 18 feet long (or even longer) and could weigh 150 pounds or more. More common was the shorter type of board called *alaia*. At 8 to 10 feet long, it was lighter and more maneuverable than the olo, and is the forerunner of the modern surfboard.

WALKING ON WATER

Surfing played a huge role in Hawaiian culture. The most revered wave riders were called *ali'i*, or "high class." They were often political leaders who competed against each other while entire communities cheered from the beach. The priests, or *kahunas*, would pray each morning for good waves. Surfboard construction also had a set of rituals, performed in beachfront temples dedicated to the art. But it wasn't just the leaders who surfed—nearly everyone in old Hawaii rode the waves, regardless of age, gender, or class.

When British explorer Captain James Cook's Third Pacific Expedition arrived there in 1778, his men thought their eyes were playing tricks on them—the natives were zipping through the sea while standing upright on wooden planks. One sailer wrote, "The boldness and address with which I saw them perform these difficult and dangerous maneuvers was altogether astonishing and is scarcely to be believed."

WIPEOUT

Although the Europeans who first landed in Hawaii were awed by the native surf culture, the missionaries who came later were not amused. They disliked the idea of scantily clad natives frolicking on the beach, so they tried to suppress the sport. In the century after Captain Cook's arrival, the native population of Hawaii dropped from an estimated 300,000 to just 40,000—and surfing nearly vanished. Fortunately, the determined Hawaiians who survived 19th-century colonialism refused to stop riding the waves.

And later visitors were just as impressed as Cook's men had been. On a trip to Hawaii in the 1860s, Mark Twain gave "surf-bathing" a try. "I got the board placed right," he wrote, "and at the right moment, too; but missed the connection myself. The board struck the shore in three-quarters of a second, without any cargo, and I struck the bottom about the same time, with a couple of barrels of water in me."

By the turn of the 20th century, tourism had become integral to the Hawaiian economy for both natives and non-natives. White businessmen romanticized the island culture, with surfing at its center. Native Hawaiians found that one of the few ways to earn a living was by providing tourists with an "authentic" island experience. One such tourist was novelist and newspaper correspondent Jack London, who took a surfing lesson at Waikiki Beach in 1907 with a 23-year-old "beach boy" of mixed Hawaiian and Irish descent named George Freeth. In a magazine article titled "The Royal Sport," London described Freeth as "a young god bronzed with sunburn" who "leaped upon the back of the sea" and stood "calm and superb, poised on the giddy summit...flying as fast as the surge on which he stands."

CALIFORNIA DREAMIN'

Twain's and London's colorful accounts caught the attention of mainlanders looking for new adventures. In a bid to bring that island culture the States, a wealthy California businessman named Henry Huntington hired Freeth to come to California and give regularly scheduled surfing demonstrations. Huntington's goal: To promote the seaside town of Redondo Beach. He'd recently built a rail line connecting it to Los Angeles, and Freeth was instrumental in convincing the citizens of L.A. that a weekend at the beach was a good way to spend their leisure money. Once the idea caught on, Huntington made a fortune selling oceanfront property. Southern Californians came out in droves to see Freeth ride the waves—and many didn't want to go back home at the end of the weekend.

Another surfing ambassador, Olympic swimming star Duke Kahanamoku, came to California in 1912 and gave similar demonstrations. He'd go on to become the most famous surfer of the early 1900s.

Solidifying its place as a viable sport, in 1928 Californians organized the Pacific Coast Surfriding Championships at Corona Del Mar and held the event annually until it was interrupted by World War II in 1941. After the war, California culture exploded. Americans from all over the country headed west in droves to take advantage of the good jobs and the booming economy. With an ever-increasing number of people on the beach, just one last piece remained to move surfing from a niche hobby to a national phenomenon: the development of cheap, lightweight, mass-produced surfboards.

BUSTIN' SURFBOARDS

Until the late 1940s, boards were made of solid wood and weighed 80 to 100 pounds. It took a great deal of physical strength and determination to wrestle one of those old planks through the waves. That all changed when board makers figured out how to seal lightweight balsa wood inside of a thin layer of fiberglass resin. These new boards were about 10 feet long, weighed only 20 to 30 pounds, and were far more buoyant than their heavier predecessors. In time, expensive balsa wood was replaced by molded plastic foam, making true mass production possible for the first time. With that, surfing suddenly became a lot cheaper...and a lot easier.

And just as it had in Hawaii centuries before, surfing became more than just a sport, but the center of an entire culture—in this case, pop culture. It began in 1957 when Hollywood screenwriter Frederick Kohner created a character based on his teenage daughter's exploits in the burgeoning surf scene at Malibu Beach. He named the character Gidget, short for "Girl Midget." The *Gidget* franchise went on to include seven novels, three films, and a television series. Surf movies became drive-in staples: Elvis Presley rode the waves in 1961 in *Blue Hawaii*; and in 1966 filmmaker

Bruce Brown made what has become the classic surf documentary, *The Endless Summer*, which followed two surfers as they spent the summer chasing waves around the globe.

By the mid-1960s, teenagers from the quiet shores of the east coast to the land-locked Midwest were watching Gidget movies and listening to the Beach Boys. Those kids dreamed of moving to California to take up the surfing lifestyle. And they did—in droves.

WAVE GOODBYE

For the old guard of surfers who'd pioneered the California version of the sport, all this new attention wasn't necessarily a good thing. More than the Hollywood sanitization of their lifestyle, they grumbled that their once-pristine beaches had become crowded overnight. Many of them left California and relocated to Hawaii...or to wherever on Earth they could find big waves.

That emigration, along with the advent of wetsuits for surfing cold waters, made the possibilities endless. In the chilly seas off Alaska, extreme surfers wait for chunks of glacier to fall into the sea and then try to ride the massive waves they cause. In the Amazon River, waves from the Atlantic Ocean, known as *tidal bores*, can roll 100 miles or more upstream from where the river meets the ocean. Surfers sometimes ride a single wave for as long as half an hour, covering distances up to seven miles.

Yet Hawaii remains the mecca to surfers the world over. Enthusiasts make pilgrimages to the islands not just for the near-perfect conditions, but also to surf the same waves where the kings of old perfected the art so many generations ago.

RANDOM FACTS

• One of the strangest surfing records was set in the summer of 2005 at a surfing competition in Australia: 47 surfers rode together on one giant, 40-foot, 1,200-pound surfboard.

• The most surfers ever to ride a single wave was 73, set in 2006 at Muizenberg Corner, a beach in Cape Town, South Africa.

• Dave "Daily" Webster of Bodega Bay, California, surfed every day from September 3, 1975 to February 29, 2009—10,407 days in a row. (He worked nights so he'd never miss an opportunity to catch a wave.)

No wonder you can see through it: Peeling Scotch Tape off its roll emits X-rays.

THE PHYSICS OF SURFING

On page 463, we told you the history of surfing. Here's how they do it.

On page 463

CATCH A WAVE

When a surfer rides a wave toward shore, it may look as though the board and rider are being propelled by the rushing water. But they're not. In fact, the act of surfing is more like riding a skateboard down a hill. The difference is that a surfer is sliding down the face of a hill made of water.

An ocean wave moves through water that stays relatively still. Think of a gull floating in the ocean. When a wave comes along, the gull floats up to the top and then back down without being carried along with it. Waves don't carry water—or anything else—with them until they break on the beach.

When a wave breaks, it's because it has run into land. Half of a wave is above the water's surface and the other half is below. As the wave approaches the beach, it moves into shallower water. The bottom of the wave slows down when it begins to run into the ocean floor, but the top keeps going just as fast. As the top of the wave outpaces the bottom, the moving hill of water gets steeper until it breaks into white water and falls in front of itself with incredible weight and force. It's as the wave stands up and gets ready to break that a surfer wants to begin sliding down its face.

GET ON BOARD

• Surf boards come in all shapes and sizes, but are divided into two broad categories: Long boards and short boards.

• Long boards generally range from 9 to 12 feet long. Because of their greater size and mass, they offer more stability but are not as maneuverable as short boards. Beginning surfers usually start with long boards and move up to smaller boards as their skills improve.

• Why is there a fin on the bottom of a surfboard? It provides stability and prevents the board from sliding sideways.

HOW TO TELL IF YOU'VE BEEN ABDUCTED BY ALIENS

Believe it or not, there is a support group called Abduct Anon for people who believe they've been kidnapped by extraterrestrials. Are you about to be abducted by aliens and subjected to medical experiments? Or has it happened already? Here are some signs that Abduct Anon and other UFO groups say you should be on the watch for.

AT BEDTIME
• You have chronic insomnia, and you hear a tapping or humming noise just as you're dropping off to sleep.

• You may dream of aliens and UFOs directly, or you may dream of vaguely mysterious beings but remember none of the details except one: The beings had very large eyes.

• You have the feeling you're being watched, especially as you're dropping off to sleep. Or you wake up in the middle of the night because you think someone—or some*thing*—is watching you. You may even see one or more shadowy figures standing around the bed, staring at you.

• You sleepwalk. You've gone to sleep in one place and woken up in another with no explanation for how it happened. (And alcohol is not involved.)

• For the first few seconds or minutes after awakening, you are paralyzed and cannot move your body.

• When you wake up you find small drops of blood on your pillow, but there's no explanation for how they got there.

ON THE ROAD
• Your car breaks down unexpectedly with no explanation, often soon after you've spotted a UFO.

• You pull over to the side of the road...and the next thing you remember is standing next to or driving your car. Hours or even

---

A bear named Voytek helped carry ammunition for Polish troops during World War II.

days may have passed, but you have no memory of what has happened in the meantime. Your "broken-down" car is running again, and you have no explanation for that, either.

• You have the sense that you have levitated or passed through solid objects such as the doors or roof of your car, perhaps as the aliens lifted you into their spacecraft.

DURING THE DAY

• You see smoke, fog, or haze at a time and in a place for which there is no logical explanation.

• You have an unexplained, irresistible desire to walk or drive to a particular location, where you believe something "familiar, yet unknown" will soon happen. You may experience a heightened level of anxiety in the days leading up to this strange happening.

PHYSICAL CHANGES

• You begin to get frequent nosebleeds and you don't know why.

• You have unexplained soreness or stiffness, or a mysterious rash on one or more parts of your body. There may also be evidence that your skin has been scraped (and a sample taken).

• You find new scars on your body and you have no idea how they got there. (And alcohol is not involved.)

• When you go in for your annual physical, your doctor finds strange, tiny probes implanted in your body.

WHAT'S UP, DOC?

• You may have a dim memory of a very *probing* (hint, hint) medical exam conducted against your will.

• You may also have memories of having your head placed in some kind of restraining device as long needles are inserted into your nostrils or ears, or something drills into your skull. These sensations may be accompanied by a burning smell. Human medical examiners who look you over after the fact find no signs that such procedures have taken place.

AFTER THE FACT

• There may be evidence that the scene of your abduction has

Only 109 of the world's mountains are higher than 24,000 feet. 96 of them are in the Himalayas.

have been "staged" to look as if nothing has happened, but a few incorrect details might be noticeable. For example, if you went to bed wearing pajamas, you may wake up nude or dressed only in underwear, with the pajamas folded neatly and placed at the foot of the bed. You may even wake up in the wrong room of the house. If you were abducted from your car, you may find that items in the car or in the trunk have been moved around.

• Your ability to remember things suddenly becomes stronger, and you may even develop psychic powers that enable you to see events in the future.

• You suddenly get a sense of mission or the feeling that you have been chosen (by the aliens) for an important purpose, but you don't know what it is. This often replaces feelings of low self-esteem that you had before the alien encounter.

• Electronic appliances behave strangely when you pass by. Computers crash, clocks lose time, radio and TV reception is distorted, and streetlights go dark as you walk under them.

• You develop a new phobia of some kind. Did you suddenly become afraid of spiders? Heights? Enclosed spaces? Crowds? The aliens may be to blame.

• You become obsessive-compulsive or develop addictions that you didn't have before.

• You become less trusting of other people, especially doctors, police, and other authority figures, than you were before.

• You have an uncontrollable urge to take vitamins.

• You develop an interest in UFOs, astronomy, or physics. Or, conversely, an aversion to being around other people when they are discussing these subjects.

...DON'T LEAVE EARTH WITHOUT IT
If this topic has unsettled you, fear not! The St. Lawrence Agency of Altamonte Springs, Florida, sells a UFO abduction insurance policy that pays out $10 million, with a double-indemnity payment of $20 million "if the aliens insist on conjugal visits." Cost: $19.95 plus $3.00 for same-day shipping. The policy pays out $1 per year for 10 million years or until the death of the policy holder, whichever comes first.

THE LIFE AND TIMES OF JAR JAR BINKS

*He could've gone down in movie history as
more than just another character in the* Star Wars
*saga, because he really was a pioneer in digital filmmaking.
In the end, Jar Jar did become a cultural phenomenon, though
for all the wrong reasons. Here's his fascinating—and tragic—story.*

WE WAITED FOR THIS?
May 19, 1999, was a pop culture milestone: *Star Wars Episode I: The Phantom Menace*, the first *Star Wars* movie in 16 years, opened in the United States. It set a single-day box-office record, bringing in $28 million. More than two million people took the day off of work to see it. And what did those fans get after all of the hype? A movie that drew mixed reviews at best.

And as the summer rolled on, one name kept popping up in news reports and on Internet message boards: Jar Jar Binks. While there was some disagreement as to whether the rest of the film worked, the alien sidekick character was almost universally reviled. A typical review came from the *Village Voice*: "Jar Jar sucks the oxygen out of every scene he's in." So what went wrong?

SUPPORTING CAST

While outlining *The Phantom Menace* in the mid-1990s, *Star Wars* creator George Lucas wanted a character that served the same purpose as R2-D2 and C-3PO had in the original trilogy—someone who had no special abilities but could comment on the proceedings, provide comic relief, and even help out in the end.

So he created Jar Jar Binks, member a race of amphibian-like creatures called Gungans who live on the planet Naboo. In the movie, we learn that Jar Jar's people banished him from their underwater city because he's clumsy. While living on the surface, Jar Jar meets two Jedi knights who are on a mission to warn the planet's human population of an imminent invasion. Jar Jar joins forces with the good guys, gets in all sorts of trouble, makes a lot

---

In 1916 Will Coltharp sent an entire building through the mail...one brick at a time.

of wisecracks, provides plot exposition for younger viewers, and ends up an unwitting hero in the final battle.

Lucas had another goal for Jar Jar: to make him the first 100 percent computer-generated character who interacts with live actors. So Jar Jar couldn't be a puppet (like Yoda) or a man in a suit (like Chewbacca). Instead, his exaggerated movements, floppy ears, and long snout were created by Industrial Light & Magic. Helping bring the character to life was a dancer named Ahmed Best, who provided Jar Jar's voice and big, loping movements. "I wore what's called a motion capture suit, which is like a tight scuba suit with a bunch of light sensors on it," he recalled. "They had infrared cameras that caught the light-sensor data and input that into a computer." Then digital animators "painted" Binks over the infrared images of Best. The process took nearly two years and resulted in the first completely digitized principle character in movie history. But that wasn't what people were talking about.

A STAR IS TORN

The first thing that annoyed viewers was Jar Jar's squeaky voice and fractured grammar: "Mesa day startin' pretty okee-day with a brisky morning munchy, then BOOM! Gettin' very scared and grabbin' that Jedi and POW! Mesa here!"

People didn't merely dislike Jar Jar Binks—they *hated* him. Several organizations sprang up calling for the alien's head, such as the "Society for the Extermination of Jar Jar Binks" and "Jar Jar Binks Must Die!"—which was also the title of a song by the rap group Damn Nation. Sample lyrics: "He's got big freakin' ears, and eyes like a bug / Every time I eat a taco I see his ugly mug." (People were also upset by the rampant use of the character in TV commercials.) One *Star Wars* fan, Mike Nichols, was so disappointed by *Episode I* that he recut the film on his home computer—removing most of Jar Jar's scenes and dialogue—and released it online as *The Phantom Edit*...to rave reviews.

And then there were the accusations of racism. To some critics, Jar Jar's dialect, combined with his long "dreadlocks-style" ears, were reminiscent of drugged-out Jamaicans. To Brent Staples of the *New York Times*, "Jar Jar lopes along in a combination shuffle and pimp walk. Binks is by far the stupidest person in the film.

His simple-minded devotion to his (white) Jedi masters has reminded people of Hollywood's most offensive racial stereotypes."

THE FILMMAKERS STRIKE BACK

Suddenly, instead of celebrating the achievement of the first digital character, Lucas was defending him. He wasn't caught completely off guard, though—many older filmgoers didn't like the "cute" Ewoks from 1983's *Return of the Jedi*, either. His standard defense: "The movies are for children but the older fans don't want to admit that. They want the films to be tough like *The Terminator*." Lucas maintained that he didn't model the alien after African Americans or Jamaicans. Jar Jar, he said, was a combination of Charlie Chaplin, Jimmy Stewart, and Danny Kaye. And his exaggerated walk wasn't a "pimp walk," it was an effect of his amphibious nature—Jar Jar walks as if he's swimming. Concerning the alien's voice, Lucas charged that those critiques were made by people "who've obviously never met a Jamaican, because it's definitely not Jamaican and if you were to say those lines in Jamaican they wouldn't be anything like that." Best, an African American, also denied the voicework was racist, explaining that he and the filmmakers wanted it to sound "fun."

DEMOTED

Jar Jar's role was greatly reduced in 2002's *Episode II: Attack of the Clones*. He appears only in a few scenes, though one is crucial to the greater story arc: He's been appointed representative of Naboo, and is unwittingly duped into making a motion in the Galactic Senate that will grant absolute power to Supreme Chancellor Palpatine. Without realizing it, Jar Jar is instrumental in turning Palpatine into the evil emperor, the saga's true villain.

In *Episode III*, Jar Jar makes only one cameo appearance. Though Lucas maintains he'd always planned to cut back on the part, movie insiders insist that it was actually done in response to the massively negative reaction.

Adding insult to injury, all of the technical accolades Lucas was expecting for Jar Jar never happened. Instead, they were bestowed upon the similarly rendered character of Gollum in 2002's *The Lord of the Rings: The Two Towers*. Gollum's creators, not Jar Jar's, won the Academy Award. (Jar Jar supporters are quick to point out that among all of the problems people have with him, most viewers take his presence on the screen for granted, at least proving the filmmakers got that part right.)

ATTACK OF THE CLOWNS

Today, Jar Jar is still disliked, having been named in several polls "the most annoying character in movie history." But he does have his supporters. In 2009 filmmaker and Huffington Post columnist Bryan Young wrote a passionate defense of the character:

> I find Jar Jar just as obnoxious as you guys do. But that doesn't mean I don't like him and that he doesn't serve a specific and brilliant purpose to the Star Wars saga. Looking to Shakespeare's *The Merchant of Venice*, we see Lancelot the Clown featuring prominently in the early act of the play, providing useful commentary, lessons, and above all, laughs—and then largely disappearing later in the body of the work. Jar Jar works the same way. His role in the second episode was particularly poignant and explored how even the most well-meaning person can, by no fault of anything but his intention to do the right thing, be manipulated into perpetrating a great evil.

Here's another view: In 2009 *New Yorker* columnist Amy Davidson used Jar Jar in a political commentary. Contrary to the popular opinion that former President George W. Bush was the Darth Vader to Vice President Dick Cheney's Emperor, she wrote, Bush was more akin to "Jar Jar Binks, who, after a buffoonish youth, improbably rises to a prominent political position and obliviously fronts for the soon-to-be emperor in getting the *Star Wars* equivalent of the PATRIOT Act passed."

A JARRING FUTURE

So Jar Jar Binks has become as well known as any other *Star Wars* character. But will audiences ever warm up to him? For many older viewers, scorn for Jar Jar runs deep. If there is any hope for the much-maligned alien, it's with children, who can now view the entire saga from beginning to end without all of the pop culture hullabaloo that surrounded it. They can just enjoy the story for what it is: a space fantasy full of corny dialogue, neat ships, cool battles, bizarre planets, and strange creatures. And to George Lucas—who modeled *Star Wars* after the 1950s *Flash Gordon* serials he enjoyed from his own childhood—that's all he was going for in the first place.

THE BROTHERS ROCKEFELLER

America has no royalty. But it does have wealthy families—some so wealthy that they're treated like royalty and become leaders in politics and society. Here are the facts behind one of the most powerful generations of one of the most powerful families in American history.

WITH GREAT POWER...
The Rockefeller dynasty began with Standard Oil founder John D. Rockefeller (1839–1937), who amassed a $1.5 billion fortune in his lifetime. By the time he died, America's first billionaire had managed to spin his image from ruthlessly ambitious businessman into philanthropist by giving away more than $500 million to charities. John D. Rockefeller Jr. followed in his father's footsteps, both building upon what remained of the family fortune and also spending an enormous amount of time furthering "the well-being of mankind." He expected his five sons—John D. III, Nelson, Laurance, Winthrop, and David, known collectively as the Rockefeller Brothers—to do the same; they were, by their own description, inheritors not just of huge wealth, but also of the responsibilities that come with it.

All five were active in the family businesses and philanthropies—the Rockefeller Family Fund, the Rockefeller Foundation, the Rockefeller Brothers Fund, and others. But while it is impossible for a Rockefeller *not* to be defined by money, the brothers were defined by more than that. Each had his own areas of expertise and special interest. "The road to happiness," said John D. III, "lies in two simple principles: Find what it is that interests you and that you can do well, and when you find it put your whole soul into it—every bit of energy and ambition and natural ability that you have."

SON #1: JOHN D. ROCKEFELLER III (1906–78)

• John III won high honors in economics at Princeton and then began working for his father in 1929. He was groomed to take the

---

In one poll, 10% of US college students thought MLK's "I Have a Dream" speech was about slavery.

lead in the family, but his brothers objected strenuously, and his own lack of confidence made it hard for him to stand up to them.

• He joined the Navy in WWII and worked on a task force planning postwar policy for Japan. Japan "became a second home" to him and his wife, Blanchette. He was a trusted advisor to several Asian governments as well as a supporter of the Asia Society (founded in 1956 to promote better understanding between the people of Asia and the U.S.), the Japan Society, the Asian Cultural Program, and the Institute of Pacific Relations.

• Amassed a major collection of Asian ceramics, metalwork, sculpture, and painting that was later donated to the San Francisco Fine Art Museum and the Asia Society. He was deeply committed to shaping public policy toward philanthropy and lobbied Congress to enact tax laws that would encourage private giving.

• He founded the nonprofit, research-based Population Council in 1952 and became an activist in the problem of world overpopulation, taking the unusual (for his time) position of advocating the use of contraception (though the family's focus on population control has sometimes been attributed to an interest in eugenics).

• In 1956 he became the first president of the Lincoln Square Renewal Project in Manhattan and the moving force behind the creation of Lincoln Center for the Performing Arts.

• Died in a car accident near the Rockefeller family estate in Pocantico Hills, in Westchester County, NY.

SON #2: NELSON ALDRICH ROCKEFELLER (1908–79)

• Even as a child, Nelson was considered the leader and most forceful personality of the brothers. He had trouble reading (probably due to undiagnosed dyslexia) and was an underachieving student.

• He married Philadelphia socialite Mary "Tod" Clark in 1930, six days after graduating from Dartmouth. They had five kids, but the marriage was not a happy one. They announced their separation in November 1961; almost simultaneously their son Michael was reported missing on an anthropological expedition in New Guinea.

• In 1932 he convinced Mexican muralist Diego Rivera to paint a a wall of the new Rockefeller Center, but when the left-wing Rivera refused to remove the figure of Lenin from his mural, Rockefeller halted the work and had the entire mural destroyed.

- His mother was a founder of the Museum of Modern Art, which opened in New York in 1929. He became president of MoMA in 1939, overseeing its expansion into a new building.

- He convinced his father to buy and donate land for the United Nations complex in order to keep the U.N. from moving to Philadelphia; the $8.5 million purchase was made in 1945.

- He was elected governor of New York in 1958 and served four terms before resigning in 1973. He was widely recognized for his achievements in education, public transportation, and massive building projects. (He was accused of having an "edifice complex.") He was also known for quadrupling the New York state budget, for the "Rockefeller drug laws" that meted out heavy prison sentences for minor offenses, and for the suppression of a riot at Attica State Prison, during which 29 inmates and 10 prison guard hostages died.

- "I'm a politician," he asserted. "That is my profession. Success in politics, real success, means only one thing in America." That one thing was the presidency, which eluded him repeatedly. He ran for the Republican nomination in 1960 (Nixon got it), in 1964 (Goldwater got it), and in 1968 (Nixon got it again).

- In 1974 he was nominated by President Gerald Ford and confirmed by Congress to be vice president. (Ford had become president after Nixon resigned.)

- He died of a heart attack, age 70, in the home of his 25-year-old aide while still married to his second wife, "Happy" Rockefeller.

SON #3: LAURANCE S. ROCKEFELLER (1910–2004)

- Laurance was known as the quiet, reserved, reclusive Rockefeller and the best businessman of the brothers. His greatest passions were venture capitalism and conservation.

- He sought out and invested heavily in unproven new businesses (especially those pushing the "frontiers of technology"), including biotechnology, aviation, electronics, and computers. A 1959 *Wall Street Journal* article reported that the $9 million Laurance had invested in the 14 years since World War II had yielded more than $28 million.

- He combined his two passions in Rockresorts, Inc., a company that developed environmentally friendly resorts in the Virgin Islands, Puerto Rico, Hawaii, and other places. Caneel Bay, on St.

According to a 1964 study, rats love scrambled eggs and mac & cheese, but hate peaches & beets.

John in the Virgin Islands, his first resort, opened in 1956. Swimming, snorkeling, and nature-walking were permitted; telephones, air conditioning, and tipping were not. Later he bought 5,000 acres surrounding the resort and gave it to the federal government to create the U.S. Virgin Islands National Park.

• An advisor to every president from Eisenhower on in matters of conservation, wilderness preservation, and ecology, he was pivotal in the movement to establish and improve national parks across the country. In 1968 he successfully negotiated a deal between the Sierra Club, the lumber companies, and the state of California to preserve 58,000 acres for Redwood National Park.

• Among the many honors he received were the Presidential Medal of Freedom, the Congressional Gold Medal, the Theodore Roosevelt National Park Medal of Honor, the National Institute of Social Sciences Gold Medal, Commander of the British Empire, and the Woodrow Wilson Award from Princeton University.

• Went to his office as usual on Wednesday, July 7, 2004, and died four days later at the age of 94.

SON #4: WINTHROP ROCKEFELLER (1912–73)

• Winthrop got off to a very different start from his brothers, dropping out of Yale in 1934 to work as a roughneck in the Texas oil fields. He returned to New York in 1937 to try settling down as an executive, but in 1941 he enlisted in the wartime Army as a private.

• After World War II, he lived a playboy lifestyle in New York. He married showgirl "Bobo" Sears in 1948; they had a son and separated within a year, and were embroiled for five more years in an acrimonious divorce.

• He moved to Arkansas in 1953 and promptly poured $8 million into Arkansas land, colleges, mental health programs, public school systems, and the arts. One newspaper called him "the Big Rock of Little Rock." In 1954 Governor Cherry said, "The people wish Winthrop Rockefeller had been quintuplets and that they had all come here."

• In 1955 Democratic Gov. Orval Faubus appointed him to head the Arkansas Industrial Development Commission; during his nine-year tenure, he brought 600 new factories, 90,000 new jobs, and $270 million in new payroll to the state.

- He recognized that real social and political change was impossible until the entrenched Democratic machine led by Faubus was ousted, and began a drive to make Arkansas a two-party state again. He won the governorship in 1966 (the first Republican governor in 94 years), with African-American voters giving him the margin of victory, and won again in 1968 (at that time Arkansas governors served two-year terms) but lost in 1970. His reform programs were repeatedly rejected by a Democratic state legislature.

- Was the only Southern governor to hold a public ceremony of mourning when Martin Luther King Jr. was assassinated in 1968.

- With a drinking problem, a dissolving second marriage, and a political agenda that Arkansans no longer wanted, he withdrew from public life. He died of pancreatic cancer in Palm Springs, California, in 1973, at the age of 60.

SON #5: DAVID ROCKEFELLER (1915–)

- David graduated from Harvard in 1936 and received a Ph.D in economics from the University of Chicago in 1940. He married Margaret McGrath the same year. (They remained married until her death in 1996.) He chose international banking and finance as his sphere of influence.

- Enlisted as a private in the Army (refusing to take the commission his family could easily have gotten for him), was discharged as a captain in 1945, and returned to New York to begin a career at Chase National Bank. He started as assistant manager, rose to senior vice president in 1952, and by 1961 he was bank president.

- In 1949 he became a director of the Council on Foreign Relations, a foreign policy study organization considered one of the world's most influential nongovernmental agencies. From 1970 to 1985 he was the council's chairperson. In 1979 he convinced President Carter to allow the shah of Iran to enter the United States for medical treatment, which led to the seizure of American hostages in Iran and ultimately to the downfall of the shah (and, in the U.S., to Ronald Reagan's defeat of Jimmy Carter in the 1980 presidential election).

- He helped found the Downtown-Lower Manhattan Association to represent and advance the interests of major downtown businesses (including Chase Manhattan Bank), and chaired it from

1958 to 1975. He was instrumental in developing the plans that led to the construction of the World Trade Center.

• In 1982 he became chairman of Rockefeller Center. In 1989 he sold an 80 percent share to Mitsubishi for $1.373 billion. In 1995 Rockefeller Center went bankrupt, and he bought it back with a group of other investors. He sold it again in 2000 for $1.85 billion.

• In 2002, contrary to the Rockefeller reticence about revealing anything personal, he published his memoirs. "Well," he explained, "it just occurred to me that I had led a rather interesting life."

NET GAINS AND LOSSES

The children of the Rockefeller Brothers (and of their sister, Abby) are the fourth generation of immensely wealthy Rockefellers. There are 23 of them, sometimes called the Cousins Generation. Although they had the advantages of wealth and power, many of the cousins felt burdened by (and angry at) their parents' and the world's expectations of them. Eventually they made peace with their parents and took their own places on the boards of the various Rockefeller foundations, trusts, and philanthropies, while continuing to pursue their own interests—and they have plenty of money to back up their chosen causes.

On the other hand, although the Rockefeller name may be synonymous with enormous wealth, each generation inherits less because more and more people have a share in it. What about the fifth generation, the grandchildren of the Rockefeller Brothers? The family has always guarded its privacy, and family members are not forthcoming about the actual value of their assets. Researchers have been unable to discern exactly how much money any individual Rockefeller has; all they know is that the trust funds that support the fifth generation don't begin to compare to the fortunes of the second, third, and fourth generations.

❋   ❋   ❋

"The penalty for success is to be bored by the people who used to snub you."

—Lady Astor

URBAN WILDLIFE

In recent years, the number of wild animal encounters in cities and suburbs has skyrocketed, prompting wildlife officials to increase efforts to educate people about the most effective methods to live with our beastly neighbors.

CROWDED HOUSE

Right now, depending on where you are, there might be a raccoon family living under your floorboards, bats sleeping in your attic, birds nesting in your trees, not to mention the squirrels, mice, and snakes that inhabit your yard and a coyote that comes around at night. (And don't forget about all of the insects and spiders.) Yet despite their greater numbers, we often don't even notice these animals until one of them has torn through our garbage cans. Can we all survive together in harmony...or does someone have to go?

Basically, there are three choices when dealing with a wild animal in an urban setting: Relocate it, exterminate it, or coexist with it. Until recently, relocation was the most common tactic, but it has serious drawbacks. According to the National Audubon Society: "In the vast majority of cases, relocation is an ineffective, inhumane, and ecologically destructive method for dealing with urban wildlife." The first problem: Unless an experienced professional sets the trap, the animal can get injured or killed—as could a curious house pet. Trying to capture the animal yourself could lead to a nasty bite (and even nastier rabies shots). There's also the potential of catching and relocating a nursing mother, leaving her orphans to fend for themselves. But of even more concern is what can occur when the wild animal is released into a brand-new area.

THERE GOES THE NEIGHBORHOOD

Take the raccoon population in the BRI's hometown of Ashland, Oregon, a valley town surrounded by forested mountains. Homeowners trap the raccoons that have invaded their yards and then release them in the woods around nearby Emigrant Lake. But raccoons are considered an *invasive species*; when they enter a new ecosystem, they tend to throw it out of balance—that is, *if* they survive. For most transplanted animals (whether they're mammals, birds, or reptiles), the stress of being trapped and released often leads to a quick death, either from starvation or predation. Those that do survive infringe on other animals' established territories and diminish the food supply. Worse yet, raccoons can spread a form of canine distemper similar to rabies. And when the native berry supply runs out, where do the transplanted raccoons go? Into the backyards of the homes surrounding the lake—as do the bears who are forced to find new food sources because the transplanted raccoons ate up all of the berries.

These kinds of scenarios are being played out every day in and around towns and cities throughout North America. And the problem is growing. According to Susan Barnes, a biologist for U.S. Fish and Wildlife, "The more urbanized we get, the more people don't know how to tolerate urban wildlife." And as more and more patches of forests turn into neighborhoods, these encounters will only increase. The Audubon Society reports that every year, Portland, Oregon, citizens capture and relocate 5,000 raccoons, opossums, foxes, coyotes, rabbits, and skunks, into the forests around nearby Mt. Hood, one of several ecosystems threatened by invasive species and their city-born diseases.

OPTIONS

So, if relocation doesn't work, what do homeowners do? In many cases, they exterminate. Companies that once specialized in moving wild animals now offer "humane methods" of disposing of them, usually by poisoning them. Coleen McIntyre, manager of Critter Control of Portland, Oregon, says there is often no other choice: "People usually say, 'Oh, don't kill it.' Then, after the animal has kept them up every morning for two months, they want me to kill it." But only a small portion of these intruders actually get exterminated. And even then, the problem doesn't go away: You can get rid of one pest, but if your yard has something desirable—shelter, warmth, food—it's a safe bet that a new one will try to take its place.

Ironically, wildlife experts maintain that the best thing citizens can do for a wild animal is to *not* give it anything to eat, even by accident. Wildlife and health officials are so serious about controlling wild populations—and in doing so, reducing vermin—that in many towns, it's illegal to feed deer in your yard, or squirrels in the park, or even ducks at the pond. Daniel Haag-Wackernagel, a biologist at the University of Basel in Switzerland, is speaking here about pigeons, but you can substitute any other wild animal: "People say it's cruel to deprive them of food, but in the wild, the sudden absence of food is a completely natural occurrence. The animals will adapt to it." Here are a few tips for keeping hungry critters out of your yard.

• Securely fasten your garbage can lids.

• Don't leave pet food outside at night.

• If you compost, bury any food scraps you toss into the pile.

• If you have fruit trees, pick up all of the fallen fruit.

• Eliminate potential den and nesting sights of small mammals by sealing up the crawl space underneath your house as well as any holes that might allow access to your attic. And regularly clean out your shed and other yard structures.

Remember, though, that wild animals are cunning and tenacious and have been known to rip away brand-new siding in order to reclaim a former den.

BIG CRITTERS

Keeping larger animals out of your yard may be difficult, but officials say it's important to both your well-being and theirs.

Deer: Feeding them disrupts their diets—they need certain native plants to aid digestion. If they only get their food from people's gardens, they run the risk of digestion problems that can lead to starvation. And as deer get more used to people, they create hazards on the roads and can become aggressive. In addition, a fed deer will view *everybody's* yard as a potential cafeteria.

Coyotes and foxes: With more of these wild canines' habitats disappearing, they're showing up in places where they've never been seen before. Although they rarely, if ever, target humans, they're very interested in your pets, which can be easy prey. That's because to a typical cat, a full-grown coyote or fox can look like a relatively harmless dog. So keep your pets inside at night (when coyotes and foxes hunt).

Other large predators: Depending on your area, you may be prone to bear and mountain lion encounters, both of which are also on the rise. The same basic rules apply to keeping them out of your yard, but if one does venture in, you can scare it away by jumping around and yelling. The same goes if you meet one on a trail or in the parking lot of your local shopping mall. But this is only if they appear to be threatening you. In most cases, you can quietly walk away from a large predator and be left alone. And officials request that every sighting of a big animal be reported.

YOUR OWN NATURAL WILDERNESS AREA

Another option when dealing with urban wildlife (of the smaller variety)—give them a home away from home. For most of the species mentioned above, officials recommend against it, but it can be effective (and rewarding) for wild birds and some smaller mammals and reptiles. "The best thing you can do for wildlife, without question," says Bob Sallinger of the Audubon Society, "is just naturescape your yard." This primarily entails planting native vegetation, removing non-native plants, avoiding the use of pesticides, and keeping dogs and cats indoors. Some yards can even be designated wildlife habitats. This tactic comes with a lot of responsibility, though, so if you're interested in naturescaping, research the bylaws of your municipality first.

And keep in mind that every action in nature has a reaction. So if you really want wild birds in your yard and decide to put up a feeder, you may get more than birds—you may get squirrels, chipmunks, or even rats feeding off the seeds that the birds drop on your lawn. It all comes down to plenty of research, a little experimentation, and a willingness to change course if you start attracting vermin (or the scorn of your neighbors).

OPPORTUNISTS

Three wild animal species have adapted so well to living with humans that about all we can do is step back and appreciate their abilities (and try not to feed them).

Common house mice: In terms of sheer numbers, these rodents have benefited more from humans than any other mammal has. Why? Because we give them two things that are in short supply in the natural world: food and protection. In the wild, mice live in burrows or under felled trees, which they must leave to forage

While only 1% of the population suffers from bipolar disorder, it's thought that as many as...

for grains, making them vulnerable to snakes, birds, foxes, and other predators. Their only way to ensure survival: produce lots and lots of offspring. In your house, however, there are few, if any, predators lurking around (except your ferocious cat, of course). And there's plenty of food in your cupboards and crumbs on your floor. So with the dangers removed, the food provided, and the reproduction rate steady, the common house mouse has become the world's second most populous mammal. (We're #1.)

Peregrine falcons: Once nearly wiped out in the U.S. because of the pesticide DDT, the world's fastest bird of prey has rebounded, thanks in large part to urbanization. Before electricity, the peregrine was a daytime hunter. It has since adapted to take advantage of streetlights to hunt bats and other small creatures of the night. They've also adapted to living in a new environment: the big city. Skyscrapers resemble the peregrines' native habitat—rocky cliffs—so today the birds can be sighted in Boston, Philadelphia, Baltimore, Seattle, Pittsburgh, Chicago, New York, and other cities, where they are welcomed by the local residents. Why? They're spectacular birds, and they eat pigeons.

Pigeons: It was an easy move for these birds to go from their rocky dwellings on cliffsides to the ledges of our buildings. Pigeons' remarkable ability to nest almost anywhere (even inside air conditioners and vending machines), combined with their easily adaptable diets (cheeseburgers, candy, and edible trash), has helped the worldwide pigeon population explode to more than 350 million. Multiply that amount by 26 pounds of bird droppings per pigeon per year, and you have...a lot of reasons to try to reduce the number of pigeons. Cities around the world have been attempting this for decades—blasting pigeons with salt, firing giant nets over the top of flocks, scaring them with loud noises, poisoning them, placing food on electrically charged platforms, and even contraception—with little or no success.

And so, the battle goes on against the pigeons...and the mice, rats, gulls, roaches, raccoons, skunks, deer, bears, alligators, and so on. As we build more communities, more of their world will cease to exist, forcing them to survive in ours—with or without our help.

RANDOM BITS ON 2000s HITS

A few short, catchy facts about a few short, catchy pop songs.

• **"Don't Know Why," by Norah Jones.** Amazingly, this old-fashioned torch song was a Top-30 hit in an era dominated by hip-hop. The album, *Come Away With Me*, became the bestselling album in the history of the legendary Blue Note Records.

• **"Lose Yourself," by Eminem.** From Eminem's semiautobio-graphical movie *8 Mile*, this was the first rap song to ever be nominated for the Oscar for Best Song. (It won the award.)

• **"Hey Ya!" by Outkast.** The repeated line "shake it like a Polaroid picture" became a catchphrase. But actually doing that damages the photo, leading Polaroid to issue a statement warning consumers to *not* shake their Polaroid pictures.

• **"Hollaback Girl," by Gwen Stefani.** The song is built around a drumline stomp and chanted lyrics, like a cheerleading routine. Stefani got the idea when Courtney Love said in *Seventeen*: "Being famous is like being in high school. I'm not interested in being the cheerleader. I'm not interested in being Gwen Stefani."

• **"Bad Day," by Daniel Powter.** It became a #1 hit after it was used as the "exit music" for eliminated contestants on *American Idol*. It's the only time a performer has had the *Billboard* Song of the Year (the top seller)…and never had another hit.

• **"Gold Digger," by Kanye West featuring Jamie Foxx.** Foxx won an Oscar for his portrayal of Ray Charles in *Ray*. "Gold Digger" features a sample of Charles's "I Got a Woman." That's really Charles singing, not Foxx, even though Foxx is credited on the song. Foxx's sole contribution: a brief spoken intro.

• **"Umbrella," by Rihanna.** The song was originally written for Britney Spears, whose management turned it down without her knowledge (which she came to regret). Mary J. Blige was the songwriter's next choice, but they were unable to arrange a meeting, so it went to up-and-coming singer Rihanna.

BELTS

Buckle up with a few of our favorite geographical (and astronomical) belts.

BELTWAY: A section of highway that loops the perimeter of a major city. In politics, it refers to the Capital Beltway, which surrounds Washington, D.C., and is used to describe the difference between political perceptions inside and outside of Washington.

BIBLE BELT: Nickname given to the American South, roughly from Florida north to Virginia and east to Oklahoma and Texas, where fundamentalist Christianity and church attendance are important aspects of local culture. The term was first used by *Chicago Daily Tribune* columnist H. L. Mencken in 1924.

BORSCHT BELT: Nickname for a region of the Catskill Mountains northwest of New York City, a popular vacation spot for wealthy New York City Jews from the 1910s until the 1970s. It was in the Borscht Belt resorts that scores of world-famous comedians got their start, including Henny Youngman, Milton Berle, Rodney Dangerfield, Lenny Bruce, and Sid Caesar.

SUN BELT: Nickname given to the American South and Southwest, from Florida and the Carolinas to Southern California, a region that's several degrees warmer year-round than the North. The term was coined by author Kevin Phillips in his 1969 book *The Emerging Republican Majority*. (According to Phillips, anyway.)

STROKE BELT: Nickname given to a region in the American Southeast, particularly Tennessee, Georgia, and the Carolinas, that has an unusually high rate of death by stroke.

KUIPER BELT: A massive ring-shaped region of our solar system beyond the planets. It's nearly two billion miles wide and contains numerous KBOs (Kuiper Belt Objects)—balls of ice, some more than 600 miles across, that orbit the sun.

BELT: A town in central Montana, population 633, named after nearby Belt Butte, a mountain that appears to have a belt of rocks around it.

98% of Ireland's schools are run by the Roman Catholic Church.

GROANERS

Faithful BRI members keep sending Uncle John their horrible puns. Of course he loves them—and then insists on "sharing" them with us. So why are we inflicting them on you? Have you ever heard the saying "misery loves company?" Feel free to groan out loud.

A MAN HEARD ABOUT the discovery of gold in California. He immediately packed up his possessions and moved out west. Six months later, he gave up and returned home. Why? It didn't pan out.

A GUY GOES INTO a hardware store and asks the manager for a tool to break up the hard ground. The manager shows him a wall of shovels, hoes, and other tools and says, "Take your pick."

A RANCHER WAS taking inventory of his livestock. He figured that it wouldn't take him too long because he knew for a fact that he had exactly 196 head of cattle. But then he discovered that he actually had 200 head? How'd he find out? He rounded them up.

"DOCTOR, DOCTOR, you've got to help me!"
"What's the trouble?"
"One night I dream that I'm a car's muffler. And then the next night, I dream that I'm part of the wheel."
"Why is that such a big deal?"
"I wake up exhausted and tired."

JOHN LOVES WHEAT—wheat bread, wheat rolls, wheat muffins—he can't get enough wheat. Only problem: He's allergic to it. Whenever he eats it, he breaks out in a rash. But does that stop him from eating it? No, he's a real gluten for punishment.

THE STATE TREASURER had to balance the budget, so he sliced a little bit off the proposed funding for schools, parks, and other services. It was the most successful fund razor of the year.

TOM IS OBSESSED with monorails. All he ever talks about is monorails—especially how amazing it is that they travel with the use of just a single rail. He has a one-track mind.

A full-body CT scan can expose you to as much radiation as being 2 miles from an atomic-bomb blast.

RETURN TO CHERNOBYL

On page 404, we told the story of the Chernobyl disaster.
What's happened in the years after the accident?
The answer may surprise you.

MELTDOWN!
More than two decades after the meltdown that made it famous, Chernobyl still stands for everything humans fear about nuclear power. On April 26, 1986, plant operators lost control of one of the reactors at the Chernobyl nuclear power station in the former Soviet Republic of Ukraine. The reactor core melted down, causing several explosions and a fire that released massive amounts of radiation directly into the environment.

Radioactive fallout from the disaster permanently displaced more than 300,000 people in the Ukraine, Belarus, and Russia. It contaminated hundreds of thousands of acres of formerly valuable cropland and continues to threaten the region's groundwater. The 1,100 square mile "exclusion zone" surrounding the ruined power plant will be uninhabitable for generations. Most frightening, scientists will likely never know how many lives were shortened by exposure to Chernobyl radiation.

SILENT SPRING

The immediate effects of the disaster were devastating to the local flora and fauna. Two square miles of pine forest adjacent to the power plant turned brown and died in a matter of days. Any farm animals unfortunate enough to be downwind within four miles of the reactor received lethal doses of radiation. But in a strange footnote to the disaster, by making a huge area of rural farm country unsafe for humans, the world's worst nuclear disaster created the world largest accidental wildlife refuge.

Within the first few years, wildlife began to return. The pine forest grew back—although its trees now have a distinctly mutant look, with odd-sized needles and strange clusters of buds and branches. Birds and rodents actually nest in the walls of the giant concrete and steel sarcophagus that was built to contain the reactor core, and there are fish in the old cooling pond.

More murders and home burglaries take place in August than in any other month.

Moving out from ground zero, wildlife reclaimed not just the forests but abandoned towns as well—including the ghost-metropolis of Pripyat, from which nearly 50,000 people were evacuated two days after the accident. The evacuated zone is now home to wild boar, deer, beaver, fox, lynx, elk, and a large wolf population. Wild horses were reintroduced and are thriving along with rare birds like the black stork, marsh hawk, golden and white-tailed eagles, and the green crane.

OPPOSING VIEWS

The exclusion zone is no Garden of Eden, not by a long shot: Dr. Timothy Mousseau, of the University of South Carolina has studied wildlife inside the zone and has found higher mortality rates, lower birthrates, and an unusually high occurrence of genetic defects among Chernobyl's bird populations. Mousseau claims that "reports of wildlife flourishing in the area are completely anecdotal," and suggests that population pressure in less contaminated areas may be causing healthy animals to migrate into the exclusion zone—giving the *appearance* of a thriving ecosystem.

NOBODY WINS

In the meantime, aside from a small handful of elderly squatters who (illegally) moved back into their old villages despite the risks, and a skeleton crew of technicians who monitor the defunct power station, the animals have Chernobyl all to themselves.

* * *

MALE CHAUVINIST SMURF

On the '80s cartoon *The Smurfs*, there was only one female character—Smurfette, who was actually created by the show's villain, the evil wizard Gargamel, to infiltrate the Smurf community. Here are the ingredients that Gargamel used to make Smurfette: "sugar and spice (but nothing nice), a dram of crocodile tears, a peck of bird brain, the tip of an adder's tongue, half a pack of lies (white, of course), the slyness of a cat, the vanity of a peacock, the chatter of a magpie, the guile of a vixen, the disposition of a shrew, and the hardest stone for her heart."

THE BALLOON MAN

It's hard to imagine birthday parties, celebrations, or political conventions without a rainbow of balloons. So considering that they're associated with joyous occasions, it's kind of ironic that if it weren't for poverty and sheer desperation, balloons never would have been invented.

FROM DEPRESSION TO INFLATION

Before the 1929 stock market crash and the Great Depression, Neil Tillotson thought he had a career that could last him a lifetime. In 1915 he dropped out of high school and began working for the Hood Rubber Company, a prosperous manufacturer of tires and rubber footwear located in Watertown, Massachusetts. In little time, he worked his way into a position as a researcher.

After serving in World War I (he was assigned to a cavalry unit that spent the war years chasing Mexican outlaw Pancho Villa around Texas and northern Mexico), he returned home and reclaimed his position at Hood. With new products and research on artificial rubber, Hood's wartime boom promised to continue into the post-war years. In the early 1920s, an industry newsletter reported that Hood had become the largest independent rubber footwear manufacturer in the country, capable of pumping out 75,000 pairs of shoes a day.

But then came the Depression. Struggling with cash flow issues and a lack of demand for its products, Hood Rubber went on hiatus for most of January 1931, locking its doors and laying off 1,200 employees. Along with everyone else, Tillotson found himself on an involuntary, unpaid vacation. To make matters worse, his brother and father-in-law had lost their jobs...and moved in with Tillotson. Trapped in a house that had become uncomfortably overcrowded, and with cabin fever setting in, he feared that Hood would not reopen. Regardless, he knew he couldn't afford to work for a company that reserved the right to lay him off periodically with little warning.

ESCAPING TO HIS LAB

So Tillotson built a makeshift laboratory in his attic and set about trying to invent something that might let him start his own business. The problem was that the only thing Tillotson knew well was rubber, and making the vulcanized rubber invented by Charles Goodyear required expensive machinery, lots of raw materials, and workers.

Tillotson pinned his hopes on something new in the field: liquid latex. A few years earlier, German scientist Peter Schidrowitz had developed a thick liquid that could be painted onto almost anything and would air dry into a rubber skin. It didn't require heat, sulfur, or molding machines, just a paintbrush or a dipping bowl, which made it theoretically possible for Tillotson to start manufacturing something (he wasn't sure what yet) with a few molds and minimal up-front costs. But what could he make?

AIR HEAD

Back at Hood Rubber, Tillotson had been lucky: He'd been allocated a supply of liquid latex and assigned the job of finding uses for it, so he already knew something about what it could do. He'd also had the opportunity to take home a quantity of liquid latex before the plant locked its doors.

His first idea was to create inexpensive inner tubes for automobile and bicycle tires. On paper, it seemed like it should work, but Tillotson quickly discovered that his latex skin wasn't as strong as molded rubber, and it wasn't durable enough for heavy-duty use. His first efforts were, quite literally, a blowout.

Frustrated, Tillotson came up with another idea—one that he thought might be an amusing novelty. He cut a piece of cardboard into the shape of a cat's head (complete with little cat ears at the top) and dipped it into the gooey latex. He had no idea what would happen, but it was a whimsical diversion from working on inner tubes. After the latex dried, he sprinkled it with talc to keep the rubber from sticking to itself, then carefully rolled the thin skin off the cardboard. It seemed to be an intact cat-head shape. Gingerly, he put it to his lips and blew a small puff of air into the hole at the bottom. It seemed to be airtight, so he blew a little more and kept repeating until the latex skin was round and dangerously taut. It was a balloon with cat ears, something he'd never seen before.

BALLOONS FROM THE BUTCHER

Not that toy balloons were anything new. For a great kids' toy in the early 1800s, you couldn't do much better than blowing up a pig's bladder: It was thin, airtight, durable, and fun to toss around. Kids who wanted a different-size balloon had plenty of choices available, from small balloons made from pig intestines or rabbit bladders to large balloons from cattle organs.

In 1824 British scientist Michael Faraday invented a rubber balloon by taking two pieces of rubber and sticking them together. It didn't require special adhesives because before Charles Goodyear invented vulcanization to fix the problem, rubber was sticky and malleable like a thick bubble gum. Faraday filled his balloon with hydrogen in order to conduct scientific experiments, but it didn't take long for the invention to become a popular plaything for his kids. Problems: The balloons couldn't be mass-produced, and they didn't last long.

A CAT KISS FOR LUCK

Tillotson had something new, and he knew it. He tied off the balloon and hand painted a cat's face on the front. When he carried it downstairs to show the rest of the family, their reaction was enough to make him completely forget about inner tubes. He went to work with his scissors, creating more cat-head molds, and recruited his brother and father-in-law to help hand dip dozens at a time. After making and painting 2,000, he sold them all to a Boston novelty company, C. Decieco & Son, who filled them with helium to sell at a parade in nearby Lexington.

Desperately curious to see how the public would respond to his cat balloons, Tillotson headed to the parade site. Besides being reassured by the brisk sales of balloons, he witnessed something that convinced him that he had a hit product on his hands: A little girl pulled her balloon down and kissed the cat's face.

That was it. Tillotson withdrew his life savings and sank the entire $720 into latex, molds, and a building, and set up production. By the end of 1931, the Tillotson Rubber Company had popped out five million cat-faced balloons and, despite the worsening Depression, generated sales of $85,000 (the equivalent of $1.2 million today).

Other companies also began making balloons and plenty of other rubbery products. Tillotson's company went on to develop the first high-speed latex dipping machine, which helped with his second invention in the early 1960s: the one-size-fits-either-hand disposable latex medical glove.

FOOTNOTE TO OBSCURITY

Tillotson became fabulously wealthy, moved to Dixville Notch, New Hampshire, and bought a hotel. There he earned his final claim to fame: For 40 years, until his death in 2001 at age 102, he was the nation's first voter in all presidential primaries and all presidential elections. He slid his paper ballot into Dixville Notch's ballot box at the stroke of midnight every Election Day, followed quickly by the three dozen other registered voters in the tiny town. Dixville Notch became famous as the first place to vote and the first to report its results a few minutes later, resulting in a crush of reporters and television cameras at every election.

Tillotson always ended up in the network news reports. But did that give him the fame he deserved as the inventor of the modern balloon and the disposable surgical glove? No. In 2007 the New Hampshire Historical Society began selling a Neil Tillotson bobblehead figure…depicting the staunch Republican dropping his ballot into the Dixville Notch ballot box. (Want one? At last report, they still have plenty on hand.)

*   *   *

LONGEST-RUNNING SITCOMS IN TV HISTORY

- *The Simpsons* (1989–present), 441 episodes (and counting)
- *The Adventures of Ozzie and Harriet* (1952–66), 435 episodes
- *My Three Sons* (1960–72), 380 episodes
- *The Danny Thomas Show* (1953–64), 336 episodes
- *Burns and Allen* (1950–58) 291, episodes
- *Cheers* (1982–93), 275 episodes
- *The Donna Reed Show* (1958–66), 275 episodes
- *The Beverly Hillbillies* (1962–71), 274 episodes
- *Frasier* (1993-2004), 264 episodes
- *Married…With Children* (1987–97), 259 episodes

The 2008 Wall Street bailout cost $200 billion more than was spent on public education in 2007.

TALK TO THE BONES

TV shows like CSI *and* Bones *make forensic science seem commonplace, but 30 years ago, one man took the practice from an obscure academic specialty to the frontlines of international crime and human rights investigations.*

BIOGRAPHY OF THE BONES

Clyde Snow stands over six feet tall, wears a cowboy hat and leather boots, and chain-smokes Cuban cigars. He drinks a lot, too. He's been described as "an unmade bed of a man." He doesn't look like an angel or a savior, but that's what many people think he is—people who've lost loved ones, especially children and grandchildren. He hardly ever has happy news for relatives, though; it's rare that a case he's involved in turns up a living person. In fact, the person is usually long dead, maybe even for decades. Snow has little more than bones—often buried in unmarked plots; sometimes in mass graves—with which to identify who people were and how they died. He says the bones "make good witnesses. They may speak softly, but they never forget." He calls his work *osteobiography*, the art and science of reading a person's bones. "There is," he says, "a brief but very informative biography contained within the skeleton, if you know how to read it."

MEASURING THE PAST

Forensics is the application of any science in a criminal or legal investigation. Forensic anthropology focuses on human skeletal remains. The long bones of the leg, for example, can determine height and weight, the bones in the arms and hands can tell whether the deceased was left- or right-handed, skull measurements can determine sex and race, and measurements of the back of the skull can determine age at time of death. In addition, forensic anthropologists can identify old fractures, scarring from wounds, and deformities from disease.

And sometimes they can determine the cause of death. Once, when investigating human rights abuses at a youth detention facility in Bolivia, Snow found metal residue from a .22 caliber rifle bullet on a boy's ribcage, indicating he'd been shot in the back, probably by a guard. Another boy had a bullet wound in a his skull, but Snow determined it wasn't the actual shot that killed him; it was lead poisoning from the bullet fragment that remained in his head. It's this kind of work that makes Snow and the other anthropologists he's trained during his long career the forensic experts of last resort, when there's no blood, soft tissue, or even teeth. "Bones can be puzzles," he says. "But they never lie."

PLANE SPEAKER

Born in 1928, Clyde Snow grew up in rural West Texas, the son of a country doctor. He was used to looking at bones at an early age as he accompanied his father on patient visits. He got his Master's Degree in Zoology and eventually a Ph.D. in Anthropology at the University of Arizona. He wound up based in Oklahoma City in 1960 when an old friend offered him a job in a new field—investigating casualties of airline crashes to help design safer airplanes at the Civil Aeromedical Institute, a subsidiary of the Federal Aviation Administration (FAA). One of the most important parts of his job was recreating what happened during an airline crash by studying the human remains at crash sites. By determining what passengers did before and during impact, he could learn where and how safety improvements could be incorporated into planes.

This combination of physical anthropology and the study of human behavior appealed to Snow, and he started offering his services to the local medical examiner's office. From the 1960s through the 1990s, if there were hard-to-identify victims anywhere in the United States, law enforcement called Clyde Snow.

FACES AND PLACES

Snow worked on some of the most notorious cases of the 20th century, including the serial killings of Ted Bundy, identifying the skull of notorious Auschwitz doctor Josef Mengele, reviewing the autopsy X-rays from John F. Kennedy's assassination, and identifying victims of the 1995 terrorist bombings in Oklahoma City. He traveled to the Little Big Horn to try and identify soldiers who died with Custer, and to Bolivia to see if the real Butch Cassidy and the Sundance Kid were buried there (they weren't). For a NASA study about what happened to bones after a high-altitude

---

American girls break their arms 56% more often today than girls did 40 years ago.

fall, he interviewed survivors of suicide jumps off the Golden Gate Bridge. (He says most of the survivors had a change of mind on the way down.) Here are some of his best-known cases:

American Airlines Flight 191: On May 25, 1979, the deadliest airline crash in American history killed all 258 passengers, 13 crew, and 2 bystanders on the ground in Chicago. Clyde Snow was called to a makeshift morgue in a hangar at O'Hare International Airport to try to identify what were essentially the unidentifiable remains of the 50 people whose bodies had not been accounted for. He worked 16-hour days with a team of medical investigators, dentists, and X-ray technicians examining more than 10,000 body parts. Snow had to create new forensic techniques on the spot, including designing the first computer database that matched information compiled from the bones with what was known about missing passengers. Over a five-week period, they identified 20 more people—an amazing outcome, considering the condition of the remains.

Serial Killer John Wayne Gacy: In 1980 Gacy was convicted of murdering 33 young men who had been found the year before, buried beneath his home in a Chicago suburb or dumped in a nearby river. The victims were not easy to identify—they were all young white males—and many were probably runaways or drifters. Using missing persons reports, dental records, X-rays, and fingerprints, police could identify only half of them.

Snow was called in by the medical examiner's office, and with the help of a forensic radiologist, they managed to identify five more victims over the next few months. But after a year, there were still nine unidentified bodies. Rather than give up, Snow enlisted the aid of medical artist Betty Pat Gatlieff to undertake the very new practice of facial reconstruction. Using Snow's precise measurements, Gatlieff painstakingly sculpted clay onto various points of each skull, recreating the nose, cheeks and mouth, and later adding prosthetic eyes and a wig. Though only one of the nine victims was identified from the recreations, the technique was further refined by Snow and Gatlieff and used successfully many times since, leading to about a 70% identification rate.

Argentina and the Disappeared: A turning point in Snow's career came in 1984 when he was alerted to the plight of relatives of *desaparecidos* (the disappeared)—thousands of people who were abducted and killed by Argentina's military junta between 1976 and 1983. Many of the bodies had been dumped in unmarked graves, and now, with a new government in power, there was an outcry from the public to try to locate the missing. Snow originally went to Argentina as part of a group advising officials how to properly exhume and identify remains, but his involvement quickly became more hands-on. He agreed to work directly on a couple of cases, and when he couldn't find enough professionals, he trained a team of six anthropology and medical students from the University of Buenos Aires. Over the next two years, they worked on dozens of exhumations together, and were able to identify the bodies of numerous *desaparecidos.*

A NEW ERA

Snow's work in Argentina went beyond merely identifying bodies; it marked the first time forensics were used to bring human-rights criminals to justice. At the 1985 trial of nine former Junta officials, Snow showed dozens of slides documenting atrocities—a sternum that clearly showed a victim had been shot in the back, a skull with fragments of shotgun pellets that had come from a standard police weapon at close range, and the skeleton of a young woman whose pelvis showed clear signs of having given birth shortly before her death. With Snow's help, the bones of three victims spoke loud and clear—and five of the nine defendants were convicted. Snow's work in Argentina has led to nearly 25 years of organized humanitarian investigations by himself and other forensic scientists, in countries such as Guatemala, Ethiopia, Iraq, Bolivia, the Philippines, Chile, and the former Yugoslavia.

❊ ❊ ❊

EVERY MAN FOR HIMSELF

From 1961 to '62, Clyde Snow developed statistical models of airline crashes that combined anthropological measurements with seating charts and statements from survivors. His shocking conclusion: Young men were twice as likely to survive as older men, women, and children. Why? "They do not act like gentlemen," Snow concluded. In other words, they didn't help others get out. Families traveling together helped each other, but strangers, for the most part, didn't help other strangers—even children.

ENGLAND'S ROSWELL, PART II

What really did happen in Rendlesham Forest in the wee hours of the morning on December 26 and 28, 1980? Here's the second installment of the story. Part I is on page 373.

NOT SO FAST

For the witnesses of the strange goings-on in Rendlesham Forest, convincing themselves that they'd seen a UFO was one thing—convincing the locals was another. When the story finally broke in the pages of the *News of the World*, a British tabloid newspaper, in October 1983, the farmers and foresters who lived around Rendlesham Forest didn't believe a word of it. *They* hadn't seen or heard anything unusual on the nights in question, and when a reporter from the *Times* of London visited the area the day the *News of the World* story broke, he had no trouble finding locals who were already laughing off some of the key elements of the story.

DUMB YANKEES

Had the American airmen ever even been in a forest before?

• Depressions in the ground of the kind described by the witnesses at the "landing site" are scattered all over the forest—not always arranged by chance into triangular patterns, but they are everywhere. Rabbits dig them, to get at roots under the ground.

• The strange marks in the trees? They were everywhere, too, not just at the landing sight. They weren't burns or scrapes made by a UFO blasting off—they were axe marks made by foresters to mark the trees that are ready to be cut down.

• The screaming animals? Those were *muntjac*, also called "barking deer," who live in Rendlesham Forest and are well known—at least to the locals—for squeaking, barking, and even screaming like human beings when startled by things like, say, bands of agitated airmen roaming through the forest at 3:00 a.m. waving flashlights and talking loudly into tape recorders as they troll for space aliens.

LARGER THAN (EXTRATERRESTRIAL) LIFE

By now the story was taking on a life of its own, helped along by the fact that the original witness statements, though unclassified, still hadn't been made public. They were gathering dust in an Air Force filing cabinet somewhere. Only the Halt memo had been leaked to the *News of the World.*

Without their original written statements to pin them down, some of the witnesses apparently began to embellish their stories. Remember how Jim Penniston reported that the closest he ever came to the object was 50 yards, or half a football field, away? In time he would claim that he not only walked right up to the craft, he examined it for 45 minutes before it finally took off, and he took notes and drew diagrams into a small notebook the entire time. John Burroughs was with Penniston, and he denies this version of the story. He says that neither of them got close to the source of the lights. He also denies that Penniston took notes. But that hasn't stopped Penniston from producing such a notebook, complete with handwritten notes and sketches of the spacecraft, in television interviews ever since.

SHINING A LIGHT ON THINGS

Lieutenant Colonel Halt's story also "improved" with age: Though he never mentioned it in his memo, he later claimed that after the UFO left the forest, it hovered over the base for a while and even shined a spotlight on the bunker where nuclear weapons were stored. (In the event of a Soviet nuclear attack on NATO countries, nuclear bombers based at RAF Bentwaters and RAF Woodbridge would have been part of a retaliatory strike).

Halt's new version of events collapses under its *own* weight: If an unidentified aircraft—human or otherwise—had entered the airspace over a military base and shined a beam of light right on the building where nuclear bombs were kept, wouldn't someone have sounded an alarm? Scrambled jets? But no one did. According to Halt—the deputy base commander—he and his men, by now "unnerved and exhausted" after spending hours in the forest, just returned to base after seeing the UFO and went to bed. The unidentified craft (if there ever really was one) was allowed to fly off unchallenged.

THE SKEPTIC

The furor surrounding the "Incident at Rendlesham" soon caught the interest of Ian Ridpath, a prominent British science writer and editor of the *Oxford Dictionary of Astronomy*. When Ridpath started asking locals for their theory on what the airmen saw in the woods, one forester named Vincent Thurkettle told him that the bright light they saw was almost certainly the lighthouse at Orford Ness, some five miles east of the forest.

A lighthouse on the coast? Ridpath paid a visit to Rendlesham Forest and, with the help of Thurkettle, made his way to the area where the UFO was first sighted. Sure enough, right at the spot where the airmen say they encountered the UFO, the light from the Orford Ness Lighthouse could be seen flashing brightly from the same direction where the witnesses say they saw the UFO.

SEEING IS BELIEVING

To be fair to the original witnesses, there were a number of things about the light coming from the lighthouse that could have made it seem odd and mysterious, especially to American airmen who may not have realized 1) that there even *was* a lighthouse on the coast, and 2) that its light could penetrate the trees and be seen five miles inland. "At the time, almost none of us knew there was a lighthouse at Orford Ness," Chris Armold admitted to an interviewer in 2000.

The Orford Ness Lighthouse is at a lower elevation than the forest. But only a little bit lower: just low enough, in fact, for the lighthouse beam, when seen from the forest, to be right at eye level. This could make it appear as if it was coming from a light source on the ground—just as the witnesses described it—and being deliberately beamed right into the eyes of people standing in the forest.

And though the light in the lighthouse rotates a full 360°, much of the landward side is shielded, preventing the light—which in 1980 was 5 million candles strong—from being seen inland. Sections of Rendlesham are close enough to the coast for the light to be seen…and other sections are not. If the airmen moved from an area where the light was shielded into one where it could be seen, the sudden sight of such a powerful beam of light would have been very shocking indeed.

MUCH ADO ABOUT...

One by one, the other details of the story became a lot less extra-terrestrial as Ridpath looked into them:

✔ The radiation levels that Halt's party picked up using their Geiger counter were nothing more than the normal background radiation that is present everywhere on Earth.

✔ The smaller, colored flashing lights could have been any number of lights that are visible from the forest. When Ridpath visited the site, he saw lights on buildings in the valley below, as well as flashing red lights on giant antenna masts at Orford Ness.

✔ What about the "star-like" lights that Halt says he saw? "They were probably just that—stars," Ridpath wrote in a 1985 article in the British newspaper *The Guardian*. Three very bright stars were visible on the nights in question: Deneb, Vega, and Sirius. Deneb and Vega were both prominent in the northern sky, where Halt says he saw two UFOs; Sirius, the brightest star in the entire sky, was visible to the south, where Halt says he saw one UFO.

✔ So if these UFOs were really just stars, how were the stars able to move "rapidly in sharp, angular movements," as Halt described it, and change color from red to green to blue? The apparent movement can be attributed to an optical phenomenon known as the "autokinetic effect." You can experience this yourself by staring at a night light or a digital clock in a dark room: if you stare at it for more than a few seconds, it will appear to move. This is because your brain perceives the movement of objects in relation to other visible reference points. In a darkened room—or a sky in which only the very brightest stars are visible—there are no other reference points; your brain perceives the objects as moving when in fact they are not. And the change in colors is caused by the same atmospheric effect that causes stars to twinkle in the night sky.

BLIND DATE

That explains what the airmen saw once they arrived in the forest, but what was it they saw that prompted them to search the forest for a downed aircraft in the first place? This would have been one of the easier pieces of the puzzle to solve, had Lieutenant Colonel Halt not gotten his dates wrong when he typed up his memo three weeks after the fact. Halt misstated the date of the first incident as December 27, 1980. Ridpath was apparently the first person to catch the mistake, when he noticed that the Suffolk Constabulary logged in the first call from RAF Woodbridge on the morning of December 26, not 27. This was important, because when Ridpath called the British Astronomical Association to ask if any meteor sightings had been reported over England at about 3:00 a.m. on the morning of December 27, the BAA found nothing.

But when Ridpath called back with the correct date, bingo! "Shortly before 3:00 a.m. on December 26th, an exceptionally brilliant meteor, almost as bright as the full moon, had been seen over southern England," Ridpath wrote in the *Guardian*. "This meteor would have been visible to the airmen at Woodbridge as though something were crashing into the forest nearby."

A LIKELY STORY

Now there was a more plausible explanation for the Incident at Rendlesham: At 3:00 a.m. on December 26, 1980, some airmen at RAF Woodbridge saw a meteor pass overhead. Mistaking it for a downed aircraft, they searched the forest for the crash site...and stumbled into a section of the forest where they could see the Orford Ness Lighthouse. Two nights later, Lieutenant Colonel Halt, his mind already primed for the possibility of seeing a UFO, went into the same section of the forest and made the same mistake.

The final blow came in 1997, when a researcher named James Easton obtained copies of the original witness statements written shortly after the incident. Not only did the statements undercut the exaggerated claims made by Penniston, Halt, and other witnesses, but they also confirmed that some witnesses had seen nothing unusual. Others who did chase strange lights had known all along that they weren't extraterrestrial. "We ran a good two miles past our vehicle, until we got to a vantage point where we could determine that what we were chasing was only a beacon light off in the distance," wrote Airman Edward Cabansag.

*   *   *

"Census workers have been attacked by the people they're trying to interview. No one knows how many."

—Jon Stewart

"THE MAINTENANCE OF WORLD PEACE"

President Harry S Truman delivered this radio speech on August 6, 1945, the day after the U.S. dropped the atomic bomb on Japan. We're including it here not only because that event was a turning point in history and represents the birth of the nuclear age, but because it portrays a different time in politics and communication. Truman did play down the devastation and play up the victory, but at the same time, he was blunt, candid...and truthful.

Sixteen hours ago, an American airplane dropped one bomb on Hiroshima, an important Japanese Army base. That bomb had more power than 20,000 tons of TNT. It had more than 2,000 times the blast power of the British "Grand Slam," which is the largest bomb ever yet used in the history of warfare.

The Japanese began the war from the air at Pearl Harbor. They have been repaid manyfold. And the end is not yet. With this bomb we have now added a new and revolutionary increase in destruction to supplement the growing power of our armed forces. In their present form, these bombs are now in production, and even more powerful forms are in development. It is an atomic bomb. It is a harnessing of the basic power of the universe. The force from which the sun draws its power has been loosed against those who brought war to the Far East.

Before 1939, it was the accepted belief of scientists that it was theoretically possible to release atomic energy, but no one knew any practical method of doing it. By 1942, however, we knew that the Germans were working feverishly to find a way to add atomic energy to the other engines of war with which they hoped to enslave the world. But they failed. The battle of the laboratories held fateful risks for us as well as the battles of the air, land, and sea, and we have now won the battle of the laboratories as we have won the other battles.

Beginning in 1940, before Pearl Harbor, scientific knowledge useful in war was pooled between the United States and Great

Britain, and many priceless helps to our victories have come from that arrangement. Under that general policy the research on the atomic bomb was begun.

The United States had available the large number of scientists of distinction in the many needed areas of knowledge. It had the tremendous industrial and financial resources necessary for the project, and they could be devoted to it without undue impairment of other vital war work. In the United States the laboratory work and the production plants, on which a substantial start had already been made, would be out of reach of enemy bombing, while at that time Britain was exposed to constant air attack and was still threatened with the possibility of invasion. For these reasons Prime Minister Churchill and President Roosevelt agreed that it was wise to carry on the project here.

We now have two great plants and many lesser works devoted to the production of atomic power. Employment during peak construction numbered 125,000 and over 65,000 individuals are even now engaged in operating the plants. Few know what they have been producing. They see great quantities of material going in and they see nothing coming out of these plants, for the physical size of the explosive charge is exceedingly small. We have spent $2 billion on the greatest scientific gamble in history—and won.

But the greatest marvel is not the size of the enterprise, its secrecy, nor its cost, but the achievement of scientific brains in putting together infinitely complex pieces of knowledge held by many men in different fields of science into a workable plan. And hardly less marvelous has been the capacity of industry to design, and of labor to operate, the machines and methods to do things never done before so that the brainchild of many minds came forth in physical shape and performed as it was supposed to do. Both science and industry worked under the direction of the United States Army, which achieved a unique success in managing so diverse a problem in the advancement of knowledge in an amazingly short time. It is doubtful if such another combination could be got together in the world. What has been done is the greatest achievement of organized science in history. It was done under high pressure and without failure.

We are now prepared to obliterate more rapidly and com-

pletely every productive enterprise the Japanese have above ground in any city. We shall destroy their docks, their factories, and their communications. Let there be no mistake; we shall completely destroy Japan's power to make war.

The secretary of war, who has kept in personal touch with all phases of the project, will immediately make public a statement giving further details. His statement will give facts concerning the sites at Oak Ridge, Tennessee, and at Richland, Washington, and an installation near Santa Fe, New Mexico. Although the workers at the sites have been making materials to be used in producing the greatest destructive force in history, they have not themselves been in danger, for the utmost care has been taken of their safety.

The fact that we can release atomic energy ushers in a new era in man's understanding of nature's forces. Atomic energy may in the future supplement the power that now comes from coal, oil, and falling water, but at present it cannot be produced on a basis to compete with them commercially. Before that comes there must be a long period of intensive research.

It has never been the habit of the scientists of this country or the policy of this government to withhold from the world scientific knowledge. Normally, everything about the work with atomic energy would be made public. But under present circumstances it is not intended to divulge the technical processes of production or all the military applications, pending further examination of possible methods of protecting us and the rest of the world from the danger of sudden destruction.

I shall recommend that the Congress of the United States consider prompt establishment of an appropriate commission to control the production and use of atomic power within the United States. I shall give further consideration and make further recommendations as to how atomic power can become a powerful and forceful influence towards the maintenance of world peace.

* * *

Even in a quarrel, leave room for reconciliation.

—*Russian proverb*

It costs a tenth of a cent to make one plastic grocery bag.

TALL TALES OF THE TOTEM POLE

The totem poles of the Pacific Northwest are impressive for their artistry. But you may be surprised at what they are…and what they aren't.

HISTORY'S MYTH-STORIES

Forget what you think you know about totem poles. They're not idols, they're not ancient, and they're not particularly rare. Totem poles are an art form created by the indigenous tribes of the Pacific Northwest, and the name comes from the Ojibwe word *odoodeman*, meaning "the mark of my kin-ship group." Because totems were made in a close collaboration of artist and buyer, they have traditionally portrayed animals, plants, birds, fish, or anything else for which the patron felt an affinity. They were meant to make an impression, and they do: Towering, intricately carved, and brightly painted, they're hard to ignore.

There's evidence that the Haida people of British Columbia's Queen Charlotte Islands were the first to carve totem poles. With time, the practice spread northward to the Tlingit of southern Alaska and westward to the Tsimshian. Totem styles evolved as the practice moved south down the coast and was adopted by the Heiltsuk, Nuxalk, Kwakiutl, Nootka, and finally the Makah, Quinault and Salish peoples of lower British Columbia and Washington. The northern grouping of tribes largely used pigments of red, black and turquoise on their poles. The southern tribes often included a spread-winged thunderbird at the totem's top and a wider color palette of black, white, red, green, yellow, and turquoise.

MYTHS AND ORIGINS

There aren't any ancient totem poles around. In fact, there are comparatively few from before 1900. Reasons for this:

• They're made of wood, which is biodegradable, especially so in the rain forests of the Northwest.

• Few stand-alone totem poles were even carved before the 1800s. Before contact with Europeans, totem poles were generally just support posts used to decorate the interiors of homes.

• Christian missionaries, thinking the poles were some sort of idols, encouraged new converts to destroy their totems and refrain from building new ones. In truth, totem poles were not worshiped. Nor were they believed to ward off evil spirits or tell the future. Nor were human-sacrifice victims buried below them. Instead, most totem poles were erected for a much less lofty, much more human reason: as a status symbol.

MINE'S BETTER THAN YOURS

In 1741 Russian explorers became the first Europeans to arrive on the North American Pacific coast. Impressed with the quality of North American furs, Russian traders began traveling the coast, buying up pelts from the coastal tribes, which brought the natives great wealth. With wealth, the people could afford to pay artists to beautify their surroundings. The wood carvings inside homes became more elaborate, and the stand-alone totems were moved outside where friends, neighbors, and rivals could see them.

The flip side of that new-found wealth was that it also led to competition between neighbors. In this case, it inspired a "totem race" among leaders of clans and rival tribes, each wanting to illustrate the superiority and affluence of its members. Totem poles, traditionally indoor decorations of modest size, became bigger, taller, and more elaborate through the 1800s. Originally small enough to be carried by two men, the poles of the era began looming as high as 40 feet and weighing many tons.

THE FIGURES

A totem pole starts as the trunk of a Western red cedar, an evergreen found in great abundance along the coast from southern Alaska to northern California. The trees' habitat can range from a few feet above sea level to about 3,000 feet up the coastal mountains. The red cedar can live 800–1,000 years, growing as high as 180–200 feet and as wide as 9–10 feet. Its trunk is tall and straight, and its wood is comparatively soft and easy to carve.

Totem images are richly varied. They can include seemingly random combinations of faces or full figures, animals, fish, birds, legendary creatures, plants, and abstract designs, all carved vertically on a single log, and usually painted with striking colors.

The apparent randomness of images up and down a totem pole has inspired assumptions about their significance. It's easy to think that, like Egyptian hieroglyphics, there's some sort of recognizable story that can be read from the presence and position of each character. For example, there's a common belief that the least important symbols are at the bottom and the most important at the top, as illustrated by the phrase about being "the low man on the totem pole." Others assume that the most important figure is the bottom one, holding all the others up. Analysis of many poles, though, shows no apparent significant meaning in positioning. The most important character appears sometimes at the bottom, sometimes at the top, and sometimes in between.

There's a similar lack of uniformity in the meanings of the totem's individual icons. True, the characteristics of certain animals have obvious symbolic meaning: a dog signifying loyalty, a bear signifying strength, etc. But the patrons usually determined the images and what significance, if any, they suggested. Artists, too, were often given a lot of latitude in what to include and where to place it. What can be surprising is how much humor is built into traditional designs. Figures can appear with intentionally comic postures and facial expressions. Even the person who commissioned the pole can't expect to be spared: they may be portrayed hanging upside down or embarrassingly naked somewhere in the design.

SHAME ON YOU

Not all totem poles were status symbols. Some were meant as memorials and markers, as reminders of history and lineage, or as illustrations for well-known stories and legends. Some were carved to put to rest or memorialize unpleasant intra-tribal conflict: murders, feuds, and other traumatic events. Perhaps the most expressive totems are "shame poles," small poles carved specifically to shame or ridicule someone. If somebody owes you a substantial amount of money and refuses to pay, you might commission an unflattering totem caricature showing the world what a crook he is and post it in a public place until he repays you.

A modern example: In 2007 Native Alaskan artist Mike Webber erected a seven-foot shame pole after the Exxon oil com-

Unlike that of most dog breeds, the Great Dane's vision is better than its sense of smell.

pany refused to pay billions of dollars in court-ordered damages for the Valdez oil spill 18 years earlier. Installed in hard-hit Cordova, Webber's pole depicted the face of Exxon CEO Lee Raymond with dollar signs for eyes, a Pinocchio nose, and an oil slick pouring from his mouth. Around the face he carved the reassuring words from an Exxon official at the time: "We will make you whole." Unfortunately, the power of a shame pole has its limits: A 2009 Supreme Court ruling cut Exxon's liability from $5 billion to $500 million.

ARTISTS AND THEIR TOOLS

Only a few totems were built during the first half of the 20th century, when Indian culture seemed on the verge of dwindling away to nothing. But the civil rights and ethnic pride movements of the 1960s and '70s brought renewed interest among Native Americans about their own culture, and since then totem pole carving has thrived.

Although totem-building tools were once bone and flint, nowadays modern hand tools such as saws, axes, chisels, and gouges make up a basic totem-carving tool kit. A scout knife is the tool most used in the process of detailing and fine carving. Before placing the totem into the ground, the artist would traditionally singe its base to provide some resistance to bugs and rot. But they don't do that anymore.

TOTEM PRESERVATION

Let's say your clan has owned a totem pole for a few generations. What are the odds that it will still be around for your great-grandchildren to see? Not too good. Totem poles will stand only as long as they remain in good shape. At some point, usually after 60 to 80 years, weather and rot gang up with gravity, and the totem meets its end with a mighty crash. This often happens during windstorms, or is done deliberately to avoid tragedy when a weakened totem begins leaning ominously.

Perhaps that natural decay and death is as it should be. But old totems are valuable, not only to their communities and to those who appreciate their history, art, and culture, but to hotels, shopping centers, and museums, as well. (Even modern, freshly carved totems are expensive—a rule of thumb is roughly $500 per foot for a new totem pole hand carved by a native artist with traditional tools; $125 per foot for a machine-assisted version.) So a lot of research has gone into preserving and rehabilitating them. Rather than letting totems rot back into the ground, current state-of-the-art methods turn them into weatherproofed, plasticized artifacts, installed by a derrick and cemented into a concrete base.

REACHING HIGHER

Totem poles began as status symbols, and the tradition continues. Several towns along the Northwest coast proudly claim to have the world's largest totem pole. The *tallest* appears to be a 173-foot pole in Alert Bay, British Columbia. The *widest*, measuring more than six feet in diameter, decorates Duncan, British Columbia. These are records likely to stand for a while, since it's gotten progressively harder to obtain red cedar logs anywhere near that size.

❈   ❈   ❈

SAY UNCLE!

Uncle John isn't the only famous uncle out there.

Uncle Herschel. Dan Evins, the founder of the Cracker Barrel restaurant chain, named one of his most popular entrées after his favorite uncle, Herschel McCartney. The dish consists of eggs, grits, biscuits and gravy, fried apples, hash browns, and a pork chop.

"Bob's your uncle!" A British slang expression which means "there you go" or "there you have it."

The Man from U.N.C.L.E. A 1964–68 TV spy show that followed Napoleon Solo (Robert Vaughan), a top secret agent of the United Network Command for Law Enforcement, in his efforts to defeat the evil criminal organization the Technological Hierarchy for the Removal of Undesirables and the Subjugation of Humanity (T.H.R.U.S.H.).

Uncle Joe. During World War II, President Franklin D. Roosevelt came up with this warm-and-fuzzy nickname for Soviet dictator (and U.S. ally) Josef Stalin in order to make him seem more trustworthy to the American public.

WHO'S LOW MAN ON THE TOTEM POLE?

The figures on totem poles can represent animals, fish, birds, plants, and mythical creatures as well. The stories behind these icons are often as interesting as the carvings themselves.

THUNDERBIRD: Carved with wings proudly outstretched on top of totem poles, thunderbirds are the grand lords of the sky realm, and war with each other above the clouds. Their beating wings are the cause of thunder, and their blinking eyes create lightning. They can make themselves invisible and have been known to kill (and eat) whales. The thunderbird's official role: the protector of the Earth.

KOLUS: The strong but dim-witted brother of the thunderbird, Kolus is a competitive show-off. He is often carved with his wings burned at the tips from flying too close to the sun. But he's not completely useless: He eats mosquitoes and sometimes helps humans with heavy lifting.

EAGLE: The eagle is the ruler of the sky, and represents divine spirit and a connection to the spiritual world. Eagles are known to turn themselves into humans and dance at tribal ceremonies.

RAVEN: Despite being a thief, liar, and trickster, the raven is considered a lovable rogue. But be careful not to cross him: When feeling vengeful, he can turn himself into the fearsome Hok Hok, a long-beaked bird monster that will gladly pluck out your eyes.

SISKIUTI: Carved in coils around the totem pole, Siskiuti is a two-headed sea serpent that encourages war and loves to see injuries and blood. He's not just a spectator, though—he pulls war canoes to battle sites, protects his crestholders during war, and with one glance of his crystal eyes, turns enemy warriors into stone.

BEAVER: Beavers, the storytellers say, have been at war with humans for hundreds of years, mostly because the fur trade of the 1800s decimated them. Beavers will gang up and occasionally murder people walking near rivers. Their vengeance knows no bounds: If slighted, they will dig underground tunnels that cause earthquakes and landslides.

BEAR: Bears are teacher symbols, believed to have taught humans to catch salmon and pick berries. They really like humans—so much so that they turn themselves into big, lumbering humans in order to marry attractive princesses.

TSONOQUA: A wild, foul-smelling woman, Tsonoqua steals fish, treasures, and—when hungry—children to eat. (But don't worry—she's also stupid, so most kids escape.) She cannot be killed permanently, but if she's burned up in a fire, her ashes fly into the air and turn into mosquitoes.

WHALE: Rulers of an underwater city, whales hate and fear thunderbirds, because thunderbirds like to eat them. When they get bored with being the rulers of the underwater world, they can scrape off their skin and become wolves. They're sometimes pictured with Komogwa, the sea king, or Copper Woman, who forges underwater metal goods and causes volcanic eruptions.

WOLF: Wolves are not just great howlers—they're good drummers as well. Because of their nocturnal nature and their love of dancing, they know many secrets and sometimes party late into the night with the Ghost People. Although it drains them physically, wolves are great healers and can turn themselves into shamans (and sometimes vice versa).

OCTOPUS: When pictured on totems, they're called Devilfish. You don't want to wear red when paddling on the sea, because it makes them want to pull you underwater and drown you.

FROG: Carved on totem poles to bring good fortune, frogs can survive bursting out of their skin or (thanks to their friendship with Copper Woman) jumping into volcanoes. They are not to be insulted or mistreated: In one myth, a frog was held in a fire and then burst, spewing out enough lava to destroy an entire village.

A 7-Eleven "X-treme Gulp" cup holds 1.5 times more liquid than the average human stomach can.

FOLLOWING PROTOCOL

*When one is addressing the exalted Uncle John at official Throne
Room functions, one must first bow, then curtsy, then jump up
and down for 10 seconds while singing "Rubber Duckie."
It may sound weird, but it's protocol.*

INTERNATIONAL INCIDENTS

In today's jet-set culture, most heads of state lead an incredibly hectic life—trips, negotiations, press conferences, speeches, and dozens of meetings every day. All of those comings and goings present some unusual scheduling problems. For instance, what would happen if a foreign leader arrived at the White House for an official visit, and the president happened to be out playing golf? Or if the president flew to a summit meeting and the host country had forgotten to book a hotel room for him? In international relations, these embarrassing situations have to be avoided at all cost. That's why governments follow "protocol"—official procedures and rules of diplomatic conduct, right down to the minutiae of how flags are displayed, how officials are addressed, who speaks first at a ceremonial event, and whether it's proper to shake hands, bow, or salute. In the United States, there is an entire State Department division devoted to the finer points of making sure our government doesn't embarrass itself: the Office of the Chief of Protocol.

WE'RE ON A MISSION

The two most important jobs of the 64-person Office of the Chief of Protocol are 1) planning the schedules of foreign leaders visiting the president and 2) accompanying the president on his official visits abroad and coordinating all travel and meeting plans with the White House, the First Lady's staff, and the host country's officials.

But that's not all the Protocol Office does. It organizes treaty-signing ceremonies, resolves diplomatic-immunity cases, and helps foreign diplomatic missions set up their embassies in the U.S. It also plans the schedules of presidential delegations at foreign inaugurals, funerals, weddings, and similar ceremonies. It organizes swearing-in ceremonies for U.S. ambassadors and other State Department officials. It arranges the arrivals of foreign dignitaries visiting the U.S., along with any foreign journalists accompanying them. It approves the credentials of foreign ambassadors and then acts as the president's liaison to them while they're in Washington. And it plans and carries out the president's and the secretary of state's visits to the United Nations General Assembly.

In brief, the Office oversees or assists with just about everything that has to do with state visits, U.S. diplomats, foreign diplomats in the U.S., and official ceremonies. Where diplomacy is concerned, it's our national concierge, party planner, travel agent, gift giver, hotelier, and mediator.

And that's still not all it does.

MANAGING THE WORLD'S MOST EXCLUSIVE HOTEL

Blair House, on Pennsylvania Avenue across the street from the Old Executive Office Building of the White House, is the president's official guesthouse for visiting heads of state and occasional domestic guests, such as presidents-elect. The Office of the Chief of Protocol maintains and manages the facility with the help of a staff (on call 24/7) that spares no effort to make each guest comfortable and provide everything he or she might need (like jelly beans for president-elect Ronald Reagan or burgers for King Hussein of Jordan).

The original building was a single townhouse constructed in 1824 by Dr. Joseph Lovell, the 8th surgeon general of the U.S. Army. In 1837 it was purchased for $6,500 by the family of Francis Preston Blair, owner of the Washington *Globe* newspaper and close friend of Andrew Jackson. The house remained in the Blair family until 1942, when the State Department bought it to provide accommodations for VIPs visiting President Roosevelt.

Today Blair House comprises the original townhouse plus three adjacent ones, which look separate from the outside but are actually connected inside—they add up to a whopping 70,000 square feet and 119 rooms. Blair House is, in fact, bigger than the White House, with 14 guest bedrooms, 9 staff bedrooms, 35 bathrooms, 4 dining rooms, many conference rooms and sitting rooms, an exercise room, a hair salon, kitchens, laundry and dry-cleaning facilities, and even a flower shop. It's decorated in the style of an elegant 19th-century home, with antiques, fine art, Oriental rugs, polished silver, and crystal chandeliers. There are 14–25 official visits to Blair House per year and 50–100 other functions, such as receptions and meetings. While a visiting president, prime minister, or monarch is in residence, his or her national flag flies over Blair House, which becomes, in effect, an embassy of that nation.

One other thing the Office of the Chief of Protocol maintains at Blair House: the official guest book. Some visitors simply sign their names—François Mitterand, Margaret Thatcher, or Jawaharlal Nehru, for example—but others leave messages. During the week of President Reagan's state funeral, Nancy Reagan stayed at Blair House and left this entry: "Many thanks for all your kindness and thoughtfulness at a very difficult time in our lives." Hamid Karzai, chairman of the Interim Administration of Afghanistan, was a little more informal: "Such a wonderful and pleasant stay at the homely Blair House. I will remember you guys."

THE GIFT UNIT

The Protocol Office's Gift Unit has a unique job. In addition to keeping track of all the gifts given to and sent by the president, vice president, secretary of state and their spouses, the Protocol Gift Unit is "the central processing point for all tangible gifts received from foreign sources by employees of the Executive Branch of the Federal government." The unit keeps a detailed list of each gift, including a description, name and title of recipient, date of acceptance, estimated value, current location, name of the donor and government, and circumstances justifying acceptance. Almost all gifts are accepted because, according to official guidelines, "non-acceptance would cause embarrassment to the donor and the U.S. Government."

In 2001, for example, more than 150 gifts were received for President Bush, and hundreds more were received for the First Lady, First Family, First Daughters, vice president, vice president's wife, secretaries of state, treasury, and defense, and dozens of other government officials. The list includes paintings, rugs, statues, books, vases, dishes, bowls, pitchers, a silver coffeepot, silver spoons, jewelry, watches, pistols, sabers, daggers, arrows, coins, plaques, carved elephant tusks, a patchwork coverlet, a drum, a briefcase, an evening purse, shawls, neckties, wine, a baseball bat, desk sets, table linens, toiletries, ornamental boxes, a silver-framed photo of Queen Elizabeth II, a silver-framed photo of the king and queen of Spain, two ceramic coffee mugs, a CD called *The Best of Western Gotaland*, a laser portrait of the president on stretch nylon fabric, a pair of brown lizard-skin boots for the First Lady, a pair of black ostrich-skin boots for the president, and an Inuit sculpture of a walrus.

A BARREL OF GAFFES

In the world of international diplomacy there are real mistakes, and then there are gaffes—moments of minor screwed-up protocol. Real mistakes rock foreign policy and can have worldwide repercussions, sometimes for decades, like the Bay of Pigs invasion. Protocol gaffes generally make headlines for a few days and then fade away...until they appear in *Uncle John's Bathroom Reader*.

• In 1981 Leonore Annenberg, President Reagan's chief of protocol, made a small curtsy to England's visiting Prince Charles. Mistake: The chief of protocol should have known that one of the rules of U.S. protocol is that no American is supposed to bend a knee to anyone.

• In 2007 President George W. Bush visited the Vatican. One of the gifts he gave Pope Benedict XVI was a walking stick with the Ten Commandments carved into it. Oops—they were the Protestant version of the Ten Commandments, which are slightly different from the Catholic version.

• In March 2009, President Barack Obama presented British Prime Minister Gordon Brown with a 25-DVD box set of classic American films collected especially for the occasion by the American Film Institute. A few days later, Brown sat down to watch *Psycho*, reported the *Telegraph*, but was disappointed to find that the U.S.-made DVDs wouldn't play in his British DVD player. (One reader wrote in to the newspaper to ask if *Clueless* was one of the movies in the box set. It wasn't.)

THE DIGITAL CAMERA REVOLUTION, PART IV

Here's a philosophical question: Just because you can make the sky in your image prettier, or remove the wrinkles from under your eyes, does it mean you should? (Part III is on page 382.)

THE DIGITAL DARKROOM

A major factor in the digital revolution has been the camera's partnership with the computer, specifically, with graphics editing software. The most popular program: Adobe Photoshop. It was invented in the late 1980s by brothers John and Thomas Knoll. The sons of a photographer, they combined their love of working in their father's darkroom with their love of computers. Ever since Photoshop 1.0 was released in 1990, the program's ability to alter the colors, tone, brightness, and elements in a photo file has advanced right alongside the digital camera's ability to take better images. By the 2000s, it had become obvious that anyone who is serious about taking and selling pictures must master both photography *and* Photoshop. Those who were able to master the latter have found their skills in great demand.

THE PHOTOSHOP EFFECT

Altering photos of celebrities, athletes, and models for use in magazines and advertising is nothing new; it's been done to some extent for much of photography's existence. But the advent of Photoshop has taken it to a whole new level—the process is much easier than working in a darkroom, cutting and pasting prints together, or airbrushing photos. Today, nearly every one of the millions of magazine and advertising photographs printed each year are first manipulated by a Photoshop artist. They're experts at removing blemishes and making hips curvier, busts bigger, and waists slimmer. In many cases, a Photoshopper will take elements from many different images of a person—the head from one shot, the nose from another, the body from yet another—and combine them all into one picture.

In the eyes of advocacy groups and government health agencies, this is having a profound effect on our culture's collective self-esteem. In short, Photoshop, they say, is changing society's definition of what is considered "beautiful" into something that cannot exist in real life. The most common sufferers: teenage girls. According to the U.S. Department of Health and Human Services, 70 percent of girls report that images of models in magazines influence their definition of a perfect female body.

The "Photoshop Effect," as it's called, affects young men, too. Being constantly bombarded by "perfect" images of male celebrities, models, and athletes may be a contributing factor in an increase in steroid usage in teenage boys who want to attain the perfect "cut body." Health officials are so concerned about these trends that they've urged lawmakers in the United States, France, and England to force magazines to disclose the extent to which their images have been retouched. Currently, no such laws are on the books.

PRESSED

On a similar note, digital manipulation can be a quick, easy way to alter journalistic images. Most news organizations around the world—worried that they'll lose the confidence of the their readers—have enforced strict no-tolerance policies toward image manipulation. Two examples:

• In 2003 the *Los Angeles Times* printed an image by staff photographer Brian Walski of an American soldier walking through a crowded Iraqi village. It turned out, though, that it was actually *two* images. In one shot, the soldier had the pose Walski wanted, but the civilians' positions didn't work. In another, the civilians were lined up to Walski's liking, but it appeared that the soldier's gun was pointed toward a child. So Walski used Photoshop to combine the soldier from one image with the civilians from the other. When the editors at the *Times* found out, they apologized to their readers and fired Walski.

• In 2006 *Charlotte Observer* photographer Patrick Schneider altered a photo he took of some firefighters silhouetted against the sky, which he changed from dull gray to deep red...and was fired. After further investigation revealed that Schneider had regularly enhanced his backgrounds and rearranged elements before turning his photos in, the North Carolina Press Photographers

---

The age at which a woman is likely to reach menopause is 85% determined by her genes.

Association rescinded his three previous "Picture of the Year" awards.

Both of the fired photographers argued that they were merely using Photoshop to make a more accurate portrayal of the scene they actually witnessed; they weren't using it to lie, but to get closer to the truth. The editors who fired them, however, viewed it differently: The journalist's job is to objectively present what he or she sees, not to create an idealistic version of it. According to John Chapnick, executive vice president of Black Star, America's oldest photojournalism agency, "The profession as we know it is threatened by technological transformation. It's under fire from a suspicious public—watchdog bloggers, cable and radio pundits, and other critics who question the profession's credibility and authority to bring us an accurate picture of the world."

A WHOLE LOT OF NOTHING

Another downside to the digital photography age: the storage and retrieval of images. The negatives, slides, and prints of yesteryear can last for a century or more if properly stored. Digital images are much more fickle—they're nothing more than electronic bits of information. As Steven Sasson, inventor of the digital camera, recently put it, "Being able to retrieve, find, and organize images is critical. There is no lack of pictures; there's a lack of being able to find them. It has to be as easy as taking a picture, and that is going to be a challenge." Sasson, who still works for Kodak, is one of many scientists working on methods to make it easier to organize digital images, make them more secure wherever or however they're stored, and make it easier to find and retrieve them. In the meantime, billions of digital pictures remain at the mercy of the world's hard drives, CDs, DVDs, and the Internet. And as the people who bought the first inkjet printers in the mid-1990s are finding out now, their prints are fading fast. But at least they have something tangible. In reality, only a tiny fraction of all of the digital pictures taken will ever get printed.

NOW MUSEUM, NOW YOU DON'T

So which digital storage system is the best? Bad news: none of them. "There isn't any computer-based storage medium that can be considered archival, irrespective of its physical longevity," said

Darin Stahl, senior research analyst at the Ontario-based Info-Tech Research Group. The problem with backing up your images on a Web site is that there's no guarantee the site won't get hacked, or that the company will stay in business. The problem with using magnetic-based storage media (disks and hard drives that use a magnetically coated surface to store information) is that they're going to last only about 25 years...if the hard drive doesn't break first or the disk doesn't get scratched. The problem with using optical storage (tiny deformations in a disk that are read by a laser beam and transferred to data) is that it's also unstable; if the disk gets scratched, much of that data—your pictures—will be gone.

So if you want your pictures to last beyond your lifetime, you have to keep up with the latest technology, transferring your files over to the next medium before your current hardware becomes obsolete. Industry experts advise people to back up their most important photos in at least two different systems. But the most stable method of all is still the old-fashioned analog one: Make archival prints, which won't fade or deteriorate, and store them in acid-free folders in a dry, dark place.

A PICTURE OF TOMORROW

What's on the horizon for digital photography? Plenty. Tech developers are hard at work on coming up with "the next big thing." Already available are 15-megapixel cameras that can take dozens of high-resolution images in less than a second, and point-and-shoots that incorporate "smile recognition technology"—they automatically take a picture when a person smiles.

In the not-too distant future, cameras may finally be able to record a scene as well as the human eye sees it. Don't they do that already? Not really. If you were standing in a room during the daytime and looked out a window, you'd see details inside *and* outside. Due to the limitations of today's cameras, a photo can only show detail in *one* of these two areas, making the other too dark or too light (unless you use a flash). A new technology under development could change all that. *High dynamic range imaging* will make cameras achieve what's called "photo-realism," recording the scene as it's seen through human eyes. Poorly exposed pictures will be a thing of the past.

The volcano under Yellowstone Park is causing it to rise an average of three inches per year.

But tomorrow's cameras will go even beyond what the eye can do—they'll record the ambient temperature, measure distances between objects in the picture, identify people and objects, and photograph full-color images in the dark without the use of flash.

And as these cameras get better, they'll get smaller, even by today's standards—some the size of credit cards, and some resembling pagers (remember those?), that will clip on to your shirt pocket. And when you want to upload your new pictures, new interactive technology will allow you to simply hold your camera a few inches away from your computer, press a button, and the images will automatically be transferred wirelessly. You'll use this same method to print your images as well. And thanks to an emerging technology called *3-D optical data storage*, you'll be able to store your entire photo library—no matter how large—on a single DVD-size disc.

FUSION
Looking beyond that, the cameras of the somewhat distant future will look less and less like a traditional camera. One that's in the planning stages will be incorporated into a pair of eyeglasses and respond to voice commands. Looking beyond even that, scientists have proposed a tiny camera that will mount onto the surface of the human eye and link up directly to the brain. So when you're walking in the park of the future and Big Foot emerges from a UFO, you can just "stare and shoot" and then download the image from your brain, sell it to the tabloids…and get rich!

Yet no matter how advanced these futuristic cameras get, they will all incorporate the same basic light-sensor technology utilized in Steven Sasson's toaster-size digital camera from 1975. Until, that is, some young digital whiz comes up with the *next* "next big thing"—perhaps the Kodak Think-and-Shoot Insta-3-D Levitation 3000. ("You think of the picture, we do the rest!")

* * *

"I have made mistakes, but have never made the mistake of claiming I never made one."

—James G. Bennett

Yo, Flipper! Scientists say that bottlenose dolphins call each other by "name" when they whistle.

DOG TIRED! THE STORY OF THE IDITAROD

Maybe it's the original extreme sport—an 1,100-mile dog race across some of the roughest, coldest terrain in the world.

MUSH!

If you don't live in a near-polar region, you probably can't really imagine how harsh the conditions can be at the annual Iditarod Trail Sled Dog Race. Wind can sweep snow off the ground and create a choking, blinding white curtain with visibility measured in inches. Temperatures can go down to –50°F, as was the case during the 2009 race. Snow can be so deep that leaving the trail buries sleds, suspends mushers (drivers) up to their chests, and forces dogs into desperate dog-paddling just to keep their heads above the surface. People get frostbite. Dogs get injured (and some die). Yet the Iditarod is also supposed to be fun—something done for recreation, prize money, and a chance to prove something about yourself.

ALL-TERRAIN VEHICLES

Long before the arrival of Europeans in the 1700s, Native Alaskans used dogsleds along sections of what became the Iditarod Trail. During the 1896 Alaskan gold rush, it was an important dogsled highway during the winter, when steamships didn't run. Sleds would haul as much as 1,100 pounds of freight between cities, making stops with goods and mail in little towns along the way.

The trail got its name from the town of Iditarod, which was a Native Alaskan village, then a mining center in the 1910 gold rush, and shortly after that, a ghost town.

By World War I, the gold rush had ended, the miners had gone home or into the military, and hauling goods by airplane was replacing dogsled travel. Towns along the trail became deserted, and the Iditarod fell into disuse. Its last hurrah was also its most famous: In the winter of 1925, the first stages of a fast-moving diphtheria epidemic threatened Nome's 1,430 residents. Nome was accustomed to being cut off from the rest of the world for much of the year. But on January 22, the town's only doctor, Curtis Welch, sent an urgent telegram to Juneau and Washington, D.C., saying that five children had died and thousands of people were in grave danger from a disease that, if left untreated, had a nearly 100 percent mortality rate:

> An epidemic of diphtheria is almost inevitable here. I am in urgent need of one million units of diphtheria antitoxin. Mail is only form of transportation…

THE DOGGY EXPRESS

At the time, there were still only three airplanes in the entire state, all of them war surplus with open cockpits and water-cooled engines, making them unsuitable for temperatures well below freezing. Dogsleds were the only answer. At 9:00 p.m. on January 27, "Wild Bill" Shannon received the first shipment of emergency serum at the train station in Nenana. He and his dogs, although inexperienced, left immediately. The temperature began to drop, and Shannon had to jog alongside the sled to stay alive. Nonetheless, he arrived at his relay stop in the town of Minto at 3:00 a.m. with hypothermia and a face blackened by frostbite.

As Pony Express riders had done decades earlier across the American West, mushers and their dogs were waiting and ready at relay stations that had been built along the trail. Over the next four days, 20 dogsleds took turns hauling the serum to Nome. Frostbite was common in the drivers and one reportedly needed hot water poured over his hands at the end of his run in order to unfreeze his gloved hands from his sled. Several dogs died of cold and exhaustion along the way, but four days later the first batch of emergency serum arrived in Nome.

GAME ON

In addition to commemorating the 1925 "Serum Run," the first race was also intended to celebrate Alaska's centennial, revive a near-dead sport, and generate enough publicity for the Iditarod to receive National Historic Trail status. The gambit worked. Dogsled racing was back, and the Iditarod Trail was designated as one of 19 National Historic Trails.

Although the creators of the race, Dorothy Page and Joe Reddington, had sponsored a much shorter 56-mile competition in

1967 and another in 1969, the first 1,100-mile Iditarod from Anchorage to Nome took place on March 3, 1973. Thirty-five sled teams started, and 22 completed the race. It took Dick Wilmarth, the winner that year, 20 days to get to the finish line.

GETTING ALL YOUR DOGS IN A ROW

Getting ready for the Iditarod can be a full-time job. Besides training dogs into a seamless team, mushers have to raise money for huge quantities of dog food, vet bills, and equipment. Most obtain multiple sponsors, as does the race itself.

The rules are pretty loose about what kind of "sled or toboggan" can be used, only that it has to be big enough to haul injured or fatigued dogs, it must have a braking device that doesn't extend beyond the back of the sled runners, and it can't be equipped with sails or wheels. The rules are much more specific about what has to be *inside* the sled: an arctic parka, eight extra booties for each dog, a heavy sleeping bag, an axe, snowshoes, a pot, a cookstove and enough fuel to boil three gallons of water, food for both musher and dogs, and promotional material provided by the race organizers. Competitors may have extra sleds dropped off along the route, as long as they don't use more than three different sleds during the race.

To qualify, mushers must have competed in three approved long-distance races of 300 miles or more and never been convicted of animal neglect or abuse. They also need money—in 2009 the organizers lost a major sponsor, causing them to raise the entrance fee from $3,000 to $4,000 and drop the total prize money 35%.

The entrance fee, it turns out, is only a small part of the cost of competing in the race. Additional costs typically include $50,000 for a year's supply of dog food and care during training, and $7,000 for race supplies (food and supplies for dogs and mushers along the route). In addition, there's the cost of transportation, which can be significant for a person coming from the lower 48 states with sleds and a dozen big dogs.

POLE POSITION

During a ceremonial welcome dinner that takes place the night before the race, the contenders draw for starting positions. But being in the front at the beginning isn't necessarily an advantage.

Originally, wedding cake was thrown at the newlyweds.

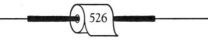

Although organizers "break" the trail with snowmobiles before the race begins, storms can drop new snow, and wind can blow drifts across the path. As a result, dogs at the front may expend energy creating an easier path for those behind them.

The race begins with a ceremonial "start" in Anchorage that doesn't really count. It gives crowds and TV cameras a chance to see the racers and the dogs, creating excitement around the world for a sporting event that's measured in weeks. (The Anchorage event is a ritual many contestants would prefer to skip, because the crowds can agitate and distress their dogs, who are more used to wide-open expanses than big cities.) The next day, the competitors reconvene in nearby Willow for the actual start. The race used to start in Wasilla, but that changed permanently in 2008 because of a lack of snow in recent years.

It would be an impossible mess if all the dogsleds lined up at a long starting line and took off at the same time. To avoid tangled leads and snarling dogs, racers leave at two-minute intervals in the order that they drew at the welcome dinner. To balance out the staggered starts, officials adjust the leaving times from the first 24-hour mandatory layover. Any penalties—up to two hours per infraction—are also added during the mandatory layovers.

AND THEY'RE OFF!

In even-numbered years, the race takes a northern branch of the Iditarod Trail for a distance of 1,112 miles; in odd years, a southern branch measuring 1,131 miles.

Who has the right of way if one sled overtakes another? Surprisingly, the one behind. The one in front must stop the dogs for up to one minute and let the other pass. More rules: Mushers—and dogs—are subject to random drug testing throughout the race. Also, a musher blood-alcohol level above .04% is grounds for disciplinary action.

And yes, dog drivers really do say "Mush!" (That's why they're called mushers.) The command, the equivalent of "Giddyup!", came from a misunderstanding. French fur trappers riding on dogsleds across the Canadian snow shouted *Marchons!* ("Let's go!"). Obscured by the ever-present sound of barking dogs, English speakers heard "Mush on!" When they trained their own dogs, they shortened the command to "Mush!"

EQUIPMENT

A good dogsled, tricked out with a harness, gang lines (the leashes that hold the dogs together), and a snow hook (the Arctic equivalent of an anchor), can cost $600 or more. Cold-weather dog booties cost $1–2 per paw. They're designed to protect paws from cold and "ice balling" between the toes while still allowing dogs to feel the terrain as they run. Made of cloth, they tend to need replacing every 100 miles.

Mushers aren't allowed to use any navigational or communication device beyond 19th-century technology. A watch, magnetic compass, pencil, map, and math skills are allowed; cell phones, GPS devices, night goggles, and speed/distance calculators are not. One exception: Mushers are allowed to carry emergency devices that broadcast a signal if they need help; however, it is their last resort, because at the moment they push the signal button, they are disqualified from the race.

THE RACERS

Iditarod racers represent a wide range of abilities and skill levels, which sometimes sparks conflict. At the top are the genuine contenders, the serious athletes, one of whom is almost certain to win. In the middle are the less experienced or less skillful contenders, who vie to place in the top 30 and win some money. At the bottom? The ones who just hope to finish: the inexperienced, the old-timers past their prime, and the amateurs, usually from the lower 48 states, who want the experience of running in the famous race and the bragging rights that come with it. The members of this last category are most likely to take unwise risks and get into life-threatening situations that require rescue by emergency snowmobile or airplane.

THE DOGS

About 1,000 dogs make the run each year. Siberian Huskies, Samoyeds, and Alaskan Malamutes have been bred over centuries for the job of pulling sleds. They are comfortable buried in snow, and they sleep with their tail over their nose for extra insulation. They are still the engines that power most dogsleds in the Iditarod.

An Iditarod dog team must consist of 12–16 dogs at the beginning of the race. Those dogs must be either on the towline or, if injured or exhausted, hauled in the sled until the next "dog-drop" site at a checkpoint. At least six of the original dogs must be pulling the sled's towline at the finish of the race. What happens to the dogs that are dropped off at the drop sites? They're transported by air to a prison in Eagle River, where inmates take care of them until their owners claim them.

At least one dog has died in almost every Iditarod race. The worst ever: 1985, when nine dogs died. To try to prevent that from happening again, organizers require certificates of dog health before the race, and rest stops and veterinary checkpoints during. However, in 2009's run, six dogs died along the course as the weather turned unusually cold. This may be the beginning of a trend. Because winter weather has been warming in Alaska, some racers have begun gambling on dog breeds that are faster or stronger, but not quite as cold-resistant as the traditional breeds.

THE FINISH LINE

• The first 30 finishers get a share of the prize money. Total purse for for 2010: $610,000. Any finisher after the 30th gets a consolation award of $1,049 to help get them and their dogs home.

• The most finishers at the end of a single race: 77 in 2004.

• Fastest winning time: 8 days, 22 hours, 46 minutes, and 2 seconds, by Martin Buser in 2002.

• Slowest winning time: 20 days, 15 hours, 2 minutes, and 7 seconds, by Carl Huntington in 1974. (Delays from weather conditions can make a huge difference in the race.)

• First woman to win the race: Libby Riddles in 1985. (Susan Butcher won the race four times—in 1986, '87, '88, and '90.)

• Often, the winner is hours ahead of the second-place competitor. That wasn't true in 1978, when two men raced to the finish neck and neck. At the end, Dick Mackey finished first, one second ahead of Rick Swenson.

• Slowest competitor ever: John Schultz, who arrived at the end of the 1973 race after 32 days, 15 hours, 9 minutes, and 1 second.

• Organizers keep a red lantern burning at the finish line until the last competitor arrives. The lantern is then extinguished and presented to the last musher to finish.

THE MAKING OF ROCKY

The movie poster for the 1976 film Rocky *had the tagline "His whole life was a million-to-one shot." It turns out that the real million-to-one shots took place behind the scenes.*

MAN OF THE HOUR

If you're old enough to remember when the sleeper hit *Rocky* arrived in theaters in November 1976, you may also remember how quickly the film's star, Sylvester Stallone, burst from obscurity to become a major Hollywood star. Before *Rocky*, not many people had heard his name; then, overnight, everyone was talking about his performance as Rocky Balboa. Suddenly the whole world knew who he was.

Though Stallone may have seemed like an instant success, he had struggled for years to make a name for himself as an actor, first in New York and then in Hollywood. But few casting directors had been able to see past his swarthy looks and muscular build to give him decent roles. On those rare occasions when he actually did land a part in a film, he was invariably cast as the heavy—in Woody Allen's 1971 film *Bananas,* he plays a thug who attacks an old lady on the subway; in the 1975 film *The Prisoner of Second Avenue*, he plays a man that Jack Lemmon mistakes for a pickpocket. And when he finally got his first supporting role, in the 1974 film *The Lords of Flatbush,* he was cast as yet another thug.

EASY WRITER

As Stallone was turned down for good parts in one film after another, he came to believe that the only way for him to get a good movie role was to write it himself. He was particularly inspired by the 1969 cult film *Easy Rider,* starring Peter Fonda, Dennis Hopper, and Jack Nicholson. Stallone didn't think much of the screenplay, which was written by Fonda, Hopper, and Terry Southern. But he figured that if something as flawed as the *Easy Rider* screenplay could find its way onto the screen, he could write something as good (or better) and it, too, would have a decent shot at getting made into a film.

Stallone quickly learned that screenwriting is a lot more difficult than it looks. His earliest scripts were so bad that he never tried to sell them. *Cry Full and Whisper Empty in the Same Breath*, for example, was about a rock musician whose career is destroyed by his insatiable craving for bananas.

As he gained experience, the quality of his work improved. *Easy Rider, Midnight Cowboy*, and other films of the period were dark and filled with doomed antiheroes—in the aftermath of Vietnam and Watergate, there was a lot to be pessimistic about, and these films fit the public mood. Stallone did his best to produce a gloomy script that the major Hollywood studios would buy, but at some point he realized that the only reason he was writing such negative stories was that they were popular, not because he was really interested in them. Besides, with every screenwriter in Hollywood producing these sad stories by the bushel, there was very little in Stallone's screenplays that was unique, original, or interesting.

CORN BRED

Stallone's own taste in films was more old-fashioned: He liked uplifting movies with *heroes*—films where the central character is a noble figure who, when challenged, struggles and wins in the end. Such films had been popular in the 1930s and '40s. Director Frank Capra, for example, spent most of his career making feel-good films like *Mr. Deeds Goes to Town* (1936), *Mr. Smith Goes to Washington* (1939), and *It's a Wonderful Life* (1946), and he had won six Academy Awards for his efforts. But by the mid-1970s, such films were decidedly out of fashion and dismissed as "Capra-corn."

Stallone decided to write one anyway. He wanted to build a story around a theme that was close to his heart: a common man's battle for recognition, dignity, and self-respect. But he didn't think his own life story, that of an actor who has trouble landing parts, and a screenwriter who has trouble selling scripts, would make for a very compelling tale. He had to find a better angle.

Then in early 1975, Muhammad Ali, the reigning World Heavyweight Champion boxer, announced that he would be fighting an unknown fighter named Chuck Wepner, a.k.a. "The Bayonne Bleeder," a nickname he earned from all the cuts (and more than 300 stitches) he'd received over the course of his 51-fight career. Wepner would be no match for Ali; both Wepner and the champ knew it. But Ali was looking for an easy fight (and a quick

At 15, Sylvester Stallone was chosen "most likely to die in the electric chair" by his classmates.

$1.5 million paycheck) between his more serious title challenges, and Wepner was happy to take the $100,000 he was offered, which was more than 10 times what he'd ever been paid for a fight. For the first time he could afford to train for a fight full-time, instead of just on weekends and before or after work.

Stallone paid $20 to see the fight, which was broadcast by closed-circuit TV to select movie theaters around the country. If Stallone knew anything about the 30–1 underdog Wepner, he must have expected him to lose early and lose big. But Wepner stunned the boxing world by lasting round after round. In the ninth round, he even managed to knock Ali down—the only fighter ever to do so while Ali was champ. Suddenly, the crowds that had been yelling "Ali! Ali! Ali!" started yelling "Chuck! Chuck! Chuck!" And though Wepner got clobbered in the later rounds and lost in a TKO just seconds before the end of the 15th and final round, he was seen as the real winner that night, because he had nearly gone the distance with the best boxer in the world when nobody thought he could do it.

Stallone had his character. After a marathon four-day writing session—he wrote in pen on a legal pad, and his wife, Sasha, typed it up—he had the first draft of the script he titled simply *Rocky*.

STARRING BURT REYNOLDS AS ROCKY

When he wasn't writing, Stallone was still auditioning for movie roles. His luck was as bad as ever, but as he was leaving yet another fruitless audition with a producer named Robert Chartoff, Stallone happened to mention that he was also a writer. Chartoff had liked Stallone's work in *Lords of Flatbush*; he thought the young actor had the potential to be another Marlon Brando. He agreed to have a look at the *Rocky* script, and enjoyed it so much that he asked his partner, Irwin Winkler, to read it, too. *Rocky* was exactly the kind of script they were in the market for, one that could serve as a big-budget vehicle for an established star like Ryan O'Neal, Steve McQueen, or Burt Reynolds. The two producers decided to buy it. They offered Stallone $75,000 for the script—a small fortune in the mid-1970s.

Stallone said no. By now he'd been turned down for so many parts that he wasn't about to let this one get away. And since he

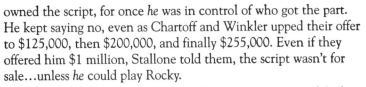

owned the script, for once *he* was in control of who got the part. He kept saying no, even as Chartoff and Winkler upped their offer to $125,000, then $200,000, and finally $255,000. Even if they offered him $1 million, Stallone told them, the script wasn't for sale...unless *he* could play Rocky.

At the time, Stallone had barely $100 to his name, and Sasha was pregnant with their first child. He was in no position to turn down $255,000, but he did it anyway and held his ground. *Rocky* was about a million-to-one shot, about an ordinary man who goes the distance. Stallone was determined to go the distance, too—he wanted his own million-to-one shot. He didn't want to spend the rest of his life wondering "What if?" Sasha backed his decision— "Go for it," she told him.

DOWNSIZING

Chartoff and Winkler didn't want to let the *Rocky* script get away. They finally agreed to Stallone's terms—he would play Rocky Balboa. But since he was an unknown actor with nonexistent box-office appeal, a big budget production was out of the question. *Rocky* would have to be a low-budget film instead. And to save on up-front expenses, Stallone let them have the script for nothing and agreed to act in the film for "scale"—the actor's equivalent of minimum wage. In exchange for accepting so little money up front, Stallone would receive a percentage of the profits if the film ever made any money, which was doubtful.

YO, PERRY!

Chartoff and Winkler had a deal with United Artists that allowed them to approve almost any film they wanted to make, as long as the budget was kept under $1 million. But the studio could still kill a project if it really wanted to.

A movie about a past-his-prime fighter who falls in love with a wallflower who works at a pet store? Who gets a shot at the world championship and *loses* the big fight? Starring a nobody? The top brass at United Artists still needed convincing. Chartoff and Winkler sent them a copy of *The Lords of Flatbush* to familiarize them with Stallone's work. The only problem: Though Stallone is identified by name in the film's credits, it's never completely clear *which* of the film's four main actors he is. One of the other actors, a man named Perry King, had light brown hair and leading-man good looks. The studio heads concluded that *he* was Stallone. He didn't look Italian—so he must be from northern Italy, they figured. Satisfied that Perry King had the star quality to carry the film, United Artists gave *Rocky* the green light. The executives didn't realize who the real Sylvester Stallone was until they saw the finished film...and Perry King wasn't in it.

PINCHING PENNIES

Making the film on such a limited budget was quite a challenge, but it is also one of the things that made the film unique.

• With no money to pay big stars, little-known actors like Talia Shire (Rocky's girlfriend, Adrian), Burt Young (Adrian's brother, Paulie), and former Oakland Raiders linebacker Carl Weathers (heavyweight champ Apollo Creed) were cast in the supporting roles. Shire was only cast after the first choice for Adrian, actress Carrie Snodgress, asked for too much money. Burgess Meredith, who played Rocky's trainer and manager, Mickey, was the only well-known actor cast in the film. And at this late stage in his career, the 69-year-old Meredith was best known for playing the Penguin in the *Batman* TV series.

• Instead of hiring a top film composer, the producers had to settle for a young composer named Bill Conti. To show Conti what kind of music he wanted, director John Avildsen played a record of Beethoven's 6th Symphony over some footage of Stallone and Weathers boxing. Conti came up with "Gonna Fly Now," one of the most memorable movie themes of all time.

• The fight scenes were filmed in an entirely new way. To save money (and because director Avildsen thought the fight scenes in other boxing films looked fake), instead of just filming Stallone and Weathers boxing away at random until there was enough usable footage to edit into a fight sequence, Stallone choreographed every individual punch in the fight. Then he and Weathers rehearsed the punches for weeks on end before filming began. The result was one of the most realistic fight scenes ever filmed; boxing movies have been filmed that way ever since.

KNOCKOUT

The entire film was shot in 28 days for just over $1 million. It was

There are approximately 1,200 peanuts in a 28-oz. jar of peanut butter.

finished on time and only a little over budget, which was a good thing, because United Artists had insisted that Chartoff and Winkler pay for any cost overruns out of their own pockets, which they did by taking mortgages out on their homes. The studio also reserved the right to fire Stallone after 10 days if they didn't like his work.

United Artists need not have worried—though even Chartoff and Winkler themselves had expected *Rocky* to be little more than a marginally successful "B movie," the kind of film that got second-billing at drive-in theaters, it became one of the hottest films of 1976, earning both critical praise and a whopping $117 million at the box office. Nominated for 10 Academy awards, *Rocky* won Oscars for Best Director, Best Editing, and Best Picture—a surprise winner over the heavily favored *All the President's Men*. The film made Sylvester Stallone a rich man and established him as one of the biggest stars in Hollywood. Together, *Rocky* and its five sequels have earned more than $1 billion at the box office, making it one of the most successful film franchises in Hollywood history.

*   *   *

STEP LIVELY

The most famous *Rocky* scene of all—Rocky running up the steps of the Philadelphia Museum of Art—came about by chance after a cameraman named Garrett Brown invented something he called the "Brown Stabilizer." The device, which held a camera steady even when the camera operator was moving, allowed for much smoother filming than was possible with traditional handheld techniques. To demonstrate the capabilities of his invention, now known as the Steadicam, Brown shot some test footage of his girlfriend running up and down the Philadelphia Museum of Art steps. When *Rocky* director John Avildsen saw the footage, he called Brown and asked him, "How did you shoot that footage, and where are those steps?" *Rocky* was one of the first films to include scenes filmed with a Steadicam, including footage of Stallone running up those same steps. More than 30 years later, the "Rocky Steps" remain the second most popular tourist destination in Philadelphia after the Liberty Bell.

ENDLESS WISDOM

Some thoughts that we hope will stay with you long after you've flushed.

"There is no way to look at the past. Don't hide from it. It will not catch you if you don't repeat it."

—Pearl Bailey

"It is curious that physical courage should be so common in the world, and moral courage so rare."

—Mark Twain

"A certain amount of opposition is a great help. Kites rise against, not with, the wind."

—John Neal

"It's useless to hold a person to anything he says while he's in love, drunk, or running for office."

—Shirley MacLaine

"We either make ourselves happy or miserable. The amount of work is the same."

—Carlos Castaneda

"If fear alters your behavior, you're already defeated."

—Brenda Hammond

"No man was ever wise by chance."

—Seneca

"There's no such thing as simple. Simple is hard."

—Martin Scorsese

"Opportunities are like buses: There's always another one coming."

—Richard Branson

"A few observations and much reasoning lead to error; many observations and a little reasoning to truth."

—Alexis Carrel

"The obscure we see eventually. The completely obvious, it seems, takes longer."

—Edward R. Murrow

"Strength is the capacity to break a chocolate bar into four pieces with your bare hands—and then eat just one of the pieces."

—Judith Viorst

"In seeking truth you have to get both sides of a story."

—Walter Cronkite

"All experience is great provided you live through it. If it kills you, you've gone too far."

—Alice Neel

Walk of fame: Actress Natalie Portman has her own line of eco-friendly "vegan" shoes.

ANSWER PAGES

NAME GAME
(Answers for page 177)

1) Salinger
2) Pei
3) Tolkien
4) Lewis
5) Barnum
6) Eliot
7) lang
8) Auden
9) Escher
10) Lovecraft

11) Skinner
12) Foyt
13) Marshall
14) Baracus (Mr. T)
15) Wells
16) Morgan
17) Sabathia
18) Knight
19) Hughley

20) Reynolds
21) cummings
22) Ewing
23) Griffith
24) Milne
25) Richardson
26) Mencken
27) O'Rourke
28) Barrie
29) Hooker

EXERCISE YOUR BRAIN
(Answers for page 381)

1. Florida and Rhode Island. (If you thought of Wyoming as well, that's incorrect, because "y" is acting as a vowel.)

2. bustle, subtle, sublet, bluest

3. Tuesday

4. The Seven Dwarfs (Grumpy, Dopey, Sneezy, Sleepy, Bashful, Doc, and Happy)

5. Donny Osmond, because unlike Marie, his name has a set of double letters, which you'll find in all of the words he likes.

6. 11 + 11/11

7. Each can be preceded by "HIGH" to form a common word or phrase.

8. The closest the pilot can be is 100 miles. However, if he flew over the North Pole, then he'd instantly be traveling south, so the farthest distance is 300 miles.

9. successfully, unsuccessfully

According to neuroscientists, only one brain cell is needed to spot a familiar face.

10. They're all movie lines:
"Show me the money." (*Jerry Maguire*)
"Hasta la vista, baby." (*Terminator 2*)
"May the Force be with you." (*Star Wars*)
"We're not in Kansas anymore." (*The Wizard of Oz*)
"Don't call me Shirley." (*Airplane!*)
11. If you're adding the numbers on a clock—starting at 4:00, if you add 9 hours, it will be 1:00.
12. You have one $50 bill, one $5 bill, and four $2 bills.
13. An equal.

"ALWAYS"...OR "NEVER"?
(Answers for page 272)

1. Always	**6.** Always	**11.** Never
2. Never	**7.** Always	**12.** Never
3. Always	**8.** Always	**13.** Always
4. Always	**9.** Never	**14.** Never
5. Never	**10.** Never	**15.** Never, Always

VERY QUIZ-LIKE
(Answers for page 317)

1. c	**6.** e	**11.** h	**16.** r	**21.** d
2. t	**7.** a	**12.** f	**17.** k	**22.** i
3. p	**8.** v	**13.** s	**18.** l	**23.** y
4. m	**9.** n	**14.** x	**19.** b	**24.** q
5. g	**10.** j	**15.** o	**20.** u	**25.** w

PORTMANTEAU MOVIE QUIZ
(Answers for page 439)

1. *WALL-E.T.: The Extra-Terrestrial* = *WALL-E* (2008) + *E.T.: The Extra-Terrestrial* (1982)
2. *No Country for Old Men in Black* = *No Country for Old Men* (2007) + *Men in Black* (1997)

Robert De Niro has died in 14 movies, a Hollywood record.

3. *His Girl Friday the 13th* = *His Girl Friday* (1940) + *Friday the 13th* (1980)

4. *A Cry in the Dark Knight* = *A Cry in the Dark* (1988) + *The Dark Knight* (2008)

5. *Lilies of the Field of Dreams* = *Lilies of the Field* (1963) + *Field of Dreams* (1989)

6. *The Lion King Ralph* = *The Lion King* (1994) + *King Ralph* (1991)

7. *Shakespeare in Love Story* = *Shakespeare in Love* (1998) + *Love Story* (1970)

8. *My Fair Lady and the Tramp* = *My Fair Lady* (1964) + *Lady and the Tramp* (1955)

9. *The Gold Rush Hour* = *The Gold Rush* (1925) + *Rush Hour* (1998)

10. *The Lost Weekend at Bernie's* = *The Lost Weekend* (1945) + *Weekend at Bernie's* (1989)

11. *Singin' in the Rain Man* = *Singin' in the Rain* (1952) + *Rain Man* (1988)

12. *The Empire Strikes Back to the Future* = *The Empire Strikes Back* (1980) + *Back to the Future* (1985)

*　　*　　*

LAST WORD

Circus promoter and public-relations genius P. T. Barnum opened a museum in Manhattan in 1841. It cost 25 cents to get in and featured thousands of exhibits, including General Tom Thumb, an erudite 25-inch-tall man; and the Fiji Mermaid, the mummified body of an unknown creature that sort of (but not really) looked like a mermaid. The museum was immensely popular, and people would stay in it for hours—much to the chagrin of Barnum, who wanted traffic to move as briskly as possible. To speed things up he had signs installed in the museum reading, "This way to the Egress." They led curious visitors down a series of hallways…and finally to a remote exit, from which they were not allowed to return unless they went back to the main entrance and paid another quarter. Barnum correctly assumed that most of his customers wouldn't know that "egress" is just a fancy word for "exit."

THE LAST PAGE

FELLOW BATHROOM READERS:
The fight for good bathroom reading should never be taken loosely—we must do our duty and sit firmly for what we believe in, even while the rest of the world is taking potshots at us.

We'll be brief. Now that we've proven we're not simply a flush-in-the-pan, we invite you to take the plunge: Sit Down and Be Counted! Become a member of the Bathroom Readers' Institute. Log on to *www.bathroomreader.com*, or send a self-addressed, stamped, business-sized envelope to: BRI, PO Box 1117, Ashland, Oregon 97520. You'll receive your free membership card, get discounts when ordering directly through the BRI, and earn a permanent spot on the BRI honor roll!

If you like reading our books...
VISIT THE BRI'S WEB SITE!
www.bathroomreader.com

- Visit "The Throne Room"—a great place to read!
- Receive our irregular newsletters via e-mail
- Order additional *Bathroom Readers*
- Become a BRI member

Go with the Flow...

Well, we're out of space, and when you've gotta go, you've gotta go. Tanks for all your support. Hope to hear from you soon. Meanwhile, remember...

Keep on flushin'!